Commercial Pilot

2023 Test Prep

Study and prepare for your pilot FAA Knowledge Exam

AVIATION SUPPLIES & ACADEMICS, INC.
NEWCASTLE, WASHINGTON

The FAA Knowledge Exam questions can change throughout the year. Stay current with test changes; sign up for ASA's free email update service at **asa2fly.com/testupdate**

Commercial Pilot Test Prep
2023 Edition

Aviation Supplies & Academics, Inc.
7005 132nd Place SE
Newcastle, Washington 98059
asa@asa2fly.com | 425.235.1500 | asa2fly.com

© 2022 Aviation Supplies & Academics, Inc.

Visit **asa2fly.com/TPC** for additional information and resources related to this book.

Sample Federal Aviation Administration (FAA) questions herein contain information as of: September 2022. Stay informed of changes since the book was printed: **asa2fly.com/testupdate**

None of the material in this publication supersedes any documents, procedures or regulations issued by the Federal Aviation Administration.

Aviation Supplies & Academics, Inc. (ASA), assumes no responsibility for any errors or omissions. Neither is any liability assumed for damages resulting from the use of the information contained herein.

Cover photo: Aleksandr Lupin/Shutterstock.com

ASA-TP-C-23
ISBN   978-1-64425-241-3

Additional format available:
eBook PDF ISBN   978-1-64425-242-0

Also sold as *Commercial Pilot Test Prep Plus*, which includes this book plus Prepware software.
ASA-TPP-C-23, ISBN 978-1-64425-255-0

Printed in the United States of America

2023   2022   5   4   3   2   1

About the Contributors

Jackie Spanitz
General Manager
Aviation Supplies & Academics, Inc.

As ASA General Manager, Jackie Spanitz oversees maintenance and development of more than 1,000 titles and pilot supplies in the ASA product line. Ms. Spanitz has worked with airman training and testing for more than 25 years, including participation in the Airman Certification Standards (ACS) development committees. Jackie holds a Bachelor of Science in Aviation Technology from Western Michigan University, a Master of Science from Embry-Riddle Aeronautical University, and Instructor and Commercial Pilot certificates. She is the author of *Guide to the Flight Review*, and the technical editor for ASA's Test Prep and FAR/AIM series.

Aviation Supplies & Academics, Inc. (ASA) is an industry leader in the development and sale of aviation supplies and publications for pilots, flight instructors, aviation maintenance technicians, aircraft dispatchers, air traffic controllers, flight attendants, and drone operators. We manufacture and publish more than 1,000 products and have been providing trusted and reliable training materials to the aviation industry for over 80 years. Visit **asa2fly.com** to learn more.

Stay informed with ASA online resources.

Website
asa2fly.com

Updates
asa2fly.com/testupdate

Follow, like, share.
twitter.com/asa2fly
instagram.com/asa2fly
facebook.com/asa2fly
youtube.com/asa2fly
linkedin.com/company/asa2fly

Contents

Instructions
Updates and Practice Tests v
Introduction vi
Description of the Tests vii
   Knowledge Test Registration vii
   Knowledge Test Eligibility viii
   Acceptable Materials ix
   Testing Procedures for Applicants
      Requesting Special Accommodations ix
   Test Reports x
   Retesting Procedures x
   Cheating or Other Unauthorized Conduct x
   Test-Taking Tips xii
Commercial Pilot Certificate Eligibility
   Requirements xiii
Knowledge Exam References xiv
Acronyms xv
ASA Test Prep Layout xvii

Chapter 1 **Basic Aerodynamics**
Aerodynamic Terms 1–3
Axes of Rotation and the Four Forces Acting
   in Flight 1–5
   Lift 1–6
   Weight 1–7
   Thrust 1–7
   Drag 1–7
Lift/Drag Ratios 1–11
The V_G Diagram 1–13
Stability 1–14
Turns, Loads, and Load Factors 1–16
Stalls and Spins 1–23
Flaps 1–24
Wing Shapes 1–25
Torque 1–26
Ground Effect 1–27
Wake Turbulence 1–28
Glider Aerodynamics 1–30

Chapter 2 **Aircraft Systems**
Ignition System 2–3
Fuel/Air Mixture 2–4
Carburetor Ice 2–6
Aviation Fuel 2–7
Engine Temperatures 2–8
Propellers 2–9
Cold Weather Operations 2–12
Rotorcraft Systems 2–13
Glider Systems 2–29
Balloon Operations 2–37
Airship Operations 2–43
Airship IFR Operations 2–45

Chapter 3 **Flight Instruments**
Airspeed Indicator 3–3
Altitudes 3–6
Magnetic Compass 3–7
Gyroscopic Instruments and Systems 3–8
Attitude Instrument Flying 3–9
Electronic Flight Instruments 3–10

Chapter 4 **Regulations**
Pilot Certificate Types and Privileges 4–3
Medical Certificates 4–6
Pilot Logbooks 4–7
High-Performance, Complex, and Tailwheel
   Airplanes 4–8
Recent Flight Experience: Pilot-In-Command 4–10
Change of Address 4–11
Towing 4–12
Responsibility and Authority of the
   Pilot-In-Command 4–13
Preflight Action 4–15
Seatbelts 4–17
Portable Electronic Devices 4–19
Fuel Requirements 4–20
Transponder and ADS-B Requirements 4–20
Supplemental Oxygen 4–22
Instrument and Equipment Requirements 4–23
Restricted, Limited, and Experimental
   Aircraft: Operating Limitations 4–24
Emergency Locator Transmitter (ELT) 4–25
Truth in Leasing 4–25
Operating Near Other Aircraft and
   Right-of-Way Rules 4–26
Speed Limits 4–29
Aircraft Lights 4–30
Minimum Altitudes 4–31
Maintenance Responsibility 4–32
Aircraft Inspections 4–33

Maintenance Records........................... 4–35
Maintenance, Preventative Maintenance,
    Rebuilding, and Alteration.......................... 4–36
NTSB Part 830 4–38
IFR Operations 4–41
Rotorcraft Regulations 4–42
Glider Regulations 4–43
Lighter-Than-Air Regulations.................. 4–43
LTA Fundamentals of Instructing 4–46

Chapter 5 **Procedures and Airport Operations**

Airspace... 5–3
Basic VFR Weather Minimums 5–14
Operations on Wet or Slippery Runways.... 5–15
Land and Hold Short Operations (LAHSO) 5–16
Airport Marking Aids and Signs............... 5–17
VFR Cruising Altitudes 5–22
Collision Avoidance 5–22
Fitness Physiology................................. 5–25
Aeronautical Decision Making (ADM)..... 5–29

Chapter 6 **Weather**

The Earth's Atmosphere......................... 6–3
Temperature 6–6
Wind 6–7
Moisture... 6–9
Stable and Unstable Air 6–10
Clouds 6–11
Air Masses and Fronts........................... 6–16
Turbulence 6–17
Icing 6–19
Thunderstorms 6–21
Fog 6–24
Wind Shear.. 6–26
Soaring Weather.................................... 6–29

Chapter 7 **Weather Services**

Aviation Routine Weather Report (METAR)........... 7–3
Pilot Report (UA) 7–5
Terminal Aerodrome Forecast (TAF) 7–8
Graphical Forecasts for Aviation (GFA) 7–9
Winds and Temperatures Aloft Forecast (FB)..... 7–10
Inflight Weather Advisories (WA, WS, WST)...... 7–10
Surface Analysis Chart........................... 7–12
Constant Pressure Chart........................ 7–13
Tropopause Height/Vertical Wind Shear
    Prognostic Chart 7–14
Significant Weather Prognostics........... 7–14
Lifted Index Chart 7–16

Chapter 8 **Aircraft Performance**

Weight and Balance 8–3
    Computing Weight and Balance 8–4
    Graph Weight and Balance Problems 8–4
    Weight Change.................................. 8–5
    Weight Shift...................................... 8–6
Rotorcraft Weight and Balance............... 8–12
Glider Weight and Balance 8–15
Headwind and Crosswind Components 8–17
Density Altitude...................................... 8–19
Takeoff and Landing Considerations 8–20
Takeoff and Landing Distance 8–22
Fuel Consumption vs. Brake Horsepower 8–26
Time, Fuel, and Distance to Climb 8–28
    Table Method.................................... 8–28
    Graph Method 8–29
Cruise Performance Table 8–33
Cruise and Range Performance Table..... 8–35
Maximum Rate of Climb 8–36
Glide Distance 8–37
Rotorcraft Performance 8–38
Glider Performance................................ 8–40
Balloon Performance 8–43

Chapter 9 **Navigation**

The Flight Computer............................... 9–3
    *Finding True Course, Time, Rate, Distance,
        and Fuel* 9–3
    Finding Density Altitude................... 9–10
    Finding Wind Direction and Velocity 9–12
VHF Omni-Directional Range (VOR) 9–14
Horizontal Situation Indicator (HSI) 9–18

Cross References

A: Question Number and Page Number............. A–1
B: Airman Knowledge Test Report
    Codes and Question Numbers B–1

FAA Figures

Airman Knowledge Testing Supplement for
Commercial Pilot (FAA-CT-8080-1E)

Updates and Practice Tests

Free Test Updates for the One-Year Life Cycle of Test Prep Books

The FAA modifies tests as needed throughout the year. ASA keeps abreast of changes to the tests and posts free Test Updates on the ASA website. Before taking your test, be certain you have the most current information by visiting the ASA Test Updates webpage: **asa2fly.com/testupdate**. Additionally, sign up for free email notifications, which are sent when new Test Updates are available.

We Invite Your Feedback

After you take your FAA exam, let us know how you did. Were you prepared? Did ASA's products meet your needs and exceed your expectations? We want to continue to improve these products to ensure applicants are prepared and become safe aviators. Send your feedback to: **cfi@asa2fly.com**.

---

prepware.com

See inside front cover for FREE account!

Helping you practice for written exams.

As the experts in FAA Knowledge Exam preparation, we want you to have the confidence needed before heading to the testing center, and help eliminate the hassle and expense of retaking exams.

> **Realistic Test Simulation**
> Test questions and time allowed replicate the official FAA exam

> **Performance Graphs**
> Review how you did, track your performance and review explanations for the questions you missed

> **Gain Confidence**
> Go into your exam fully prepared after practicing up to 5 simulated tests

> **Succeed**
> Pass your exam, achieve your goals, and set new ones

Remote Pilot • Sport Pilot • Private Pilot • Instrument Rating • Commercial Pilot • Flight Instructor • Ground Instructor
Fundamentals of Instructing • Flight Engineer • Airline Transport Pilot • Aviation Mechanic General • Airframe • Powerplant
Practice tests are also available as an app! **asa2fly.com/apps**

Introduction

Welcome to the Aviation Supplies & Academics, Inc., (ASA) Test Prep Series. This series has been helping pilots prepare for the FAA Knowledge Tests for more than 60 years with great success. We are confident that with proper use of this book you will score very well on your Commercial Pilot certificate test.

Begin your studies with a classroom or home-study ground school course, which will involve reading a comprehensive textbook. Visit the Reader Resources for this Test Prep (**asa2fly.com/TPC**) and become familiar with the FAA guidance materials available for this certification exam. Then use this Test Prep to prepare for your exam: read the question, select your choice for the correct answer, and then read the explanation. Use the references that conclude each explanation to identify additional resources for further study of a subject. Upon completion of your studies, take practice tests at **prepware.com** (see inside the front cover for your activation code).

The questions in this book have been arranged into chapters based on subject matter to promote better understanding, aid recall, and provide a more efficient study guide. Place emphasis on questions most likely to be included in your test (identified by the aircraft category above each question). For example, a pilot preparing for the Commercial Airplane test would focus on the questions marked "ALL" and "AIR," and a pilot preparing for the Commercial Helicopter test would focus on the questions marked "ALL" and "RTC."

Prior to taking an FAA Airman Knowledge Test, all applicants must establish an FAA Tracking Number (FTN) by creating a profile in the Integrated Airman Certification and Rating Application (IACRA) system at **iacra.faa.gov**. Then visit **faa.psiexams.com** to register for your exam and take FAA-created practice tests to become familiar with the computer testing platform.

It is important to answer every question assigned on your FAA Knowledge Test. If in their ongoing review, the FAA decides a question has no correct answer, is no longer applicable, or is otherwise defective, your answer will be marked correct no matter which one you chose. However, you will not be given the automatic credit if you have not marked an answer. Unlike some other exams you may have taken, there is no penalty for guessing in this instance.

The FAA exams are "closed tests" which means the exact database of questions is not available to the public. The question and answer choices in this book are based on our extensive history and experience with the FAA testing and airman certification process. You might see similarly worded questions on your official FAA exam, or answer stems might be rearranged from the order you see in this book. Therefore, be sure to fully understand the intent of each question and corresponding answer while studying, rather than memorizing the letter associated with the correct response. You may be asked a question that has unfamiliar wording; studying and understanding the information in this book and the associated references will give you the tools to answer question variations with confidence.

If your study leads you to question an answer choice, we recommend you seek the assistance of a local instructor. We welcome your questions, recommendations, and concerns—send them to:

Aviation Supplies & Academics, Inc.
7005 132nd Place SE
Newcastle, WA 98059-3153
Voice: 425.235.1500   Fax: 425.235.0128
Email: cfi@asa2fly.com   Website: asa2fly.com

The FAA appreciates testing experience feedback. You can contact them at:

Federal Aviation Administration
AFS-630, Airman Testing Standards Branch
PO Box 25082
Oklahoma City, OK 73125
Email: afs630comments@faa.gov

Description of the Tests

The FAA Knowledge Exam is an objective, multiple choice test. Each question can be answered by one of the three choices. Each test question is independent of the others—a correct response to one question does not depend on the correct response to another. You must score at least 70 percent to pass the test.

As stated in 14 CFR §61.63, an applicant need not take an additional knowledge test provided the applicant holds an airplane, rotorcraft, powered-lift, or airship rating at that pilot certificate level. For example, an applicant transitioning from gliders to airplanes will need to take the 100-question test. But an applicant transitioning from airplanes to gliders, or airplanes to helicopters, will *not* be required to take the Knowledge Exam.

Military applicants should refer to the *Commercial Pilot – Military Competence Airman Certification Standards* (FAA-S-ACS-12) for information on the expected knowledge in preparation for the Military Competence Knowledge Exam. Additionally, applicants should review §61.73. Military pilots or former military pilots: Special rules, which provides information to military pilots who are interested in acquiring their civilian pilot certificate.

The table below lists the number of questions and the allotted time for each test. Each question in this book is preceded by a category. Use these categories to study the content that may appear on your test. Study all the questions first, then refer to the following table, placing emphasis on those questions most likely to be included on your test (identified by the test prep category above each question number).

Test Code	Test Name	Test Prep Study	Number of Questions	Min. Age	Allotted Time (hrs)
CAX	Commercial Pilot—Airplane	ALL, AIR	100	16	3.0
CRH	Commercial Pilot—Helicopter	ALL, RTC	100	16	3.0
CRG	Commercial Pilot—Gyroplane	ALL, RTC	100	16	3.0
CGX	Commercial Pilot—Glider	ALL, GLI	100	16	3.0
CBH	Commercial Pilot—Balloon–Hot Air	ALL, LTA	100	16	3.0
CLA	Commercial Pilot—Airship	ALL, LTA	100	16	3.0
CBG	Commercial Pilot—Balloon–Gas	ALL, LTA	60	16	2.5
MCN	Military Competency—Non-Category	MIL	50	18	2.0
CCP	Commercial Pilot—Airplane Canadian Conversion*	ALL, AIR	40	18	2.0
CCH	Commercial Pilot—Helicopter Canadian Conversion*	ALL, RTC	40	18	2.0

* This test focuses on U.S. regulations, procedures, and operations.

Knowledge Test Registration

The FAA testing providier authorizes hundreds of test center locations that offer a full range of airman knowledge tests. For information on authorized testing centers and to register for the knowledge test, visit **faa.psiexams.com**.

When you contact a knowledge testing center, be prepared to select a test date and make payment. You may register for test(s) several weeks in advance online or by phone, and you may cancel in accordance with the testing center's cancellation policy.

Regardless of your registration method, you will need an FAA Tracking Number (FTN) prior to registering for the FAA Airman Knowledge Test. This FTN will follow you throughout your aviation career. You will obtain your FTN as part of the test registration process, by creating a profile in the Integrated Airman Certificate and Rating Application (IACRA) system at iacra.faa.gov/IACRA. This FTN will be printed on your Airman Knowledge Test Report (AKTR).

The test registration process includes collection of this information: name, FTN, physical address, date of birth, email address, photo identification, phone number, test authorization (credentials of the individual such as an instructor endorsement), and previous number of test attempts.

Step 1: Create a profile using the IACRA system and login to obtain your FTN.
Step 2: Register for your knowledge test with PSI by phone or online.

For more information, contact:
PSI Services LLC
844-704-1487 or examschedule@psionline.com
faa.psiexams.com

Knowledge Test Eligibility

All Commercial Pilot Tests

You will be required to show proper identification and the following:

1. Certificate of graduation or a statement of accomplishment certifying the satisfactory completion of the ground school portion of a course for the certificate or rating sought. The certificate or statement may be issued by a Federal Aviation Administration certified pilot school or an agency such as a high school, college, adult education program, Civil Air Patrol, or Reserve Officers Training Corp (ROTC) flight training school.

2. Written statement or logbook endorsement from an authorized ground or flight instructor certifying that the applicant completed an applicable ground training or home study course and is prepared for the knowledge test.

Ground schools will issue an endorsement when you complete their course. If you choose to home-study, you can either get an endorsement from your instructor or submit your home-study materials to an FAA Office for review and approval prior to taking the test.

Complete two Prepware practice tests with scores of 80% or higher to get your knowledge test endorsement for any pilot rating directly from ASA. Visit **asa2fly.com/prepware** or **prepware.com** for more details.

If a flight or ground instructor is providing your endorsement, you may use the following template:

Commercial Pilot Endorsement

I certify that *(First name, MI, Last name)* _____ has received the required training of 14 CFR §61.125. I have determined he/she is prepared for the *(Test name; e.g., Commercial Pilot – Airplane)* _____ knowledge test.

Signed _____ Date _____

CFI Number _____ Expires _____

Military Competency Tests

Requires *no* instructor endorsements or other form of written authorization.

Acceptable Materials

The applicant may use test aids and materials within the guidelines listed below during the test, if actual test questions or answers are not revealed.

Acceptable Materials	Unacceptable Materials	Notes
Supplement book provided by proctor.	Written materials that are handwritten, printed, or electronic.	Testing centers may provide calculators and/or deny the use of personal calculators.
All models of aviation-oriented calculators or small electronic calculators that perform only arithmetic functions.	Electronic calculators incorporating permanent or continuous type memory circuits without erasure capability.	Test proctor may prohibit the use of your calculator if he or she is unable to determine the calculator's erasure capability.
Calculators with simple programmable memories, which allow addition to, subtraction from, or retrieval of one number from the memory; or simple functions, such as square root and percentages.	Magnetic cards, magnetic tapes, modules, computer chips, or any other device upon which pre-written programs or information related to the test can be stored and retrieved.	Printouts of data must be surrendered at the completion of the test if the calculator incorporates this design feature.
Scales, straight-edges, protractors, plotters, navigation computers, blank log sheets, holding pattern entry aids, and electronic or mechanical calculators that are directly related to the test.	Dictionaries.	Before, and upon completion of the test, while in the presence of the test proctor, actuate the ON/OFF switch or RESET button, and perform any other function that ensures erasure of any data stored in memory circuits.
Manufacturer's permanently inscribed instructions on the front and back of such aids, such as formulas, conversions, regulations, signals, weather data, holding pattern diagrams, frequencies, weight and balance formulas, and ATC procedures.	Any booklet or manual containing instructions related to use of test aids.	Test proctor makes the final determination regarding aids, reference materials, and test materials.

Testing Procedures for Applicants Requesting Special Accommodations

If you are an applicant with a learning or reading disability, you may request approval from the local FAA office to take an airman knowledge test, using the special accommodations procedures outlined in the most current version of FAA Order 8080.6 Conduct of Airman Knowledge Tests.

Prior to approval of any option, the FAA Aviation Safety Inspector must advise you of the regulatory certification requirement of being able to read, write, speak, and understand the English language.

Test Reports

Your test will be graded immediately upon completion and your score will display on the computer screen. You will receive your Airman Knowledge Test Report (AKTR), which will state your score. See sample AKTR on the next page.

Visit **faa.psiexams.com** to request a duplicate or replacement AKTR due to loss or destruction.

Airman Knowledge Test Reports are valid for 24 calendar months preceding the month you complete the practical test. If the AKTR expires before completion of the practical test, you must retake the knowledge test.

The AKTR lists the Airman Certification Standard (ACS) code (if an Airman Certification Standard is available for the certificate and rating specific to the test) or Learning Statement Code (LSC) (if a Practical Test Standard is in effect for the certificate and rating specific to the test) for questions answered incorrectly. The total number of ASCs/LSCs shown on the AKTR is not necessarily an indication of the total number of questions answered incorrectly. Study these knowledge areas to improve your understanding of the subject matter. See Cross-Reference B in the back of this book for a listing of ASCs/LSCs and their associated questions.

Your instructor is required to provide instruction on each of the knowledge areas listed on your AKTR and to complete an endorsement of this instruction. You must present this to the examiner prior to taking the practical test. During the oral portion of the practical test, the examiner is required to evaluate the noted areas of deficiency.

Retesting Procedures

Applicants retesting *after failure* are required to submit the applicable AKTR indicating failure, along with an endorsement (on the test report) from an authorized instructor, who gave the applicant the additional training, certifying the applicant is competent to pass the test. The original failed AKTR and retest endorsement presented as authorization shall be retained by the proctor and attached to the applicable sign-in/out log. The latest test taken will reflect the official score.

Applicants retesting *in an attempt to achieve a higher passing score* may retake the same test for a better grade after 30 days. The latest test taken will reflect the official score. Applicants are required to submit the original applicable AKTR indicating previous passing score to the testing center prior to testing. Testing center personnel must collect and destroy this report prior to issuing the new test report.

Cheating or Other Unauthorized Conduct

Computer testing centers must follow strict security procedures to avoid test compromise. These procedures are established by the FAA and are covered in FAA Order 8080.6 Conduct of Airman Knowledge Tests. The FAA has directed testing centers to terminate a test at any time a test proctor suspects a cheating incident has occurred. An FAA investigation will then be conducted. If the investigation determines that cheating or unauthorized conduct has occurred, then any airman certificate or rating that you hold may be revoked, and you will be prohibited for one year from applying for or taking any test for a certificate or rating under 14 CFR Part 61.

U.S. DEPARTMENT OF TRANSPORTATION
Federal Aviation Administration
Airman Knowledge Test Report

NAME: TAYLOR SMITH

FAA TRACKING NUMBER (FTN): C1234567   **EXAM ID:** 98765432109876543

EXAM: Commercial Pilot – Airplane (CAX)

EXAM DATE: 09/15/2022   **EXAM SITE:** ABC12345

SCORE: 88%   **GRADE:** Pass   **TAKE:** 1

The Airman Certification Standards (ACS) codes listed below represent incorrectly answered questions. These ACS codes and their associated Areas of Operation/Tasks/Elements may be found in the appropriate ACS document at http://www.faa.gov/training_testing/testing/acs.

A single code may represent more than one incorrect response.

CA.I.F.K3   CA.I.G.R1   CA.III.A.K8   CA.IV.A.R2d   CA.V.A.K2e   CA.VII.B.K1   CA.IX.D.K3c

EXPIRATION DATE: 09/30/2024

DO NOT LOSE THIS REPORT

AUTHORIZED INSTRUCTOR'S STATEMENT: (if applicable)

On _____ (date) I gave the above named applicant _____ hours of additional instruction, covering each subject area shown to be deficient, and consider the applicant competent to pass the knowledge test.

Name _____

Cert. No. _____ *(print clearly)*

Type of instructor certificate _____

Signature _____

FRAUDULENT ALTERATION OF THIS FORM BY ANY PERSON IS A BASIS FOR SUSPENSION OR REVOCATION OF ANY CERTIFICATES OR RATINGS HELD BY THAT PERSON.
ISSUED BY: PSI Services LLC
FEDERAL AVIATION ADMINISTRATION

THIS INFORMATION IS PROTECTED BY THE PRIVACY ACT. FOR OFFICIAL USE ONLY.

Sample Airman Knowledge Test Report

Test-Taking Tips

Prior to launching the actual test, the test proctor's testing software will provide you with an opportunity to practice navigating through the test. This practice (or tutorial) session may include a "sample" question(s). These sample questions have no relation to the content of the test, but are meant to familiarize you with the look and feel of the system screens, including selecting an answer, marking a question for later review, time remaining for the test, and other features of the testing software.

Follow these time-proven tips, which will help you develop a skillful, smooth approach to test-taking:

- Visit **faa.psiexams.com** to take a small sample test to become familiar with the latest PSI exam interface you will see on your actual FAA knowledge test.
- Be careful to fully understand the intent of each question and corresponding answer while studying, rather than memorize the A, B, C answer choice—answer stems may appear in a different order than you studied and have some wording differences.
- Take with you to the testing center a sign-off from an instructor (except for military competency test candidates), photo I.D., the testing fee, calculator, flight computer (ASA's E6-B or CX-3 Flight Computer), plotter, magnifying glass, and a sharp pointer, such as a safety pin.
- Your first action when you sit down should be to write on the scratch paper the weight and balance and any other formulas and information you can remember from your study. Remember, some of the formulas may be on your E6-B.
- Answer each question in accordance with the latest regulations and guidance publications.
- Read each question carefully before looking at the possible answers. You should clearly understand the problem before attempting to solve it.
- After formulating an answer, determine which answer choice corresponds the closest with your answer. The answer chosen should completely resolve the problem.
- From the answer choices given, it may appear that there is more than one possible answer. However, there is only one answer that is correct and complete. The other answers are either incomplete, erroneous, or represent popular misconceptions.
- Answer each question in accordance with the latest regulations and guidance publications.
- If a certain question is difficult for you, it is best to mark it for REVIEW and proceed to the other questions. After you answer the less difficult questions, return to those which you marked for review and answer them. The review marking procedure will be explained to you prior to starting the test. Although the computer should alert you to unanswered questions, make sure every question has an answer recorded. This procedure will enable you to use the available time to the maximum advantage.
- Perform each math calculation twice to confirm your answer. If adding or subtracting a column of numbers, reverse your direction the second time to reduce the possibility of error.
- When solving a calculation problem, select the answer nearest to your solution. The problem has been checked with various types of calculators; therefore, if you have solved it correctly, your answer will be closer to the correct answer than any of the other choices.
- Remember that information is provided in the Legends and Figures contained within the Airman Knowledge Testing Supplement (FAA-CT-8080 document) you'll be using during the test.
- Remember to answer every question, even the ones with no completely correct answer, to ensure the FAA gives you credit for a bad question.
- Take your time and be thorough but relaxed. Take a minute off every half-hour or so to relax the brain and the body. Get a drink of water halfway through the test.
- Your test will be graded immediately upon completion.

Commercial Pilot Certificate Eligibility Requirements

The general prerequisites for a Commercial Pilot Certificate require that the applicant have a combination of experience, knowledge, risk management, and skill. For specific information pertaining to certification, an applicant should carefully review the appropriate sections of Part 61 for Commercial Pilot Certification, including 14 CFR §61.23 "Medical Certificates: Requirement and Duration," and §61.35, "Knowledge Test: Prerequisites and Passing Grades."

Additionally, to be eligible for a Commercial Pilot Certificate, applicants must:

- Be at least 18 years of age (16 to take the knowledge test).
- Be able to read, speak, write, and understand English or have a limitation placed on the certificate.
- Hold a current medical certificate issued under Part 67. No medical certificate is required for a glider or balloon rating.
- Pass a knowledge test appropriate to the aircraft rating sought on the subjects in which ground instruction is required. Applicants for a knowledge test must show evidence of completing ground training or a home study course and be prepared for the knowledge test.
- Pass an oral and flight test appropriate to the rating they seek, covering items selected by the inspector or examiner from those on which training is required.
- Hold at least a Private Pilot Certificate.
- Comply with the provisions of Part 61 which apply to the rating they seek.

Knowledge Exam References

The FAA references the following documents to write the FAA Knowledge Exam questions. You should be familiar with all of these as part of your ground school studies, which you should complete before starting test preparation.

FAA-H-8083-1 *Aircraft Weight and Balance Handbook*
FAA-H-8083-3 *Airplane Flying Handbook*
FAA-H-8083-13 *Glider Flying Handbook*
FAA-H-8083-21 *Helicopter Flying Handbook*
FAA-H-8083-25 *Pilot's Handbook of Aeronautical Knowledge*
FAA-H-8083-15 *Instrument Flying Handbook*
FAA-H-8083-11 *Balloon Flying Handbook*
(Note: LTA applicants should also review FAA-H-8083-9 *Aviation Instructor's Handbook, How to Fly a Balloon, Balloon Digest, Balloon Ground School, Powerline Excerpts*, and *Goodyear Airship Operations Manual*)

FAA-S-ACS-7 *Commercial Pilot Airplane Airman Certification Standards*
FAA-S-ACS-12 *Commercial Pilot Military Competence Airman Certification Standards*
FAA-S-8081-16 *Commercial Pilot Helicopter Practical Test Standards*

AC 00-6 *Aviation Weather*
AC 00-30 *Atmospheric Turbulence Avoidance*
AC 00-45 *Aviation Weather Services*
AC 60-22 *Aeronautical Decision Making*
AC 90-48 *Pilot's Role in Collision Avoidance*
AC 91-13 *Cold Weather Operation of Aircraft*
AC 91-51 *Effect of Icing on Aircraft Control and Airplane Deice and Anti-Ice Systems*

Chart Supplement U.S.
Sectional Aeronautical Chart (SAC)
U.S. Terminal Procedures

Aeronautical Information Manual (AIM)
14 CFR Part 1, 23, 29, 39, 43, 61, 68, 71, 73, 91, 117, 119
49 CFR Part 830 (NTSB)

Visit **asa2fly.com** for these and many more titles and pilot supplies for your aviation endeavors.
Visit **asa2fly.com/TPC** for reader resources useful to commercial pilots.

Acronyms

For reference, acronyms appearing in this book are defined below.

AC	Convective Outlook	IFR	instrument flight rules
AD	Airworthiness Directive	IR	Instrument Route (MTR)
ADC	air data computer	KIAS	knots indicated airspeed
ADM	aeronautical decision making	L/D	lift-to-drag ratio
ADS-B	Automatic Dependent Surveillance–Broadcast	LAHSO	land and hold short operation
		LLWAS	Low-Level Wind Shear Alert System
AGL	above ground level	LOA	Letter of Agreement
AGL	above ground level	LOC	localizer (ILS)
AIRMET	airman's meteorological information	LTA	lighter than air
AME	aviation medical examiner	LTE	loss of tail rotor effectiveness
ARTCC	air traffic control center	MAP	manifold pressure
ATC	air traffic control	MEF	maximum elevation figure
ATIS	Automatic Terminal Information Service	METAR	aviation routine weather report
AWC	aviation weather center	MOA	Memorandum of Agreement
AWOS	Automated Surface Weather Observing System	MOA	Military Operation Area
		MSL	mean sea level
AWW	Severe Weather Forecast Alert	MTR	Military Training Route
BHP	brake horsepower	NM	nautical mile
BTU	British thermal unit	NMAC	near midair collision
CAMI	Civil Aeromedical Institute	NOTAM	Notice to Air Missions
CAT	clear air turbulence	NTSB	National Transportation Safety Board
CDI	course deviation indicator	OAT	outside air temperature
CG	center of gravity	OBS	omni bearing selector
CL	center of lift	PA	pressure altitude
CONUS	continental/contiguous United States	PATWAS	pilots' automatic telephone weather answering service
CWA	Center Weather Advisory	PFD	primary flight display
ELT	emergency locator transmitter	PIC	pilot-in-command
FA	area forecast	PIREP	pilot report
FAR	Federal Aviation Regulation	PT	procedure turn
FB	winds and temperatures aloft forecast	RAIM	receiver autonomous integrity monitoring
FL	flight level	SIC	second-in-command
FSDO	Flight Standards District Office	SIGMET	significant meteorological information
FSS	Flight Service Station	SM	statute mile
GFA	Graphical Forecasts for Aviation	TAF	terminal aerodrome forecast
GMT	Greenwich Mean Time	TAS	true airspeed
GPH	gallons per hour	TC	true course
GPS	Global Positioning System	TH	true heading
HIS	horizontal situation indicator		

TI	thermal index
TIBS	Telephone Information Briefing Service
TIS-B	Traffic Information Service–Broadcast
UAT	Universal Access Transceiver
VFR	visual flight rules
VOR	VHF Omnidirectional Range
VOT	VOR Test Facility
VR	Visual Route (MTR)
WCA	wind correction angle
WSFO	Weather Service Forecast Office

ASA Test Prep Layout

Sample FAA questions have been sorted into chapters according to subject matter. Within each chapter, similar questions are grouped together following introductory chapter text. Figures referenced in the chapter text are numbered with the appropriate chapter number, e.g., "Figure 1-1" is Chapter 1's first chapter text figure.

Some sample FAA questions refer to Figures or Legends immediately following the question number, e.g., "5201. (Refer to Figure 14.)." These are FAA Figures and Legends from the Airman Knowledge Testing Supplement (FAA-CT-8080-1E) that can be found at the back of this book. This supplement will be provided to you as a separate booklet when you take your FAA test.

Following each sample FAA test question is ASA's explanation in italics. The last line of the explanation contains a Learning Statement Code (LSC), for those tests referencing an FAA Practical Test Standard (PTS), or Airman Certification Standards (ACS) code, for those tests with an ACS, as well as a reference for further study. Some questions include an explanation for the incorrect answers for added clarity. When you encounter a difficult question, find the LSC or ACS code in Cross-Reference B, and then look for material relating to the subject description within the given reference(s). Refer to Cross-Reference B for more information on how to use LSCs or ACS codes for effective studying.

Answers to each question are found at the bottom of each page.

EXAMPLE:

Chapter text →

Four aerodynamic forces are considered to be basic because they act upon an aircraft during all flight maneuvers. There is the downward-acting force called WEIGHT which must be overcome by the upward-acting force called LIFT, and there is the rearward-acting force called DRAG, which must be overcome by the forward-acting force called THRUST.

Category rating. This question may be found on tests for these ratings.*

ALL, AIR, RTC, GLI, LTA, MIL

5201. (Refer to Figure 14.) The four forces acting on an airplane in flight are

See the Airman Knowledge Testing Supplement at the back of the book.

A— lift, weight, thrust, and drag.
B— lift, weight, gravity, and thrust.
C— lift, gravity, power, and friction.

Question and answer choices

Lift, weight, thrust, and drag are the four basic aerodynamic forces acting on an aircraft in flight. (PLT235, IR.IV.A.K1) — FAA-H-8083-25

Explanation

Code line. FAA LSC and ACS codes in parentheses, followed by references for further study.

Answer (B) is incorrect because the force of gravity is always the same number and reacts with the airplane's mass to produce a different weight for almost every airplane. Answer (C) is incorrect because weight is the final product of gravity, thrust is the final product of power, and drag is the final product of friction. Power, gravity, and friction are only parts of the aerodynamic forces of flight.

Incorrect answer explanation. Reasons why answer choices are *incorrect* explained here.

*****Note:** The FAA does *not* identify which questions are on the different ratings' tests. Unless the wording of a question is pertinent to only one rating category, it may be found on *any* of the tests.

ALL = All aircraft **AIR** = Airplane **GLI** = Glider **LTA** = Lighter-than-air (applies to hot air balloon, gas balloon and airship)
RTC = Rotorcraft (applies to both helicopter and gyroplane) **MIL** = Military Competency

Commercial Pilot Test Prep ASA xvii

Chapter 1
Basic Aerodynamics

Aerodynamic Terms   *1–3*

Axes of Rotation and the Four Forces Acting in Flight   *1–5*

   Lift   *1–6*

   Weight   *1–7*

   Thrust   *1–7*

   Drag   *1–7*

Lift/Drag Ratios   *1–11*

The V_G Diagram   *1–13*

Stability   *1–14*

Turns, Loads, and Load Factors   *1–16*

Stalls and Spins   *1–23*

Flaps   *1–24*

Wing Shapes   *1–25*

Torque   *1–26*

Ground Effect   *1–27*

Wake Turbulence   *1–28*

Glider Aerodynamics   *1–30*

Aerodynamic Terms

An airfoil is a structure of body which produces a useful reaction to air movement. Airplane wings, helicopter rotor blades, and propellers are airfoils. See Figure 1-1.

The chord line is a straight reference line from the leading edge to the trailing edge of an airfoil. See Figure 1-2.

Changing the shape of an airfoil (by lowering flaps, for example) will change the chord line. See Figure 1-3.

In aerodynamics, relative wind is the wind felt by an airfoil. It is created by the movement of air past an airfoil, by the motion of an airfoil through the air, or by a combination of the two. Relative wind is parallel to and in the opposite direction of the flight path of the airfoil. See Figure 1-4.

Figure 1-1. A typical airfoil cross-section

Figure 1-2. Chord line

Figure 1-3. Changing shape of wing changes the chord line

Figure 1-4. Relative wind

Chapter 1 **Basic Aerodynamics**

The angle of attack is the angle between the chord line of the airfoil and the relative wind. The pilot can vary the angle of attack by manipulating aircraft controls. See Figure 1-5. When the angle of attack of a symmetrical airfoil is increased, the center of pressure movement is very limited.

The angle of incidence is the angle between the wing chord line and the center line of the fuselage. The pilot has no control over the angle of incidence. See Figure 1-6.

Figure 1-5. Angle of attack

Figure 1-6. Angle of incidence

AIR, GLI

5198. By changing the angle of attack of a wing, the pilot can control the airplane's

A—lift, airspeed, and drag.
B—lift, airspeed, and CG.
C—lift and airspeed, but not drag.

By changing the angle of attack, the pilot can control lift, airspeed, and drag. (PLT168, CA.I.F.K3) — FAA-H-8083-25

Answer (B) is incorrect because the angle of attack does not affect the CG. Answer (C) is incorrect because the angle of attack also determines drag.

ALL

5198-1. An aircraft airfoil is designed to produce lift resulting from a difference in the

A—negative air pressure below and a vacuum above the airfoil's surface.
B—vacuum below the airfoil's surface and greater air pressure above the airfoil's surface.
C—higher air pressure below the airfoil's surface and lower air pressure above the airfoil's surface.

The highest velocity is at the top of the airfoil with the lowest velocity at the bottom. Because there is a difference of velocity above and below the wing, the result is a higher pressure at the bottom of the wing and a lower pressure on the top of the wing. This low-pressure area produces an upward force known as the Magnus Effect, the physical phenomenon whereby an object's rotation affects its path through a fluid, including air. (PLT242, CA.I.F.K3) — FAA-H-8083-25

Answers

5198 [A]   5198-1 [C]

AIR, GLI
5199. The angle of attack of a wing directly controls the

A—angle of incidence of the wing.
B—amount of airflow above and below the wing.
C—distribution of pressures acting on the wing.

The angle of attack of an airfoil directly controls the distribution of pressure below and above it. By changing the angle of attack, the pilot can control lift, airspeed, and drag. (PLT168, CA.I.F.K3) — FAA-H-8083-25

Answer (A) is incorrect because the angle of incidence is a fixed angle between the chordline of the aircraft and the aircraft's longitudinal axis. Answer (B) is incorrect because the amount of airflow above and below the wing stays constant.

RTC
5239. When the angle of attack of a symmetrical airfoil is increased, the center of pressure will

A—have very limited movement.
B—move aft along the airfoil surface.
C—remain unaffected.

On a symmetrical airfoil, center of pressure movement is very limited. (PLT236) — FAA-H-8083-21

Axes of Rotation and the Four Forces Acting in Flight

An airplane has three axes of rotation: lateral, longitudinal, and vertical. See Figure 1-7.

The lateral axis is an imaginary line from wing tip to wing tip. The rotation about this axis is called pitch. Pitch is controlled by the elevators, and this type of rotation is referred to as longitudinal control or longitudinal stability. See Figure 1-8.

The longitudinal axis is an imaginary line from the nose to the tail. Rotation about the longitudinal axis is called roll. Roll is controlled by the ailerons, and this type of rotation is referred to as lateral control, or lateral stability. See Figure 1-9.

The vertical axis is an imaginary line extending vertically through the intersection of the lateral and longitudinal axes. Rotation about the vertical axis is called yaw. Yaw is controlled by the rudder, and this type of rotation is referred to as directional control or directional stability. See Figure 1-10.

Figure 1-7. Axes of rotation

Figure 1-8. Effect of elevators

Answers
5199 [C]   5239 [A]

Chapter 1 **Basic Aerodynamics**

Figure 1-9. Effect of ailerons

Figure 1-10. Effect of rudder

The center of gravity (CG) is the point at which an airplane would balance if suspended from that point. The three axes intersect at the center of gravity. Movement of the center of gravity can affect the stability of the airplane.

Four aerodynamic forces are considered basic because they act upon an aircraft during all flight maneuvers. The downward-acting force called weight is counteracted by the upward-acting force called lift. The rearward-acting force called drag is counteracted by the forward-acting force called thrust. See Figure 1-11.

Figure 1-11. Relationship of forces in flight

Lift

Air is a gas that can be compressed or expanded. When compressed, more air can occupy a given volume and air density is increased. When allowed to expand, air occupies a greater space and density is decreased. Temperature, atmospheric pressure, and humidity all affect air density. Air density has significant effects on an aircraft's performance.

As the velocity of a fluid (gas or liquid) increases, its pressure decreases. This is known as Bernoulli's principle. See Figure 1-12.

Lift is the result of a pressure difference between the top and the bottom of the wing. A wing is designed to accelerate air over the top camber of the wing, thereby decreasing the pressure on the top and producing lift. See Figure 1-13.

Several factors are involved in the creation of lift: angle of attack, wing area and shape (planform), air velocity, and air density. All of these factors have an effect on the amount of lift produced at any given moment. The pilot can actively control the angle of attack and the airspeed, and increasing either of these will result in an increase in lift.

Figure 1-12. Flow of air through a constriction

Figure 1-13. Development of lift

Weight
Weight is the force with which gravity attracts all bodies (masses) vertically toward the center of the Earth.

Thrust
Thrust is the forward force produced by the propeller acting as an airfoil to displace a large mass of air rearward.

Drag
Drag, the force acting parallel to the flight path, resists the forward movement of an airplane through the air. Drag may be classified into two main types: parasite drag and induced drag.

Parasite drag is the resistance of the air produced by any part of an airplane that does not produce lift (antennae, landing gear, etc.). Parasite drag will increase as airspeed increases. If the airspeed of an airplane is doubled, parasite drag will be quadrupled.

Induced drag is a by-product of lift. In other words, this drag is generated as the wing develops lift. The high-pressure air beneath the wing trying to flow around and over the wing tips into the area of low pressure causes a vortex behind the wing tip. This vortex causes a spanwise flow and creates vortices along the trailing edge of the wing. As angle of attack is increased (up to the critical angle), lift will increase and so will the vortices and downwash. This downwash redirects the lift vector rearward, causing a rearward component of lift (induced drag). Induced drag will increase as airspeed decreases. See Figure 1-14.

During unaccelerated (straight-and-level) flight, the four aerodynamic forces which act on an airplane are said to be in equilibrium, or: lift = weight, and thrust = drag.

Figure 1-14. Drag curve diagram

Chapter 1 Basic Aerodynamics

AIR

5200. In theory, if the angle of attack and other factors remain constant and the airspeed is doubled, the lift produced at the higher speed will be

A—the same as at the lower speed.
B—two times greater than at the lower speed.
C—four times greater than at the lower speed.

Lift is proportional to the square of the airplane's velocity. For example, an airplane traveling at 200 knots has four times the lift as the same airplane traveling at 100 knots, if the angle of attack and other factors remain constant. (PLT168, CA.I.F.K3) — FAA-H-8083-25

Answers (A) and (B) are incorrect because as airspeed doubles, lift will be four times greater than at the lower speed.

AIR

5203. Which statement is true, regarding the opposing forces acting on an airplane in steady-state level flight?

A—These forces are equal.
B—Thrust is greater than drag and weight and lift are equal.
C—Thrust is greater than drag and lift is greater than weight.

During straight-and-level flight at constant airspeed, thrust and drag are equal and lift and weight are equal. (PLT246, CA.I.F.K3) — FAA-H-8083-25

AIR

5223. To generate the same amount of lift as altitude is increased, an airplane must be flown at

A—the same true airspeed regardless of angle of attack.
B—a lower true airspeed and a greater angle of attack.
C—a higher true airspeed for any given angle of attack.

In order to maintain its lift at a higher altitude, an airplane must fly at a greater true airspeed for any given angle of attack. (PLT242, CA.I.F.K3) — FAA-H-8083-25

Answers (A) and (B) are incorrect because true airspeed must be increased as altitude increases to generate the same amount of lift.

AIR

5229. What changes in airplane longitudinal control must be made to maintain altitude while the airspeed is being decreased?

A—Increase the angle of attack to produce more lift than drag.
B—Increase the angle of attack to compensate for the decreasing lift.
C—Decrease the angle of attack to compensate for the increasing drag.

As the airplane slows down, the decreasing airspeed or velocity requires increasing the angle of attack to produce the constant lift needed to maintain altitude. (PLT237, CA.I.F.K3) — FAA-H-8083-25

Answer (A) is incorrect because if you are generating more lift than drag, an increase in the angle of attack will cause the airplane to climb. Answer (C) is incorrect because the angle of attack must be increased in order to maintain altitude, if airspeed is being decreased.

AIR

5161. In theory, if the airspeed of an airplane is doubled while in level flight, parasite drag will become

A—twice as great.
B—half as great.
C—four times greater.

Parasite drag has more influence at high speed, and induced drag has more influence at low speed. For example, if an airplane in a steady flight condition at 100 knots is then accelerated to 200 knots, the parasite drag becomes four times as great. (PLT237, CA.I.F.K3) — FAA-H-8083-25

AIR

5161-1. In theory, if the airspeed of an aircraft in level flight is cut in half, parasite drag will become

A—one-third as much.
B—one-half as much.
C—one-fourth as much.

Parasite drag increases as the square of the airspeed. (PLT237, CA.I.F.K3) — FAA-H-8083-25

Answers

5200 [C]   5203 [A]   5223 [C]   5229 [B]   5161 [C]   5161-1 [C]

AIR

5162. As airspeed decreases in level flight below that speed for maximum lift/drag ratio, total drag of an airplane

A—decreases because of lower parasite drag.
B—increases because of increased induced drag.
C—increases because of increased parasite drag.

Parasite drag is greatest at higher airspeeds. Induced drag is the by-product of lift and becomes a greater influence at higher angles of attack and slower airspeeds. It increases in direct proportion to increases in the angle of attack. Any angle of attack lower or higher than that for L/D$_{MAX}$ reduces the lift-drag ratio and consequently increases the total drag. (PLT237, CA.I.F.K3) — FAA-H-8083-25

Answer (A) is incorrect because total drag increases when airspeed decreases below L/D$_{MAX}$ due to increased induced drag. Answer (C) is incorrect because parasite drag decreases with speeds below L/D$_{MAX}$.

AIR

5220. When transitioning from straight-and-level flight to a constant airspeed climb, the angle of attack and lift

A—are increased and remain at a higher lift-to-weight ratio to maintain the climb.
B—remain the same and maintain a steady state lift-to-weight ratio during the climb.
C—are momentarily increased and lift returns to a steady state during the climb.

When transitioning from level flight to a climb, the forces acting on the airplane go through certain changes. The first change, an increase in lift, occurs when back pressure is applied to the elevator control. This initial change is a result of the increase in the angle of attack which occurs when the airplane's pitch attitude is raised. This results in a climbing attitude. When the inclined flight path and the climb speed are established, the angle of attack and the corresponding lift stabilize at approximately the original value. (PLT168, CA.I.F.K3) — FAA-H-8083-25

AIR

5220-1. To hold an airplane in level flight at airspeeds from very slow to very fast, a pilot must coordinate thrust and

A—angle of incidence.
B—gross weight.
C—angle of attack.

Straight-and-level flight may be sustained at a wide range of speeds. The pilot coordinates angle of attack and thrust in all speed regimes if the aircraft is to be held in level flight. (PLT168, CA.I.F.K3) — FAA-H-8083-25

AIR, GLI

5158. Lift on a wing is most properly defined as the

A—force acting perpendicular to the relative wind.
B—differential pressure acting perpendicular to the chord of the wing.
C—reduced pressure resulting from a laminar flow over the upper camber of an airfoil, which acts perpendicular to the mean camber.

Lift opposes the downward force of weight. It is produced by the dynamic effect of the air acting on the wing, and acts perpendicular to the flight path (relative wind) through the wing's center of lift. (PLT242, CA.I.F.K3) — FAA-H-8083-25

AIR, GLI

5201. An aircraft wing is designed to produce lift resulting from a difference in the

A—negative air pressure below and a vacuum above the wing's surface.
B—vacuum below the wing's surface and greater air pressure above the wing's surface.
C—higher air pressure below the wing's surface and lower air pressure above the wing's surface.

The wing is designed to provide actions greater than its weight by shaping it to develop a relatively positive (high)-pressure lifting action from the air mass below the wing and a negative (low)-pressure lifting action from lowered pressure above the wing. The increased speed of the air over the top of the airfoil produces the drop in pressure. The pressure difference between the upper and lower surface does not account for all the lift produced. Air also strikes the lower surface of the wing, and the reaction of this downward-backward flow results in an upward-forward force on the wing. (PLT242, CA.I.F.K3) — FAA-H-8083-25

Answers

5162 [B]   5220 [C]   5220-1 [C]   5158 [A]   5201 [C]

Chapter 1 **Basic Aerodynamics**

AIR, GLI

5219. Which is true regarding the force of lift in steady, unaccelerated flight?

A—At lower airspeeds the angle of attack must be less to generate sufficient lift to maintain altitude.
B—There is a corresponding indicated airspeed required for every angle of attack to generate sufficient lift to maintain altitude.
C—An airfoil will always stall at the same indicated airspeed; therefore, an increase in weight will require an increase in speed to generate sufficient lift to maintain altitude.

To maintain the lift and weight forces in balance, and to keep the airplane straight-and-level in a state of equilibrium, as velocity increases, angle of attack must be decreased. Conversely, as the airplane slows, the decreasing velocity requires the angle of attack be increased enough to create sufficient lift to maintain flight. Therefore, for every angle of attack, there is a corresponding indicated airspeed required to maintain altitude in steady, unaccelerated flight—all other factors being constant. (PLT242, CA.I.F.K3) — FAA-H-8083-25

Answer (A) is incorrect because to provide sufficient lift, the angle of attack must be increased as the airspeed is reduced. Answer (C) is incorrect because the angle of attack must be increased to compensate for the decreased lift.

AIR, GLI

5167. Which statement is true relative to changing angle of attack?

A—A decrease in angle of attack will increase pressure below the wing, and decrease drag.
B—An increase in angle of attack will increase drag.
C—An increase in angle of attack will decrease pressure below the wing, and increase drag.

Air striking the underside of the wing is deflected downward, producing an opposite reaction which pushes (lifts) the wing upward. To increase lift, the wing is tilted upward, increasing the angle of attack and deflecting more air downward. The larger the angle of attack, the more the lift force tilts toward the rear of the aircraft, increasing drag. (PLT168, CA.I.F.K3) — FAA-H-8083-25

AIR, GLI

5202. On a wing, the force of lift acts perpendicular to and the force of drag acts parallel to the

A—chord line.
B—flightpath.
C—longitudinal axis.

Lift acts upward and perpendicular to the relative wind. Drag acts parallel to, and in the same direction as the relative wind, which is parallel to the flightpath. (PLT242, CA.I.F.K3) — FAA-H-8083-25

Answers (A) and (C) are incorrect because there is not a fixed relationship between lift and drag with respect to the airplane's chord line or longitudinal axis.

AIR, GLI, RTC

5218. Which is true regarding the forces acting on an aircraft in a steady-state descent? The sum of all

A—upward forces is less than the sum of all downward forces.
B—rearward forces is greater than the sum of all forward forces.
C—forward forces is equal to the sum of all rearward forces.

In steady-state flight, the sum of the opposing forces is equal to zero. The sum of all upward forces equals the sum of all downward forces. The sum of all forward forces equals the sum of all backward forces. (PLT242, CA.I.F.K3) — FAA-H-8083-25

GLI

5280. Which is true regarding aerodynamic drag?

A—Induced drag is created entirely by air resistance.
B—All aerodynamic drag is created entirely by the production of lift.
C—Induced drag is a by-product of lift and is greatly affected by changes in airspeed.

When an aircraft develops lift, the upward force on the aircraft results in an equal and downward force on the air which is then set in motion, generally downward. It takes energy to do this, and the transfer of energy from the aircraft to the air implies the existence of drag on the aircraft. This lift-related part of the total drag is called induced drag. The induced drag varies inversely with the square of the velocity. (PLT241) — FAA-H-8083-13

Answer (A) is incorrect because skin friction drag (a form of parasite drag), is created by air resistance. Answer (B) is incorrect because aerodynamic drag (a form of parasite drag), is created by friction between the air and the surface over which it is flowing.

Answers

5219 [B]   5167 [B]   5202 [B]   5218 [C]   5280 [C]

Chapter 1 **Basic Aerodynamics**

Lift/Drag Ratios

The lift-to-drag (L/D) ratio is the lift required for level flight (weight) divided by the drag produced at the airspeed and angle of attack required to produce that lift. The L/D ratio for a particular angle of attack is equal to the power-off glide ratio.

Problem:

Refer to FAA Figure 3. If an airplane glides at an angle of attack of 10°, how much altitude will it lose in 1 mile?

Solution:

1. Enter the L/D chart from the bottom at a 10° angle of attack.
2. Proceed vertically upward until intersecting the L/D curve.
3. Follow the horizontal reference lines to the right to the point of intersection with the glide ratio scale. L/D at 10° angle of attack = 11.0.
4. 5,280 feet ÷ 11 = 480 foot altitude loss.

L/D_{MAX} occurs at the angle of attack that gives maximum glide performance and maximum range in a propeller driven aircraft. At an airspeed slower (or at a higher angle of attack) than needed for L/D_{MAX}, the glide distance will be reduced due to the increase in induced drag.

ALL
5505. Which maximum range factor decreases as weight decreases?

A—Altitude.
B—Airspeed.
C—Angle of attack.

The maximum range condition is obtained at maximum L/D ratio which occurs at a particular angle of attack and lift coefficient. As gross weight decreases, the airspeed for maximum L/D decreases. (PLT017, CA.I.F.K3) — FAA-H-8083-25

Answer (A) is incorrect because as weight decreases, the maximum range altitude may increase. Answer (C) is incorrect because angle of attack does not play a role in determining maximum range factor.

AIR
5165. (Refer to Figure 1.) At the airspeed represented by point A, in steady flight, the airplane will

A—have its maximum L/D ratio.
B—have its minimum L/D ratio.
C—be developing its maximum coefficient of lift.

At point A, the total drag curve is at its lowest point. When an aircraft is flown at the airspeed and angle of attack that results in the lowest total drag possible, then the resulting L/D ratio is at its maximum. (PLT017, CA.I.F.K3) — FAA-H-8083-25

Answer (B) is incorrect because the minimum L/D ratio occurs when parasite drag is very high, a result of high airspeeds. Answer (C) is incorrect because the maximum coefficient of lift occurs at slower airspeeds, which results in higher induced drag and a lower L/D ratio.

AIR
5166. (Refer to Figure 1.) At an airspeed represented by point B, in steady flight, the pilot can expect to obtain the airplane's maximum

A—endurance.
B—glide range.
C—coefficient of lift.

Point B represents the airspeed that results in the greatest L/D ratio. At this point the aircraft will have its maximum glide range. (PLT017, CA.I.F.K3) — FAA-H-8083-25

Answer (A) is incorrect since only jet aircraft will obtain maximum endurance at L/D_{MAX}. Answer (C) is incorrect because the critical angle of attack and the maximum coefficient of lift occur at the same point, where total drag is also high because of an increase in induced drag.

Answers

5505 [B]   5165 [A]   5166 [B]

Chapter 1 **Basic Aerodynamics**

AIR

5213. (Refer to Figure 3.) If an airplane glides at an angle of attack of 10°, how much altitude will it lose in 1 mile?

A—240 feet.
B—480 feet.
C—960 feet.

To find the glide ratio (L/D) at an angle of attack of 10°, move upward from the angle of attack scale to the L/D curve. Then move horizontally to the right to find the value located on the L/D scale. This gives an 11:1 glide ratio. The question only deals with glide ratio, so that is the only scale needed. With this glide ratio, the airplane will descend 1 foot of altitude for every 11 feet covered horizontally.

$$\frac{L}{D} = \frac{11}{1} = \frac{\text{horizontal distance}}{\text{vertical distance}}$$

$$\frac{11}{1} = \frac{5{,}280 \text{ feet (1 SM)}}{X}$$

$$X = 480 \text{ feet}$$

(PLT015, CA.I.F.K3) — FAA-H-8083-25

AIR

5214. (Refer to Figure 3.) How much altitude will this airplane lose in 3 miles of gliding at an angle of attack of 8°?

A—440 feet.
B—880 feet.
C—1,320 feet.

To find the glide ratio (L/D) at an angle of attack of 8°, move upward from the angle of attack scale to the L/D curve. Then move horizontally to the right to find the value located on the L/D scale. This gives a 12:1 glide ratio. The question only deals with glide ratio, so that is the only scale needed. With this glide ratio, the airplane will descend 1 foot of altitude for every 12 feet covered horizontally.

$$\frac{L}{D} = \frac{12}{1} = \frac{\text{horizontal distance}}{\text{vertical distance}}$$

$$\frac{12}{1} = \frac{5{,}280 \text{ feet (3 SM)}}{X}$$

$$X = 1{,}320 \text{ feet}$$

(PLT015, CA.I.F.K3) — FAA-H-8083-25

AIR

5217. What performance is characteristic of flight at maximum lift/drag ratio in a propeller-driven airplane? Maximum

A—gain in altitude over a given distance.
B—range and maximum distance glide.
C—coefficient of lift and minimum coefficient of drag.

Maximum range condition would occur where the proportion between speed and power required is greatest. The maximum range condition (of propeller driven airplanes) is obtained at maximum lift-drag ratio (L/D$_{MAX}$). The best angle of glide is one that allows the airplane to travel the greatest distance over the ground with the least loss of altitude. This is also the airplane's maximum L/D and is usually expressed as a ratio. This implies that the airplane should be flown at L/D$_{MAX}$ to obtain the greatest glide distance. (PLT351, CA.I.F.K3) — FAA-H-8083-25

AIR, GLI

5215. (Refer to Figure 3.) The L/D ratio at a 2° angle of attack is approximately the same as the L/D ratio for a

A—9.75° angle of attack.
B—10.5° angle of attack.
C—16.5° angle of attack.

The glide ratio (L/D) at a 2° angle of attack is about 7.6:1, which is the same glide ratio (L/D) as at a 16.5° angle of attack. (PLT015, CA.I.F.K3) — FAA-H-8083-25

Answers

5213 [B]   5214 [C]   5217 [B]   5215 [C]

The V_G Diagram

FAA Figure 5 is a V_G diagram which plots load factor against indicated airspeed and shows the pilot the limits within which the aircraft will safely handle structural loads. Point C is maneuvering speed (V_A). Any plotted combination of load factor and airspeed which falls in the shaded area may result in structural damage.

V_{NO}, the maximum speed for normal operations, is shown by the vertical line from point D to point G on the V_G diagrams, and is marked as the upper limit of the green arc on the airspeed indicator. The red line on the airspeed indicator is represented by the line from point E to point F. The line connecting points C, D, and E represents the limit load factor above which structural damage may occur.

AIR, GLI
5231. (Refer to Figure 5.) The horizontal dashed line from point C to point E represents the

A—ultimate load factor.
B—positive limit load factor.
C—airspeed range for normal operations.

C to E is the maximum positive load limit. In this case it is 3.8 Gs, which is appropriate for normal category airplanes. (PLT312, CA.I.F.K1) — FAA-H-8083-25

AIR, GLI
5232. (Refer to Figure 5.) The vertical line from point E to point F is represented on the airspeed indicator by the

A—upper limit of the yellow arc.
B—upper limit of the green arc.
C—blue radial line.

V_{NE} (never exceed airspeed), the vertical line from point E to F, is marked on airspeed indicators with a red radial line, the upper limit of the yellow arc. (PLT074, CA.I.F.K1) — FAA-H-8083-25

AIR, GLI
5979. (Refer to Figure 5.) What does the intersection of the dashed line at point C represent?

A—V_A.
B—Negative limit load factor.
C—Positive limit load factor.

Point C represents the intersection of the positive limit load factor and the line of maximum positive lift capability. The airspeed at this point is the minimum airspeed at which the limit load can be developed aerodynamically. Any airspeed greater than this provides a positive lift capability sufficient to damage the aircraft. Conversely, any airspeed less than this does not provide positive lift capability sufficient to cause damage from excessive flight loads. This point is commonly referred to as "maneuvering speed" or V_A. (PLT074, CA.I.F.K1) — FAA-H-8083-25

Answers

5231 [B]   5232 [A]   5979 [A]

Stability

Stability is the inherent ability of an airplane to return, or not return, to its original flight condition after being disturbed by an outside force, such as rough air.

Positive static stability is the initial tendency of an aircraft to return to its original position. See Figure 1-15.

Positive dynamic stability is the tendency of an oscillating airplane (with positive static stability) to return to its original position relative to time. See Figure 1-16.

Aircraft design normally assures that the aircraft will be stable in pitch. The pilot can adversely affect this longitudinal stability by allowing the center of gravity (CG) to move forward or aft of specified CG limits through improper loading procedures. One undesirable flight characteristic a pilot might experience in an airplane loaded with the CG located behind the aft CG limit would be the inability to recover from a stalled condition.

The location of the CG with respect to the center of lift (CL) will determine the longitudinal stability of an airplane. See Figure 1-17.

An airplane will be less stable at all airspeeds if it is loaded to the most aft CG. An advantage of an airplane said to be inherently stable is that it will require less effort to control.

Changes in pitch can also be experienced with changes in power setting (except in T-tail airplanes). When power is reduced, there is a corresponding reduction in downwash on the tail, which results in the nose "pitching" down.

Figure 1-15. Static stability

Figure 1-16. Positive static stability relative to dynamic stability

Effects of Forward CG

1. Increased longitudinal stability.
2. Lower cruise speed. The wing flies at a higher angle of attack to create more lift to counter the added downward forces produced by the tail, therefore the wing also produces more induced drag.
3. Higher stall speed. The wing flies at a higher angle of attack to create more lift to counter the added downward forces produced by the tail, therefore the wing also produces more induced drag.

Effects of Aft CG

1. Decreased longitudinal stability.
2. Higher cruise speed (for just the opposite reason listed above).
3. Lower stall speed.
4. Poor stall/spin recovery.

Figure 1-17. Effects of CG on aircraft stability

AIR
5205. In small airplanes, normal recovery from spins may become difficult if the

A—CG is too far rearward and rotation is around the longitudinal axis.
B—CG is too far rearward and rotation is around the CG.
C—spin is entered before the stall is fully developed.

The recovery from a stall in any airplane becomes progressively more difficult as its center of gravity moves aft. This is particularly important in spin recovery, as there is a point in rearward loading of any airplane at which a "flat" spin will develop. (PLT240, CA.VII.E.K1) — FAA-H-8083-25

Answer (A) is incorrect because rotation is around the CG in a spin. Answer (C) is incorrect because an airplane must first stall in order to spin.

AIR
5974. A sweptwing airplane with weak static directional stability and increased dihedral causes an increase in

A—Mach tuck tendency.
B—Dutch roll tendency.
C—longitudinal stability.

When the dihedral effect is large in comparison with static direction stability, the dutch roll motion has weak dampening and is increased. (PLT214, CA.I.F.K3) — FAA-H-8083-25

Answer (A) is incorrect because Mach tuck tendency occurs when going through the sound barrier. Answer (C) is incorrect because longitudinal stability is not affected by directional stability or dihedral.

AIR
5207. If an airplane is loaded to the rear of its CG range, it will tend to be unstable about its

A—vertical axis.
B—lateral axis.
C—longitudinal axis.

Lateral stability is controlled by the CG along the longitudinal axis. An airplane will become less laterally stable as the CG is moved further rearward along the longitudinal axis. Longitudinal stability (pitching) is stability about the lateral axis. (PLT240, CA.I.F.K2e) — FAA-H-8083-25

Answer (A) is incorrect because the CG has little to do with the vertical axis. Answer (C) is incorrect because lateral stability is not greatly affected by the CG location.

AIR
5212. An airplane will stall at the same

A—angle of attack regardless of the attitude with relation to the horizon.
B—airspeed regardless of the attitude with relation to the horizon.
C—angle of attack and attitude with relation to the horizon.

The definition of a stall is when the airplane exceeds the critical angle of attack. This happens because the smooth airflow over the airplane's wing is disrupted and the lift degenerates rapidly. This can occur at any airspeed, in any attitude, with any power setting. (PLT240, CA.VII.C.K1) — FAA-H-8083-25

AIR
5228. Longitudinal stability involves the motion of the airplane controlled by its

A—rudder.
B—elevator.
C—ailerons.

Longitudinal stability or pitching is the motion around the lateral axis. Pitch is controlled by the elevator. (PLT213, CA.I.F.K3) — FAA-H-8083-25

Answer (A) is incorrect because the rudder affects directional stability. Answer (C) is incorrect because the ailerons affect lateral stability.

Answers

| 5205 | [B] | 5974 | [B] | 5207 | [B] | 5212 | [A] | 5228 | [B] |

Chapter 1 **Basic Aerodynamics**

AIR

5230. If the airplane attitude initially tends to return to its original position after the elevator control is pressed forward and released, the airplane displays

A—positive dynamic stability.
B—positive static stability.
C—neutral dynamic stability.

Static stability deals with initial tendencies. Positive static stability is the initial tendency of the airplane to return to its original state after being disturbed. (PLT480, CA.I.F.K3) — FAA-H-8083-25

AIR, GLI

5226. If the airplane attitude remains in a new position after the elevator control is pressed forward and released, the airplane displays

A—neutral longitudinal static stability.
B—positive longitudinal static stability.
C—neutral longitudinal dynamic stability.

Neutral static stability is the initial tendency of the airplane to remain in the new condition after its equilibrium has been disturbed. When an airplane's attitude is momentarily displaced and it remains at the new attitude, it is displaying neutral longitudinal static stability.

Longitudinal stability makes an airplane stable about its lateral axis (pitch). (PLT213, CA.I.F.K3) — FAA-H-8083-25

Answer (B) is incorrect because positive longitudinal static stability is the initial tendency of the airplane to return to its original attitude after the elevator control is pressed forward and released. Answer (C) is incorrect because neutral longitudinal dynamic stability is the overall tendency for the airplane to remain in the new condition over a period of time.

AIR, GLI

5227. Longitudinal dynamic instability in an airplane can be identified by

A—bank oscillations becoming progressively steeper.
B—pitch oscillations becoming progressively steeper.
C—Trilatitudinal roll oscillations becoming progressively steeper.

Longitudinal stability, or pitching about the lateral axis, is considered to be the most affected by certain variables in various flight conditions. A longitudinally unstable airplane has a tendency to dive or climb progressively into a steep dive or climb which may result in a stall. A longitudinally unstable airplane is difficult and sometimes dangerous to fly. (PLT213, CA.I.F.K3) — FAA-H-8083-25

Answers (A) and (C) are incorrect because roll oscillations refer to lateral stability.

Turns, Loads, and Load Factors

When an airplane is banking into a turn, a portion of the lift developed is diverted into a horizontal component of lift. It is this horizontal (sideward) force that forces the airplane from straight-and-level flight and causes it to turn. The reduced vertical lift component results in a loss of altitude unless total lift is increased by increasing the angle of attack, increasing airspeed or both.

In aerodynamics, load is the force, or imposed stress, that must be supported by an airplane structure in flight. The loads imposed on the wings in flight are stated in terms of load factor.

In straight-and-level flight, the wings of an airplane support a load equal to the sum of the weight of the airplane plus its contents. This particular load factor is equal to "one G," where "G" refers to the pull of gravity.

However, a force which acts toward the outside of the curve, called centrifugal force, is generated any time an airplane is flying a curved path (turns, climbs, or descents).

Whenever the airplane is flying in a curved flight path with a positive load, the load that the wings must support will be equal to the weight of the airplane plus the load imposed by centrifugal force; therefore, it can be said that turns increase the load factor on an airplane.

As the angle of bank of a turn increases, the load factor increases, as shown in Figure 1-18.

The amount of excess load that can be imposed on the wing of an airplane depends on the speed of the airplane. An example of this would be a change in direction made at high speed with forceful control movement, which results in a high load factor being imposed.

Answers

5230 [B]   5226 [A]   5227 [B]

An increased load factor (weight) will cause an airplane to stall at a higher airspeed, as shown in Figure 1-19.

Some conditions that increase the weight (load) of an aircraft are: overloading the airplane, too steep an angle of bank, turbulence and abrupt movement of the controls.

Because different types of operations require different maneuvers (and therefore varying bank angles and load factors), aircraft are separated into categories determined by the loads that their wing structures can support:

Category	Positive Limit Load
Normal (nonacrobatic) (N)	3.8 times gross weight
Utility (normal operations and limited acrobatic maneuvers)	4.4 times gross weight
Acrobatic (A)	6.0 times gross weight

The limit loads should not be exceeded in actual operation, even though a safety factor of 50% above limit loads is incorporated into the strength of an airplane.

Figure 1-18. Increase in load on wings as angle of bank increases

Figure 1-19. Effect of angle of bank on stall speed

Chapter 1 Basic Aerodynamics

AIR
5193. Which is correct with respect to rate and radius of turn for an airplane flown in a coordinated turn at a constant altitude?

A—For a specific angle of bank and airspeed, the rate and radius of turn will not vary.
B—To maintain a steady rate of turn, the angle of bank must be increased as the airspeed is decreased.
C—The faster the true airspeed, the faster the rate and larger the radius of turn regardless of the angle of bank.

At a specific angle of bank and a specific airspeed, the radius of the turn and the rate of turn would remain constant if the altitude were maintained. Rate of turn varies with airspeed, or bank angle. If the angle of bank is held constant and the airspeed is increased, the rate of turn will decrease, and the radius of turn will increase. To maintain a constant rate of turn as the airspeed is increased, the angle of bank must be increased. (PLT348, CA.V.A.K2e) — FAA-H-8083-3

Answer (B) is incorrect because you must decrease the angle of bank when the airspeed is decreased if you are to maintain a steady rate of turn. Answer (C) is incorrect because for a given bank angle a faster airspeed gives a slower rate of turn.

AIR
5194. Why is it necessary to increase back elevator pressure to maintain altitude during a turn? To compensate for the

A—loss of the vertical component of lift.
B—loss of the horizontal component of lift and the increase in centrifugal force.
C—rudder deflection and slight opposite aileron throughout the turn.

Lift during a bank is divided into two components, one vertical and the other horizontal. The vertical component of lift must be equal to the weight to maintain altitude. Since the vertical component of lift decreases as the bank angle increases, the angle of attack must be progressively increased to produce sufficient vertical lift to support the airplane's weight. The increased back elevator pressure provides the increased angle of attack. (PLT348, CA.I.F.K3) — FAA-H-8083-3

Answer (B) is incorrect because this describes a skidding turn. Answer (C) is incorrect because slight opposite aileron pressure may be required to compensate for the overbanking tendency, not to maintain altitude.

AIR
5195. To maintain altitude during a turn, the angle of attack must be increased to compensate for the decrease in the

A—forces opposing the resultant component of drag.
B—vertical component of lift.
C—horizontal component of lift.

Lift during a bank is divided into two components, one vertical and the other horizontal. The vertical component of lift must be equal to the weight to maintain altitude. Since the vertical component of lift decreases as the bank angle increases, the angle of attack must be progressively increased to produce sufficient vertical lift to support the airplane's weight. The increased back elevator pressure provides the increased angle of attack. (PLT348, CA.I.F.K3) — FAA-H-8083-3

Answer (A) is incorrect because the phrase "the resultant component of drag" has no meaning. Answer (C) is incorrect because as the horizontal component of lift decreases, the vertical component of lift increases, therefore the angle of attack must be decreased.

AIR
5210. If airspeed is increased during a level turn, what action would be necessary to maintain altitude? The angle of attack

A—and angle of bank must be decreased.
B—must be increased or angle of bank decreased.
C—must be decreased or angle of bank increased.

To compensate for added lift which would result if the airspeed were increased during a turn, the angle of attack must be decreased, or the angle of bank increased, if a constant altitude is to be maintained. (PLT168, CA.I.F.K3) — FAA-H-8083-25

Answer (A) is incorrect because either the angle of attack can be decreased or the angle of bank increased to maintain altitude as airspeed is increased. Answer (B) is incorrect because to maintain constant altitude in a turn as the airspeed increases, the angle of bank must decrease.

AIR
5210-1. To maintain a standard rate turn as the airspeed increases, the bank angle of the aircraft will need to

A—remain constant.
B—increase.
C—decrease.

Answers

5193 [A]   5194 [A]   5195 [B]   5210 [C]   5210-1 [B]

As airspeed is increased in a constant bank angle the rate of turn will decrease. For example, in a 30° bank at 100 knots your rate of turn will equal 6.5° degrees per second. If you maintain the 30° bank angle and increase speed to 150 knots your rate of turn will decrease to 4.4° degrees per second. Therefore, to maintain a standard rate turn of either 3° or 1.5° per second (high-speed aircraft), as airspeed is increased bank angle will need to be increased. (PLT118, CA.V.A.K2e) — FAA-H-8083-25

AIR
5153. For a given angle of bank, in any airplane, the load factor imposed in a coordinated constant-altitude turn

A—is constant and the stall speed increases.
B—varies with the rate of turn.
C—is constant and the stall speed decreases.

In an airplane at any airspeed, if a constant altitude is maintained during the turn, the load factor for a given degree of bank is the same, which is the resultant of gravity and centrifugal force. Load supported by the wings increases as the angle of bank increases. Stall speeds increase in proportion to the square root of the load factor. (PLT309, CA.I.F.K3) — FAA-H-8083-25

Answer (B) is incorrect because rate of turn does not affect the load factor. Answer (C) is incorrect because stall speed will increase with an increase in bank.

AIR
5154. Airplane wing loading during a level coordinated turn in smooth air depends upon the

A—rate of turn.
B—angle of bank.
C—true airspeed.

For any given angle of bank, the rate of turn varies with the airspeed. If the angle of bank is held constant and the airspeed is increased, the rate of turn will decrease. Because of this, there is no change in centrifugal force for any given bank angle. Therefore, the load factor remains the same. Load factor varies with changing bank angle and increases at a rapid rate after the angle of bank reaches 50°. (PLT309, CA.I.F.K3) — FAA-H-8083-25

Answers (A) and (C) are incorrect because rate of turn and true airspeed do not have an impact on wing loading in a coordinated turn.

AIR
5163. If the airspeed is increased from 90 knots to 135 knots during a level 60° banked turn, the load factor will

A—increase as well as the stall speed.
B—decrease and the stall speed will increase.
C—remain the same but the radius of turn will increase.

At a given angle of bank, a higher airspeed will make the radius of the turn larger and the airplane will be turning at a slower rate. This compensates for added centrifugal force, allowing the load factor to remain the same. (PLT018, CA.V.A.K2) — FAA-H-8083-25

ALL
5163-1. A load factor of 1.2 means the total load on an aircraft's structure is 1.2 times its

A—gross weight.
B—load limit.
C—gust factor.

In aerodynamics, load factor is the ratio of the maximum load an aircraft can sustain to the gross weight of the aircraft. For example, a load factor of 1.2 means the total load on an aircraft's structure is 1.2 times its gross weight. (PLT310, CA.I.F.K3) — FAA-H-8083-25

AIR
5179. (Refer to Figure 2.) Select the correct statement regarding stall speeds.

A—Power-off stalls occur at higher airspeeds with the gear and flaps down.
B—In a 60° bank the airplane stalls at a lower airspeed with the gear up.
C—Power-on stalls occur at lower airspeeds in shallower banks.

Power-on stalls occur at lower airspeeds than power-off stalls because of increased airflow over the wing and because some lift is produced by the vertical component of thrust, reducing the lift needed to be produced by velocity. Power-on or -off stalls occur at a lower airspeed in a shallower bank. (PLT002, CA.VII.C.K1) — FAA-H-8083-25

Answer (A) is incorrect because stall speed is lower with power-off stalls, with gear and flaps down. Answer (B) is incorrect because the gear position alone will not affect stall speed in a 60° bank.

Answers

| 5153 [A] | 5154 [B] | 5163 [C] | 5163-1 [A] | 5179 [C] |

Chapter 1 **Basic Aerodynamics**

AIR

5180. (Refer to Figure 2.) Select the correct statement regarding stall speeds. The airplane will stall

A—10 knots higher in a power-on 60° bank with gear and flaps up than with gear and flaps down.
B—25 knots lower in a power-off, flaps-up, 60° bank, than in a power-off, flaps-down, wings-level configuration.
C—10 knots higher in a 45° bank, power-on stall than in a wings-level stall with flaps up.

The stalling speed (in knots) for a power-on, 60° bank, with gear and flaps up is 76 knots. For a power-on, 60° bank, and gear and flaps down, the stalling speed is 66 knots, which is 10 knots slower. (PLT002, CA.VII.C.K1) — FAA-H-8083-25

Answer (B) is incorrect because the airplane will stall 35 knots higher (not 25) in this specified configuration. Answer (C) is incorrect because this configuration is not specified in the question.

AIR

5978. If the airspeed is decreased from 98 knots to 85 knots during a coordinated level 45° banked turn, the load factor will

A—remain the same, but the radius of turn will decrease.
B—decrease, and the rate of turn will decrease.
C—remain the same, but the radius of turn will increase.

At a given angle of bank, a lower airspeed will make the radius of the turn smaller and the airplane will be turning at a faster rate. This compensates for the reduced centrifugal force, allowing the load factor to remain the same. (PLT018, CA.V.A.K2d) — FAA-H-8083-25

AIR

5978-1. If the airspeed is increased from 89 knots to 98 knots during a coordinated level 45° banked turn, the load factor will

A—decrease, and the radius of turn will decrease.
B—remain the same, but the radius of turn will increase.
C—increase, but the rate of turn will decrease.

When a turn is made at a higher true airspeed at a given bank angle, the inertia is greater and the horizontal lift component required for the turn is greater, causing the turning rate to become slower. Therefore, at a given angle of bank, a higher true airspeed will make the radius of turn larger because the airplane will be turning at a slower rate. This compensates for added centrifugal force, allowing the load factor to remain the same. (PLT018, CA.V.A.K2d) — FAA-H-8083-25

AIR

5221. (Refer to Figure 4.) What is the stall speed of an airplane under a load factor of 2 Gs if the unaccelerated stall speed is 60 knots?

A—66 knots.
B—74 knots.
C—84 knots.

From a load factor of 2, go horizontally to the curved line labeled "Load Factor." From that point of intersection, go up to the curve labeled "Stall Speed Increase." From there, go to the left and read the increase: 40%. The new accelerated stall speed will be 140%, or 1.4 times, the original value. 60 × 1.4 = 84 knots. (PLT002, CA.I.F.K3) — FAA-H-8083-25

AIR

5221-1. (Refer to Figure 4.) What is the stall speed of an airplane under a load factor of 2.5 G's if the unaccelerated stall speed is 60 knots?

A—62 knots.
B—84 knots.
C—96 knots.

From a load factor of 2.5, go horizontally to the curved line labeled "Load Factor." From that point of intersection, go up to the curve labeled "Stall Speed Increase." From there, go to the left and read the increase: 60%. The new accelerated stall speed will be 160%, or 1.6 times the original value. 60 × 1.6 = 96 knots. (PLT002, CA.I.F.K3) — FAA-H-8083-25

AIR, GLI, RTC

5192. To increase the rate of turn and at the same time decrease the radius, a pilot should

A—maintain the bank and decrease airspeed.
B—increase the bank and increase airspeed.
C—increase the bank and decrease airspeed.

The horizontal component of lift will equal the centrifugal force of steady, turning flight. To increase the rate of turn, the angle of bank may be increased and the airspeed may be decreased. (PLT348, CA.I.F.K3) — FAA-H-8083-25

Answer (A) is incorrect because although at a given angle of bank a decrease in airspeed will increase the rate of turn and decrease the radius, it will not be as effective as steepening the bank and decreasing the airspeed. Answer (B) is incorrect because the pilot should decrease airspeed to decrease the turn radius.

Answers

5180 [A]   5978 [A]   5978-1 [B]   5221 [C]   5221-1 [C]   5192 [C]

Chapter 1 Basic Aerodynamics

AIR, GLI, RTC

5225. As the angle of bank is increased, the vertical component of lift

A—decreases and the horizontal component of lift increases.
B—increases and the horizontal component of lift decreases.
C—decreases and the horizontal component of lift remains constant.

Lift during a bank is divided into two components, one vertical and the other horizontal. The vertical component of lift must be equal to the weight to maintain altitude. Since the vertical component of lift decreases as the bank angle increases, the angle of attack must be progressively increased to produce sufficient vertical lift to support the airplane's weight. The increased back elevator pressure provides the increased angle of attack. (PLT309, CA.I.F.K3) — FAA-H-8083-25

AIR, GLI

5181. Which is true regarding the use of flaps during level turns?

A—The lowering of flaps increases the stall speed.
B—The raising of flaps increases the stall speed.
C—Raising flaps will require added forward pressure on the yoke or stick.

If flaps are raised, the stall speed increases. (PLT305, CA.I.F.K3) — FAA-H-8083-25

Answer (A) is incorrect because flaps decrease the stall speed. Answer (C) is incorrect because raising the flaps decreases the lift provided, therefore, back pressure is required to maintain altitude.

AIR, RTC, GLI

5151. The ratio between the total airload imposed on the wing and the gross weight of an aircraft in flight is known as

A—load factor and directly affects stall speed.
B—aspect load and directly affects stall speed.
C—load factor and has no relation with stall speed.

The load factor is the ratio between the total airload imposed on the wings of an airplane and the gross weight of the airplane. An increased load factor increases stalling speed and a decreased load factor decreases stalling speed. (PLT310, CA.I.F.K3) — FAA-H-8083-25

AIR, GLI

5152. Load factor is the lift generated by the wings of an aircraft at any given time

A—divided by the total weight of the aircraft.
B—multiplied by the total weight of the aircraft.
C—divided by the basic empty weight of the aircraft.

Load factor is the ratio between the total airload supported by the wing to the total weight of the airplane; i.e., the total airload supported by the wings divided by the total weight of the airplane. (PLT310, CA.I.F.K3) — FAA-H-8083-25

Answer (B) is incorrect because load factor multiplied by airplane weight equals required lift. Answer (C) is incorrect because load factor is lift divided by the total weight of the airplane.

AIR, GLI

5152-1. While executing a 60° level turn, your aircraft is at a load factor of 2.0. What does this mean?

A—The total load on the aircraft's structure is two times its weight.
B—The load factor is over the load limit.
C—The gust factor is two times the total load limit.

Load factor is the ratio between the total airload supported by the wing to the total weight of the airplane; i.e., the total airload supported by the wings divided by the total weight of the airplane. (PLT310, CA.I.F.K3) — FAA-H-8083-25

ALL

5977. What is the best indicator to the pilot of the load factor on the airplane?

A—How firmly the pilot is pressed into the seat during a maneuver.
B—Amount of pressure required to operate the controls.
C—Airspeed when pulling out of a descent.

Load factor can be detected by noting how firmly the pilot is pressed into the seat during a maneuver. If an aircraft is pulled up from a dive, subjecting the pilot to 3 Gs, he or she would be pressed down into the seat with a force equal to three times his or her weight. (PLT140, CA.I.F.K3) — AIM ¶4-3-11

Answers

| 5225 [A] | 5181 [B] | 5151 [A] | 5152 [A] | 5152-1 [A] | 5977 [A] |

Chapter 1 Basic Aerodynamics

AIR, GLI

5155. In a rapid recovery from a dive, the effects of load factor would cause the stall speed to

A—increase.
B—decrease.
C—not vary.

There is a direct relationship between the load factor imposed upon the wing and its stalling characteristics. The stalling speed increases in proportion to the square root of the load factor. (PLT312, CA.VII.C.K4) — FAA-H-8083-25

AIR, GLI

5156. (Refer to Figure 4.) If an aircraft with a gross weight of 2,000 pounds was subjected to a 60° constant-altitude bank, the total load would be

A—3,000 pounds.
B—4,000 pounds.
C—12,000 pounds.

The load factor in a 60° bank is 2 Gs. Load Factor = G Load × Aircraft Weight. Therefore, 2,000 × 2 = 4,000 pounds. (PLT018, CA.I.F.K3) — FAA-H-8083-25

AIR, GLI, RTC

5157. While maintaining a constant angle of bank and altitude in a coordinated turn, an increase in airspeed will

A—decrease the rate of turn resulting in a decreased load factor.
B—decrease the rate of turn resulting in no change in load factor.
C—increase the rate of turn resulting in no change in load factor.

For any given angle of bank the rate of turn varies with the airspeed. In other words, if the angle of bank is held constant and the airspeed is increased, the rate of turn will decrease, or if the airspeed is decreased, the rate of turn will increase. Because of this, there is no change in centrifugal force for any given bank. Therefore, the load factor remains the same. (PLT309, CA.I.F.K3) — FAA-H-8083-25

Answer (A) is incorrect because load factor remains the same at a constant angle of bank. Answer (C) is incorrect because the rate of turn in a constant angle of bank will decrease with an increase in airspeed, and the load factor will remain the same.

AIR, GLI

5159. While holding the angle of bank constant in a level turn, if the rate of turn is varied the load factor would

A—remain constant regardless of air density and the resultant lift vector.
B—vary depending upon speed and air density provided the resultant lift vector varies proportionately.
C—vary depending upon the resultant lift vector.

For any given angle of bank the rate of turn varies with the airspeed. In other words, if the angle of bank is held constant and the airspeed is increased, the rate of turn will decrease, or if the airspeed is decreased, the rate of turn will increase. Because of this, there is no change in centrifugal force for any given bank. Therefore, the load factor remains the same. (PLT309, CA.I.F.K3) — FAA-H-8083-25

Answer (B) is incorrect because rate of turn will vary based on airspeed with a constant angle of bank. Answer (C) is incorrect because load factor varies based on the resultant load vector.

AIR, GLI, RTC

5222. (Refer to Figure 4.) What increase in load factor would take place if the angle of bank were increased from 60° to 80°?

A—3 Gs.
B—3.5 Gs.
C—4 Gs.

Proceed vertically along the line above 60° angle of bank to where it intersects the curve labeled "Load Factor." Next, proceed along this line to the left to the corresponding load factor or "G" unit, which is 2 Gs in this case. Now, repeat the procedure using 80° of bank, which should yield a load factor of 6, which is a difference of 4 Gs. (PLT018, CA.V.A.K2d) — FAA-H-8083-25

AIR

5017. If an airplane category is listed as utility, it would mean that this airplane could be operated in which of the following maneuvers?

A—Limited acrobatics, excluding spins.
B—Limited acrobatics, including spins (if approved).
C—Any maneuver except acrobatics or spins.

Utility category airplanes can do all normal category maneuvers plus limited acrobatics, including spins (if approved). (PLT113, CA.I.F.R2) — FAA-H-8083-3

Answer (A) is incorrect because the utility category includes spins. Answer (C) is incorrect because the normal category prohibits acrobatics and spins.

Answers

| 5155 | [A] | 5156 | [B] | 5157 | [B] | 5159 | [A] | 5222 | [C] | 5017 | [B] |

Stalls and Spins

As the angle of attack is increased (to increase lift), the air will no longer flow smoothly over the upper wing surface, but instead will become turbulent or "burble" near the trailing edge. A further increase in the angle of attack will cause the turbulent area to expand forward. At an angle of attack of approximately 18° to 20° (for most wings), turbulence over the upper wing surface decreases lift so drastically that flight cannot be sustained and the wing stalls. See Figure 1-20.

The angle at which a stall occurs is called the critical angle of attack. An airplane can stall at any airspeed or any attitude, but will always stall at the same critical angle of attack. The indicated airspeed at which a given airplane will stall in a particular configuration, however, will remain the same regardless of altitude. Because air density decreases with an increase in altitude, the airplane has to be flown faster at higher altitudes to cause the same pressure difference between pitot impact pressure and static pressure. The recovery from a stall in any airplane becomes progressively more difficult as its center of gravity moves aft.

An aircraft will spin only after it has stalled, and will continue to spin as long as the outside wing continues to provide more lift than the inside wing, and the aircraft remains stalled.

Figure 1-20. Flow of air over wing at various angles of attack

AIR
5196. Stall speed is affected by

A—weight, load factor, and power.
B—load factor, angle of attack, and power.
C—angle of attack, weight, and air density.

The indicated stalling speed is affected by:
1. *Weight. As the weight is increased, the stall speed also increases.*
2. *Bank angle (load factor). As the bank angle increases, so does the stalling speed.*
3. *Power. An increase in power will decrease the stalling speed.*

A change in density altitude (air density) or angle of attack has no effect on the indicated stalling speed, since for a given airplane, the stalling or critical angle of attack remains constant. (PLT242, CA.I.F.K3) — FAA-H-8083-25

AIR
5211. The stalling speed of an airplane is most affected by

A—changes in air density.
B—variations in flight altitude.
C—variations in airplane loading.

The indicated stalling speed is most affected by load factor. The airplane's stalling speed increases in proportion to the square root of the load factor, whereas a change in altitude (air density) has no effect on the indicated stalling speed. (PLT477, CA.I.F.K3) — FAA-H-8083-25

AIR
5206. Recovery from a stall in any airplane becomes more difficult when its

A—center of gravity moves aft.
B—center of gravity moves forward.
C—elevator trim is adjusted nosedown.

The recovery from a stall in any airplane becomes progressively more difficult as its center of gravity moves aft. (PLT240, CA.I.F.K3) — FAA-H-8083-25

Answers

5196 [A]   5211 [C]   5206 [A]

Chapter 1 **Basic Aerodynamics**

AIR, GLI
5160. The need to slow an aircraft below V_A is brought about by the following weather phenomenon:

A—High density altitude which increases the indicated stall speed.
B—Turbulence which causes an increase in stall speed.
C—Turbulence which causes a decrease in stall speed.

When severe turbulence is encountered, the airplane should be flown at or below maneuvering speed. This is the speed least likely to result in structural damage to the airplane, even if full control travel is used, and yet allows a sufficient margin of safety above stalling speed in turbulent air. When an airplane is flying at a high speed with a low angle of attack, and suddenly encounters a vertical current of air moving upward, the relative wind changes to an upward direction as it meets the airfoil. This increases the angle of attack on the wings and has the same effect as applying a sharp back pressure on the elevator control. It increases the load factor which in turn increases the stall speed. (PLT120, CA.I.F.K3) — FAA-H-8083-25

Answer (A) is incorrect because indicated stall speed is not affected by changes in density altitude. Answer (C) is incorrect because the higher load factors imposed on the aircraft by turbulence increases stall speed.

AIR, GLI
5204. The angle of attack at which a wing stalls remains constant regardless of

A—weight, dynamic pressure, bank angle, or pitch attitude.
B—dynamic pressure, but varies with weight, bank angle, and pitch attitude.
C—weight and pitch attitude, but varies with dynamic pressure and bank angle.

When the angle of attack becomes so great that the air can no longer flow smoothly over the top wing surface, it becomes impossible for the air to follow the contour of the wing. This is the stalling or critical angle of attack. For any given airplane, the stalling or critical angle of attack remains constant regardless of weight, dynamic pressure, bank angle, or pitch attitude. These factors will affect the speed at which the stall occurs, but not the angle. (PLT168, CA.I.F.K3) — FAA-H-8083-25

Answers (B) and (C) are incorrect because the stall speed varies with weight and bank angle.

Flaps

Extending the flaps increases the wing camber and the angle of attack of a wing. This increases wing lift and also increases induced drag. The increased lift enables the pilot to make steeper approaches to a landing without an increase in airspeed. Spoilers, unlike flaps, do not change the wing camber. Their primary purpose is to decrease or "spoil" lift (increase drag) of the wing. See Figure 1-21.

Figure 1-21. Use of flaps increases lift and drag

AIR, GLI
5182. One of the main functions of flaps during the approach and landing is to

A—decrease the angle of descent without increasing the airspeed.
B—provide the same amount of lift at a slower airspeed.
C—decrease lift, thus enabling a steeper-than-normal approach to be made.

Extending the flaps increases wing lift and also increases induced drag. The increased drag enables the pilot to make steeper approaches without an increase in airspeed. (PLT473, CA.I.F.K3) — FAA-H-8083-25

Answer (A) is incorrect because the flaps will increase the angle of descent without increasing the airspeed. Answer (C) is incorrect because the flaps increase lift and induced drag.

Answers

5160 [B]   5204 [A]   5182 [B]

GLI
5276. The primary purpose of wing spoilers is to decrease

A—the drag.
B—landing speed.
C—the lift of the wing.

Deployable spoilers added to the upper wing surface "spoil" lift. These devices, when deployed, also increase drag. (PLT473) — FAA-H-8083-13

GLI
5282. Both lift and drag would be increased when which of these devices are extended?

A—Flaps.
B—Spoilers.
C—Slats.

Spoilers decrease a wing's lift whereas flaps increase lift. Both spoilers and flaps increase the drag. (PLT519) — FAA-H-8083-13

Wing Shapes

It is desirable for a wing to stall in the root area before it stalls near the tips. This provides a warning of an impending stall and allows the ailerons to be effective during the stall. A rectangular wing stalls in the root area first. The stall begins near the tip and progresses inboard on a highly tapered wing or a wing with sweepback. See Figure 1-22.

Aspect ratio is the ratio of the span of an aircraft wing to its mean, or average, chord. Generally speaking, the higher the aspect ratio, the more efficient the wing. But for practical purposes, structural considerations normally limit the aspect ratio for all except high-performance sailplanes. A high-aspect-ratio wing has a low stall speed, and at a constant air velocity and high angle of attack has less drag than a low-aspect-ratio wing.

Figure 1-22. Wing shapes

Answers
5276 [C]   5282 [A]

Chapter 1 Basic Aerodynamics

AIR, GLI

5197. A rectangular wing, as compared to other wing planforms, has a tendency to stall first at the

A—wingtip, with the stall progression toward the wing root.
B—wing root, with the stall progression toward the wing tip.
C—center trailing edge, with the stall progression outward toward the wing root and tip.

The rectangular wing has a tendency to stall first at the wing root with the stall pattern progressing outward to the tip. This type of stall pattern decreases undesirable rolling tendencies and increases lateral control when approaching a stall. (PLT242, CA.I.F.K3) — FAA-H-8083-25

Torque

In an airplane of standard configuration there is an inherent tendency for the airplane to turn to the left. This tendency, called torque, is a combination of the following four forces:

- reactive force
- spiraling slipstream
- gyroscopic precession
- "P" factor

Spiraling slipstream is the only one addressed in this test. A spiraling slipstream is the reaction of the air to a rotating propeller, which forces the air to spiral in a clockwise direction around the fuselage. This tends to rotate the airplane right around the longitudinal axis.

AIR

5238. A propeller rotating clockwise as seen from the rear, creates a spiraling slipstream. The spiralling slipstream, along with torque effect, tends to rotate the airplane to the

A—right around the vertical axis, and to the left around the longitudinal axis.
B—left around the vertical axis, and to the right around the longitudinal axis.
C—left around the vertical axis, and to the left around the longitudinal axis.

The slipstream strikes the vertical fin on the left causing a yaw to the left, at the same time it causes a rolling moment to the right. (PLT243, CA.I.F.K3) — FAA-H-8083-25

Answers

5197 [B]   5238 [B]

Chapter 1 **Basic Aerodynamics**

Ground Effect

Ground effect occurs when flying within one wingspan or less above the surface. The airflow around the wing and wing tips is modified and the resulting pattern reduces the downwash which reduces the induced drag. These changes can result in an aircraft either becoming airborne before reaching recommended takeoff speed or floating during an approach to land. See Figure 1-23.

An airplane leaving ground effect after takeoff will require an increase in angle of attack to maintain the same lift coefficient, which in turn will cause an increase in induced drag and therefore, require increased thrust.

Figure 1-23. Ground effect phenomenon

AIR
5209. An airplane leaving ground effect will

A—experience a reduction in ground friction and require a slight power reduction.
B—experience an increase in induced drag and require more thrust.
C—require a lower angle of attack to maintain the same lift coefficient.

As the wing encounters ground effect and is maintained at a constant lift coefficient, there is a reduction in the upwash, downwash, and wing-tip vortices. This causes a reduction in induced drag. While in ground effect, the airplane requires less thrust to maintain lift. It will also require a lower angle of attack. When an airplane leaves ground effect, there is an increase in drag which will require a higher angle of attack. Additional thrust will be required to compensate for the loss. (PLT131, CA.I.F.K3) — FAA-H-8083-25

Answer (A) is incorrect because ground friction is reduced when breaking ground. Answer (C) is incorrect because a higher angle of attack is required to maintain the same lift coefficient when leaving the ground.

AIR
5224. To produce the same lift while in ground effect as when out of ground effect, the airplane requires

A—a lower angle of attack.
B—the same angle of attack.
C—a greater angle of attack.

If the airplane is brought into ground effect with a constant angle of attack, it will experience an increase in lift coefficient and a reduction in the thrust required. The reduction of the wing-tip vortices due to ground effect alters the spanwise lift distribution and reduces the induced flow. The reduction in induced flow causes a significant reduction in induced drag, but has no direct effect on parasite drag. (PLT131, CA.I.F.K3) — FAA-H-8083-25

AIR, GLI
5216. If the same angle of attack is maintained in ground effect as when out of ground effect, lift will

A—increase, and induced drag will decrease.
B—decrease, and parasite drag will increase.
C—increase, and induced drag will increase.

If the airplane is brought into ground effect with a constant angle of attack, it will experience an increase in lift coefficient and a reduction in the thrust required. The reduction of the wing-tip vortices due to ground effect alters the spanwise lift distribution and reduces the induced flow. The reduction in induced flow causes a significant reduction in induced drag, but has no direct effect on parasite drag. (PLT131, CA.I.F.K3) — FAA-H-8083-25

Answers

5209 [B]   5224 [A]   5216 [A]

Chapter 1 **Basic Aerodynamics**

Wake Turbulence

All aircraft leave behind two types of wake turbulence: prop or jet blast, and wing-tip vortices.

Prop or jet blast could be hazardous to light aircraft on the ground behind large aircraft that are either taxiing or running-up their engines. In the air, prop or jet blast dissipates rapidly.

Wing-tip vortices are a by-product of lift. When a wing is flown at a positive angle of attack, a pressure differential is created between the upper and lower wing surfaces, and the pressure above the wing will be lower than the pressure below the wing. In attempting to equalize the pressure, air moves outward, upward, and around the wing tip, setting up a vortex which trails behind each wing. See Figure 1-24.

The strength of a vortex is governed by the weight, speed, and the shape of the wing of the generating aircraft. Maximum vortex strength occurs when the generating aircraft is heavy, clean, and slow.

Vortices generated by large aircraft in flight tend to sink below the flight path of the generating aircraft. A pilot should fly at or above the larger aircraft's flight path in order to avoid the wake turbulence created by the wing-tip vortices. See Figure 1-25.

Close to the ground, vortices tend to move laterally. A crosswind will tend to hold the upwind vortex over the landing runway, while a tailwind may move the vortices of a preceding aircraft forward into the touchdown zone.

To avoid wake turbulence when landing, a pilot should note the point where a preceding large aircraft touched down and then land past that point. See Figure 1-26.

On takeoff, a pilot should lift off prior to reaching the rotation point of a preceding large aircraft; the flight path should then remain upwind and above the preceding aircraft's flight path. See Figure 1-27.

Figure 1-25. Vortices in cruise flight

Figure 1-26. Touchdown and wake end

Figure 1-24. Wing-tip vortices

Figure 1-27. Rotation and wake beginning

ALL

5750. Choose the correct statement regarding wake turbulence.

A—Vortex generation begins with the initiation of the takeoff roll.
B—The primary hazard is loss of control because of induced roll.
C—The greatest vortex strength is produced when the generating airplane is heavy, clean, and fast.

Vortices sink at 400–500 fpm. Vortex generation begins when lift is being produced at takeoff. Greatest vortex strength is produced when the airplane is heavy, clean, and slow. The primary hazard is loss of control due to induced roll caused by the spinning vortices. (PLT509, CA.IV.A.R2d) — AIM ¶7-4-3

Answer (A) is incorrect because vortex generation begins at the rotation point when the airplane takes off. Answer (C) is incorrect because the greatest vortex strength is when the generating aircraft is heavy, clean, and slow.

ALL

5751. During a takeoff made behind a departing large jet airplane, the pilot can minimize the hazard of wingtip vortices by

A—being airborne prior to reaching the jet's flightpath until able to turn clear of its wake.
B—maintaining extra speed on takeoff and climbout.
C—extending the takeoff roll and not rotating until well beyond the jet's rotation point.

Vortices begin to form when the jet rotates. Plan to be off the runway prior to reaching the jet's point of rotation, then fly above or turn away from the jet's flight path. (PLT509, CA.IV.A.R2d) — AIM ¶7-4-4

ALL

5752. Your flight takes you in the path of a large aircraft. In order to avoid the vortices you should fly

A—at the same altitude as the large aircraft.
B—below the altitude of the large aircraft.
C—above the flight path of the large aircraft.

Fly above the jet's flight path whenever possible, because the vortices descend. Avoid flight below and behind a large aircraft's path. (PLT509, CA.IV.A.R2d) — AIM ¶7-4-6

ALL

5753. To avoid possible wake turbulence from a large jet aircraft that has just landed prior to your takeoff, at which point on the runway should you plan to become airborne?

A—Past the point where the jet touched down.
B—At the point where the jet touched down, or just prior to this point.
C—Approximately 500 feet prior to the point where the jet touched down.

Vortices cease to be generated when the aircraft lands. Plan to become airborne beyond this point. (PLT509, CA.IV.A.R2d) — AIM ¶7-4-6

ALL

5754. When landing behind a large aircraft, which procedure should be followed for vortex avoidance?

A—Stay above its final approach flightpath all the way to touchdown.
B—Stay below and to one side of its final approach flightpath.
C—Stay well below its final approach flightpath and land at least 2,000 feet behind.

Stay at or above the large aircraft's final approach flight path. Note the touchdown point and land beyond it. (PLT509, CA.IV.A.R2d) — AIM ¶7-4-6

ALL

5655. Which is true with respect to vortex circulation in the wake turbulence generated by an aircraft?

A—Helicopters generate downwash turbulence only, not vortex circulation.
B—The vortex strength is greatest when the generating aircraft is heavy, clean, and slow.
C—When vortex circulation sinks into ground effect, it tends to dissipate rapidly and offer little danger.

The strength of a vortex is governed by the weight, speed, and the shape of the wing of the generating aircraft. Maximum vortex strength occurs when the generating aircraft is heavy, clean, and slow. (PLT509, CA.IV.A.R2d) — AIM ¶7-4-3

Answers

| 5750 [B] | 5751 [A] | 5752 [C] | 5753 [A] | 5754 [A] | 5655 [B] |

Glider Aerodynamics

GLI
5053. GIVEN:

Glider's maximum certificated
operating weight .... 1,140 lb
Towline breaking strength .... 3,050 lb

Which meets the requirement for one of the safety links? A breaking strength of

A—812 pounds installed where the towline is attached to the towplane.
B—912 pounds installed where the towline is attached to the glider.
C—2,300 pounds installed where the towline is attached to the glider.

The breaking strength of the safety link between the towline and the glider must be between 80% of the maximum operating weight of the glider and twice that weight (or it must be between 912 and 2,280 pounds). A towplane-towline safety link strength must be greater than the glider-towline link which, in this case, cannot be less than 912 pounds. (PLT373) — 14 CFR §91.309

GLI
5054. During aerotow of a glider that weighs 940 pounds, which towrope tensile strength would require the use of safety links at each end of the rope?

A—752 pounds.
B—1,500 pounds.
C—2,000 pounds.

A towline of up to 1,880 pounds breaking strength may be used without safety links in this case since this is twice the weight of the glider. (PLT373) — 14 CFR §91.309

GLI
5277. That portion of the glider's total drag created by the production of lift is called

A—induced drag, and is not affected by changes in airspeed.
B—induced drag, and is greatly affected by changes in airspeed.
C—parasite drag, and is greatly affected by changes in airspeed.

When a sailplane develops lift, the upward force on the sailplane results in an equal and downward force on the air which is then set in motion, generally downward. It takes energy to do this, and the transfer of energy from the sailplane to the air implies the existence of drag on the sailplane. This part of the total drag is called induced drag. The induced drag varies inversely with the square of the velocity. (PLT257) — FAA-H-8083-13

GLI
5278. The best L/D ratio of a glider occurs when parasite drag is

A—equal to induced drag.
B—less than induced drag.
C—greater than induced drag.

L/D$_{MAX}$ is the airspeed where parasite drag and induced drag are equal. (PLT257) — FAA-H-8083-13

GLI
5279. A glider is designed for an L/D ratio of 22:1 at 50 MPH in calm air. What would the approximate GLIDE RATIO be with a direct headwind of 25 MPH?

A—44:1.
B—22:1.
C—11:1.

$$\text{Glide ratio} = \frac{88\,(V_C + V_W)}{R_S}$$

Where V_C = gliding airspeed
V_W = wind speed (+ = tailwind, – = head wind)
R_S = rate of sink

Thus, if V_W = 0 in calm air, V_W = -25 MPH, V_C is fixed at 50 MPH. Glide ratio would be reduced in the ratio of:

$$\frac{V_C + V_W}{V_C + V_W} = \frac{50 - 25}{50 - 0} = \frac{1}{2}$$

and would become 11:1.

(PLT257) — FAA-H-8083-13

GLI
5281. At a given airspeed, what effect will an increase in air density have on lift and drag of a glider?

A—Lift and drag will decrease.
B—Lift will increase but drag will decrease.
C—Lift and drag will increase.

Lift and drag vary directly with the density of the air. As air density increases, lift and drag increase. (PLT237) — FAA-H-8083-13

Answers

5053 [B]   5054 [C]   5277 [B]   5278 [A]   5279 [C]   5281 [C]

Chapter 1 Basic Aerodynamics

GLI

5283. If the airspeed of a glider is increased from 45 MPH to 90 MPH, the parasite drag will be

A—two times greater.
B—four times greater.
C—six times greater.

As speed increases, the amount of parasite drag increases as the square of the velocity. If the speed is doubled, four times as much drag is produced. (PLT237) — FAA-H-8083-13

GLI

5284. If the indicated airspeed of a glider is decreased from 90 MPH to 45 MPH, the induced drag will be

A—four times less.
B—two times greater.
C—four times greater.

The induced drag varies inversely with the square of the velocity. Airspeed is decreased, so induced drag will increase. Velocity is changed by a factor of two; induced drag will vary as two squared or a factor of four. (PLT237) — FAA-H-8083-13

GLI

5285. Which is true regarding wing camber of a glider's airfoil? The camber is

A—the same on both the upper and lower wing surface.
B—less on the upper wing surface than it is on the lower wing surface.
C—greater on the upper wing surface than it is on the lower wing surface.

Camber is the curvature of the upper and lower surfaces of an airfoil from the leading edge to the trailing edge. The upper surface normally has a greater camber than the lower wing surface. (PLT236) — FAA-H-8083-13

GLI

5286. If the glider's radius of turn is 175 feet at 40 MPH, what would the radius of turn be if the TAS is increased to 80 MPH while maintaining a constant angle of bank?

A—350 feet.
B—525 feet.
C—700 feet.

At a given angle of bank, the radius of the turn increases in proportion to the square of the velocity. If the velocity is doubled, the radius will increase four times.

$175 \times 4 = 700$ *feet*

(PLT309) — FAA-H-8083-13

GLI

5290. With regard to the effects of spoilers and wing flaps, which is true if the glider's pitch attitude is held constant when such devices are being operated? (Disregard negative flap angles above neutral position.) Retracting flaps

A—will reduce the glider's stall speed.
B—or extending spoilers will increase the glider's rate of descent.
C—or extending spoilers will decrease the glider's rate of descent.

Opening the spoilers causes the glider to sink faster while decelerating, whereas raising the flaps will increase the rate of descent without a speed increase. (PLT519) — FAA-H-8083-13

GLI

5291. If the angle of attack is increased beyond the critical angle of attack, the wing will no longer produce sufficient lift to support the weight of the glider

A—regardless of airspeed or pitch attitude.
B—unless the airspeed is greater than the normal stall speed.
C—unless the pitch attitude is on or below the natural horizon.

A glider can be stalled in any attitude and at any airspeed. (PLT242) — FAA-H-8083-13

GLI

5292. What force causes the glider to turn in flight?

A—Vertical component of lift.
B—Horizontal component of lift.
C—Positive yawing movement of the rudder.

The horizontal component of lift is the force that pulls the glider from a straight flight path to make it turn. (PLT235) — FAA-H-8083-13

Answers

| 5283 | [B] | 5284 | [C] | 5285 | [C] | 5286 | [C] | 5290 | [B] | 5291 | [A] |
| 5292 | [B] | | | | | | | | | | |

Chapter 1 **Basic Aerodynamics**

GLI
5293. GIVEN:

Glider A
Wingspan .... 51 ft
Average wing chord .... 4 ft

Glider B
Wingspan .... 48 ft
Average wing chord .... 3.5 ft

Determine the correct aspect ratio and its effect on performance at low speeds.

A—Glider A has an aspect ratio of 13.7, and will generate less lift with greater drag than glider B.
B—Glider B has an aspect ratio of 13.7, and will generate greater lift with less drag than glider A.
C—Glider B has an aspect ratio of 12.7, and will generate less lift with greater drag than glider A.

Aspect ratio is defined as the ratio between the glider's span and the mean chord of its wings. High-aspect ratio in a glider is associated with a high glide ratio (higher lift/lower drag), other factors being equal.

Wingspan ÷ Average Wing Chord = Aspect Ratio
51 ÷ 4 = 12.75 (Glider A)
48 ÷ 3.5 = 13.7 (Glider B)
(PLT238) — FAA-H-8083-13

GLI
5294. GIVEN:

Glider A
Wingspan .... 48 ft
Average wing chord .... 4.5 ft

Glider B
Wingspan .... 54 ft
Average wing chord .... 3.7 ft

Determine the correct aspect ratio and its effect on performance at low speeds.

A—Glider A has an aspect ratio of 10.6, and will generate greater lift with less drag than will glider B.
B—Glider B has an aspect ratio of 14.5, and will generate greater lift with less drag than will glider A.
C—Glider B has an aspect ratio of 10.6, and will generate less lift with greater drag than will glider A.

Aspect ratio is defined as the ratio between the glider's span and the mean chord of its wings. High-aspect ratio in a glider is associated with a high glide ratio (higher lift/lower drag), other factors being equal.

Wingspan ÷ Average Wing Chord = Aspect Ratio
48 ÷ 4.5 =10.67 (Glider A)
54 ÷ 3.7 =14.59 (Glider B)
(PLT238) — FAA-H-8083-13

GLI
5295. The best L/D ratio of a glider is a value that

A—varies depending upon the weight being carried.
B—remains constant regardless of airspeed changes.
C—remains constant and is independent of the weight being carried.

A heavily loaded glider goes forward and down faster than when lightly loaded. The glide ratios are the same for both loading conditions, but occur at different airspeeds. (PLT303) — FAA-H-8083-13

GLI
5296. A glide ratio of 22:1 with respect to the air mass will be

A—11:1 in a tailwind and 44:1 in a headwind.
B—22:1 regardless of wind direction and speed.
C—11:1 in a headwind and 44:1 in a tailwind.

Glide ratio may be taken as the ratio of forward to downward motion and is numerically the same as the lift to drag ratio (L/D). Within the air mass this value remains unchanged. However, glide ratio, when expressed in terms of motion over the ground, will vary as a function of wind velocity. (PLT124) — FAA-H-8083-13

Answers

5293 [B]   5294 [B]   5295 [C]   5296 [B]

Chapter 2
Aircraft Systems

Ignition System *2–3*

Fuel/Air Mixture *2–4*

Carburetor Ice *2–6*

Aviation Fuel *2–7*

Engine Temperatures *2–8*

Propellers *2–9*

Cold Weather Operations *2–12*

Rotorcraft Systems *2–13*

Glider Systems *2–29*

Balloon Operations *2–37*

Airship Operations *2–43*

Airship IFR Operations *2–45*

Ignition System

Most reciprocating engines used to power small aircraft incorporate two separate magneto ignition systems. The primary advantages of the dual ignition system are increased safety and improved engine performance.

A magneto ("mag") is a self-contained source of electrical energy, so even if an aircraft loses total electric power, the engine will continue to run. For electrical energy, magnetos depend upon a rotating magnet and a coil.

When checking for magneto operation prior to flight, the engine should run smoothly when operating with the magneto selector set on BOTH, and should experience a slight drop in revolutions per minute (RPM) when running on only one or the other magneto. The drop in RPM is caused by reduced efficiency of a single spark plug, as opposed to two.

If the ground wire between the magneto and the ignition switch becomes disconnected or broken, the engine cannot be shut down by turning off the ignition switch.

AIR, RTC
5169. Before shutdown, while at idle, the ignition key is momentarily turned OFF. The engine continues to run with no interruption; this

A—is normal because the engine is usually stopped by moving the mixture to idle cut-off.
B—should not normally happen. Indicates a magneto not grounding in OFF position.
C—is an undesirable practice, but indicates that nothing is wrong.

If the magneto switch ground wire is disconnected, the magneto is ON even though the ignition switch is in the OFF position. The engine could fire if the propeller is moved from outside the airplane. (PLT478, CA.I.G.R1) — FAA-H-8083-25

Answer (A) is incorrect because the engine should stop when the ignition key is turned to the OFF position. Answer (C) is incorrect because this indicates there is a faulty ground wire.

AIR, RTC
5171. A way to detect a broken magneto primary grounding lead is to

A—idle the engine and momentarily turn the ignition off.
B—add full power, while holding the brakes, and momentarily turn off the ignition.
C—run on one magneto, lean the mixture, and look for a rise in manifold pressure.

If the magneto switch ground wire is disconnected, the magneto is ON even though the ignition switch is in the OFF position. The engine could fire if the propeller is moved from outside the airplane. (PLT343, CA.I.G.R1) — FAA-H-8083-25

Answer (B) is incorrect because it is not necessary to add full power when performing the check. Answer (C) is incorrect because the way to detect a broken magneto ground wire is to turn the ignition to the OFF position; if the engine continues to run, the problem is confirmed.

AIR, RTC
5173. The most probable reason an engine continues to run after the ignition switch has been turned off is

A—carbon deposits glowing on the spark plugs.
B—a magneto ground wire is in contact with the engine casing.
C—a broken magneto ground wire.

If the magneto switch ground wire is disconnected, the magneto is ON even though the ignition switch is in the OFF position. The engine could fire if the propeller is moved from outside the airplane. (PLT343, CA.I.G.R1) — FAA-H-8083-25

Answer (A) is incorrect because glowing carbon deposits is a result of preignition. Answer (B) is incorrect because a magneto ground wire should be in contact with the engine casing to provide grounding.

Answers

5169 [B]   5171 [A]   5173 [C]

AIR, RTC
5174. If the ground wire between the magneto and the ignition switch becomes disconnected, the engine

A—will not operate on one magneto.
B—cannot be started with the switch in the BOTH position.
C—could accidentally start if the propeller is moved with fuel in the cylinder.

If the magneto switch ground wire is disconnected, the magneto is ON even though the ignition switch is in the OFF position. The engine could fire if the propeller is moved from outside the airplane. (PLT343, CA.I.G.R1) — FAA-H-8083-25

Answer (A) is incorrect because both magnetos remain on when the ground wire is disconnected. Answer (B) is incorrect because the engine can still be started, and the magnetos cannot be turned off.

Fuel/Air Mixture

Carburetors are normally set to deliver the correct fuel/air mixture (fuel/air ratio) at sea level. This fuel/air ratio is the ratio of the weight of fuel to the weight of air entering the cylinder. The ratio is determined by the setting of the mixture control in both fuel injection and carburetor-equipped engines.

When climbing, the mixture control allows the pilot to decrease fuel flow as altitude increases (air density decreases), thus maintaining the correct fuel/air ratio. If fuel flow is allowed to remain constant by not leaning the mixture, the fuel/air ratio will become too rich as the density of air decreases with increased altitude, resulting in a loss of efficiency. Operating with an excessively rich mixture may cause fouling of spark plugs.

When descending, air density increases. Unless fuel flow is increased, the mixture may become excessively lean; i.e., the weight of fuel will be too low for the weight of air reaching the cylinders. This may result in the creation of high engine temperatures and pressures.

The best power mixture is the fuel/air ratio from which the most power can be obtained for any given throttle setting.

AIR, RTC, LTA
5172. Fouling of spark plugs is more apt to occur if the aircraft

A—gains altitude with no mixture adjustment.
B—descends from altitude with no mixture adjustment.
C—throttle is advanced very abruptly.

If the fuel/air mixture is too rich, excessive fuel consumption, rough engine operation, and appreciable loss of power will occur. Because of excessive fuel, a cooling effect takes place which causes below normal temperatures in the combustion chambers. This cooling results in spark plug fouling. Unless the mixture is leaned with a gain in altitude, the mixture becomes excessively rich. (PLT343, CA.I.G.R1) — FAA-H-8083-25

Answer (B) is incorrect because descending without a mixture adjustment (operating with an excessively lean mixture) would result in overheating, rough engine operation, a loss of power, and detonation. Answer (C) is incorrect because advancing the throttle abruptly may cause the engine to hesitate or stop.

AIR, RTC, LTA
5176. The pilot controls the air/fuel ratio with the

A—throttle
B—manifold pressure
C—mixture control

The fuel/air ratio of the combustible mixture delivered to the engine is controlled by the mixture control. (PLT249, CA.I.G.K1e) — FAA-H-8083-25

Answer (A) is incorrect because the throttle regulates the total volume of fuel and air entering the combustion chamber. Answer (B) is incorrect because the manifold pressure indicates the engine's power output.

Answers

5174 [C]   5172 [A]   5176 [C]

Chapter 2 Aircraft Systems

AIR, RTC, LTA
5187. Fuel/air ratio is the ratio between the

A—volume of fuel and volume of air entering the cylinder.
B—weight of fuel and weight of air entering the cylinder.
C—weight of fuel and weight of air entering the carburetor.

The mixture control is used to change the fuel to air mixture entering the combustion chamber (cylinder). Fuel-to-air ratio is the weight of fuel to a given weight of air. (PLT249, CA.I.G.K1e) — FAA-H-8083-25

Answer (A) is incorrect because, as altitude increases, the amount of air in a fixed volume decreases. Answer (C) is incorrect because the carburetor is where the fuel/air ratio is established prior to entering the cylinders.

AIR, RTC, LTA
5188. The mixture control can be adjusted, which

A—prevents the fuel/air combination from becoming too rich at higher altitudes.
B—regulates the amount of air flow through the carburetor's venturi.
C—prevents the fuel/air combination from becoming lean as the airplane climbs.

As the aircraft climbs, the fuel/air mixture becomes richer and the excessive fuel causes the engine to lose power and to run rougher. The mixture control provides a means for the pilot to decrease fuel to compensate for this imbalance in mixture as altitude increases. (PLT343, CA.I.G.R1) — FAA-H-8083-25

Answer (B) is incorrect because the throttle regulates the airflow through the carburetor's venturi. Answer (C) is incorrect because the fuel/air ratio becomes richer as the aircraft climbs.

AIR, RTC, LTA
5298. The best power mixture is that fuel/air ratio at which

A—cylinder head temperatures are the coolest.
B—the most power can be obtained for any given throttle setting.
C—a given power can be obtained with the highest manifold pressure or throttle setting.

The throttle setting determines the amount of air flowing into the engine. The mixture control is then adjusted to get the best fuel/air ratio, resulting in the best power the engine can develop at this particular throttle setting. (PLT249, CA.I.G.K1c) — FAA-H-8083-25

Answer (A) is incorrect because the cylinder heads will be the coolest when mixture is richest. Answer (C) is incorrect because this describes the highest power setting.

AIR, RTC, LTA
5608. What will occur if no leaning is made with the mixture control as the flight altitude increases?

A—The volume of air entering the carburetor decreases and the amount of fuel decreases.
B—The density of air entering the carburetor decreases and the amount of fuel increases.
C—The density of air entering the carburetor decreases and the amount of fuel remains constant.

Fuel flow remains constant if no adjustments are made. The same volume of air goes into the carburetor, but the weight and density of the air is less, causing an excessively rich mixture, which causes spark plug fouling and decreased power. (PLT249, CA.I.G.K1c) — FAA-H-8083-25

AIR, RTC, LTA
5609. Unless adjusted, the fuel/air mixture becomes richer with an increase in altitude because the amount of fuel

A—decreases while the volume of air decreases.
B—remains constant while the volume of air decreases.
C—remains constant while the density of air decreases.

Fuel flow remains constant if no adjustments are made. The same volume of air goes into the carburetor, but the weight and density of the air is less, causing an excessively rich mixture, which causes spark plug fouling and decreased power. (PLT249, CA.I.G.K1c) — FAA-H-8083-25

AIR, RTC, LTA
5610. The basic purpose of adjusting the fuel/air mixture control at altitude is to

A—decrease the fuel flow to compensate for decreased air density.
B—decrease the amount of fuel in the mixture to compensate for increased air density.
C—increase the amount of fuel in the mixture to compensate for the decrease in pressure and density of the air.

Fuel flow remains constant if no adjustments are made. The same volume of air goes into the carburetor, but the weight and density of the air is less, causing an excessively rich mixture, which causes spark plug fouling and decreased power. (PLT249, CA.I.G.K1c) — FAA-H-8083-25

Answers

| 5187 [B] | 5188 [A] | 5298 [B] | 5608 [C] | 5609 [C] | 5610 [A] |

AIR, RTC, LTA
5611. At high altitudes, an excessively rich mixture will cause the

A—engine to overheat.
B—fouling of spark plugs.
C—engine to operate smoother even though fuel consumption is increased.

Fuel flow remains constant if no adjustments are made. The same volume of air goes into the carburetor, but the weight and density of the air is less, causing an excessively rich mixture, which causes spark plug fouling and decreased power. (PLT343, CA.I.G.K1c) — FAA-H-8083-25

Answer (A) is incorrect because a lean mixture will cause the engine to overheat. Answer (C) is incorrect because an engine runs smoother when the mixture is adjusted for the altitude.

Carburetor Ice

As air flows through a carburetor, it expands rapidly. At the same time, fuel entering the airstream is vaporized. Expansion of the air and vaporization of the fuel causes a sudden cooling of the mixture which may cause ice to form inside the carburetor. The possibility of icing should always be considered when operating in conditions where the outside air temperature is between 20°F and 70°F and the relative humidity is high.

Carburetor heat preheats the air before it enters the carburetor and either prevents carburetor ice from forming or melts any ice which may have formed. When carburetor heat is applied, the heated air that enters the carburetor is less dense. This causes the air/fuel mixture to become enriched, and this in turn decreases engine output (less engine horsepower) and increases engine operating temperatures.

During engine run-up, prior to departure from a high-altitude airport, the pilot may notice a slight engine roughness which is not affected by the magneto check but grows worse during the carburetor heat check. In this case the air/fuel mixture may be too rich due to the lower air density at the high altitude, and applying carburetor heat decreases the air density even more. A leaner setting of the mixture control may correct this problem.

In an airplane with a fixed-pitch propeller, the first indication of carburetor ice will likely be a decrease in RPM as the air supply is choked off. Application of carburetor heat will decrease air density, causing the RPM to drop even lower. Then, as the carburetor ice melts, the RPM will rise gradually.

Fuel injection systems, which do not utilize a carburetor, are generally considered to be less susceptible to icing than carburetor systems are.

AIR, RTC, LTA
5170. Leaving the carburetor heat on while taking off

A—leans the mixture for more power on takeoff.
B—will decrease the takeoff distance.
C—will increase the ground roll.

Use of carburetor heat enriches the mixture, which tends to reduce the output of the engine and also increases the operating temperature. Therefore, the heat should not be used when full power is required (such as during takeoff) or during normal engine operations except to check for the presence of, or removal of carburetor ice. A decrease in engine output will increase distance required to reach lift off speed. Therefore, it will increase ground roll. (PLT189, CA.I.G.K1e) — FAA-H-8083-25

AIR, RTC, LTA
5189. Which statement is true concerning the effect of the application of carburetor heat?

A—It enriches the fuel/air mixture.
B—It leans the fuel/air mixture.
C—It has no effect on the fuel/air mixture.

Use of carburetor heat enriches the mixture which tends to reduce the output of the engine and also increases the operating temperature. (PLT189, CA.I.G.K1e) — FAA-H-8083-25

Answers

5611 [B]   5170 [C]   5189 [A]

Chapter 2 Aircraft Systems

AIR, RTC, LTA
5606. Applying carburetor heat will

A—not affect the mixture.
B—lean the fuel/air mixture.
C—enrich the fuel/air mixture.

Use of carburetor heat enriches the mixture which tends to reduce the output of the engine and also increases the operating temperature. (PLT343, CA.I.G.K1e) — FAA-H-8083-25

Aviation Fuel

Fuel does two things for the engine; it acts both as an agent for combustion and as an agent for cooling (based on the mixture setting of the engine).

Aviation fuel is available in several grades. The proper grade for a specific engine will be listed in the aircraft flight manual. If the proper grade of fuel is not available, it is possible to use the next higher grade. A lower grade of fuel should never be used.

The use of low-grade fuel or a too lean air/fuel mixture may cause detonation, which is the uncontrolled spontaneous explosion of the mixture in the cylinder, instead of burning progressively and evenly. Detonation produces extreme heat.

Preignition is the premature uncontrolled firing of the fuel/air mixture. It is caused by an incandescent area (such as a carbon or lead deposit heated to a red hot glow) serving as an ignitor in advance of normal ignition.

Fuel can be contaminated by water and/or dirt. The air inside the aircraft fuel tanks can cool at night, which allows formation of water droplets (through condensation) on the insides of the fuel tanks. These droplets then fall into the fuel. To avoid this problem, always fill the tanks completely when parking overnight.

Thoroughly drain all of the aircraft's sumps, drains, and strainers before a flight to get rid of any water that may have collected.

Dirt can get into the fuel if refueling equipment is poorly maintained or if the refueling operation is sloppy. Use care when refueling an aircraft.

On aircraft equipped with fuel pumps, the practice of running a fuel tank dry before switching tanks is considered unwise because the engine-driven fuel pump or electric fuel boost pump may draw air into the fuel system and cause vapor lock.

AIR, RTC, LTA
5185-1. Detonation may occur at high-power settings when

A—the fuel mixture ignites instantaneously instead of burning progressively and evenly.
B—an excessively rich fuel mixture causes an explosive gain in power.
C—the fuel mixture is ignited too early by hot carbon deposits in the cylinder.

Detonation or knock is a sudden explosion or shock to a small area of the piston top, rather than the normal smooth burn in the combustion chamber. (PLT115, CA.I.G.K1e) — FAA-H-8083-25

Answer (B) is incorrect because detonation may occur with an excessively lean fuel mixture and a loss in power. Answer (C) is incorrect because this describes preignition.

Answers
5606 [C] 5185-1 [A]

Chapter 2 Aircraft Systems

AIR, RTC, LTA

5186. The uncontrolled firing of the fuel/air charge in advance of normal spark ignition is known as

A—instantaneous combustion.
B—detonation.
C—pre-ignition.

When the cylinder head gets too hot, it can ignite the fuel/air mixture before the spark. This condition is called preignition. (PLT115, CA.I.G.K1e) — FAA-H-8083-25

Answers (A) and (B) are incorrect because detonation is an instantaneous combustion of the fuel/air mixture, which is caused by using too lean a mixture, using too low a grade of fuel, or operating with temperatures that are too high.

AIR, RTC, LTA

5190. Detonation occurs in a reciprocating aircraft engine when

A—there is an explosive increase of fuel caused by too rich a fuel/air mixture.
B—the spark plugs receive an electrical jolt caused by a short in the wiring.
C—the unburned fuel/air charge in the cylinders is subjected to instantaneous combustion.

Detonation is a sudden explosion, or instantaneous combustion, of the fuel/air mixture in the cylinders, producing extreme heat and severe structural stresses on the engine. (PLT115, CA.I.G.K1c) — FAA-H-8083-25

Answer (A) is incorrect because detonation is caused by too lean a mixture. Answer (B) is incorrect because detonation does not have anything to do with the wiring.

AIR, RTC, LTA

5299. Consider a reciprocating engine. Detonation can be caused by

A—a "rich" mixture.
B—low engine temperatures.
C—using a lower grade fuel than recommended.

Detonation is a sudden explosion or shock to a small area of the piston top, rather than the normal smooth burn in the combustion chamber. It can be caused by low grade fuel or a lean mixture. (PLT251, CA.I.G.K1c) — FAA-H-8083-25

Engine Temperatures

Most light aircraft engines are cooled externally by air. For internal cooling and lubrication, an engine depends on circulating oil. Engine lubricating oil not only prevents direct metal-to-metal contact of moving parts, it also absorbs and dissipates part of the engine heat produced by internal combustion. If the engine oil level is too low, an abnormally high engine oil temperature indication may result.

On the ground or in the air, excessively high engine temperatures can cause excessive oil consumption, loss of power, and possible permanent internal engine damage.

If the engine oil temperature and cylinder head temperature gauges have exceeded their normal operating range, or if the pilot suspects that the engine (with a fixed-pitch propeller) is detonating during climb-out, the pilot may have been operating with either too much power and the mixture set too lean, using fuel of too low a grade, or operating the engine with not enough oil in it. Reducing the rate of climb and increasing airspeed, enriching the fuel mixture, or retarding the throttle will help cool an overheating engine. Also, rapid throttle operation can induce detonation, which may detune the crankshaft.

The most important rule to remember in the event of a power failure after becoming airborne is to maintain safe airspeed.

Answers

5186 [C]   5190 [C]   5299 [C]

AIR
5175. For internal cooling, reciprocating aircraft engines are especially dependent on

A—a properly functioning cowl flap augmenter.
B—the circulation of lubricating oil.
C—the proper freon/compressor output ratio.

Lubricating oil serves two purposes:

1. It furnishes a coating of oil over the surfaces of the moving parts, preventing metal-to-metal contact and the generation of heat; and

2. It absorbs and dissipates, through the oil cooling system, part of the engine heat produced by the internal combustion process.

(PLT343, CA.I.G.R1) — FAA-H-8083-25

Answer (A) is incorrect because although cowl flaps aid internal cooling, they are not the primary cooling source. Answer (C) is incorrect because the proper freon/compressor output ratio controls cabin cooling.

AIR
5271. A detuning of engine crankshaft counterweights is a source of overstress that may be caused by

A—rapid opening and closing of the throttle.
B—carburetor ice forming on the throttle valve.
C—operating with an excessively rich fuel/air mixture.

Rapid throttle operation can induce detonation, which may detune the crankshaft. (PLT343, CA.I.G.R1) — AC 20-103

Answer (B) is incorrect because carburetor ice can cause the engine to stop running, but it will not affect the engine crankshaft counterweights. Answer (C) is incorrect because operating with an excessively rich mixture fouls the spark plugs, but does not affect the crankshaft.

AIR, RTC, LTA
5607. An abnormally high engine oil temperature indication may be caused by

A—a defective bearing.
B—the oil level being too low.
C—operating with an excessively rich mixture.

The oil pressure indication varies inversely with the oil temperature. High temperature and low-pressure usually indicate low oil level. (PLT343, CA.I.G.R1) — FAA-H-8083-25

Answer (A) is incorrect because a defective bearing will increase metal particles in the oil, but will not significantly affect the oil temperature. Answer (C) is incorrect because a rich mixture results in lower engine operating temperatures; therefore, it would not increase engine oil temperature.

Propellers

The propeller is a rotating airfoil which produces thrust by creating a positive dynamic pressure, usually on the engine side.

When a propeller rotates, the tips travel at a greater speed than the hub. To compensate for the greater speed at the tips, the blades are twisted slightly. The propeller blade angles decrease from the hub to the tips with the greatest angle of incidence, or highest pitch, at the hub and the smallest at the tip. This produces a relatively uniform angle of attack (uniform lift) along the blade's length in cruise flight.

No propeller is 100% efficient. There is always some loss of power when converting engine output into thrust. This loss is primarily due to propeller slippage. A propeller's efficiency is the ratio of thrust horsepower (propeller output) to brake horsepower (engine output). A fixed propeller will have a peak (best) efficiency at only one combination of airspeed and RPM.

A constant-speed (controllable-pitch) propeller allows the pilot to select the most efficient propeller blade angle for each phase of flight. In this system, the throttle controls the power output as registered on the manifold pressure gauge, and the propeller control regulates the engine RPM (propeller RPM). The pitch angle of the blades is changed by governor regulated oil pressure which keeps engine speed at a constant selected RPM. A constant-speed propeller allows the pilot to select a small propeller blade angle (flat pitch) and high RPM to develop maximum power and thrust for takeoff.

To reduce the engine output to climb power after takeoff, a pilot should decrease the manifold pressure. The RPM is decreased by increasing the propeller blade angle. When the throttle is advanced

Answers

5175 [B]   5271 [A]   5607 [B]

(increased) during cruise, the propeller pitch angle will automatically increase to allow engine RPM to remain the same. A pilot should avoid a high manifold pressure setting with low RPM on engines equipped with a constant-speed propeller to prevent placing undue stress on engine components. To avoid high manifold pressure combined with low RPM, the manifold pressure should be reduced before reducing RPM when decreasing power settings, and the RPM increased before increasing the manifold pressure when increasing power settings.

AIR

5183. Which statement best describes the operating principle of a constant-speed propeller?

A—As throttle setting is changed by the pilot, the prop governor causes pitch angle of the propeller blades to remain unchanged.
B—A high blade angle, or increased pitch, reduces the propeller drag and allows more engine power for takeoffs.
C—The propeller control regulates the engine RPM and in turn the propeller RPM.

The propeller control regulates the engine RPM and in turn, the propeller RPM. The RPM is registered on the tachometer. (PLT350, CA.I.G.K1c) — FAA-H-8083-25

Answer (A) is incorrect because the prop governor causes the pitch angle of the prop blades to change to help maintain a specified airspeed. Answer (B) is incorrect because a high blade angle will increase propeller drag with less engine power.

AIR

5184. In aircraft equipped with constant-speed propellers and normally-aspirated engines, which procedure should be used to avoid placing undue stress on the engine components? When power is being

A—decreased, reduce the RPM before reducing the manifold pressure.
B—increased, increase the RPM before increasing the manifold pressure.
C—increased or decreased, the RPM should be adjusted before the manifold pressure.

Power change procedure on a constant-speed propeller is to increase RPM before manifold pressure. To decrease power, reduce manifold pressure before reducing RPM. This will help avoid placing undue stress on the engine components. (PLT350, CA.I.G.K1c) — FAA-H-8083-25

Answers (A) and (C) are incorrect because when power is being decreased, the manifold pressure should be reduced before reducing the RPM.

AIR

5235. Propeller efficiency is the

A—ratio of thrust horsepower to brake horsepower.
B—actual distance a propeller advances in one revolution.
C—ratio of geometric pitch to effective pitch.

Since the efficiency of any machine is the ratio of useful power output to actual power input, propeller efficiency is the ratio of thrust horsepower to brake horsepower. (PLT351, CA.I.G.K1c) — FAA-H-8083-25

Answer (B) is incorrect because effective pitch is the actual distance a propeller advances in one revolution. Answer (C) is incorrect because the ratio of geometric pitch to effective pitch is called slippage.

AIR

5236. A fixed-pitch propeller is designed for best efficiency only at a given combination of

A—altitude and RPM.
B—airspeed and RPM.
C—airspeed and altitude.

Fixed-pitch propellers are most efficient only at a given combination of airspeed and RPM. (PLT351, CA.I.G.K1c) — FAA-H-8083-25

Answers (A) and (C) are incorrect because altitude does not affect propeller efficiency.

Answers

5183 [C]   5184 [B]   5235 [A]   5236 [B]

AIR
5237. The reason for variations in geometric pitch (twisting) along a propeller blade is that it

A—permits a relatively constant angle of incidence along its length when in cruising flight.
B—prevents the portion of the blade near the hub from stalling during cruising flight.
C—permits a relatively constant angle of attack along its length when in cruising flight.

Twisting, or variations in the geometric pitch of the blades, permits the propeller to operate with a relatively constant angle of attack along its length when in cruising flight. (PLT243, CA.I.G.K1c) — FAA-H-8083-25

Answer (A) is incorrect because variations in geometric pitch permit a constant angle of attack along its length. Answer (B) is incorrect because the propeller tips would be stalled during cruising flight if there was no variation in geometric pitch.

AIR
5654. To establish a climb after takeoff in an aircraft equipped with a constant-speed propeller, the output of the engine is reduced to climb power by decreasing manifold pressure and

A—increasing RPM by decreasing propeller blade angle.
B—decreasing RPM by decreasing propeller blade angle.
C—decreasing RPM by increasing propeller blade angle.

A low-pitch, high RPM setting is utilized to obtain maximum power for takeoff. Then, after the airplane is airborne, an increasing blade angle/pitch will cause lower RPM which provides adequate thrust and better economy while maintaining the proper airspeed. (PLT350, CA.I.G.K1c) — FAA-H-8083-25

Answer (A) is incorrect because RPM is decreased to reduce power, by increasing propeller blade angle. Answer (B) is incorrect because blade angle must be increased to decrease RPM.

AIR
5667. To develop maximum power and thrust, a constant-speed propeller should be set to a blade angle that will produce a

A—large angle of attack and low RPM.
B—small angle of attack and high RPM.
C—large angle of attack and high RPM.

Smaller angle of attack makes the blades take smaller amounts of air, which in turn allows the engine to run at higher RPM, producing more power. (PLT350, CA.I.G.K1c) — FAA-H-8083-25

AIR
5668. For takeoff, the blade angle of a controllable-pitch propeller should be set at a

A—small angle of attack and high RPM.
B—large angle of attack and low RPM.
C—large angle of attack and high RPM.

Smaller angle of attack makes the blades take smaller amounts of air, which in turn allows the engine to run at higher RPM, producing more power. (PLT350, CA.I.G.K1c) — FAA-H-8083-25

Answers

5237 [C] 5654 [C] 5667 [B] 5668 [A]

Cold Weather Operations

At low temperatures, changes occur in the viscosity of engine oil, batteries can lose a high percentage of their effectiveness, instruments can stick, and warning lights can stick in the pushed position when "pushed to test." Therefore, preheating the engines, as well as the cockpit, before starting is advisable in low temperatures. The pilot should also be aware that at extremely low temperatures, the engine can develop more than rated takeoff power even though the manifold pressure (MAP) and RPM readings are normal.

Overpriming is a frequent cause of difficult starting in cold weather because oil is washed off the cylinder walls and poor compression results. The manufacturer's instructions should be followed for starting an overprimed engine.

During cold weather preflight operations, be sure to check the oil breather lines. Vapors caused by combustion may condense and then freeze, clogging these lines.

Since most aircraft heaters work by using the engine to heat outside air, a pilot should frequently inspect a manifold type heating system to minimize the possibility of hazardous exhaust gases leaking into the cockpit.

AIR, RTC
5653. Your aircraft has an exhaust manifold type heating system. The exhaust manifold should be periodically inspected to avoid

A—carbon monoxide poisoning.
B—overheating in the cockpit.
C—extremely cold temperatures in the cabin.

Carbon monoxide poisoning from exhaust gases leaking into the cockpit from a faulty exhaust manifold has been linked to several fatal aircraft accidents. (PLT343, CA.I.G.K1i) — FAA-H-8083-25

AIR, RTC
5766. During preflight in cold weather, crankcase breather lines should receive special attention because they are susceptible to being clogged by

A—congealed oil from the crankcase.
B—moisture from the outside air which has frozen.
C—ice from crankcase vapors that have condensed and subsequently frozen.

The crankcase breather requires special consideration when preparing for cold weather. Frozen breather lines can create numerous problems. When crankcase vapors cool, they may condense in the breather line and subsequently freeze it closed. Special care is recommended during the preflight to ensure that the breather system is free of ice. (PLT136, CA.I.G.R1) — AC 91-13

Answer (A) is incorrect because oil that lays in the bottom of the crankcase never gets into the breather lines. Answer (B) is incorrect because a low air temperature is usually associated with a low moisture content.

AIR, RTC
5767. Which is true regarding preheating an aircraft during cold weather operations?

A—The cabin area as well as the engine should be preheated.
B—The cabin area should not be preheated with portable heaters.
C—Hot air should be blown directly at the engine through the air intakes.

Low temperatures may cause a change in the viscosity of engine oils, batteries may lose a high percentage of their effectiveness, and instruments may stick. Because of the above, preheating the engines as well as the cabin before starting is desirable in low temperatures. Extreme caution should be used in the preheat process to avoid fire. (PLT126, CA.I.G.K1) — AC 91-13

Answers

5653 [A]   5766 [C]   5767 [A]

Rotorcraft Systems

The pitch angle of a helicopter rotor blade is the acute angle between the chord line of the blade and the plane of rotor rotation.

In a semirigid rotor system, the rotor blades are rigidly interconnected to the hub, but the hub is free to tilt and rock with respect to the rotor shaft. In this system in which only two-bladed rotors are used, the blades flap as a unit; that is, as one blade flaps up, the other blade flaps down an equal amount. The hinge which permits the flapping or see-saw effect is called a teetering hinge.

A rocking hinge, perpendicular to the teetering hinge and parallel to the rotor blades, allows the head to rock in response to tilting of the swash plate by the cyclic pitch control. This changes the pitch angle an equal amount on each blade—decreasing it on one blade and increasing it on the other.

In a fully articulated rotor system, each blade is attached to the hub by three hinges, oriented at approximately right angles to each other. A horizontal hinge, called the flapping hinge, allows the blades to move up and down independently. A vertical hinge, called a drag, or lag hinge, allows each blade to move back and forth in the plane of the rotor disk. This movement is called dragging, or hunting. The blades can also rotate about their spanwise axis to change their individual blade pitch angle, or feather.

Fully articulated helicopter rotor systems generally use three or more blades, and each blade can flap, drag, and feather independently of the other blades.

The freewheeling unit in a helicopter rotor system allows the engine to automatically disengage from the rotor when the engine stops or slows below the corresponding rotor RPM. This makes autorotation possible.

Because a helicopter rotor system weighs so much more than a propeller, a helicopter (except for those with free turbine engines) must have some way to disconnect the engine from the rotor to relieve the starter load. For this reason, it is necessary to have a clutch between the engine and the rotor. The clutch in a helicopter rotor system allows the engine to be started without the load, and when the engine is running properly, the rotor load can be gradually applied.

High-frequency vibrations are associated with the engine in most helicopters and are impossible to count, because of their high frequency. A high-frequency vibration that suddenly occurs during flight could be an indication of a transmission bearing failure. Such a failure will result in vibrations whose frequencies are directly related to the engine speed. Abnormal low-frequency vibrations in a helicopter are always associated with the main rotor.

RTC
5168. For gyroplanes with constant-speed propellers, the first indication of carburetor icing is usually

A—a decrease in engine RPM.
B—a decrease in manifold pressure.
C—engine roughness followed by a decrease in engine RPM.

For gyroplanes with controllable-pitch (constant speed) propellers, the first indication of carburetor icing is usually a drop in manifold pressure. There will be no reduction in RPM with constant-speed propellers, since propeller pitch is automatically adjusted to compensate for the loss of power, thus maintaining constant RPM. (PLT253) — FAA-H-8083-21

RTC
5240. Coning is caused by the combined forces of

A—drag, weight, and translational lift.
B—lift and centrifugal force.
C—flapping and centrifugal force.

Coning is the upward bending of the blades caused by the combined forces of lift and centrifugal force. (PLT027) — FAA-H-8083-21

Answers

5168 [B]   5240 [B]

Chapter 2 **Aircraft Systems**

RTC
5241. The forward speed of a rotorcraft is restricted primarily by

A—dissymmetry of lift.
B—transverse flow effect.
C—high-frequency vibrations.

A tendency for the retreating blade to stall in forward flight is inherent in all present-day helicopters and is a major factor in limiting their forward airspeed. Retreating blade stall is caused by the dissymmetry of lift created when the airflow over the retreating blade of the helicopter slows down as forward speed of the helicopter increases. (PLT235) — FAA-H-8083-21

RTC
5242. When hovering, a helicopter tends to move in the direction of tail rotor thrust. This statement is

A—true; the movement is called transverse tendency.
B—true; the movement is called translating tendency.
C—false; the movement is opposite the direction of tail rotor thrust, and is called translating tendency.

Due to translating tendency or drift, the entire helicopter has a tendency to move in the direction of tail rotor thrust (to the right) when hovering. (PLT268) — FAA-H-8083-21

RTC
5243. The purpose of lead-lag (drag) hinges in a three-bladed, fully articulated helicopter rotor system is to compensate for

A—Coriolis effect.
B—dissymmetry of lift.
C—blade flapping tendency.

When a rotor blade of a three-bladed rotor system flaps upward, the center of mass of the blade moves closer to the axis of rotation and blade acceleration takes place. This acceleration and deceleration action (often referred to as leading, lagging or hunting) in the plane of rotation is due to "Coriolis effect." (PLT470) — FAA-H-8083-21

RTC
5244. What happens to the helicopter as it experiences translating tendency?

A—It tends to dip slightly to the right as the helicopter approaches approximately 15 knots in takeoff.
B—It gains increased rotor efficiency as air over the rotor system reaches approximately 15 knots.
C—It moves in the direction of tail rotor thrust.

Due to translating tendency or drift, the entire helicopter has a tendency to move in the direction of tail rotor thrust (to the right) when hovering. (PLT235) — FAA-H-8083-21

RTC
5245. The unequal lift across the rotor disc that occurs in horizontal flight as a result of the difference in velocity of the air over the advancing half of the disc area and the air passing over the retreating half of the disc area is known as

A—coning.
B—disc loading.
C—dissymmetry of lift.

Dissymmetry of lift is created by horizontal flight or by wind during hovering flight, and is the difference in lift that exists between the advancing blade half of the disc area and the retreating blade half. (PLT242) — FAA-H-8083-21

RTC
5246. The lift differential that exists between the advancing blade and the retreating blade is known as

A—Coriolis effect.
B—translational lift.
C—dissymmetry of lift.

Dissymmetry of lift is created by horizontal flight or by wind during hovering flight, and is the difference in lift that exists between the advancing blade half of the disc area and the retreating blade half. (PLT235) — FAA-H-8083-21

Answers

5241 [A]   5242 [B]   5243 [A]   5244 [C]   5245 [C]   5246 [C]

RTC
5247. Most helicopters, by design tend to drift to the right when hovering in a no-wind condition. This statement is

A—false; helicopters have no tendency to drift, but will rotate in that direction.
B—true; the mast or cyclic pitch system of most helicopters is rigged forward, this with gyroscopic precession will overcome this tendency.
C—true; the mast or cyclic pitch system of most helicopters is rigged to the left to overcome this tendency.

The entire helicopter has a tendency to move in the direction of tail rotor thrust (to the right) when hovering. To counteract this drift, the rotor mast in some helicopters is rigged slightly to the left side. (PLT268) — FAA-H-8083-21

RTC
5248. When a rotorcraft transitions from straight-and-level flight into a 30° bank while maintaining a constant altitude, the total lift force must

A—increase and the load factor will increase.
B—increase and the load factor will decrease.
C—remain constant and the load factor will decrease.

The steeper the angle of bank, the greater the angle of attack of the rotor blades required to maintain altitude. Thus, with an increase in bank and a greater angle of attack, the resultant lifting force will be increased. The load factor and hence, apparent gross weight increase, is relatively small in banks up to 30°. (PLT219) — FAA-H-8083-21

RTC
5249. Cyclic control pressure is applied during flight that results in a maximum increase in main rotor blade pitch angle at the "three o'clock" position. Which way will the rotor disc tilt?

A—Aft.
B—Left.
C—Right.

Because of the gyroscopic precession property, the blades do not rise or lower to maximum deflection until a point approximately 90° later in the plane of rotation. (PLT235) — FAA-H-8083-21

RTC
5250. Cyclic control pressure is applied during flight that results in a maximum decrease in pitch angle of the rotor blades at the "12 o'clock" position. Which way will the rotor disc tilt?

A—Aft.
B—Left.
C—Forward.

Because of the gyroscopic precession property, the blades do not rise or lower to maximum deflection until a point approximately 90° later in the plane of rotation. (PLT235) — FAA-H-8083-21

RTC
5251. The primary purpose of the tail rotor system is to

A—assist in making coordinated turns.
B—maintain heading during forward flight.
C—counteract the torque effect of the main rotor.

The force that compensates for torque and keeps the fuselage from turning in the direction opposite to the main rotor is produced by means of an auxiliary rotor located on the end of the tail boom. (PLT470) — FAA-H-8083-21

RTC
5252. Can the tail rotor produce thrust to the left?

A—No; the right thrust can only be reduced, causing tail movement to the left.
B—Yes; primarily so that hovering turns can be accomplished to the right.
C—Yes; primarily to counteract the drag of the transmission during autorotation.

The maximum positive-pitch angle of the tail rotor is generally somewhat greater than the maximum negative pitch angle available. This is because the primary purpose of the tail rotor is to counteract the torque of the main rotor. The capability for tail rotors to produce thrust to the left (negative-pitch angle) is necessary because, during autorotation, the drag of the transmission tends to yaw the nose to the left—in the same direction that the main rotor is turning. (PLT470) — FAA-H-8083-21

Answers

| 5247 [C] | 5248 [A] | 5249 [A] | 5250 [B] | 5251 [C] | 5252 [C] |

RTC

5253. The main rotor blades of a fully-articulated rotor system can

A—flap and feather collectively.
B—flap, drag, and feather independently.
C—feather independently, but cannot flap or drag.

Each blade of a fully articulated rotor system can flap, drag, and feather independently of the other blades. (PLT470) — FAA-H-8083-21

RTC

5254. A reciprocating engine in a helicopter is more likely to stop due to in-flight carburetor icing than will the same type engine in an airplane. This statement

A—has no basis in fact. The same type engine will run equally well in either aircraft.
B—is true. The freewheeling unit will not allow windmilling (flywheel) effect to be exerted on a helicopter engine.
C—is false. The clutch will immediately release the load from the helicopter engine under engine malfunctioning conditions.

Carburetor icing is a frequent cause of engine failure. Even a slight accumulation of this deposit will reduce power and may lead to complete engine failure, particularly when the throttle is partly or fully closed. (PLT343) — FAA-H-8083-21

RTC

5255. What is the primary purpose of the clutch?

A—It allows the engine to be started without driving the main rotor system.
B—It provides disengagement of the engine from the rotor system for autorotation.
C—It transmits engine power to the main rotor, tail rotor, generator/alternator, and other accessories.

Because of the much greater weight of a helicopter rotor in relation to the power of the engine, than the weight of a propeller in relation to the power of the engine in an airplane, it is necessary to have the rotor disconnected from the engine to relieve the starter load. For this reason, a clutch is needed between the engine and rotor. The clutch allows the engine to be started and gradually assume the load of driving the heavy rotor. (PLT471) — FAA-H-8083-21

RTC

5256. What is the primary purpose of the freewheeling unit?

A—It allows the engine to be started without driving the main rotor system.
B—It provides speed reduction between the engine, main rotor system, and tail rotor system.
C—It provides disengagement of the engine from the rotor system for autorotation purposes.

The freewheeling coupling provides for autorotative capabilities by automatically disconnecting the rotor system from the engine when the engine stops or slows below the equivalent of rotor RPM. When the engine is disconnected from the rotor system through the automatic action of the freewheeling coupling, the transmission continues to rotate with the main rotor thereby enabling the tail rotor to continue turning at its normal rate. This permits the pilot to maintain directional control during autorotation. (PLT471) — FAA-H-8083-21

RTC

5257. The main rotor blades of a semi-rigid rotor system can

A—flap together as a unit.
B—flap, drag, and feather independently.
C—feather independently, but cannot flap or drag.

A semi-rigid rotor system can flap together as a unit. (PLT470) — FAA-H-8083-21

RTC

5258. Rotorcraft climb performance is most adversely affected by

A—higher than standard temperature and low relative humidity.
B—lower than standard temperature and high relative humidity.
C—higher than standard temperature and high relative humidity.

High elevations, high temperatures, and high moisture content, all of which contribute to a high density altitude condition, lessen helicopter performance. (PLT127) — FAA-H-8083-21

Answers

| 5253 | [B] | 5254 | [B] | 5255 | [A] | 5256 | [C] | 5257 | [A] | 5258 | [C] |

Chapter 2 **Aircraft Systems**

RTC
5259. The most unfavorable combination of conditions for rotorcraft performance is

A—low density altitude, low gross weight, and calm wind.
B—high density altitude, high gross weight, and calm wind.
C—high density altitude, high gross weight, and strong wind.

The most adverse conditions for helicopter performance are the combination of a high density altitude, heavy gross weight, and calm or no wind. (PLT127) — FAA-H-8083-21

RTC
5260. How does high density altitude affect rotorcraft performance?

A—Engine and rotor efficiency is reduced.
B—Engine and rotor efficiency is increased.
C—It increases rotor drag, which requires more power for normal flight.

Helicopter performance is reduced because the thinner air at high density altitudes reduces the amount of lift of the rotor blades. Also, the (unsupercharged) engine does not develop as much power because of the thinner air and the decreased atmospheric pressure. (PLT127) — FAA-H-8083-21

RTC
5261. A medium-frequency vibration that suddenly occurs during flight could be indicative of a defective

A—main rotor system.
B—tail rotor system.
C—transmission system.

Medium-frequency vibrations are a result of trouble with the tail rotor in most helicopters. Improper rigging, imbalance, defective blades, or bad bearings in the tail rotor are all sources of these vibrations. If the vibration occurs only during turns, the trouble may be caused by insufficient tail rotor flapping action. (PLT472) — FAA-H-8083-21

RTC
5262. In most helicopters, medium-frequency vibrations indicate a defective

A—engine.
B—main rotor system.
C—tail rotor system.

Medium-frequency vibrations are a result of trouble with the tail rotor in most helicopters. Improper rigging, imbalance, defective blades, or bad bearings in the tail rotor are all sources of these vibrations. If the vibration occurs only during turns, the trouble may be caused by insufficient tail rotor flapping action. (PLT472) — FAA-H-8083-21

RTC
5263. Abnormal helicopter vibrations in the low-frequency range are associated with which system or component?

A—Tail rotor.
B—Main rotor.
C—Transmission.

Abnormal vibrations in this category are always associated with the main rotor. The vibration will be some frequency related to the rotor RPM and the number of blades of the rotor, such as one vibration per revolution, two per revolution, or three per revolution. Low-frequency vibrations are slow enough that they can be counted. (PLT472) — FAA-H-8083-21

RTC
5264. Helicopter low-frequency vibrations are always associated with the

A—main rotor.
B—tail rotor.
C—transmission.

Abnormal vibrations in this category are always associated with the main rotor. The vibration will be some frequency related to the rotor RPM and the number of blades of the rotor, such as one vibration per revolution, two per revolution, or three per revolution. Low-frequency vibrations are slow enough that they can be counted. (PLT472) — FAA-H-8083-21

Answers

5259 [B]   5260 [A]   5261 [B]   5262 [C]   5263 [B]   5264 [A]

Chapter 2 **Aircraft Systems**

RTC
5265. A high-frequency vibration that suddenly occurs during flight could be an indication of a defective

A—transmission.
B—freewheeling unit.
C—main rotor system.

High-frequency vibrations are associated with the engine in most helicopters, and will be impossible to count due to the high rate of vibration. However, they could be associated with the tail rotor for helicopters in which the tail rotor RPM is approximately equal to or greater than the engine RPM. A defective clutch, or missing or bent fan blades will cause vibrations which should be corrected. Any bearings in the engine or in the transmission or the tail rotor drive shaft that go bad will result in vibrations with frequencies directly related to the speed of the engine. (PLT472) — FAA-H-8083-21

RTC
5266-1. Ground resonance is more likely to occur with helicopters that are equipped with

A—rigid rotor systems.
B—semi-rigid rotor systems.
C—fully articulated rotor systems.

In general, if ground resonance occurs, it will occur only in helicopters possessing three-bladed, fully articulated rotor systems and landing wheels. (PLT259) — FAA-H-8083-21

RTC
5266-2. Ground resonance is less likely to occur with helicopters that are not equipped with

A—rigid rotor systems.
B—fully articulated rotor systems.
C—semi-rigid rotor systems.

Ground resonance is an aerodynamic phenomenon associated with fully-articulated rotor systems. This situation does not occur in rigid or semirigid rotor systems, because there is no drag hinge. (PLT259) — FAA-H-8083-21

RTC
5267. The proper action to initiate a quick stop is to apply

A—forward cyclic, while raising the collective and applying right antitorque pedal.
B—aft cyclic, while raising the collective and applying left antitorque pedal.
C—aft cyclic, while lowering the collective and applying right antitorque pedal.

The deceleration is initiated by applying aft cyclic to reduce forward speed. Simultaneously, the collective pitch should be lowered as necessary to counteract any climbing tendency. The timing must be exact. If too little down collective is applied for the amount of aft cyclic applied, a climb will result. If too much down collective is applied for the amount of aft cyclic applied, a descent will result. A rapid application of aft cyclic requires an equally rapid application of down collective. As collective pitch is lowered, right pedal should be increased to maintain heading and throttle should be adjusted to maintain RPM. (PLT217) — FAA-H-8083-21

RTC
5671. During the flare portion of a power-off landing, the rotor RPM tends to

A—remain constant.
B—increase initially.
C—decrease initially.

Forward speed during autorotation descent permits a pilot to incline the rotor disc rearward, thus causing a flare. The additional induced lift created by the greater volume of air momentarily checks forward speed as well as descent. The greater volume of air acting on the rotor disc will normally increase rotor RPM during the flare. (PLT470) — FAA-H-8083-21

RTC
5672. Which would produce the slowest rotor RPM?

A—A vertical descent with power.
B—A vertical descent without power.
C—Pushing over after a steep climb.

A pushover out of a steep climb will produce the lowest rotor RPM. (PLT470) — FAA-H-8083-21

Answers

5265 [A]   5266-1 [C]   5266-2 [B]   5267 [C]   5671 [B]   5672 [C]

Chapter 2 **Aircraft Systems**

RTC
5673. If the RPM is low and the manifold pressure is high, what initial corrective action should be taken?

A—Increase the throttle.
B—Lower the collective pitch.
C—Raise the collective pitch.

Problem: RPM low, manifold pressure high.

Solution: Lowering the collective pitch will reduce the manifold pressure, decrease drag on the rotor, and therefore, increase the RPM.

(PLT112) — FAA-H-8083-21

RTC
5674. During climbing flight, the manifold pressure is low and the RPM is high. What initial corrective action should be taken?

A—Increase the throttle.
B—Decrease the throttle.
C—Raise the collective pitch.

Problem: RPM high, manifold pressure low.

Solution: Raising the collective pitch will increase the manifold pressure, increase drag on the rotor, and therefore decrease the RPM.

(PLT112) — FAA-H-8083-21

RTC
5675. During level flight, if the manifold pressure is high and the RPM is low, what initial corrective action should be made?

A—Decrease the throttle.
B—Increase the throttle.
C—Lower the collective pitch.

Problem: RPM low, manifold pressure high.

Solution: Lowering the collective pitch will reduce the manifold pressure, decrease drag on the rotor, and therefore, increase the RPM.

(PLT112) — FAA-H-8083-21

RTC
5676. When operating a helicopter in conditions favorable for carburetor icing, the carburetor heat should be

A—adjusted to keep the carburetor air temperature gauge indicating in the green arc at all times.
B—OFF for takeoffs, adjusted to keep the carburetor air temperature gauge indicating in the green arc at all other times.
C—OFF during takeoffs, approaches, and landings; adjusted to keep the carburetor air temperature gauge indicating in the green arc at all other times.

When a carburetor temperature gauge is used, the carburetor heat should be adjusted to keep the temperature in the green band. (PLT190) — FAA-H-8083-21

RTC
5686. As altitude increases, the V_{NE} of a helicopter will

A—increase.
B—decrease.
C—remain the same.

As the altitude increases, the never-exceed airspeed (red line) for most helicopters decreases. (PLT127) — FAA-H-8083-21

RTC
5695. The antitorque system fails during cruising flight and a powered approach landing is commenced. If the helicopter yaws to the right just prior to touchdown, what could the pilot do to help swing the nose to the left?

A—Increase the throttle.
B—Decrease the throttle.
C—Increase collective pitch.

Directional control should be maintained primarily with cyclic control and secondarily, by gently applying throttle momentarily, with needles joined, to swing the nose to the right, or decreasing throttle to swing the nose to the left. (PLT169) — FAA-H-8083-21

Answers

| 5673 | [B] | 5674 | [C] | 5675 | [C] | 5676 | [A] | 5686 | [B] | 5695 | [B] |

Chapter 2 **Aircraft Systems**

RTC
5696. If antitorque failure occurred during cruising flight, what could be done to help straighten out a left yaw prior to touchdown?

A—A normal running landing should be made.
B—Make a running landing using partial power and left cyclic.
C—Apply available throttle to help swing the nose to the right just prior to touchdown.

Directional control should be maintained primarily with cyclic control and secondarily, by gently applying throttle momentarily, with needles joined, to swing the nose to the right. (PLT169) — FAA-H-8083-21

RTC
5697. Should a helicopter pilot ever be concerned about ground resonance during takeoff?

A—No; ground resonance occurs only during an autorotative touchdown.
B—Yes; although it is more likely to occur on landing, it can occur during takeoff.
C—Yes; but only during slope takeoffs.

Ground resonance occurs when the helicopter makes contact with the surface during landing or while in contact with the surface during an attempted takeoff. (PLT265) — FAA-H-8083-21

RTC
5698. An excessively steep approach angle and abnormally slow closure rate should be avoided during an approach to a hover, primarily because

A—the airspeed indicator would be unreliable.
B—a go-around would be very difficult to accomplish.
C—vortex ring state could develop, particularly during the termination.

Situations that are conducive to a vortex ring state condition are:

1. *Attempting to hover out of ground effect at altitudes above the hovering ceiling of the helicopter;*
2. *Attempting to hover out of ground effect without maintaining precise altitude control; or*
3. *A steep power approach in which airspeed is permitted to drop nearly to zero.*

(PLT264) — FAA-H-8083-21

RTC
5699. During a near-vertical power approach into a confined area with the airspeed near zero, what hazardous condition may develop?

A—Ground resonance.
B—Vortex ring state.
C—Blade stall vibration.

Situations that are conducive to a vortex ring state condition are:

1. *Attempting to hover out of ground effect at altitudes above the hovering ceiling of the helicopter;*
2. *Attempting to hover out of ground effect without maintaining precise altitude control; or*
3. *A steep power approach in which airspeed is permitted to drop nearly to zero.*

(PLT264) — FAA-H-8083-21

RTC
5700. Which procedure will result in recovery from a vortex ring state?

A—Increase collective pitch and power.
B—Maintain constant collective pitch and increase throttle.
C—Increase forward speed and reduce collective pitch.

When recovering from a vortex ring state condition, pilots tend to try to stop the descent by increasing collective pitch. However, this only results in increasing the stalled area of the rotor, thus increasing the rate of descent. Since inboard portions of the blades are stalled, cyclic control is limited. Recovery is accomplished by increasing forward speed, and/or partially lowering collective pitch. (PLT264) — FAA-H-8083-21

Answers

| 5696 | [C] | 5697 | [B] | 5698 | [C] | 5699 | [B] | 5700 | [C] |

Chapter 2 **Aircraft Systems**

RTC
5701. The addition of power in a vortex ring state situation produces an

A—increase in airspeed.
B—even greater rate of descent.
C—increase in cyclic control effectiveness.

When recovering from a vortex ring state condition, pilots tend to try to stop the descent by increasing collective pitch. However, this only results in increasing the stalled area of the rotor, thus increasing the rate of descent. Since inboard portions of the blades are stalled, cyclic control is limited. Recovery is accomplished by increasing forward speed, and/or partially lowering collective pitch. (PLT341) — FAA-H-8083-21

RTC
5702. Under which situation is accidental vortex ring state likely to occur?

A—A steep approach in which the airspeed is permitted to drop to nearly zero.
B—A shallow approach in which the airspeed is permitted to drop below 10 MPH.
C—Hovering in ground effect during calm wind, high-density altitude conditions.

Situations that are conducive to a vortex ring state condition are:

1. *Attempting to hover out of ground effect at altitudes above the hovering ceiling of the helicopter;*
2. *Attempting to hover out of ground effect without maintaining precise altitude control; or*
3. *A steep power approach in which airspeed is permitted to drop nearly to zero.*

(PLT264) — FAA-H-8083-21

RTC
5703. To recover from a vortex ring state condition, the pilot should

A—apply forward cyclic and simultaneously reduce collective, if altitude permits.
B—not apply antitorque pedal during the recovery.
C—increase rotor RPM, reduce forward airspeed, and minimize maneuvering.

When recovering from a vortex ring state condition, pilots tend to try to stop the descent by increasing collective pitch. However, this only results in increasing the stalled area of the rotor, thus increasing the rate of descent. Since inboard portions of the blades are stalled, cyclic control is limited. Recovery is accomplished by increasing forward speed, and/or partially lowering collective pitch. In a fully developed vortex ring state, the only recovery may be to enter autorotation to break the vortex ring state. When cyclic authority is regained, you can then increase forward airspeed. (PLT264) — FAA-H-8083-21

RTC
5703-1. Loss of tail rotor effectiveness (LTE) is caused by

A—a main rotor disk vortex causes the tail rotor to operate in an extremely turbulent environment.
B—the failure of the power drive portion of the tail rotor disk, resulting in a complete loss of antitorque.
C—an aerodynamic interaction between the main rotor and tail rotor and not caused from a mechanical failure.

LTE is caused by an aerodynamic interaction between the main rotor and tail rotor and not caused by mechanical failure. Some helicopter types are more likely to encounter LTE due to the normal thrust produced by having a tail rotor that, although meeting certification standards, is not always able to produce the additional thrust demanded by the pilot. (PLT262) — FAA-H-8083-21

RTC
5704. When operating at high forward airspeed, retreating blade stall is more likely to occur under conditions of

A—low gross weight, high density altitude, and smooth air.
B—high gross weight, low density altitude, and smooth air.
C—high gross weight, high density altitude, and turbulent air.

When operating at high forward airspeeds, stalls are more likely to occur under conditions of:

1. *High gross weight.*
2. *Low RPM.*
3. *High density altitude.*
4. *Steep or abrupt turns.*
5. *Turbulent air.*

(PLT470) — FAA-H-8083-21

Answers

5701 [B]   5702 [A]   5703 [A]   5703-1 [C]   5704 [C]

Chapter 2 **Aircraft Systems**

RTC
5705. What are the major indications of an incipient retreating blade stall situation, in order of occurrence?

A—Low-frequency vibration, pitchup of the nose, and a roll in the direction of the retreating blade.
B—Slow pitchup of the nose, high-frequency vibration, and a tendency for the helicopter to roll.
C—Slow pitchup of the nose, tendency for the helicopter to roll, followed by a medium-frequency vibration.

The major warnings of approaching retreating blade stall conditions, in the order in which they will generally be experienced, are:

1. *Abnormal two-per-revolution vibration in two-bladed rotors or three-per-revolution vibration in three-bladed rotors.*
2. *Pitchup of the nose.*
3. *Tendency for the helicopter to roll.*

(PLT470) — FAA-H-8083-21

RTC
5706. How should a pilot react at the onset of retreating blade stall?

A—Reduce collective pitch, rotor RPM, and forward airspeed.
B—Reduce collective pitch, increase rotor RPM, and reduce forward airspeed.
C—Increase collective pitch, reduce rotor RPM, and reduce forward airspeed.

At the onset of blade stall vibration, the pilot should take the following corrective measures:

1. *Reduce collective pitch.*
2. *Increase rotor RPM.*
3. *Reduce forward airspeed.*
4. *Minimize maneuvering.*

(PLT470) — FAA-H-8083-21

RTC
5707. The most power will be required to hover over which surface?

A—High grass.
B—Concrete ramp.
C—Rough/uneven ground.

Tall grass will tend to disperse or absorb the ground effect. More power will be required to hover, and takeoff may be very difficult. (PLT268) — FAA-H-8083-21

RTC
5708. Which flight technique is recommended for use during hot weather?

A—During takeoff, accelerate quickly into forward flight.
B—During takeoff, accelerate slowly into forward flight.
C—Use minimum allowable RPM and maximum allowable manifold pressure during all phases of flight.

Flight technique in hot weather:

1. *Make full use of wind and translational lift.*
2. *Hover as low as possible and no longer than necessary.*
3. *Maintain maximum allowable engine RPM.*
4. *Accelerate very slowly into forward flight.*
5. *Employ running takeoffs and landings when necessary.*
6. *Use caution in maximum performance takeoffs and steep approaches.*

(PLT486) — FAA-H-8083-21

RTC
5709. To taxi on the surface in a safe and efficient manner, helicopter pilots should use the

A—cyclic pitch to control starting, taxi speed, and stopping.
B—collective pitch to control starting, taxi speed, and stopping.
C—antitorque pedals to correct for drift during crosswind conditions.

The collective pitch controls starting, stopping and rate of speed while taxiing. The higher the collective pitch, the faster will be the taxi speed. Taxi at a speed no greater than that of a normal walk. (PLT112) — FAA-H-8083-21

RTC
5710. During surface taxiing, the cyclic pitch stick is used to control

A—heading.
B—ground track.
C—forward movement.

Move the cyclic slightly forward of the neutral position and apply a gradual upward pressure on the collective pitch to move the helicopter forward along the surface. Use pedals to maintain heading and cyclic to maintain ground track. (PLT112) — FAA-H-8083-21

Answers

| 5705 | [A] | 5706 | [B] | 5707 | [A] | 5708 | [B] | 5709 | [B] | 5710 | [B] |

RTC

5711. To taxi on the surface in a safe and efficient manner, one should use the cyclic pitch to

A—start and stop aircraft movement.
B—maintain heading during crosswind conditions.
C—correct for drift during crosswind conditions.

During crosswind taxi, the cyclic should be held into the wind a sufficient amount to eliminate any drifting movement. (PLT112) — FAA-H-8083-21

RTC

5712. A pilot is hovering during calm wind conditions. The greatest amount of engine power will be required when

A—ground effect exists.
B—making a left-pedal turn.
C—making a right-pedal turn.

During a hovering turn to the left, the RPM will decrease if throttle is not added. In a hovering turn to the right, RPM will increase if throttle is not reduced slightly. This is due to the amount of engine power that is being absorbed by the tail rotor which is dependent upon the pitch angle at which the tail rotor blades are operating. Avoid making large corrections in RPM while turning, since the throttle adjustment will result in erratic nose movements due to torque changes. (PLT268) — FAA-H-8083-21

RTC

5713. Which statement is true about an autorotative descent?

A—Generally, only the cyclic control is used to make turns.
B—The pilot should use the collective pitch control to control the rate of descent.
C—The rotor RPM will tend to decrease if a tight turn is made with a heavily loaded helicopter.

When making turns during an autorotative descent, generally use cyclic control only. Use of antitorque pedals to assist or speed the turn causes loss of airspeed and downward pitching of the nose, especially when the left pedal is used. When the autorotation is initiated, sufficient right pedal pressure should be used to maintain straight flight and prevent yawing to the left. This pressure should not be changed to assist the turn. (PLT208) — FAA-H-8083-21

RTC

5714. Using right pedal to assist a right turn during an autorotative descent will probably result in what actions?

A—A decrease in rotor RPM, pitch up of the nose, decrease in sink rate, and increase in indicated airspeed.
B—An increase in rotor RPM, pitch up of the nose, decrease in sink rate, and increase in indicated airspeed.
C—An increase in rotor RPM, pitch down of the nose, increase in sink rate, and decrease in indicated airspeed.

Using right pedal to assist a right turn during an autorotative descent will probably result in an increase in rotor RPM, pitch down of the nose, increase in sink rate, and decrease in indicated airspeed. (PLT175) — FAA-H-8083-21

RTC

5715. Using left pedal to assist a left turn during an autorotative descent will probably cause the rotor RPM to

A—increase and the airspeed to decrease.
B—decrease and the aircraft nose to pitch down.
C—increase and the aircraft nose to pitch down.

Use of antitorque pedals to assist or speed the turn causes loss of airspeed and downward pitching of the nose, especially when the left pedal is used. (PLT175) — FAA-H-8083-21

RTC

5716. When planning slope operations, only slopes of 5° gradient or less should be considered, primarily because

A—ground effect is lost on slopes of steeper gradient.
B—downwash turbulence is more severe on slopes of steeper gradient.
C—most helicopters are not designed for operations on slopes of steeper gradient.

As collective pitch is lowered, continue to move the cyclic stick toward the slope to maintain a fixed position and use cyclic as necessary to stop forward or aft movement of the helicopter. The slope must be shallow enough to allow the pilot to hold the helicopter against it with the cyclic stick during the entire landing. A slope of 5° is considered maximum for normal operation of most helicopters. Each make of helicopter will generally have its own peculiar way of indicating to the pilot when lateral cyclic stick travel is about to run out: i.e., the rotor hub

Answers

| 5711 [C] | 5712 [B] | 5713 [A] | 5714 [C] | 5715 [C] | 5716 [C] |

Chapter 2 Aircraft Systems

hitting the rotor mast, vibrations felt through the cyclic stick, and others. A landing should not be made in these instances since this indicates to the pilot that the slope is too steep. (PLT113) — FAA-H-8083-21

RTC
5717. When making a slope landing, the cyclic pitch control should be used to

A—lower the downslope skid to the ground.
B—hold the upslope skid against the slope.
C—place the rotor disc parallel to the slope.

As collective pitch is lowered, continue to move the cyclic stick toward the slope to maintain a fixed position and use cyclic as necessary to stop forward or aft movement of the helicopter. The slope must be shallow enough to allow the pilot to hold the helicopter against it with the cyclic stick during the entire landing. A slope of 5° is considered maximum for normal operation of most helicopters. Each make of helicopter will generally have its own peculiar way of indicating to the pilot when lateral cyclic stick travel is about to run out: i.e., the rotor hub hitting the rotor mast, vibrations felt through the cyclic stick, and others. A landing should not be made in these instances since this indicates to the pilot that the slope is too steep. (PLT336) — FAA-H-8083-21

RTC
5718. Takeoff from a slope is normally accomplished by

A—making a downslope running takeoff if the surface is smooth.
B—simultaneously applying collective pitch and downslope cyclic control.
C—bringing the helicopter to a level attitude before completely leaving the ground.

As the downslope skid is rising and the helicopter approaches a level attitude, move the cyclic stick back to the neutral position keeping the rotor disc parallel to the true horizon. Continue to apply collective pitch and take the helicopter straight up to a hover before moving away from the slope. In moving away from the slope, the tail should not be turned upslope because of the danger of the tail rotor striking the surface. (PLT486) — FAA-H-8083-21

RTC
5719. What is the procedure for a slope landing?

A—Use maximum RPM and maximum manifold pressure.
B—If the slope is 10° or less, the landing should be made perpendicular to the slope.
C—When parallel to the slope, slowly lower the upslope skid to the ground prior to lowering the downslope skid.

A downward pressure on the collective pitch will start the helicopter descending. As the upslope skid touches the ground, apply cyclic stick in the direction of the slope. This will hold the skid against the slope while the downslope skid is continuing to be let down with the collective pitch. (PLT129) — FAA-H-8083-21

RTC
5720. You are hovering during calm wind conditions and decide to make a right-pedal turn. In most helicopters equipped with reciprocating engines, the engine RPM will tend to

A—increase.
B—decrease.
C—remain unaffected.

During a hovering turn to the left, the RPM will decrease if throttle is not added. In a hovering turn to the right, RPM will increase if throttle is not reduced slightly. This is due to the amount of engine power that is being absorbed by the tail rotor which is dependent upon the pitch angle at which the tail rotor blades are operating. Avoid making large corrections in RPM while turning, since the throttle adjustment will result in erratic nose movements due to torque changes. (PLT268) — FAA-H-8083-21

Answers

5717 [B]   5718 [C]   5719 [C]   5720 [A]

RTC
5721. During calm wind conditions, in most helicopters, which of these flight operations would require the most power?

A—A left-pedal turn.
B—A right-pedal turn.
C—Hovering in ground effect.

During a hovering turn to the left, the RPM will decrease if throttle is not added. In a hovering turn to the right, RPM will increase if throttle is not reduced slightly. This is due to the amount of engine power that is being absorbed by the tail rotor which is dependent upon the pitch angle at which the tail rotor blades are operating. Avoid making large corrections in RPM while turning, since the throttle adjustment will result in erratic nose movements due to torque changes. (PLT268) — FAA-H-8083-21

RTC
5722. If complete power failure should occur while cruising at altitude, the pilot should

A—partially lower the collective pitch, close the throttle, then completely lower the collective pitch.
B—lower the collective pitch as necessary to maintain proper rotor RPM, and apply right pedal to correct for yaw.
C—close the throttle, lower the collective pitch to the full-down position, apply left pedal to correct for yaw, and establish a normal power-off glide.

By immediately lowering collective pitch (which must be done in case of engine failure), lift and drag will be reduced and the helicopter will begin an immediate descent, thus producing an upward flow of air through the rotor system. (PLT175) — FAA-H-8083-21

RTC
5723. When making an autorotation to touchdown, what action is most appropriate?

A—A slightly nose-high attitude at touchdown is the proper procedure.
B—The skids should be in a longitudinally level attitude at touchdown.
C—Aft cyclic application after touchdown is desirable to help decrease ground run.

As the helicopter approaches normal hovering altitude, maintain a landing attitude with cyclic control, maintain heading with pedals, apply sufficient collective pitch (while holding the throttle in the closed position) to cushion the touchdown and be sure the helicopter is landing parallel to its direction of motion upon contact with the surface. Avoid landing on the heels of the skid gear. (PLT175) — FAA-H-8083-21

RTC
5724. During the entry into a quick stop, how should the collective pitch control be used? It should be

A—lowered as necessary to prevent ballooning.
B—raised as necessary to prevent a rotor overspeed.
C—raised as necessary to prevent a loss of altitude.

The deceleration is initiated by applying aft cyclic to reduce forward speed. Simultaneously, the collective pitch should be lowered as necessary to counteract any climbing tendency. (PLT217) — FAA-H-8083-21

RTC
5725. During a normal approach to a hover, the collective pitch control is used primarily to

A—maintain RPM.
B—control the rate of closure.
C—control the angle of descent.

The angle of descent is primarily controlled by collective pitch. The airspeed is primarily controlled by the cyclic control. Heading on final approach is maintained with pedal control. However, the approach can only be accomplished successfully by the coordination of all controls. (PLT336) — FAA-H-8083-21

Answers

5721 [A]   5722 [B]   5723 [B]   5724 [A]   5725 [C]

Chapter 2 **Aircraft Systems**

RTC

5726. During a normal approach to a hover, the cyclic pitch is used primarily to

A—maintain heading.
B—control rate of closure.
C—control angle of descent.

The angle of descent is primarily controlled by collective pitch. The airspeed, or rate of closure, is primarily controlled by the cyclic control. Heading on final approach is maintained with pedal control. However, the approach can only be accomplished successfully by the coordination of all controls. (PLT336) — FAA-H-8083-21

RTC

5727. Normal RPM should be maintained during a running landing primarily to ensure

A—adequate directional control until the helicopter stops.
B—that sufficient lift is available should an emergency develop.
C—longitudinal and lateral control, especially if the helicopter is heavily loaded or high density altitude conditions exist.

After surface contact, the cyclic control should be placed slightly forward of neutral to tilt the main rotor away from the tail boom, antitorque pedals should be used to maintain heading, throttle should be used to maintain RPM, and cyclic stick should be used to maintain surface track. Normally, the collective pitch is held stationary after touchdown until the helicopter comes to a complete stop. However, if braking is desired or required, the collective pitch may be lowered cautiously. To ensure directional control, normal rotor RPM must be maintained until the helicopter stops. (PLT170) — FAA-H-8083-21

RTC

5728. Which is true concerning a running takeoff?

A—If a helicopter cannot be lifted vertically, a running takeoff should be made.
B—One advantage of a running takeoff is that the additional airspeed can be converted quickly to altitude.
C—A running takeoff may be possible when gross weight or density altitude prevents a sustained hover at normal hovering altitude.

A running takeoff is used when conditions of load and/or density altitude prevent a sustained hover at normal hovering altitude. It is often referred to as a high-altitude takeoff. (PLT201) — FAA-H-8083-21

RTC

5729. When conducting a confined area-type operation, the primary purpose of the high reconnaissance is to determine the

A—power requirements for the approach.
B—suitability of the area for landing.
C—amount of slope in the landing area.

The purpose of a high reconnaissance is to determine the wind direction and speed, a point for touchdown, the suitability of the landing area, the approach and departure axes, obstacles and their effect on wind patterns, and the most suitable flight paths into and out of the area. When conducting a high reconnaissance, give particular consideration to forced landing areas in case of an emergency. (PLT349) — FAA-H-8083-21

RTC

5730. During a pinnacle approach under conditions of high wind and turbulence, the pilot should make a

A—shallow approach, maintaining a constant line of descent with cyclic applications.
B—normal approach, maintaining a slower-than-normal rate of descent with cyclic applications.
C—steeper-than-normal approach, maintaining the desired angle of descent with collective applications.

A steep approach is used primarily when there are obstacles in the approach path that are too high to allow a normal approach. A steep approach will permit entry into most confined areas and is sometimes used to avoid areas of turbulence around a pinnacle. (PLT170) — FAA-H-8083-21

RTC

5731. What type approach should be made to a pinnacle under conditions of relatively high wind and turbulence?

A—A normal approach.
B—A steeper-than-normal approach.
C—A shallower-than-normal approach.

A steep approach is used primarily when there are obstacles in the approach path that are too high to allow a normal approach. A steep approach will permit entry into most confined areas and is sometimes used to avoid areas of turbulence around a pinnacle. (PLT420) — FAA-H-8083-21

Answers

| 5726 | [B] | 5727 | [A] | 5728 | [C] | 5729 | [B] | 5730 | [C] | 5731 | [B] |

RTC
5732. If turbulence and downdrafts are expected during a pinnacle approach, plan to make a

A—steeper-than-normal approach.
B—normal approach, maintaining a lower-than-normal airspeed.
C—shallow approach, maintaining a higher-than-normal airspeed.

A steep approach is used primarily when there are obstacles in the approach path that are too high to allow a normal approach. A steep approach will permit entry into most confined areas and is sometimes used to avoid areas of turbulence around a pinnacle. (PLT170) — FAA-H-8083-21

RTC
5733. If ground resonance is experienced during rotor spin-up, what action should you take?

A—Taxi to a smooth area.
B—Make a normal takeoff immediately.
C—Close the throttle and slowly raise the spin-up lever.

A corrective action for ground resonance is an immediate takeoff if RPM is in proper range (for helicopters) or an immediate closing of the throttle and placing the blades in low pitch if the RPM is low. "During spin-up" implies low RPM, so closing the throttle is appropriate. (PLT265) — FAA-H-8083-21

RTC
5734. The principal factor limiting the never-exceed speed (V_{NE}) of a gyroplane is

A—turbulence and altitude.
B—blade-tip speed, which must remain below the speed of sound.
C—lack of sufficient cyclic stick control to compensate for dissymmetry of lift or retreating blade stall, depending on which occurs first.

Retreating blade stall is the principal factor limiting the never-exceed speed. (PLT373) — FAA-H-8083-21

RTC
5735. Why should gyroplane operations within the cross-hatched portion of a Height vs. Velocity chart be avoided?

A—The rotor RPM may build excessively high if it is necessary to flare at such low altitudes.
B—Sufficient airspeed may not be available to ensure a safe landing in case of an engine failure.
C—Turbulence near the surface can dephase the blade dampers causing geometric unbalanced conditions on the rotor system.

A rotorcraft or gyroplane pilot must become familiar with this chart for the particular gyroplane he or she is flying. From it, the pilot can determine what altitudes and airspeeds are required to safely make an autorotative landing in case of an engine failure. The chart can be used to determine altitude-airspeed combinations from which it would be nearly impossible to successfully complete an autorotative landing. The altitude-airspeed combinations that should be avoided are represented by the shaded areas of the chart. (PLT123) — FAA-H-8083-21

RTC
5736. The principal reason the shaded area of a Height vs. Velocity chart should be avoided is

A—rotor RPM may decay before ground contact is made if an engine failure should occur.
B—rotor RPM may build excessively high if it is necessary to flare at such low altitudes.
C—insufficient airspeed would be available to ensure a safe landing in case of an engine failure.

A rotorcraft or gyroplane pilot must become familiar with this chart for the particular gyroplane he or she is flying. From it, the pilot can determine what altitudes and airspeeds are required to safely make an autorotative landing in case of an engine failure. The chart can be used to determine altitude-airspeed combinations from which it would be nearly impossible to successfully complete an autorotative landing. The altitude-airspeed combinations that should be avoided are represented by the shaded areas of the chart. (PLT123) — FAA-H-8083-21

Answers

| 5732 | [A] | 5733 | [C] | 5734 | [C] | 5735 | [B] | 5736 | [C] |

Chapter 2 **Aircraft Systems**

RTC
5737. During the transition from pre-rotation to flight, all rotor blades change pitch

A—simultaneously to the same angle of incidence.
B—simultaneously but to different angles of incidence.
C—to the same degree at the same point in the cycle of rotation.

Compensation for dissymmetry of lift requires constant change in the blade angle of incidence, with one increasing as another simultaneously decreases. During the transition from prerotation to flight (or any time there is dissymmetry of lift) all rotor blades change pitch simultaneously, but to different angles of incidence. (PLT470) — FAA-H-8083-21

RTC
5737-1. The greatest angle of incidence on a rotor blade can be found near

A—the hub.
B—the tip.
C—the root.

Angle of incidence is the angle between the chord line of a main or tail rotor blade and the rotor hub. It is a mechanical angle rather than an aerodynamic angle and is sometimes referred to as blade pitch angle. Blade twist provides higher pitch angles at the root where velocity is low and lower pitch angles nearer the tip where velocity is higher. (PLT470) — FAA-H-8083-21

RTC
5738. Select the true statement concerning gyroplane taxi procedures.

A—Avoid abrupt control movements when blades are turning.
B—The cyclic stick should be held in the neutral position at all times.
C—The cyclic stick should be held slightly aft of neutral at all times.

Avoid abrupt control motions while taxiing. (PLT149) — FAA-H-8083-21

RTC
5755. With respect to vortex circulation, which is true?

A—Helicopters generate downwash turbulence, not vortex circulation.
B—The vortex strength is greatest when the generating aircraft is flying fast.
C—Vortex circulation generated by helicopters in forward flight trail behind in a manner similar to wingtip vortices generated by airplanes.

In forward flight, departing or landing helicopters produce a pair of high velocity trailing vortices similar to wing-tip vortices of large fixed-wing aircraft. Pilots of small aircraft should use caution when operating behind or crossing behind landing and departing helicopters. (PLT509) — AIM ¶7-4-7

RTC
5756. Which is true with respect to vortex circulation?

A—Helicopters generate downwash turbulence only, not vortex circulation.
B—The vortex strength is greatest when the generating aircraft is heavy, clean, and slow.
C—When vortex circulation sinks into ground effect, it tends to dissipate rapidly and offer little danger.

The strength of the vortex is governed by the weight, speed, and shape of the airfoil of the generating aircraft. The greatest vortex strength occurs when the generating aircraft is heavy, clean, and slow. (PLT509) — AIM ¶7-4-7

Answers

5737 [B]   5737-1 [C]   5738 [A]   5755 [C]   5756 [B]

Glider Systems

Variometers used in gliders are so sensitive that they indicate climbs and descents as a result of changes in airspeed. A total energy compensator for a variometer reduces the climb and dive errors that are caused by airspeed changes and cancels out errors caused by "stick thermals" and changes in airspeed. The variometer shows only when the glider is climbing in rising air currents.

GLI
5273. Which is true regarding electric variometers?

A—Are generally considered to be less sensitive and has a slower response time than a vertical-speed indicator.
B—The sensitivity can be adjusted in flight to suit existing air conditions.
C—They do not utilize outside air static pressure lines.

Variometers are so sensitive they indicate climbs and descents as a result of changes in airspeed. A total energy compensator is used to cancel out errors caused by thermals and changes in airspeed. (PLT216) — FAA-H-8083-13

GLI
5274. Which is true regarding variometers?

A—An electric variometer does not utilize outside air static pressure lines.
B—One of the advantages of the pellet variometer over the vane variometer, is that dirt, moisture, or static electricity will not affect its operation.
C—A total energy system senses airspeed changes and tends to cancel out the resulting variometer climb or dive indications.

A total energy variometer has been compensated so it only responds to changes in total energy, there by canceling out false indications of climbs or descents. (PLT216) — FAA-H-8083-13

GLI
5275. Which is true concerning variometers with total energy systems? These instruments

A—sense airspeed changes and tend to cancel resulting climb and dive indications.
B—will consistently register climbs that result from stick thermals.
C—react to air mass climbs and descents like a conventional rate-of-climb indicator.

A total energy variometer has been compensated so it only responds to changes in total energy of the sailplane; thus, a change in altitude and airspeed due to stick deflection does not register as lift or sink on the variometer. If the system is properly designed, the false climb or descent will be canceled out. (PLT216) — FAA-H-8083-13

GLI
5297. The advantage of a total energy compensator is that this system

A—includes a speed ring around the rim of the variometer.
B—adds the effect of stick thermals to the total energy produced by thermals.
C—reduces climb and dive errors on variometer indications caused by airspeed changes.

A total energy variometer has been compensated so it responds only to changes in total energy of the sailplane; thus, a change in altitude and airspeed due to stick deflection does not register as lift or sink on the variometer. If the system is properly designed, the false climb or descent will be canceled out. (PLT216) — FAA-H-8083-13

Answers

5273 [B]   5274 [C]   5275 [A]   5297 [C]

Chapter 2 **Aircraft Systems**

GLI

5612. In the Northern Hemisphere, if a sailplane is accelerated or decelerated, the magnetic compass will normally indicate

A—correctly, only when on a north or south heading.
B—a turn toward south while accelerating on a west heading.
C—a turn toward north while decelerating on an east heading.

When on a north or south heading, there is no acceleration or deceleration error. (PLT215) — FAA-H-8083-25

GLI

5613. When flying on a heading of west from one thermal to the next, the airspeed is increased to the "speed-to-fly" with the wings level. What will the conventional magnetic compass indicate while the airspeed is increasing?

A—A turn toward the south.
B—A turn toward the north.
C—Straight flight on a heading of 270°.

When on an east or west heading, an acceleration will cause the compass to indicate a turn to the north. (PLT215) — FAA-H-8083-25

GLI

5792. Select the true statement concerning oxygen systems that are often installed in sailplanes.

A—Most civilian aircraft oxygen systems use low-pressure cylinders for oxygen storage.
B—When aviation breathing oxygen is not available, hospital or welder's oxygen serves as a good substitute.
C—In case of a malfunction of the main oxygen system a bailout bottle may serve as an emergency oxygen supply.

A bail-out bottle is an emergency oxygen supply and can be used in the event of a malfunction in the main system. (PLT326) — FAA-H-8083-13

GLI

5794. Which is true regarding the assembly of a glider for flight?

A—It may be accomplished by the pilot.
B—It is not required by regulations for a glider pilot to know this.
C—It must be accomplished under the supervision of an FAA maintenance inspector.

The removal or installation of glider wings and tail surfaces may be accomplished by a certificated (private or better) pilot. (PLT445) — FAA-H-8083-13

GLI

5973. Which of the following elements should be considered when preparing to assemble a glider for flight?

A—Whether seat belts and shoulder harnesses are fastened and tightened.
B—Availability of water for ballast.
C—Checklists that detail the appropriate assembly procedures.

While preparing to assemble a glider, consider the following elements: location, number of crewmembers, tools and parts necessary, and checklists that detail the appropriate assembly procedures. (PLT445) — FAA-H-8083-13

GLI

5769. What corrective action should be taken during a landing if the glider pilot makes the roundout too soon while using spoilers?

A—Leave the spoilers extended and lower the nose slightly.
B—Retract the spoilers and leave them retracted until after touchdown.
C—Retract the spoilers until the glider begins to settle again, then extend the spoilers.

During the round-out, if spoilers are being used and it becomes apparent that the round-out was made too soon or too late, the spoilers should be retracted. Once retracted under either of these conditions, they should not be extended again until the wheel is on the ground, because opening the spoilers close to the ground may cause the sailplane to drop to the runway. (PLT170) — FAA-H-8083-13

Answers

5612 [A]   5613 [B]   5792 [C]   5794 [A]   5973 [C]   5769 [B]

GLI
5770. What consideration should be given in the choice of a towplane for use in aerotows?

A—L/D ratio of the glider to be towed.
B—Gross weight of the glider to be towed.
C—Towplane's low-wing loading and low-power loading.

A good towplane has low wing loading and low power loading, with sufficient excess power to get off the ground in much less than runway length and give a reasonable and safe rate and angle of climb, considering the local terrain and gross weight of the sailplane. (PLT496) — FAA-H-8083-13

GLI
5771. Looseness in a glider's flight control linkage or attachments could result in

A—increased stalling speed.
B—loss of control during an aerotow in turbulence.
C—flutter while flying at near maximum speed in turbulence.

Flutter may be caused by looseness in control cables, linkages, hinges, or play in the wing or empennage attachments. (PLT496) — FAA-H-8083-13

GLI
5772. A left side slip is used to counteract a crosswind drift during the final approach for landing. An over-the-top spin would most likely occur if the controls were used in which of the following ways? Holding the stick

A—too far back and applying full right rudder.
B—in the neutral position and applying full right rudder.
C—too far to the left and applying full left rudder.

The spin will be in the direction of the applied rudder. Just before the nose drops, the control stick is brought to the aft stop and full rudder is applied in the desired spin direction. Rotation begins immediately and continues as long as the controls are held in this position. (PLT245) — FAA-H-8083-13

GLI
5791. When flying on a heading of east from one thermal to the next, the airspeed is increased to the speed-to-fly with wings level. What will the conventional magnetic compass indicate while the airspeed is increasing?

A—A turn toward the south.
B—A turn toward the north.
C—Straight flight on a heading of 090°.

When on an east or west heading, an acceleration will cause the compass to indicate a turn to the north. (PLT215) — FAA-H-8083-13

GLI
5793. The spoilers should be in what position when operating in a strong wind?

A—Extended during both a landing roll or ground operation.
B—Retracted during both a landing roll or ground operation.
C—Extended during a landing roll, but retracted during a ground operation.

The spoilers should remain open during ground operations in strong wind conditions. (PLT011) — FAA-H-8083-13

GLI
5795. The primary cause of towline slack during aerotows is

A—glider acceleration.
B—poor coordination.
C—positioning the glider too high.

Slack in the towline can only occur when the glider has a faster speed than the towplane. The most common time to have towline slack is during, and especially after turns. The glider is flying a greater distance, and therefore will have to fly a faster airspeed. (PLT298) — FAA-H-8083-13

GLI
5796. To signal the glider pilot during an aerotow to release immediately, the tow pilot will

A—fishtail the towplane.
B—rock the towplane's wings.
C—alternately raise and lower the towplane's pitch attitude.

The mandatory release signal is the rocking of the towplane's wings. (PLT401) — FAA-H-8083-13

Answers

| 5770 | [B] | 5771 | [C] | 5772 | [A] | 5791 | [B] | 5793 | [A] | 5795 | [A] |
| 5796 | [B] | | | | | | | | | | |

GLI

5797. During an aerotow, moving from the inside to the outside of the towplane's flightpath during a turn will cause the

A—towline to slacken.
B—glider's airspeed to increase, resulting in a tendency to climb.
C—glider's airspeed to decrease, resulting in a tendency to descend.

When a glider turns on a radius outside that of the towplane, it not only goes faster but also farther. Any increase in speed will cause a climb, assuming there is no change in pitch. (PLT257) — FAA-H-8083-13

GLI

5798. During an aerotow, is it good operating practice to release from a low-tow position?

A—No. The tow ring may strike and damage the glider after release.
B—No. The towline may snap forward and strike the towplane after release.
C—Yes. Low-tow position is the correct position for releasing from the towplane.

In the low-tow position, upon release, the tow ring may snap back and strike the glider. (PLT496) — FAA-H-8083-13

GLI

5799. During an aerotow, if slack develops in the towline, the glider pilot should correct this situation by

A—making a shallow-banked coordinated turn to either side.
B—increasing the glider's pitch attitude until the towline becomes taut.
C—yawing the glider's nose to one side with rudder while keeping the wings level with the ailerons.

Yawing should be used to remove slack from the towline. (PLT496) — FAA-H-8083-13

GLI

5800. During aerotow takeoffs in crosswind conditions, the glider starts drifting downwind after becoming airborne and before the towplane lifts off. The glider pilot should

A—not correct for a crosswind during this part of the takeoff.
B—crab into the wind to remain in the flightpath of the towplane.
C—hold upwind rudder in order to crab into the wind and remain in the flightpath of the towplane.

A crabbing heading should be held to make it easier for the towplane to stay lined up with the runway. (PLT496) — FAA-H-8083-13

GLI

5801. When should the wing runner raise the glider's wing to the level position in preparation for takeoff?

A—When the towplane pilot fans the towplane's rudder.
B—When the glider pilot is seated and has fastened the safety belt.
C—After the glider pilot gives a thumbs-up signal to take up towline slack.

This indicates the pilot is fully ready to take control of the glider for takeoff. (PLT222) — FAA-H-8083-13

GLI

5802. During an aerotow, the glider moves to one side of the towplane's flightpath. This was most likely caused by

A—variations in the heading of the towplane.
B—entering wingtip vortices created by the towplane.
C—flying the sailplane in a wing-low attitude or holding unnecessary rudder pressure.

Flying with a wing low, or with unnecessary rudder pressure, can cause a glider to move off centerline. (PLT304) — FAA-H-8083-13

Answers

5797 [B]   5798 [A]   5799 [C]   5800 [B]   5801 [C]   5802 [C]

Chapter 2 Aircraft Systems

GLI

5803. In which manner should the glider be flown while turning during an aerotow? By

A—flying inside the towplane's flightpath.
B—flying outside the towplane's flightpath.
C—banking at the same point in space where the towplane banked and using the same degree of bank and rate of roll.

The bank angle of the glider should be the same as that of the towplane. (PLT298) — FAA-H-8083-13

GLI

5804. What corrective action should a glider pilot take during takeoff if the towplane is still on the ground and the glider is airborne and drifting to the left?

A—Crab into the wind to maintain a position directly behind the towplane.
B—Establish a right wing-low drift correction to remain in the flightpath of the towplane.
C—Wait until the towplane becomes airborne before attempting to establish a drift correction.

A crabbing heading should be held to make it easier for the towplane to stay lined up with the runway. (PLT401) — FAA-H-8083-13

GLI

5805. At what point during an autotow should the glider pilot establish the maximum pitch attitude for the climb?

A—Immediately after takeoff.
B—100 feet above the ground.
C—200 feet above the ground.

The pitch angle should not exceed 15° at 50 feet (indicated altitude), 30° at 100 feet, and 45° at 200 feet. (PLT304) — FAA-H-8083-13

GLI

5806. When preparing for an autotow with a strong crosswind, where should the glider and towrope be placed?

A—Straight behind the tow car.
B—Obliquely to the line of takeoff on the upwind side of the tow car.
C—Obliquely to the line of takeoff on the downwind side of the tow car.

The tow rope should be laid obliquely to the line of takeoff, to preclude the possibility of the glider over-running the rope during takeoff. (PLT496) — FAA-H-8083-13

GLI

5807. Which is true regarding the use of glider tow hooks?

A—The use of a CG hook for auto or winch tows allows the sailplane greater altitude for a given line length.
B—The use of a CG hook for aerotows allows better directional control at the start of the launch than the use of a nose hook.
C—The use of a nose hook for an auto or winch launch reduces structural loading on the tail assembly compared to the use of a CG hook.

There is a tendency to pitchup when using a belly hook on a winch tow. The CG hook allows the sailplane to gain a greater altitude with a given length of line. (PLT304) — FAA-H-8083-13

GLI

5146. What factors affect glider performance during launch?

A—Density altitude at the launch airport and towline strength.
B—Pressure altitude at the launch airport and the temperature sounding at 1,000 feet AGL.
C—Power output of the launch mechanism and aerodynamic efficiency of the glider.

Glider performance during launch depends on the power output of the launch mechanism and on the aerodynamic efficiency of the glider itself. The three major factors that affect performance are density altitude, weight, and wind. (PLT304) — FAA-H-8083-13

Answers

5803 [C] 5804 [A] 5805 [C] 5806 [C] 5807 [A] 5146 [C]

Chapter 2 **Aircraft Systems**

GLI
5808. GIVEN:

Glider's max auto/winch tow speed .... 66 MPH
Surface wind (direct headwind) .... 5 MPH
Wind gradient .... 4 MPH

When the glider reaches an altitude of 200 feet the auto/winch speed should be

A—42 MPH.
B—46 MPH.
C—56 MPH.

The tow speed for straight auto tow may be calculated as follows:

1. *Subtract the surface wind from the placard speed.*
2. *Subtract an additional 5 miles per hour as a safety factor.*
3. *After the sailplane has climbed to an altitude between 100 and 200 feet, the tow speed should be reduced an additional 10 MPH.*
4. *Subtract the surface wind again to accommodate wind gradient increases.*

(PLT012) — FAA-H-8083-13

GLI
5809. The towrope breaks when at the steepest segment of the climb during a winch launch. To recover to a normal gliding attitude, the pilot should

A—relax the back stick pressure to avoid excessive loss of altitude.
B—apply forward pressure until the buffeting sound and vibration disappear.
C—move the stick fully forward immediately and hold it there until the nose crosses the horizon.

If the power fails or the towline breaks below 200 feet, the pilot should quickly and smoothly lower the nose until it crosses the horizon, pull the release handle, and land straight ahead making turns only to avoid objects on the ground. (PLT304) — FAA-H-8083-13

GLI
5810. Which would cause pitch oscillations or porpoising during a winch launch?

A—Excessive winch speed.
B—Insufficient winch speed.
C—Excessive slack in the towline.

Porpoising or a rapid pitch oscillation may occur as the sailplane approaches the top of the climb. This phenomenon occurs as a result of the horizontal stabilizer stalling and unstalling in combination with the downward pull of the tow cable. Launching into rough air, jerky movements of the elevator, or too fast a tow can lead to or aggravate porpoising. (PLT304) — FAA-H-8083-13

GLI
5811. During a ground tow, the pitch angle of the glider should not exceed

A—10° at 50 feet, 20° at 100 feet, and 45° at 200 feet.
B—15° at 50 feet, 30° at 100 feet, and 45° at 200 feet.
C—15° at 50 feet, 20° at 100 feet, and 40° at 200 feet.

The pitch angle should not exceed 15° at 50 feet (indicated altitude), 30° at 100 feet, and 45° (maximum) at 200 feet. (PLT304) — FAA-H-8083-13

GLI
5812. To stop pitch oscillation during a winch launch, the pilot should

A—increase the back pressure on the control stick and steepen the angle of climb.
B—relax the back pressure on the control stick and shallow the angle of climb.
C—extend and retract the spoilers several times until the oscillations subside.

With full-up elevator (stick back) the angle of attack of the horizontal tail surface becomes so great that it stalls, thus reducing the downward force and allowing the sailplane nose to pitch down. This eventually results in a decrease in the angle of attack of the horizontal tail surface, reinstating the downward forces which pitches the sailplane nose-up. This develops into a cycling situation and the pilot finds the sailplane is porpoising. The recommended corrective procedure is to release a portion of the back pressure to reduce the angle of climb until the oscillation dampens; then add only part of the back pressure which was released, and thus climb less rapidly without porpoising. (PLT304) — FAA-H-8083-13

Answers

5808 [A]   5809 [C]   5810 [A]   5811 [B]   5812 [B]

GLI
5814. What corrective action should be taken, if while thermalling at minimum sink speed in turbulent air, the left wing drops while turning to the left?

A—Apply right rudder pressure to slow the rate of turn.
B—Lower the nose before applying right aileron pressure.
C—Apply right aileron pressure to counteract the overbanking tendency.

The left wing is starting to stall, so airspeed should be increased before starting any rolling maneuvers. (PLT257) — FAA-H-8083-13

GLI
5815. A rule of thumb for flying a final approach is to maintain a speed that is

A—twice the glider's stall speed, regardless of windspeed.
B—twice the glider's stall speed plus half the estimated windspeed.
C—50 percent above the glider's stall speed plus half the estimated windspeed.

Pattern airspeed should be a minimum of stalling speed plus one-half stalling speed plus one-half estimated wind velocity. (PLT170) — FAA-H-8083-13

GLI
5816. To stop a ground loop to the left after landing a glider, it would be best to lower the

A—right wing in order to shift the CG.
B—left wing to compensate for crosswind.
C—nose skid to the ground and apply wheel brake.

The nose skid is helpful until the glider starts to swerve, when it may dig in and pivot the glider into a ground loop. Once the swerve is underway, locking the wheel will help—use the brakes hard. (PLT474) — FAA-H-8083-13

GLI
5817. In which situation is a hazardous stall more likely to occur if inadequate airspeed allowance is made for wind velocity gradient?

A—During the approach to a landing.
B—While thermalling at high altitudes.
C—During takeoff and climb while on aerotow.

An unintentional stall is most likely to occur during thermalling or in the landing pattern. Because of the glider's proximity to the ground in the pattern, insufficient altitude may remain for recovery. (PLT477) — FAA-H-8083-13

GLI
5818. With regard to two or more gliders flying in the same thermal, which is true?

A—All turns should be to the right.
B—Turns should be in the same direction as the highest glider.
C—Turns should be made in the same direction as the first glider to enter the thermal.

If more than one sailplane is circling in the same direction, the first sailplane in the thermal establishes the direction of turn. Each pilot must constantly be alert for other traffic while thermalling. (PLT474) — FAA-H-8083-13

GLI
5819. Which is true regarding the direction in which turns should be made during slope soaring?

A—All reversing turns should be made to the left.
B—All reversing turns should be made into the wind away from the slope.
C—The upwind turn should be made to the left; the downwind turn should be made to the right.

A downwind turn toward the slope may force the glider into the hillside. Make all turns away from the ridge into the wind. (PLT474) — FAA-H-8083-13

Answers

5814 [B]   5815 [C]   5816 [C]   5817 [A]   5818 [C]   5819 [B]

Chapter 2 **Aircraft Systems**

GLI

5820. Which airspeed should be used when circling within a thermal?

A—Best L/D speed.
B—Maneuvering speed.
C—Minimum sink speed for the angle of bank.

Minimum sink speed allows for the least rate of descent, which in turn allows for maximum climb in lift. The minimum sink speed for the bank angle being flown should be utilized. (PLT474) — FAA-H-8083-13

GLI

5821. Which is a recommended procedure for an off-field landing?

A—A recommended landing site would be a pasture.
B—Always land into the wind even if you have to land downhill on a sloping field.
C—If the field slopes, it is usually best to land uphill, even with a tailwind.

The beneficial effects of an uphill landing make such a procedure preferable even in a tail wind. (PLT208) — FAA-H-8083-13

GLI

5822. What would be a proper action or procedure to use if you are getting too low on a cross-country flight in a glider?

A—Fly directly into the wind and make a straight-in approach at the end of the glide.
B—Have a suitable landing area selected upon reaching 2,000 feet AGL, and a specific field chosen upon reaching 1,500 feet AGL.
C—Continue on course until descending to 500 feet, then select a field and confine the search for lift to an area within gliding range of a downwind leg for the field you have chosen.

Always have a suitable landing area in sight and specific field at low altitude. The choices should be narrowed down at 2,000 feet AGL and a specific field chosen upon reaching 1,500 feet AGL. (PLT474) — FAA-H-8083-13

GLI

5823. What is the proper speed to fly when passing through lift with no intention to work the lift?

A—Best L/D speed.
B—Maximum safe speed.
C—Minimum sink speed.

Even if not stopping to work a thermal, it is advisable to slow to the minimum sink airspeed when passing through the area of lift. (PLT474) — FAA-H-8083-13

GLI

5824. What is the proper airspeed to use when flying between thermals on a cross-country flight against a headwind?

A—The best L/D speed increased by one-half the estimated wind velocity.
B—The best L/D speed decreased by one-half the estimated wind velocity.
C—The minimum sink speed increased by one-half the estimated wind velocity.

Fly at best L/D or faster. When flying cross-country, it is good practice to increase speed-to-fly by one-half of the estimated wind velocity. (PLT474) — FAA-H-8083-13

Answers

5820 [C]   5821 [C]   5822 [B]   5823 [C]   5824 [A]

Balloon Operations

LTA
5825. What should a pilot do if a small hole is seen in the fabric during inflation?

A—Continue the inflation and make a mental note of the location of the hole for later repair.
B—Instruct a ground crewmember to inspect the hole, and if under 5 inches in length, continue the inflation.
C—Consult the flight manual to determine if the hole is within acceptable damage limits established for the balloon being flown.

Any hole in the fabric is dangerous because it is a weak point, and any stress on the fabric will allow a larger hole to tear in the fabric. Preventive maintenance in the form of mending rips and tears in the bag may be done by the owners, but major repairs must be done by a certificated airframe and powerplant mechanic, who also performs the annual checkup. Local unfamiliarity with the equipment often makes it advisable to contact the manufacturer for maintenance assistance. Consult the flight manual to determine if the hole is within acceptable damage limits established for the balloon being flown. (PLT182) — How to Fly a Balloon

LTA
5826. Propane is preferred over butane for fuel in hot air balloons because

A—it has a higher boiling point.
B—it has a lower boiling point.
C—butane is very explosive under pressure.

Propane is preferred over butane and other hydrocarbons in balloon design because propane has a lower boiling point (propane -44°F, butane 32°F) and, therefore, a consistently higher vapor pressure for a given temperature. (PLT130) — Balloon Digest

LTA
5827. On a balloon equipped with a blast valve, the blast valve is used for

A—climbs only.
B—emergencies only.
C—control of altitude.

The blast valve allows control of the fuel used to heat the air. (PLT346) — Balloon Ground School

LTA
5828. It may be possible to make changes in the direction of flight in a hot air balloon by

A—using the maneuvering vent.
B—operating at different flight altitudes.
C—flying a constant atmospheric pressure gradient.

The pilot might accomplish a change of direction in flight by changing altitude. (PLT219) — How to Fly a Balloon

LTA
5829. Regarding lift as developed by a hot air balloon, which is true?

A—The higher the temperature of the ambient air, the greater the lift for any given envelope temperature.
B—The greater the difference between the temperature of the ambient air and the envelope air, the greater the lift.
C—The smaller the difference between the temperature of the ambient air and the envelope air, the greater the lift.

The primary lifting force is brought about because of a temperature differential, and therefore a density differential, between the outside air and the air inside the envelope. (PLT180) — How to Fly a Balloon

LTA
5830. What causes false lift which sometimes occurs during launch procedures?

A—Closing the maneuvering vent too rapidly.
B—Excessive temperature within the envelope.
C—Venturi effect of the wind on the envelope.

False lift is created when there is a wind blowing across the top of an inflated envelope, causing a venturi effect. This lowers the pressure above the balloon, creating a dynamic lifting force. As the balloon is accelerated by the wind, this force decreases. (PLT180) — Balloon Ground School

Answers

| 5825 [C] | 5826 [B] | 5827 [C] | 5828 [B] | 5829 [B] | 5830 [C] |

Chapter 2 **Aircraft Systems**

LTA
5831. The lifting forces which act on a hot air balloon are primarily the result of the interior air

A—pressure being greater than ambient pressure.
B—temperature being less than ambient temperature.
C—temperature being greater than ambient temperature.

The theory of balloon flight is basically the theory of lift as applied to an envelope which traps a gas that is lighter, or less dense, than the ambient atmosphere. Hot air is less dense than cool air. (PLT180) — Balloon Ground School

LTA
5832. While in flight, ice begins forming on the outside of the fuel tank in use. This would most likely be caused by

A—water in the fuel.
B—a leak in the fuel line.
C—vaporized fuel instead of liquid fuel being drawn from the tank into the main burner.

Vaporized fuel being drawn off reduces the tank pressure, allowing liquid fuel in the tank to boil off, reducing the temperature of the tank. (This is a good procedure for reducing tank pressure on a hot day.) (PLT254) — How to Fly a Balloon

LTA
5833. If ample fuel is available, within which temperature range will propane fuel vaporize sufficiently to provide enough fuel pressure for burner operation during flight?

A—0°F to 30°F.
B—10°F to 30°F.
C—30°F to 90°F.

When ample liquid propane is available, propane will vaporize sufficiently to provide proper operation between 30° and 90°F. (PLT251) — How to Fly a Balloon

LTA
5834. When landing a balloon, what should the occupant(s) do to minimize landing shock?

A—Be seated on the floor of the basket.
B—Stand back-to-back and hold onto the load ring.
C—Stand with knees slightly bent facing the direction of movement.

By facing forward, the body is best balanced against tipping, and the bent legs will absorb the landing shock. (PLT221) — How to Fly a Balloon

LTA
5835. Vertical control of a gas balloon is accomplished by

A—using the rip panel rope.
B—valving gas or releasing ballast.
C—opening and closing the appendix.

Altitude in a gas balloon is controlled by valving gas or releasing ballast. (PLT244) — How to Fly a Balloon

LTA
5836. To perform a normal descent in a gas balloon, it is necessary to release

A—air.
B—gas.
C—ballast.

By releasing gas, a balloon will have reduced lift and will descend. (PLT183) — Balloon Digest

LTA
5837. What would cause a gas balloon to start a descent if a cold air mass is encountered and the envelope becomes cooled?

A—The expansion of the gas.
B—The contraction of the gas.
C—A barometric pressure differential.

As gas cools, it contracts, reducing its lift capacity. (PLT183) — Balloon Digest

LTA
5838. If a balloon inadvertently descends into stratus clouds and is shielded from the Sun, and if no corrections are made, one can expect to descend

A—more slowly.
B—more rapidly.
C—at an unchanged rate.

In order for clouds to form, water vapor condenses to liquid. During this process, the latent heat of condensation of water is about 600 calories per gram. This heat released during condensation is an important source of energy for the maintenance of thunderstorms, etc. While descending into a cloud layer, a temperature rise can be expected, reducing the difference in temperature between the balloon and the atmosphere increasing the descent. The rate of descent will also increase because of the loss of solar heating. (PLT180) — Balloon Ground School

Answers

| 5831 | [C] | 5832 | [C] | 5833 | [C] | 5834 | [C] | 5835 | [B] | 5836 | [B] |
| 5837 | [B] | 5838 | [B] | | | | | | | | | | |

LTA
5839. What action is most appropriate when an envelope overtemperature condition occurs?

A—Turn the main burner OFF.
B—Land as soon as practical.
C—Throw all unnecessary equipment overboard.

Overtemping the envelope is dangerous because it weakens the fabric; land as soon as possible if this condition occurs. (PLT208) — Balloon Ground School

LTA
5840. Which is the proper way to detect a fuel leak?

A—Sight.
B—Use of smell and sound.
C—Check fuel pressure gauge.

Propane under pressure will cause a hissing sound when leaking and it has an artificial odor added to aid in detection. (PLT251) — Balloon Ground School

LTA
5841. What is the weight of propane?

A—4.2 pounds per gallon.
B—6.0 pounds per gallon.
C—7.5 pounds per gallon.

Propane weighs 4.2 pounds per gallon. (PLT021) — FAA-H-8083-11

LTA
5842. What effect, if any, does ambient temperature have on propane tank pressure?

A—It has no effect.
B—As temperature decreases, propane tank pressure decreases.
C—As temperature decreases, propane tank pressure increases.

Propane boils at -40°F. The colder the ambient air, the colder the tank and the less pressure the tank will have. The greater the pressure, the greater the volume of fuel to the burner. (PLT253) — Balloon Ground School

LTA
5843. Why is it considered a good practice to blast the burner after changing fuel tanks?

A—To check for fuel line leaks.
B—It creates an immediate source of lift.
C—To ensure the new tank is functioning properly.

This check will ensure that a full, properly functioning tank has been selected before its use becomes critical. (PLT253) — Balloon Ground School

LTA
5844. For what reason is methanol added to the propane fuel of hot air balloons?

A—As a fire retardant.
B—As an anti-icing additive.
C—To reduce the temperature.

Methanol mixes with water and acts as an antifreeze. (PLT251) — Balloon Ground School

LTA
5845. To respond to a small leak around the stem of a Rego blast valve in a single-burner system balloon, one should

A—turn off the fuel system and make an immediate landing.
B—continue operating the blast valve making very small quick blasts until a good landing field appears.
C—continue operating the blast valve, making long infrequent blasts and opening the handle slightly to reduce leakage until a good landing field appears.

If a propane leak develops anywhere in the fuel system during flight, the pilot should, as soon as possible, close the main tank valves, set open all of the other control valves in the fuel system, and pilot the balloon to a more or less normal landing by opening and closing the main tank valve to control the heat output of the burners. (PLT208) — Balloon Digest

Answers

| 5839 [B] | 5840 [B] | 5841 [A] | 5842 [B] | 5843 [C] | 5844 [B] |
| 5845 [A] | | | | | |

LTA
5846. Which action would be appropriate if a small leak develops around the stem of the tank valve, and no other tanks have sufficient fuel to reach a suitable landing field?

A—Warm the tank valve leak with your bare hand.
B—Turn the leaking tank handle to the full-open position.
C—Turn off the tank, then slowly reopen to reseat the seal.

Tank valves have a stem seal built in, when the valve is wide open. (PLT251) — Balloon Digest

LTA
5847. Why should propane lines be bled after use?

A—Fire may result from spontaneous combustion.
B—The propane may expand and rupture the lines.
C—If the temperature is below freezing, the propane may freeze.

The fuel in the lines is in a liquid state. Any heating would cause the fuel to expand and possibly rupture the line. (PLT253) — Balloon Ground School

LTA
5848. The purpose of the preheating coil as used in hot air balloons is to

A—prevent ice from forming in the fuel lines.
B—warm the fuel tanks for more efficient fuel flow.
C—vaporize the fuel for more efficient burner operation.

Hot air balloon burners perform the following three functions:

1. *Vaporize the liquid propane supplied to them;*
2. *Mix the propane vapor with air to form a combustible mixture; and*
3. *Burn the resulting mixture to form an essentially directional flow of very hot gases.*

All burners commonly in use on hot air balloons have preheat coils surrounding the base of the flame. The liquid propane flows through these coils on its way through the burner. Since the coils are heated directly by the flame, they are hot enough to vaporize the liquid propane flowing through them. If the propane is not vaporized, it does not mix well with the air, and burns in a long, yellow flame which radiates a great amount of heat. Properly vaporized propane burns with a mostly blue flame. (PLT253) — Balloon Digest

LTA
5849. The best way to determine burner BTU availability is the

A—burner sound.
B—tank quantity.
C—fuel pressure gauge.

BTUs (British Thermal Units) are the quantity of heat required to raise the temperature of one pound of water from 60° to 61°F at a constant pressure of one atmosphere. The greater the pressure the greater the rate of flow of propane (fuel) to the burner and therefore the greater the availability of the quantity of heat. (PLT253) — Balloon Digest

LTA
5850. The practice of allowing the ground crew to lift the balloon into the air is

A—a safe way to reduce stress on the envelope.
B—unsafe because it can lead to a sudden landing at an inopportune site just after lift-off.
C—considered to be a good operating practice when obstacles must be cleared shortly after lift-off.

The practice of allowing ground crew to lift the balloon in an attempt to shove it up into the air is unsafe, for it can lead to a sudden landing at an inopportune site just after lift off. (PLT221) — Powerline Excerpts

LTA
5851. Why is false lift dangerous?

A—Pilots are not aware of its effect until the burner sound changes.
B—To commence a descent, the venting of air will nearly collapse the envelope.
C—When the balloon's horizontal speed reaches the windspeed, the balloon could descend into obstructions downwind.

Sometimes false lift occurs, caused by the venturi effect produced by the wind blowing across an inflated, but stationary, envelope. This is known as aerodynamic lift, created by relative air movement. When the balloon is released, the relative wind decreases as the balloon accelerates to the wind's speed, and false lift decreases. (PLT180) — Powerline Excerpts

Answers

5846 [B]   5847 [B]   5848 [C]   5849 [C]   5850 [B]   5851 [C]

LTA
5852. If you are over a heavily-wooded area with no open fields in the vicinity and have only about 10 minutes of fuel remaining, you should

A—stay low and keep flying in hope that you will find an open field.
B—climb as high as possible to see where the nearest landing field is.
C—land in the trees while you have sufficient fuel for a controlled landing.

A controlled landing is always best, to minimize damage and injury. (PLT184) — Powerline Excerpts

LTA
5853. Which precaution should be exercised if confronted with the necessity of having to land when the air is turbulent?

A—Land in the center of the largest available field.
B—Throw propane equipment overboard immediately prior to touchdown.
C—Land in the trees to absorb shock forces, thus cushioning the landing.

Turbulent air can and will suddenly change direction. If the air is turbulent, land in the center of the largest available field. (PLT170) — FAA-H-8083-11

LTA
5854. False lift occurs whenever a balloon

A—ascends rapidly.
B—ascends due to solar assistance.
C—ascends into air moving faster than the air below.

Sometimes false lift occurs, caused by the venturi effect produced by the wind blowing across an inflated, but stationary, envelope. This is known as aerodynamic lift, created by relative air movement. When the balloon is released, the relative wind decreases as the balloon accelerates to the wind's speed, and false lift decreases. (PLT030) — Powerline Excerpts

LTA
5855. What is the relationship of false lift to the wind? False lift

A—exists only if the surface winds are calm.
B—increases if the vertical velocity of the balloon increases.
C—decreases as the wind accelerates the balloon to the same speed as the wind.

Sometimes false lift occurs, caused by the venturi effect produced by the wind blowing across an inflated, but stationary, envelope. This is known as aerodynamic lift, created by relative air movement. When the balloon is released, the relative wind decreases as the balloon accelerates to the wind's speed, and false lift decreases. (PLT030) — Powerline Excerpts

LTA
5856. The weigh-off procedure is useful because the

A—pilot can adjust the altimeter to the correct setting.
B—ground crew can assure that downwind obstacles are cleared.
C—pilot will learn what the equilibrium conditions are prior to being committed to fly.

The weigh-off procedure allows a pilot to determine the equilibrium of the balloon before lift-off. (PLT221) — Powerline Excerpts

LTA
5857. One characteristic of nylon rope is that it

A—flexes.
B—stretches.
C—splinters easily.

Nylon stretches and is strong. (PLT177) — FAA-H-8083-11

LTA
5858. Why is nylon rope good for tethering a balloon?

A—It does not stretch under tension.
B—It is not flexible and therefore can withstand greater tension without breaking.
C—It stretches under tension, but recovers to normal size when tension is removed, giving it excellent shock absorbing qualities.

Nylon has great elasticity; therefore it is a good shock absorber. (PLT177) — FAA-H-8083-11

Answers

| 5852 [C] | 5853 [A] | 5854 [C] | 5855 [C] | 5856 [C] | 5857 [B] |
| 5858 [C] | | | | | |

Chapter 2 **Aircraft Systems**

LTA
5859. One advantage nylon rope has over manila rope is that it

A—will not stretch.
B—is nearly three times as strong.
C—does not tend to snap back if it breaks.

Nylon is a synthetic material and is not as affected by sunlight, and is nearly 3 times as strong as manila rope. (PLT473) — FAA-H-8083-11

LTA
5860. A pilot should be aware that drag ropes constructed of hemp or nylon

A—should be a maximum of 100 feet long and used only in gas balloons.
B—can be considered safe because they will not conduct electricity.
C—can conduct electricity when contacting powerlines carrying 600 volts or more current if they are not clean and dry.

Any material will conduct electricity through the dirt and water on it. (PLT473) — FAA-H-8083-11

LTA
5861. If powerlines become a factor during a balloon flight, a pilot should know that

A—it is safer to contact the lines than chance ripping.
B—contact with powerlines creates no great hazard for a balloon.
C—it is better to chance ripping at 25 feet above the ground than contacting the lines.

Powerlines are the most hazardous obstacle to ballooning. (PLT208) — FAA-H-8083-11

LTA
5862. The windspeed is such that it is necessary to deflate the envelope as rapidly as possible during a landing. When should the deflation port (rip panel) be opened?

A—Prior to ground contact.
B—The instant the gondola contacts the surface.
C—As the balloon skips off the surface the first time and the last of the ballast has been discharged.

In a high-wind landing, ripping out at one foot above the ground for each mile per hour of speed will minimize ground slide and potential damage to the balloon. (PLT184) — FAA-H-8083-11

LTA
5863. The term "to weigh off" as used in ballooning means to determine the

A—standard weight and balance of the balloon.
B—neutral buoyancy by taking weight off at launch.
C—amount of gas required for an ascent to a preselected altitude.

The weigh-off procedure allows a pilot to determine the neutral buoyancy by taking weight off at launch. (PLT184) — FAA-H-8083-11

LTA
5864. Superheat is a term used to describe the condition which exists

A—when the surrounding air is at least 10° warmer than the gas in the envelope.
B—when the Sun heats the envelope surface to a temperature at least 10° greater than the surrounding air.
C—relative to the difference in temperature between the gas in the envelope and the surrounding air caused by the Sun.

Superheat is the term used to describe the difference in temperature between the gas in the envelope and the surrounding air. (PLT159) — Goodyear Airship Operations Manual

LTA
5865. How does the pilot know when pressure height has been reached? Liquid in the gas

A—and air manometers will fall below the normal level.
B—manometer will fall and the liquid in the air manometer will rise above normal levels.
C—manometer will rise and the liquid in the air manometer will fall below normal levels.

The pilot will know when pressure height has been reached when liquid in the gas manometer rises and the liquid in the air manometer falls below normal levels. (PLT153) — Goodyear Airship Operations Manual

Answers

| 5859 | [B] | 5860 | [C] | 5861 | [C] | 5862 | [A] | 5863 | [B] | 5864 | [C] |
| 5865 | [C] | | | | | | | | | | |

Airship Operations

LTA
5866. The ballonet volume of an airship envelope with respect to the total gas volume is approximately

A—15 percent.
B—25 percent.
C—30 percent.

Ballonet volume is about 25% of total gas volume. (PLT153) — Goodyear Airship Operations Manual

LTA
5867. The pressure height with any airship is that height at which

A—both ballonets are empty.
B—both ballonets are inflated.
C—gas pressure is 3 inches of water.

Pressure height is reached when the ballonets are deflated. (PLT159) — Goodyear Airship Operations Manual

LTA
5868. If both engines fail while en route, an airship should be

A—brought to a condition of equilibrium as soon as possible and free-ballooned.
B—trimmed nose-heavy to use the airship's negative dynamic lift to fly the airship down to the landing site.
C—trimmed nose-light to use the airship's positive dynamic lift to control the angle and rate of descent to the landing site.

An airship without engine power must be flown as a free balloon. (PLT208) — Goodyear Airship Operations Manual

LTA
5869. If an airship in flight is either light or heavy, the unbalanced condition must be overcome

A—by valving air.
B—aerodynamically.
C—by releasing ballast.

A light or heavy condition must be overcome aerodynamically. (PLT152) — Goodyear Airship Operations Manual

LTA
5870. Maximum headway in an airship is possible only under which condition?

A—Slightly nosedown.
B—Slightly tail down.
C—Flying in equilibrium.

Flying in equilibrium will produce the smallest frontal area and least drag. (PLT153) — Goodyear Airship Operations Manual

LTA
5871. To accomplish maximum headway, the airship must be kept

A—at equilibrium.
B—heavy and flown dynamically positive.
C—heavy by the bow and light by the stern.

Flying in equilibrium will produce the smallest frontal area and least drag. (PLT152) — Goodyear Airship Operations Manual

LTA
5872. Damper valves should normally be kept closed during a maximum rate climb to altitude because any air forced into the system would

A—decrease the volume of gas within the envelope.
B—decrease the purity of the gas within the envelope.
C—increase the amount of air to be exhausted, resulting in a lower rate of ascent.

Air entering through the damper valves would have to be exhausted as well as the air in the ballonets. (PLT473) — Goodyear Airship Operations Manual

LTA
5873. When checking gas pressure (pressure height) of an airship during a climb, the air damper valves should be

A—opened.
B—closed.
C—opened aft and closed forward.

Any ram pressure will keep the ballonet pressure too high and prevent deflation at pressure height. Therefore, the air damper valves should be closed when checking gas pressure during a climb. (PLT157) — Goodyear Airship Operations Manual

Answers

| 5866 | [B] | 5867 | [A] | 5868 | [A] | 5869 | [B] | 5870 | [C] | 5871 | [A] |
| 5872 | [C] | 5873 | [B] | | | | | | | | |

Chapter 2 **Aircraft Systems**

LTA
5874. Which take-off procedure is considered to be most hazardous?

A—Failing to apply full engine power properly on all takeoffs, regardless of wind.
B—Maintaining only 50 percent of the maximum permissible positive angle of inclination.
C—Maintaining a negative angle of inclination during takeoff after elevator response is adequate for controllability.

The most hazardous takeoff condition would be maintaining a negative angle of inclination during takeoff, after elevator response is adequate for stability. (PLT221) — Goodyear Airship Operations Manual

LTA
5875. The purpose of a ground weigh-off is to determine the

A—useful lift of the airship.
B—gross weight of the airship.
C—static condition of the airship and the condition of trim.

The purpose of the ground weigh-off is to determine the static condition of the airship and the condition of trim. (PLT154) — Goodyear Airship Operations Manual

LTA
5876. When operating an airship with the ballonet air valve in the automatic forward position, the aft valve locks should not be engaged with either after-damper open because

A—ballonet overinflation and rupture may occur.
B—the aircraft will enter an excessive bow-high attitude.
C—the aircraft will enter an excessive stern-high attitude.

Under the conditions described, the aft ballonet could inflate, causing a bow-high condition. (PLT473) — Goodyear Airship Operations Manual

LTA
5877. Which action is necessary to perform a normal descent in an airship?

A—Valve gas.
B—Valve air.
C—Take air into the aft ballonets.

An airship is normally flown heavy and so a decrease in power will result in a descent. Valving gas will also cause a descent. (PLT133) — Goodyear Airship Operations Manual

LTA
5878. To land an airship that is 250 pounds heavy when the wind is calm, the best landing can usually be made if the airship is

A—in trim.
B—nose-heavy approximately 20°.
C—tail-heavy approximately 20°.

A heavy airship should be landed tail heavy. (PLT221) — Goodyear Airship Operations Manual

LTA
5879. A heavy airship flying dynamically with air ballasted forward to overcome a climbing tendency and slowed down for a weigh-off in the air prior to landing, will be very bow heavy. This condition must be corrected prior to landing by

A—ballasting air aft.
B—discharging forward ballast.
C—dumping fuel from the forward tanks.

Air must be ballasted aft to overcome the bow-heavy condition. (PLT153) — Goodyear Airship Operations Manual

Answers

5874 [C]   5875 [C]   5876 [B]   5877 [A]   5878 [C]   5879 [A]

LTA
5880. If an airship should experience failure of both engines during flight and neither engine can be restarted, what initial immediate action must the pilot take?

A—Immediate preparations to operate the airship as a balloon are necessary.
B—The airship must be driven down to a landing before control and envelope shape are lost.
C—The emergency auxiliary power unit must be started for electrical power to the airscoop blowers so that ballonet inflation can be maintained.

An airship without engine power must be flown as a balloon. (PLT208) — Goodyear Airship Operations Manual

LTA
5881. Critical factors affecting the flight characteristics and controllability of an airship are

A—airspeed and power.
B—static and dynamic trim.
C—temperature and atmospheric density.

Critical factors affecting the flight characteristics and controllability of an airship are airspeed and power. (PLT244) — Goodyear Airship Operations Manual

Airship IFR Operations

LTA
5562. When operating an airship under IFR with a VFR-on-top clearance, what altitude should be maintained?

A—The last IFR altitude assigned by ATC.
B—An IFR cruising altitude appropriate to the magnetic course being flown.
C—A VFR cruising altitude appropriate to the magnetic course being flown and as restricted by ATC.

When operating in VFR conditions with an ATC authorization to "Maintain VFR-On-Top/maintain VFR conditions," pilots on IFR flight plans must fly at the appropriate VFR altitude as prescribed in 14 CFR §91.159. When operating below 18,000 feet MSL and:

1. On a magnetic course of 0° through 179°, any odd thousand-foot MSL altitude plus 500 feet.

2. On a magnetic course of 180° through 359°, any even thousand-foot MSL altitude plus 500 feet.

(PLT298) — 14 CFR §91.179 and §91.159

LTA
5563. Does the ATC term, "cruise 3000", apply to airship IFR operations?

A—No, this term applies to airplane IFR operations only.
B—Yes, it means that any assigned altitude can be vacated without notifying ATC.
C—Yes, in part, it authorizes the pilot to commence the approach at the destination airport at the pilot's discretion.

The term "cruise" may be used instead of "maintain" to assign a block of airspace to a pilot, from the minimum IFR altitude up to and including the altitude specified in the cruise clearance. The pilot may level off at any intermediate altitude within this block of airspace. Climb/descent within the block is to be made at the discretion of the pilot. However, once the pilot starts descent and verbally reports leaving an altitude in the block, he may not return to that altitude without additional ATC clearance. Also, it is approval for the pilot to proceed to and make an approach to the destination airport. (PLT044) — AIM ¶4-4-3

LTA
5603. You are flying an airship under an IFR flight plan and experience two-way communications radio failure while in VFR conditions. In this situation, you should continue your flight under

A—VFR and land as soon as practicable.
B—VFR and proceed to your flight-plan destination.
C—IFR and maintain the last assigned route and altitude to your flight-plan destination.

A radio failure in VFR conditions requires that the aircraft remain VFR and land as soon as practicable. (PLT391) — 14 CFR §91.185

Answers

| 5880 [A] | 5881 [A] | 5562 [C] | 5563 [C] | 5603 [A] |

Chapter 3
Flight Instruments

Airspeed Indicator   *3–3*

Altitudes   *3–6*

Magnetic Compass   *3–7*

Gyroscopic Instruments and Systems   *3–8*

Attitude Instrument Flying   *3–9*

Electronic Flight Instruments   *3–10*

Chapter 3 **Flight Instruments**

Airspeed Indicator

The airspeed indicator in a light airplane shows some of the airspeed limitations of the aircraft by means of colored arcs. On aircraft manufactured prior to 1978, these arcs are calibrated airspeed. The arcs on later aircraft are indicated airspeed.

The white arc is the flap operating range. The low-speed end of the white arc is V_{S0}, the stalling speed or the minimum steady-flight speed in the landing configuration. The high-speed end of the white arc is V_{FE}, the maximum flap extended speed. Flight at airspeeds greater than V_{FE} with the flaps extended can impose excessive loads on the flaps and wing structure.

The green arc is the normal operating range. The low-speed end is V_{S1}, the stalling speed or the minimum steady-flight speed in a specified configuration. The high-speed end of the green arc is V_{NO}, maximum structural cruising speed.

The yellow arc begins at V_{NO} and continues to the red line, which represents V_{NE}, the never exceed speed. Operations at speeds in the yellow arc may be conducted only in smooth air and with caution.

Other speed limitations which are not color-coded on the airspeed indicator include:

V_S—stalling speed or minimum steady flight speed at which the airplane is controllable.

V_F—design flap speed.

V_{LE}—maximum landing gear extended speed.

V_A—design maneuvering speed. If severe turbulence is encountered during flight, the pilot should reduce the airspeed to the design maneuvering speed. In addition to setting the power and trimming to obtain an airspeed at or below maneuvering speed, the wings should be kept level, and allow slight variations of airspeed and altitude. This technique will help minimize the wing load factor in severe turbulence. Maneuvering speed is also the maximum speed at which full or abrupt control movements may be made. Maneuvering speed decreases as gross weight decreases. See Figure 3-1.

Figure 3-1. Airspeed indicator

ALL
5604. Why should flight speeds above V_{NE} be avoided?

A—Excessive induced drag will result in structural failure.
B—Design limit load factors may be exceeded, if gusts are encountered.
C—Control effectiveness is so impaired that the aircraft becomes uncontrollable.

Any speed above V_{NE} can cause damage; therefore, flight above this speed should be avoided even in smooth air. (PLT466, CA.I.F.R2) — FAA-H-8083-25

Answer (A) is incorrect because induced drag decreases with increased airspeed. Answer (C) is incorrect because control effectiveness increases with increased airspeed.

Answers

5604 [B]

Chapter 3 Flight Instruments

ALL
5604-1. Structural damage or failure is more likely to occur in smooth air at speeds above

A—V_{NO}.
B—V_A.
C—V_{NE}.

Any speed above V_{NE} can cause damage; therefore, flight above this speed should be avoided even in smooth air. (PLT113, CA.I.F.R2) — FAA-H-8083-25

ALL
5601. Calibrated airspeed is best described as indicated airspeed corrected for

A—installation and instrument error.
B—instrument error.
C—non-standard temperature.

Calibrated airspeed is the indicated airspeed corrected for position (or installation), and instrument errors. (PLT123, CA.I.F.K3) — FAA-H-8083-25

ALL
5602. True airspeed is best described as calibrated airspeed corrected for

A—installation or instrument error.
B—non-standard temperature.
C—altitude and non-standard temperature.

True airspeed is indicated airspeed after it has been corrected for nonstandard temperature and pressure altitude. (PLT123, CA.I.F.K3) — FAA-H-8083-25

AIR
5605. Maximum structural cruising speed is the maximum speed at which an airplane can be operated during

A—abrupt maneuvers.
B—normal operations.
C—flight in smooth air.

The maximum structural cruising speed (V_{NO}) is the speed at which exceeding the load limit factor may cause permanent deformation of the airplane structure. This is the maximum speed for normal operation. (PLT466, CA.I.F.R2) — FAA-H-8083-25

Answer (A) is incorrect because design maneuvering speed (V_A) is the maximum speed for abrupt maneuvers. Answer (C) is incorrect because the yellow arc identifies the range where flight is only recommended in smooth air.

AIR
5669. A pilot is entering an area where significant clear air turbulence has been reported. Which action is appropriate upon encountering the first ripple?

A—Maintain altitude and airspeed.
B—Adjust airspeed to that recommended for rough air.
C—Enter a shallow climb or descent at maneuvering speed.

In an area where significant clear air turbulence (CAT) has been reported or is forecast, it is suggested that the pilot adjust the speed to fly at the recommended rough air speed on encountering the first ripple, since the intensity of such turbulence may build up rapidly. (PLT120, CA.I.C.K3g) — FAA-H-8083-25

Answers (A) and (C) are incorrect because the appropriate action is to adjust airspeed to design maneuvering speed (V_A).

AIR
5670. If severe turbulence is encountered during flight, the pilot should reduce the airspeed to

A—minimum control speed.
B—design-maneuvering speed.
C—maximum structural cruising speed.

Design maneuvering speed (V_A) is the maximum speed at which the maximum load limit can be imposed (either by gust or full deflection of the control surfaces) without causing structural damage. (PLT120, CA.I.F.R2) — FAA-H-8083-25

Answer (A) is incorrect because in turbulence, minimum control speed would result in the airplane stalling or significant control problems. Answer (C) is incorrect because the maximum structural cruising speed is faster than V_A.

AIR
5741. Which is the best technique for minimizing the wing-load factor when flying in severe turbulence?

A—Change power settings, as necessary, to maintain constant airspeed.
B—Control airspeed with power, maintain wings level, and accept variations of altitude.
C—Set power and trim to obtain an airspeed at or below maneuvering speed, maintain wings level, and accept variations of airspeed and altitude.

In severe turbulence, set power and trim to obtain an airspeed at or below maneuvering speed; this helps avoid exceeding the aircraft's maximum load factor. Attempt to maintain constant attitude, and accept airspeed and altitude variations caused by gusts. (PLT501, CA.I.F.R2) — AC 00-6

Answers (A) and (B) are incorrect because it is not possible to maintain a constant airspeed in severe turbulence.

Answers

| 5604-1 | [C] | 5601 | [A] | 5602 | [C] | 5605 | [B] | 5669 | [B] | 5670 | [B] |
| 5741 | [C] |

AIR, GLI

5233. (Refer to Figure 5.) The vertical line from point D to point G is represented on the airspeed indicator by the maximum speed limit of the

A—green arc.
B—yellow arc.
C—white arc.

The high speed limit of the green arc is the maximum speed for normal operation. This is designated as maximum structural cruising speed (V_{NO}), which is line D to G. (PLT312, CA.I.F.R2) — FAA-H-8083-25

Answer (B) is incorrect because the high speed limit of the yellow arc is the never exceed speed (V_{NE}), which is line E to F. Answer (C) is incorrect because the high speed limit of the white arc is the maximum flap extended speed (V_{FE}), which is not indicated on the chart.

AIR, GLI

5013. Which is the correct symbol for the stalling speed or the minimum steady flight speed in a specified configuration?

A—V_S.
B—V_{S1}.
C—V_{S0}.

V_{S1} is the stalling speed or the minimum steady flight speed obtained in a specific configuration. (PLT466, CA.VII.B.K1) — 14 CFR §1.2

Answer (A) is incorrect because V_S is the stalling speed or the minimum steady flight speed at which the airplane is controllable. Answer (C) is incorrect because V_{S0} is the stalling speed or the minimum steady flight speed in the landing configuration.

AIR, GLI

5014. Which is the correct symbol for the stalling speed or the minimum steady flight speed at which the airplane is controllable?

A—V_S.
B—V_{S1}.
C—V_{S0}.

V_S is the stalling speed or the minimum steady flight speed at which the airplane is controllable. (PLT466, CA.VII.B.K1) — 14 CFR §1.2

Answer (B) is incorrect because V_{S1} is the stalling speed or the minimum steady flight speed obtained in a specified configuration. Answer (C) is incorrect because V_{S0} is the stalling speed or the minimum steady flight speed in the landing configuration.

AIR, GLI

5015-1. 14 CFR Part 1 defines V_F as

A—design flap speed.
B—flap operating speed.
C—maximum flap extended speed.

V_F is the design flap speed. (PLT395, CA.I.F.K3) — 14 CFR §1.2

Answer (B) is incorrect because the flap operating range is indicated by the white arc on the airspeed indicator. Answer (C) is incorrect because V_{FE} is the maximum flap extended speed.

AIR, GLI

5015-2. 14 CFR Part 1 defines V_{NO} as

A—maximum structural cruising speed.
B—never exceed speed.
C—maximum operating limit speed.

V_{NO} means maximum structural cruising speed. (PLT395, CA.I.F.R2) — 14 CFR §1.2

AIR, GLI

5016-2. 14 CFR Part 1 defines V_{NE} as

A—maximum nose wheel extend speed.
B—never-exceed speed.
C—maximum landing gear extended speed.

V_{NE} is the never-exceed speed. (PLT466, CA.I.F.R2) — 14 CFR §1.2

Answer (A) is incorrect because this speed is not defined in 14 CFR Part 1. Answer (C) is incorrect because this is V_{LE}.

AIR, GLI

5016-3. 14 CFR Part 1 defines V_Y as

A—speed for best rate of descent.
B—speed for best angle of climb.
C—speed for best rate of climb.

V_Y is the speed for best rate of climb. (PLT395, CA.IV.A.K2) — 14 CFR §1.2

Answer (A) is incorrect because this is not defined in 14 CFR Part 1. Answer (B) is incorrect because this is V_X.

Answers

| 5233 | [A] | 5013 | [B] | 5014 | [A] | 5015-1 | [A] | 5015-2 | [A] | 5016-2 | [B] |
| 5016-3 | [C] |

AIR, GLI

5177. Which airspeed would a pilot be unable to identify by the color coding of an airspeed indicator?

A—The never-exceed speed.
B—The power-off stall speed.
C—The maneuvering speed.

Maneuvering speed is not color-coded on airspeed indicators. (PLT088, CA.I.G.K1h) — FAA-H-8083-25

Answer (A) is incorrect because the never-exceed speed is identified by the red line at the high-speed end of the yellow arc. Answer (B) is incorrect because the power-off stall speed is identified by the low-speed end of the white arc for landing configuration (V_{S0}), and the low-speed end of the green arc for clean configuration (V_{S1}).

AIR

5177-1. The ratio of an airplane's true airspeed to the speed of sound in the same atmospheric conditions is

A—equivalent airspeed.
B—transonic airflow.
C—Mach number.

Mach number means the ratio of true airspeed to the speed of sound. (PLT132, CA.I.F.K3) — 14 CFR §1.1

AIR

5177-2. What could be one result of exceeding critical Mach number?

A—Propeller stall.
B—Reduction in drag.
C—Aircraft control difficulties.

Critical Mach number is the boundary between subsonic and transonic flight. When shock waves form on the aircraft, airflow separation followed by buffet and aircraft control difficulties can occur. Shock waves, buffet, and airflow separation take place above critical Mach number. (PLT123, CA.I.F.K3) — FAA-H-8083-25

AIR

5016-1. 14 CFR Part 1 defines V_{LE} as

A—maximum landing gear extended speed.
B—maximum landing gear operating speed.
C—maximum leading edge flaps extended speed.

V_{LE} is the maximum landing gear extended speed. (PLT395, CA.I.F.R2) — 14 CFR §1.2

Answer (B) is incorrect because V_{LO} is the maximum landing gear operating speed. Answer (C) is incorrect because maximum leading edge flaps extended speed is not defined in 14 CFR Part 1.

ALL

5016-4. Newer airplanes have a design maneuvering speed that can generally be calculated as follows:

A—1.2 V_{S0}.
B—1.7 V_{S0}.
C—half the stall speed.

The maximum speed at which an aircraft may be stalled safely is now determined for all new designs. This speed is called the "design maneuvering speed" (V_A) and must be entered in the AFM/POH of all recently designed aircraft. For older general aviation aircraft, this speed is approximately 1.7 times the normal stalling speed. For example, an older aircraft that normally stalls at 60 knots must never be stalled at above 102 knots (60 knots × 1.7 = 102 knots). An aircraft with a normal stalling speed of 60 knots stalled at 102 knots undergoes a load factor equal to the square of the increase in speed, or 2.89 Gs (1.7 × 1.7 = 2.89 Gs). (PLT088, CA.I.F.R2) — FAA-H-8083-25

Altitudes

Indicated altitude—the altitude indicated on an altimeter set to the current local altimeter setting.

Pressure altitude—the altitude indicated on an altimeter when it is set to the standard sea level pressure of 29.92 inches of mercury (29.92 "Hg). Above 18,000 feet MSL, flight levels, which are pressure altitudes, are flown.

Density altitude—pressure altitude corrected for a nonstandard temperature. The performance tables of an aircraft are based on density altitude.

Answers

| 5177 | [C] | 5177-1 | [C] | 5177-2 | [C] | 5016-1 | [A] | 5016-4 | [B] |

True altitude—the exact height above mean sea level (MSL). Calculation of true altitude does not always yield a correct figure. Atmospheric conditions may deviate from the standard temperature and pressure lapse rates used in the computation of true altitude.

ALL
5740. To determine pressure altitude prior to takeoff, the altimeter should be set to

A—the current altimeter setting.
B—29.92" Hg and the altimeter indication noted.
C—the field elevation and the pressure reading in the altimeter setting window noted.

Pressure altitude can be determined by setting the altimeter to 29.92" Hg and reading the altimeter indication. (PLT166, CA.I.G.K1h) — FAA-H-8083-25

Answers (A) and (C) are incorrect because these would indicate field elevation, or true altitude.

ALL
5114. What altimeter setting is required when operating an aircraft at 18,000 feet MSL?

A—Current reported altimeter setting of a station along the route.
B—29.92" Hg.
C—Altimeter setting at the departure or destination airport.

Each person operating an aircraft shall maintain the cruising altitude or flight level of that aircraft, as the case may be, by reference to an altimeter that is set, when operating at or above 18,000 feet MSL, to 29.92" Hg. (PLT041, CA.I.G.K1h) — 14 CFR §91.121

ALL
5408. An airplane is located at an airport with an elevation of 5,000 feet MSL and a temperature of 90°F. The altimeter is set to airport elevation. Later that night the temperature plummets to 50°F. Unless the altimeter setting is changed, it will read

A—4,800 feet.
B—5,000 feet.
C—5,200 feet.

A decrease in air temperature will increase the density of the air and decrease the density altitude of a given airport. If the altimeter setting isn't adjusted for the change in pressure, the altimeter will read higher than the field elevation. (PLT167, CA.I.G.K1h) — FAA-H-8083-25

Magnetic Compass

The magnetic compass is the only self-contained directional instrument in the aircraft. It is affected by deviation error. Magnetic disturbances (magnetic fields) within an aircraft deflect the compass needles from alignment with magnetic north. Each aircraft will affect a magnetic compass differently, and the direction and magnitude of the error will vary with heading and the electrical systems in use. Compensating magnets are used to minimize this type of error as much as possible. Any remaining error is noted on the compass correction card.

ALL
5178. Which statement is true about magnetic deviation of a compass? Deviation

A—varies over time as the agonic line shifts.
B—varies for different headings of the same aircraft.
C—is the same for all aircraft in the same locality.

Deviation depends, in part, on the heading of the aircraft. The difference between the direction indicated by a magnetic compass not installed in an airplane, and one that is installed in an airplane, is deviation. (PLT215, CA.VI.A.K2) — FAA-H-8083-25

Answer (A) is incorrect because variation varies over time as the agonic line shifts. Answer (C) is incorrect because deviation varies from aircraft to aircraft.

Answers

5740 [B]   5114 [B]   5408 [C]   5178 [B]

Gyroscopic Instruments and Systems

Gyroscopes ("gyros") exhibit two important principles—rigidity in space and precession. Of the seven basic flight instruments, three are controlled by gyroscopes:

- Attitude indicator
- Turn coordinator/turn-and-slip indicator
- Heading indicator

The turn coordinator/turn-and-slip indicator is the only one addressed on the test. The turn coordinator is designed to show roll rate, rate of turn, and quality of turn. See Figure 3-2. The turn-and-slip indicators are gyroscopically-operated instruments designed to show the rate of turn and quality of turn. The turn-and-slip indicator does not show roll rate. See Figure 3-3.

A single needle-width deflection on the 2-minute indicator means that the aircraft is turning at 3° per second, or standard rate (2 minutes for a 360° turn). On the 4-minute indicator, a single needle-width deflection shows when the aircraft is turning at 1-1/2° per second, or half-standard rate (4 minutes for a 360° turn).

Before starting the engine, the turn needle should be centered and the race full of fluid. During a taxiing turn, the needle will indicate a turn in the proper direction and the ball will show a skid. An electric turn-and-slip, or turn coordinator, acts as a backup system in case of a failure of the vacuum-powered gyros.

Figure 3-2. Turn coordinator

Figure 3-3. Turn-and-slip indicator

AIR, RTC

5268. What is an operational difference between the turn coordinator and the turn-and-slip indicator? The turn coordinator

A—is always electric; the turn-and-slip indicator is always vacuum-driven.
B—indicates bank angle only; the turn-and-slip indicator indicates rate of turn and coordination.
C—indicates roll rate, rate of turn, and coordination; the turn-and-slip indicator indicates rate of turn and coordination.

The turn coordinator indicates roll rate in addition to rate of turn and coordination. The turn-and-slip indicator only indicates rate of turn and coordination. (PLT187, CA.I.G.K1h) — FAA-H-8083-25

Answer (A) is incorrect because both these instruments are usually electrically driven. Answer (B) is incorrect because a turn coordinator does not indicate bank angle.

AIR, RTC, LTA

5269. What is an advantage of an electric turn coordinator if the airplane has a vacuum system for other gyroscopic instruments?

A—It is a backup in case of vacuum system failure.
B—It is more reliable than the vacuum-driven indicators.
C—It will not tumble as will vacuum-driven turn indicators.

An electric turn coordinator provides a backup in case the vacuum system fails. (PLT118, CA.I.G.K1h) — FAA-H-8083-25

Answers (B) and (C) are incorrect because both the vacuum-driven and electrically-driven indicators are reliable, and both can tumble.

AIR, RTC, LTA

5270. If a standard rate turn is maintained, how long would it take to turn 360°?

A—1 minute.
B—2 minutes.
C—3 minutes.

A standard rate turn means the aircraft is turning at a rate of 3° per second. 360° divided by 3° per second is equal to 120 seconds, or 2 minutes. (PLT187, CA.V.A.K2e) — FAA-H-8083-25

Attitude Instrument Flying

The four flight fundamentals involved in maneuvering an aircraft are straight-and-level flight, turns, climbs, and descents.

ALL

5191. Name the four fundamentals involved in maneuvering an aircraft.

A—Power, pitch, bank, and trim.
B—Thrust, lift, turns, and glides.
C—Straight-and-level flight, turns, climbs, and descents.

Maneuvering the airplane is generally divided into four flight fundamentals:

1. *Straight-and-level*
2. *Turns*
3. *Climbs*
4. *Descents*

(PLT219, CA.V.A.K2e) — FAA-H-8083-3

Answers

5268 [C]   5269 [A]   5270 [B]   5191 [C]

Electronic Flight Instruments

Electronic flight instrument systems integrate many individual instruments into a single presentation called a primary flight display (PFD). Flight instrument presentations on a PFD differ from conventional instrumentation not only in format, but sometimes in location as well. For example, the attitude indicator on the PFD is often larger than conventional round-dial presentations of an artificial horizon. Airspeed and altitude indications are presented on vertical tape displays that appear on the left and right sides of the primary flight display. The vertical speed indicator is depicted using conventional analog presentation. Turn coordination is shown using a segmented triangle near the top of the attitude indicator. The rate-of-turn indicator appears as a curved line display at the top of the heading/navigation instrument in the lower half of the PFD.

Figure 3-4. A typical primary flight display (PFD)

ALL
5999-2. What is a consideration when using a hand-held GPS for VFR navigation?

A—Position accuracy may degrade without notification.
B—RAIM capability will be maintained for entire flight.
C—Waypoints will still be accurate even if database is not current.

While a hand-held GPS receiver can provide excellent navigation capability to VFR pilots, be prepared for intermittent loss of navigation signal, possibly with no RAIM warning to the pilot. (PLT354, CA.VI.B.K2) — FAA-H-8083-25

ALL
5999-3. You are flying an aircraft equipped with an electronic flight display and the air data computer fails. What instrument is affected?

A—ADS-B In capability.
B—Airspeed indicator.
C—Attitude indicator.

The pitot-static inputs are received by the air data computer (ADC). If the ADC fails, the airspeed indicator will be affected. (PLT337, CA.IX.C.K2d) — FAA-H-8083-25

Answers
5999-2 [A]   5999-3 [B]

Chapter 4
Regulations

Pilot Certificate Types and Privileges   *4–3*

Medical Certificates   *4–6*

Pilot Logbooks   *4–7*

High-Performance, Complex, and Tailwheel Airplanes   *4–8*

Recent Flight Experience: Pilot-In-Command   *4–10*

Change of Address   *4–11*

Towing   *4–12*

Responsibility and Authority of the Pilot-In-Command   *4–13*

Preflight Action   *4–15*

Seatbelts   *4–17*

Portable Electronic Devices   *4–19*

Fuel Requirements   *4–20*

Transponder and ADS-B Requirements   *4–20*

Supplemental Oxygen   *4–22*

Instrument and Equipment Requirements   *4–23*

Restricted, Limited, and Experimental Aircraft: Operating Limitations   *4–24*

Emergency Locator Transmitter (ELT)   *4–25*

Truth in Leasing   *4–25*

Operating Near Other Aircraft and Right-of-Way Rules   *4–26*

Speed Limits   *4–29*

Aircraft Lights   *4–30*

Minimum Altitudes   *4–31*

Maintenance Responsibility   *4–32*

Aircraft Inspections   *4–33*

Maintenance Records   *4–35*

Maintenance, Preventative Maintenance, Rebuilding, and Alteration   *4–36*

NTSB Part 830   *4–38*

IFR Operations   *4–41*

Chapter 4 Regulations

Rotorcraft Regulations   *4–42*

Glider Regulations   *4–43*

Lighter-Than-Air Regulations   *4–43*

LTA Fundamentals of Instructing   *4–46*

Chapter 4 **Regulations**

Pilot Certificate Types and Privileges

Although FAR is used as the acronym for Federal Aviation Regulations, and can be seen used throughout the regulations themselves and hundreds of other publications, the FAA is now actively discouraging its use. FAR also stands for Federal Acquisition Regulations. To eliminate any possible confusion, the FAA cites the Federal Aviation Regulations with reference to Title 14 of the Code of Federal Regulations. For example, "FAR Part 91.3" is referred to as "14 CFR Part 91 Section 3" or "14 CFR §91.3."

The holder of a **Student Pilot Certificate** is limited to flight with an instructor until certain requirements are met, after which solo flight may be authorized. A student pilot may neither carry passengers nor fly for compensation or hire.

A **Private Pilot Certificate** grants almost unlimited solo, passenger carrying, and cargo transport privileges, as long as the flying is not done for compensation or hire. A private pilot may share the operating expenses of a flight with their passengers. A private pilot may also act as pilot-in-command (PIC) in connection with business or employment if the flight is only incidental to that business.

The holder of a **Commercial Pilot Certificate** may act as PIC of an aircraft carrying persons or property for compensation or hire. To carry passengers for hire on cross-country flight of more than 50 NM, or at night, a commercial airplane pilot must hold an appropriate Instrument Rating.

An **airline transport pilot (ATP)** has the privileges of a commercial pilot with an Instrument Rating. They may also instruct other pilots in air transportation service in aircraft of the category, class, and type for which the ATP is rated. Part 121 and Part 135 regulations address the situations in which an ATP Rating is required, such as when acting as PIC of a multi-engine commuter flight.

Aircraft category and class ratings in which a pilot is qualified are placed on the pilot's certificate. A type rating is also required to act as PIC of a large aircraft (in excess of 12,500 pounds maximum gross takeoff weight) or of a turbojet-powered aircraft of any weight. Private or commercial pilots wishing to fly under instrument flight rules must also have an Instrument Rating placed on their certificates.

Additional ratings may be granted when a pilot has achieved the required level of skill and knowledge and has successfully completed an inflight test. In the case of an Instrument Rating, the pilot must also pass an FAA Knowledge Exam.

All pilot certificates (except student) are valid indefinitely unless surrendered, suspended, or revoked. There are no expiration dates.

A pilot must have in their possession, or readily accessible in the aircraft, the following documents when operating an aircraft:

1. A pilot's certificate; and
2. A current medical certificate (except for glider and free balloon pilots).

ALL
5022. When is the pilot-in-command required to hold a category and class rating appropriate to the aircraft being flown?

A—All solo flights.
B—On practical tests given by an examiner or FAA Inspector.
C—On flights when carrying another person.

Unless a person holds a category, class, and type rating (if a class and type rating is required) that applies to the aircraft, that person may not act as pilot-in-command of an aircraft that is carrying another person, or is operated for compensation or hire. (PLT443, CA.I.A.K2) — 14 CFR §61.31

Answer (A) is incorrect because a pilot can solo an aircraft with an authorized instructor's logbook endorsement. Answer (B) is incorrect because a pilot may act as pilot-in-command when testing for a category and class rating with a duly authorized examiner.

Answers

5022 [C]

ALL

5966. In what type of operation, not regulated by 14 CFR part 119, may a commercial pilot act as pilot-in-command and receive compensation for services?

A—Part-time contract pilot.
B—Nonstop flights within a 25 SM radius of an airport to carry persons for intentional parachute jumps.
C—Nonstop flights within a 25 SM radius of an airport to carry cargo only.

Part 119 does not apply to nonstop flights conducted within a 25 SM radius of the airport of takeoff carrying persons or objects for the purpose of conducting intentional parachute operations. (PLT444, CA.I.A.K2) — 14 CFR §119.1

Answers (A) and (C) are incorrect because these operations are regulated by Part 119.

ALL

5967. You are acting as a commercial pilot, but are not operating under the regulations of 14 CFR Part 119. Which of these operations are you authorized to conduct?

A—Aerial application and aerial photography.
B—On-demand, passenger carrying flights of nine persons or less.
C—On-demand cargo flights.

Part 119 does not apply to crop dusting, seeding, spraying, and bird chasing. (PLT389, CA.I.A.K2) — 14 CFR §119.1

Answers (B) and (C) are incorrect because these operations are regulated by Part 119.

ALL, MIL

5020. Does a commercial pilot certificate have a specific expiration date?

A—No, it is issued without a specific expiration date.
B—Yes, it expires at the end of the 24th month after the month in which it was issued.
C—No, but commercial privileges expire if a flight review is not satisfactorily completed each 12 months.

Any pilot certificate, other than a student pilot certificate, is issued without a specific expiration date. (PLT386, CA.I.A.K2) — 14 CFR §61.19

ALL, MIL

5018. Commercial pilots are required to have a valid and appropriate pilot certificate in their physical possession or readily accessible in the aircraft when

A—piloting for hire only.
B—carrying passengers only.
C—acting as pilot-in-command.

No person may act as pilot-in-command or in any other capacity as a required pilot flight crew member of a civil aircraft unless a current pilot certificate and, except for glider and balloon pilots, an appropriate current medical certificate is in his/her possession or readily accessible in the aircraft. (PLT444, CA.I.A.K4) — 14 CFR §61.3

Answers (A) and (B) are incorrect because having the appropriate pilot and medical certificates is required regardless of the type of operation.

ALL, MIL

5111. No person may operate an aircraft in simulated instrument flight conditions unless the

A—other control seat is occupied by at least an appropriately rated commercial pilot.
B—pilot has filed an IFR flight plan and received an IFR clearance.
C—other control seat is occupied by a safety pilot, who holds at least a private pilot certificate and is appropriately rated.

No person may operate a civil aircraft in simulated instrument flight unless the other control seat is occupied by a safety pilot who possesses at least a private pilot certificate with category and class ratings appropriate to the aircraft being flown. (PLT444, CA.I.A.K2) — 14 CFR §91.109

ALL, MIL

5126. A person with a commercial pilot certificate may act as pilot-in-command of an aircraft carrying persons or property for compensation or hire, if that person

A—holds appropriate category, class ratings, and meets the recent flight experience requirements of 14 CFR part 61.
B—is qualified in accordance with 14 CFR part 61 and with the applicable parts that apply to the operation.
C—is qualified in accordance with 14 CFR part 61 and has passed a pilot competency check given by an authorized check pilot.

Not only must the pilot be qualified in accordance with Part 61, the pilot must also comply with Part 91, the regulations which govern the operation of the flight. (PLT448, CA.I.A.K2) — 14 CFR §61.31

Answers

5966 [B]   5967 [A]   5020 [A]   5018 [C]   5111 [C]   5126 [B]

Chapter 4 **Regulations**

AIR, RTC, MIL
5023. Unless otherwise authorized, the pilot-in-command is required to hold a type rating when operating any

A—aircraft that is certificated for more than one pilot.
B—aircraft of more than 12,500 pounds maximum certificated takeoff weight.
C—multiengine airplane having a gross weight of more than 12,000 pounds.

A person may not act as pilot-in-command of any of the following aircraft unless he/she holds a type rating for that aircraft:

1. *A large aircraft (except lighter-than-air), more than 12,500 pounds maximum certificated takeoff weight.*
2. *A helicopter, for operations requiring an airline transport pilot certificate.*
3. *A turbojet-powered airplane.*
4. *Other aircraft specified by the Administrator through aircraft type certificate procedures.*

(PLT443, CA.I.A.K2) — 14 CFR §1.1, §61.31

AIR, MIL
5039. What limitation is imposed on a newly certificated commercial pilot–airplane, if that person does not hold an instrument rating? The carriage of passengers

A—for hire on cross-country flights is limited to 50 NM for night flights, but not limited for day flights.
B—or property for hire on cross-country flights at night is limited to a radius of 50 NM.
C—for hire on cross-country flights in excess of 50 NM or for hire at night is prohibited.

A person who applies for a commercial pilot certificate with an airplane category and does not hold an instrument rating in the same category and class will be issued a commercial pilot certificate that contains the limitation, "The carriage of passengers for hire in (airplanes) on cross-country flights in excess of 50 NM or at night is prohibited." (PLT443, CA.I.A.K2) — 14 CFR §61.133

AIR, RTC, LTA, MIL
5019. Which of the following are considered aircraft class ratings?

A—Transport, normal, utility, and acrobatic.
B—Airplane, rotorcraft, glider, and lighter-than-air.
C—Single-engine land, multiengine land, single-engine sea, and multiengine sea.

Aircraft class ratings, with respect to airmen, include single-engine land, multi-engine land, single-engine sea, and multi-engine sea, helicopter, gyroplane, airship, and free balloon. (PLT371, CA.I.A.K2) — 14 CFR §1.1, §61.5

Answer (A) is incorrect because these are aircraft categories with respect to the certification of aircraft. Answer (B) is incorrect because these are categories of aircraft with respect to airmen.

RTC
5968. In what type of operation, not regulated by 14 CFR part 119, may a commercial pilot act as pilot-in-command of a helicopter and receive compensation for services?

A—Military contract rescue flights.
B—On-demand charter flights.
C—Carriage of candidates in a Federal election.

An aircraft operator, other than one operating an aircraft under Part 121, 125, or 135, may receive payment for the carriage of a candidate in a Federal election, an agent of the candidate, or a person traveling on behalf of the candidate, if—

1. *That operator's primary business is not as an air carrier or commercial operator;*
2. *The carriage is conducted under the rules of Part 91; and*
3. *The payment for the carriage is required, and does not exceed the amount required to be paid, by regulations of the Federal Election Commission.*

(PLT389) — 14 CFR §91.321

Answers (A) and (B) are incorrect because these operations are regulated by Part 119.

RTC
5969. In what type of operation, not regulated by 14 CFR part 119, may a commercial pilot act as pilot-in-command of a helicopter and receive compensation for services?

A—On-demand charter flights.
B—Helicopter flights with two passengers or less, within 25 SM radius of the departure heliport.
C—Military contract rescue flights.

Part 119 does not apply to helicopter flights with two passengers or less, within 25 SM radius of the departure heliport. (PLT389) — 14 CFR §119.1

Answers (A) and (C) are incorrect because these operations are regulated by Part 119.

Answers

5023 [B]   5039 [C]   5019 [C]   5968 [C]   5969 [B]

Chapter 4 **Regulations**

AIR, MIL
5545. As a commercial pilot, you decide to start a small business flying non-stop tours to look at Christmas lights during the holiday season. What authorizations, if any, are required to conduct Christmas light tours?

A—No authorizations or approvals are required if you hold the appropriate category and class rating for the aircraft that will be flown.
B—You must apply for and receive a Letter of Authorization from a Flight Standards District Office.
C—You must apply to the FAA to receive an exemption to carry passengers at night within a 50 mile radius of your departure airport.

A Letter of Authorization must be obtained from your local Flight Standards District Office (FSDO) prior to conducting commercial air tours. These regulations can be found under 14 CFR §91.146 and §91.147. (PLT448, CA.I.A.K2) — 14 CFR §61.133, §119.1

Medical Certificates

Student pilot, recreational pilot, and private pilot operations in aircraft other than glider or balloon require a Third Class Medical Certificate, or if operating without a medical certificate, compliance with 14 CFR Part 68—referred to as BasicMed. A Third Class Medical Certificate or compliance with BasicMed does not authorize the PIC to exercise commercial pilot privileges. To operate as a commercial pilot you are required to hold either a first or Second Class Medical Certificate. A Third Class Medical Certificate expires at the end of:

1. The 60th month after the month of the date of the examination shown on the certificate if the person has not reached their 40th birthday on or before the date of examination; or
2. The 24th month after the month of the date of examination shown on the certificate if the person has reached their 40th birthday on or before the date of the examination.

The holder of a Second Class Medical Certificate may exercise commercial privileges during the first 12 calendar months, but the certificate is valid only for private pilot privileges during the following (12 or 48) calendar months, depending on the applicant's age.

The holder of a First Class Medical Certificate may exercise airline transport pilot privileges during the first (6 or 12) calendar months, commercial privileges during the following (6 or 0) calendar months, and private pilot privileges during the following (12 or 48) calendar months, depending on the applicant's age. To state another way, a medical certificate may last 6 months to a year with first-class privileges, 12 months (from the date of the examination) with second-class privileges, and 2 or 5 years with third-class privileges—depending on whether the applicant is above or below 40 years of age.

Each type of medical certificate is valid through the last day of the month (of the month it expires), regardless of the day the physical examination was given.

Answers
5545 [B]

Chapter 4 **Regulations**

AIR, RTC, LTA, MIL

5021. A second-class medical certificate issued to a commercial pilot on April 10, this year, permits the pilot to exercise which of the following privileges?

A—Commercial pilot privileges through April 30, next year.
B—Commercial pilot privileges through April 10, 2 years later.
C—Private pilot privileges through, but not after, March 31, next year.

A second-class medical certificate expires at the end of the last day of:

1. *The 12th month after the month of the date of examination shown on the certificate, for operations requiring a commercial pilot certificate or an air traffic control tower operator certificate, and*

2. *The 24th or 60th (depending on the applicant's age) month after the month of the date of examination shown on the certificate, for operations requiring a private, recreational, or student pilot certificate.*

(PLT447, CA.I.A.K3) — 14 CFR §61.23

Answer (B) is incorrect because a second-class medical is valid for commercial operations for 12 months, and expires on the last day of the month. Answer (C) is incorrect because a second-class medical is valid for private pilot operations for 24 or 60 months (depending on the applicant's age).

AIR, RTC, LTA, MIL

5021-1. The holder of a commercial pilot certificate while exercising commercial pilot privileges is restricted from operating under BasicMed

A—at anytime.
B—for flights over 18,000 FT MSL.
C—if carrying more than 5 passengers.

A third-class medical certificate or compliance with BasicMed does not authorize the PIC to exercise commercial pilot privileges. To operate as a commercial pilot you are required to hold either a first- or second-class medical certificate. (PLT427, CA.I.A.K5) — 14 CFR Parts 61 and 68

MIL

5021-2. May a pilot in the U.S. military use a current U.S. armed forces medical examination to exercise the privileges of an FAA Commercial Pilot Certificate?

A—Yes, the military examination may be used for any civilian flight operations.
B—No, the medical examination may not be used to exercise the privileges of an FAA Commercial Pilot Certificate.
C—No, a military medical examination may not be used for any civilian flight operations.

A U.S. Armed Forces medical examination may be substituted for a FAA medical certificate when the flight does not require higher than a third-class medical certificate and the flight is conducted as a domestic flight operation within U.S. airspace. A Commercial Pilot Certificate requires at minimum a second-class medical certificate. Therefore, an armed forces medical examination may not be used in place of an FAA medical. (PLT447, CA.I.A.K3) — 14 CFR §61.23

Pilot Logbooks

A pilot must log:
- The time required for an added certificate or rating; or
- The time necessary for meeting their recent flight experience requirements.

The logging of other flight time is not required.

A pilot may log flight time as PIC only that flight time during which they act as the sole manipulator of the controls, or during the time they are acting as PIC on an aircraft which requires more than one pilot due to the aircraft's certification or the regulations under which the flight is conducted.

A pilot may log as second-in-command (SIC) time all flight time during which they act as SIC of an aircraft in which more than one pilot is required due to the aircraft's certification or the regulations under which the flight is conducted.

An airline transport pilot may log as PIC time all the flight time during which they act as PIC.

Answers

5021 [A]   5021-1 [A]   5021-2 [B]

Chapter 4 **Regulations**

ALL, MIL

5026. What flight time must be documented and recorded, by a pilot exercising the privileges of a commercial certificate?

A—Flight time showing training and aeronautical experience to meet requirements for a certificate, rating, or flight review.
B—All flight time flown for compensation or hire.
C—Only flight time for compensation or hire with passengers aboard which is necessary to meet the recent flight experience requirements.

The aeronautical training and experience needed to meet the requirements for a certificate or rating, and/or the recent flight experience requirements, must be documented and recorded. The logging of other flight time is not required. (PLT448, CA.I.A.K2) — 14 CFR §61.51

AIR, RTC, MIL

5025. What flight time may a pilot log as second-in-command?

A—All flight time while acting as second-in-command in aircraft configured for more than one pilot.
B—All flight time when qualified and occupying a crewmember station in an aircraft that requires more than one pilot.
C—Only that flight time during which the second-in-command is the sole manipulator of the controls.

A person may log second-in-command time only for that flight time during which that person is qualified in accordance with the second-in-command requirements of this part, and occupies a crewmember station in an aircraft that requires more than one pilot by the aircraft's type certificate. (PLT448, CA.I.A.K2) — 14 CFR §61.51

High-Performance, Complex, and Tailwheel Airplanes

To act as PIC of an airplane that has more than 200 horsepower, or is equipped with retractable landing gear, flaps, and a controllable propeller, a person must receive flight instruction and obtain a logbook endorsement of competency from a certified flight instructor. This endorsement is required only one time.

No person may serve as SIC of a large airplane, or a turbojet-powered airplane type certificated for more than one required flight crew member unless the person holds:

1. At least a current private pilot certificate with appropriate category and class ratings; and
2. An appropriate Instrument Rating, in the case of flight under IFR.

AIR, MIL

5024. To act as pilot-in-command of an airplane that is equipped with retractable landing gear, flaps, and controllable-pitch propeller, a person is required to

A—make at least six takeoffs and landings in such an airplane within the preceding 6 months.
B—receive and log ground and flight training in such an airplane, and obtain a logbook endorsement certifying proficiency.
C—hold a multiengine airplane class rating.

No person may act as PIC of a complex airplane (an airplane that has a retractable landing gear, flaps, and a controllable pitch propeller), unless the person has received and logged ground and flight training from an authorized instructor in a complex airplane, or in a flight simulator or flight training device that is representative of a complex airplane, and has been found proficient in the operation and systems of the airplane; and received a one-time endorsement in the pilot's logbook from an authorized instructor who certifies the person is proficient to operate a complex airplane. (PLT448, CA.I.A.K2) — 14 CFR §61.31

Answers

5026 [A]   5025 [B]   5024 [B]

AIR, MIL
5106. To act as pilot-in-command of an airplane with more than 200 horsepower, a person is required to

A—receive and log ground and flight training from a qualified pilot in such an airplane.
B—obtain an endorsement from a qualified pilot stating that the person is proficient to operate such an airplane.
C—receive and log ground and flight training from an authorized instructor in such an airplane.

To act as pilot-in-command of a high-performance airplane (an airplane with an engine of more than 200 horsepower), the person must receive and log ground and flight training from an authorized instructor in a high-performance airplane and has been found proficient in the operation and systems of the airplane. In addition, the pilot must receive a one-time endorsement in the pilot's logbook from an authorized instructor who certifies that the person is proficient to operate a high-performance airplane. The training and endorsement is not required if the person has logged flight time as pilot-in-command of a high-performance airplane prior to August 4, 1997. (PLT448, CA.I.A.K2) — 14 CFR §61.31

Answers (A) and (B) are incorrect because the required training and endorsement must be provided by an authorized instructor, not a qualified pilot.

AIR, MIL
5107. To serve as pilot-in-command of an airplane that is certified for more than one pilot crewmember, and operated under Part 91, a person must

A—complete a flight review within the preceding 24 calendar months.
B—receive and log ground and flight training from an authorized flight instructor.
C—complete a pilot-in-command proficiency check within the preceding 12 calendar months in an airplane that is type certificated for more than one pilot.

To serve as PIC of an aircraft that is type certificated for more than one required pilot flight crewmember, a person must complete a PIC proficiency check in the aircraft that is type certificated for more than one required pilot flight crewmember within the preceding 12 calendar months. Additionally, the pilot must complete a PIC proficiency check in the particular type of aircraft in which that person will serve as PIC within the preceding 24 calendar months. (PLT448, CA.I.A.K2) — 14 CFR §61.58

AIR, MIL
5108. To serve as second-in-command of an airplane that is certificated for more than one pilot crewmember, and operated under Part 91, a person must

A—receive and log flight training from an authorized flight instructor in the type of airplane for which privileges are requested.
B—hold at least a commercial pilot certificate with an airplane category rating.
C—within the last 12 months become familiar with the required information, and perform and log pilot time in the type of airplane for which privileges are requested.

Under Part 91 no person may serve as a second-in-command of an aircraft type certificated for more than one required pilot flight crewmember unless that person has within the previous 12 calendar months become familiar with information for the specific type aircraft for which second-in-command privileges are requested and performed and logged pilot time in the type of aircraft or in a flight simulator that represents the type of aircraft for which second-in-command privileges are requested. Also, no person may serve as a second-in-command of an aircraft type certificated for more than one required pilot flight crewmember unless that person holds at least a current private pilot certificate with the appropriate category and class rating. (PLT448, CA.I.A.K2) — 14 CFR §61.55

AIR, MIL
5128. To act as pilot-in-command of a tailwheel airplane, without prior experience, a pilot must

A—log ground and flight training from an authorized instructor.
B—pass a competency check and receive an endorsement from an authorized instructor.
C—receive and log flight training from an authorized instructor as well as receive a logbook endorsement from an authorized instructor who finds the person proficient in a tailwheel airplane.

No person may act as pilot-in-command of a tailwheel airplane unless that person has received and logged flight training from an authorized Instructor in a tailwheel airplane and received an endorsement in the person's logbook from an authorized instructor who found the person proficient in the operation of a tailwheel airplane. (PLT448, CA.I.A.K2) — 14 CFR §61.31

Answers

5106 [C]   5107 [C]   5108 [C]   5128 [C]

Chapter 4 Regulations

AIR, MIL

5539. To act as PIC of a high performance airplane, which training or experience would meet the additional requirements?

A—Logged at least five hours as SIC in a high-performance or turbine-powered airplane in the last 12 calendar months.
B—Received and logged ground and flight training in an airplane with retractable landing gear, flaps, and controllable-pitch propeller.
C—Received and logged ground and flight training in a high-performance airplane and a received a logbook endorsement.

To act as pilot-in-command of a high-performance airplane (an airplane with an engine of more than 200 horsepower), the pilot must receive and log ground and flight training from an authorized instructor in a high-performance airplane and must be found proficient in the operation and systems of the airplane. In addition, the pilot must receive a one-time endorsement in the pilot's logbook from an authorized instructor who certifies that the pilot is proficient in operating a high-performance airplane. The training and endorsement is not required if the pilot has logged flight time as pilot-in-command of a high-performance airplane prior to August 4, 1997. (PLT451, CA.I.A.K1) — 14 CFR §61.31

Recent Flight Experience: Pilot-In-Command

No person may act as PIC of an aircraft unless, within the preceding 24 calendar months, they have accomplished a **flight review**. This review is given in an aircraft for which the person is rated by an appropriately certificated instructor or other person designated by the FAA. Satisfactory accomplishment of this flight review will be endorsed in the pilot's logbook. If the pilot takes a proficiency check (for a certificate or a new rating), it counts for the flight review. A biennial flight review would then be required at the end of the 24th calendar month following that proficiency check. The review must include a minimum of 1 hour flight instruction and 1 hour ground instruction.

No person may act as PIC of an aircraft carrying passengers unless, within the preceding 90 days, they have made three takeoffs and landings (touch-and-go landings are allowed if the aircraft is not a tailwheel airplane) as the sole manipulator of the controls in an aircraft of the same category, class, and type (if required). In order to carry passengers in a tailwheel (conventional gear) airplane, the takeoffs and landings must be made to a full stop, and they must be in a tailwheel airplane.

No person may act as PIC of an aircraft carrying passengers during the period from 1 hour after sunset to 1 hour before sunrise unless, within the preceding 90 days, they have made at least three takeoffs and three landings to a full stop during that period in the same category and class of aircraft to be used.

ALL, MIL

5027. If a pilot does not meet the recency of experience requirements for night flight and official sunset is 1900 CST, the latest time passengers should be carried is

A—1959 CST.
B—1900 CST.
C—1800 CST.

No person may act as PIC of an aircraft carrying passengers during the period beginning 1 hour after sunset and ending 1 hour before sunrise, unless within the preceding 90 days that person has made at least three takeoffs and three landings to a full stop during the period beginning 1 hour after sunset and ending 1 hour before sunrise. (PLT220, CA.I.A.K1) — 14 CFR §61.57

ALL, MIL

5028. Prior to carrying passengers at night, the pilot-in-command must have accomplished the required takeoffs and landings in

A—any category aircraft.
B—the same category and class of aircraft to be used.
C—the same category, class, and type of aircraft (if a type rating is required).

No person may act as pilot-in-command of an aircraft carrying passengers during the period beginning 1 hour after sunset and ending 1 hour before sunrise unless within the preceding 90 days, he/she has made at least three takeoffs and three landings to a full stop during that period in the same category, class, and type (if a type rating is required) of aircraft to be used. (PLT442, CA.I.A.K1) — 14 CFR §61.57

Answers

5539 [C]   5027 [A]   5028 [C]

Chapter 4 **Regulations**

ALL, MIL

5031. To act as pilot-in-command of an aircraft under 14 CFR Part 91, a commercial pilot must have satisfactorily accomplished a flight review or completed a proficiency check within the preceding

A—6 calendar months.
B—12 calendar months.
C—24 calendar months.

No person may act as pilot-in-command of an aircraft unless, within the preceding 24 calendar months, he/she has accomplished a flight review, completed a pilot proficiency check, or has completed one or more phases of an FAA-sponsored pilot proficiency award program. (PLT442, CA.I.A.K1) — 14 CFR §61.56

ALL, MIL

5030. No pilot may act as pilot-in-command of an aircraft under IFR or in weather conditions less than the minimums prescribed for VFR unless that pilot has, within the past 6 months, performed and logged under actual or simulated instrument conditions, at least

A—six instrument approaches, holding procedures, intercepting and tracking courses, or passed an instrument proficiency check in an aircraft that is appropriate to the aircraft category.
B—three instrument approaches and logged 3 hours of instruments.
C—six instrument flights and six approaches.

To act as pilot-in-command under IFR, the pilot must, within the preceding 6 calendar months, have performed and logged under actual or simulated instrument conditions at least six instrument approaches, holding procedures, and intercepting and tracking of courses through the use of navigation systems. (PLT442, CA.I.A.K1) — 14 CFR §61.57

ALL, MIL

5477. You have accomplished 25 takeoffs and landings in multi-engine land airplanes in the previous 45 days. For a flight you plan to conduct today, this meets the PIC recency of experience requirements to carry passengers in which airplanes?

A—Multi- or single-engine land.
B—Single-engine land airplane.
C—Multi-engine land airplane.

No person may act as PIC of an aircraft carrying passengers unless, within the preceding 90 days, he or she has made three takeoffs and landings as the sole manipulator of the controls in an aircraft of the same category, class, and type (if required). (PLT442, CA.I.A.K1) — 14 CFR §61.57

Change of Address

If a pilot changes their permanent address without notifying the FAA Airman Certification Branch within 30 days, they may not exercise the privileges of their certificate. For notification of address change, a pilot may do so online at **faa.gov/licenses_certificates/airmen_certification/airmen_services** or by mail to:

Federal Aviation Administration
Airman Certification Branch, AFS-760
PO Box 25082
Oklahoma City, OK 73125-0082

ALL, MIL

5032. Pilots who change their permanent mailing address and fail to notify the FAA Airmen Certification Branch of this change, are entitled to exercise the privileges of their pilot certificate for a period of

A—30 days.
B—60 days.
C—90 days.

The holder of a pilot or flight instructor certificate who has made a change in his/her permanent mailing address may not after 30 days from the date he/she moved, exercise the privileges of his/her certificate unless he/she has notified the FAA in writing. (PLT387, CA.I.A.K1) — 14 CFR §61.60

Answers

| 5031 | [C] | 5030 | [A] | 5477 | [C] | 5032 | [A] |

Chapter 4 **Regulations**

Towing

A certificated pilot may not act as pilot-in-command of an aircraft towing a glider unless there is a minimum of 100 hours of pilot flight time in powered aircraft entered in the pilot's logbook, and within the preceding 24 months, that pilot has made at least three actual or simulated glider tows while accompanied by a qualified pilot.

No pilot may tow anything other than a glider with an aircraft, except in accordance with the terms of a certificate of waiver issued by the Administrator.

AIR, MIL
5055. Which is required to operate an aircraft towing an advertising banner?

A—Approval from ATC to operate in Class E airspace.
B—A certificate of waiver issued by the Administrator.
C—A safety link at each end of the towline which has a breaking strength not less than 80 percent of the aircraft's gross weight.

A certificate of waiver is required for towing objects other than gliders. (PLT389, CA.I.A.K2) — 14 CFR §91.311

Answer (A) is incorrect because approval from ATC to operate in Class E airspace is only required in IFR conditions. Answer (C) is incorrect because the towline breaking strength requirement is for towing gliders.

AIR, GLI, MIL
5033. To act as pilot-in-command of an airplane towing a glider, the tow pilot is required to have

A—a logbook endorsement from an authorized glider instructor certifying receipt of ground and flight training in gliders, and be proficient with techniques and procedures for safe towing of gliders.
B—at least a private pilot certificate with a category rating for powered aircraft, and made and logged at least three flights as pilot or observer in a glider being towed by an airplane.
C—a logbook record of having made at least three flights as sole manipulator of the controls of a glider being towed by an airplane.

To act as pilot-in-command of an aircraft towing a glider, a person must have a logbook endorsement from an authorized instructor who certifies that the person has received ground and flight training in gliders and is proficient in the techniques and procedures essential to the safe towing of gliders, including airspeed limitations. (PLT442, CA.I.A.K1) — 14 CFR §61.69

Answer (B) is incorrect because the PIC must have logged at least three flights as the sole manipulator of the controls, not as an observer, of an aircraft towing a glider or simulating glider-towing flight procedures while accompanied by an authorized pilot. Answer (C) is incorrect because any person who, before May 17, 1967, has made and logged 10 or more flights as PIC of an aircraft towing a glider in accordance with a certificate of waiver need not comply with this rule.

AIR, GLI, MIL
5034. To act as pilot-in-command of an airplane towing a glider, a pilot must have accomplished, within the preceding 24 months, at least

A—three actual glider tows under the supervision of a qualified tow pilot.
B—three actual or simulated glider tows while accompanied by a qualified tow pilot.
C—ten flights as pilot-in-command of an aircraft while towing a glider.

To act as PIC, the pilot must make at least three actual or simulated glider tows while accompanied by a qualified pilot or make at least three flights as pilot-in-command of a glider towed by an aircraft. (PLT442, CA.I.A.K1) — 14 CFR §61.69

GLI
5127. To act as pilot-in-command of a glider, using self-launch procedures, that person must hold a pilot certificate with a glider rating and have accomplished

A—a competency flight check given by an authorized flight instructor.
B—ground and flight training in self-launch procedures and operations, and possess a logbook endorsement from a flight instructor certifying such proficiency.
C—appropriate flight training and meet recent experience in self-launch operations.

No person may act as pilot-in-command of a glider using self-launch procedures, unless that person has satisfactorily accomplished ground and flight training on self-launch procedures and operations and has received an endorsement from an authorized instructor who certifies in that pilot's logbook that the pilot has been found proficient in self-launch procedures and operations. (PLT448) — 14 CFR §61.31

Answers

5055 [B]   5033 [A]   5034 [B]   5127 [B]

Responsibility and Authority of the Pilot-In-Command

The pilot-in-command is directly responsible for the safety of his/her aircraft. The PIC is the final authority as to the operation of the aircraft. In the interest of safety, the PIC can deviate from any of these regulations to the extent necessary to meet an emergency. Each pilot-in-command who deviates from a regulation must, if requested, send a written report of that deviation to the Administrator.

No pilot-in-command may allow any object to be dropped from an aircraft in flight that creates a hazard to persons or property. However, this does not prohibit the dropping of objects if reasonable precautions are taken to avoid injury or damage to persons or property.

Operate, with respect to aircraft, means use, cause to use, or authorize to use aircraft, for the purpose of air navigation including the piloting of aircraft, with or without the right of legal control (as owner, lessee, or otherwise).

Operational control, with respect to a flight, means the exercise of authority over initiating, conducting or terminating a flight.

Commercial operator means a person who, for compensation or hire, engages in the carriage by aircraft in air commerce of persons or property, other than as an air carrier or foreign air carrier. Where it is doubtful that an operation is for compensation or hire, the test applied is whether the carriage by air is merely incidental to the person's other business or is, in itself, a major enterprise for profit.

ALL, MIL
5044. What action must be taken when a pilot-in-command deviates from any rule in 14 CFR Part 91?

A—Upon landing, report the deviation to the nearest FAA Flight Standards District Office.
B—Advise ATC of the pilot-in-command's intentions.
C—Upon the request of the Administrator, send a written report of that deviation to the Administrator.

Each pilot-in-command who deviates from a rule in an emergency shall, upon request, send a written report of that deviation to the Administrator. (PLT444, CA.I.A.K2) — 14 CFR §91.3

ALL, MIL
5047. A pilot-in-command (PIC) of a civil aircraft may not allow any object to be dropped from that aircraft in flight

A—if it creates a hazard to persons and property.
B—unless the PIC has permission to drop any object over private property.
C—unless reasonable precautions are taken to avoid injury to property.

No pilot-in-command of a civil aircraft may allow any object to be dropped from an aircraft in flight that creates a hazard to persons or property. However, this does not prohibit the dropping of objects if reasonable precautions are taken to avoid injury or damage to persons or property. (PLT401, CA.I.A.K2) — 14 CFR §91.15

ALL, MIL
5011. Regulations which refer to operate relate to that person who

A—acts as pilot-in-command of the aircraft.
B—is the sole manipulator of the aircraft controls.
C—causes the aircraft to be used or authorizes its use.

"Operate," with respect to aircraft, means use, cause to use, or authorize to use aircraft. (PLT395, CA.I.A.K2) — 14 CFR §1.1

Answer (A) is incorrect because the pilot-in-command may not necessarily be the operator of the aircraft. Answer (B) is incorrect because the sole manipulator may not necessarily be the operator of the aircraft.

ALL, MIL
5012. Regulations which refer to the operational control of a flight are in relation to

A—the specific duties of any required crewmember.
B—acting as the sole manipulator of the aircraft controls.
C—exercising authority over initiating, conducting, or terminating a flight.

"Operational control," with respect to a flight, means the exercise of authority over initiating, conducting, or terminating a flight. (PLT395, CA.I.A.K2) — 14 CFR §1.1

Answer (A) is incorrect because assigning specific duties to a crew member is only a small part of exercising operational control. Answer (B) is incorrect because acting as sole manipulator of an aircraft is a flight crew responsibility.

Answers

5044 [C]   5047 [A]   5011 [C]   5012 [C]

Chapter 4 **Regulations**

ALL, MIL
5010. Regulations which refer to "commercial operators" relate to that person who

A—is the owner of a small scheduled airline.
B—for compensation or hire, engages in the carriage by aircraft in air commerce of persons or property, as an air carrier.
C—for compensation or hire, engages in the carriage by aircraft in air commerce of persons or property, other than as an air carrier.

"Commercial operator" means a person who, for compensation or hire, engages in the carriage by aircraft in air commerce of persons or property, other than as an air carrier. (PLT395, CA.I.A.K2) — 14 CFR §1.1

ALL, MIL
5109. What person is directly responsible for the final authority as to the operation of the airplane?

A—Certificate holder.
B—Pilot-in-command.
C—Airplane owner/operator.

The pilot-in-command of an aircraft is directly responsible for, and is the final authority as to, the operation of that aircraft. (PLT444, CA.I.A.K2) — 14 CFR §91.3

ALL, MIL
5141. A pilot convicted of operating a motor vehicle while either intoxicated by, impaired by, or under the influence of alcohol or a drug is required to provide a

A—written report to the FAA Civil Aeromedical Institute (CAMI) within 60 days after the motor vehicle action.
B—written report to the FAA Civil Aviation Security Division (AMC-700) not later than 60 days after the conviction.
C—notification of the conviction to an FAA Aviation Medical Examiner (AME) not later than 60 days after the motor vehicle action.

Each person holding a pilot certificate shall provide a written report of each motor vehicle action to the FAA, Civil Aviation Security Division (AMC-700), not later than 60 days after the motor vehicle action. (PLT463, CA.I.H.K2) — 14 CFR §61.15

ALL, MIL
5142. A pilot convicted of a motor vehicle offense involving alcohol or drugs is required to provide a written report to the

A—nearest FAA Flight Standards District Office (FSDO) within 60 days after such action.
B—FAA Civil Aeromedical Institute (CAMI) within 60 days after the conviction.
C—FAA Civil Aviation Security Division (AMC-700) within 60 days after such action.

Each person holding a pilot certificate shall provide a written report of each motor vehicle action to the FAA, Civil Aviation Security Division (AMC-700), not later than 60 days after the motor vehicle action. (PLT463, CA.I.H.K2) — 14 CFR §61.15

ALL, MIL
5143. A pilot convicted for the violation of any Federal or State statute relating to the process, manufacture, transportation, distribution, or sale of narcotic drugs is grounds for

A—a written report to be filed with the FAA Civil Aviation Security Division (AMC-700) not later than 60 days after the conviction.
B—notification of this conviction to the FAA Civil Aeromedical Institute (CAMI) within 60 days after the conviction.
C—suspension or revocation of any certificate, rating, or authorization issued under 14 CFR Part 61.

A conviction for the violation of any Federal or State statute relating to the growing, processing, manufacture, sale, disposition, possession, transportation, or importation of narcotic drugs, marijuana, or depressant or stimulant drugs or substances is grounds for: (1) Denial of an application for any certificate, rating, or authorization for a period of up to 1 year after the date of final conviction; or (2) Suspension or revocation of any certificate, rating, or authorization. (PLT463, CA.I.H.K2) — 14 CFR §61.15

Answers

5010 [C]   5109 [B]   5141 [B]   5142 [C]   5143 [C]

ALL, MIL

5144. A pilot convicted of operating an aircraft as a crewmember under the influence of alcohol, or using drugs that affect the person's faculties, is grounds for a

A—written report to be filed with the FAA Civil Aviation Security Division (AMC-700) not later than 60 day after the conviction.
B—written notification to the FAA Civil Aeromedical Institute (CAMI) within 60 days after the conviction.
C—denial of an application for an FAA certificate, rating, or authorization issued under 14 CFR part 61.

No person may act or attempt to act as a crewmember of a civil aircraft within 8 hours after the consumption of any alcoholic beverage, while under the influence of alcohol, while using any drug that affects the person's faculties in any way contrary to safety; or while having 0.04 percent by weight or more alcohol in the blood. Committing any of these acts is grounds for: (1) Denial of an application for a certificate, rating, or authorization for a period of up to 1 year after the date of that act; or (2) Suspension or revocation of any certificate, rating, or authorization. (PLT463, CA.I.H.K2) — 14 CFR §61.15

Preflight Action

Each pilot-in-command, before starting a flight, shall familiarize him/herself with all available information concerning that flight. This information must include runway lengths and takeoff and landing distance information for airports of intended use. If the flight will not be in the vicinity of an airport or will be under IFR, the PIC must also check:

- Available weather reports and forecasts
- Fuel requirements
- Alternatives available if the flight cannot be completed as planned
- Any known traffic delays as advised by ATC

No person may operate an aircraft unless it has within it:

1. An appropriate and current airworthiness certificate, displayed at the cabin or cockpit entrance so that it is legible to passengers or crew.
2. A registration certificate issued to its owner.
3. An approved flight manual, manual material, markings, and placards or any combination of these, showing the operating limitations of the aircraft.

A mnemonic aid to remembering the documentation required on board an aircraft prior to flight is:

A irworthiness certificate

R egistration certificate

O wner's manual or operating limitations

W eight and balance data

ALL, MIL

5045. Who is responsible for determining if an aircraft is in condition for safe flight?

A—A certificated aircraft mechanic.
B—The pilot-in-command.
C—The owner or operator.

The pilot-in-command of an aircraft is responsible for determining whether that aircraft is in condition for safe flight. The pilot shall discontinue the flight when unairworthy mechanical, electrical, or structural conditions occur. (PLT444, CA.II.A.K2) — 14 CFR §91.7

Answers

5144 [C]   5045 [B]

Chapter 4 **Regulations**

ALL, MIL
5046. When operating a U.S.-registered civil aircraft, which document is required by regulation to be available in the aircraft?

A—A manufacturer's Operations Manual.
B—A current, approved Airplane (or Rotorcraft) Flight Manual.
C—An Owner's Manual.

No person may operate an aircraft unless it has within it:

1. *An appropriate and current airworthiness certificate, displayed at the cabin or cockpit entrance so that it is legible to passengers or crew.*
2. *A registration certificate issued to its owner.*
3. *An approved flight manual, manual material, markings and placards or any combination of these, showing the operating limitations of the aircraft.*

(PLT400, CA.I.B.K1a) — 14 CFR §91.203

ALL, MIL
5046-1. Which of the following preflight actions is the pilot-in-command required to take in order to comply with the United States Code of Federal Regulations regarding day Visual Flight Rules (VFR)?

A—File a VFR flight plan with a Flight Service Station.
B—Verify the airworthiness certificate is legible to passengers.
C—Verify approved position lights are not burned out.

No person may operate an aircraft unless it has within it:

1. *An appropriate and current Airworthiness Certificate, displayed at the cabin or cockpit entrance so that it is legible to passengers or crew.*
2. *A Registration Certificate issued to its owner.*
3. *An approved flight manual, manual material, markings and placards or any combination of these, showing the operating limitations of the aircraft.*

(PLT444, CA.I.B.K1a) — 14 CFR §91.203

Answer (A) is incorrect because it is not mandatory to file a flight plan. Answer (C) is incorrect because regulations only specify approved position lights must be installed.

ALL, MIL
5046-2. You are taking a 123 nautical mile VFR flight from one airport to another. Which of the following actions must the pilot-in-command take?

A—Ensure each passenger has a legible photo identification.
B—Verify the airworthiness certificate is legible to passengers.
C—File a VFR flight plan with a Flight Service Station.

No person may operate an aircraft unless it has within it:

1. *An appropriate and current Airworthiness Certificate, displayed at the cabin or cockpit entrance so that it is legible to passengers or crew.*
2. *A Registration Certificate issued to its owner.*
3. *An approved flight manual, manual material, markings and placards or any combination of these, showing the operating limitations of the aircraft.*

(PLT444, CA.I.B.K1a) — 14 CFR §91.203

ALL, MIL
5049-1. When is preflight action required, relative to alternatives available, if the planned flight cannot be completed?

A—IFR flights only.
B—any flight not in the vicinity of an airport.
C—any flight conducted for compensation or hire.

For a flight under IFR or flight not in the vicinity of an airport, the pilot must be familiar with weather reports and forecasts, fuel requirements, alternatives available if the planned flight cannot be completed, and any known traffic delays of which he/she has been advised by ATC. (PLT444, CA.I.D.R3) — 14 CFR §91.103

ALL, MIL
5049-2. The required preflight action relative to weather reports and fuel requirements is applicable to

A—any flight conducted for compensation or hire.
B—any flight not in the vicinity of an airport.
C—IFR flights only.

Before beginning a flight under IFR or a flight not in the vicinity of an airport, each PIC shall become familiar with all available information concerning that flight, including weather reports and forecasts, fuel requirements, alternatives available if the planned flight cannot be completed, and any known traffic delays of which the pilot-in-command has been advised by ATC. (PLT444, CA.I.D.R3) — 14 CFR §91.103

Answers

| 5046 | [B] | 5046-1 | [B] | 5046-2 | [B] | 5049-1 | [B] | 5049-2 | [B] |

Chapter 4 Regulations

ALL, MIL

5049-3. You are pilot-in-command of a VFR flight that you think will be within the fuel range of your aircraft. As part of your preflight planning you must

A—be familiar with all instrument approaches at the destination airport.
B—list an alternate airport on the flight plan and confirm adequate takeoff and landing performance at the destination airport.
C—obtain weather reports, forecasts, and fuel requirements for the flight.

Before beginning a flight under IFR or a flight not in the vicinity of an airport, each PIC shall become familiar with all available information concerning that flight, including weather reports and forecasts, fuel requirements, available alternatives if the planned flight cannot be completed, and any known traffic delays of which the pilot-in-command has been advised by ATC. (PLT445, CA.I.C.K3) — 14 CFR §91.103

ALL, MIL

5050. Before beginning any flight under IFR, the pilot-in-command must become familiar with all available information concerning that flight. In addition, the pilot must

A—be familiar with all instrument approaches at the destination airport.
B—list an alternate airport on the flight plan and confirm adequate takeoff and landing performance at the destination airport.
C—be familiar with the runway lengths at airports of intended use, weather reports, fuel requirements, and alternatives available, if the flight cannot be completed.

For a flight under IFR or flight not in the vicinity of an airport, the pilot must be familiar with weather reports and forecasts, fuel requirements, alternatives available if the planned flight cannot be completed, and any known traffic delays of which he/she has been advised by ATC. For any flight, the pilot must be familiar with runway lengths at airports of intended use, and the following takeoff and landing distance information: For civil aircraft for which an approved airplane or rotorcraft flight manual containing takeoff and landing distance data is required, the takeoff and landing distance data contained therein. (PLT444, CA.II.A.K4) — 14 CFR §91.103

Answer (A) is incorrect because only pilots filing an IFR flight must be familiar with the instrument approaches at their destination airport and possible alternates. Answer (B) is incorrect because an alternate is not required if weather is VFR at the destination.

ALL, MIL

5050-1. Which list accurately reflects some of the documents required to be current and carried in a U.S. registered civil airplane flying in the United States under day Visual Flight Rules (VFR)?

A—Proof of insurance certificate, VFR flight plan or flight itinerary, and the aircraft logbook.
B—VFR sectional(s) chart(s) for the area in which the flight occurs, aircraft logbook, and engine logbook.
C—Airworthiness certificate, approved airplane flight manual, and aircraft registration certificate.

No person may operate an aircraft unless it has within it:

1. *An appropriate and current Airworthiness Certificate, displayed at the cabin or cockpit entrance so that it is legible to passengers or crew.*
2. *A Registration Certificate issued to its owner.*
3. *An approved flight manual, manual material, markings and placards or any combination thereof, which show the operating limitations of the aircraft.*

(PLT400, CA.I.B.K1a) — 14 CFR §91.203

Seatbelts

During takeoff and landing and while en route, each required flight crewmember shall be at their station with seatbelt fastened, unless the crewmember has to leave in connection with the operation of the aircraft or physiological needs. Also, each required flight crewmember must keep the shoulder harness fastened during takeoff and landing, unless the crewmember would be unable to perform their duties with the shoulder harness fastened.

No pilot may takeoff or land a civil aircraft unless the PIC ensures that each person on board has been notified to fasten their safety belt and ensures that each person on board knows how to operate the

Answers

5049-3 [C]   5050 [C]   5050-1 [C]

safely belt. Each person on board must occupy a seat with a seatbelt properly secured during takeoffs and landings. (A person who has not reached their second birthday may be held by an adult.)

Free balloons and some airships are exempted from these requirements.

ALL, MIL
5051-1. Required flight crewmembers' safety belts must be fastened

A—only during takeoff and landing.
B—while the crewmembers are at their stations.
C—only during takeoff and landing when passengers are aboard the aircraft.

Required flight crewmembers must keep their safety belts fastened while at their stations. (PLT464, CA.II.B.K1) — 14 CFR §91.105

ALL, MIL
5051-2. Each required flight crewmember is required to keep his or her shoulder harness fastened

A—during takeoff and landing only when passengers are aboard the aircraft.
B—while the crewmembers are at their stations, unless he or she is unable to perform required duties.
C—during takeoff and landing, unless he or she is unable to perform required duties.

Each required flight crewmember of a U.S.-registered civil aircraft shall, during takeoff and landing, keep his or her shoulder harness fastened while at his or her assigned duty station. This rule does not apply if the seat at the crewmember's station is not equipped with a shoulder harness, or the crewmember would be unable to perform required duties with the shoulder harness fastened. (PLT464, CA.II.B.K1) — 14 CFR §91.105

Answer (A) is incorrect because the shoulder harness must be used on takeoff and landing regardless of the passenger complement. Answer (B) is incorrect because the regulation specifies shoulder harness use during takeoff and landing.

AIR, MIL
5052. With U.S.-registered civil airplanes, the use of safety belts is required during movement on the surface, takeoffs, and landings for

A—safe operating practice, but not required by regulations.
B—each person over 2 years of age on board.
C—commercial passenger operations only.

No pilot may cause to be moved on the surface, take-off, or land a U.S.-registered civil aircraft unless the PIC of that aircraft ensures that each person on board has been notified to fasten his or her safety belt and, if installed, his or her shoulder harness. A person who has not reached his/her second birthday may be held by an adult. (PLT465, CA.II.B.K1) — 14 CFR §91.107

AIR, MIL
5110-1. Operating regulations for U.S.-registered civil airplanes require that during movement on the surface, takeoffs, and landings, a seat belt and shoulder harness (if installed) must be properly secured about each

A—flight crewmember only.
B—person on board.
C—flight and cabin crewmembers.

No pilot may cause to be moved on the surface, takeoff, or land a U.S.-registered civil aircraft unless the pilot-in-command of that aircraft ensures that each person on board (over two years of age) has been notified to fasten his or her safety belt and, if installed, his or her shoulder harness. (PLT465, CA.II.B.K1) — 14 CFR §91.107

RTC, MIL
5110-2. Operating regulations for U.S.-registered civil helicopters require that during movement on the surface, takeoffs, and landings, a seat belt and shoulder harness (if installed) must be properly secured about each

A—person on board.
B—flight and cabin crewmembers.
C—flight crew member only.

No pilot may cause to be moved on the surface, takeoff, or land a U.S.-registered civil aircraft unless the pilot-in-command of that aircraft ensures that each person on board (over two years of age) has been notified to fasten his or her safety belt and, if installed, his or her shoulder harness. (PLT464, MC.I.A.K3) — 14 CFR §91.107

Answers

5051-1   [B]   5051-2   [C]   5052   [B]   5110-1   [B]   5110-2   [A]

ALL, MIL

5051-3. During preflight, you discover one of the passenger seats has a defective shoulder harness. All of the seats will be occupied. This flight is

A—allowed.
B—not allowed.
C—allowed so long as the passenger is notified of the defective shoulder harness.

No pilot may cause to be moved on the surface, takeoff, or land a U.S.-registered civil aircraft unless the PIC of that aircraft ensures that each person on board has been notified to fasten his or her safety belt and, if installed, his or her shoulder harness. (PLT464, CA.II.B.K1) — 14 CFR §91.107

ALL, MIL

5051-4. You are planning a trip and one of your passengers states that he prefers not to use his shoulder harness because it is uncomfortable. You should

A—explain that it is a mandatory requirement and that he use the shoulder harness during takeoff, landing, and movement on the surface.
B—allow him to use his seat belt for the entire trip without the shoulder harness.
C—allow him to use his seat belt for takeoff and landing and the shoulder harness while en route.

If installed, a shoulder harness must be worn during movement on the surface, takeoff, and landing. (PLT464, CA.II.B.K1) — 14 CFR §91.107

Portable Electronic Devices

No person may operate or allow the operation of any portable electronic device on board an aircraft:

1. Operated by an air carrier or commercial operator; or
2. While the aircraft is operated under IFR.

   Exceptions to this regulation are:

- Voice recorders
- Hearing aids
- Heart pacemakers
- Electric shavers
- Anything else the PIC has determined will not cause interference with navigation or communications systems.

ALL, MIL

5056-1. Portable electronic devices which may cause interference with the navigation or communication system may not be operated on a U.S.-registered civil aircraft being flown

A—along Federal airways.
B—within the U.S.
C—in air carrier operations.

Portable electronic devices may not be operated on aircraft operated by a holder of an air carrier operating certificate. (PLT392, CA.II.B.R1) — 14 CFR §91.21
Answers (A) and (B) are incorrect because this rule pertains only to IFR and commercial flights.

ALL, MIL

5056-2. Portable electronic devices which may cause interference with the navigation or communication system may not be operated on U.S.-registered civil aircraft being operated

A—under IFR.
B—in passenger carrying operations.
C—along Federal airways.

Any portable electronic device that the operator of the aircraft has determined could cause interference with the navigation or communication systems may not be used on any aircraft operated under IFR. (PLT392, CA.II.B.R1) — 14 CFR §91.21

Answers

5051-3 [B]   5051-4 [A]   5056-1 [C]   5056-2 [A]

Chapter 4 **Regulations**

Fuel Requirements

No person may begin a flight in an airplane under VFR unless there is enough fuel to get to the first point of intended landing and, assuming normal cruise speed:

- During the day, to fly after that for at least 30 minutes
- At night, to fly after that for at least 45 minutes.

No person may operate an airplane in IFR conditions unless it carries enough fuel (considering available weather reports and forecasts) to:

1. Fly to the first airport of intended landing;
2. Fly from that airport to the alternate, if required; and
3. Fly thereafter for 45 minutes at normal cruising speed;
4. If a standard instrument approach is prescribed for the first airport of intended landing; and
5. For at least 1 hour before to 1 hour after the ETA at the airport, weather reports and forecasts indicate:
    a. The ceiling will be at least 2,000 feet above the airport elevation; and
    b. Visibility will be at least 3 miles.

AIR, LTA, MIL
5059. If weather conditions are such that it is required to designate an alternate airport on your IFR flight plan, you should plan to carry enough fuel to arrive at the first airport of intended landing, fly from that airport to the alternate airport, and fly thereafter for

A—30 minutes at slow cruising speed.
B—45 minutes at normal cruising speed.
C—1 hour at normal cruising speed.

Civil airplanes in IFR conditions must have sufficient fuel (considering weather reports, forecasts, and conditions) to fly to the first airport of intended landing, then to an alternate, then to fly for 45 minutes at normal cruising speed. (PLT224, CA.I.D.K3c) — 14 CFR §91.167

Transponder and ADS-B Requirements

A coded transponder with altitude reporting capability is required for flight in all airspace over the 48 contiguous states and the District of Columbia; at and above 10,000 feet MSL; and below the floor of a Class A airspace, excluding the airspace at and below 2,500 feet AGL.

ATC may authorize deviations on a continuing basis or for individual flights. To operate an aircraft without a transponder, a request must be submitted at least 1 hour before the proposed operation to the ATC facility that has jurisdiction over the airspace.

As of January 1, 2020, aircraft operating in airspace previously requiring the use of a transponder will in addition be required to have an Automatic Dependent Surveillance–Broadcast (ADS-B) system that includes a certified position source capable of meeting requirements defined in 14 CFR §91.227. For altitudes below FL180, this system can be either a 1090-ES or Universal Access Transceiver (UAT). Operations in Class A airspace require the use of extended squitter ADS-B and Traffic Information Services–Broadcast (TIS-B) equipment operating on the radio frequency of 1090 MHz. This combination of equipment is simply referred to as 1090-ES.

All aircraft equipped with functioning ADS-B Out must operate in transmit mode at all times, unless otherwise authorized by the FAA. Authorization may be approved when the aircraft is performing a sensitive government mission for national defense, homeland security, intelligence, or law enforcement purposes when transmitting would compromise the operations security and safety of the mission.

Answers

5059 [B]

ALL, MIL
5060. A coded transponder equipped with altitude reporting equipment is required for

1. Class A, Class B, and Class C airspace areas.
2. all airspace of the 48 contiguous U.S. and the District of Columbia at and above 10,000 feet MSL (including airspace at and below 2,500 feet above the surface).

A—1.
B—2.
C—Both 1 and 2.

Mode C (encoding) transponders are required in Class A, B, and C airspace. (PLT405, CA.I.E.K1) — 14 CFR §91.215

Answers (B) and (C) are incorrect because a transponder is required in all airspace of the 48 contiguous U.S. and the District of Columbia at and above 10,000 feet MSL, excluding airspace at and below 2,500 feet AGL.

ALL, MIL
5060-1. Your transponder is inoperative. In order to enter Class B airspace, you must submit a request for a deviation from the

A—ATC facility no less than 24 hours before the proposed operation.
B—nearest FSDO 24 hours before the proposed operation.
C—controlling ATC facility at any time prior to entering the controlled airspace.

Mode C (encoding) transponders are required in Class A, B, and C airspace. (PLT161, CA.I.E.K1) — 14 CFR §91.215

ALL, MIL
5072-2. What transponder equipment is required for airplane operations within Class B airspace? A transponder

A—with 4096 code or Mode S, and Mode C capability.
B—with 4096 code capability is required except when operating at or below 1,000 feet AGL under the terms of a letter of agreement.
C—is required for airplane operations when visibility is less than 3 miles.

Unless otherwise authorized or directed by ATC, no person may operate an aircraft in a Class B airspace area unless the aircraft is equipped with an operating transponder and automatic altitude reporting equipment that has an operable coded radar beacon transponder having either Mode 3/A 4096 code capability, or a Mode S capability, and that aircraft is equipped with automatic pressure altitude reporting equipment having a Mode C capability. (PLT161, CA.I.E.K1) — 14 CFR §91.131 and §91.215

AIR, RTC, MIL
5061. In the contiguous U.S., excluding the airspace at and below 2,500 feet AGL, an operable coded transponder equipped with Mode C capability is required in all airspace above

A—10,000 feet MSL.
B—12,500 feet MSL.
C—14,500 feet MSL.

With some balloon, glider, and no-electrical-system exceptions, Mode C (encoding) transponders are required in all airspace above 10,000 feet MSL excluding airspace at or below 2,500 feet AGL. (PLT497, CA.I.E.K1) — 14 CFR §91.215

ALL, MIL
5061-1. What type of ADS-B equipment is required for aircraft operating in class A airspace?

A—1090-ES.
B—Universal Access Transceiver.
C—1090-ES or Universal Access Transceiver.

For flights at and above 18,000 feet MSL in Class A airspace, the aircraft must be equipped with 1090-ES and meet the performance requirements outlined in 14 CFR §91.227. For flights below 18,000 feet MSL, either 1090-ES or UAT equipment can be used. (PLT497, CA.VI.B.K4) – 14 CFR §91.225

ALL, MIL
5061-2. Operations in Class A airspace require the aircraft be equipped with

A—ADS-B and FIS-B.
B—ADS-B and TIS-B.
C—ADS-B.

No person may operate an aircraft in Class A airspace unless that aircraft is equipped with an extended squitter ADS-B and TIS-B operating on the radio frequency 1090 MHz. (PLT497, CA.VI.B.K4) – 14 CFR §91.225

Answers

5060 [A]   5060-1 [C]   5072-2 [A]   5061 [A]   5061-1 [A]   5061-2 [B]

Chapter 4 Regulations

ALL, MIL
5061-3. When may an aircraft equipped with ADS-B Out not operate in transmit mode?

A—Anytime the aircraft is operating in Class G airspace.
B—If the aircraft is being operated for law enforcement purposes and transmitting would jeopardize the safety of the mission.
C—If the aircraft was not originally certificated with an electrical system.

If transmitting would jeopardize the safety or security of a law enforcement mission, the FAA may approve the flight to be conducted without ADS-B Out equipment in transmit mode. (PLT497, CA.VI.B.K4) – 14 CFR §91.225

Answers (A) and (C) are incorrect. Regardless of airspace or whether the aircraft was originally certificated with an electrical system, it must operate any installed ADS-Out equipment in transmit mode.

ALL
5061-4. Unless otherwise authorized by ATC, which airspace requires the appropriate Automatic Dependent Surveillance–Broadcast (ADS-B) Out equipment installed?

A—Within Class E airspace below the upper shelf of Class C Airspace.
B—Above the ceiling and within the lateral boundaries of Class D airspace up to 10,000 feet MSL.
C—Within Class G airspace 25 nautical miles from a Class B airport.

Any airspace that requires the use of a transponder also requires aircraft to be equipped with an ADS-B Out system. ADS-B is required when operating within 30 NM of an airport listed in appendix D of Part 91 from the surface up to 10,000 feet MSL. (PLT497, CA.I.E.K1) — 14 CFR §91.225

Supplemental Oxygen

No person may operate a civil aircraft:

1. At cabin pressure altitudes above 12,500 feet MSL up to and including 14,000 feet MSL, unless the required minimum flight crew uses supplemental oxygen for that part of the flight that is more than 30 minutes duration;

2. At cabin pressure altitudes above 14,000 feet MSL, unless the required minimum flight crew uses supplemental oxygen during the entire flight at those altitudes; and

3. At cabin pressure altitudes above 15,000 feet MSL, unless each occupant of the aircraft is provided with oxygen.

ALL, MIL
5063. In accordance with 14 CFR Part 91, supplemental oxygen must be used by the required minimum flight-crew for that time exceeding 30 minutes while at cabin pressure altitudes of

A—10,500 feet MSL up to and including 12,500 feet MSL.
B—12,000 feet MSL up to and including 18,000 feet MSL.
C—12,500 feet MSL up to and including 14,000 feet MSL.

No person may operate a civil aircraft of U.S. registry:

1. *At cabin pressure altitudes above 12,500 feet MSL up to and including 14,000 feet MSL, unless the required minimum flight crew is provided with and uses supplemental oxygen for that part of the flight at those altitudes that is of more than 30 minutes duration;*

2. *At cabin pressure altitudes above 14,000 feet MSL, unless the required minimum flight crew is provided with and uses supplemental oxygen during the entire flight time at those altitudes; and*

3. *At cabin pressure altitudes above 15,000 feet MSL, unless each occupant of the aircraft is provided with supplemental oxygen.*

(PLT438, CA.VIII.A.K1) — 14 CFR §91.211

Answers
5061-3 [B]   5061-4 [C]   5063 [C]

Chapter 4 **Regulations**

ALL, MIL

5064. What are the oxygen requirements when operating at cabin pressure altitudes above 15,000 feet MSL?

A—Oxygen must be available for the flightcrew.
B—Oxygen is not required at any altitude in a balloon.
C—The flightcrew and passengers must be provided with supplemental oxygen.

No person may operate a civil aircraft of U.S. registry:

1. At cabin pressure altitudes above 12,500 feet MSL up to and including 14,000 feet MSL, unless the required minimum flight crew is provided with and uses supplemental oxygen for that part of the flight at those altitudes that is of more than 30 minutes duration;

2. At cabin pressure altitudes above 14,000 feet MSL, unless the required minimum flight crew is provided with and uses supplemental oxygen during the entire flight time at those altitudes; and

3. At cabin pressure altitudes above 15,000 feet MSL, unless each occupant of the aircraft is provided with supplemental oxygen.

(PLT438, CA.VIII.A.K1) — 14 CFR §91.211

Answer (A) is incorrect because the flight crew must use oxygen above 14,000 feet MSL. Answer (B) is incorrect because oxygen requirements apply to all aircraft.

Instrument and Equipment Requirements

If a flight is being conducted for hire over water and beyond power-off gliding distance from shore, approved flotation gear readily available to each occupant and at least one pyrotechnic signaling device are required. Also, if the flight is conducted for hire at night, one electric landing light is needed. An operating anti-collision system is required for all night flights. This equipment is in addition to that required for noncommercial operations.

ALL, MIL

5067. Approved flotation gear, readily available to each occupant, is required on each aircraft if it is being flown for hire over water,

A—in amphibious aircraft beyond 50 NM from shore.
B—beyond power-off gliding distance from shore.
C—more than 50 statute miles from shore.

Approved flotation gear readily available to each occupant is required on each aircraft if it is being flown for hire over water beyond power-off gliding distance from shore. "Shore" is defined as the area of the land adjacent to the water that is above the high water mark, excluding land areas which are intermittently under water. (PLT417, CA.IX.D.K3c) — 14 CFR §91.205

Answer (A) is incorrect because the flotation gear requirement applies to all aircraft operated for hire when flying beyond power-off gliding distance from shore. Answer (C) is incorrect because flotation gear is not required if the aircraft remains within power-off gliding distance from shore.

AIR, RTC, MIL

5066. Which is required equipment for powered aircraft during VFR night flights?

A—Flashlight with red lens if the flight is for hire.
B—An electric landing light if the flight is for hire.
C—Sensitive altimeter adjustable for barometric pressure.

An electric landing light is required only if the night flight is for hire. (PLT405, CA.I.B.K3) — 14 CFR §91.205

Answer (A) is incorrect because there is no specific requirement for flashlights and the color of the lens. Answer (C) is incorrect because sensitive altimeters are only required for IFR flight.

Answers

5064 [C]   5067 [B]   5066 [B]

Chapter 4 **Regulations**

Restricted, Limited, and Experimental Aircraft: Operating Limitations

No person may operate a restricted, limited, or experimentally certificated civil aircraft carrying passengers or property for compensation or hire. In addition, no person may operate a restricted category aircraft:

- Over a densely populated area
- In a congested airway
- Near a busy airport where passenger transport operations are conducted

ALL, MIL
5069. The carriage of passengers for hire by a commercial pilot is

A—not authorized in a "utility" category aircraft.
B—not authorized in a "limited" category aircraft.
C—authorized in "restricted" category aircraft.

Operations for compensation or hire are not authorized in limited category aircraft, experimental aircraft, and restricted category aircraft. Operations using utility category aircraft (such as Cessna 152) are authorized. (PLT373, CA.I.A.K2) — 14 CFR §91.315

Answer (A) is incorrect because the carriage of passengers for hire is permitted in normal and utility category aircraft. Answer (C) is incorrect because the carriage of passengers for hire is not permitted in restricted category aircraft.

ALL, MIL
5129. No person may operate an aircraft that has an experimental airworthiness certificate

A—under instrument flight rules (IFR).
B—when carrying property for hire.
C—when carrying persons or property for hire.

No person may operate an aircraft that has an experimental certificate while carrying persons or property for compensation or hire. (PLT373, CA.I.A.K2) — 14 CFR §91.319

AIR, MIL
5068-2. Which is true with respect to operating limitations of a "restricted" category airplane?

A—A pilot of a "restricted" category airplane is required to hold a commercial pilot certificate.
B—A "restricted" category airplane is limited to an operating radius of 25 miles from its home base.
C—No person may operate a "restricted" category airplane carrying passengers or property for compensation or hire.

No person may operate a restricted category civil aircraft carrying persons or property for compensation or hire. (PLT373, CA.I.A.K2) — 14 CFR §91.313

AIR, MIL
5068-3. Which is true with respect to operating limitations of a "primary" category airplane?

A—A "primary" category airplane is limited to a specified operating radius from its home base.
B—No person may operate a "primary" category airplane carrying passengers or property for compensation or hire.
C—A pilot of a "primary" category airplane must hold a commercial pilot certificate when carrying passengers for compensation or hire.

No person may operate a primary category aircraft carrying persons or property for compensation or hire. (PLT373, CA.I.A.K2) — 14 CFR §91.325

AIR, MIL
5068-4. An aircraft's operating limitations may be found in the

A—FAA-approved aircraft flight manual.
B—owner's handbook published by the aircraft manufacturer.
C—aircraft flight manual, approved manual material, markings and placards, or any combination thereof.

As required by 14 CFR §21.5, no person may operate a U.S.-registered civil unless there is a current approved flight manual, approved manual material, markings and placards, or any combination thereof available in the aircraft. (PLT373, CA.I.A.K2) — 14 CFR §91.9

Answers

5069 [B]   5129 [C]   5068-2 [C]   5068-3 [B]   5068-4 [C]

Emergency Locator Transmitter (ELT)

Except as listed below, all airplanes must have on board an ELT that:

1. Is attached to the airplane in such a manner as to minimize the possibility of damage in a crash;
2. Transmits on 121.5 and 243.0 MHz;
3. Has batteries which must be replaced (or recharged, if the battery is rechargeable) after 1 hour of cumulative use, or when 50% of their useful shelf life has expired (or in the case or rechargeable batteries, when 50% of the useful life of the charge has expired). This date must be stamped on the outside of the battery case and entered in the aircraft logbook.

   Aircraft and operations that do not need ELTs are:

1. Those ferrying an aircraft for an ELT installation or repair;
2. Training flights within a 50-mile radius from the airport;
3. Turbojet-powered aircraft; or
4. Agricultural operations.

   Testing of ELTs should be carried out only during the first 5 minutes of any hour for no more than three sweeps, unless coordinated with ATC.

AIR, RTC, MIL
5070. The maximum cumulative time that an emergency locator transmitter may be operated before the rechargeable battery must be recharged is

A—30 minutes.
B—45 minutes.
C—60 minutes.

ELT batteries must be replaced or recharged when the transmitter has been in use for more than one cumulative hour. (PLT446, CA.IX.D.K1) — 14 CFR §91.207

Truth in Leasing

To operate a large civil U.S. aircraft that is leased, the lessee must mail a copy of the lease to the Aircraft Registry Technical Section, Box 25724, Oklahoma City, Oklahoma, 73125, within 24 hours of its execution.

AIR, MIL
5071. No person may operate a large civil aircraft of U.S. registry which is subject to a lease, unless the lessee has mailed a copy of the lease to the FAA Aircraft Registration Branch, Technical Section, Oklahoma City, OK within how many hours of its execution?

A—24.
B—48.
C—72.

The lessee must mail a copy of the lease to the Aircraft Registry Technical Section, Box 25724, Oklahoma City, Oklahoma, 73125, within 24 hours of its execution. (PLT392, CA.I.A.K2) — 14 CFR §91.23

Answers

5070 [C]   5071 [A]

Chapter 4 **Regulations**

Operating Near Other Aircraft and Right-of-Way Rules

No person may operate an aircraft so close to another aircraft as to create a collision hazard. Aircraft carrying passengers for hire may not be flown in formation. Formation flying on flights not carrying passengers for hire is allowed, if the pilots of all the aircraft involved are in agreement.

When weather conditions permit, it is each pilot's responsibility to see and avoid other traffic, regardless of whether the flight is being conducted under VFR or IFR. An aircraft in distress has the right-of-way over all others.

Aircraft on final approach to land, or while landing, have the right-of-way over other aircraft in flight or on the surface. If two aircraft are approaching the airport for the purpose of landing, the lower aircraft has the right-of-way, but the pilot shall not take advantage of this rule to cut in front of or to overtake the other aircraft.

When aircraft of the same category are converging, the aircraft to the other's right has the right-of-way. If the aircraft are of different categories, the order of right-of-way is:

1. Balloon
2. Glider
3. Airship
4. Airplane or rotorcraft

If two aircraft are approaching head-on, each pilot shall alter course to the right. See Figure 4-1. If two aircraft of the same category are converging because one is overtaking the other, the one being overtaken has the right-of-way and the overtaking aircraft must pass well clear to the right. See Figure 4-2.

Any aircraft towing another aircraft or refueling in flight has the right-of-way over all other engine-driven aircraft.

Figure 4-1. Aircraft approaching head-on

Figure 4-2. One aircraft overtaking another

ALL, MIL
5073-1. Which is true with respect to formation flights? Formation flights are

A—authorized when carrying passengers for hire with prior arrangement with the pilot-in-command of each aircraft in the formation.
B—not authorized when visibilities are less than 3 SM.
C—not authorized when carrying passengers for hire.

No person may operate an aircraft carrying passengers for hire in formation flight. (PLT431, CA.I.A.K2) — 14 CFR §91.111

Answer (A) is incorrect because when carrying passengers for hire, formation flights are prohibited. Answer (B) is incorrect because formation flights are authorized regardless of visibility.

Answers

5073-1 [C]

ALL, MIL

5073-2. Which is true with respect to operating near other aircraft in flight? They are

A—not authorized, when operated so close to another aircraft they can create a collision hazard.
B—not authorized, unless the pilot-in-command of each aircraft is trained and found competent in formation.
C—authorized when carrying passengers for hire, with prior arrangement with the pilot-in-command of each aircraft in the formation.

No person may operate an aircraft so close to another aircraft as to create a collision hazard. No person may operate an aircraft in formation flight except by arrangement with the pilot-in-command of each aircraft in the formation. No person may operate an aircraft, carrying passengers for hire, in formation flight. (PLT431, CA.I.A.K2) — 14 CFR §91.111

ALL, MIL

5073-3. Which is true with respect to formation flights? Formation flights are

A—not authorized, except by arrangement with the pilot-in-command of each aircraft.
B—not authorized, unless the pilot-in-command of each aircraft is trained and found competent in formation.
C—authorized when carrying passengers for hire, with prior arrangement with the pilot-in-command of each aircraft in the formation.

No person may operate an aircraft so close to another aircraft as to create a collision hazard. No person may operate an aircraft in formation flight except by arrangement with the pilot-in-command of each aircraft in the formation. No person may operate an aircraft, carrying passengers for hire, in formation flight. (PLT431, CA.I.A.K2) — 14 CFR §91.111

ALL, MIL

5075. Two aircraft of the same category are approaching an airport for the purpose of landing. The right-of-way belongs to the aircraft

A—at the higher altitude.
B—at the lower altitude, but the pilot shall not take advantage of this rule to cut in front of or to overtake the other aircraft.
C—that is more maneuverable, and that aircraft may, with caution, move in front of or overtake the other aircraft.

When two or more aircraft are approaching an airport for the purpose of landing, the lower aircraft has the right-of-way. However, a pilot shall not take advantage of this rule to overtake or cut in front of another aircraft that is on final approach to land. (PLT414, CA.III.B.K3) — 14 CFR §91.113

AIR, RTC, MIL

5074. While in flight a helicopter and an airplane are converging at a 90° angle, and the helicopter is located to the right of the airplane. Which aircraft has the right-of-way, and why?

A—The helicopter, because it is to the right of the airplane.
B—The helicopter, because helicopters have the right-of-way over airplanes.
C—The airplane, because airplanes have the right-of-way over helicopters.

When aircraft of the same category are converging at approximately the same altitude (except head-on, or nearly so) the aircraft to the other's right has the right-of-way. Aircraft and rotorcraft are treated as equally maneuverable, so neither aircraft has right-of-way over the other. (PLT414, CA.III.B.K3) — 14 CFR §91.113

Answers

5073-2   [A]   5073-3   [A]   5075   [B]   5074   [A]

Chapter 4 **Regulations**

AIR, RTC, MIL
5076-1. Airplane A is overtaking airplane B. Which airplane has the right-of-way?

A—Airplane A; the pilot should alter course to the right to pass.
B—Airplane B; the pilot should expect to be passed on the right.
C—Airplane B; the pilot should expect to be passed on the left.

Each aircraft that is being overtaken has the right-of-way, and each pilot of an overtaking aircraft shall alter course to the right to pass well clear. (PLT414, CA.III.B.K3) — 14 CFR §91.113

AIR, RTC, MIL
5076-2. An airplane is overtaking a helicopter. Which aircraft has the right-of-way?

A—Helicopter; the pilot should expect to be passed on the right.
B—Airplane; the airplane pilot should alter course to the left to pass.
C—Helicopter; the pilot should expect to be passed on the left.

When weather conditions permit, regardless of whether an operation is conducted under instrument flight rules or visual flight rules, vigilance shall be maintained by each person operating an aircraft so as to see and avoid other aircraft. Each aircraft that is being overtaken has the right-of-way and each pilot of an overtaking aircraft shall alter course to the right to pass well clear. (PLT414, CA.III.B.K3) — 14 CFR §91.113

AIR, RTC, MIL
5076-3. During a night operation, the pilot of aircraft #1 sees only the green light of aircraft #2. If the aircraft are converging, which pilot has the right-of-way? The pilot of aircraft

A—#2; aircraft #2 is to the left of aircraft #1.
B—#2; aircraft #2 is to the right of aircraft #1
C—#1; aircraft #1 is to the right of aircraft #2.

When aircraft of the same category are converging at approximately the same altitude (except head-on, or nearly so), the aircraft to the other's right has the right-of-way. The green light indicates aircraft #1 is looking at the right wing of aircraft #2, which means aircraft #1 is to the right of aircraft #2. (PLT414, CA.III.B.K3) — 14 CFR §91.113

AIR, RTC, MIL
5076-4. A pilot flying a single-engine airplane observes a multiengine airplane approaching from the left. Which pilot should give way?

A—The pilot of the multiengine airplane should give way; the single-engine airplane is to its right.
B—The pilot of the single-engine airplane should give way; the other airplane is to the left.
C—Each pilot should alter course to the right.

When aircraft of the same category are converging at approximately the same altitude (except head-on, or nearly so), the aircraft to the other's right has the right-of-way. (PLT414, CA.III.B.K3) — 14 CFR §91.113

AIR, RTC, MIL
5076-5. An airplane is converging with a helicopter. Which aircraft has the right-of-way?

A—The aircraft on the left.
B—The aircraft on the right.
C—The faster of the two aircraft.

If aircraft of the same category (or an airplane and rotorcraft) are converging, the aircraft to the other's right has the right-of-way. (PLT414, CA.III.B.K3) — 14 CFR §91.113

Answers

5076-1   [B]   5076-2   [A]   5076-3   [C]   5076-4   [A]   5076-5   [B]

Chapter 4 **Regulations**

Speed Limits

If ATC assigned an airspeed, it must be maintained within plus or minus 10 knots. All aircraft must observe the speed limits (all speeds are shown in knots and are indicated airspeed) as illustrated in Figure 4-3.

Figure 4-3. Maximum speed limits

ALL, MIL
5112. If the minimum safe speed for any particular operation is greater than the maximum speed prescribed in 14 CFR Part 91, the

A—operator must have a Memorandum of Agreement (MOA) with the controlling agency.
B—aircraft may be operated at that speed.
C—operator must have a Letter of Agreement with ATC.

If the minimum safe airspeed for any particular operation is greater than the maximum speed prescribed in Part 91, the aircraft may be operated at that minimum speed. (PLT161, CA.I.E.K1) — 14 CFR §91.117

AIR, RTC, MIL
5077. What is the maximum indicated airspeed authorized in the airspace underlying Class B airspace?

A—156 knots.
B—200 knots.
C—230 knots.

No person may operate an aircraft in the airspace underlying Class B airspace, or in a VFR corridor designated through Class B airspace, at an indicated airspeed of more than 200 knots (230 MPH). (PLT161, CA.I.E.K1) — 14 CFR §91.117

Answers
5112 [B]   5077 [B]

Chapter 4 **Regulations**

AIR, RTC, MIL

5078. Unless otherwise authorized or required by ATC, the maximum indicated airspeed permitted when at or below 2,500 feet AGL within 4 NM of the primary airport within Class C or D airspace is

A—180 knots.
B—200 knots.
C—230 knots.

Unless otherwise authorized or required by ATC, no person may operate an aircraft within 4 NM of the primary airport of Class C or D airspace at an indicated airspeed of more than 200 knots (230 MPH). (PLT161, CA.I.E.K1) — 14 CFR §91.117

Aircraft Lights

No person may, during the period from sunset to sunrise, operate an aircraft unless it has lighted position lights. The right wing-tip position light is green, the left is red and the tail white. Each aircraft must also have an approved anti-collision light system.

ALL

5666. What is the general direction of movement of the other aircraft if during a night flight you observe a steady white light and a rotating red light ahead and at your altitude? The other aircraft is

A—headed away from you.
B—crossing to your left.
C—approaching you head-on.

The pilot is seeing the rotating beacon and the white light on the tail. The other aircraft is headed away. (PLT119, CA.I.B.K3) — FAA-H-8083-3

Answer (B) is incorrect because you would see a steady red light if the other aircraft was crossing to your left. Answer (C) is incorrect because you would see both the red and green wing-tip position lights if the other aircraft were approaching you head-on.

ALL, MIL

5080-1. If not equipped with required position lights, an aircraft must terminate flight

A—at sunset.
B—30 minutes after sunset.
C—1 hour after sunset.

No person may, during the period from sunset to sunrise (or, in Alaska, during the period a prominent unlighted object cannot be seen from a distance of 3 statute miles or the sun is more than 6° below the horizon) operate an aircraft unless it has lighted position lights. (PLT220, CA.I.B.K3) — 14 CFR §91.209

ALL, MIL

5080-2. If an aircraft is not equipped with an electrical or anticollision light system, no person may operate that aircraft

A—after sunset to sunrise.
B—after dark.
C—1 hour after sunset.

No person may during the period from sunset to sunrise operate an aircraft that is equipped with an anticollision light system, unless it has lighted anticollision lights. However, the anticollision lights need not be lighted when the pilot-in-command determines that, because of operating conditions, it would be in the interest of safety to turn the lights off. (PLT220, CA.I.B.K3) — 14 CFR §91.209

LTA

5080-3. Operation of a balloon, during the period of sunset to sunrise, requires that it be equipped and lighted with

A—red and green position lights.
B—approved aviation red and white lights.
C—a steady aviation white position light and a red or white anticollision light.

No person may, during the period from sunset to sunrise, operate an aircraft unless it has lighted position lights. If position lights are installed, there must be one steady aviation white position light, and one flashing aviation red (or flashing aviation white) position light. (PLT220) — 14 CFR §91.209 and §31.65

Answers

5078 [B]   5666 [A]   5080-1 [A]   5080-2 [A]   5080-3 [C]

LTA
5080-4. Operation of a lighter-than-air airship, during the period of sunset to sunrise, requires it be equipped and lighted with

A—position lights and aviation red or white anticollision light system.
B—approved aviation red and white lights.
C—position lights.

No person may, during the period from sunset to sunrise, operate an aircraft unless it has lighted position lights. The airplane must have an approved anticollision light system and each anticollision light must be either aviation red or aviation white. (PLT220) — 14 CFR §25.1401

AIR, RTC, MIL
5065. Which is required equipment for powered aircraft during VFR night flights?

A—Anticollision light system.
B—Gyroscopic direction indicator.
C—Gyroscopic bank-and-pitch indicator.

An approved anticollision light system is required for flight under VFR between sunset and sunrise. (PLT405, CA.I.B.K3) — 14 CFR §91.205

Answers (B) and (C) are incorrect because a gyroscopic direction indicator and gyroscopic bank-and-pitch indicator is required for IFR flights.

Minimum Altitudes

Except when necessary for takeoff or landing, no person may operate an aircraft below an altitude allowing, if a power unit fails, an emergency landing without undue hazard to persons or property on the surface. Except when necessary for takeoff or landing, no person may operate an aircraft over any congested area of a city, town, or settlement, or over any open air assembly of persons, below an altitude of 1,000 feet above the highest obstacle within a horizontal radius of 2,000 feet of the aircraft. Except when necessary for takeoff or landing, no person may operate an aircraft over other than congested areas below an altitude of 500 feet above the surface except over open water or sparsely populated areas. In that case, the aircraft may not be operated closer than 500 feet to any person, vessel, vehicle, or structure.

Except when necessary for takeoff or landing, or unless otherwise authorized by the Administrator, the minimum altitude for IFR flight is:

1. 2,000 feet above the highest obstacle within a horizontal distance of 4 NM from the course to be flown over an area designated as a mountainous area; or
2. 1,000 feet above the highest obstacle within a horizontal distance of 4 NM from the course to be flown over terrain in other areas.

ALL, MIL
5092. Except when necessary for takeoff or landing or unless otherwise authorized by the Administrator, the minimum altitude for IFR flight is

A—2,000 feet over all terrain.
B—3,000 feet over designated mountainous terrain; 2,000 feet over terrain elsewhere.
C—2,000 feet above the highest obstacle over designated mountainous terrain; 1,000 feet above the highest obstacle over terrain elsewhere.

At a minimum, IFR flight must remain at 2,000 feet AGL in mountainous areas and 1,000 feet AGL elsewhere. (PLT224, CA.I.D.K2) — 14 CFR §91.177

RTC, MIL
5113-1. Minimum safe altitude rules require that helicopter pilots

A—not fly lower than 500 feet, except when necessary for takeoff or landing.
B—comply with routes and altitudes prescribed by the FAA.
C—not fly closer than 500 feet to any person, vessel, vehicle, or structure.

Helicopters may be operated at less than minimum altitudes if the operation is conducted without hazard to persons or property on the surface. In addition, each person operating a helicopter shall comply with any routes or altitudes specifically prescribed for helicopters by the Administrator. (PLT430, MC.II.A.K4) — 14 CFR §91.119

Answers

5080-4 [A]   5065 [A]   5092 [C]   5113-1 [B]

Chapter 4 **Regulations**

RTC, MIL

5113-2. Minimum safe altitude rules authorize helicopter pilots to

A—fly at less than 500 feet.
B—fly at less than 500 feet if they do not create a hazard to persons or property on the surface.
C—fly closer than 500 feet to any person, vehicle, vessel, or structure on the surface.

Helicopters may be operated at less than minimum altitudes if the operation is conducted without hazard to persons or property on the surface. In addition, each person operating a helicopter shall comply with any routes or altitudes specifically prescribed for helicopters by the Administrator. (PLT430, MC.II.A.K4) — 14 CFR §91.119

ALL, MIL

5992. According to 14 CFR Part 91, at what minimum altitude may an airplane be operated unless necessary for takeoff and landing?

A—In congested areas, you must maintain 500 feet over obstacles and no closer than 500 feet to any person, vessel, vehicle, or structure.
B—In uncongested areas, 1,000 feet over any obstacle within a horizontal radius of 2,000 feet.
C—An altitude allowing for an emergency landing without undue hazard, if a power unit fails.

Except when necessary for takeoff or landing, no person may operate an aircraft below an altitude allowing, if a power unit fails, an emergency landing without undue hazard to persons or property on the surface. (PLT430, CA.I.D.K2) — 14 CFR §91.119

Answer (A) is incorrect because except when necessary for takeoff or landing, no person may operate an aircraft over any congested area of a city, town, or settlement, or over any open air assembly of persons, below an altitude of 1,000 feet above the highest obstacle within a horizontal radius of 2,000 feet of the aircraft. Answer (B) is incorrect because except when necessary for takeoff or landing, no person may operate an aircraft over other than congested areas below an altitude of 500 feet above the surface except over open water or sparsely populated areas. In that case, the aircraft may not be operated closer than 500 feet to any person, vessel, vehicle, or structure.

Maintenance Responsibility

The owner or operator of an aircraft holds primary responsibility for:

1. Maintaining that aircraft in an airworthy condition;
2. Having required inspections performed; and
3. Ensuring that maintenance personnel make the required entries in the aircraft maintenance records indicating that the aircraft has been approved for return to service.

   Operation of an aircraft after maintenance, rebuilding or alteration is prohibited unless:
   - The aircraft has been approved for return to service by authorized maintenance personnel
   - The required maintenance record entry has been made

In addition, after any major alteration or repair that may have substantially affected an aircraft's flight characteristics or flight operation, it must be test flown before passengers may be carried. The test pilot must be appropriately rated and must hold at least a Private Pilot Certificate. The aircraft's documents must indicate that it was test flown and approved for return to service by an appropriately rated pilot.

Answers

5113-2 [B]   5992 [C]

ALL, MIL

5093. Who is primarily responsible for maintaining an aircraft in an airworthy condition?

A—The lead mechanic responsible for that aircraft.
B—Pilot-in-command or operator.
C—Owner or operator of the aircraft.

The owner or operator of an aircraft is primarily responsible for maintaining that aircraft in an airworthy condition, including compliance with Airworthiness Directives. (PLT374, CA.II.A.K3d) — 14 CFR §91.403

Answer (A) is incorrect because mechanics work under the advisement of the owner/operator. Answer (B) is incorrect because the pilot is only responsible for determining airworthiness before flight.

ALL, MIL

5097. If an aircraft's operation in flight was substantially affected by an alteration or repair, the aircraft documents must show that it was test flown and approved for return to service by an appropriately-rated pilot prior to being operated

A—under VFR or IFR rules.
B—with passengers aboard.
C—for compensation or hire.

No person may carry any person (meaning passengers) other than crewmembers in an aircraft that has been maintained, rebuilt, or altered in a manner that may have appreciably changed its flight characteristics or substantially affected its operation in flight, until an appropriately-rated pilot with at least a private pilot certificate flies the aircraft, makes an operational check of the maintenance performed or alteration made, and logs the flight in the aircraft records. (PLT426, CA.I.B.K1b) — 14 CFR §91.407

Aircraft Inspections

Each aircraft must have had an **annual inspection** performed within the preceding 12 calendar months. That inspection must be recorded in the aircraft and engine logbooks, and is valid through the last day of the month, regardless of the issuance date.

In addition to an annual inspection, if an aircraft is used to carry passengers for hire or is used for flight instruction, it must have an inspection every 100 hours. The **100-hour limitation** may be exceeded by not more than 10 hours, if necessary, to reach a location where the inspection can be done. The excess time, however, must be included in calculating the following 100 hours of time in service. An annual inspection may be substituted for 100-hour inspection.

A **progressive maintenance program** requires that an aircraft be maintained and inspected at specified intervals (for example, every 50 hours) and according to a specific sequence (for example, four operations per cycle). A typically approved progressive maintenance program meets the requirements of both annual and 100-hour inspections when the scheduled operations are completed within 12 months.

In order to be approved for operation at all, each transponder must be inspected and tested within 24 calendar months. This inspection must be noted in the appropriate logbooks.

The validity of an airworthiness certificate is maintained by an appropriate return-to-service notation in the aircraft maintenance records at the completion of any required inspections and maintenance.

Answers

5093 [C]   5097 [B]

Chapter 4 **Regulations**

ALL, MIL
5096. A standard airworthiness certificate remains in effect as long as the aircraft receives

A—required maintenance and inspections.
B—an annual inspection.
C—an annual inspection and a 100-hour inspection prior to their expiration dates.

No person may operate an aircraft unless, within the preceding 12 calendar months, it has had an annual inspection and has been approved for return to service by an authorized person or an inspection for the issuance of an airworthiness certificate. No person may operate an aircraft carrying passengers for hire or give flight instruction for hire in an aircraft which that person provides, unless within the preceding 100 hours of time in service the aircraft has received an annual or 100-hour inspection. An aircraft inspected in accordance with an approved aircraft progressive inspection program may be authorized as compliant. (PLT377, CA.I.B.K1a) — 14 CFR §91.409

ALL, MIL
5096-1. What regulations are in the terms and conditions of a Standard Airworthiness Certificate?

A—Parts 21, 31, 43, and 91.
B—Parts 21, 61, and 91.
C—Parts 21, 43, and 91.

A Standard Airworthiness Certificate is issued for aircraft type certificated in the normal, utility, acrobatic, commuter, transport categories, and manned free balloons. The Airworthiness Certificate is in effect indefinitely if the aircraft is maintained in accordance with 14 CFR parts 21, 43, and 91, and the aircraft is registered in the United States. (PLT377, CA.I.B.K1a) — FAA-H-8083-25

ALL, MIL
5099. An aircraft carrying passengers for hire has been on a schedule of inspection every 100 hours of time in service. Under which condition, if any, may that aircraft be operated beyond 100 hours without a new inspection?

A—The aircraft may be flown for any flight as long as the time in service has not exceeded 110 hours.
B—The aircraft may be dispatched for a flight of any duration as long as 100 hours has not been exceeded at the time it departs.
C—The 100-hour limitation may be exceeded by not more than 10 hours if necessary to reach a place at which the inspection can be done.

The 100-hour limitation may be exceeded by not more than 10 hours if necessary to reach a place the inspection can be done. The excess time, however, is included in computing the next 100 hours of time in service. (PLT372, CA.I.B.K1b) — 14 CFR §91.409

Answers (A) and (B) are incorrect because the 10-hour grace period only applies to ferrying an aircraft to a maintenance facility, for the 100-hour inspection.

ALL, MIL
5100. Which is true concerning required maintenance inspections?

A—A 100-hour inspection may be substituted for an annual inspection.
B—An annual inspection may be substituted for a 100-hour inspection.
C—An annual inspection is required even if a progressive inspection system has been approved.

The annual is considered the more rigorous inspection and can be substituted for the 100-hour, not vice versa. (PLT372, CA.I.B.K1b) — 14 CFR §91.409

Answer (A) is incorrect because an annual inspection may be substituted for a 100-hour inspection. Answer (C) is incorrect because a progressive inspection can be done in place of an annual inspection.

ALL, MIL
5101. An ATC transponder is not to be used unless it has been tested, inspected, and found to comply with regulations within the preceding

A—30 days.
B—12 calendar months.
C—24 calendar months.

No person may use an ATC transponder unless, within the preceding 24 calendar months, that ATC transponder has been tested, inspected, and found to comply with regulations. (PLT454, CA.I.B.K1b) — 14 CFR §91.413

ALL, MIL
5105. If an ATC transponder installed in an aircraft has not been tested, inspected, and found to comply with regulations within a specified period, what is the limitation on its use?

A—Its use is not permitted.
B—It may be used when in Class G airspace.
C—It may be used for VFR flight only.

No person may use an ATC transponder unless, within the preceding 24 calendar months, that ATC transponder has been tested, inspected and found to comply with regulations. (PLT454, CA.I.B.K1b) — 14 CFR §91.413

Answers

5096 [A]   5096-1 [C]   5099 [C]   5100 [B]   5101 [C]   5105 [A]

ALL, MIL
5534. A transponder will become unserviceable when it is off by more than

A—125 feet.
B—50 feet.
C—20 feet.

The difference between the automatic reporting output and the altitude displayed at the altimeter shall not exceed 125 feet. (PLT454, CA.VI.B.K4) — 14 CFR §91.217

ALL, MIL
5547. You are conducting your preflight of an aircraft and notice that the last inspection of the emergency locator transmitter was 11 calendar months ago. You may

A—depart if you get a special flight permit.
B—depart because the ELT is within the inspection requirements.
C—not depart until a new inspection is conducted.

Emergency locator transmitters (ELTs) must be inspected within 12 calendar months after the last inspection. (PLT377, CA.I.B.K1b) — 14 CFR §91.207

Maintenance Records

With the exception of work performed under 14 CFR §91.171, records of the following work must be kept until the work is repeated or superseded by other work or for one year after the work is performed:

- Records of maintenance or alterations
- Records of 100-hour, annual, progressive, and other required or approved inspections

The records of the following must be retained and transferred with the aircraft at the time the aircraft is sold:

- Total time in service of the airframe
- Current status of life-limited parts of each airframe, engine, propeller, rotor, and appliance
- Current status of inspections and Airworthiness Directives (ADs)
- A list of all current major alterations

A recording tachometer cannot be substituted for required aircraft maintenance records.

Each manufacturer or agency that grants zero time to a rebuilt engine shall enter, in a new record:

- A signed statement of the date the engine was rebuilt
- Each change made as required by ADs
- Each change made in compliance with manufacturer service bulletins

Old maintenance records may be discarded when an engine is rebuilt.

ALL, MIL
5095. After an annual inspection has been completed and the aircraft has been returned to service, an appropriate notation should be made

A—on the airworthiness certificate.
B—in the aircraft maintenance records.
C—in the FAA-approved flight manual.

Each owner or operator of an aircraft shall have that aircraft inspected as prescribed by regulations and shall, between required inspections, have discrepancies repaired as prescribed in 14 CFR Part 43. In addition, each owner or operator shall ensure that maintenance personnel make appropriate entries in the aircraft maintenance records indicating that the aircraft has been approved for return to service. (PLT425, CA.I.B.K1b) — 14 CFR §91.405

Answers

5534 [A]   5477 [B]   5095 [B]

Chapter 4 **Regulations**

ALL, MIL
5102. Aircraft maintenance records must include the current status of the

A—applicable airworthiness certificate.
B—life-limited parts of only the engine and airframe.
C—life-limited parts of each airframe, engine, propeller, rotor, and appliance.

Each registered owner or operator shall keep records containing the following information: the current status of life-limited parts of each airframe, engine, propeller, rotor, and appliance. (PLT425, CA.I.B.K1b) — 14 CFR §91.417

AIR, RTC, MIL
5104. A new maintenance record being used for an aircraft engine rebuilt by the manufacturer must include previous

A—operating hours of the engine.
B—annual inspections performed on the engine.
C—changes as required by Airworthiness Directives.

Each manufacturer or agency that grants zero time to an engine rebuilt by it shall enter, in the new record, each change made as required by Airworthiness Directives. (PLT425, CA.I.B.K1c) — 14 CFR §91.421

Answer (A) is incorrect because a rebuilt engine is considered to start with zero time. Answer (B) is incorrect because a record of previous maintenance is not required for a rebuilt engine.

ALL, MIL
5535. For the purpose of airworthiness, a dealer registration certificate is the same as the owner's certificate when

A—the aircraft is old and moved.
B—traveling more than 150 NM.
C—required for flight testing.

A dealer's aircraft registration certificate may be used in lieu of the owner's registration if the flight is required for flight testing the aircraft or is necessary for, or incident to, the sale of the aircraft. (PLT425, CA.I.B.K1a) — 14 CFR §47.69

ALL, MIL
5535-1. Under what condition could an aircraft's engine logbook show no previous operating history?

A—If the aircraft had been imported from a foreign country.
B—This would indicate an error by maintenance personnel.
C—After the aircraft's engine has been rebuilt by the manufacturer.

The owner or operator may use a new maintenance record without previous operating history for an aircraft engine rebuilt by the manufacturer or by an agency approved by the manufacturer. (PLT425, CA.I.B.K1b) — 14 CFR §91.421

Maintenance, Preventative Maintenance, Rebuilding, and Alteration

The holder of a pilot certificate issued under Part 61 may perform preventative maintenance (in accordance with Part 43, Appendix A) on any aircraft owned or operated by that certificate holder that is not in air carrier service. Two of the conditions that apply are as follows:

1. Preventive maintenance performed by a certificated pilot must be logged, and kept in the aircraft maintenance records; and
2. Work considered as preventive maintenance is generally that which does nothing to alter the weight, CG, or flight controls, and does not require tampering with key components (prop, struts, etc.).

Part 39 prescribes ADs that apply to an aircraft and its parts. When aircraft operational or mechanical problems are discovered, manufacturers may issue service bulletins recommending corrective measures. However, when an unsafe condition exists and that condition is likely to exist or develop in other products of the same or similar type or design, the FAA will issue an Airworthiness Directive. ADs are considered to be amendments to regulations. Compliance is mandatory and is the responsibility of the owner or operator of that aircraft. Noncompliance with ADs renders an aircraft unairworthy. No person may operate an aircraft to which an AD applies, except in accordance with the requirements of that AD. Compliance with the provisions of each AD must be recorded in the aircraft maintenance records.

Answers

5102 [C]   5104 [C]   5535 [C]   5535-1 [C]

ALL, MIL
5098. Which is correct concerning preventive maintenance, when accomplished by a pilot?

A—A record of preventive maintenance is not required.
B—A record of preventive maintenance must be entered in the maintenance records.
C—Records of preventive maintenance must be entered in the FAA-approved flight manual.

A person holding at least a private pilot certificate may approve an aircraft for return to service after performing preventative maintenance under the provisions of Part 43.3(g) and shall make an entry in the maintenance record of that maintenance. (PLT446, CA.I.B.K2) — 14 CFR §43.5, §43.9

ALL, MIL
5094. Assuring compliance with an Airworthiness Directive is the responsibility of the

A—pilot-in-command and the FAA certificated mechanic assigned to that aircraft.
B—pilot-in-command of that aircraft.
C—owner or operator of that aircraft.

The owner or operator of an aircraft is primarily responsible for maintaining that aircraft in an airworthy condition, including compliance with Part 39 (Airworthiness Directives). (PLT374, CA.I.B.K1c) — 14 CFR §91.403

Answers (A) and (B) are incorrect because the pilots are responsible for determining airworthiness before flight, and the mechanics work under the advisement of the owner/operator.

ALL, MIL
5103. Which is true relating to Airworthiness Directives (ADs)?

A—ADs are advisory in nature and are, generally, not addressed immediately.
B—Noncompliance with ADs renders an aircraft unairworthy.
C—Compliance with ADs is the responsibility of maintenance personnel.

No person may operate a product to which an Airworthiness Directive applies except in accordance with the requirements of that Airworthiness Directive. (PLT378, CA.I.B.K1c) — 14 CFR §39.3

Answer (A) is incorrect because ADs are mandatory. Answer (C) is incorrect because compliance with ADs, along with other maintenance regulations, is the responsibility of the owner/operator.

ALL, MIL
5987. You are PIC of a flight and determine that the aircraft you planned to fly has an overdue Airworthiness Directive (AD). Which of the following is an appropriate decision?

A—No maintenance is available so you wait until after the trip to comply with the AD.
B—You make the flight because you can overfly an AD by 10 hours.
C—You cancel the flight and have the aircraft scheduled for maintenance.

No person may operate a product to which an Airworthiness Directive (AD) applies except in accordance with the requirements of that AD. (PLT377, CA.I.B.K1c) — 14 CFR §39.3

Answers
5098 [B] 5094 [C] 5103 [B] 5987 [C]

Chapter 4 **Regulations**

NTSB Part 830

49 CFR Part 830 deals with the reporting of aircraft accidents and incidents. An operator is responsible to the NTSB, not the FAA, for all rules pertaining to this part. Part 830 also deals with the preservation of aircraft wreckage, mail, cargo, and records. An operator will notify the nearest NTSB office immediately if any of the following occur:

1. An aircraft accident, meaning—
   a. A fatality or serious injury; or
   b. Any substantial damage. This means any damage which adversely affects the structural strength, performance, or flight characteristics of the aircraft; (damage to the landing gear, wheels, tires, flaps, engine accessories, brakes, wing tips or small puncture holes in the skin or fabric are not considered substantial damage);
2. An aircraft overdue and believed to have been involved in an accident; or
3. Any of the following incidents:
   a. An inflight fire;
   b. Aircraft collision in flight;
   c. Inability of a flight crew member to perform his/her duties due to illness or injury; or
   d. Flight control system malfunction or failure.

In addition to the immediate notification, the pilot or operator will file a written report:
- In the case of an accident, within 10 days
- In the case of an overdue aircraft, within 7 days if the aircraft is still missing
- In the case of an incident, upon request

ALL, MIL
5965. What period of time must a person be hospitalized before an injury may be defined by the NTSB as a "serious injury"?

A—10 days, with no other extenuating circumstances.
B—48 hours; commencing within 7 days after date of the injury.
C—72 hours; commencing within 10 days after date of the injury.

"Serious injury" means any injury requiring hospitalization for more than 48 hours, commencing within 7 days from the date the injury was received. (PLT395, CA.III.A.K8) — 49 CFR §830.2

ALL, MIL
5001. Notification to the NTSB is required when there has been substantial damage

A—which requires repairs to landing gear.
B—to an engine caused by engine failure in flight.
C—which adversely affects structural strength or flight characteristics.

The operator of an aircraft shall immediately, and by the most expeditious means available, notify the nearest NTSB field office when an aircraft accident occurs. An aircraft accident is an occurrence associated with the operation of an aircraft which takes place between the time any person boards the aircraft with the intention of flight and all such persons have disembarked, and in which any person suffers death or serious injury, or in which the aircraft receives substantial damage which adversely affects the structural strength, performance, or flight characteristics of the aircraft. (PLT366, CA.III.A.K8) — 49 CFR §830.2, §830.5

Answers
5965 [B]   5001 [C]

Chapter 4 **Regulations**

ALL, MIL

5002. NTSB Part 830 requires an immediate notification as a result of which incident?

A—Engine failure for any reason during flight.
B—Damage to the landing gear as a result of a hard landing.
C—Any required flight crewmember being unable to perform flight duties because of illness.

The operator of an aircraft shall immediately, and by the most expeditious means available, notify the nearest NTSB field office of the inability of any required flight crew member to perform normal flight duties as a result of injury or illness. (PLT416, CA.III.A.K8) — 49 CFR §830.2, §830.5

Answers (A) and (B) are incorrect because these are not considered "substantial damage" requiring immediate notification.

ALL, MIL

5003-1. Which incident would require that the nearest NTSB field office be notified immediately?

A—In-flight fire.
B—Ground fire resulting in fire equipment dispatch.
C—Fire of the primary aircraft while in a hangar which results in damage to other property of more than $25,000.

The operator of an aircraft shall immediately and by the most expeditious means available notify the nearest NTSB field office of any inflight fire. (PLT416, CA.III.A.K8) — 49 CFR §830.5

Answers (B) and (C) are incorrect because the regulation specifies "inflight" fires only.

ALL, MIL

5003-2. Which airborne incident would require that the nearest NTSB field office be notified immediately?

A—Cargo compartment door malfunction or failure.
B—Cabin door opened in-flight.
C—Flight control system malfunction or failure.

Immediate notification is required by the operator of any civil aircraft when a flight control system malfunction or failure occurs. (PLT416, CA.III.A.K8) — 49 CFR §830.5

Answers (A) and (B) are incorrect because neither a cargo compartment door malfunction nor a cabin door opening would require immediate notification to the NTSB, unless substantial damage affecting the structural integrity of the aircraft resulted.

ALL, MIL

5004-1. While taxiing for takeoff, a small fire burned the insulation from a transceiver wire. What action would be required to comply with NTSB Part 830?

A—No notification or report is required.
B—A report must be filed with the avionics inspector at the nearest FAA field office within 48 hours.
C—An immediate notification must be filed by the operator of the aircraft with the nearest NTSB field office.

The operator of an aircraft shall immediately and by the most expeditious means available notify the nearest NTSB field office of any inflight fire. This rule specifies "inflight" fires only. (PLT366, CA.III.A.K8) — 49 CFR §830.5

Answers (B) and (C) are incorrect because an immediate report is only required if certain items occur, such as an inflight fire, and reports are made to the NTSB, not the FAA.

ALL, MIL

5004-2. While taxiing on the parking ramp, the landing gear, wheel, and tire are damaged by striking ground equipment. What action would be required to comply with NTSB Part 830?

A—An immediate notification must be filed by the operator of the aircraft with the nearest NTSB field office.
B—A report must be filed with the nearest FAA field office within 7 days.
C—No notification or report is required.

An accident is defined as the occurrence of a fatality or serious injury or substantial damage to the aircraft. Substantial damage specifically excludes damage to the landing gear, wheels and tires. (PLT366, CA.III.A.K8) — 49 CFR §830.2

Answer (A) is incorrect because no notification is required due to damaged landing gear alone. Answer (B) is incorrect because notification of an overdue aircraft requires a report within 7 days if the aircraft is still missing, not damage to the landing gear.

ALL, MIL

5004-3. On a post-flight inspection of your aircraft after an aborted takeoff due to an elevator malfunction, you find that the elevator control cable has broken. According to NTSB 830, you

A—must immediately notify the nearest NTSB office.
B—should notify the NTSB within 10 days.
C—must file a NASA report immediately.

Immediate notification is required by the operator of any civil aircraft when a flight control system malfunction or failure occurs. (PLT366, CA.III.A.K8) — 49 CFR §830.5

Answers

5002 [C]   5003-1 [A]   5003-2 [C]   5004-1 [A]   5004-2 [C]   5004-3 [A]

Chapter 4 **Regulations**

ALL, MIL
5005. During flight a fire which was extinguished burned the insulation from a transceiver wire. What action is required by regulations?

A—No notification or report is required.
B—A report must be filed with the avionics inspector at the nearest FAA Flight Standards District Office within 48 hours.
C—An immediate notification by the operator of the aircraft to the nearest NTSB field office.

The operator of an aircraft shall immediately and by the most expeditious means available notify the nearest NTSB field office of any inflight fire. (PLT366, CA.III.A.K8) — 49 CFR §830.5

Answer (A) is incorrect because only an inflight fire requires immediate notification. Answer (B) is incorrect because no report to the avionics inspector is required.

ALL, MIL
5006. When should notification of an aircraft accident be made to the NTSB if there was substantial damage and no injuries?

A—Immediately.
B—Within 10 days.
C—Within 30 days.

The operator of an aircraft shall immediately, and by the most expeditious means available, notify the nearest NTSB field office when an aircraft accident occurs. An aircraft accident is an occurrence associated with the operation of an aircraft which takes place between the time any person boards the aircraft with the intention of flight and all such persons have disembarked, and in which any person suffers death or serious injury, or in which the aircraft receives substantial damage which adversely affects the structural strength, performance, or flight characteristics of the aircraft. (PLT377, CA.III.A.K8) — 49 CFR §830.2, §830.5

Answer (B) is incorrect because 10 days is the time specified to file a detailed aircraft accident report with the NTSB. Answer (C) is incorrect because 30 days is not a deadline specified in NTSB Part 830.

ALL, MIL
5007. The operator of an aircraft that has been involved in an incident is required to submit a report to the nearest field office of the NTSB

A—within 7 days.
B—within 10 days.
C—only if requested to do so.

A written report of an incident need be filed only if requested by the NTSB. (PLT366, CA.III.A.K8) — 49 CFR §830.2, §830.15

Answer (A) is incorrect because 7 days is the time limitation for reporting overdue (missing) aircraft. Answer (B) is incorrect because 10 days is the limitation on filing a report for accidents.

ALL, MIL
5008. How many days after an accident is a report required to be filed with the nearest NTSB field office?

A—2.
B—7.
C—10.

The operator of an aircraft shall file a report within 10 days after an accident. (PLT366, CA.III.A.K8) — 49 CFR §830.2, §830.15

Answer (A) is incorrect because 2 days is not a reporting requirement in NTSB Part 830. Answer (B) is incorrect because 7 days is the limitation with respect to an overdue aircraft that is missing.

ALL, MIL
5985. Pilots and/or flight crew members involved in near midair collision (NMAC) occurrences are urged to report each incident immediately

A—by cell phone to the nearest Flight Standards District Office, as this is an emergency.
B—to local law enforcement.
C—by radio or telephone to the nearest FAA ATC facility or FSS.

The primary purpose of the Near Midair Collision (NMAC) Reporting Program is to provide information for use in enhancing the safety and efficiency of the National Airspace System. Pilots and/or flight crew members involved in NMAC occurrences are urged to report each incident immediately by radio or telephone to the nearest FAA ATC facility or FSS. (PLT526, CA.III.A.K8) — AIM ¶7-7-3

ALL, MIL
5986. Who is responsible for filing a Near Midair Collision (NMAC) Report?

A—A passenger on board the involved aircraft.
B—Local law enforcement.
C—Pilot and/or Flight Crew of the aircraft involved in the incident.

It is the responsibility of the pilot and/or flight crew to determine whether a near midair collision did actually occur and, if so, to initiate an NMAC report. (PLT526, CA.III.A.K8) — AIM ¶7-7-3

Answers

| 5005 | [C] | 5006 | [A] | 5007 | [C] | 5008 | [C] | 5985 | [C] | 5986 | [C] |

Chapter 4 **Regulations**

IFR Operations

The pilot-in-command of each aircraft operated in controlled airspace under IFR shall report as soon as practical to ATC any malfunctions of navigational approach, or communication equipment occurring in flight.

No pilot operating an aircraft, except a United States military aircraft, may land that aircraft when the flight visibility is less than the visibility prescribed in the standard instrument approach procedure being used.

The limitation on procedure turns states that in the case of a radar vector to a final approach course or fix, a timed approach from a holding fix, or an approach for which the procedure specifies "No PT," no pilot may make a procedure turn unless cleared to do so by ATC.

ALL
5125-2. The pilot-in-command of an aircraft operated under IFR, in controlled airspace, shall report as soon as practical to ATC when

A—climbing or descending to assigned altitudes.
B—experiencing any malfunctions of navigational, approach, or communications equipment, occurring in flight.
C—requested to contact a new controlling facility.

The pilot-in-command of each aircraft operated in controlled airspace under IFR shall report as soon as practical to ATC any malfunctions of navigational, approach, or communication equipment occurring in flight. (PLT393, CA.IX.C.K2) — 14 CFR §91.187

RTC
5124-2. Pilots are not authorized to land an aircraft from an instrument approach unless the

A—flight visibility is at, or exceeds the visibility prescribed in the approach procedure being used.
B—flight visibility and ceiling are at, or exceeds the minimums prescribed in the approach being used.
C—visual approach slope indicator and runway references are distinctly visible to the pilot.

No pilot operating an aircraft, except a military aircraft of the United States, may land that aircraft when the flight visibility is less than the visibility prescribed in the standard instrument approach procedure being used. (PLT170) — 14 CFR §91.175

RTC
5124-3. A pilot performing a published instrument approach is not authorized to perform a procedure turn when

A—receiving a radar vector to a final approach course or fix.
B—maneuvering at minimum safe altitudes.
C—maneuvering at radar vectoring altitudes.

A limitation on procedure turns states that in the case of a radar vector to a final approach course or fix, a timed approach from a holding fix, or an approach for which the procedure specifies "No PT," no pilot may make a procedure turn unless cleared to do so by ATC. (PLT420) — 14 CFR §91.175

Answers

5125-2 [B]   5124-2 [A]   5124-3 [A]

Chapter 4 **Regulations**

Rotorcraft Regulations

RTC
5029. To act as pilot-in-command of a gyroplane carrying passengers, what must the pilot accomplish in that gyroplane to meet recent daytime flight experience requirements?

A—Make nine takeoffs and landings within the preceding 30 days.
B—Make three takeoffs and landings to a full stop within the preceding 90 days.
C—Make three takeoffs and landings within the preceding 90 days.

No person may act as pilot-in-command carrying passengers unless within the preceding 90 days he/she has made three takeoffs and three landings in the category and class of aircraft to be used. (PLT442) — 14 CFR §61.57

RTC
5058. To begin a flight in a rotorcraft under VFR, there must be enough fuel to fly to the first point of intended landing and, assuming normal cruise speed, to fly thereafter for at least

A—20 minutes.
B—30 minutes.
C—45 minutes.

Twenty minutes of fuel is required for rotorcraft beyond the first point of intended landing, assuming normal cruising speed. (PLT413) — 14 CFR §91.151

RTC
5068-1. Which is true with respect to operating limitations of a "restricted" category helicopter?

A—A "restricted" category helicopter is limited to an operating radius of 25 miles from its home base.
B—A pilot of a "restricted" category helicopter is required to hold a commercial pilot certificate.
C—No person may operate a "restricted" category helicopter carrying passengers or property for compensation or hire.

No person may operate a restricted category civil aircraft carrying persons or property for compensation or hire. (PLT373) — 14 CFR §91.313

RTC
5072-1. What transponder equipment is required for helicopter operations within Class B airspace? A transponder

A—with 4096 code and Mode C capability.
B—is required for helicopter operations when visibility is less than 3 miles.
C—with 4096 code capability is required except when operating at or below 1,000 feet AGL under the terms of a letter of agreement.

Helicopters must use Mode C transponders in Class B airspace. (PLT161) — 14 CFR §91.215

Answer (B) is incorrect because transponder regulations are not tied to visibility. Answer (C) is incorrect because the Mode C requirement would also require a waiver.

RTC
5087. Basic VFR weather minimums require at least what visibility for operating a helicopter within Class D airspace?

A—1 mile.
B—2 miles.
C—3 miles.

Visibility in controlled airspace below 10,000 feet is 3 miles. (PLT163) — 14 CFR §91.155

RTC
5086. Which minimum flight visibility and distance from clouds is required for a day VFR helicopter flight in Class G airspace at 3,500 feet MSL over terrain with an elevation of 1,900 feet MSL?

A—Visibility–3 miles; distance from clouds–1,000 feet below, 1,000 feet above, and 1 mile horizontally.
B—Visibility–3 miles; distance from clouds–500 feet below, 1,000 feet above, and 2,000 feet horizontally.
C—Visibility–1 mile; distance from clouds–500 feet below, 1,000 feet above, and 2,000 feet horizontally.

The chopper is at 1,600 feet AGL. In Class G airspace, more than 1,200 feet above the surface but less than 10,000 feet MSL, during day VFR operations, helicopters are required to maintain 1 mile visibility, and 500 feet below, 1,000 above, and 2,000 feet horizontal distance from clouds. (PLT163) — 14 CFR §91.155

Answers

5029 [C]　　5058 [A]　　5068-1 [C]　　5072-1 [A]　　5087 [C]　　5086 [C]

Glider Regulations

GLI
5038. To exercise the privileges of a commercial pilot certificate with a glider category rating, what medical certification is required?

A—No medical certification is required.
B—At least a second-class medical certificate when carrying passengers for hire.
C—A statement by the pilot certifying he/she has no known physical defects that makes him/her unable to pilot a glider.

A person is not required to hold a medical certificate when exercising the privileges of a pilot certificate with a glider category rating. (PLT447) — 14 CFR §61.23

GLI
5084. When flying a glider above 10,000 feet MSL and more than 1,200 feet AGL, what minimum flight visibility is required?

A—3 NM.
B—5 NM.
C—5 SM.

The only area requiring 5 statute miles visibility is 10,000 feet MSL and up, when above 1,200 feet AGL. (PLT163) — 14 CFR §91.155, §61.3

GLI, LTA
5035-1. What is the minimum age requirement for a person to be issued a commercial pilot certificate for the operation of gliders?

A—17 years.
B—18 years.
C—16 years.

A person must be at least 18 years of age to hold a commercial pilot certificate. (PLT457) — 14 CFR §61.123

Lighter-Than-Air Regulations

LTA
5035-2. What is the minimum age requirement for a person to be issued a student pilot certificate for the operation of balloons?

A—16 years.
B—15 years.
C—14 years.

A person must be at least 14 years of age to hold a student pilot certificate for the operation of a glider or balloon. (PLT457) — 14 CFR §61.83

LTA
5036. To operate a balloon in solo flight, a student pilot must have received a logbook endorsement by an authorized instructor who gave the flight training within the preceding

A—30 days.
B—60 days.
C—90 days.

A student pilot may not operate an aircraft in solo flight unless his/her student pilot certificate is endorsed, and unless within the preceding 90 days his/her pilot logbook has been endorsed, by an authorized flight instructor. (PLT457) — 14 CFR §61.87

LTA
5037. To exercise the privileges of a commercial pilot certificate with a lighter-than-air category, balloon class rating, what medical certification is required?

A—Statement by pilot certifying that he/she has no known physical defects that makes him/her unable to act as pilot of a balloon.
B—At least a current second-class medical certificate when carrying passengers for hire.
C—No medical certification is required.

A person is not required to hold a medical certificate when exercising the privileges of a pilot certificate with a balloon class rating. (PLT447) — 14 CFR §61.23

Answers

5038 [A]　　5084 [C]　　5035-1 [B]　　5035-2 [C]　　5036 [C]　　5037 [C]

Chapter 4 **Regulations**

LTA

5131. A person with a commercial pilot certificate with a lighter-than-air, balloon rating may give

A—flight training and conduct practical tests for balloon certification.
B—balloon ground and flight training and endorsements that are required for a flight review, or recency-of-experience requirements.
C—ground and flight training and endorsements that are required for balloon and airship ratings.

A person with a commercial pilot certificate with a lighter-than-air, balloon rating may: give flight and ground training in a balloon for the issuance of a certificate or rating, give an endorsement for a pilot certificate with a balloon rating, endorse a student pilot certificate or logbook for solo operating privileges in a balloon, and give flight and ground training and endorsements that are required for a flight review, an operating privilege, or recency-of-experience requirements. (PLT448) — 14 CFR §61.133

LTA

5132. A person who makes application for a commercial pilot certificate with a balloon rating, using a balloon with an airborne heater, will be

A—limited to balloon, with an airborne heater.
B—authorized to conduct ground and flight training in a balloon with an airborne heater or gas balloon.
C—authorized both airborne heater or gas balloon.

A person who applies for commercial pilot certificate with a balloon rating, using a balloon with an airborne heater, will be restricted to exercising the privileges of that certificate to a balloon with an airborne heater. (PLT448) — 14 CFR §61.133

LTA

5040. A commercial pilot who gives flight instruction in lighter-than-air category aircraft must keep a record of such instruction for a period of

A—1 year.
B—2 years.
C—3 years.

The records of instruction given shall be retained by the flight instructor separately or in his/her logbook for at least three years. (PLT419) — 14 CFR §61.189

LTA

5041. What is the maximum amount of flight instruction an authorized instructor may give in any 24 consecutive hours?

A—4 hours.
B—6 hours.
C—8 hours.

An instructor may not conduct more than eight hours of flight instruction in any period of 24 consecutive hours. (PLT419) — 14 CFR §61.195

LTA

5042. A student pilot may not operate a balloon in solo flight unless that pilot has

A—made and logged at least 10 balloon flights under the supervision of an authorized instructor.
B—received and logged flight training from an authorized instructor and demonstrated satisfactory proficiency and safety on the required maneuvers and procedures.
C—received a minimum of 5 hours of flight training in a balloon from an authorized instructor.

A student pilot who is receiving training in a balloon must receive and log flight training for the following maneuvers and procedures:

1. *Layout and assembly procedures;*
2. *Proper flight preparation procedures, including pre-flight planning and preparation, and aircraft systems;*
3. *Ascents and descents;*
4. *Landing and recovery procedures;*
5. *Emergency procedures and equipment malfunctions;*
6. *Operation of hot air or gas source, ballast, valves, vents, and rip panels, as appropriate;*
7. *Use of deflation valves or rip panels for simulating an emergency;*
8. *The effects of wind on climb and approach angles; and*
9. *Obstruction detection and avoidance techniques.*

(PLT457) — 14 CFR §61.87

Answers

5131 [B]   5132 [A]   5040 [C]   5041 [C]   5042 [B]

Chapter 4 Regulations

LTA
5048. Which person is directly responsible for the prelaunch briefing of passengers for a balloon flight?

A—Crew chief.
B—Safety officer.
C—Pilot-in-command.

The pilot-in-command of an aircraft is directly responsible for, and is the final authority as to, the operation of that aircraft. As part of crew briefing and preparation, the pilot-in-command briefs crewmembers and occupants on their duties and responsibilities in all areas of the flight including inflation, tether, inflight, landing, emergency, and recovery procedures. (PLT384) — 14 CFR §61.189

LTA
5057. The use of certain portable electronic devices is prohibited on airships that are being operated under

A—IFR.
B—VFR.
C—DVFR.

Certain portable electronic devices may not be operated on any aircraft which is operating under IFR. (PLT415) — 14 CFR §91.21

LTA
5081. If a balloon is not equipped for night flight and official sunset is 1730 EST, the latest a pilot may operate that balloon and not violate regulations is

A—1629 EST.
B—1729 EST.
C—1829 EST.

No person may, during the period from sunset to sunrise (or, in Alaska, during the period a prominent unlighted object cannot be seen from a distance of 3 statute miles or the sun is more than 6° below the horizon) operate an aircraft unless it has lighted position lights. The glow from the burner is not enough; balloons can be equipped for night flight with unique dangling position lights. (PLT220) — 14 CFR §91.209

LTA
5590. A balloon flight through a restricted area is

A—never permitted.
B—permitted anytime, but caution should be exercised because of high-speed military aircraft.
C—permitted at certain times, but only with prior permission by the appropriate authority.

No person may operate an aircraft within a restricted area contrary to the restrictions imposed, or within a prohibited area, unless he/she has the permission of the using or controlling agency. (PLT161) — 14 CFR §73.13

LTA
5554. (Refer to Figure 52, point 2.)
GIVEN:

Sacramento Executive (SAC) tower
   reports wind ....290 at 10 kts
Highest balloon flight altitude ....1,200 MSL

If you depart for a 2-hour balloon flight from SAC airport (point 2), which response best describes what ATC requires of you?

A—You will have to contact Sacramento Approach Control.
B—You must communicate with Sacramento Approach Control because you will enter the Alert Area.
C—Your flightpath will require communications with Sacramento Executive (SAC) control tower and not with Sacramento Approach Control.

The floor of the Class C airspace here is 1,600 feet MSL, the top is 4,100 feet MSL. The flight path of the balloon will pass under the floor of Class B airspace; therefore, no communication is required with Sacramento Approach Control. However, communications must be established with SAC tower since the balloon will be flying through the Class D airspace. (PLT040) — Sectional Chart Legend

Answers

| 5048 [C] | 5057 [A] | 5081 [B] | 5590 [C] | 5554 [C] |

LTA Fundamentals of Instructing

LTA
5882. A change in behavior as a result of experience can be defined as

A—learning.
B—knowledge.
C—understanding.

As a result of a learning experience, an individual's way of perceiving, thinking, feeling, and doing may change. Thus, learning can be defined as a change in behavior as a result of experience. (PLT308) — FAA-H-8083-9

LTA
5883. In levels of learning, what are the steps of progression?

A—Application, understanding, rote, and correlation.
B—Rote, understanding, application, and correlation.
C—Correlation, rote, understanding, and application.

The lowest level, rote learning, is the ability to repeat back something which one has been taught, without understanding or being able to apply what has been learned. Progressively higher levels of learning are understanding what has been taught, achieving the skill to apply what has been learned to perform correctly, and associating and correlating what has been learned with things previously learned or subsequently encountered. (PLT306) — FAA-H-8083-9

LTA
5884. In the learning process, fear or the element of threat will

A—inspire the learner to improve.
B—narrow the learner's perceptual field.
C—decrease the rate of associative reactions.

Fear adversely affects learners' perception by narrowing their perceptual field. Confronted with threat, learners tend to limit their attention to the threatening object or condition. (PLT308) — FAA-H-8083-9

LTA
5885. What is the basis of all learning?

A—Insight.
B—Perception.
C—Motivation.

Initially, all learning comes from perceptions directed to the brain by one or more of the five senses (sight, hearing, touch, smell, and taste). (PLT308) — FAA-H-8083-9

LTA
5886. While material is being taught, learners may be learning other things as well. What is the additional learning called?

A—Residual learning.
B—Conceptual learning.
C—Incidental learning.

Learning is multifaceted. While learning the subject at hand, learners may be learning other things as well. They may be developing attitudes about aviation—good or bad—depending on what they experience. Under a skillful instructor, for example, they may learn self-reliance. This learning is sometimes called "incidental," but it may have a great impact on the total development of the learner. (PLT306) — FAA-H-8083-9

LTA
5887. Individuals learn best when they are willing to learn. This feature of LAWS OF LEARNING is referred to as the law of

A—recency.
B—readiness.
C—willingness.

Individuals learn best when they are ready to learn, and they do not learn much if they see no reason for learning. (PLT308) — FAA-H-8083-9

LTA
5888. Perceptions result when a person

A—gives meaning to sensations.
B—groups together bits of information.
C—responds to visual cues first, then aural cues, and relates these cues to ones previously learned.

Perceptions result when a person gives meaning to sensations. (PLT308) — FAA-H-8083-9

Answers

5882 [A]   5883 [B]   5884 [B]   5885 [B]   5886 [C]   5887 [B]
5888 [A]

LTA
5889. Which is true? Motivations

A—should be obvious to be useful.
B—must be tangible to be effective.
C—may be very subtle and difficult to identify.

Motivations may be very subtle and difficult to identify or they may be obvious. (PLT308) — FAA-H-8083-9

LTA
5890. To effectively motivate learners, an instructor should

A—promise rewards.
B—appeal to their pride and self-esteem.
C—maintain pleasant personal relationships, even if necessary to lower standards.

Positive motivations are provided by the promise or achievement of rewards. (PLT490) — FAA-H-8083-9

LTA
5891. Motivations in the form of reproof and threats should be avoided with all but the learner who is

A—bored.
B—discouraged.
C—overconfident.

Negative motivations in the form of reproof and threats should be avoided with all but the most overconfident and impulsive learners. (PLT490) — FAA-H-8083-9

LTA
5892. The level of learning at which a person can repeat something without understanding is called

A—rote learning.
B—basic learning.
C—random learning.

The lowest level, rote learning, is the ability to repeat back something which one has been taught, without understanding or being able to apply what has been learned. (PLT306) — FAA-H-8083-9

LTA
5893. The level of learning at which the learner becomes able to associate an element which has been learned with other blocks of learning is called the level of

A—application.
B—association.
C—correlation.

The highest level of learning, which should be the objective of all instruction, is that level at which the learner becomes able to associate an element which has been learned with other segments or "blocks" of learning or accomplishment. This level is called "correlation." (PLT306) — FAA-H-8083-9

LTA
5894. To ensure proper habits and correct techniques during training, an instructor should

A—never repeat subject matter already taught.
B—use the "building-block" technique of instruction.
C—introduce tasks which are difficult and challenging to the learner.

It is the instructor's responsibility to insist on correct techniques and procedures from the outset of training to provide proper habit patterns. It is much easier to foster proper habits from the beginning of training than to correct faulty ones later. This is the basic reason for the building block technique of instruction, in which each simple task is performed acceptably and correctly before the next learning task is introduced. (PLT295) — FAA-H-8083-9

LTA
5895. Before an individual can concentrate on learning, which of these human needs must be satisfied first?

A—Social needs.
B—Safety needs.
C—Physical needs.

At the broadest level are the physical needs. Individuals are first concerned with their need for food, rest, exercise, and protection from the elements. Until these needs are satisfied to a reasonable degree, they cannot concentrate on learning or self-expression. (PLT270) — FAA-H-8083-9

LTA
5896. Although defense mechanisms can serve a useful purpose, they can also be a hindrance because they

A—alleviate the cause of problems.
B—can result in delusional behavior.
C—involve self-deception and distortion of reality.

Because they involve some self-deception and distortion of reality, defense mechanisms do not solve problems. (PLT269) — FAA-H-8083-9

Answers

| 5889 | [C] | 5890 | [A] | 5891 | [C] | 5892 | [A] | 5893 | [C] | 5894 | [B] |
| 5895 | [C] | 5896 | [C] | | | | | | | | | | |

Chapter 4 Regulations

LTA
5897. When a learner asks irrelevant questions or refuses to participate in class activities, it usually is an indication of the defense mechanism known as

A—aggression.
B—resignation.
C—substitution.

An aggressive learner may ask irrelevant questions, refuse to participate in the activities of the class, or disrupt activities within their own group. (PLT269) — FAA-H-8083-9

LTA
5898. Taking physical or mental flight is a defense mechanism that learners use when they

A—want to escape from frustrating situations.
B—become bewildered and lost in the advanced phase of training.
C—attempt to justify actions that otherwise would be unacceptable.

Learners often escape from frustrating situations by taking flight, physical or mental. (PLT269) — FAA-H-8083-9

LTA
5899. When a learner uses excuses to justify inadequate performance, it is an indication of the defense mechanism known as

A—aggression.
B—resignation.
C—rationalization.

If learners cannot accept the real reasons for their behavior, they may rationalize. This device permits them to substitute excuses for reasons. Moreover, they can make those excuses plausible and acceptable to themselves. (PLT269) — FAA-H-8083-9

LTA
5900. When learners become so frustrated they no longer believe it possible to work further, they usually display which defense mechanism?

A—Aggression.
B—Resignation.
C—Rationalization.

Learners may become so frustrated that they lose interest and give up. They may no longer believe it profitable or even possible to work further. (PLT233) — FAA-H-8083-9

LTA
5901. A learner who is daydreaming is engaging in the defense mechanism known as

A—flight.
B—substitution.
C—rationalization.

Learners often escape from frustrating situations by taking flight, physical or mental. (PLT233) — FAA-H-8083-9

LTA
5902. Which of these instructor actions would more likely result in learners becoming frustrated?

A—Presenting a topic or maneuver in great detail.
B—Covering up instructor mistakes or bluffing when the instructor is in doubt.
C—Telling the learners that their work is unsatisfactory without explanation.

If a learner has made an earnest effort but is told that the work is not satisfactory, with no other explanation, frustration occurs. (PLT419) — FAA-H-8083-9

LTA
5903. The effectiveness of communication between the instructor and the learner is measured by the degree of

A—motivation manifested by the learner.
B—similarity between the idea transmitted and the idea received.
C—attention the learner gives to the instructor during a lesson.

Communication's effectiveness is measured by the similarity between the idea transmitted and the idea received. (PLT204) — FAA-H-8083-9

LTA
5904. To communicate effectively, instructors must

A—utilize highly organized notes.
B—display an authoritarian attitude.
C—display a positive, confident attitude.

An instructor's attitude must be positive if he/she is to communicate effectively. Communicators must be confident. (PLT204) — FAA-H-8083-9

Answers

5897 [A]	5898 [A]	5899 [C]	5900 [B]	5901 [A]	5902 [C]
5903 [B]	5904 [C]				

Chapter 4 **Regulations**

LTA
5905. Probably the greatest single barrier to effective communication is the

A—use of inaccurate statements.
B—use of abstractions by the communicator.
C—lack of a common core of experience between communicator and receiver.

Probably the greatest single barrier to effective communication is the lack of a common core of experience between communicator and receiver. (PLT204) — FAA-H-8083-9

LTA
5906. What is the proper sequence in which the instructor should employ the four basic steps in the teaching process?

A—Explanation, demonstration, practice, and evaluation.
B—Explanation, trial and practice, evaluation, and review.
C—Preparation, presentation, application, and review and evaluation.

The teaching of new materials, as reflected in any of the lists, can be broken down into the steps of:

1. Preparation;

2. Presentation;

3. Application; and

4. Review and evaluation.

(PLT481) — FAA-H-8083-9

LTA
5907. Evaluation of learner performance and accomplishment during a lesson should be based on the

A—learner's background and past experiences.
B—objectives and goals that were established in the lesson plan.
C—learner's actual performance as compared to an arbitrary standard.

The evaluation of learner performance and accomplishment during a lesson should be based on the objectives and goals that were established in the instructor's lesson plan. (PLT491) — FAA-H-8083-9

LTA
5908. To enhance a learner's acceptance of further instruction, the instructor should

A—keep the learner informed of his/her progress.
B—continually prod the learner to maintain motivational levels.
C—establish performance standards a little above the learner's actual ability.

The failure of the instructor to ensure that learners are cognizant of their progress, or lack of it, may impose a barrier between them. Though it may be slight, it may make further instruction more difficult. (PLT482) — FAA-H-8083-9

LTA
5909. The method of arranging lesson material from the simple to complex, past to present, and known to unknown, is one that

A—the instructor should avoid.
B—creates learner thought pattern departures.
C—indicates the relationship of the main points of the lesson.

The instructor must logically organize the material to show the relationships of the main points. The instructor usually shows these primary relationships by developing the main points in one of the following ways: From the past to the present; from the simple to the complex; from the known to the unknown; and from the more frequently used to the least frequently used. (PLT489) — FAA-H-8083-9

LTA
5910. The KNOWN to UNKNOWN pattern helps the instructor lead the learner into new ideas and concepts by

A—anxieties and insecurities.
B—using something the learner already knows.
C—previously held opinions, both valid and invalid.

From known to unknown—by using something the learner already knows as the point of departure, the instructor can lead into new ideas and concepts. (PLT489) — FAA-H-8083-9

Answers

| 5905 [C] | 5906 [C] | 5907 [B] | 5908 [A] | 5909 [C] | 5910 [B] |

Chapter 4 **Regulations**

LTA

5911. In developing a lesson, the instructor must logically organize explanations and demonstrations to help the learner

A—understand the separate items of knowledge.
B—understand the relationships of the main points of the lesson.
C—learn by rote so that performance of the procedure will become automatic.

The instructor must logically organize the material to show the relationships of the main points. (PLT491) — FAA-H-8083-9

LTA

5912. Which should be the first step in preparing a lecture?

A—Organizing the material.
B—Researching the subject.
C—Establishing the objective and desired outcome.

The following four steps should be followed in the planning phase of preparation:

1. *Establishing the objective and desired outcomes;*
2. *Researching the subject;*
3. *Organizing the material; and*
4. *Planning productive classroom activities.*

(PLT491) — FAA-H-8083-9

LTA

5913. What is one advantage of a lecture?

A—It provides for learner participation.
B—Many ideas can be presented in a short time.
C—Maximum attainment in all types of learning outcomes is possible.

In a lecture, the instructor can present many ideas in a relatively short time. (PLT488) — FAA-H-8083-9

LTA

5914. In a "guided discussion," lead-off questions should usually begin with

A—"why…"
B—"when…"
C—"where…"

Lead-off questions should usually begin with "how" or "why." (PLT488) — FAA-H-8083-9

LTA

5915. What are the essential steps in the "demonstration/performance" method of teaching?

A—Demonstration, practice, and evaluation.
B—Demonstration, learner performance, and evaluation.
C—Explanation, demonstration, learner performance, instructor supervision, and evaluation.

The demonstration—performance method of teaching has five essential phases:

1. *Explanation;*
2. *Demonstration;*
3. *Learner performance;*
4. *Instructor supervision; and*
5. *Evaluation.*

(PLT487) — FAA-H-8083-9

LTA

5916. Which is true about an instructor's critique of a learner's performance?

A—It must be given in written form.
B—It should be subjective rather than objective.
C—It is a step in the learning process, not in the grading process.

A critique is not a step in the grading process. It is a step in the learning process. (PLT482) — FAA-H-8083-9

LTA

5917. The purpose of a critique is to

A—identify only the learner's faults and weaknesses.
B—give a delayed evaluation of the learner's performance.
C—provide direction and guidance to raise the level of the learner's performance.

A critique should provide direction and guidance to raise the level of the learner's performance. (PLT481) — FAA-H-8083-9

Answers

| 5911 | [B] | 5912 | [C] | 5913 | [B] | 5914 | [A] | 5915 | [C] | 5916 | [C] |
| 5917 | [C] | | | | | | | | | | |

LTA
5918. When an instructor critiques a learner, it should always be

A—done in private.
B—subjective rather than objective.
C—conducted immediately after the learner's performance.

A critique should come immediately after a learner's individual or group performance, while the details of the performance are easy to recall. (PLT482) — FAA-H-8083-9

LTA
5919. Proper quizzing by the instructor during a lesson can have which of these results?

A—It identifies points which need emphasis.
B—It encourages rote response from learners.
C—It permits the introduction of new material which was not covered previously.

A quiz identifies points which need more emphasis. (PLT482) — FAA-H-8083-9

LTA
5920. For oral quizzing to be effective during a lesson, a question should

A—center on only one idea.
B—include a combination of where, how, and why.
C—be easy for the learner at that particular stage of training.

Effective questions center on only one idea. (PLT482) — FAA-H-8083-9

LTA
5921. A written test has validity when it

A—yields consistent results.
B—samples liberally whatever is being measured.
C—actually measures what it is supposed to measure and nothing else.

A measuring instrument, including a written test, is valid when it actually measures what it is supposed to measure and nothing else. (PLT211) — FAA-H-8083-9

LTA
5922. A written test which has reliability is one which

A—yields consistent results.
B—measures small differences in the achievement of learners.
C—actually measures what it is supposed to measure and nothing else.

A reliable measuring instrument, including a written test, is one which yields consistent results. (PLT211) — FAA-H-8083-9

LTA
5923. A written test is said to be comprehensive when it

A—yields consistent results.
B—includes all levels of difficulty.
C—liberally samples whatever is being measured.

To be comprehensive, a measuring instrument, including a written test, must sample liberally whatever is being measured. (PLT211) — FAA-H-8083-9

LTA
5924. Which is true concerning the use of visual aids? They

A—should be used to emphasize key points in a lesson.
B—ensure getting and holding the learner's attention.
C—should not be used to cover a subject in less time.

The aids should be concentrated on the key points. (PLT505) — FAA-H-8083-9

LTA
5925. Instructional aids used in the teaching/learning process should be

A—self-supporting and should require no explanation.
B—compatible with the learning outcomes to be achieved.
C—selected prior to developing and organizing the lesson plan.

Aids should be simple and compatible with the learning outcomes to be achieved. (PLT505) — FAA-H-8083-9

Answers

5918 [C]	5919 [A]	5920 [A]	5921 [C]	5922 [A]	5923 [C]
5924 [A]	5925 [B]				

Chapter 4 **Regulations**

LTA
5926. The professional relationship between the instructor and the learner should be based upon

A—the need to disregard the learner's personal faults, interests, or problems.
B—setting the learning objectives very high so that the learner is continually challenged.
C—the mutual acknowledgment that they are important to each other and both are working toward the same objective.

The professional relationship of the instructor with the learner should be based on a mutual acknowledgment that both the learner and the instructor are important to each other, and that both are working toward the same objective. (PLT229) — FAA-H-8083-9

LTA
5927. Which is true regarding professionalism as an instructor?

A—Professionalism demands a code of ethics.
B—To achieve professionalism, actions and decisions must be limited to standard patterns and practices.
C—Professionalism does not require extended training and preparation.

Professionalism demands a code of ethics. Professionals must be true to themselves and to those they serve. Anything less than a sincere performance is quickly detected, and immediately destroys their effectiveness. (PLT229) — FAA-H-8083-9

LTA
5928. An instructor can most effectively maintain a high level of learner motivation by

A—making each lesson a pleasurable experience.
B—easing the standards for an apprehensive learner.
C—continually challenging the learner to meet the highest objectives of training.

By making each lesson a pleasurable experience for the learner, the flight instructor can maintain a high-level of learner motivation. (PLT490) — FAA-H-8083-9

LTA
5929. The overconfidence of fast learners should be corrected by

A—high praise when no errors are made.
B—raising the standard of performance for each lesson.
C—providing strong, negative evaluation at the end of each lesson.

Apt learners can also create problems. Because they make few mistakes, they may assume that the correction of errors is unimportant. Such overconfidence soon results in faulty performance. For such learners, a good instructor will constantly raise the standard of performance for each lesson, demanding greater effort. (PLT232) — FAA-H-8083-9

LTA
5930. What should an instructor do with a learner who assumes that correction of errors is unimportant?

A—Invent learner deficiencies.
B—Try to reduce the learner's overconfidence.
C—Raise the standards of performance, demanding greater effort.

Apt learners can also create problems. Because they make few mistakes, they may assume that the correction of errors is unimportant. Such overconfidence soon results in faulty performance. For such learners, a good instructor will constantly raise the standard of performance for each lesson, demanding greater effort. (PLT232) — FAA-H-8083-9

LTA
5931. What should an instructor do if a learner's slow progress is due to discouragement and lack of confidence?

A—Assign subgoals which can be attained more easily than the normal learning goals.
B—Emphasize the negative aspects of poor performance by pointing out the serious consequences.
C—Raise the performance standards so the learner will gain satisfaction in meeting higher standards.

A learner whose slow progress is due to discouragement and a lack of confidence should be assigned "subgoals" which can be attained more easily than the normal learning goals. For this purpose, complex flight maneuvers can be separated into their elements, and each element practiced until an acceptable performance is achieved before the whole maneuver or operation is attempted. (PLT490) — FAA-H-8083-9

Answers

5926 [C]   5927 [A]   5928 [A]   5929 [B]   5930 [C]   5931 [A]

Chapter 4 Regulations

LTA
5932. Should an instructor be concerned about an apt learner who makes very few mistakes?

A—No. Some learners have an innate, natural aptitude for flight.
B—Yes. The learner may assume that the correction of errors is unimportant.
C—Yes. The learner will lose confidence in the instructor if the instructor does not invent deficiencies in the learner's performance.

Apt learners can also create problems. Because they make few mistakes, they may assume that the correction of errors is unimportant. Such overconfidence soon results in faulty performance. For such learners, a good instructor will constantly raise the standard of performance for each lesson, demanding greater effort. (PLT232) — FAA-H-8083-9

LTA
5933. When a learner correctly understands the situation and knows the correct procedure for the task, but fails to act at the proper time, the learner most probably

A—lacks self-confidence.
B—will be unable to cope with the demands of flying.
C—is handicapped by indifference or lack of interest.

A learner may fail to act at the proper time due to lack of self-confidence, even though the situation is correctly understood. (PLT490) — FAA-H-8083-9

LTA
5934. What should an instructor do if a learner is suspected of not fully understanding the principles involved in a task, even though the learner can correctly perform the task?

A—Require the learner to apply the same elements to the performance of other tasks.
B—Require the learner to repeat the task, as necessary, until the principles are understood.
C—Repeat demonstrating the task as necessary until the learner understands the principles.

A learner may perform a procedure or maneuver correctly and not fully understand the principles and objectives involved. When this is suspected by the instructor, the learner should be required to vary the performance of the maneuver slightly, combine it with other operations, or apply the same elements to the performance of other maneuvers. (PLT227) — FAA-H-8083-9

LTA
5935. When under stress, normal individuals usually react

A—with marked changes in mood on different lessons.
B—with extreme overcooperation, painstaking self-control, and laughing or singing.
C—by responding rapidly and exactly, often automatically, within the limits of their experience and training.

Normal individuals begin to respond rapidly and exactly, within the limits of their experience and training. Many responses are automatic. (PLT231) — FAA-H-8083-9

LTA
5936. The instructor can counteract anxiety in a learner by

A—treating learner fear as a normal reaction.
B—allowing the learner to select tasks to be performed.
C—continually citing the unhappy consequences of faulty performance.

An effective technique is to treat fears as a normal reaction. (PLT231) — FAA-H-8083-9

LTA
5937. Which would most likely indicate that a learner is reacting abnormally to stress?

A—Thinks and acts rapidly.
B—Extreme overcooperation.
C—Extreme sensitivity to surroundings.

Abnormal reaction to stress would be indicated by inappropriate reactions such as extreme over-cooperation, painstaking self-control, inappropriate laughter, singing, very rapid changes in emotions, or motion sickness. (PLT231) — FAA-H-8083-9

Answers

| 5932 | [B] | 5933 | [A] | 5934 | [A] | 5935 | [C] | 5936 | [A] | 5937 | [B] |

Chapter 4 **Regulations**

LTA

5938. What is the primary consideration in determining the length and frequency of flight instruction periods?

A—Fatigue.
B—Mental acuity.
C—Physical conditioning.

Fatigue is the primary consideration in determining the length and frequency of flight instruction periods. The amount of training which can be absorbed by one learner without incurring fatigue does not necessarily indicate the capacity of another learner. Fatigue which results from training operations may be either physical or mental, or both. (PLT295) — FAA-H-8083-9

LTA

5939. Learners quickly become apathetic when they

A—understand the objective toward which they are working.
B—are assigned goals that are difficult, but possible to attain.
C—recognize that their instructor is poorly prepared to conduct the lesson.

Learners quickly become apathetic when they recognize that the instructor has made inadequate preparations for the instruction being given, or when the instruction appears to be deficient, contradictory, or insincere. (PLT295) — FAA-H-8083-9

LTA

5940. In planning any instructional activity, the instructor's first consideration should be to

A—determine the overall objectives and standards.
B—identify the blocks of learning which make up the overall objective.
C—establish common ground between the instructor and learners.

Before any important instruction can begin, a determination of standards and objectives is necessary. (PLT491) — FAA-H-8083-9

Answers

5938 [A]   5939 [C]   5940 [A]

Chapter 5
Procedures and Airport Operations

Airspace   *5–3*

Basic VFR Weather Minimums   *5–14*

Operations on Wet or Slippery Runways   *5–15*

Land and Hold Short Operations (LAHSO)   *5–16*

Airport Marking Aids and Signs   *5–17*

VFR Cruising Altitudes   *5–22*

Collision Avoidance   *5–22*

Fitness Physiology   *5–25*

Aeronautical Decision Making (ADM)   *5–29*

Chapter 5 **Procedures and Airport Operations**

Airspace

Figure 5-1. Airspace

Controlled airspace, that is, airspace within which some or all aircraft may be subject to ATC, consists of those areas designated as Class A, Class B, Class C, Class D, and Class E airspace.

Much of the controlled airspace begins at either 700 feet or 1,200 feet above the ground. The 700-foot lateral limits and floors of Class E airspace are defined by a magenta vignette; while the 1,200-foot lateral limits and floors are defined by a blue vignette if it abuts uncontrolled airspace. Floors other than 700 feet or 1,200 feet are shown by a number indicating the floor.

Class A—Class A airspace extends from 18,000 feet MSL up to and including FL600 and is not depicted on VFR sectional charts. No flight under VFR, including VFR-on-top, is authorized in Class A airspace.

Class B—Class B airspace consists of controlled airspace extending upward from the surface or higher to specified altitudes. Each Class B airspace sector, outlined in blue on the sectional aeronautical chart, is labeled with its delimiting altitudes. On the Terminal Area Chart, each Class B airspace sector is also outlined in blue and labeled with its delimiting arcs, radials, and altitudes. Each Class B airspace location will contain at least one primary airport. An ATC clearance is required prior to operating within Class B airspace.

A pilot landing or taking off from one of a group of 12 specific, busy airports must hold at least a Private Pilot Certificate. At other airports, a student pilot may not operate an aircraft on a solo flight within Class B airspace or to, from, or at an airport located within Class B airspace unless both ground and flight instruction has been received from an authorized instructor to operate within that Class B airspace or at that airport, and the flight and ground instruction has been received within that Class B airspace or at the specific airport for which the solo flight is authorized. The student's logbook must be endorsed within the preceding 90 days by the instructor who gave the flight training and the endorsement must specify that the student has been found competent to conduct solo flight operations in that Class B airspace or at that specific airport.

Chapter 5 **Procedures and Airport Operations**

Each airplane operating within Class B airspace must be equipped with a two-way radio with appropriate ATC frequencies, and a 4096 code transponder with Mode C automatic altitude-reporting capability.

Class C—Class C airspace is controlled airspace surrounding designated airports within which ATC provides radar vectoring and sequencing for all IFR and VFR aircraft. Each airplane operating within Class C airspace must be equipped with a two-way radio with appropriate frequencies and a 4096 code transponder with Mode C automatic altitude-reporting capability. Communications with ATC must be established prior to entering Class C airspace.

Class C airspace consists of two circles, both centered on the primary airport. The surface area has a radius of 5 NM. The airspace of the surface area normally extends from the surface of Class C airspace airport up to 4,000 feet above that airport. Some situations require different boundaries. The shelf area has a radius of 10 NM. The airspace between the 5 and 10 NM rings begins at a height of 1,200 feet and extends to the same altitude cap as the inner circle. An outer area with a normal radius of 20 NM surrounds the surface and shelf areas. Within the outer area, pilots are encouraged to participate but it is not a VFR requirement.

Class C airspace service to aircraft proceeding to a satellite airport will be terminated at a sufficient distance to allow time to change to the appropriate tower or advisory frequency. Aircraft departing satellite airports within Class C airspace shall establish two-way communication with ATC as soon as practicable after takeoff. On aeronautical charts, Class C airspace is depicted by solid magenta lines.

Class D—Class D airspace extends upward from the surface to approximately 2,500 feet AGL (the actual height is as needed). Class D airspace may include one or more airports and is normally 4 NM in radius. The actual size and shape is depicted by a blue dashed line and numbers showing the top. When the ceiling of Class D airspace is less than 1,000 feet and/or the visibility is less than 3 SM, pilots wishing to takeoff or land must hold an instrument rating, must have filed an instrument flight plan, and must have received an appropriate clearance from ATC. In addition, the aircraft must be equipped for instrument flight.

At some locations, a pilot who does not hold an instrument rating may be authorized to takeoff or land when the weather is less than that required for visual flight rules. When special VFR (SFVR) flight is prohibited, it will be depicted by "No SVFR" above the airport information on the chart. Special VFR requires the aircraft to be operated clear of clouds with flight visibility of at least 1 SM. For Special VFR operations between sunset and sunrise, the pilot must hold an instrument rating and the airplane must be equipped for instrument flight. Requests for Special VFR arrival or departure clearance should be directed to the airport traffic control tower.

Class E—Magenta shading identifies Class E airspace starting at 700 feet AGL, and an area with no shading (or blue shading if next to Class G airspace) identifies Class E airspace starting at 1,200 feet AGL. It may also start at other altitudes. All airspace from 14,500 feet to 17,999 feet is Class E airspace. It also includes the surface area of some airports with an instrument approach but no control tower. An **airway** is a corridor of controlled airspace extending from 1,200 feet above the surface (or as designated) up to and including 17,999 feet MSL, and 4 NM either side of the centerline. The airway is indicated by a centerline, shown in blue.

Class G—Class G is airspace within which ATC has neither the authority nor responsibility to exercise any control over air traffic.

Prohibited Areas are blocks of airspace within which the flight of aircraft is prohibited.

Restricted Areas denote the presence of unusual, often invisible, hazards to aircraft such as artillery firing, aerial gunnery, or guided missiles. Penetration of Restricted Areas without authorization of the using or controlling agency may be extremely hazardous to the aircraft and its occupants.

Chapter 5 Procedures and Airport Operations

Warning Areas contain the same hazardous activities as those found in Restricted Areas, but are located in international airspace.

Military Operations Areas (MOAs) consist of airspace established for the purpose of separating certain military training activities from instrument flight rules (IFR) traffic. Pilots operating under VFR should exercise extreme caution while flying within an active MOA. Any Flight Service Station (FSS) within 100 miles of the area will provide information concerning MOA hours of operation. Prior to entering an active MOA, pilots should contact the controlling agency for traffic advisories.

Alert Areas may contain a high volume of pilot training activities or an unusual type of aerial activity, neither of which is hazardous to aircraft. Pilots of participating aircraft, as well as pilots transiting the area, are equally responsible for collision avoidance.

An **Airport Advisory Area** is the area within 10 statute miles of an airport where a control tower is not in operation but where a Flight Service Station (FSS) is located. The FSS provides advisory service to aircraft arriving and departing. It is not mandatory for pilots to use the advisory service, but it is strongly recommended that they do so.

Aircraft are requested to remain at least 2,000 feet above the surface of National Parks, National Monuments, Wilderness and Primitive Areas, and National Wildlife Refuges.

Military Training Routes (MTRs) have been developed for use by the military for the purpose of conducting low-altitude, high-speed training. Generally, MTRs are established below 10,000 feet MSL for operations at speeds in excess of 250 knots.

IFR Military Training Routes (IR) operations are conducted in accordance with instrument flight rules, regardless of weather conditions. VFR Military Training Routes (VR) operations are conducted in accordance with visual flight rules. IR and VR at and below 1,500 feet AGL (with no segment above 1,500) will be identified by four digit numbers, e.g., VR1351, IR1007. IR and VR above and below 1,500 feet AGL (segments of these routes may be below 1,500) will be identified by three digit numbers, e.g., IR341, VR426. MTRs are charted on IFR low altitude enroute charts, VFR sectional charts and area planning charts.

ALL, MIL

5115. After an ATC clearance has been obtained, a pilot may not deviate from that clearance, unless the pilot

A—requests an amended clearance.
B—is operating VFR on top.
C—receives an amended clearance or has an emergency.

When an ATC clearance has been obtained, no pilot-in-command may deviate from that clearance unless an amended clearance is obtained, an emergency exists, or the deviation is in response to a traffic alert and collision avoidance system resolution advisory. (PLT444, CA.III.A.K2) — 14 CFR §91.123

ALL, MIL

5043. Excluding Hawaii, the vertical limits of the Federal Low Altitude airways extend from

A—700 feet AGL up to, but not including, 14,500 feet MSL.
B—1,200 feet AGL up to, but not including, 18,000 feet MSL.
C—1,200 feet AGL up to, but not including, 14,500 feet MSL.

Each Federal airway includes that airspace extending upward from 1,200 feet above the surface up to but not including 18,000 feet MSL. Federal airways for Hawaii have no upper limits. (PLT393, CA.I.E.K1) — 14 CFR §61.87

Answers

5115 [C]   5043 [B]

Chapter 5 Procedures and Airport Operations

ALL, MIL
5082-1. Which is true regarding flight operations in Class B airspace?

A—Flight under VFR is not authorized unless the pilot-in-command is instrument rated.
B—The pilot must receive an ATC clearance before operating an aircraft in that area.
C—Solo student pilot operations are not authorized.

No person may operate an aircraft within a Class B airspace area unless the operator receives an ATC clearance from the ATC facility having jurisdiction for that area before operating an aircraft in that area. (PLT162, CA.I.E.K1) — 14 CFR §91.131

Answer (A) is incorrect because a private pilot's certificate without an instrument rating is sufficient to operate in Class B airspace. Answer (C) is incorrect because with the proper training and endorsements a student pilot may operate in Class B airspace.

ALL, MIL
5082-2. Which is true regarding pilot certification requirements for operations in Class B airspace?

A—The pilot-in-command must hold at least a private pilot certificate with an instrument rating.
B—The pilot-in-command must hold at least a private pilot certificate.
C—Solo student pilot operations are not authorized.

No person may operate an aircraft within a Class B airspace area unless the pilot-in-command holds at least a private pilot certificate. (PLT161, CA.I.E.K1) — 14 CFR §91.131

Answer (A) is incorrect because a private pilot certificate without an instrument rating is sufficient to operate in Class B airspace. Answer (C) is incorrect because with the proper training and endorsements, a student pilot may operate in Class B airspace.

ALL, MIL
5082-3. Which is true regarding flight operations in Class B airspace?

A—The aircraft must be equipped with an ATC transponder and altitude reporting equipment.
B—The pilot-in-command must hold at least a private pilot certificate with an instrument rating.
C—The pilot-in-command must hold at least a student pilot certificate.

A student pilot may only operate an aircraft on a solo flight in Class B airspace if the student pilot has received both ground and flight training from an authorized instructor and has received a logbook endorsement. No person may operate an aircraft in a Class B airspace area unless the aircraft is equipped with the applicable operating transponder and automatic altitude reporting equipment. Requests for ATC authorized deviations for operation of an aircraft that is not equipped with a transponder must be made at least one hour before the proposed operation. (PLT162, CA.I.E.K2) — 14 CFR §91.131, §91.215 and §61.95

ALL, MIL
5082-4. You would like to enter Class B airspace and contact the approach controller. The controller responds to your initial radio call with "N125HF standby." May you enter the Class B airspace?

A—You must remain outside Class B airspace until controller gives you a specific clearance.
B—You may continue into the Class B airspace and wait for further instructions.
C—You may continue into the Class B airspace without a specific clearance, if the aircraft is ADS-B equipped.

No. You are not to enter the Class B airspace until you have received authorization from ATC. "Standby" simply means the controller has your request, it does not give you permission to enter the airspace. (PLT161, CA.I.E.K1) – AIM ¶3-2-3

ALL, MIL
5009. What designated airspace associated with an airport becomes inactive when the control tower at that airport is not in operation?

A—Class D, which then becomes Class C.
B—Class D, which then becomes Class E.
C—Class B.

Class D airspace exists only when the control tower is operating. It reverts to Class E when the tower closes if there is an instrument approach and a weather observer. (PLT161, CA.I.E.K1) — 14 CFR §1.1

Answer (A) is incorrect because Class D airspace will revert to Class E airspace when the control tower closes. Answer (C) is incorrect because the primary airport of Class B airspace will have a control tower that operates full-time.

Answers

5082-1 [B]   5082-2 [B]   5082-3 [A]   5082-4 [A]   5009 [B]

ALL, MIL
5564. Which is true concerning the blue and magenta colors used to depict airports on Sectional Aeronautical Charts?

A—Airports with control towers underlying Class A, B, and C airspace are shown in blue, Class D and E airspace are magenta.
B—Airports with control towers underlying Class C, D, and E airspace are shown in magenta.
C—Airports with control towers underlying Class B, C, D, and E airspace are shown in blue.

Airports having Control Towers (Class B, C, D or E airspace) are shown in blue. All others are shown in magenta. (PLT040, CA.I.E.K2) — Sectional Chart Legend

ALL, MIL
5117. When operating an aircraft in the vicinity of an airport with an operating control tower, in Class E airspace, a pilot must establish communications prior to

A—8 NM, and up to and including 3,000 feet AGL.
B—5 NM, and up to and including 3,000 feet AGL.
C—4 NM, and up to and including 2,500 feet AGL.

Unless otherwise authorized or required by ATC, no person may operate an aircraft to, from, through, or on an airport having an operational control tower unless two-way radio communications are maintained between that aircraft and the control tower. Communications must be established prior to 4 NM from the airport, up to and including 2,500 feet AGL. (PLT434, CA.I.E.K1) — 14 CFR §91.127

ALL, MIL
5118. When approaching to land at an airport with an ATC facility, in Class D airspace, the pilot must establish communications prior to

A—10 NM, up to and including 3,000 feet AGL.
B—30 SM, and be transponder equipped.
C—4 NM, up to and including 2,500 feet AGL.

Unless otherwise authorized or required by ATC, no person may operate an aircraft to, from, through, or on an airport having an operational control tower unless two-way radio communications are maintained between that aircraft and the control tower. Communications must be established prior to 4 NM from the airport, up to and including 2,500 feet AGL. (PLT044, CA.I.E.K1) — 14 CFR §91.127

ALL, MIL
5119-1. Which is true regarding flight operations to or from a satellite airport, without an operating control tower, within the Class C airspace area?

A—Prior to takeoff, a pilot must establish communication with the ATC controlling facility.
B—Aircraft must be equipped with an ATC transponder and altitude reporting equipment.
C—Prior to landing, a pilot must establish and maintain communication with an ATC facility.

Unless otherwise authorized or directed by ATC, no person may operate an aircraft in Class C airspace unless that aircraft is equipped with an operable transponder and altitude reporting equipment. (PLT434, CA.I.E.K1) — 14 CFR §91.130

Answer (A) is incorrect because pilots must establish communication with the ATC controlling facility as soon as practicable, which may not be prior to takeoff. Answer (C) is incorrect because communications must be established prior to entering Class C airspace, well before a "prior to landing" point.

ALL, MIL
5119-2. Which is true regarding flight operations to or from a satellite airport, without an operating control tower, within the Class C airspace area?

A—Prior to entering that airspace, a pilot must establish and maintain communication with the ATC serving facility.
B—Aircraft must be equipped with an ATC transponder.
C—Prior to takeoff, a pilot must establish communication with the ATC controlling facility.

No person may take off or land an aircraft at a satellite airport within a Class C airspace area except in compliance with FAA arrival and departure traffic patterns. Each person must establish two-way radio communications with the ATC facility providing air traffic services prior to entering that airspace and thereafter maintain those communications while within that airspace. (PLT434, CA.I.E.K1) — 14 CFR §91.130

Answers (B) and (C) are incorrect because unless otherwise authorized or directed by ATC, no person may operate an aircraft in Class C airspace unless that aircraft is equipped with an operable transponder and altitude reporting equipment; from a satellite airport without an operating control tower within Class C airspace, the pilot must establish and maintain two-way radio communications with the controlling ATC facility as soon as practicable after departing.

Answers

5564 [C]   5117 [C]   5118 [C]   5119-1 [B]   5119-2 [A]

Chapter 5 **Procedures and Airport Operations**

ALL
5119-3. The radius of the uncharted Outer Area of Class C airspace is normally

A—20 NM.
B—30 NM.
C—40 NM.

The normal radius of the outer area will be 20 NM. This is the area where separation is provided after two-way communication is established. It is only a requirement to contact ATC before entering the 10 NM Class C airspace depicted on the sectional chart. (PLT 161, CA.I.E.K1) — AIM ¶3-2-4

ALL, MIL
5120-1. Which is true regarding flight operations in Class A airspace?

A—Aircraft must be equipped with approved distance measuring equipment (DME).
B—Must conduct operations under instrument flight rules.
C—Aircraft must be equipped with an approved ATC transponder.

Each person operating an aircraft in Class A airspace must conduct that operation under instrument flight rules. (PLT162, CA.I.E.K1) — 14 CFR §91.135

Answer (A) is incorrect because if VOR navigational equipment is required, no person may operate a U.S.-registered civil aircraft at or above FL240 unless that aircraft is equipped with approved distance measuring equipment (DME). Answer (C) is incorrect because all aircraft must be equipped with an approved ATC transponder and altitude reporting equipment in airspace at and above 10,000 feet MSL, excluding the airspace at and below 2,500 feet above the surface.

ALL, MIL
5120-2. Which is true regarding flight operations in Class A airspace?

A—Aircraft must be equipped with approved distance measuring equipment (DME).
B—Aircraft must be equipped with an ATC transponder and altitude reporting equipment.
C—May conduct operations under visual flight rules.

Unless otherwise authorized by ATC, no person may operate an aircraft within Class A airspace unless that aircraft is equipped with an approved transponder and altitude reporting equipment. (PLT162, CA.I.E.K1) — 14 CFR §91.135

ALL, MIL
5576. The thinner outer magenta circle depicted around Class B Airspace is

A—the outer segment of Class B Airspace.
B—an area within which an appropriate transponder must be used from outside of the Class B Airspace from the surface to 10,000 feet MSL.
C—a Mode C "veil" boundary where a balloon may penetrate without a transponder, provided it remains below 10,000 feet MSL.

A balloon or glider may conduct operations in the airspace below the altitude of the ceiling of a Class B or Class C airspace area designated for an airport, or 10,000 feet MSL, whichever is lower. (PLT161, CA.I.E.K2) — Sectional Chart Legend

ALL, MIL
5572. (Refer to Figure 54, point 1.) What minimum altitude is required to avoid the Livermore Airport (LVK) Class D airspace?

A—2,503 feet MSL.
B—2,901 feet MSL.
C—3,297 feet MSL.

The Class D airspace at Livermore has a top of 2,900 feet MSL, indicated by the [29] within the blue segmented circle. Therefore, the minimum altitude to fly over and avoid the Class D airspace is 2,901 feet MSL. (PLT040, CA.I.E.K2) — AIM ¶3-2-5

Answer (A) is incorrect because 2,503 feet MSL would place you within the Class D airspace. Answer (C) is incorrect because although 3,297 feet MSL would keep you outside the Class D airspace, it is not the minimum altitude required to avoid it.

ALL, MIL
5572-1. (Refer to Figure 54.) What is the ceiling of the Class D Airspace of the Byron (C83) airport (area 2)?

A—2,900 feet.
B—7,600 feet.
C—Class D Airspace does not exist at Byron (C83).

Byron airport is surrounded by magenta shading, indicating Class E airspace with floor 700 feet above the surface. (PLT040, CA.I.E.K2) — Sectional Chart Legend

Answers

5119-3 [A]   5120-1 [B]   5120-2 [B]   5576 [C]   5572 [B]   5572-1 [C]

Chapter 5 **Procedures and Airport Operations**

ALL, MIL

5583. (Refer to Figure 52, point 6.) Van Vleck Airport is

A—an airport restricted to use by private and recreational pilots.
B—a restricted military stage field within restricted airspace.
C—a nonpublic use airport.

The "Pvt" after the airport name indicates Van Vleck Airport is a restricted or non-public use airport. (PLT101, CA.I.E.K2) — Sectional Chart Legend

Answer (A) is incorrect because the R in the circle indicates the airport is a nonpublic-use airport. Answer (B) is incorrect because the blue box near Van Vleck Airport indicates an alert area.

ALL, MIL

5584. (Refer to Figure 54, point 2.) After departing from Byron Airport (C83) with a northeast wind, you discover you are approaching Livermore Class D airspace and flight visibility is approximately 2-1/2 miles. You must

A—stay below 700 feet to remain in Class G and land.
B—stay below 1,200 feet to remain in Class G.
C—contact Livermore ATCT on 119.65 and advise of your intentions.

The magenta shading indicates Class E airspace begins at 700 feet. The VFR minimum in controlled airspace below 10,000 feet is 3 SM. Therefore, with 2-1/2 miles visibility, you must stay below 700 feet to remain in Class G airspace. (PLT064, CA.I.E.K2) — AIM ¶3-2-1

Answer (B) is incorrect because Class E space begins at 1,200 feet when surrounded by blue shading. Answer (C) is incorrect because 119.65 is ATIS for Livermore, not ATCT.

ALL, MIL

5587. (Refer to Figure 54, point 6.) The Class C airspace at Metropolitan Oakland International (OAK) which extends from the surface upward has a ceiling of

A—both 2,100 feet and 3,000 feet MSL.
B—10,000 feet MSL.
C—2,100 feet AGL.

The letter "T" denotes the ceiling of the Class C airspace which extends up to, but does not include the floor of the overlying Class B airspace. The Class C airspace normally extends upward to 4,000 feet AGL. However, in this case the Class C airspace extends upward to the base of the Class B airspace. The overlying Class B airspace has bases of 2,100 feet MSL, and 3,000 feet MSL. (PLT040, CA.I.E.K2) — Sectional Chart Legend

Answer (B) is incorrect because 10,000 feet is the ceiling of the Class B airspace over OAK. Answer (C) is incorrect because the Class C airspace ceiling on the west side of OAK is 2,100 feet MSL, and the ceiling on the east side is 3,000 feet MSL.

ALL, MIL

5569. (Refer to Figure 53, point 1.) This thin black shaded line is most likely

A—an arrival route.
B—a military training route.
C—a state boundary line.

The thin black shaded line is most likely a military training route (MTR). MTRs are normally labeled on sectional charts with either IR (IFR operations) or VR (VFR operations), followed by either three or four numbers. (PLT101, CA.I.E.K2) — Sectional Chart Legend

Answer (A) is incorrect because arrival routes are found on IFR charts. Answer (C) is incorrect because state boundaries are indicated by a thin black broken line.

ALL, MIL

5569-1. (Refer to Figure 53.) What is indicated by the star next to the "L" in the airport information box for the MADERA (MAE) airport north of area 2?

A—Special VFR is prohibited.
B—There is a rotating beacon at the field.
C—Lighting limitations exist.

The "L" with an asterisk indicates lighting limitations exist. Pilots should refer to the Chart Supplement for this airport for details on these limitations. (PLT162, CA.I.E.K2) — Sectional Chart Legend

ALL, MIL

5575. An alert area is an area in which

A—the flight of aircraft, while not prohibited, is subject to restriction.
B—the flight of aircraft is prohibited.
C—there is a high volume of pilot training activities or an unusual type of aerial activity, neither of which is hazardous to aircraft.

Alert Areas inform pilots of airspace that may contain a high volume of pilot training or an unusual type of aerial activity. While pilots should be particularly alert in these areas, there are no restrictions on flying through them. (PLT040, CA.I.E.K2) — Pilot/Controller Glossary

Answer (A) is incorrect because this describes a Restricted Area. Answer (B) is incorrect because this describes a Prohibited Area.

Answers

| 5583 | [C] | 5584 | [A] | 5587 | [A] | 5569 | [B] | 5569-1 | [C] | 5575 | [C] |

Chapter 5 **Procedures and Airport Operations**

ALL, MIL
5575-1. What must a pilot do or be aware of when transitioning an Alert Area?

A—All pilots must contact the controlling agency to ensure aircraft separation.
B—Non-participating aircraft may transit the area as long as they operate in accordance with their waiver.
C—Be aware that the area may contain unusual aeronautical activity or a high volume of pilot training.

Alert Areas inform pilots of airspace that may contain a high volume of pilot training or an unusual type of aerial activity. While pilots should be particularly alert in these areas, there are no restrictions on flying through them. (PLT376, CA.I.E.K3) — Pilot/Controller Glossary

ALL, MIL
5565. (Refer to Figure 52, point 1.) The floor of the Class E airspace above Georgetown Airport (Q61) is at

A—the surface.
B—700 feet AGL.
C—3,823 feet MSL.

Georgetown Airport is outside the magenta shaded area, which indicates the floor of Class E airspace is at 1,200 feet AGL. The airport elevation is given in the airport data as 2,623 feet MSL. Therefore, the Class E airspace above Georgetown Airport is 3,823 feet MSL (2,623 + 1,200). (PLT040, CA.I.E.K2) — Sectional Chart Legend

Answer (A) is incorrect because Class E airspace only begins at the surface when surrounded by a magenta segmented circle. Answer (B) is incorrect because Class E airspace begins at 700 feet AGL inside the magenta shaded areas.

ALL, MIL
5566. (Refer to Figure 52, point 7.) The floor of Class E airspace over the town of Woodland is

A—700 feet AGL over part of the town and no floor over the remainder.
B—1,200 feet AGL over part of the town and no floor over the remainder.
C—both 700 feet and 1,200 feet AGL.

Woodland has magenta shading over part of the town. Inside this magenta shading, Class E airspace begins at 700 feet AGL. Outside the magenta area, Class E airspace begins at 1,200 feet AGL. (PLT040, CA.I.E.K2) — Sectional Chart Legend

ALL, MIL
5567. (Refer to Figure 52, point 5.) The floor of the Class E airspace over University Airport (O05) is

A—the surface.
B—700 feet AGL.
C—1,200 feet AGL.

University Airport is within the magenta shading, which indicates the floor of the Class E airspace begins at 700 feet AGL. (PLT040, CA.I.E.K2) — Sectional Chart Legend

Answer (A) is incorrect because the Class E airspace would begin at the surface if the airport were surrounded by a magenta segmented circle. Answer (C) is incorrect because the Class E airspace would begin at 1,200 feet AGL if the airport were outside the magenta shaded area.

ALL, MIL
5568. (Refer to Figure 52, point 8.) The floor of the Class E airspace over the town of Auburn is

A—1,200 feet MSL.
B—700 feet AGL.
C—1,200 feet AGL.

Auburn is inside the magenta shading, which indicates the Class E airspace begins at 700 feet AGL. (PLT040, CA.I.E.K2) — Sectional Chart Legend

Answers (A) and (C) are incorrect because the Class E airspace would begin at 1,200 feet AGL (not MSL) if the airport were outside the magenta shaded area.

ALL, MIL
5570. (Refer to Figure 53, point 2.) The 16 indicates

A—an antenna top at 1,600 feet AGL.
B—the maximum elevation figure for that quadrangle.
C—the minimum safe sector altitude for that quadrangle.

The number 16 is a maximum elevation figure (MEF) which approximate and round-up from the highest known feature within each quadrangle. (PLT064, CA.I.E.K2) — Sectional Chart Legend

Answer (A) is incorrect because antennas are identified by obstruction symbols with the height above ground given in parentheses. Answer (C) is incorrect because minimum safe altitudes are not depicted on sectional charts.

Answers

| 5575-1 | [C] | 5565 | [C] | 5566 | [C] | 5567 | [B] | 5568 | [B] | 5570 | [B] |

Chapter 5 Procedures and Airport Operations

ALL, MIL
5581. (Refer to Figure 52, point 4.) The obstruction within 10 NM closest to Lincoln Regional Airport (LHM) is how high above the ground?

A—1,254 feet.
B—662 feet.
C—296 feet.

The obstruction south of the airport is 296 feet above the ground, which is the number in parenthesis. (PLT064, CA.I.E.K2) — Sectional Chart Legend

Answer (A) is incorrect because 1,245 is the height above sea level of the obstruction 8.5 NM east of the airport. Answer (B) is incorrect because 662 feet is the height above ground of the obstructions 8 NM southwest of the airport.

ALL, MIL
5581-1. (Refer to Figure 52, area 6.) What is the purpose of the star that follows the CT-120.65 in the information box for Sacramento Mather Airport (MHR)?

A—It means that the control tower has limited hours of operation.
B—The airport has maintenance facilities.
C—There is a rotating beacon on the field.

The star symbol indicates that control tower operation is part time only. (PLT484, CA.I.E.K2) — Sectional Chart Legend

ALL, MIL
5585. (Refer to Figure 52, point 4.) The terrain at the obstruction approximately 8 NM east southeast of the Lincoln Airport is approximately how much higher than the airport elevation?

A—376 feet.
B—827 feet.
C—1,135 feet.

```
  1,245 feet   MSL obstruction height
 –  297 feet   AGL
    948 feet   MSL terrain height at obstruction
 –  121 feet   MSL airport elevation
    827 feet   terrain height higher than airport elevation
```
(PLT064, CA.I.E.K2) — Sectional Chart Legend

ALL, MIL
5993. (Refer to Figure 52, Area 8). The traffic pattern altitude at the Auburn Airport (AUN) is 1,000 feet AGL. Can you practice landings under VFR when the AWOS is reporting a ground visibility of 2 miles?

A—Yes, you will be operating in a combination of Class E and G airspace.
B—No, the reported ground visibility must be at least 3 miles.
C—No, the Class E airspace extends to the airport surface.

Auburn is inside the magenta shading, which indicates that Class E airspace begins at 700 feet AGL. Therefore, you are operating in a combination of Class E and G airspace since the traffic pattern altitude is given to be 1,000 feet AGL. With no other visibility information given, other than 2 SM reported by the AWOS, you will need to assume that visibility in the Class E airspace above AUB will be less than the prescribed 3 SM minimum for VFR flight. (PLT163, CA.I.E.K2) – Sectional Chart Legend

ALL, MIL
5570-1. (Refer to Figure 53, Area 4.) You plan to depart on a day VFR flight from the Firebaugh (F34) airport. What is the floor of controlled airspace above this airport?

A—1,200 feet above the airport.
B—700 feet above the airport.
C—1,500 feet above the airport.

Firebaugh (F34) is inside the magenta shading, which indicates the Class E airspace begins at 700 feet AGL. (PLT161, CA.I.E.K2) — Sectional Chart Legend

ALL, MIL
5994. (Refer to Figure 52, Area 2.) When departing the Rio Linda Airport (L36) to the northwest at an altitude of 1,000 feet AGL, you

A—must make contact with the McClellan (MCC) control tower as soon as practical after takeoff.
B—are not required to contact any ATC facilities if you do not enter the Class C Airspace.
C—must make contact with the Sacramento Intl (SMF) control tower immediately after takeoff.

Rio Linda (L36) is within Class E airspace at the surface and within Class C airspace starting at 1,600 feet MSL. Departing to the northwest, you will enter Class C airspace at the surface and must contact Sacramento Intl (SMF) control tower immediately after takeoff prior to entering the Class C airspace. (PLT370, CA.I.E.K2) — Sectional Chart Legend

Answers

| 5581 | [C] | 5581-1 | [A] | 5585 | [B] | 5993 | [B] | 5570-1 | [B] | 5994 | [C] |

ALL, MIL

5577. When a dashed blue circle surrounds an airport on a sectional aeronautical chart, it will depict the boundary of

A—Special VFR airspace.
B—Class B airspace
C—Class D airspace.

Class D airspace areas are depicted on Sectional and Terminal charts with blue segmented lines. (PLT064, CA.I.E.K2) — AIM ¶3-2-5

Answer (A) is incorrect because no special VFR airspace is designated by a "NO SVFR" notation in the airport data block of the sectional. Answer (B) is incorrect because Class B airspace is depicted by a solid blue line.

AIR, MIL

5088. When operating an airplane for the purpose of landing or takeoff within Class D airspace under special VFR, what minimum distance from clouds and what visibility are required?

A—Remain clear of clouds, and the ground visibility must be at least 1 SM.
B—500 feet beneath clouds, and the ground visibility must be at least 1 SM.
C—Remain clear of clouds, and the flight visibility must be at least 1 NM.

No person may operate an airplane within Class D airspace under Special VFR unless they remain clear of clouds and the ground visibility must be at least 1 SM. (PLT163, CA.I.E.K1) — 14 CFR §91.157

Answer (B) is incorrect because the cloud clearance for Special VFR is clear of clouds. Answer (C) is incorrect because if ground visibility is not reported, flight visibility during landing or takeoff must be at least 1 SM.

AIR, MIL

5089. At some airports located in Class D airspace where ground visibility is not reported, takeoffs and landings under special VFR are

A—not authorized.
B—authorized by ATC if the flight visibility is at least 1 SM.
C—authorized only if the ground visibility is observed to be at least 3 SM.

No person may operate an airplane within Class D airspace under Special VFR unless they remain clear of clouds and the ground visibility must be at least 1 SM. If ground visibility is not reported at that airport, flight visibility during landing or takeoff must be at least 1 SM. (PLT467, CA.I.E.K1) — 14 CFR §91.157

Answer (A) is incorrect because Special VFR is authorized if flight visibility is at least 1 SM. Answer (C) is incorrect because the visibility requirement for Special VFR is 1 SM.

AIR, MIL

5090. To operate an airplane under SPECIAL VFR (SVFR) within Class D airspace at night, which is required?

A—The pilot must hold an instrument rating, but the airplane need not be equipped for instrument flight, as long as the weather will remain at or above SVFR minimums.
B—The Class D airspace must be specifically designated as a night SVFR area.
C—The pilot must hold an instrument rating and the airplane must be equipped for instrument flight.

No person may operate an airplane in Class D airspace under Special VFR at night unless that person is instrument rated, and the airplane is equipped for instrument flight. (PLT467, CA.I.E.K1) — 14 CFR §91.157

Answer (A) is incorrect because the airplane must be equipped for instrument flight. Answer (B) is incorrect because there is no such designation as "night SVFR area."

AIR, GLI, LTA, MIL

5116-1. When approaching to land at an airport, without an operating control tower, in Class G airspace, the pilot should

A—make all turns to the left, unless otherwise indicated.
B—fly a left-hand traffic pattern at 800 feet AGL.
C—enter and fly a traffic pattern at 800 feet AGL.

When approaching to land at an airport without an operating control tower in a Class G airspace area each pilot of an airplane must make all turns of that airplane to the left unless the airport displays approved light signals or visual markings indicating that turns should be made to the right, in which case the pilot must make all turns to the right. (PLT435, CA.I.E.K1) — 14 CFR §91.126

Answers

5577 [C]   5088 [A]   5089 [B]   5090 [C]   5116-1 [A]

Chapter 5 **Procedures and Airport Operations**

RTC, MIL

5116-2. When approaching to land at an airport, without an operating control tower, in Class G airspace, a helicopter pilot should

A—avoid the flow of fixed-wing aircraft.
B—make all turns to the left, unless otherwise indicated.
C—enter and fly a traffic pattern at 800 feet AGL.

Each pilot of a helicopter must avoid the flow of fixed-wing aircraft. (PLT435, MC.II.A.K1) — 14 CFR §91.126

LTA

5574-1. (Refer to Figure 54, point 1.) A balloon flight over Livermore Airport (LVK) at 3,000 feet MSL

A—requires a transponder, but ATC communication is not necessary.
B—does not require a transponder or ATC communication.
C—cannot be accomplished without meeting all Class B airspace requirements.

Aircraft operating within the Mode C veil must be equipped with automatic pressure altitude reporting requirement having Mode C capability. However, aircraft that was not originally certificated with an engine-driven electrical system or which has not subsequently been certified with a system installed, may conduct operations within a Mode C veil provided the aircraft remains outside Class A, B, or C airspace, and below the altitude of the ceiling of a Class B or Class C airspace area designated for an airport or 10,000 feet MSL, whichever is lower. (PLT040) — AIM ¶3-2-1

RTC, MIL

5574-2. (Refer to Figure 54, point 1.) A helicopter flight over Livermore Airport (LVK) at 3,000 feet MSL

A—requires a transponder, but ATC communication is not necessary.
B—does not require a transponder or ATC communication.
C—cannot be accomplished without meeting all Class B airspace requirements.

At 3,000 feet MSL, the flight is above the Class D airspace, but within the 30-mile ring of San Francisco. Therefore, a transponder is required since the flight is in Class E airspace, but no communication is required since the flight is outside the Class B airspace (PLT040) — AIM ¶3-2-1

ALL, MIL

5574-3. If a military training route has flights operating at or below 1,500 feet AGL, it will be designated by

A—VR and a three digit number only.
B—IR or VR and a four digit number.
C—IR or VR and a three digit number.

Military Training Routes (MTRs) in which flights are conducted at or below 1,500 feet AGL are designated by the letters IR or VR and a four-digit number. (PLT393, MC.II.A.K1) — AIM ¶3-5-2

ALL, MIL

5995. (Refer to Figure 53.) You are planning a VFR westbound flight departing the Fresno Chandler Executive Airport (FCH) and you will be passing through the active Lemoore C and A MOAs. What action should you take?

A—Exercise extreme caution while in the boundaries of the MOA.
B—Avoid the MOA, VFR, and IFR flights are prohibited during day light hours.
C—Contact the aircraft operating in the MOA on the Guard frequency of 121.5.

Pilots operating under VFR should exercise extreme caution while flying within an MOA when military activity is being conducted. The activity status (active/inactive) of MOAs may change frequently. Therefore, pilots should contact any FSS within 100 miles of the area to obtain accurate real-time information concerning the MOA hours of operation. Prior to entering an active MOA, pilots should contact the controlling agency for traffic advisories. (PLT376, CA.I.E.K3) – AIM ¶3-4-5

ALL, MIL

5996. (Refer to Figure 54, Area 3.) What is the significance of R-2531? This is a restricted area

A—for IFR aircraft.
B—where aircraft may never operate.
C—where often invisible hazards exist.

Restricted Areas denote the presence of unusual, often invisible, hazards to aircraft such as artillery firing, aerial gunnery, or guided missiles. Penetration of Restricted Areas without authorization of the using or controlling agency may be extremely hazardous to the aircraft and its occupants. (PLT376, CA.I.E.K3) — AIM ¶3-4-3

Answers

| 5116-2 [A] | 5574-1 [B] | 5574-2 [A] | 5574-3 [B] | 5995 [A] | 5996 [C] |

Chapter 5 **Procedures and Airport Operations**

ALL, MIL
5083-1. Your VFR flight will be conducted above 10,000 MSL in Class E airspace. What is the minimum flight visibility?

A—3 NM.
B—5 SM.
C—1 SM.

The only area requiring 5 statute miles visibility is 10,000 feet MSL and up (when above 1,200 feet AGL). (PLT163, CA.I.E.K1) — 14 CFR §91.155

Basic VFR Weather Minimums

Rules governing flight under VFR have been adopted to assist the pilot in meeting their responsibility to see and avoid other aircraft. Minimum weather conditions and distance from clouds required for VFR flight are listed in Figure 5-2.

When operating within a Class B, C, D, or E airspace designated for an airport, the ceiling must not be less than 1,000 feet. If the pilot intends to land, take off, or enter a traffic pattern at an airport within the lateral boundaries of Class B, C, D, or E airspace designated for an airport, the ground visibility must be at least 3 miles at that airport. If ground visibility is not reported, 3 miles flight visibility is required.

Airspace	Flight Visibility	Distance from Clouds
Class A	Not Applicable	Not Applicable
Class B	3 statute miles	Clear of clouds
Class C	3 statute miles	500 feet below 1,000 feet above 2,000 feet horizontal
Class D	3 statute miles	500 feet below 1,000 feet above 2,000 feet horizontal
Class E Less than 10,000 feet MSL	3 statute miles	500 feet below 1,000 feet above 2,000 feet horizontal
At or above 10,000 feet MSL	5 statute miles	1,000 feet below 1,000 feet above 1 statute mile horizontal
Class G 1,200 feet or less above the surface (regardless of MSL altitude) Day, except as provided in § 91.155(b)	1 statute mile	Clear of clouds
Night, except as provided in § 91.155(b)	3 statute miles	500 feet below 1,000 feet above 2,000 feet horizontal
More than 1,200 feet above the surface but less than 10,000 feet MSL Day	1 statute mile	500 feet below 1,000 feet above 2,000 feet horizontal
Night	3 statute miles	500 feet below 1,000 feet above 2,000 feet horizontal
More than 1,200 feet above the surface and at or above 10,000 feet MSL	5 statute miles	1,000 feet below 1,000 feet above 1 statute mile horizontal

Figure 5-2. Basic VFR weather minimums

ALL, MIL
5083. The minimum flight visibility for VFR flight increases to 5 statute miles beginning at an altitude of

A—14,500 feet MSL.
B—10,000 feet MSL if above 1,200 feet AGL.
C—10,000 feet MSL regardless of height above ground.

The only area requiring 5 statute miles visibility is 10,000 feet MSL and up (when above 1,200 feet AGL). (PLT161, CA.I.E.K1) — 14 CFR §91.155

ALL, MIL
5121. When weather information indicates that abnormally high barometric pressure exists, or will be above _____ inches of mercury, flight operations will not be authorized contrary to the requirements published in NOTAMs.

A—31.00
B—32.00
C—30.50

Special flight restrictions exist when any information indicates that barometric pressure on the route of flight currently exceeds or will exceed 31 inches of mercury, and no person may operate an aircraft or initiate a flight contrary to the requirements established by the Administrator and published in a Notice to Air Missions. (PLT323, CA.I.E.K1) — 14 CFR §91.144

Answers

5083-1 [B]   5083 [B]   5121 [A]

Chapter 5 **Procedures and Airport Operations**

ALL, MIL
5588. (Refer to Figure 53.)
GIVEN:

Location .... Madera Airport (MAE)
Altitude .... 1,000 ft AGL
Position .... 7 NM north of Madera (MAE)
Time .... 3 p.m. local
Flight visibility .... 1 SM

You are VFR approaching Madera Airport for a landing from the north. You

A—are in violation of the CFRs; you need 3 miles of visibility under VFR.
B—are required to descend to below 700 feet AGL to remain clear of Class E airspace and may continue for landing.
C—may descend to 800 feet AGL (Pattern Altitude) after entering Class E airspace and continue to the airport.

At 7 NM north of Madera, you are outside the magenta shading, which indicates the floor of the Class E airspace is 1,200 feet AGL. At 1,000 feet, you are in Class G airspace. During daylight hours, the minimum flight visibility for VFR flight is 1 SM. Inside the magenta shading, the floor of the Class E airspace drops to 700 feet. Therefore, to remain VFR, you must remain in Class G airspace, which requires you to descend below 700 feet before entering the Class E airspace to continue for landing. (PLT040, CA.I.E.K2) — 14 CFR §91.155

Answer (A) is incorrect because only 1 SM visibility is necessary to remain VFR in Class G airspace at 1,000 feet AGL during daylight hours. Answer (C) is incorrect because you must descend below 700 feet AGL before entering Class E airspace to remain VFR.

AIR, LTA, GLI, MIL
5085. What is the minimum flight visibility and proximity to cloud requirements for VFR flight, at 6,500 feet MSL, in Class C, D, and E airspace?

A—1 mile visibility; clear of clouds.
B—3 miles visibility; 1,000 feet above and 500 feet below.
C—5 miles visibility; 1,000 feet above and 1,000 feet below.

In Class C, D, or E airspace at 6,500 feet MSL, the VFR flight visibility requirement is 3 SM. The distance from cloud requirement is 500 feet below, 1,000 feet above, and 2,000 feet horizontal. (PLT163, CA.I.E.K1) — 14 CFR §91.155

Answer (A) is incorrect because 1 SM visibility and clear of clouds is the VFR weather minimum when at or below 1,200 feet AGL in Class G airspace during the day. Answer (C) is incorrect because 5 SM visibility and cloud clearance of 1,000 feet above and below is the VFR weather minimum in Class E airspace at or above 10,000 feet MSL.

Operations on Wet or Slippery Runways

When taking off from a slippery runway, delay full-power checks until the aircraft is lined up on the runway and ready for takeoff.

After takeoff from a slushy runway, the landing gear should be cycled up and down to minimize the possibility of the gear being frozen in the up position. If departing from an airstrip with wet snow or slush on the takeoff surface, the gear should not be retracted immediately so that any wet snow or slush is allowed to air-dry.

AIR
5768. When departing from a runway that is covered with snow or slush, what can a pilot do to prevent damage to the landing gear due to the conditions?

A—Do not retract the landing gear immediately to allow the gear to air-dry.
B—Immediately retract the landing gear so it can be heated in the gear wells.
C—Fly at a speed above the green arc of the airspeed indicator can remove the snow and slush.

If departing from an airstrip with wet snow or slush on the takeoff surface, the gear should not be retracted immediately so that any wet snow or slush is allowed to air-dry (PLT126, CA.I.G.K1d) — FAA-H-8083-3

Answers

5588 [B]   5085 [B]   5768 [A]

Land and Hold Short Operations (LAHSO)

LAHSO operations include landing and holding short of an intersecting runway, an intersecting taxiway, or some other designated point on a runway other than an intersecting runway or taxiway. LAHSO is an ATC procedure that requires pilot participation to balance the needs for increased airport capacity and system efficiency, consistent with safety. Student pilots or pilots not familiar with LAHSO should not participate in the program. The pilot-in-command has the final authority to accept or decline any land and hold short clearance. The safety and operation of the aircraft remain the responsibility of the pilot. Pilots are expected to decline a LAHSO clearance if they determine it will compromise safety. Available landing distance (ALD) data is published in the special notices section of the Chart Supplements U.S. and in the U.S. Terminal Procedures Publications. Pilots should only receive a LAHSO clearance when there is a minimum ceiling of 1,000 feet and 3 statute miles visibility. The intent of having "basic" VFR weather conditions is to allow pilots to maintain visual contact with other aircraft and ground vehicle operations.

ALL
5138. Who has the final authority to accept or decline any "land and hold short" (LAHSO) clearance?

A—ATC tower controller.
B—ATC approach controller.
C—Pilot-in-command.

The pilot-in-command has the final authority to accept or decline any land and hold short clearance. The safety and operation of the aircraft remain the responsibility of the pilot. (PLT444, CA.IV.B.R3b) — AIM ¶4-3-11

ALL
5139. When should pilots decline a "land and hold short" (LAHSO) clearance?

A—When it will compromise safety.
B—If runway surface is contaminated.
C—Only when the tower controller concurs.

Pilots are expected to decline a LAHSO clearance if they determine it will compromise safety. (PLT140, CA.IV.B.R3b) — AIM ¶4-3-11

ALL
5139-1. A "land and hold short" (LAHSO) clearance

A—precludes a "Go Around" by ATC.
B—does not preclude a rejected landing.
C—requires a runway exit at the first taxiway.

A LAHSO clearance, once accepted, must be adhered to, just as any other ATC clearance, unless an amended clearance is obtained or an emergency occurs. A LAHSO clearance does not preclude a rejected landing. (PLT140, CA.IV.B.R3b) — AIM ¶4-3-11

ALL
5140. What is the minimum visibility and ceiling required for a pilot to receive a "land and hold short" clearance?

A—3 statute miles and 1,000 feet.
B—3 nautical miles and 1,000 feet.
C—3 statute miles and 1,500 feet.

Pilots should only receive a LAHSO clearance when there is a minimum ceiling of 1,000 feet and 3 statute miles visibility. The intent of having "basic" VFR weather conditions is to allow pilots to maintain visual contact with other aircraft and ground vehicle operations. (PLT140, CA.IV.B.R3b) — AIM ¶4-3-11

ALL
5972. Once a pilot-in-command accepts a "land and hold short" (LAHSO) clearance, the clearance must be adhered to, just as any other ATC clearance, unless

A—an amended clearance is obtained or an emergency occurs.
B—the wind changes or Available Landing Distance decreases.
C—Available Landing Distance decreases or density altitude increases.

Once accepted, a LAHSO clearance must be adhered to unless an amended clearance is obtained or an emergency occurs. (PLT140, CA.IV.B.R3b) — AIM ¶4-3-11

ALL
5656-1. When should pilots decline a "land and hold short" (LAHSO) clearance?

A—Only when the tower controller concurs.
B—If runway surface is contaminated.
C—When it will compromise safety.

Answers

| 5138 | [C] | 5139 | [A] | 5139-1 | [B] | 5140 | [A] | 5972 | [A] | 5656-1 | [C] |

Pilots are expected to decline a LAHSO clearance if they determine it will compromise safety. (PLT140, CA.IV.B.R3b) — AIM ¶4-3-11

ALL
5656-2. What is the minimum visibility and ceiling required for a pilot to receive a "land and hold short" clearance?

A—3 statute miles and 1,500 feet.
B—3 nautical miles and 1,000 feet.
C—3 statute miles and 1,000 feet.

Pilots should only receive a LAHSO clearance when there is a minimum ceiling of 1,000 feet and 3 statute miles visibility. The intent of having "basic" VFR weather conditions is to allow pilots to maintain visual contact with other aircraft and ground vehicle operations. (PLT140, CA.IV.B.R3b) — AIM ¶4-3-11

ALL
5976. What should you consider when planning to land at another airport?

A—Land and hold short procedures.
B—Check for airport and touchdown markings.
C—Airport lighting using continuous wiring.

As part of the preflight planning process, pilots should determine if their destination airport has LAHSO. If so, their preflight planning process should include an assessment of which LAHSO combinations would work given their aircraft's required landing distance. Good pilot decision making is knowing in advance whether or not one can accept a LAHSO clearance if it is offered. (PLT140, CA.IV.B.R3b) — AIM ¶4-3-11

ALL
5656-3. What should you expect when you are told that LAHSO operations are in effect at your destination airport?

A—All aircraft must operate on an IFR clearance due to high traffic volume.
B—That ATC will give you a clearance to land and hold short of a specified point on the runway.
C—Delays due to low IFR conditions and high traffic volume.

Land and Hold Short Operations (LAHSO) are air traffic control procedures to balance the needs for increased airport capacity and system efficiency, consistent with safety. (PLT140, CA.IV.B.R3b) — AIM ¶4-3-11

Answer (A) is incorrect because LAHSO clearances are also available to aircraft operating VFR. Answer (C) is incorrect because LAHSO are found at high density airports and are not due to IFR conditions.

Airport Marking Aids and Signs

You must be familiar with the markings and signs used at airports, which provide directions and assist pilots in airport operations. Chapter 12 of the *Pilot's Handbook of Aeronautical Knowledge* (FAA-H-8083-25) and Chapter 2, Section 3 of the *Aeronautical Information Manual* are excellent resources for learning this subject. Some of the most common markings and signs are included in the Airman Knowledge Testing Supplement for Commercial Pilot (CT-8080-1D) that shipped with this Test Prep. You can expect questions that will test your knowledge of Figures 56 through 65:

Figure 56 #1 depicts an outbound destination sign, which defines directions to takeoff runways. #2 is a mandatory instruction sign, typically used as a holding position sign at the beginning of takeoff runways.

Figure 57 depict direction and destination signs, which provide information on locating areas such as runways, terminals, cargo areas, and the intersecting taxiway(s) leading out of an intersection.

Figure 58 shows an airport diagram with a mandatory instruction sign. This sign denotes an entrance to a runway, a critical area, or a prohibited area. It is frequently used as a taxiway/runway hold position sign.

Figure 59 shows a taxiway diagram and a direction sign array, which identifies location in conjunction with multiple intersecting taxiways. When more than one taxiway designation is shown on the sign, each designation and its associated arrow is separated from the other taxiway designations by either a vertical message divider or a taxiway location sign.

Answers

5656-2 [C]   5976 [A]   5656-3 [B]

Chapter 5 **Procedures and Airport Operations**

Figure 60 #1 is a taxiway ending marker, which indicates the taxiway does not continue. #2 is a direction sign array, which identifies location in conjunction with multiple intersecting taxiways.

Figure 61 is a direction sign array, with the boxed A in the middle being the taxiway location sign.

Figure 62 is a direction sign array without a location sign included. Direction signs have a yellow background with a black inscription. The black inscription identifies the designation(s) of the intersecting taxiway(s) leading out of the intersection that a pilot would normally be expected to turn onto or hold short of. Each designation is accompanied by an arrow indicating the direction of the turn.

Figure 63 is a direction sign array, with the boxed A in the middle being the taxiway location sign. Orientation of signs are from left to right in a clockwise manner. Left turn signs are on the left of the location sign and right turn signs are on the right side of the location sign.

Figure 64 is a mandatory instruction sign. It is a runway/runway hold position sign, which includes where you must hold short of intersecting runway.

Figure 65 is a taxiway ending marker, which indicates the taxiway does not continue.

A hot spot is a location on an airport movement area with a history or potential risk of collision or runway incursion, and where heightened attention by pilots and drivers is necessary. The FAA depicts hot spots in Chart Supplements with symbols using three shapes with two distinct meanings: a circle or ellipse for ground movement hot spots and a cylinder for wrong-surface hot spots. To address wrong-surface events where an aircraft lines up to or lands on the incorrect runway, taxiway, or airport, the FAA is releasing Arrival Alert Notices (AANs) at several airports with a history of misalignment risk. AANs include graphics that visually depict the approach to a particular airport with a history of misalignment risk and language that describes the misalignment risk. AANs incorporate the standardized hot spot symbology.

ALL
5964. The "taxiway ending" marker

A—indicates taxiway does not continue.
B—identifies area where aircraft are prohibited.
C—provides general taxiing direction to named taxiway.

Taxiway ending markers are used to indicate the taxiway does not continue. (PLT141, CA.II.D.K3) — FAA-H-8083-25

ALL
5970. (Refer to Figure 58.) You have requested taxi instructions for takeoff using Runway 16. The controller issues the following taxi instructions: "N123, Taxi to runway 16." Where are you required to stop in order to be in compliance with the controller's instructions?

A—5 (Five).
B—6 (Six).
C—9 (Nine).

When ATC clears an aircraft to "taxi to" an assigned takeoff runway, the absence of holding instructions does not authorize the aircraft to "cross" all runways which the taxi route intersects except the assigned takeoff runway. A clearance must be obtained prior to crossing any runway. It does not include authorization to "taxi onto" or "cross" the assigned takeoff runway at any point. You should taxi and hold short of runway 16, which is position 5. (PLT141, CA.II.D.K2) — AIM ¶4-3-18

Answer (B) is incorrect because "taxi to" does not authorize the aircraft to "taxi onto" the assigned takeoff runway. Answer (C) is incorrect because the airplane should taxi the most direct route to the assigned runway unless instructed otherwise; position 9 would not be encountered for the airplane at the west ramp to taxi to runway 16.

Answers

5964 [A]   5970 [A]

ALL
5659-1. (Refer to Figure 51.) While clearing an active runway you are most likely clear of the ILS critical area when you pass which sign?

A—Illustration D.
B—Illustration G.
C—Illustration H.

While clearing an active runway, you are most likely to be clear of the ILS critical area when you pass the sign depicted in illustration H. This is the ILS critical area boundary sign. (PLT141, CA.II.D.K3) — AIM ¶2-3-8, 2-3-9

Answer (A) is incorrect because this symbol prohibits aircraft entry into an area. Answer (B) is incorrect because Illustration G indicates you are most likely clear of the runway.

ALL
5145. (Refer to Figure 60.) Sign "1" is an indication

A—of an area where aircraft are prohibited.
B—that the taxiway does not continue.
C—of the general taxiing direction to a taxiway.

The black and yellow diagonal striped sign is a taxiway ending marker, which indicates the taxiway does not continue. (PLT141, CA.II.D.K3) — FAA-H-8083-25

AIR, RTC
5657. (Refer to Figure 51.) The pilot generally calls ground control after landing when the aircraft is completely clear of the runway. This is when the aircraft

A—passes the red symbol shown in illustration D.
B—is on the dashed-line side of Illustration G.
C—is past the solid-line side of Illustration G.

After landing, the pilot generally calls ground control when the aircraft is completely clear of the runway. This is when the aircraft is on the solid-line side of Illustration G. The solid lines always indicate the side on which the aircraft is to hold. (PLT141, CA.II.D.K3) — AIM ¶2-3-8, 2-3-9

Answer (A) is incorrect because Illustration D prohibits aircraft entry into an area. Answer (B) is incorrect because you are still on the runway if you are on the dashed-line side of Illustration G.

AIR, RTC
5658. (Refer to Figure 51.) Illustration D would most likely be found

A—upon exiting all runways prior to calling ground control.
B—at an intersection where a roadway may be mistaken as a taxiway.
C—near the approach end of ILS runways.

This sign prohibits an aircraft from entering an area. Typically, this sign would be located on a taxiway intended to be used in only one direction or at the intersection of vehicle roadways with runways, taxiways, or aprons where the roadway may be mistaken as a taxiway or other aircraft movement surface. (PLT141, CA.II.D.K3) — AIM ¶2-3-8, 2-3-9

Answer (A) is incorrect because this refers to Illustration G. Answer (C) is incorrect because this refers to Illustration H.

AIR, RTC
5659-2. (Refer to Figure 51.) When taxiing up to an active runway, you are likely to be clear of the ILS critical area when short of which sign?

A—Illustration H.
B—Illustration D.
C—Illustration G.

Illustration H is located adjacent to the ILS holding position marking on the pavement and can be seen by pilots leaving the critical area. The sign is intended to provide pilots with another visual cue which they can use as a guide in deciding when they are clear of the ILS critical area. (PLT141, CA.II.D.K3) — AIM ¶2-3-8, 2-3-9

Answer (B) is incorrect because this is the sign prohibiting aircraft entry into an area. Answer (C) is incorrect because this is a runway boundary sign.

AIR, RTC
5660. (Refer to Figure 51.) Which symbol does not directly address runway incursion with other aircraft?

A—Illustration D.
B—Illustration G.
C—Illustration H.

Illustration D prohibits an aircraft from entering an area. This sign would typically be located on one-way taxiways or a vehicle roadway. Thus, this sign does not directly address runway incursions with other aircraft. (PLT141, CA.II.D.K3) — AIM ¶2-3-8, 2-3-9

Answer (B) is incorrect because Illustration G is used to indicate when you are clear of the runway. Answer (C) is incorrect because Illustration H is used to indicate when you are clear of the ILS critical area.

Answers

| 5659-1 | [C] | 5145 | [B] | 5657 | [C] | 5658 | [B] | 5659-2 | [A] | 5660 | [A] |

Chapter 5 Procedures and Airport Operations

AIR, RTC, MIL

5748. Pilots are required to have the anti-collision light system operating

A—anytime an engine is in operation.
B—anytime the pilot is in the cockpit.
C—during all types of operations, both day and night.

Pilots of aircraft equipped with rotating beacons are encouraged to turn them on when intending to fly, as an alert to other aircraft and ground personnel. (PLT461, CA.II.D.K5) — AIM ¶4-3-23

Answers (A) and (B) are incorrect because lights are not needed if the pilot is simply sitting in the cockpit, or for example, if a mechanic is working on the aircraft and does not intend to taxi or fly.

ALL

5975. When turning onto a taxiway from another taxiway, what is the purpose of the taxiway directional sign?

A—Indicates direction to take-off runway.
B—Indicates designation and direction of exit taxiway from runway.
C—Indicates designation and direction of taxiway leading out of an intersection.

The taxiway directional sign identifies the designation(s) of the intersecting taxiway(s) leading out of the intersection that a pilot would normally be expected to turn onto or hold short of. (PLT141, CA.II.D.K3) — AIM ¶2-3-10

Answer (A) is incorrect because this is the purpose of the runway location sign. Answer (B) is incorrect because this is the purpose of the destination sign.

ALL

5980. The "yellow demarcation bar" marking indicates

A—runway with a displaced threshold that precedes the runway.
B—a hold line from a taxiway to a runway.
C—the beginning of available runway for landing on the approach side.

A demarcation bar delineates a runway with a displaced threshold from a blast pad, stopway or taxiway that precedes the runway. A demarcation bar is 3 feet (1 m) wide and yellow, since it is not located on the runway. (PLT141, CA.II.D.K3) — AIM ¶2-3-3

ALL

5981. The runway holding position sign is located on

A—runways that intersect other runways.
B—taxiways protected from an aircraft approaching a runway.
C—runways that intersect other taxiways.

Mandatory instruction signs are used to denote an entrance to a runway or critical area and areas where an aircraft is prohibited from entering. The runway holding position sign is located at the holding position on taxiways that intersect a runway or on runways that intersect other runways. (PLT141, CA.II.D.K3) — AIM ¶2-3-8

ALL

5982. "Runway Holding Position Markings" on taxiways

A—identify where aircraft are prohibited to taxi when not cleared to proceed by ground control.
B—identify where aircraft are supposed to stop when not cleared to proceed onto the runway.
C—allow an aircraft permission onto the runway.

Runway holding position markings indicate where an aircraft is supposed to stop. When used on a taxiway, these markings identify the locations where an aircraft is supposed to stop when it does not have clearance to proceed onto the runway. (PLT141, CA.II.D.K3) — AIM ¶2-3-8

ALL

5983. (Refer to Figure 57.) You are directed to taxi to runway 10. You see this sign at a taxiway intersection while taxiing. Which way should you proceed?

A—Left.
B—Right.
C—Straight ahead.

This destination sign indicates runway 10 is straight ahead. (PLT141, CA.II.D.K3) — AIM ¶2-3-11

Answers

| 5748 [C] | 5975 [C] | 5980 [A] | 5981 [A] | 5982 [B] | 5983 [C] |

ALL
5983-1. (Refer to Figure 51, A.) This taxiway sign would be expected

A—at the intersection of runway 04/22 departure end and the taxiway.
B—near the intersection of runways 04 and 22.
C—at a taxiway intersecting runway 04/22.

This question will likely include an onscreen graphic of a taxiway location sign with a direction sign or runway holding position sign. This type of sign is used at a taxiway intersection of runways. (PLT141, CA.II.D.K3) — AIM ¶2-3-9

ALL
5983-2. (Refer to Figure 61.) Ground control has instructed you to taxi from Alfa to Foxtrot to the active runway. According to the sign in the figure, which direction would you turn at this intersection to comply with ATC?

A—No turn is required.
B—The turn will be made to the right.
C—The turn will be made to the left.

Left turn signs are on the left of the location sign and right turn signs are on the right side of the location sign. Figure 61 indicates taxiway Foxtrot will be a left turn from Alfa. (PLT141, CA.II.D.K3) — AIM ¶2-3-10

ALL
5984. (Refer to Figure 64.) You see this sign when holding short of the runway. You receive clearance to back taxi on the runway for a full-length runway 8 departure. Which way should you turn when first taxiing on to the runway for takeoff?

A—Left.
B—Right.
C—Need more information.

The runway holding position sign contains the designation of the intersecting runways. The runway numbers are arranged to correspond to the respective runway threshold. For example, "26-8" indicates that the threshold for Runway 26 is to the left and the threshold for Runway 8 is to the right. (PLT141, CA.II.D.K3) — AIM ¶2-3-8

ALL
5999. You are preflight planning in the morning before an afternoon flight. Where would you find information regarding an "airport surface hot spot"?

A—Call the Automated Flight Service Station.
B—In the *Chart Supplements U.S.*
C—In the NOTAMs during your preflight briefing.

A hot spot is defined as a location on an airport movement area with a history of potential risk of collision or runway incursion, and where heightened attention by pilots and drivers is necessary. Hot spots are depicted on airport charts in the Chart Supplements U.S. (PLT281, CA.II.D.K1) — FAA-H-8083-25

ALL, MIL
5999-4. (Refer to Figure.) The segmented circle indicates that the airport traffic is

A—left-hand for runway 36 and right-hand for runway 18.
B—left-hand for runway 18 and right-hand for runway 36.
C—right-hand for runway 9 and left-hand for runway 27.

The traffic pattern indicators on a segmented circle are used to indicate the direction of turns. The traffic pattern indicators, shown as extensions from the segmented circle, represent the base and final approach legs. (PLT141, CA.II.D.K3) — AIM ¶4-3-3

Answers

5983-1   [C]   5983-2   [C]   5984   [B]   5999   [B]   5999-4   [A]

Chapter 5 **Procedures and Airport Operations**

VFR Cruising Altitudes

When operating an aircraft under VFR in level cruising flight more than 3,000 feet above the surface and below 18,000 feet MSL, a pilot is required to maintain an appropriate altitude in accordance with certain rules. This requirement is sometimes called the hemispherical cruising rule, and is based on magnetic course. See Figure 5-3.

Figure 5-3. VFR cruising altitudes

ALL, MIL

5091. VFR cruising altitudes are required to be maintained when flying

A—at 3,000 feet or more AGL, based on true course.
B—more than 3,000 feet AGL, based on magnetic course.
C—at 3,000 feet or more above MSL, based on magnetic heading.

In level cruise at more than 3,000 feet AGL, magnetic course determines proper altitude. (PLT467, CA.I.D.K2) — 14 CFR §91.159

Answers (A) and (C) are incorrect because VFR cruising altitudes are based on magnetic course and apply for flights above 3,000 feet AGL.

Collision Avoidance

Vision is the most important physical sense for safe flight. Two major factors that determine how effectively vision can be used are the level of illumination, and the technique of scanning the sky for other aircraft.

Scanning the sky for other aircraft is a key factor in collision avoidance. Pilots must develop an effective scanning technique, one that maximizes visual capabilities. Because the eyes focus on only a narrow viewing area, effective scanning is accomplished by systematically focusing with a series of short, regularly spaced eye movements. Each movement should not exceed 10°, and each area should be observed for at least one second. At night, scan slowly to permit off-center viewing (peripheral vision). Prior to starting any maneuver, a pilot should visually scan the entire area for other aircraft. Any aircraft that appears to have no relative motion and stays in one scan quadrant is likely to be on a collision course. If a target shows neither lateral or vertical motion, but increases in size, take evasive action.

When climbing or descending VFR on an airway, execute gentle banks, right and left, to provide for visual scanning of the airspace. Particular vigilance should be exercised when operating in areas where aircraft tend to converge, such as near airports and over VOR stations.

Atmospheric haze reduces the ability to see traffic or terrain during flight, making all features appear to be farther away than their actual distance.

In preparation for a **night flight**, the pilot should avoid bright white lights for at least 30 minutes before the flight.

Answers

5091 [B]

Chapter 5 Procedures and Airport Operations

ALL
5272. How can you determine if another aircraft is on a collision course with your aircraft?

A—The nose of each aircraft is pointed at the same point in space.
B—The other aircraft will always appear to get larger and closer at a rapid rate.
C—There will be no apparent relative motion between your aircraft and the other aircraft.

It is essential to remember that if another aircraft appears to have no relative motion, it is likely to be on a collision course with you. If the other aircraft shows no lateral or vertical motion, but increases in size, take evasive action. (PLT194, CA.VI.A.R1) — AC 90-48

ALL
5133. When planning a night cross-country flight, a pilot should check for

A—availability and status of en route and destination airport lighting systems.
B—red en route course lights.
C—location of rotating light beacons.

Prior to a night flight, and particularly a cross-country night flight, pilots should check the availability and status of lighting systems at the destination airport. (PLT141, CA.II.D.K3) — FAA-H-8083-3

ALL
5134. Light beacons producing red flashes indicate

A—end of runway warning at departure end.
B—a pilot should remain clear of an airport traffic pattern and continue circling.
C—obstructions or areas considered hazardous to aerial navigation.

Beacons producing red flashes indicate obstructions or areas considered hazardous to aerial navigation. (PLT141, CA.II.D.K3) — FAA-H-8083-3

ALL
5135. What is the first indication of flying into restricted visibility conditions when operating VFR at night?

A—Ground lights begin to take on an appearance of being surrounded by a halo or glow.
B—A gradual disappearance of lights on the ground.
C—Cockpit lights begin to take on an appearance of a halo or glow around them.

Generally, at night it is difficult to see clouds and restrictions to visibility, particularly on dark nights or under overcast. Usually, the first indication of flying into restricted visibility conditions is the gradual disappearance of lights on the ground. (PLT220, CA.I.C.K3l) — FAA-H-8083-3

Answers (A) and (C) are incorrect because ground (not cockpit) lights taking on the appearance of a halo or glow indicate ground fog.

ALL
5490. For night flying operations, the best night vision is achieved when the

A—pupils of the eyes have become dilated in approximately 10 minutes.
B—rods in the eyes have become adjusted to the darkness in approximately 30 minutes.
C—cones in the eyes have become adjusted to the darkness in approximately 5 minutes.

When entering a dark room, it is difficult to see anything until the eyes become adjusted to the darkness. After approximately 5 to 10 minutes, the cones become adjusted to the dim light and the eyes become 100 times more sensitive to the light than they were before the dark room was entered. Much more time, about 30 minutes, is needed for the rods to become adjusted to darkness; but when they do adjust, they are about 100,000 times more sensitive to light than they were in the lighted area. (PLT333, CA.I.H.K1) — FAA-H-8083-3

ALL
5491-2. When planning a night cross-country flight, a pilot should check for the availability and status of

A—all VORs to be used en route.
B—airport rotating light beacons.
C—destination airport lighting systems.

It is recommended that prior to a night flight, and particularly a cross-country night flight, the pilot check the availability and status of lighting systems at the destination airport. (PLT141, CA.I.D.K1) — FAA-H-8083-3

Answers

5272 [C] 5133 [A] 5134 [C] 5135 [B] 5490 [B] 5491-2 [C]

Chapter 5 **Procedures and Airport Operations**

ALL

5493. After experiencing a powerplant failure at night, one of the primary considerations should include

A—turning off all electrical switches to save battery power for landing.
B—maneuvering to, and landing on a lighted highway or road.
C—planning the emergency approach and landing to an unlighted portion of an area.

If the engine fails at night, one of the primary considerations includes planning an emergency approach and landing to an unlighted portion of the area. (PLT220, CA.IX.C.K1) — FAA-H-8083-3

ALL

5494. When planning for an emergency landing at night, on of the primary considerations should include

A—landing without flaps to ensure a nose-high landing attitude at touchdown.
B—turning off all electrical switches to save battery power for the landing.
C—selecting a landing area close to public access, if possible.

If the engine fails at night, one of the primary considerations includes selecting an emergency landing area close to public access if possible. This may facilitate rescue or help, if needed. (PLT220, CA.IX.B.K1) — FAA-H-8083-3

ALL, MIL

5749. When in the vicinity of a VOR which is being used for navigation on VFR flights, it is important to

A—make 90° left and right turns to scan for other traffic.
B—exercise sustained vigilance to avoid aircraft that may be converging on the VOR from other directions.
C—pass the VOR on the right side of the radial to allow room for aircraft flying in the opposite direction on the same radial.

Pilots should exercise increased caution when entering high use airspace; this includes the airspace around VORs. (PLT194, CA.VI.A.R1) — AIM ¶8-1-8

Answer (A) is incorrect because 90° turns are not appropriate while en route. Answer (C) is incorrect because you should try to maintain the center of the radial.

ALL

5758. To scan properly for traffic, a pilot should

A—slowly sweep the field of vision from one side to the other at intervals.
B—concentrate on any peripheral movement detected.
C—use a series of short, regularly spaced eye movements that bring successive areas of the sky into the central visual field.

Because the eyes can focus on only a narrow viewing area, effective scanning is accomplished with a series of short, regularly-spaced eye movements that bring successive areas of the sky into the central visual field. (PLT194, CA.VI.A.R1) — AIM ¶8-1-6

Answer (A) is incorrect because a pilot should systematically concentrate on different segments. Answer (B) is incorrect because peripheral movement is not easily detected, especially under adverse conditions; therefore this would not be an effective scanning technique.

Answers

5493 [C]   5494 [C]   5749 [B]   5758 [C]

Fitness Physiology

Pilot performance can be seriously degraded by a number of physiological factors. While some of the factors may be beyond the control of the pilot, awareness of cause and effect will minimize any adverse effects. The body has no built-in alarm system to alert the pilot of many of these factors.

Hypoxia, a state of oxygen deficiency (insufficient supply), impairs functions of the brain and other organs. Headache, sleepiness, dizziness, and euphoria are all symptoms of hypoxia. For optimum protection, pilots should avoid flying above 10,000 feet MSL for prolonged periods without breathing supplemental oxygen. Part 91 requires that when operating an aircraft at cabin pressure altitudes above 12,500 feet MSL up to and including 14,000 feet MSL, supplemental oxygen shall be used by the minimum flight crew during that time in excess of 30 minutes at those altitudes. Every occupant of the aircraft must be provided with supplemental oxygen above 15,000 feet. If under the effects of hypoxia, time of useful consciousness decreases with altitude.

If rapid decompression occurs in a pressurized aircraft above 30,000 feet, a pilot's time of useful consciousness is about 30 seconds. During a rapid decompression at high altitudes, the pilot should don the oxygen mask and begin a rapid descent to an appropriate lower altitude.

Aviation breathing oxygen should be used to replenish an aircraft oxygen system for high altitude flight. Oxygen used for medical purposes or welding should not be used because it may contain too much water. The excess water could condense and freeze in oxygen lines when flying at high altitudes, and this could block oxygen flow. Also, constant use of oxygen containing too much water may cause corrosion in the system. Specifications for aviator's breathing oxygen are 99.5% pure oxygen and not more than .005 mg of water per liter of oxygen. Never use grease- or oil-covered hands, rags, or tools while working with oxygen systems.

Hyperventilation, a deficiency (insufficient supply) of carbon dioxide within the body, can be the result of rapid or extra deep breathing due to emotional tension, anxiety, or fear. The common symptoms of hyperventilation include drowsiness, and tingling of the hands, legs, and feet. A pilot should be able to overcome the symptoms or avoid future occurrences of hyperventilation by talking aloud, breathing into a bag, or slowing the breathing rate.

Carbon monoxide is a colorless, odorless, and tasteless gas contained in exhaust fumes. Symptoms of **carbon monoxide poisoning** include headache, drowsiness, or dizziness. Large accumulations of carbon monoxide in the human body result in a loss of muscular power. Susceptibility to hypoxia due to inhalation of carbon monoxide increases as altitude increases. A pilot who detects symptoms of carbon monoxide poisoning should immediately shut off the heater and open the air vents.

Various complex motions, forces, and visual scenes encountered in flight may result in various sensory organs sending misleading information to the brain. **Spatial disorientation** may result if these body signals are used to interpret flight attitude. The best way to overcome spatial disorientation is by relying on aircraft instrument indications rather than taking a chance on the sensory organs.

Extensive research has provided a number of facts about the hazards of alcohol consumption and flying. Even a small amount of **alcohol** present in the human body can impair flying skills, judgment and decision-making abilities. Alcohol also renders a pilot much more susceptible to disorientation and hypoxia. The regulations prohibit pilots from performing crew member duties within 8 hours after drinking any alcoholic beverage (bottle to throttle) or while under the influence of alcohol. However, due to the slow destruction of alcohol, a pilot may still be under influence more than 8 hours after drinking a moderate amount of alcohol.

Fatigue is one of the most treacherous hazards to flight safety because it might not be discernible to a pilot until serious errors are made. Fatigue can be either acute (short-term) or chronic (long-term). Acute fatigue, a normal occurrence of everyday living, is the tiredness felt after long periods of physical and mental strain, including strenuous muscular effort, immobility, heavy mental workload, strong emotional pressure, monotony, and lack of sleep. Chronic fatigue occurs when there is not enough time for a full recovery from repeated episodes of acute fatigue. The underlying cause of chronic fatigue is generally not rest-related and may have deeper points of origin.

Rapid acceleration during takeoff can create the illusion of being in a nose-up attitude, and a disoriented pilot will push the aircraft into a nose-low, or dive attitude. Rapid deceleration caused by a quick reduction of the throttles can have the opposite effect, with the disoriented pilot pulling the aircraft into a nose-up, or stall attitude. An upsloping runway, upsloping terrain, or both, can create the illusion that the aircraft is at a higher altitude than it actually is. The pilot who does not recognize this illusion will fly a lower approach. A downsloping runway, downsloping approach terrain, or both can have the opposite effect.

Rain on the windscreen can create the illusion of greater height, and atmospheric haze causes the illusion of being a greater distance from the runway. The pilot who does not recognize these illusions will fly a lower approach.

In darkness, vision becomes more sensitive to light, a process called **dark adaptation**. Dark adaptation is impaired by exposure to cabin pressure altitudes above 5,000 feet, by carbon monoxide inhaled by smoking or from exhaust fumes, by deficiency in Vitamin A in the diet, and by prolonged exposure to bright sunlight.

ALL
5757. As hyperventilation progresses, a pilot can experience

A—decreased breathing rate and depth.
B—heightened awareness and feeling of well being.
C—symptoms of suffocation and drowsiness.

The common symptoms of hyperventilation are dizziness, nausea, hot and cold sensations, tingling of the hands, legs and feet, sleepiness, and finally, unconsciousness. (PLT332, CA.I.H.K1b) — AIM ¶8-1-3

Answer (A) is incorrect because hyperventilation is an increase of the breathing rate and depth. Answer (B) is incorrect because heightened awareness and feeling of well-being are symptoms of hypoxia.

ALL
5759. Which is a common symptom of hyperventilation?

A—Drowsiness.
B—Decreased breathing rate.
C—A sense of well-being.

The common symptoms of hyperventilation are dizziness, nausea, hot and cold sensations, tingling of the hands, legs and feet, sleepiness and finally unconsciousness. (PLT332, CA.I.H.K1b) — AIM ¶8-1-3

Answer (B) is incorrect because hyperventilation is an increase of the breathing rate. Answer (C) is incorrect because a feeling of well-being, or euphoria, is a symptom of hypoxia.

ALL
5760. Which would most likely result in hyperventilation?

A—Insufficient oxygen.
B—Excessive carbon monoxide.
C—Insufficient carbon dioxide.

As hyperventilation "blows off" excessive carbon dioxide from the body, a pilot can experience symptoms of light-headedness, suffocation, drowsiness, tingling of the extremities, and coolness and react to them with even greater hyperventilation. (PLT332, CA.I.H.K1b) — FAA-H-8083-25

Answer (A) is incorrect because insufficient oxygen is a symptom of hypoxia. Answer (B) is incorrect because excessive carbon monoxide will lead to carbon monoxide poisoning.

ALL
5761. Hypoxia is the result of which of these conditions?

A—Excessive oxygen in the bloodstream.
B—Insufficient oxygen reaching the brain.
C—Excessive carbon dioxide in the bloodstream.

Hypoxia is the result of insufficient oxygen in the bloodstream going to the brain. (PLT096, CA.I.H.K1a) — AIM ¶8-1-2

Answer (A) is incorrect because hypoxia is a lack of oxygen in the bloodstream. Answer (C) is incorrect because excessive carbon dioxide in the bloodstream is not a symptom of hypoxia.

Answers

5757 [C]   5759 [A]   5760 [C]   5761 [B]

ALL
5762. To overcome the symptoms of hyperventilation, a pilot should

A—swallow or yawn.
B—slow the breathing rate.
C—increase the breathing rate.

Hyperventilation can be relieved by consciously slowing the breathing rate. Talking loudly or breathing into a bag to restore carbon dioxide will effectively slow the breathing rate. (PLT332, CA.I.H.K1b) — FAA-H-8083-25

Answer (A) is incorrect because swallowing or yawning is used to relieve ear block. Answer (C) is incorrect because the breathing rate should be slowed to increase the amount of carbon dioxide in the blood.

ALL
5763. Which is true regarding the presence of alcohol within the human body?

A—A small amount of alcohol increases vision acuity.
B—An increase in altitude decreases the adverse effect of alcohol.
C—Judgment and decision-making abilities can be adversely affected by even small amounts of alcohol.

As little as one ounce of liquor, one bottle of beer, or four ounces of wine can impair flying skills. (PLT503, CA.I.H.K3) — AIM ¶8-1-1

Answer (A) is incorrect because all mental and physical activities will be decreased with even small amounts of alcohol in the bloodstream. Answer (B) is incorrect because the adverse effects of alcohol are increased as altitude is increased.

ALL
5763-1. To rid itself of all the alcohol contained in one beer, the human body requires about

A—1 hour.
B—3 hours.
C—4 hours.

As little as one ounce of liquor, one bottle of beer or four ounces of wine can impair flying skills, with the alcohol consumed in these drinks being detectable in the breath and blood for at least 3 hours. (PLT205, CA.I.H.K3) — AIM ¶8-1-1

ALL
5763-2. To rid itself of all the alcohol contained in one mixed drink, the human body requires about

A—1 hour.
B—2 hours.
C—3 hours.

As little as one ounce of liquor, one bottle of beer or four ounces of wine can impair flying skills, with the alcohol consumed in these drinks being detectable in the breath and blood for at least 3 hours. (PLT205, CA.I.H.K3) — AIM ¶8-1-1

ALL
5763-3. With a blood alcohol level below .04 percent, a pilot cannot fly sooner than

A—4 hours after drinking alcohol.
B—12 hours after drinking alcohol.
C—8 hours after drinking alcohol.

It is against regulations to operate an aircraft while under the influence of alcohol or drugs, or with an alcohol concentration of .04 percent or above, or within 8 hours of consuming alcohol. (PLT463, CA.I.H.K3) — 14 CFR §91.17

ALL
5763-4. You attended a party last night and consumed several glasses of wine. You are planning to fly your aircraft home and have been careful to make sure 8 hours have passed since your last alcoholic drink. You can make the flight now only if you are not under the influence of alcohol and your blood alcohol level is

A—below .04%.
B—below .08%.
C—0.0%.

It is against regulations to operate an aircraft while under the influence of alcohol or drugs, or with an alcohol concentration of .04 percent or above, or within 8 hours of consuming alcohol. (PLT463, CA.I.H.K3) — 14 CFR §91.17

Answers

| 5762 [B] | 5763 [C] | 5763-1 [B] | 5763-2 [C] | 5763-3 [C] | 5763-4 [A] |

Chapter 5 **Procedures and Airport Operations**

ALL
5764. Hypoxia susceptibility due to inhalation of carbon monoxide increases as

A—humidity decreases.
B—altitude increases.
C—oxygen demand increases.

Carbon monoxide inhaled in smoking or from exhaust fumes, lowered hemoglobin (anemia), and certain medications can reduce the oxygen-carrying capacity of the blood to the degree that the amount of oxygen provided to body tissues will already be equivalent to the oxygen provided to the tissues when exposed to a cabin pressure altitude of several thousand feet. (PLT330, CA.I.H.K1a) — AIM ¶8-1-4

Answer (A) is incorrect because the humidity level does not have a bearing on carbon monoxide or oxygen levels. Answer (C) is incorrect because oxygen demand does not change.

AIR, RTC, LTA
5765. To best overcome the effects of spatial disorientation, a pilot should

A—rely on body sensations.
B—increase the breathing rate.
C—rely on aircraft instrument indications.

Spatial disorientation can be prevented only by visual reference to reliable fixed points on the ground or to flight instruments. (PLT334, CA.I.H.K1d) — FAA-H-8083-25

Answer (A) is incorrect because body sensations must be ignored. Answer (B) is incorrect because an increase in breathing rate could cause hyperventilation.

ALL
5765-1. To cope with spatial disorientation, pilots should rely on

A—body sensations and outside visual references.
B—adequate food, rest, and night adaptation.
C—proficient use of the aircraft instruments.

Spatial disorientation cannot be completely prevented, but it can and must be ignored or sufficiently suppressed by developing absolute reliance upon what the flight instruments are telling about the attitude of the aircraft. (PLT280, CA.I.H.K1d) — FAA-H-8083-25

ALL
5765-2. A pilot flying in a fatigued state is a hazard because

A—flying fatigued is flying impaired.
B—the pilot will hurry through checks and neglect items.
C—the pilot will exceed aircraft limitations to complete the flight.

Fatigue means a physiological state of reduced mental or physical performance capability resulting from lack of sleep or increased physical activity that can reduce a flightcrew member's alertness and ability to safely operate an aircraft or perform safety-related duties. (PLT104, CA.I.H.K1h) — 14 CFR §117.3

ALL
5998. You are most likely to experience somatogravic illusion during

A—a rapid descent.
B—deceleration upon landing.
C—rapid acceleration during takeoff.

A rapid acceleration during takeoff can create the illusion of being in a nose-up attitude. The disoriented pilot will push the aircraft into a nose-low, or dive attitude. This is called a somatogravic illusion. (PLT334, CA.I.H.K1d) — FAA-H-8083-25

Answers

| 5764 | [B] | 5765 | [C] | 5765-1 | [C] | 5765-2 | [A] | 5998 | [C] |

Chapter 5 **Procedures and Airport Operations**

Aeronautical Decision Making (ADM)

ADM is a systematic approach to the mental process used by aircraft pilots to consistently determine the best course of action in response to a given set of circumstances.

Risk management is the part of the decision making process which relies on situational awareness, problem recognition, and good judgment to reduce risks associated with each flight.

The ADM process addresses all aspects of decision making in the cockpit and identifies the steps involved in good decision making. Steps for good decision making are:

1. Identifying personal attitudes hazardous to safe flight.
2. Learning behavior modification techniques.
3. Learning how to recognize and cope with stress.
4. Developing risk assessment skills.
5. Using all resources in a multicrew situation.
6. Evaluating the effectiveness of one's ADM skills.

There are a number of classic behavioral traps into which pilots have been known to fall. Pilots, particularly those with considerable experience, as a rule always try to complete a flight as planned, please passengers, meet schedules, and generally demonstrate that they have the "right stuff." These tendencies ultimately may lead to practices that are dangerous and often illegal, and may lead to a mishap. All experienced pilots have fallen prey to, or have been tempted by, one or more of these tendencies in their flying careers. These dangerous tendencies or behavior patterns, which must be identified and eliminated, include:

- **Peer pressure.** Poor decision making based upon emotional response to peers rather than evaluating a situation objectively.
- **Mind set.** The inability to recognize and cope with changes in the situation different from those anticipated or planned.
- **Get-there-itis.** This tendency, common among pilots, clouds the vision and impairs judgment by causing a fixation on the original goal or destination combined with a total disregard for any alternative course of action.
- **Duck-under syndrome.** The tendency to sneak a peek by descending below minimums during an approach. Based on a belief that there is always a built-in "fudge" factor that can be used or on an unwillingness to admit defeat and shoot a missed approach.
- **Scud running.** Pushing the capabilities of the pilot and the aircraft to the limits by trying to maintain visual contact with the terrain while trying to avoid physical contact with it. This attitude is characterized by the old pilot's joke: "If it's too bad to go IFR, we'll go VFR."
- **Continuing VFR into IMC.** Often leads to spatial disorientation or collision with ground/obstacles. It is even more dangerous if the pilot is not instrument qualified or current.
- **Getting behind the aircraft.** Allowing events or the situation to control your actions rather than the other way around. Characterized by a constant state of surprise at what happens next.
- **Loss of positional or situation awareness.** Another case of getting behind the aircraft which results in not knowing where you are, an inability to recognize deteriorating circumstances, and/or the misjudgment of the rate of deterioration.
- **Operating without adequate fuel reserves.** Ignoring minimum fuel reserve requirements, either VFR or IFR, is generally the result of overconfidence, lack of flight planning, or ignoring the regulations.

- **Descent below the minimum enroute altitude.** The duck-under syndrome (mentioned above) manifesting itself during the enroute portion of an IFR flight.
- **Flying outside the envelope.** Unjustified reliance on the (usually mistaken) belief that the aircraft's high performance capability meets the demands imposed by the pilot's (usually overestimated) flying skills.
- **Neglect of flight planning, preflight inspections, checklists, etc.** Unjustified reliance on the pilot's short and long term memory, regular flying skills, repetitive and familiar routes, etc.

Each ADM student should take the Self-Assessment Hazardous Attitude Inventory Test in order to gain a realistic perspective on his/her attitudes toward flying. The inventory test requires the pilot to provide a response which most accurately reflects the reasoning behind his/her decision. The pilot must choose one of the five given reasons for making that decision, even though the pilot may not consider any of the five choices acceptable. The inventory test presents extreme cases of incorrect pilot decision making in an effort to introduce the five types of hazardous attitudes.

ADM addresses the following five hazardous attitudes:

1. **Antiauthority (don't tell me!).** This attitude is found in people who do not like anyone telling them what to do. In a sense they are saying "no one can tell me what to do." They may be resentful of having someone tell them what to do or may regard rules, regulations, and procedures as silly or unnecessary. However, it is always your prerogative to question authority if you feel it is in error. The antidote for this attitude is: Follow the rules. They are usually right.

2. **Impulsivity (do something quickly!)** is the attitude of people who frequently feel the need to do something—*anything*—immediately. They do not stop to think about what they are about to do, they do not select the best alternative, and they do the first thing that comes to mind. The antidote for this attitude is: Not so fast. Think first.

3. **Invulnerability (it won't happen to me).** Many people feel that accidents happen to others, but never to them. They know accidents can happen, and they know that anyone can be affected. They never really feel or believe that they will be personally involved. Pilots who think this way are more likely to take chances and increase risk. The antidote for this attitude is: It could happen to me.

4. **Macho (I can do it).** Pilots who are always trying to prove that they are better than anyone else are thinking "I can do it—I'll show them." Pilots with this type of attitude will try to prove themselves by taking risks in order to impress others. While this pattern is thought to be a male characteristic, women are equally susceptible. The antidote for this attitude is: taking chances is foolish.

5. **Resignation (what's the use?).** Pilots who think "what's the use?" do not see themselves as being able to make a great deal of difference in what happens to them. When things go well, the pilot is apt to think that's good luck. When things go badly, the pilot may feel that "someone is out to get me," or attribute it to bad luck. The pilot will leave the action to others, for better or worse. Sometimes, such pilots will even go along with unreasonable requests just to be a "nice guy." The antidote for this attitude is: I'm not helpless. I can make a difference.

Hazardous attitudes which contribute to poor pilot judgment can be effectively counteracted by redirecting that hazardous attitude so that appropriate action can be taken. Recognition of hazardous thoughts is the first step in neutralizing them in the ADM process. Pilots should become familiar with a means of counteracting hazardous attitudes with an appropriate antidote thought. When a pilot recognizes a thought as hazardous, the pilot should label that thought as hazardous, then correct that thought by stating the corresponding antidote.

If you hope to succeed at reducing stress associated with crisis management in the air or with your job, it is essential to begin by making a personal assessment of stress in all areas of your life. Good cockpit stress management begins with good life stress management. Many of the stress coping techniques practiced for life stress management are not usually practical in flight. Rather, you must condition yourself to relax and think rationally when stress appears. The following checklist outlines some thoughts on cockpit stress management.

1. Avoid situations that distract you from flying the aircraft.
2. Reduce your workload to reduce stress levels. This will create a proper environment in which to make good decisions.
3. If an emergency does occur, be calm. Think for a moment, weigh the alternatives, then act.
4. Maintain proficiency in your aircraft; proficiency builds confidence. Familiarize yourself thoroughly with your aircraft, its systems, and emergency procedures.
5. Know and respect your own personal limits.
6. Do not let little mistakes bother you until they build into a big thing. Wait until after you land, then "debrief" and analyze past actions.
7. If flying is adding to your stress, either stop flying or seek professional help to manage your stress within acceptable limits.

The DECIDE Model, comprised of a six-step process, is intended to provide the pilot with a logical way of approaching decision making. The six elements of the DECIDE Model represent a continuous loop decision process which can be used to assist a pilot in the decision making process when they are faced with a change in a situation that requires a judgment. This DECIDE Model is primarily focused on the intellectual component, but can have an impact on the motivational component of judgment as well. If a pilot practices the DECIDE Model in all decision making, its use can become very natural and could result in better decisions being made under all types of situations.

1. **D**etect. The decisionmaker detects the fact that change has occurred.
2. **E**stimate. The decisionmaker estimates the need to counter or react to the change.
3. **C**hoose. The decisionmaker chooses a desirable outcome (in terms of success) for the flight.
4. **I**dentify. The decisionmaker identifies actions which could successfully control the change.
5. **D**o. The decisionmaker takes the necessary action.
6. **E**valuate. The decisionmaker evaluates the effect(s) of his/her action countering the change.

ALL
5941. Risk management, as part of the Aeronautical Decision Making (ADM) process, relies on which features to reduce the risks associated with each flight?

A—The mental process of analyzing all information in a particular situation and making a timely decision on what action to take.
B—Application of stress management and risk element procedures.
C—Situational awareness, problem recognition, and good judgment.

Risk Management is the part of the decision making process which relies on situational awareness, problem recognition, and good judgment to reduce risks associated with each flight. (PLT022, CA.I.H.K4) — FAA-H-8083-2

Answers

5941 [C]

Chapter 5 **Procedures and Airport Operations**

ALL
5941-1. Risk management by the pilot

A—applies only on passenger/cargo IFR flights.
B—requires continuing education and certified academic training to understand the principles.
C—is improved with practice and consistent use of risk management tools.

Pilot management of risk is improved with practice and consistent use of basic and practical risk management tools. (PLT104, CA.I.H.K4) — FAA-H-8083-2

ALL
5942. Aeronautical Decision Making (ADM) is a

A—systematic approach to the mental process used by pilots to consistently determine the best course of action for a given set of circumstances.
B—decision making process which relies on good judgment to reduce risks associated with each flight.
C—mental process of analyzing all information in a particular situation and making a timely decision on what action to take.

ADM is a systematic approach to the mental process used by aircraft pilots to consistently determine the best course of action in response to a given set of circumstances. (PLT022, CA.I.H.K4) — FAA-H-8083-2

ALL
5943. The Aeronautical Decision Making (ADM) process identifies the steps involved in good decision making. One of these steps includes a pilot

A—making a rational evaluation of the required actions.
B—developing the "right stuff" attitude.
C—identifying personal attitudes hazardous to safe flight.

Steps for good decision making are: identifying personal attitudes hazardous to safe flight, learning behavior modification techniques, learning how to recognize and cope with stress, developing risk assessment skills, using all resources in a multicrew situation, and evaluating the effectiveness of one's ADM skills. (PLT022, CA.I.H.K4) — FAA-H-8083-2

ALL
5944. Examples of classic behavioral traps that experienced pilots may fall into are: trying to

A—assume additional responsibilities and assert PIC authority.
B—promote situational awareness and then necessary changes in behavior.
C—complete a flight as planned, please passengers, meet schedules, and demonstrate the "right stuff."

There are a number of classic behavioral traps into which pilots have been known to fall. Pilots, particularly those with considerable experience, as a rule always try to complete a flight as planned, please passengers, meet schedules, and generally demonstrate that they have the "right stuff." (PLT103, CA.I.H.R2) — FAA-H-8083-2

Answers (A) and (B) are incorrect because promoting situation awareness and then necessary changes in behavior and asserting PIC authority are positive pilot behaviors.

ALL
5945. The basic drive for a pilot to demonstrate the "right stuff" can have an adverse effect on safety, by

A—a total disregard for any alternative course of action.
B—generating tendencies that lead to practices that are dangerous, often illegal, and may lead to a mishap.
C—imposing a realistic assessment of piloting skills under stressful conditions.

Pilots, particularly those with considerable experience, as a rule always try to complete a flight as planned, please passengers, meet schedules, and generally demonstrate that they have the "right stuff." These tendencies ultimately may lead to practices that are dangerous and often illegal, and may lead to a mishap. (PLT103, CA.I.H.R2) — FAA-H-8083-2

Answers

5941-1 [C]   5942 [A]   5943 [C]   5944 [C]   5945 [B]

ALL
5946. Most pilots have fallen prey to dangerous tendencies or behavior problems at some time. Some of these dangerous tendencies or behavior patterns which must be identified and eliminated include:

A—Deficiencies in instrument skills and knowledge of aircraft systems or limitations.
B—Performance deficiencies from human factors such as, fatigue, illness or emotional problems.
C—Peer pressure, get-there-itis, loss of positional or situation awareness, and operating without adequate fuel reserves.

There are a number of classic behavioral traps into which pilots have been known to fall. These dangerous tendencies or behavior patterns, which must be identified and eliminated, include: peer pressure, mind set, get-there-itis, duck-under syndrome, scud running, continuing visual flight rules into instrument conditions, getting behind the aircraft, loss of positional or situation awareness, operating without adequate fuel reserves, descent below the minimum enroute altitude, flying outside the envelope, neglect of flight planning, preflight inspections, checklists, etc. (PLT103, CA.I.H.R2) — FAA-H-8083-2

ALL
5947. An early part of the Aeronautical Decision Making (ADM) process involves

A—taking a self-assessment hazardous attitude inventory test.
B—understanding the drive to have the "right stuff."
C—obtaining proper flight instruction and experience during training.

Each ADM student should take the Self-Assessment Hazardous Attitude Inventory Test in order to gain a realistic perspective on his/her attitudes toward flying. (PLT022, CA.I.H.R2) — FAA-H-8083-2

ALL
5948. Hazardous attitudes which contribute to poor pilot judgment can be effectively counteracted by

A—early recognition of hazardous thoughts.
B—taking meaningful steps to be more assertive with attitudes.
C—redirecting that hazardous attitude so that appropriate action can be taken.

Pilots should become familiar with a means of counteracting hazardous attitudes with an appropriate antidote thought. (PLT103, CA.I.H.R2) — FAA-H-8083-2

ALL
5949. What are some of the hazardous attitudes dealt with in Aeronautical Decision Making (ADM)?

A—Antiauthority (don't tell me), impulsivity (do something quickly without thinking), macho (I can do it).
B—Risk management, stress management, and risk elements.
C—Poor decision making, situational awareness, and judgment.

ADM addresses the following five hazardous attitudes: Antiauthority (don't tell me!), Impulsivity (do something quickly!), Invulnerability (it won't happen to me), Macho (I can do it), Resignation (what's the use?). (PLT022, CA.I.H.R2) — FAA-H-8083-2

ALL
5950. When a pilot recognizes a hazardous thought, he or she then should correct it by stating the corresponding antidote. Which of the following is the antidote for MACHO?

A—Follow the rules. They are usually right.
B—Not so fast. Think first.
C—Taking chances is foolish.

Macho pilots who are always trying to prove that they are better than anyone else are thinking "I can do it—I'll show them." Pilots with this type of attitude will try to prove themselves by taking risks in order to impress others. While this pattern is thought to be a male characteristic, women are equally susceptible. The antidote for this attitude is: taking chances is foolish. (PLT103, CA.I.H.R2) — FAA-H-8083-2

Answer (A) is incorrect because this is the antidote for an antiauthority attitude. Answer (B) is incorrect because this is the antidote for an impulsivity attitude.

ALL
5951. What is the first step in neutralizing a hazardous attitude in the ADM process?

A—Recognition of invulnerability in the situation.
B—Dealing with improper judgment.
C—Recognition of hazardous thoughts.

Hazardous attitudes which contribute to poor pilot judgment can be effectively counteracted by redirecting that hazardous attitude so that appropriate action can be taken. Recognition of hazardous thoughts is the first step in neutralizing them in the ADM process. (PLT103, CA.I.H.R2) — FAA-H-8083-2

Answers

| 5946 | [C] | 5947 | [A] | 5948 | [C] | 5949 | [A] | 5950 | [C] | 5951 | [C] |

Chapter 5 **Procedures and Airport Operations**

ALL
5952. What should a pilot do when recognizing a thought as hazardous?

A—Avoid developing this hazardous thought.
B—Develop this hazardous thought and follow through with modified action.
C—Label that thought as hazardous, then correct that thought by stating the corresponding learned antidote.

When a pilot recognizes a thought as hazardous, the pilot should label that thought as hazardous, then correct that thought by stating the corresponding antidote. (PLT103, CA.I.H.R2) — FAA-H-8083-2

ALL
5953. To help manage cockpit stress, pilots must

A—be aware of life stress situations that are similar to those in flying.
B—condition themselves to relax and think rationally when stress appears.
C—avoid situations that will improve their abilities to handle cockpit responsibilities.

Good cockpit stress management begins with good life stress management. Many of the stress coping techniques practiced for life stress management are not usually practical in flight. Rather, you must condition yourself to relax and think rationally when stress appears. (PLT272, CA.I.H.K1g) — FAA-H-8083-2

ALL
5954. What does good cockpit stress management begin with?

A—Knowing what causes stress.
B—Eliminating life and cockpit stress issues.
C—Good life stress management.

If you hope to succeed at reducing stress associated with crisis management in the air or with your job, it is essential to begin by making a personal assessment of stress in all areas of your life. (PLT272, CA.I.H.K1g) — FAA-H-8083-2

ALL
5955. The passengers for a charter flight have arrived almost an hour late for a flight that requires a reservation. Which of the following alternatives best illustrates the ANTIAUTHORITY reaction?

A—Those reservation rules do not apply to this flight.
B—If the pilot hurries, he or she may still make it on time.
C—The pilot can't help it that the passengers are late.

The antiauthority attitude is found in people who do not like anyone telling them what to do. In a sense, they are saying "no one can tell me what to do." They may be resentful of having someone tell them what to do or may regard rules, regulations, and procedures as silly or unnecessary. (PLT103, CA.I.H.R2) — FAA-H-8083-2

ALL
5956. While conducting an operational check of the cabin pressurization system, the pilot discovers that the rate control feature is inoperative. He knows that he can manually control the cabin pressure, so he elects to disregard the discrepancy. Which of the following alternatives best illustrates the INVULNERABILITY reaction?

A—What is the worst that could happen.
B—He can handle a little problem like this.
C—It's too late to fix it now.

The invulnerability attitude is found in people who feel accidents happen to others, but never to them. They know accidents can happen, and they know that anyone can be affected, but they never really feel or believe that they will be personally involved. Pilots who think this way are more likely to take chances and increase risk. (PLT103, CA.I.H.R2) — FAA-H-8083-2

ALL
5957. The pilot and passengers are anxious to get to their destination for a business presentation. Level IV thunderstorms are reported to be in a line across their intended route of flight. Which of the following alternatives best illustrates the IMPULSIVITY reaction?

A—They want to hurry and get going, before things get worse.
B—A thunderstorm won't stop them.
C—They can't change the weather, so they might as well go.

Answers

| 5952 | [C] | 5953 | [B] | 5954 | [C] | 5955 | [A] | 5956 | [A] | 5957 | [A] |

Impulsivity is the attitude of people who frequently feel the need to do something, anything, immediately. They do not stop to think about what they are about to do, they do not select the best alternative, and they do the first thing that comes to mind. (PLT103, CA.I.H.R2) — FAA-H-8083-2

ALL
5958. While on an IFR flight, a pilot emerges from a cloud to find himself within 300 feet of a helicopter. Which of the following alternatives best illustrates the MACHO reaction?

A—He is not too concerned; everything will be alright.
B—He flies a little closer, just to show him.
C—He quickly turns away and dives, to avoid collision.

The macho attitude is found in people who are always trying to prove they are better than anyone else. They are always thinking "I can do it, I'll show them." Pilots with this type of attitude will try to prove themselves by taking risks in order to impress others. (PLT104, CA.I.H.R2) — FAA-H-8083-2

ALL
5959. When a pilot recognizes a hazardous thought, he or she then should correct it by applying the corresponding antidote. Which of the following is the antidote for ANTIAUTHORITY hazardous attitude?

A—Not so fast. Think first.
B—It won't happen to me. It could happen to me.
C—Don't tell me. Follow the rules. They are usually right.

The antiauthority (don't tell me!) attitude is found in people who do not like anyone telling them what to do. The antidote for this attitude is: follow the rules, they are usually right. (PLT103, CA.I.H.R2) — FAA-H-8083-2

Answer (A) is incorrect because this is the antidote for the impulsivity attitude. Answer (B) is incorrect because this is the antidote for the invulnerability attitude.

ALL
5960. A pilot and friends are going to fly to an out-of-town football game. When the passengers arrive, the pilot determines that they will be over the maximum gross weight for takeoff with the existing fuel load. Which of the following alternatives best illustrates the RESIGNATION reaction?

A—Well, nobody told him about the extra weight.
B—Weight and balance is a formality forced on pilots by the FAA.
C—He can't wait around to de-fuel, they have to get there on time.

The resignation attitude is found in pilots who think, "what's the use?" They do not see themselves as being able to make a great deal of difference in what happens to them. When things go well, the pilot is apt to think that's good luck. When things go badly, the pilot may feel someone is out to get them, or attribute it to bad luck. The pilot will leave the action to others, for better or worse. Sometimes, such pilots will even go along with unreasonable requests just to be a "nice guy." (PLT103, CA.I.H.R2) — FAA-H-8083-2

ALL
5961. Which of the following is the final step of the Decide Model for effective risk management and Aeronautical Decision Making?

A—Estimate.
B—Evaluate.
C—Eliminate.

The DECIDE Model, comprised of a six-step process, is intended to provide the pilot with a logical way of approaching decision making: Detect, Estimate, Choose, Identify, Do, and Evaluate. (PLT022, CA.I.H.K4) — FAA-H-8083-2

ALL
5962. Which of the following is the first step of the Decide Model for effective risk management and Aeronautical Decision Making?

A—Detect.
B—Identify.
C—Evaluate.

The DECIDE Model, comprised of a six-step process, is intended to provide the pilot with a logical way of approaching decision making: Detect, Estimate, Choose, Identify, Do, and Evaluate. (PLT022, CA.I.H.K4) — FAA-H-8083-2

Answers

5958 [B]   5959 [C]   5960 [A]   5961 [B]   5962 [A]

Chapter 5 **Procedures and Airport Operations**

ALL
5963. The Decide Model is comprised of a 6-step process to provide a pilot a logical way of approaching Aeronautical Decision Making. These steps are:

A—Detect, estimate, choose, identify, do, and evaluate.
B—Determine, evaluate, choose, identify, do, and eliminate.
C—Determine, eliminate, choose, identify, detect, and evaluate.

The DECIDE Model, comprised of a six step process, is intended to provide the pilot with a logical way of approaching decision making: Detect, Estimate, Choose, Identify, Do, and Evaluate. (PLT022, CA.I.H.K4) — FAA-H-8083-2

Answers

5963 [A]

Chapter 6
Weather

The Earth's Atmosphere **6–3**

Temperature **6–6**

Wind **6–7**

Moisture **6–9**

Stable and Unstable Air **6–10**

Clouds **6–11**

Air Masses and Fronts **6–16**

Turbulence **6–17**

Icing **6–19**

Thunderstorms **6–21**

Fog **6–24**

Wind Shear **6–26**

Soaring Weather **6–29**

The Earth's Atmosphere

The major source of all weather is the sun. Every physical process of weather is accompanied by, or is a result of, unequal heating (heat exchange) of the Earth's surface. The heating of the Earth (and therefore the heating of the air in contact with the Earth) is unequal around the entire planet. Either north, south, east or west of a point directly under the sun, one square foot of sunrays is not concentrated over one square foot of the surface, but over a larger area. This lower concentration of sunrays produces less radiation (absorption) of heat over a given surface area and therefore, less atmospheric heating takes place in that area.

The unequal heating of the Earth's atmosphere creates a large air cell circulation pattern (wind) because the warmer air has a tendency to rise (low pressure) and the colder air has a tendency to settle or descend (high pressure) and replace the rising warmer air. This unequal heating, which causes pressure variations, will also cause variations in altimeter settings between weather reporting points.

Because the Earth rotates, this large, simple air cell circulation pattern is greatly distorted by a phenomenon known as the **Coriolis force**. When wind—which is created by pressure differences, horizontal pressure gradient, and high pressure trying to flow into low pressure—first begins to move at higher altitudes, the Coriolis force deflects it to the right (in the Northern Hemisphere). This causes it to flow parallel to the isobars (lines of equal pressure). The Coriolis force prevents air from flowing directly from high-pressure areas to low-pressure areas because it tends to counterbalance the horizontal pressure gradient. These deflections of the large-cell circulation pattern create general wind patterns as depicted in Figure 6-1.

The **jet stream** is a river of high-speed winds (by definition, 50 knots or more) associated with a layer of atmosphere called the tropopause. The tropopause is actually the boundary layer between the troposphere and the stratosphere. Within the troposphere, temperature decreases with altitude, while the stratosphere is characterized by relatively small temperature changes. The tropopause itself is found between the two layers and is marked by an abrupt change in the temperature lapse rate.

The troposphere varies in height from around 65,000 feet at the equator to about 20,000 feet over the poles, averaging about 37,000 feet in the mid-latitudes. It also is higher in the summer than in the winter. The height of the tropopause does not change uniformly, but rather tends to change in

Figure 6-1. Prevailing wind systems

"steps." The jet stream is often found at or near these steps. Since the tropopause height also changes with the seasons, the location of the jet stream changes seasonally. In the winter, the jet stream moves south and increases in speed, and during the summer, the jet stream moves north and decreases in speed.

The strong winds of the jet stream create narrow zones of wind shear which often generate hazardous turbulence. The jet stream maximum is not constant; rather, it is broken into segments, shaped something like a boomerang. Jet stream segments move with pressure ridges and troughs in the upper atmosphere.

A common location of **clear air turbulence (CAT)** and strong wind shear exists with a curving jet stream. This curve is created by an upper or lower low-pressure trough. The wind speed, shown by isotachs (lines of constant wind speed), decreases outward from the jet core. The greatest rate of decrease of wind speed is on the polar side as compared to the equatorial side. Strong wind shear and CAT can be expected on the low-pressure side or polar side of a jet stream where the speed at the core is greater than 110 knots. Air travels in a corkscrew path around the jet core with upward motion on the equatorial side. When high-level moisture is present, cirriform (cirrus) clouds may be visible, identifying the jet stream along with its associated turbulence.

ALL
5301. Every physical process of weather is accompanied by or is the result of

A—a heat exchange.
B—the movement of air.
C—a pressure differential.

The amount of solar energy received by any region varies with time of day, with seasons and with latitude. These differences in solar energy create temperature variation. Temperatures also vary with differences in topographical surface and with altitude. This temperature variation, or heat exchange, creates forces that drive the atmosphere in its endless motion. (PLT492, CA.I.C.K3) — AC 00-6

Answers (B) and (C) are incorrect because the movement of air and pressure differentials are caused by heat exchanges.

ALL
5310. What causes wind?

A—The Earth's rotation.
B—Air mass modification.
C—Pressure differences.

Differences in temperature create differences in pressure. These pressure differences drive a complex system of winds in a never-ending attempt to reach equilibrium. (PLT516, CA.I.C.K3b) — AC 00-6

ALL
5310-1. Density altitude is the vertical distance above mean sea level in the standard atmosphere at which

A—pressure altitude is corrected for standard temperature.
B—a given atmospheric density is to be found.
C—temperature, pressure, altitude, and humidity are considered.

Density altitude is the vertical distance above sea level in the standard atmosphere at which a given density is to be found. The density of air has significant effects on the aircraft's performance. (PLT127, CA.I.C.K3) — FAA-H-8083-25

ALL
5311. In the Northern Hemisphere, the wind is deflected to the

A—right by Coriolis force.
B—right by surface friction.
C—left by Coriolis force.

The Coriolis force deflects air to the right in the Northern Hemisphere. (PLT197, CA.I.C.K3b) — AC 00-6

ALL
5312. Why does the wind have a tendency to flow parallel to the isobars above the friction level?

A—Coriolis force tends to counterbalance the horizontal pressure gradient.
B—Coriolis force acts perpendicular to a line connecting the highs and lows.
C—Friction of the air with the Earth deflects the air perpendicular to the pressure gradient.

The pressure gradient force drives the wind and is perpendicular to isobars. When a pressure gradient force is first established, wind begins to blow from higher to lower pressure directly across the isobars. However, the instant air begins moving, Coriolis force deflects it to the right. Soon the wind is deflected a full 90° and is parallel to the isobars or contours. At this time, Coriolis force exactly balances pressure gradient force. With the forces in balance, wind will remain parallel to isobars or contours. (PLT197, CA.I.C.K3b) — AC 00-6

Answers

5301 [A]   5310 [C]   5310-1 [B]   5311 [A]   5312 [A]

ALL

5315. What prevents air from flowing directly from high-pressure areas to low-pressure areas?

A—Coriolis force.
B—Surface friction.
C—Pressure gradient force.

The pressure gradient force drives the wind and is perpendicular to isobars. When a pressure gradient force is first established, wind begins to blow from higher to lower pressure directly across the isobars. However, the instant air begins moving, Coriolis force deflects it to the right. Soon the wind is deflected a full 90° and is parallel to the isobars or contours. At this time, Coriolis force exactly balances pressure gradient force. With the forces in balance, wind will remain parallel to isobars or contours. (PLT197, CA.I.C.K3b) — FAA-H-8083-25

Answer (B) is incorrect because surface friction moves air from highs to lows by decreasing wind speed, which decreases the effect of the Coriolis force. Answer (C) is incorrect because the pressure gradient force causes the initial movement from high-pressure areas to low-pressure areas.

ALL

5356. Convective currents are most active on warm summer afternoons when winds are

A—light.
B—moderate.
C—strong.

Convective currents are most active on warm summer afternoons when winds are light. Heated air at the surface creates a shallow, unstable layer and the warm air is forced upward. Convection increases in strength and to greater heights as surface heating increases. (PLT516, CA.I.C.K3b) — AC 00-6

Answers (B) and (C) are incorrect because moderate and strong winds disrupt the vertical movement of convective currents.

ALL

5381. Which feature is associated with the tropopause?

A—Constant height above the Earth.
B—Abrupt change in temperature lapse rate.
C—Absolute upper limit of cloud formation.

As the thin boundary layer between the troposphere and the stratosphere, the tropopause signals an abrupt change in temperature lapse rate. (PLT203, CA.I.C.K3a) — AC 00-6

Answer (A) is incorrect because the tropopause is farther away from the Earth's surface at the equator than the poles. Answer (C) is incorrect because clouds may form above the tropopause.

ALL

5382. A common location of clear air turbulence is

A—in an upper trough on the polar side of a jet stream.
B—near a ridge aloft on the equatorial side of a high-pressure flow.
C—south of an east/west oriented high-pressure ridge in its dissipating stage.

Clear air turbulence (CAT) is greatest near the wind speed maxima, usually on the polar sides where there is a combination of strong wind shear, curvature in the flow, and cold air advection associated with sharply curved contours of strong lows, troughs and ridges aloft. A frequent location of CAT is in an upper trough on the cold, or polar side of the jet stream. (PLT263, CA.I.C.K3g) — AC 00-6

ALL

5383. The jet stream and associated clear air turbulence can sometimes be visually identified in flight by

A—dust or haze at flight level.
B—long streaks of cirrus clouds.
C—a constant outside air temperature.

Long streaks of cirrus clouds can sometimes help the pilot to visually identify the jet stream and associated clear air turbulence (CAT). (PLT076, CA.I.C.K3g) — AC 00-6

Answer (A) is incorrect because dust or haze indicates there is not enough wind or air movement to dissipate the particles. Answer (C) is incorrect because CAT is caused by mixing different air temperatures at different pressure levels.

ALL

5384. During the winter months in the middle latitudes, the jet stream shifts toward the

A—north and speed decreases.
B—south and speed increases.
C—north and speed increases.

In middle latitudes, the wind speed of the jet stream averages considerably higher in the winter months as it shifts farther south. (PLT302, CA.I.C.K3a) — AC 00-6

Answers

| 5315 | [A] | 5356 | [A] | 5381 | [B] | 5382 | [A] | 5383 | [B] | 5384 | [B] |

Chapter 6 **Weather**

ALL
5385. The strength and location of the jet stream is normally

A—weaker and farther north in the summer.
B—stronger and farther north in the winter.
C—stronger and farther north in the summer.

The jet stream is considerably weaker in the middle latitudes during the summer months, and is further north than in the winter. (PLT302, CA.I.C.K3a) — AC 00-6

ALL
5447. Which type of jetstream can be expected to cause the greater turbulence?

A—A straight jetstream associated with a low-pressure trough.
B—A curving jetstream associated with a deep low-pressure trough.
C—A jetstream occurring during the summer at the lower latitudes.

Curving jet streams, especially those which curve around a deep pressure trough, are more apt to have turbulent edges than straight jet streams. (PLT302, CA.I.C.K3g) — AC 00-30

Answer (A) is incorrect because a curving jet stream is stronger than a straight jet stream. Answer (C) is incorrect because the jet stream is weaker in the summer.

Temperature

In aviation, temperature is measured in degrees Celsius (°C). The standard temperature at sea level is 15°C (59°F). The average decrease in temperature with altitude (standard lapse rate) is 2°C (3.5°F) per 1,000 feet. Since this is an average, the exact value seldom exists; in fact, temperature sometimes increases with altitude—this is known as an inversion. The most frequent type of ground- or surface-based temperature inversion is one that is produced on clear, cool nights, with calm or light wind. See Figure 6-2.

ALL
5304. Which conditions are favorable for the formation of a surface based temperature inversion?

A—Clear, cool nights with calm or light wind.
B—Area of unstable air rapidly transferring heat from the surface.
C—Broad areas of cumulus clouds with smooth, level bases at the same altitude.

An inversion often develops near the ground on clear, cool nights when the wind is light. (PLT301, CA.I.C.K3c) — AC 00-6

Answer (B) is incorrect because the air near the surface must be stable to permit the cool ground to lower the temperature of the surrounding air. Answer (C) is incorrect because cumulus clouds are well above the surface.

Figure 6-2. Temperature inversions

Answers

5385   [A]   5447   [B]   5304   [A]

Wind

The circulation patterns for high- and low-pressure areas are caused by the Coriolis force.

The general circulation and wind rules in the Northern Hemisphere are:

- Air circulates in a clockwise direction around a high.
- Air circulates in a counterclockwise direction around a low.
- The closer the isobars are together, the greater the pressure gradient force, and the stronger the wind speed.
- Due to surface friction (up to about 2,000 feet AGL), surface winds do not exactly parallel the isobars, but move outward from the center of the high toward lower pressure. See Figure 6-3.

For preflight planning, it is useful to know that air flows out and downward (or descends) from a high-pressure area in a clockwise direction and flows upward (rises) and into a low-pressure area in a counterclockwise direction. Assume a flight from point A to point B as shown in Figure 6-4. Going direct would involve fighting the wind flowing around the low. However, by traveling south of the low-pressure area, the circulation pattern could help instead of hinder. Generally speaking, in the Northern Hemisphere, when traveling west to east, the most favorable winds can be found by flying north of high-pressure areas and south of low-pressure areas. Conversely, when flying east to west, the most favorable winds can be found south of high-pressure areas and north of low-pressure areas. If flying directly into a low-pressure area in the Northern Hemisphere, the wind direction and speed will be from the left and increasing.

Figure 6-3. Gradient and surface wind

Figure 6-4. Circulation and wind

ALL
5313. The wind system associated with a low-pressure area in the Northern Hemisphere is

A—an anticyclone and is caused by descending cold air.
B—a cyclone and is caused by Coriolis force.
C—an anticyclone and is caused by Coriolis force.

The storms that develop between high-pressure systems are characterized by low pressure. As winds try to blow inward toward the center of low pressure, they are also deflected to the right. Thus, the wind around a low moves in a counterclockwise direction. The low pressure and its wind system is a cyclone. (PLT511, CA.I.C.K3a) — FAA-H-8083-25

Answers (A) and (C) are incorrect because they describe a high-pressure system.

Answers
5313 [B]

Chapter 6 Weather

ALL
5314. With regard to windflow patterns shown on surface analysis charts; when the isobars are

A—close together, the pressure gradient force is slight and wind velocities are weaker.
B—not close together, the pressure gradient force is greater and wind velocities are stronger.
C—close together, the pressure gradient force is greater and wind velocities are stronger.

The closer the spacing of isobars, the stronger is the pressure gradient force. The stronger the pressure gradient force, the stronger is the wind. Thus, closely spaced isobars mean strong winds; widely spaced isobars mean lighter wind. (PLT287, CA.I.C.K3a) — AC 00-6

ALL
5316. While flying cross-country, in the Northern Hemisphere, you experience a continuous left cross-wind which is associated with a major wind system. This indicates that you

A—are flying toward an area of generally unfavorable weather conditions.
B—have flown from an area of unfavorable weather conditions.
C—cannot determine weather conditions without knowing pressure changes.

When flying in the Northern Hemisphere experiencing a continuous left crosswind indicates that you are entering a low-pressure system. Wind blows counterclockwise around a low which accounts for the left crosswind. In general, a low-pressure system is associated with bad weather. (PLT517, CA.I.C.K3b) — AC 00-6

Answer (B) is incorrect because if you have flown from an area of unfavorable weather conditions, you are flying out of the low, which means you would have a right crosswind. Answer (C) is incorrect because the wind can provide an indication of pressure changes and weather.

ALL
5317. Which is true with respect to a high- or low-pressure system?

A—A high-pressure area or ridge is an area of rising air.
B—A low-pressure area or trough is an area of descending air.
C—A high-pressure area or ridge is an area of descending air.

Air moving out of a high or ridge depletes the quantity of air. Highs and ridges, therefore, are areas of descending air. (PLT511, CA.I.C.K3a) — FAA-H-8083-25, Chapter 10

Answer (A) is incorrect because high-pressure air descends. Answer (B) is incorrect because low-pressure air rises.

ALL
5318. Which is true regarding high- or low-pressure systems?

A—A high-pressure area or ridge is an area of rising air.
B—A low-pressure area or trough is an area of rising air.
C—Both high- and low-pressure areas are characterized by descending air.

At the surface when air converges into a low, it cannot go outward against the pressure gradient, nor can it go downward into the ground. It must go upward. Therefore, a low or trough is an area of rising air. (PLT511, CA.I.C.K3a) — AC 00-6

Answers (A) and (C) are incorrect because high-pressure air descends and low-pressure air rises.

ALL
5319. When flying into a low-pressure area in the Northern Hemisphere, the wind direction and velocity will be from the

A—left and decreasing.
B—left and increasing.
C—right and decreasing.

In the Northern Hemisphere the wind around a low is counterclockwise. Thus, when flying to the center of a low, the wind will be from the left. When flying into a pressure system, spacing between isobars will decrease with increasing wind velocity. (PLT517, CA.I.C.K3a) — AC 00-6

ALL
5321. The general circulation of air associated with a high-pressure area in the Northern Hemisphere is

A—outward, downward, and clockwise.
B—outward, upward, and clockwise.
C—inward, downward, and clockwise.

As the air tries to blow outward from the high pressure, it is deflected to the right by the Coriolis force. Thus, the wind around a high blows clockwise. Air moving out of a high depletes the quantity of air. Highs and ridges are areas of descending air. (PLT511, CA.I.C.K3a) — AC 00-6

Answers

| 5314 [C] | 5316 [A] | 5317 [C] | 5318 [B] | 5319 [B] | 5321 [A] |

Chapter 6 Weather

ALL
5991. There is a high pressure system that is located south of your planned route in the Northern Hemisphere on a west-to-east cross-country flight. To take advantage of favorable winds, you would plan your route

A—on the north side of the high pressure area.
B—on the south side of the high pressure area.
C—through the middle of the high pressure area.

High pressure flows outward in a clockwise direction so pilot will gain tailwinds by flying on the north side of the high pressure system. (PLT517, CA.I.D.K2) — AC 00-6

Moisture

Air contains invisible water vapor. Water vapor content or air can be expressed in two different ways—relative humidity and dew point.

Relative humidity relates the actual water vapor present in the air to that which could be present in the air. Temperature largely determines the maximum amount of water vapor air can hold. Warm air can hold more water vapor than cold air. See Figure 6-5. Air with 100 percent relative humidity is said to be saturated, and air with less than 100 percent is unsaturated.

Dew point is the temperature to which air must be cooled to become saturated by the water already present in the air. See Figure 6-6.

Water vapor can be added to the air by either evaporation or sublimation. Water vapor is removed from the air by either condensation or sublimation.

When water vapor condenses on large objects, such as leaves, windshields, or airplanes, it will form dew, and when it condenses on microscopic particles (condensation nuclei), such as salt, dust, or combustion by-products, it will form clouds or fog.

If the temperature and dew point spread is small and decreasing, condensation is about to occur. If the temperature is above freezing, the weather most likely to develop will be fog or low clouds.

To summarize, relative humidity can be increased either by lowering the air temperature or by increasing the amount of water vapor in the air. This causes a decreased air temperature and temperature/dew point spread as the relative humidity increases.

Figure 6-5. Capacity of air to hold water

Figure 6-6. Relative humidity and dew point

Answers
5991 [A]

Chapter 6 Weather

ALL
5320. Which is true regarding actual air temperature and dewpoint temperature spread? The temperature spread

A—decreases as the relative humidity decreases.
B—decreases as the relative humidity increases.
C—increases as the relative humidity increases.

The difference between air temperature and dewpoint temperature is called the "spread." As the spread becomes less, relative humidity increases. (PLT492, CA.I.C.K3d) — AC 00-6

ALL
5323. Moisture is added to air by

A—sublimation and condensation.
B—evaporation and condensation.
C—evaporation and sublimation.

Evaporation is the changing of liquid water to invisible water vapor. Sublimation is the changing of ice directly to water vapor. (PLT512, CA.I.C.K3d) — AC 00-6

Answers (A) and (B) are incorrect because condensation removes moisture from the air.

Stable and Unstable Air

Atmospheric stability is defined as the resistance of the atmosphere to vertical motion. A stable atmosphere resists an upward or downward movement. An unstable atmosphere allows an upward or downward disturbance to grow into a vertical (convective) current.

Determining the stability of the atmosphere requires measuring the difference between the actual existing (ambient) temperature lapse rate of a given parcel of air and the dry adiabatic rate (a constant 3°C per 1,000 feet lapse rate).

A stable layer of air would be associated with a temperature inversion. Warming from below, on the other hand, would decrease the stability of an air mass.

The conditions shown in Figure 6-7 are characteristic of stable or unstable air masses.

Unstable Air	Stable Air
Cumuliform clouds	Stratiform clouds and fog
Showery precipitation	Continuous precipitation
Rough air (turbulence)	Smooth air
Good visibility except in blowing obstructions	Fair to poor visibility in haze and smoke

Figure 6-7. Characteristics of air masses

ALL
5333. Which would decrease the stability of an air mass?

A—Warming from below.
B—Cooling from below.
C—Decrease in water vapor.

A change in ambient temperature lapse rate of an air mass will determine its stability. Surface heating or cooling aloft can make the air more unstable. (PLT173, CA.I.C.K3a) — AC 00-6

Answer (B) is incorrect because cooling from below increases stability. Answer (C) is incorrect because a decrease in water vapor lowers the dew point of the air, but does not affect stability.

Answers

5320 [B]   5323 [C]   5333 [A]

ALL

5336. Which would increase the stability of an air mass?

A—Warming from below.
B—Cooling from below.
C—Decrease in water vapor.

A change in ambient temperature lapse rate of an air mass will determine its stability. Surface cooling or warming aloft often tips the balance toward greater stability. (PLT173, CA.I.C.K3a) — AC 00-6

Answer (A) is incorrect because warming from below decreases stability. Answer (C) is incorrect because a decrease in water vapor lowers the dew point of the air, but does not affect stability.

ALL

5334. From which measurement of the atmosphere can stability be determined?

A—Atmospheric pressure.
B—The ambient lapse rate.
C—The dry adiabatic lapse rate.

A change in ambient temperature lapse rate of an air mass will determine its stability. Surface heating or cooling aloft can make the air more unstable. On the other hand, surface cooling or warming aloft often tips the balance toward greater stability. (PLT492, CA.I.C.K3a) — AC 00-6

Answer (A) is incorrect because atmospheric pressure affects temperature and air movements, but does not determine the stability of the atmosphere. Answer (C) is incorrect because the dry adiabatic lapse rate is a constant rate.

Clouds

Stability determines which of two types of clouds will be formed: cumuliform or stratiform.

Cumuliform clouds are the billowy-type clouds having considerable vertical development, which enhances the growth rate of precipitation. They are formed in unstable conditions, and they produce showery precipitation made up of large water droplets. See Figure 6-8.

Stratiform clouds are the flat, more evenly based clouds formed in stable conditions. They produce steady, continuous light rain and drizzle made up of much smaller raindrops. See Figure 6-9.

Steady precipitation (in contrast to showery) preceding a front is an indication of stratiform clouds with little or no turbulence.

Figure 6-8. Cumulus clouds

Figure 6-9. Stratiform clouds

Answers

5336 [B]   5334 [B]

Clouds are divided into four families according to their height range: low, middle, high, and clouds with extensive vertical development. See Figure 6-10.

The first three families—low, middle, and high—are further classified according to the way they are formed. Clouds formed by vertical currents (unstable) are cumulus (heap) and are billowy in appearance. Clouds formed by the cooling of a stable layer are stratus (layered) and are flat and sheet-like in appearance. A further classification is the prefix "nimbo-" or suffix "-nimbus," which means raincloud. High clouds, called cirrus, are composed mainly of ice crystals; therefore, they are least likely to contribute to structural icing (since it requires water droplets).

The base of a cloud (AGL) that is formed by vertical currents (cumuliform clouds) can be roughly calculated by dividing the difference between the surface temperature and dew point by 4.4 and multiplying the remainder by 1,000. The convergence of the temperature and the dewpoint lapse rate is 4.4°F per 1,000 feet.

Figure 6-10. Cloud families

Problem:

What is the approximate base of the cumulus clouds if the temperature at 2,000 feet MSL is 10°C and the dew point is 1°C?

Solution:

In a convection current, the temperature and dew point converge at about 2.5°C per 1,000 feet. An estimate of convective cloud bases can be found by dividing the convergence into the temperature spread.

1. (10 − 1) ÷ 2.5 = 3.6 × 1,000 = 3,600 feet base
2. 2,000 feet MSL + 3,600 feet AGL = 5,600 feet MSL

ALL

5330. What determines the structure or type of clouds which will form as a result of air being forced to ascend?

A—The method by which the air is lifted.
B—The stability of the air before lifting occurs.
C—The relative humidity of the air after lifting occurs.

Whether the air is stable or unstable within a layer largely determines cloud structure. When stable air is forced upward the air tends to retain horizontal flow and any cloudiness is flat and stratified. When unstable air is forced upward, the disturbance grows and any resulting cloudiness shows extensive vertical development. (PLT192, CA.I.C.K3f) — AC 00-6

Answer (A) is incorrect because the stability determines the type of clouds that form. Answer (C) is incorrect because the relative humidity determines the amount of clouds that form.

ALL

5340. The formation of either predominantly stratiform or predominantly cumuliform clouds is dependent upon the

A—source of lift.
B—stability of the air being lifted.
C—temperature of the air being lifted.

When stable air is forced upward, the air tends to retain horizontal flow. Any cloudiness is flat and stratified. When unstable air is forced upward, the disturbance grows, and any resulting cloudiness shows extensive vertical development. (PLT192, CA.I.C.K3f) — AC 00-6

Answer (A) is incorrect because the stability of the air determines the type of clouds that form. Answer (C) is incorrect because the temperature of the air determines the altitude of clouds that form.

ALL

5327. When conditionally unstable air with high-moisture content and very warm surface temperature is forecast, one can expect what type of weather?

A—Strong updrafts and stratonimbus clouds.
B—Restricted visibility near the surface over a large area.
C—Strong updrafts and cumulonimbus clouds.

Characteristics of unstable air include cumuliform clouds, showery precipitation, turbulence, and good visibility, except in blowing obstructions. (PLT192, CA.I.C.K3f) — FAA-H-8083-25

Answer (A) is incorrect because stratonimbus clouds are characteristic of stable air. Answer (B) is incorrect because restricted visibility is characteristic of stable air.

ALL

5329. If clouds form as a result of very stable, moist air being forced to ascend a mountain slope, the clouds will be

A—cirrus type with no vertical development or turbulence.
B—cumulus type with considerable vertical development and turbulence.
C—stratus type with little vertical development and little or no turbulence.

Stable air resists upward movement; therefore, stratified clouds are produced. (PLT192, CA.I.C.K3f) — AC 00-6

Answer (A) is incorrect because cirrus clouds are high and composed of ice crystals. Answer (B) is incorrect because unstable air causes vertical development.

Answers

| 5330 | [B] | 5340 | [B] | 5327 | [C] | 5329 | [C] |

Chapter 6 Weather

ALL
5335. What type weather can one expect from moist, unstable air, and very warm surface temperatures?

A—Fog and low stratus clouds.
B—Continuous heavy precipitation.
C—Strong updrafts and cumulonimbus clouds.

Characteristics of unstable air include cumuliform clouds, showery precipitation, turbulence, and good visibility, except in blowing obstructions. (PLT173, CA.I.C.K3f) — AC 00-6

Answer (A) is incorrect because fog and stratus clouds are characteristics of stable air. Answer (B) is incorrect because continuous precipitation is characteristic of stable air.

ALL
5337. The conditions necessary for the formation of stratiform clouds are a lifting action and

A—unstable, dry air.
B—stable, moist air.
C—unstable, moist air.

Stable, moist air and adiabatic cooling is necessary to form stratiform clouds. (PLT192, CA.I.C.K3f) — AC 00-6

ALL
5338. Which cloud types would indicate convective turbulence?

A—Cirrus clouds.
B—Nimbostratus clouds.
C—Towering cumulus clouds.

Billowy fair weather cumulus clouds, usually seen on sunny afternoons, are signposts in the sky indicating convective turbulence. Vertical heights range from the shallow fair weather cumulus to the giant thunderstorm cumulonimbus. (PLT192, CA.I.C.K3f) — AC 00-6

Answer (A) is incorrect because cirrus clouds are high clouds made of ice crystals, and are not generated by any convective activity. Answer (B) is incorrect because nimbostratus clouds are flat rain clouds, formed in stable air and do not produce convective activity or turbulence.

ALL
5341. Which combination of weather-producing variables would likely result in cumuliform-type clouds, good visibility, and showery rain?

A—Stable, moist air and orographic lifting.
B—Unstable, moist air and orographic lifting.
C—Unstable, moist air and no lifting mechanism.

Characteristics of unstable, moist air include cumuliform clouds, showery precipitation, turbulence, and good visibility, except in blowing obstructions. "Orographic lifting" is the lifting action produced by a physical object, such as a mountain slope, forcing air upward. (PLT173, CA.I.C.K3f) — AC 00-6

Answer (A) is incorrect because if the air is stable, steady precipitation and stratiform clouds will form. Answer (C) is incorrect because a lifting mechanism must exist to form cumuliform clouds and showery rain.

ALL
5332. What are the characteristics of stable air?

A—Good visibility; steady precipitation; stratus clouds.
B—Poor visibility; steady precipitation; stratus clouds.
C—Poor visibility; intermittent precipitation; cumulus clouds.

Characteristics of stable air include stratiform clouds and fog, continuous precipitation, smooth air, and fair to poor visibility in haze and smoke. (PLT173, CA.I.C.K3a) — AC 00-6

Answer (A) is incorrect because good visibility is characteristic of unstable air. Answer (C) is incorrect because intermittent precipitation and cumulus clouds are characteristic of unstable air.

ALL
5342. What is a characteristic of stable air?

A—Stratiform clouds.
B—Fair weather cumulus clouds.
C—Temperature decreases rapidly with altitude.

Characteristics of stable air include stratiform clouds and fog, continuous precipitation, smooth air, and fair to poor visibility in haze and smoke. (PLT173, CA.I.C.K3a) — AC 00-6

Answer (B) is incorrect because cumulus clouds are characteristic of unstable air. Answer (C) is incorrect because a rapid temperature decrease with altitude indicates a high lapse rate and is characteristic of unstable air.

Answers

| 5335 | [C] | 5337 | [B] | 5338 | [C] | 5341 | [B] | 5332 | [B] | 5342 | [A] |

ALL
5343. A moist, unstable air mass is characterized by

A—poor visibility and smooth air.
B—cumuliform clouds and showery precipitation.
C—stratiform clouds and continuous precipitation.

Characteristics of unstable air include cumuliform clouds, showery precipitation, turbulence, and good visibility, except in blowing obstructions. (PLT511, CA.I.C.K3a) — AC 00-6

Answer (A) is incorrect because poor visibility and smooth air are characteristic of stable air. Answer (C) is incorrect because stratiform clouds and continuous precipitation are characteristic of stable air.

ALL
5343-1. What are the characteristics of an unstable atmosphere?

A—A cool, dry air mass.
B—A warm, humid air mass.
C—Descending air in the northern hemisphere.

Characteristics of unstable air include cumuliform clouds, showery precipitation, turbulence, and good visibility, except in blowing obstructions. (PLT511, CA.I.C.K3a) — AC 00-6

ALL
5344. When an air mass is stable, which of these conditions are most likely to exist?

A—Numerous towering cumulus and cumulonimbus clouds.
B—Moderate to severe turbulence at the lower levels.
C—Smoke, dust, haze, etc., concentrated at the lower levels with resulting poor visibility.

Characteristics typical of a stable air mass are:
- *Stratiform clouds and fog*
- *Continuous precipitation*
- *Smooth air*
- *Fair to poor visibility in haze and smoke*

(PLT173, CA.I.C.K3a) — AC 00-6

Answers (A) and (B) are incorrect because towering cumulus, cumulonimbus clouds, and turbulence are characteristic of an unstable air mass.

ALL
5345. Which is a characteristic of stable air?

A—Cumuliform clouds.
B—Excellent visibility.
C—Restricted visibility.

Characteristics typical of a stable air mass are:
- *Stratiform clouds and fog*
- *Continuous precipitation*
- *Smooth air*
- *Fair to poor visibility in haze and smoke*

(PLT173, CA.I.C.K3a) — AC 00-6

Answers (A) and (B) are incorrect because cumuliform clouds and excellent visibility are characteristic of an unstable air mass.

ALL
5346. Which is a characteristic typical of a stable air mass?

A—Cumuliform clouds.
B—Showery precipitation.
C—Continuous precipitation.

Characteristics typical of a stable air mass are:
- *Stratiform clouds and fog*
- *Continuous precipitation*
- *Smooth air*
- *Fair to poor visibility in haze and smoke*

(PLT173, CA.I.C.K3a) — AC 00-6

Answers (A) and (B) are incorrect because cumuliform clouds and showery precipitation are characteristic of an unstable air mass.

ALL
5348. Which are characteristics of a cold air mass moving over a warm surface?

A—Cumuliform clouds, turbulence, and poor visibility.
B—Cumuliform clouds, turbulence, and good visibility.
C—Stratiform clouds, smooth air, and poor visibility.

Cool air moving over a warm surface is heated from below, generating instability and increasing the possibility of showers. Unstable air is characterized by cumuliform clouds, turbulence and good visibility. (PLT511, CA.I.C.K3a) — AC 00-6

Answers

5343 [B]   5343-1 [B]   5344 [C]   5345 [C]   5346 [C]   5348 [B]

ALL
5349. The conditions necessary for the formation of cumulonimbus clouds are a lifting action and

A—unstable, dry air.
B—stable, moist air.
C—unstable, moist air.

For cumulonimbus clouds to form, the air must have sufficient water vapor, an unstable lapse rate, and an initial upward boost (lifting) to start the storm process in motion. (PLT192, CA.I.C.K3f) — AC 00-6

ALL
5328. What is the approximate base of the cumulus clouds if the temperature at 2,000 feet MSL is 10°C and the dewpoint is 1°C?

A—3,000 feet MSL.
B—4,000 feet MSL.
C—6,000 feet MSL.

In a convection current, the temperature and dew point converge at about 2.5°C per 1,000 feet. An estimate of convective cloud bases can be found by dividing the convergence into the temperature spread.

1. $(10 - 1) \div 2.5 = 3.6 \times 1,000 = 3,600$ feet base
2.
   ```
      2,000   feet MSL
   + 3,600   feet AGL
   ─────────
      5,600   feet MSL
   ```

(PLT192, CA.I.C.K3f) — AC 00-6

ALL
5331. Refer to the excerpt from the following METAR report:

KTUS.....08004KT 4SM HZ .....26/04 A2995 RMK RAE36

At approximately what altitude AGL should bases of convective-type cumuliform clouds be expected?

A—4,400 feet.
B—8,800 feet.
C—17,600 feet.

The reported temperature is 26°C, and the dew point is 4°C. In a convection current, the temperature and dew point converge at about 4.4°F (2.5°C) per 1,000 feet. An estimate of convective cloud bases can be found by dividing the convergence into the temperature spread.

$(26 - 4) \div 2.5 = 8.8 \times 1,000 = 8,800$ feet base

(PLT059, CA.I.C.K2) — FAA-H-8083-25

Air Masses and Fronts

When a body of air comes to rest on, or moves slowly over, an extensive area having fairly uniform properties of temperature and moisture, the air takes on these properties. The area from which the air mass acquires its identifying distribution of temperature and moisture is its source region. As this air mass moves from its source region, it tends to take on the properties of the new underlying surface. The trend toward change is called air mass modification.

A **ridge** is an elongated area of high pressure. A **trough** is an elongated area of low pressure. All fronts lie in troughs. A **cold front** is the leading edge of an advancing cold air mass. A **warm front** is the leading edge of an advancing warm air mass. Warm fronts move about half as fast as cold fronts. Frontal waves and cyclones (areas of low pressure) usually form on slow-moving cold fronts or stationary fronts. Figure 6-11 shows the symbols that would appear on a weather map.

The physical manifestations of a warm or cold front can be different with each front. They vary with the speed of the air mass on the move and the degree of stability of the air mass being overtaken. A stable air mass forced aloft will continue to exhibit stable characteristics, while an unstable air mass forced to ascend will continue to be characterized by cumulus clouds, turbulence, showery precipitation, and good visibility.

Answers

5349 [C]   5328 [C]   5331 [B]

Chapter 6 **Weather**

Occlusions form because cold fronts move faster than warm fronts. In a cold front occlusion, the coldest air is under the cold front. When it overtakes the warm front, it lifts the warm front aloft and the cold air replaces cool air at the surface.

Frontal passage will be indicated by the following discontinuities:

1. A temperature change (the most easily recognizable discontinuity);
2. A continuous decrease in pressure followed by an increase as the front passes; and
3. A shift in the wind direction, speed, or both.

Symbols on Surface Analysis (Surface Weather Maps)

Color	Symbol	Description
Blue	▼▼▼	Cold front
Blue	▽▽▽	Cold front aloft
Red	⌒⌒⌒	Warm front
Red/Blue	⌒▼⌒	Stationary front
Purple	⌒▲⌒	Occluded front
Purple	—·—·—	Squall line
Brown	— — —	Trough
Yellow	∿∿∿	Ridge

Figure 6-11. Weather map symbols

ALL
5347. Which is true regarding a cold front occlusion? The air ahead of the warm front

A—is colder than the air behind the overtaking cold front.
B—is warmer than the air behind the overtaking cold front.
C—has the same temperature as the air behind the overtaking cold front.

In the cold front occlusion, the coldest air is under the cold front. When it overtakes the warm front, it lifts the warm front aloft and cold air replaces cool air at the surface. (PLT511, CA.I.C.K3e) — AC 00-6

ALL
5347-1. You have delayed your flight to allow a fast moving cold front to clear your destination airport before your arrival. What type of flying conditions would you expect after the front has passed?

A—A fast moving squall line with high winds and thunderstorms.
B—Clear skies with gusty, turbulent winds and cooler temperatures.
C—Low clouds, reduced visibility, and showery, misty conditions.

Thunderstorms and heavy rain are common although not always associated with cold fronts. (PLT511, CA.I.C.K3e) — AC 00-6

Turbulence

Cumulus clouds are formed by convective currents (heating from below). Therefore, a pilot can expect turbulence below or inside cumulus clouds, especially towering cumulus clouds. The greatest turbulence could be expected inside cumulonimbus clouds. Strong winds (35+ knots) across ridges and mountain ranges can also cause severe turbulence and severe downdrafts on the lee side. The greatest potential danger from turbulent air currents exists when flying into the wind while on the leeward side of ridges and mountain ranges. See Figure 6-12.

Winds blowing across a mountain may produce an almond- or lens-shaped cloud (lenticular cloud), which appears stationary, but which may contain winds of 50 knots or more. The presence of these clouds is an indication of very strong turbulence.

Figure 6-12. Mountain turbulence

Answers
5347 [B]   5347-1 [A]

Chapter 6 Weather

The stationary crests of standing mountain waves downwind of a mountain also resemble the almond or lens shape and are referred to as standing lenticular clouds. Favorable conditions for a strong mountain wave consist of a stable layer of air being disturbed by the mountains with winds of at least 20 knots across the ridge. One of the most dangerous features of mountain waves is the turbulent areas in and below rotor clouds that form under lenticular clouds.

ALL
5339. The presence of standing lenticular altocumulus clouds is a good indication of

A—lenticular ice formation in calm air.
B—very strong turbulence.
C—heavy icing conditions.

Standing lenticular and/or rotor clouds suggest a mountain wave; expect turbulence many miles to the lee of mountains. (PLT192, CA.I.C.K3g) — AC 00-6

ALL
5357. When flying low over hilly terrain, ridges, or mountain ranges, the greatest potential danger from turbulent air currents will usually be encountered on the

A—leeward side when flying with a tailwind.
B—leeward side when flying into the wind.
C—windward side when flying into the wind.

Dangerous downdrafts may be encountered on the lee side. (PLT501, CA.I.C.K3g) — AC 00-6

Answer (A) is incorrect because with a tailwind you would be flying away from the mountain with the wind. Answer (C) is incorrect because you would be flying in air that is rising up on the windward side.

ALL
5393. The conditions most favorable to wave formation over mountainous areas are a layer of

A—stable air at mountaintop altitude and a wind of at least 20 knots blowing across the ridge.
B—unstable air at mountaintop altitude and a wind of at least 20 knots blowing across the ridge.
C—moist, unstable air at mountaintop altitude and a wind of less than 5 knots blowing across the ridge.

A strong mountain wave requires:

1. *Marked stability in the airstream disturbed by the mountains;*
2. *Wind speed at the level of the summit should exceed a minimum which varies from 15 to 25 knots, depending on the height of the range; and*
3. *Wind direction within 30° to the range. Lift diminishes as winds more closely parallel the range.*

(PLT510, CA.I.C.K3b) — AC 00-6

ALL
5450. One of the most dangerous features of mountain waves is the turbulent areas in and

A—below rotor clouds.
B—above rotor clouds.
C—below lenticular clouds.

"Rotor clouds" appear to remain stationary, parallel the range, and stand a few miles leeward of the mountains. Turbulence is most frequent and most severe in and below the standing rotors just beneath the wave crests at or below mountaintop levels. (PLT501, CA.I.C.K3b) — AC 00-6

Answers

5339 [B]   5357 [B]   5393 [A]   5450 [A]

Icing

Structural icing occurs on an aircraft whenever supercooled droplets of water make contact with any part of the aircraft that is also at a temperature below freezing. An inflight condition necessary for structural icing to form is visible moisture (clouds or raindrops).

Icing in precipitation (rain) is of concern to the VFR pilot because it can occur outside of clouds. Aircraft structural ice will most likely have the highest accumulation in freezing rain, which indicates warmer temperature (more than 32°F) at a higher altitude. See Figures 6-13 and 6-14. But the air temperature at the point where freezing precipitation is encountered is 32°F or less, causing the supercooled droplet to freeze on impact with the aircraft's surface.

If rain falling through colder air freezes during descent, **ice pellets** form. The presence of ice pellets at the surface is evidence that there is freezing rain at a higher altitude, while wet snow indicates that the temperature at your altitude is above freezing.

Chances for structural icing increase in the vicinity of fronts.

Frost is described as ice deposits formed by sublimation on a surface when the temperature of the collecting surface is at or below the dew point of the adjacent air, and the dew point is below freezing. Frost causes early airflow separation on an airfoil that results in a loss of lift, causing the airplane to stall at an angle of attack lower than normal. Therefore, all frost should be removed from the lifting surfaces of an airplane before flight, or it may prevent the airplane from becoming airborne.

Clear – Hard and Glossy
Temperature 0° to -15°C
Large water droplets
Cumuliform clouds

Rime – Brittle and Frost-like
Temperature 0° to -10°C
Small water droplets
Stratiform clouds

Figure 6-13. Clear and rime ice

Lift lessens
Drag increases
Weight grows
Stalling speed increases
Thrust falls off

Effects of icing are cumulative

Figure 6-14. Effects of structural icing

ALL
5324. Ice pellets encountered during flight normally are evidence that

A—a warm front has passed.
B—a warm front is about to pass.
C—there are thunderstorms in the area.

Rain falling from warm air above through colder air below may freeze during its descent, falling as ice pellets. This can happen any time a warmer layer of air exists above a colder layer (i.e., a warm front or a cold front). (PLT344, CA.I.C.K3i) — AC 00-6

Answer (A) is incorrect because after the warm front has passed there will no longer be a layer of warm air above a layer of cold air, which is required for the formation of ice pellets. Answer (C) is incorrect because ice pellets do not necessarily come from thunderstorms, but from rain freezing at a higher altitude.

Answers
5324 [B]

Chapter 6 **Weather**

ALL
5325. What is indicated if ice pellets are encountered at 8,000 feet?

A—Freezing rain at higher altitude.
B—You are approaching an area of thunderstorms.
C—You will encounter hail if you continue your flight.

Rain falling from warm air above through colder air below may freeze during its descent, falling as ice pellets. This can happen any time a warmer layer of air exists above a colder layer (i.e., a warm front or a cold front). (PLT511, CA.I.C.K3i) — AC 00-6

Answer (B) is incorrect because freezing rain can be encountered without thunderstorms. Answer (C) is incorrect because ice pellets are a form of hail.

ALL
5326. Ice pellets encountered during flight are normally evidence that

A—a cold front has passed.
B—there are thunderstorms in the area.
C—freezing rain exists at higher altitudes.

Rain falling from warm air above through colder air below may freeze during its decent, falling as ice pellets. This can happen any time a warmer layer of air exists above a colder layer (i.e., a warm front or a cold front). (PLT511, CA.I.C.K3i) — AC 00-6

ALL
5360. Which situation would most likely result in freezing precipitation? Rain falling from air which has a temperature of

A—32°F or less into air having a temperature of more than 32°F.
B—0°C or less into air having a temperature of 0°C or more.
C—more than 32°F into air having a temperature of 32°F or less.

Rain falling through colder air may become supercooled, freezing on impact as freezing rain, or it may freeze during its descent, falling as ice pellets. Water can freeze at 0°C or 32°F. (PLT511, CA.I.C.K3i) — AC 00-6

ALL
5971. During an IFR cross-country flight you picked up rime icing which you estimate is 1/2" thick on the leading edge of the wings. You are now below the clouds at 2000 feet AGL and are approaching your destination airport under VFR. Visibility under the clouds is more than 10 miles, winds at the destination airport are 8 knots right down the runway, and the surface temperature is 3 degrees Celsius. You decide to:

A—use a faster than normal approach and landing speed.
B—approach and land at your normal speed since the ice is not thick enough to have any noticeable effect.
C—fly your approach slower than normal to lessen the "wind chill" effect and break up the ice.

Ice will accumulate unevenly on the airplane. It will add weight and drag, and decrease thrust and lift. With ice accumulations, landing approaches should be made with a minimum wing flap setting and with an added margin of airspeed. Sudden and large configuration and airspeed changes should be avoided. (PLT511, CA.I.C.R1c) — FAA-H-8083-3

Answer (B) is incorrect because ice having a thickness similar to sandpaper on the leading edge and upper surface of a wing can reduce wing lift by as much as 30% and increase drag by 40%. Answer (C) is incorrect because ice will increase drag, requiring additional lift (airspeed); "wind chill" effect cannot be relied upon to melt/remove the ice that has already accumulated; flying slower than normal increases the possibility of a stall due to the decreased lift.

AIR
5739. Frost covering the upper surface of an airplane wing usually will cause

A—the airplane to stall at an angle of attack that is higher than normal.
B—the airplane to stall at an angle of attack that is lower than normal.
C—drag factors so large that sufficient speed cannot be obtained for takeoff.

The frost on the wing causes airflow disturbances. This will cause airflow separation (stall) at a lower angle of attack, resulting in a tendency to stall during takeoff. (PLT493, CA.I.C.R1c) — AC 00-6

Answer (A) is incorrect because frost on the wing surface will usually cause the airplane to stall at a lower angle of attack. Answer (C) is incorrect because the drag will usually not be enough to prevent the aircraft from obtaining takeoff speed.

Answers

5325 [A]   5326 [C]   5360 [C]   5971 [A]   5739 [B]

Thunderstorms

Thunderstorms present many hazards to flying. Three conditions necessary to the formation of a thunderstorm are:

- Sufficient water vapor
- An unstable lapse rate
- An initial upward boost (lifting)

The initial upward boost can be caused by heating from below, frontal lifting, or by mechanical lifting (wind blowing air upslope on a mountain). There are three stages of a thunderstorm: cumulus, mature, and dissipating. See Figure 6-15.

The cumulus stage consists of continuous updrafts, and these updrafts create low-pressure areas. Thunderstorms reach their greatest intensity during the mature stage, which is characterized by updrafts and downdrafts inside the cloud. Precipitation inside the cloud assists the development of these downdrafts, and the start of rain at the Earth's surface signals the beginning of the mature stage. Precipitation that evaporates before it reaches the ground is called virga.

When **lightning** occurs, the cloud is classified as a thunderstorm. Very frequent lightning, cumulonimbus clouds, and roll clouds indicate extreme turbulence in a thunderstorm. The dissipating stage of a thunderstorm features mainly downdrafts. Lightning is always associated with a thunderstorm.

Figure 6-15. Stages of a thunderstorm

Hail is formed inside thunderstorms (or cumulonimbus clouds) by the constant freezing, melting, and refreezing of water as it is carried about by the up- and downdrafts. Hailstones may be thrown outward from a storm cloud for several miles.

A pilot should always expect the hazardous and invisible atmospheric phenomena called **wind shear turbulence** when operating anywhere near a thunderstorm (within 20 NM). Wind shear is thought to be the most hazardous condition associated with a thunderstorm.

Thunderstorms that generally produce the most intense hazard to aircraft are called **squall-line thunderstorms**. These non-frontal, narrow bands of thunderstorms often contain severe steady-state thunderstorms that develop ahead of a cold front. The intense hazards found in these storms include destructive winds, heavy hail, and tornadoes. Embedded thunderstorms are those that are obscured by massive cloud layers and cannot be seen visually.

Airborne weather avoidance radar detects only precipitation drops; it does not detect minute cloud droplets. Therefore, the radar scope provides no assurance of avoiding instrument weather in clouds and fog. Weather radar precisely measures rainfall density which can be related to turbulence associated with the radar echoes. The most intense echoes are severe thunderstorms, and should be avoided by at least 20 miles. You should avoid flying between these intense echoes unless they are separated by at least 40 miles.

Chapter 6 Weather

ALL
5322. Virga is best described as

A—streamers of precipitation trailing beneath clouds which evaporates before reaching the ground.
B—wall cloud torrents trailing beneath cumulonimbus clouds which dissipate before reaching the ground.
C—turbulent areas beneath cumulonimbus clouds.

"Virga" refers to the streamers of precipitation trailing beneath clouds that evaporate before reaching the ground. (PLT344, CA.I.C.K3d) — AC 00-6

Answer (B) is incorrect because virga is usually thin and wispy. Answer (C) is incorrect because virga is a form of precipitation.

ALL
5361. Which statement is true concerning the hazards of hail?

A—Hail damage in horizontal flight is minimal due to the vertical movement of hail in the clouds.
B—Rain at the surface is a reliable indication of no hail aloft.
C—Hailstones may be encountered in clear air several miles from a thunderstorm.

Hailstones can fall some distance from the storm core. Hail has been observed in clear air several miles from the parent thunderstorm. (PLT261, CA.I.C.R1c) — AC 00-6

Answer (A) is incorrect because hail is one of the greatest hazards to aircraft. Answer (B) is incorrect because rain at the surface does not mean the absence of hail aloft.

ALL
5362. Hail is most likely to be associated with

A—cumulus clouds.
B—cumulonimbus clouds.
C—stratocumulus clouds.

You should anticipate possible hail with any thunderstorm, especially beneath the anvil of a large cumulonimbus. (PLT261, CA.I.C.K3d) — AC 00-6

ALL
5363. The most severe weather conditions, such as destructive winds, heavy hail, and tornadoes, are generally associated with

A—slow-moving warm fronts which slope above the tropopause.
B—squall lines.
C—fast-moving occluded fronts.

A squall line is a non-frontal, narrow band of active thunderstorms. It often contains severe steady-state thunderstorms and presents the single most intense weather hazard to aircraft. (PLT475, CA.I.C.K3h) — AC 00-6

Answer (A) is incorrect because warm fronts do not usually produce severe weather. Answer (C) is incorrect because the weather produced by occluded fronts is not as severe as a squall line.

ALL
5364. Of the following, which is accurate regarding turbulence associated with thunderstorms?

A—Outside the cloud, shear turbulence can be encountered 50 miles laterally from a severe storm.
B—Shear turbulence is encountered only inside cumulonimbus clouds or within a 5-mile radius of them.
C—Outside the cloud, shear turbulence can be encountered 20 miles laterally from a severe storm.

Hazardous turbulence is present in all thunderstorms, and a severe thunderstorm can damage an airframe. Strongest turbulence within the clouds occurs with shear between updrafts and downdrafts. Outside the cloud, shear turbulence has been encountered several thousand feet above and 20 miles laterally from a severe storm. (PLT495, CA.I.C.K3h) — AC 00-6

ALL
5365. If airborne radar is indicating an extremely intense thunderstorm echo, this thunderstorm should be avoided by a distance of at least

A—20 miles.
B—10 miles.
C—5 miles.

If the use of airborne radar indicates extremely intense echoes, they should be avoided by at least 20 miles. (PLT105, CA.I.C.K4) — AC 00-6

ALL
5366. Which statement is true regarding squall lines?

A—They are always associated with cold fronts.
B—They are slow in forming, but rapid in movement.
C—They are nonfrontal and often contain severe, steady-state thunderstorms.

A squall line is a non-frontal, narrow band of active thunderstorms. It often contains severe steady-state thunderstorms and presents the single most intense weather hazard to aircraft. (PLT475, CA.I.C.K3h) — AC 00-6

Answer (A) is incorrect because squall lines can form in any area of unstable air, but usually are found ahead of cold fronts. Answer (B) is incorrect because squall lines usually form quickly.

Answers

| 5322 | [A] | 5361 | [C] | 5362 | [B] | 5363 | [B] | 5364 | [C] | 5365 | [A] |
| 5366 | [C] |

ALL
5367. Which statement is true concerning squall lines?

A—They form slowly, but move rapidly.
B—They are associated with frontal systems only.
C—They offer the most intense weather hazards to aircraft.

A squall line is a non-frontal, narrow band of active thunderstorms. It often contains severe steady-state thunderstorms and presents the single most intense weather hazard to aircraft. (PLT475, CA.I.C.K3h) — AC 00-6

Answer (A) is incorrect because squall lines usually form rapidly. Answer (B) is incorrect because squall lines can form in any area of unstable air, but usually are found ahead of cold fronts.

ALL
5368. Select the true statement pertaining to the life cycle of a thunderstorm.

A—Updrafts continue to develop throughout the dissipating stage of a thunderstorm.
B—The beginning of rain at the Earth's surface indicates the mature stage of the thunderstorm.
C—The beginning of rain at the Earth's surface indicates the dissipating stage of the thunderstorm.

The mature stage of a thunderstorm starts when precipitation begins to fall from the cloud base. The downdrafts reach speeds that may exceed 2,500 feet per minute. Meanwhile, updrafts reach a maximum with speeds possibly exceeding 6,000 feet per minute. Updrafts and downdrafts in close proximity create strong vertical shear and a very turbulent environment. (PLT495, CA.I.C.K3h) — AC 00-6

Answer (A) is incorrect because updrafts do not continue through the dissipating stage of a thunderstorm. Answer (C) is incorrect because this indicates the beginning of the mature stage.

ALL
5369. What visible signs indicate extreme turbulence in thunderstorms?

A—Base of the clouds near the surface, heavy rain, and hail.
B—Low ceiling and visibility, hail, and precipitation static.
C—Cumulonimbus clouds, very frequent lightning, and roll clouds.

Cumulonimbus clouds represent an unstable air mass which indicates turbulent conditions. The more frequent the lightning, the more severe the thunderstorm. The roll cloud is most prevalent with cold frontal or squall line thunderstorms and signifies an extremely turbulent zone. (PLT495, CA.I.C.K3h) — AC 00-6

ALL
5370. Which weather phenomenon signals the beginning of the mature stage of a thunderstorm?

A—The start of rain.
B—The appearance of an anvil top.
C—Growth rate of cloud is maximum.

The mature stage of a thunderstorm starts when precipitation begins to fall from the cloud base. The downdrafts reach speeds that may exceed 2,500 feet per minute. Meanwhile, updrafts reach a maximum with speeds possibly exceeding 6,000 feet per minute. (PLT495, CA.I.C.K3h) — AC 00-6

Answer (B) is incorrect because the anvil top appears during the mature stage, but not necessarily at the beginning. Answer (C) is incorrect because maximum cloud growth rate occurs in the middle to the end of the mature stage.

ALL
5371. What feature is normally associated with the cumulus stage of a thunderstorm?

A—Roll cloud.
B—Continuous updraft.
C—Beginning of rain at the surface.

The key feature of the cumulus stage of a thunderstorm is a continuous updraft. (PLT495, CA.I.C.K3h) — AC 00-6

Answers (A) and (C) are incorrect because the roll cloud and the beginning of rain at the surface are features of the mature stage.

ALL
5372. During the life cycle of a thunderstorm, which stage is characterized predominately by downdrafts?

A—Mature.
B—Developing.
C—Dissipating.

Downdrafts characterize the dissipating stage of the thunderstorm cell. (PLT495, CA.I.C.K3h) — AC 00-6

Answer (A) is incorrect because the mature stage has both updrafts and downdrafts. Answer (B) is incorrect because the developing stage primarily has updrafts.

Answers

5367 [C]   5368 [B]   5369 [C]   5370 [A]   5371 [B]   5372 [C]

Chapter 6 Weather

ALL
5373. What minimum distance should exist between intense radar echoes before any attempt is made to fly between these thunderstorms?

A—20 miles.
B—30 miles.
C—40 miles.

A pilot should avoid flying between very intense echoes unless they are separated by at least 40 miles. (PLT495, CA.I.C.K3h) — AC 00-6

ALL
5373-1. Thunderstorms identified as severe or giving an intense radar echo should be avoided by what distance?

A—5 miles.
B—At least 25 miles.
C—At least 20 miles.

Avoid by at least 20 miles any thunderstorm identified as severe or giving an intense radar echo. This is especially true under the anvil of a large cumulonimbus. (PLT495, CA.I.C.K3h) — AIM ¶7-1-28

ALL
5373-2. The greatest threats to an aircraft operating in the vicinity of thunderstorms are:

A—thunder and heavy rain.
B—hail and turbulence.
C—precipitation static and low visibility.

Hazardous turbulence is present in all thunderstorms; in a severe thunderstorm, it can damage an airframe. Hail competes with turbulence as the greatest thunderstorm hazard to aircraft. (PLT495, CA.I.C.K3h) — AC 00-6

ALL
5373-3. You are avoiding a thunderstorm that is in your flightpath. You are over 20 miles from the cell however, you are under the anvil of the cell. Is this a hazard?

A—No, you are at a safe distance from the cell.
B—Yes, hail can be discharged from the anvil.
C—Yes, this is still in the area of dissipation.

Avoid by at least 20 miles any thunderstorm identified as severe or giving an intense radar echo. This is especially true under the anvil of a large cumulonimbus where hail can be discharged. (PLT495, CA.I.C.K3h) — AC 00-6

ALL
5375. Which is true regarding the use of airborne weather-avoidance radar for the recognition of certain weather conditions?

A—The radarscope provides no assurance of avoiding instrument weather conditions.
B—The avoidance of hail is assured when flying between and just clear of the most intense echoes.
C—The clear area between intense echoes indicates that visual sighting of storms can be maintained when flying between the echoes.

Weather radar detects only precipitation drops. It does not detect minute cloud droplets. Therefore, the radar scope provides no assurance of avoiding instrument weather in clouds and fog. (PLT105, CA.I.C.K4) — AC 00-6

Answer (B) is incorrect because hail can be thrown several miles from the intense echoes. Answer (C) is incorrect because clouds without precipitation may exist between the echoes.

Fog

Fog is a surface-based cloud which restricts visibility, composed of either water droplets or ice crystals. Fog may form by cooling the air to its dew point or by adding moisture to the air near the ground. A small temperature/dewpoint spread is essential to the formation of fog. An abundance of condensation nuclei from combustion products makes fog prevalent in industrial areas.

Fog is classified by the way it is formed:

Radiation fog (ground fog) is formed when terrestrial radiation cools the ground (land areas only), which in turn cools the air in contact with it. When the air is cooled to its dew point, or within a few degrees, fog will form. This fog will form most readily in warm, moist air over low, flatland areas on clear, calm (no wind) nights.

Answers

5373 [C]   5373-1 [C]   5373-2 [B]   5373-3 [B]   5375 [A]

Advection fog (sea fog) is formed when warm, moist air moves (wind is required) over colder ground or water; for example, an air mass moving inland from the coast in winter. Advection fog is usually more extensive and much more persistent than radiation fog. It can move in rapidly regardless of the time of day or night. This fog deepens as wind speed increases up to about 15 knots. Winds much stronger than 15 knots lift the fog into a layer of low stratus clouds.

Upslope fog is formed when moist, stable air is cooled to its dew point as it moves up sloping terrain (wind is required). Cooling will be at the dry adiabatic lapse rate of approximately 3°C per 1,000 feet.

Precipitation-induced fog (frontal fog) is formed when relatively warm rain or drizzle falls through cool air; evaporation from precipitation saturates cool air and forms fog. It is most commonly associated with warm fronts, but can occur with slow moving cold fronts and with stationary fronts.

Steam fog forms in winter when cold, dry air passes from land areas over comparatively warm ocean waters. Condensation takes place just above the surface of the water and appears as steam rising from the ocean.

ALL
5350. Fog produced by frontal activity is a result of saturation due to

A—nocturnal cooling.
B—adiabatic cooling.
C—evaporation of precipitation.

When relatively warm rain or drizzle falls through cool air, evaporation from the precipitation saturates the cool air and forms fog. (PLT226, CA.I.C.K3j) — AC 00-6

Answer (A) is incorrect because nocturnal cooling produces radiation fog. Answer (B) is incorrect because adiabatic cooling produces upslope fog.

ALL
5374. Which in-flight hazard is most commonly associated with warm fronts?

A—Advection fog.
B—Radiation fog.
C—Precipitation-induced fog.

When relatively warm rain or drizzle falls through cool air, evaporation from the precipitation saturates the cool air and forms fog. Precipitation-induced fog can become quite dense and continue for an extended period of time. This fog may cover large areas, completely suspending air operations. It is most commonly associated with warm fronts, but can occur with slow moving cold fronts and with stationary fronts. (PLT263, CA.I.C.K3j) — AC 00-6

Answer (A) is incorrect because advection fog forms from the movement of warm, humid air over a cold water surface. Answer (B) is incorrect because radiation fog forms from terrestrial cooling of the Earth's surface on clear, calm nights.

ALL
5376. A situation most conducive to the formation of advection fog is

A—a light breeze moving colder air over a water surface.
B—an air mass moving inland from the coastline during the winter.
C—a warm, moist air mass settling over a cool surface under no-wind conditions.

Advection fog forms when warm, moist air moves over colder ground or water. The fog forms offshore and is then carried inland by the wind. It is most common along coastal areas but often develops deep in continental areas. (PLT226, CA.I.C.K3j) — AC 00-6

Answer (A) is incorrect because this describes steam fog. Answer (C) is incorrect because this describes radiation fog.

ALL
5377. Advection fog has drifted over a coastal airport during the day. What may tend to dissipate or lift this fog into low stratus clouds?

A—Nighttime cooling.
B—Surface radiation.
C—Wind 15 knots or stronger.

Advection fog deepens as wind speed increases up to about 15 knots. Winds much stronger than 15 knots lift the fog into a layer of low stratus clouds or stratocumulus. (PLT263, CA.I.C.K3j) — AC 00-6

Answers (A) and (B) are incorrect because nighttime cooling and surface radiation form radiation fog.

Answers

| 5350 | [C] | 5374 | [C] | 5376 | [B] | 5377 | [C] |

ALL
5378. What lifts advection fog into low stratus clouds?

A—Nighttime cooling.
B—Dryness of the underlying land mass.
C—Surface winds of approximately 15 knots or stronger.

Advection fog deepens as wind speed increases up to about 15 knots. Winds much stronger than 15 knots lift the fog into a layer of low stratus clouds or stratocumulus. (PLT226, CA.I.C.K3j) — AC 00-6

Answers (A) and (B) are incorrect because nighttime cooling and dryness of the underlying land mass lead to radiation fog.

ALL
5379. In what ways do advection fog, radiation fog, and steam fog differ in their formation or location?

A—Radiation fog is restricted to land areas; advection fog is most common along coastal areas; steam fog forms over a water surface.
B—Advection fog deepens as windspeed increases up to 20 knots; steam fog requires calm or very light wind; radiation fog forms when the ground or water cools the air by radiation.
C—Steam fog forms from moist air moving over a colder surface; advection fog requires cold air over a warmer surface; radiation fog is produced by radiational cooling of the ground.

Radiation fog is restricted to land areas because water surfaces cool little from nighttime radiation. Advection fog is most common along coastal areas but often develops deep in continental areas. Steam fog, also known as "sea smoke," forms in the winter when cold, dry air passes from land areas over comparatively warm ocean waters. (PLT226, CA.I.C.K3j) — AC 00-6

ALL
5380. With respect to advection fog, which statement is true?

A—It is slow to develop, and dissipates quite rapidly.
B—It forms almost exclusively at night or near daybreak.
C—It can appear suddenly during day or night, and it is more persistent than radiation fog.

Advection fog is more persistent than radiation fog and can move in rapidly regardless of the time of day or night. (PLT226, CA.I.C.K3j) — AC 00-6

Answer (A) is incorrect because advection fog can move in rapidly regardless of the time of day or night and is persistent. Answer (B) is incorrect because this describes radiation fog.

Wind Shear

Wind shear is defined as a change in wind direction and/or speed in a very short distance in the atmosphere. This can occur at any level of the atmosphere and can exist in both horizontal and vertical direction. The amount of wind shear can be detected by the pilot as a sudden change in airspeed.

Low-level (low-altitude) wind shear can be expected during strong temperature inversions, on all sides of a thunderstorm and directly below the cell. Low-level wind shear can also be found near frontal activity because winds can be significantly different in the two air masses which meet to form the front.

In warm front conditions, the most critical period is before the front passes. Warm front shear may exist below 5,000 feet for about 6 hours before surface passage of the front. The wind shear associated with a warm front is usually more extreme than that found in cold fronts.

The shear associated with cold fronts is usually found behind the front. If the front is moving at 30 knots or more, the shear zone will be 5,000 feet above the surface 3 hours after frontal passage.

Potentially hazardous wind shear may be encountered during periods of a strong temperature inversion with calm or light surface winds, and strong winds above the inversion. Eddies (turbulence) in the shear zone cause airspeed fluctuation as an aircraft climbs or descends through the inversions. During an approach, the most easily recognized means of detecting possible windshear conditions includes monitoring the rate of descent (vertical velocity) and power required. The power needed to hold the glide slope will be different from a no-shear situation.

Answers

5378 [C]   5379 [A]   5380 [C]

There are two potentially hazardous shear situations:

1. **Loss of tailwind**—a tailwind may shear to either a calm or headwind component. In this instance, initially the airspeed will increase by an amount equal to the change of wind velocity, the aircraft pitches up, and altitude increases. Lower than normal power would be required initially, followed by a further decrease as the shear is encountered, and then an increase as glide slope is regained. See Figure 6-16.

2. **Loss of headwind**—a headwind may shear to a calm or tailwind component. The decrease in headwind will cause a loss in airspeed equal to the decrease in wind velocity. Initially, the airspeed decreases, the aircraft pitches down, and altitude decreases. See Figure 6-17.

Some airports can report **boundary winds** as well as the wind at the tower. When a tower reports a boundary wind which is significantly different from the airport wind, there is a possibility of hazardous wind shear.

Figure 6-16. Tailwind shearing to headwind or calm

Figure 6-17. Headwind shearing to tailwind or calm

ALL
5351. What is an important characteristic of wind shear?

A—It is present at only lower levels and exists in a horizontal direction.
B—It is present at any level and exists in only a vertical direction.
C—It can be present at any level and can exist in both a horizontal and vertical direction.

Wind shear may be associated with either a wind shift or a wind speed gradient at any level in the atmosphere. It may be associated with a low-level temperature inversion, in a frontal zone, or clear air turbulence (CAT) at high levels associated with a jet stream or strong circulation. (PLT518, CA.I.C.K3b) — AC 00-6

Answers (A) and (B) are incorrect because wind shear occurs both vertically and horizontally, and at all altitudes.

ALL
5449. The low-level wind shear Alert System (LLWAS) provides wind data and software process to detect the presence of a

A—rotating column of air extending from a cumulonimbus cloud.
B—change in wind direction and/or speed within a very short distance above the airport.
C—downward motion of the air associated with continuous winds blowing with an easterly component due to the rotation of the Earth.

Wind shear may be associated with either a wind shift or a wind speed gradient at any level in the atmosphere. It may be associated with a low-level temperature inversion, in a frontal zone, or clear air turbulence (CAT) at high levels associated with a jet stream or strong circulation. (PLT518, CA.I.C.K4) — AC 00-6

Answer (A) is incorrect because this describes a tornado. Answer (C) is incorrect because LLWAS detects wind changes close to the airport.

Answers

5351 [C]   5449 [B]

ALL
5352. Hazardous wind shear is commonly encountered

A—near warm or stationary frontal activity.
B—when the wind velocity is stronger than 35 knots.
C—in areas of temperature inversion and near thunderstorms.

Often there is a strong wind just above the top of an inversion layer. Flying into or out of this wind induces a shear situation. The most prominent meteorological phenomena that cause significant low-level wind shear problems are thunderstorms and certain frontal systems at or near the airport. (PLT518, CA.I.C.K3b) — AC 00-6

Answer (A) is incorrect because hazardous wind shear is more commonly found near inversions and thunderstorms. Answer (B) is incorrect because strong wind does not mean that there will always be wind shear; the wind must be in different directions.

ALL
5353. Low-level wind shear may occur when

A—surface winds are light and variable.
B—there is a low-level temperature inversion with strong winds above the inversion.
C—surface winds are above 15 knots and there is no change in wind direction and windspeed with height.

When taking off or landing in calm wind under clear skies within a few hours before or after sunrise, be prepared for a temperature inversion near the ground. You can be relatively certain of a shear zone in the inversion if you know the wind at 2,000 to 4,000 feet is 25 knots or more. Allow a margin of airspeed above normal climb or approach speed to alleviate the danger of a stall in event of turbulence or sudden change in wind velocity. (PLT518, CA.I.C.K3b) — AC 00-6

Answer (A) is incorrect because light surface winds alone would not cause wind shear. Answer (C) is incorrect because wind shear refers to an abrupt change in wind speed and/or direction.

ALL
5354. If a temperature inversion is encountered immediately after takeoff or during an approach to a landing, a potential hazard exists due to

A—wind shear.
B—strong surface winds.
C—strong convective currents.

You can be relatively certain of a shear zone in the inversion if you know the wind at 2,000 to 4,000 feet is 25 knots or more. Allow a margin of airspeed above normal climb or approach speed to alleviate the danger of a stall in event of turbulence or sudden change in wind velocity. (PLT518, CA.I.C.K3b) — AC 00-6

Answer (B) is incorrect because strong surface winds do not present as great a danger as wind shear. Answer (C) is incorrect because a temperature inversion does not generate strong convective currents.

ALL
5355. GIVEN:

Winds at 3,000 feet AGL .... 30 kts
Surface winds..Calm

While on approach for landing under clear skies with convective turbulence a few hours after sunrise, one should

A—increase approach airspeed slightly above normal to avoid stalling.
B—keep the approach airspeed at or slightly below normal to compensate for floating.
C—not alter the approach airspeed, these conditions are nearly ideal.

When taking off or landing in calm wind under clear skies within a few hours before or after sunrise, be prepared for a temperature inversion near the ground. You can be relatively certain of a shear zone in the inversion if you know the wind at 2,000 to 4,000 feet is 25 knots or more. Increase airspeed slightly above normal climb or approach speed to alleviate the danger of a stall in event of turbulence or sudden change in wind velocity. (PLT518, CA.IV.B.R2b) — AC 00-6

Answer (B) is incorrect because the hazard is wind shear. Answer (C) is incorrect because these conditions are not ideal—wind shear may be present.

ALL
5359. During departure, under conditions of suspected low-level wind shear, a sudden decrease in headwind will cause

A—a loss in airspeed equal to the decrease in wind velocity.
B—a gain in airspeed equal to the decrease in wind velocity.
C—no change in airspeed, but groundspeed will decrease.

Answers

5352 [C] 5353 [B] 5354 [A] 5355 [A] 5359 [A]

The worst situation on departure occurs when the aircraft encounters a rapidly increasing tailwind, decreasing headwind, and/or downdraft. Taking off under these circumstances would lead to a decreased performance condition. An increasing tailwind or decreasing headwind, when encountered, will cause a decrease in indicated airspeed. The aircraft will initially pitch down due to the decreased lift in proportion to the airspeed loss. After encountering the shear, if the wind remains constant, aircraft ground speed will gradually increase and indicated airspeed will return to its original value. (PLT518, CA.IV.A.R2b) — AC 00-6

Answer (B) is incorrect because a sudden decrease in headwind will cause a loss in airspeed. Answer (C) is incorrect because there is an initial loss of airspeed, followed by an increase in ground speed.

ALL
5448. A strong wind shear can be expected

A—in the jetstream front above a core having a speed of 60 to 90 knots.
B—if the 5°C isotherms are spaced between 7° to 10° of latitude.
C—on the low-pressure side of a jetstream core where the speed at the core is stronger than 110 knots.

Jet streams stronger than 110 knots (at the core) are apt to have areas of significant turbulence near them in the sloping tropopause above the core, in the jet stream front below the core and on the low-pressure side of the core. In these areas there are frequently strong wind shears. (PLT302, CA.I.C.K3b) — AC 00-30

Answer (A) is incorrect because 60 to 90 knots is common for the jet stream and if turbulence were to be found it would be to the sides and bottom of the core. Answer (B) is incorrect because these conditions do not exclusively create wind shear.

AIR, RTC
5358. During an approach, the most important and most easily recognized means of being alerted to possible wind shear is monitoring the

A—amount of trim required to relieve control pressures.
B—heading changes necessary to remain on the runway centerline.
C—power and vertical velocity required to remain on the proper glidepath.

Since rate of descent on the glide slope is directly related to ground speed, a high descent rate would indicate a strong tailwind. Conversely, a low descent rate indicates a strong headwind. The power needed to hold the glide slope also will be different from typical, no-shear conditions. Less power than normal will be needed to maintain the glide slope when a tailwind is present and more power is needed for strong headwind. (PLT518, CA.IV.B.R2b) — AC 00-6

Answer (A) is incorrect because trim adjustments are a function of power settings, airspeeds, and aircraft configuration. Answer (B) is incorrect because heading changes are due to the crosswind component.

Soaring Weather

GLI
5386. Select the true statement concerning thermals.

A—Thermals are unaffected by winds aloft.
B—Strong thermals have proportionately increased sink in the air between them.
C—A thermal invariably remains directly above the surface area from which it developed.

For every rising current there is a compensating downward current. The downward currents frequently occur over broader areas than do the upward currents; therefore, they have a slower vertical speed than do rising currents. A thermal is simply the updraft in a small-scale convective current. (PLT494) — AC 00-6

Answers

5448 [C]   5358 [C]   5386 [B]

Chapter 6 Weather

GLI

5387. A thermal column is rising from an asphalt parking lot and the wind is from the south at 12 knots. Which statement would be true?

A—As altitude is gained, the best lift will be found directly above the parking lot.
B—As altitude is gained, the center of the thermal will be found farther north of the parking lot.
C—The slowest rate of sink would be close to the thermal and the fastest rate of sink farther from it.

Wind causes a thermal to lean with altitude. When seeking the thermal supporting soaring birds or aircraft, you must make allowance for the wind. The thermal at lower levels usually is upwind from your high-level visual cue. (PLT494) — AC 00-6

GLI

5388. Which is true regarding the development of convective circulation?

A—Cool air must sink to force the warm air upward.
B—Warm air is less dense and rises on its own accord.
C—Warmer air covers a larger surface area than the cool air; therefore, the warmer air is less dense and rises.

Warm air does expand when heated, but the convective circulation or lifting force comes from the dense, cool air drawn to the ground by gravity and forcing the warm air upward. (PLT510) — AC 00-6

GLI

5389. Which is generally true when comparing the rate of vertical motion of updrafts with that of downdrafts associated with thermals?

A—Updrafts and downdrafts move vertically at the same rate.
B—Downdrafts have a slower rate of vertical motion than do updrafts.
C—Updrafts have a slower rate of vertical motion than do downdrafts.

For every rising current there is a compensating downward current. The downward currents frequently occur over broader areas than do the upward currents; therefore, they have a slower vertical speed than do rising currents. A thermal is simply the updraft in a small-scale convective current. (PLT494) — AC 00-6

GLI

5390. Which thermal index would predict the best probability of good soaring conditions?

A— -10.
B— -5.
C— +20.

Strength of thermals is proportional to the magnitude of the negative value of the thermal index (TI). A TI of -8 or -10 predicts very good lift and a long soaring day. (PLT494) — FAA-H-8083-13

GLI

5391. Which is true regarding the effect of fronts on soaring conditions?

A—A slow moving front provides the strongest lift.
B—Good soaring conditions usually exist after passage of a warm front.
C—Frequently, the air behind a cold front provides excellent soaring for several days.

In the central and eastern United States, the most favorable weather for cross-country soaring occurs behind a cold front.

1. *The cold polar air is usually dry, and thermals can build to relatively high altitudes.*
2. *The polar air is colder than the ground and thus the warm ground aids solar radiation in heating the air. Thermals begin earlier in the morning and last later in the evening. On occasions, soarable lift has been found at night.*
3. *Quite often, colder air at high altitudes moves over the cold, low-level outbreak intensifying the instability and strengthening the thermals.*
4. *The wind profile frequently favors thermal streeting—a real benefit to speed and distance.*

The same four factors may occur with cold frontal passages over mountainous regions in the western United States. (PLT511) — AC 00-6

GLI

5394. When soaring in the vicinity of mountain ranges, the greatest potential danger from vertical and rotor-type currents will usually be encountered on the

A—leeward side when flying with a tailwind.
B—leeward side when flying into the wind.
C—windward side when flying into the wind.

Dangerous downdrafts may be encountered on the lee side. (PLT494) — AC 00-6

Answers

5387 [B]   5388 [A]   5389 [B]   5390 [A]   5391 [C]   5394 [B]

GLI
5395. Which is true regarding ridge soaring with the wind direction perpendicular to the ridge?

A—When flying between peaks along a ridge, the pilot can expect a significant decrease in wind and lift.
B—When very close to the surface of the ridge, the glider's speed should be reduced to the minimum sink speed.
C—If the glider drifts downwind from the ridge and sinks slightly lower than the crest of the ridge, the glider should be turned away from the ridge and a high speed attained.

The glider pilot would want to get out of the area of strong sink as rapidly as possible. Prompt and drastic action is required. Considerable altitude may be lost in the process. Occasionally a very strong wind will sweep down the lee side of the ridge. (PLT494) — AC 00-6

GLI
5396. (Refer to Figure 6.) With regard to the soundings taken at 1400 hours, between what altitudes could optimum thermalling be expected at the time of the sounding?

A—From 2,500 to 6,000 feet.
B—From 6,000 to 10,000 feet.
C—From 13,000 to 15,000 feet.

The actual lapse rate must exceed the dry adiabatic rate of cooling for air to be unstable. That is, the line representing the lapse rate must slope parallel to, or slope more than, the dry adiabats. The 1400 GMT sounding slopes more than the adiabats from 2,500 to 6,000 feet, parallels the adiabats from 6,000 to 10,000 feet and slopes less than the adiabats from 10,000 to 13,000 and from 13,000 to 15,000 feet. (PLT062) — AC 00-6

GLI
5397. (Refer to Figure 6.) With regard to the soundings taken at 0900 hours, from 2,500 feet to 15,000 feet, as shown on the Adiabatic Chart, what minimum surface temperature is required for instability to occur and for good thermals to develop from the surface to 15,000 feet MSL?

A—58°F.
B—68°F.
C—80°F.

The actual lapse rate must exceed the adiabatic rate for good thermals to develop. Find the intersection of 0900 GMT (Greenwich Mean Time) sounding and 15,000 feet. Draw a line parallel to the diagonals (dry adiabatic lapse rate) back to the surface at 2,500 feet MSL. The surface temperature must exceed about 80°F. (PLT062) — AC 00-6

GLI
5742. (Refer to Figure 6.) At the 0900 hours sounding and the line plotted from the surface to 10,000 feet, what temperature must exist at the surface for instability to take place between these altitudes? Any temperature

A—less than 68°F.
B—more than 68°F.
C—less than 43°F.

Note that the actual lapse rate must exceed the adiabatic rate for good thermals to develop.

1. *Locate the intersection of the 0900 GMT sounding and the 10,000-foot altitude.*
2. *Draw a line parallel to the diagonals and downward to the right to intercept the line representing the surface, 2,500 feet MSL.*
3. *From that intercept draw a line downward and read the temperature, 20°C or 68°F. Temperatures greater than this will result in instability.*

(PLT062) — AC 00-6

GLI
5744. (Refer to Figure 6.) At the soundings taken at 1400 hours, is the atmosphere stable or unstable and at what altitudes?

A—Stable from 6,000 to 10,000 feet.
B—Stable from 10,000 to 13,000 feet.
C—Unstable from 10,000 to 13,000 feet.

If the sounding line is parallel to, or has less slope than the diagonals, the air is stable. (PLT062) — AC 00-6

GLI
5745. Which thermal index would predict the best probability of good soaring conditions?

A— +5.
B— -5.
C— -10.

A negative thermal index indicates unstable air. (PLT494) — FAA-H-8083-13

Answers

5395 [C]   5396 [A]   5397 [C]   5742 [B]   5744 [B]   5745 [C]

Chapter 6 Weather

GLI
5746. Which is true regarding the effect of fronts on soaring conditions?

A—Good soaring conditions usually exist after passage of a warm front.
B—Excellent soaring conditions usually exist in the cold air ahead of a warm front.
C—Frequently the air behind a cold front provides excellent soaring for several days.

Frequently, the unstable air behind a cold front provides good soaring conditions. (PLT511) — AC 00-6

GLI
5747. Which is true regarding ridge soaring with the wind direction perpendicular to the ridge?

A—When very close to the surface of the ridge, the glider's speed should be reduced to the minimum sink speed.
B—When the wind and lift are very strong on the windward side of the ridge, a weak sink condition will exist on the leeward side.
C—If the glider drifts downwind from the ridge and sinks slightly lower than the crest of the ridge, the glider should be turned away from the ridge and a high speed attained.

The glider pilot would want to get out of the area of strong sink as rapidly as possible. (PLT494) — AC 00-6

GLI
5392. Convective circulation patterns associated with sea breezes are caused by

A—water absorbing and radiating heat faster than the land.
B—land absorbing and radiating heat faster than the water.
C—cool and less dense air moving inland from over the water, causing it to rise.

Land is warmer than the sea during the day; wind blows from the cool water to warm land. (PLT510) — AC 00-6

Answer (A) is incorrect because water absorbs and radiates heat slower than land. Answer (C) is incorrect because cool air is more dense, therefore it will sink.

Answers

5746 [C]   5747 [C]   5392 [B]

Chapter 7
Weather Services

Aviation Routine Weather Report (METAR) *7–3*

Pilot Report (UA) *7–5*

Terminal Aerodrome Forecast (TAF) *7–8*

Graphical Forecasts for Aviation (GFA) *7–9*

Winds and Temperatures Aloft Forecast (FB) *7–10*

Inflight Weather Advisories (WA, WS, WST) *7–10*

Surface Analysis Chart *7–12*

Constant Pressure Chart *7–13*

Tropopause Height/Vertical Wind Shear Prognostic Chart *7–14*

Significant Weather Prognostics *7–14*

Lifted Index Chart *7–16*

Aviation Routine Weather Report (METAR)

An international weather reporting code is used for weather reports (METAR) and forecasts (TAFs) worldwide. The reports follow the format shown in Figure 7-1.

For aviation purposes, the ceiling is the lowest broken or overcast layer, or vertical visibility into an obscuration.

Figure 7-1. TAF/METAR weather card

ALL
5398. During preflight preparation, weather report forecasts can best be obtained by means of contacting the

A—weather forecast office (WFD).
B—air route traffic control center.
C—pilot's automatic telephone answering service.

Reports and forecasts are available through the request/reply service at all FSS's, WSOs and WSFOs. (PLT514, CA.I.C.K1) — AC 00-45

Answer (B) is incorrect because ARTCC deals with air traffic control. Answer (C) is incorrect because PATWAS is limited in the number of route forecasts and synopses it can provide.

Answers
5398 [A]

Chapter 7 **Weather Services**

ALL
5399. The most current en route and destination weather information for an instrument flight should be obtained from the

A—Flight Service.
B—ATIS broadcast.
C—Notices to Air Missions publications.

The FAA Flight Service provides more aviation weather briefing service than any other government service outlet. The FSS provides weather briefings, scheduled and unscheduled weather broadcasts, and furnishes weather support to flight in its area. (PLT515, CA.I.C.K1) — AC 00-45

Answer (B) is incorrect because ATIS provides information for operations at a specific airport and does not provide information for enroute operations. Answer (C) is incorrect because NOTAMs is a publication containing information on airport operations, and would not have information for en route and destination weather.

ALL
5405. What wind conditions would you anticipate when squalls are reported at your destination?

A—Rapid variations in windspeed of 15 knots or more between peaks and lulls.
B—Peak gusts of at least 35 knots combined with a change in wind direction of 30° or more.
C—Sudden increases in windspeed of at least 16 knots to a sustained speed of 22 knots or more for at least 1 minute.

A squall is a sudden increase in wind speed of 16 knots to a sustained speed of 22 knots, or more, lasting for at least 1 minute. (PLT475, CA.I.C.K3b) — AC 00-45

Answer (A) is incorrect because this describes gusts. Answer (B) is incorrect because this describes wind shear.

ALL
5402. The remarks section of the Aviation Routine Weather Report (METAR) contains the following coded information. What does it mean?

RMK FZDZB42 WSHFT 30 FROPA

A—Freezing drizzle with cloud bases below 4,200 feet.
B—Freezing drizzle below 4,200 feet and wind shear.
C—Wind shift at three zero due to frontal passage.

RMK—remarks follow

FZDZB42—freezing drizzle began 42 minutes after the hour

WSHFT 30 FROPA—wind shift at three zero due to frontal passage

(PLT059, CA.I.C.K2) — AIM ¶7-1-29

ALL
5403. What is meant by the Special METAR weather observation for KBOI?

SPECI KBOI 091854Z 32005KT 1 1/2SM RA BR OVC007 17/16 A2990 RMK RAB12

A—Rain and fog obscuring two-tenths of the sky; rain began at 1912Z.
B—Rain and mist obstructing visibility; rain began at 1812Z.
C—Rain and overcast at 1200 feet AGL.

SPECI KBOI—special report for KBOI

091854Z—the date and time the observation is taken is the 9th of the month, 1854 Zulu time

32005KT—winds are 320° true at 5 knots

1-1/2 SM RA BR—visibilities are 1-1/2 statute miles in rain and mist

OVC 007—ceiling is 700 feet overcast

17/16—temperature is 17°C and the dew point is 16°C

A2990—altimeter is 29.90

RMK RAB12—remarks, rain began 12 minutes past the hour

(PLT059, CA.I.C.K2) — FAA-H-8083-25

ALL
5404. The station originating the following METAR observation has a field elevation of 3,500 feet MSL. If the sky cover is one continuous layer, what is the thickness of the cloud layer? (Top of overcast reported at 7,500 feet MSL).

METAR KHOB 151250Z 17006KT 4SM OVC005 13/11 A2998

A—2,500 feet.
B—3,500 feet.
C—4,000 feet.

KHOB reports a ceiling of 500 feet (OVC005). This means the bottom of the overcast layer is 4,000 feet (3,500 MSL + 500 feet AGL). The top of the overcast is reported at 7,500 feet MSL. Therefore, the overcast layer is 3,500 feet thick (7,500 – 4,000). (PLT059, CA.I.C.K2) — AIM ¶7-1-29

Answers

| 5399 | [A] | 5405 | [C] | 5402 | [C] | 5403 | [B] | 5404 | [B] |

ALL

5988. Given the following METAR, what is the maximum altitude to maintain VFR below the ceiling in Class E airspace below 10,000 feet MSL?

METAR KHOB 151250Z, 17006KT 4SM BKN025 OVC040 13/11 A2998

A—2,000 feet AGL.
B—3,500 feet AGL.
C—3,900 feet AGL.

KHOB reports a broken ceiling at 2,500 feet (BKN025) and ceiling of 4,000 feet (OVC040). VFR in Class E airspace below 10,000 feet requires the pilot to maintain 1,000 feet above and 500 feet below distance from clouds. In this instance, the maximum altitude to maintain VFR is 3,500 feet AGL. (PLT059, CA.I.C.K2) — AIM ¶7-1-29

Pilot Report (UA)

Cloud tops, icing, and turbulence can only be observed directly from the cockpit. While the FAA encourages pilots to report inflight weather, a report of any unforecast weather is required by regulation. A pilot report, or PIREP (UA), is usually transmitted in a prescribed format. See Figure 7-2.

Turbulence and icing should be reported by using the intensity tables shown in Figure 7-3 and Figure 7-4.

Figure 7-2. Pilot report form

Answers

5988 [B]

Chapter 7 **Weather Services**

Icing Intensities

Intensity	Airframe ice accumulation	Pilot report
Trace	Ice becomes noticeable. The rate of accumulation is slightly greater than the rate of sublimation. A representative accretion rate for reference purposes is less than 1/4 inch (6 mm) per hour on the outer wing. The pilot should consider exiting the icing conditions before they become worse.	Aircraft identification, location, time (UTC), intensity of type*, altitude/FL, aircraft type, indicated air speed (IAS), and outside air temperature (OAT).
Light	The rate of accumulation requires occasional cycling of manual deicing systems to minimize ice accretions on the airframe. A representative accretion rate for reference purposes is 1/4 inch to 1 inch (0.6 to 2.5 cm) per hour on the unprotected part of the outer wing. The pilot should consider exiting the icing conditions.	
Moderate	The rate of ice accumulation requires frequent cycling of manual deicing systems to minimize ice accretions on the airframe. A representative accretion rate for reference purposes is 1 to 3 inches (2.5 to 7.5 cm) per hour on the unprotected part of the outer wing. The pilot should consider exiting the icing condition as soon as possible.	
Severe	The rate of ice accumulation is such that ice protection systems fail to remove the accumulation of ice and ice accumulates in locations not normally prone to icing, such as areas aft of protected surfaces and any other areas identified by the manufacturer. A representative accretion rate for reference purposes is more than 3 inches (7.5 cm) per hour on the unprotected part of the outer wing. By regulation, immediate exit is required.	

*Icing may be rime, clear, and mixed.
Rime ice: Rough, milky, opaque ice formed by the instantaneous freezing of small supercooled water droplets.
Clear ice: A glossy, clear, or translucent ice formed by the relatively slow freezing of large supercooled water droplets.
Mixed ice: A combination of rime and clear ice.

Figure 7-3. Icing intensities

Turbulence Intensities

Intensity	Aircraft reaction	Reaction inside aircraft	Reporting term definition
Light	Turbulence that momentarily causes slight, erratic changes in altitude and/or attitude (pitch, roll, yaw). Report as *Light Turbulence;* * or Turbulence that causes slight, rapid and somewhat rhythmic bumpiness without appreciable changes in altitude or attitude. Report as *Light Chop.*	Occupants may feel a slight strain against belts or shoulder straps. Unsecured objects may be displaced slightly. Food service may be conducted and little or no difficulty is encountered in walking.	Occasional – less than 1/3 of the time. Intermittent – 1/3 to 2/3 of the time. Continuous – More than 2/3 of the time.
Moderate	Turbulence that is similar to Light Turbulence but of greater intensity. Changes in altitude and/or attitude occur but the aircraft remains in positive control at all times. It usually causes variations in indicated airspeed. Report as *Moderate Turbulence;* * or Turbulence that is similar to Light Chop but of greater intensity. It causes rapid bumps or jolts without appreciable changes in aircraft altitude or attitude. Report as *Moderate Chop.*	Occupants feel definite strains against seat belts or shoulder straps. Unsecured objects are dislodged. Food service and walking are difficult.	Note: 1. Pilots should report location(s), time (UTC), intensity, whether in or near clouds, altitude, type of aircraft and, when applicable, duration of turbulence. 2. Duration may be based on time between two locations or over a single location. All locations should be readily identifiable.
Severe	Turbulence that causes large, abrupt changes in altitude and/or attitude. It usually causes large variations in indicated airspeed. Aircraft may be momentarily out of control. Report as *Severe Turbulence.* *	Occupants are forced violently against seat belts or shoulder straps. Unsecured objects are tossed about. Food service and walking are impossible.	
Extreme	Turbulence in which the aircraft is violently tossed about and is practically impossible to control. It may cause structural damage. Report as *Extreme Turbulence.* *		

* High level turbulence (normally above 15,000 feet AGL) that is not associated with cumuliform cloudiness, including thunderstorms, should be reported as CAT (clear air turbulence) preceded by the appropriate intensity, or light or moderate chop.

Figure 7-4. Turbulence reporting criteria

Chapter 7 Weather Services

ALL
5407. To best determine observed weather conditions between weather reporting stations, the pilot should refer to

A—pilot reports.
B—Area Forecasts.
C—prognostic charts.

Pilot weather reports are the best means to determine observed weather conditions between weather-reporting stations. It is also the only method of directly observing cloud tops, icing and turbulence. (PLT514, CA.I.C.K2) — AC 00-45

Answers (B) and (C) are incorrect because Area Forecasts and prognostic charts are forecasts and not observed weather.

ALL
5444. A pilot reporting turbulence that momentarily causes slight, erratic changes in altitude and/or attitude should report it as

A—light chop.
B—light turbulence.
C—moderate turbulence.

Turbulence that momentarily causes slight, erratic changes in altitude and/or attitude (pitch, roll, yaw) is reported as light turbulence. (PLT501, CA.I.C.K2) — AC 00-45

Answer (A) is incorrect because light chop is slight, rapid, somewhat rhythmic bumpiness. Answer (C) is incorrect because moderate turbulence causes changes in altitude and/or attitude, and variations in indicated airspeed.

ALL
5445. When turbulence causes changes in altitude and/or attitude, but aircraft control remains positive, that should be reported as

A—light.
B—severe.
C—moderate.

Moderate turbulence is similar to light turbulence but of greater intensity. Changes in altitude and/or attitude occur but the aircraft remains in positive control at all times. It usually causes variations in indicated airspeed. Moderate chop is similar to light chop but of greater intensity. It causes rapid bumps or jolts without appreciable changes in aircraft altitude or attitude. (PLT501, CA.I.C.K2) — AC 00-45

Answer (A) is incorrect because light turbulence momentarily causes slight, erratic changes in altitude and/or attitude. Answer (B) is incorrect because severe turbulence causes large, abrupt changes in altitude and/or attitude and the aircraft may be momentarily out of control.

ALL
5446. Turbulence that is encountered above 15,000 feet AGL not associated with cumuliform cloudiness, including thunderstorms, should be reported as

A—severe turbulence.
B—clear air turbulence.
C—convective turbulence.

High-level turbulence (normally above 15,000 feet AGL) not associated with cumuliform cloudiness, including thunderstorms, should be reported as CAT (clear air turbulence) preceded by the appropriate intensity, or light or moderate chop. (PLT501, CA.I.C.K2) — AC 00-45

Answer (A) is incorrect because severe turbulence is not dependent on altitude. Answer (C) is incorrect because convective turbulence refers to the lifting action related to turbulence with cumulus clouds.

ALL
5406. What significant cloud coverage is reported by this pilot report?

KMOB
UA/OV 15NW MOB 1340Z/SK OVC-TOP025 /
OVC045-TOP090

A—Three (3) separate overcast layers exist with bases at 250, 7,500 and 9,000 feet.
B—The top of the lower overcast is 2,500 feet; base and top of second overcast layer is 4,500 and 9,000 feet, respectively.
C—The base of the second overcast layer is 2,500 feet; top of second overcast layer is 7,500 feet; base of third layer is 9,000 feet.

UA—pilot report

/OV 15NW MOB—pilot was 15 miles northwest of Mobile, at 1340 UTC time

/SK OVC-TOP025—sky coverage, overcast layer top at 2,500 feet

/OVC045-TOP090—a second layer is at 4,500 feet with the top at 9,000 feet MSL

(PLT061, CA.I.C.K2) — AIM ¶7-1-19

Answers

| 5407 | [A] | 5444 | [B] | 5445 | [C] | 5446 | [B] | 5406 | [B] |

Chapter 7 **Weather Services**

ALL
5989. What is the bottom of the lowest overcast layer in the following pilot report?

KMOB UA /OV APE230010/TM 1515/FL085/TP BE20/ SK BKN065/WX FV03SM HZ FU/TA 20/TB LGT

A—There is not a defined ceiling in this report.
B—There is a layer reported at 8,500 feet.
C—There is a broken layer at 6,500 feet.

The sky cover portion of the report states "SK BKN 065" which means sky cover is broken at 6,500 feet. (PLT061, CA.I.C.K2) — AIM ¶7-1-19

Answer (A) is incorrect because the ceiling is defined in the "SK" section of the report. Answer (B) is incorrect because "FL085" is detailing the flight level the report was given at, not the sky coverage.

Terminal Aerodrome Forecast (TAF)

A TAF is a concise statement of the expected meteorological conditions at an airport during a specified period (usually 24 hours). TAFs use the same code used in the METAR weather reports (See Figure 7-1 on page 7-3).

TAFs are issued in the following format:

TYPE / LOCATION / ISSUANCE TIME / VALID TIME / FORECAST

Note: The "/" above are for separation purposes and do not appear in the actual TAFs.

ALL
5409. What is the meaning of the terms PROB40 2102 +TSRA as used in a Terminal Aerodrome Forecasts (TAF)?

A—Probability of heavy thunderstorms with rain showers below 4000 feet at time 2102.
B—Between 2100Z and 0200Z there is a forty percent (40%) probability of thunderstorms with heavy rain.
C—Beginning at 2102Z forty percent (40%) probability of heavy thunderstorms and rain showers.

The TAF reports there is a 40% probability (PROB40) between 2100Z and 0200Z (2102) of thunderstorms and heavy rain (+TSRA). (PLT288, CA.I.C.K2) — AIM ¶7-1-29

ALL
5410. What does the contraction VRB in the Terminal Aerodrome Forecast (TAF) mean?

A—Wind speed is variable throughout the period.
B—Cloud base is variable.
C—Wind direction is variable.

A variable wind direction is noted by "VRB" where the three-digit direction usually appears. (PLT288, CA.I.C.K2) — FAA-H-8083-25

ALL
5411. Which statement pertaining to the following Terminal Aerodrome Forecast (TAF) is true?

TAF
KMEM 091135Z 0915 15005KT 5SM HZ BKN060 FM1600 VRB04KT P6SM SKC

A—Wind in the valid period implies surface winds are forecast to be greater than 5 KTS.
B—Wind direction is from 160° at 4 KTS and reported visibility is 6 statute miles.
C—SKC in the valid period indicates no significant weather and sky clear.

TAF KMEM—terminal aerodrome forecast for Memphis

091135Z—observation is taken on the 9th of the month at 1135 Zulu time

15005KT—winds are from 150° at 5 knots

5SM HZ—visibility is 5 statute miles in haze

BKN060—ceiling is 6,000 feet broken

FM1600—from 1600Z

VRB04KT—wind is variable at 4 knots

P6SM—visibility is greater than 6 statute miles

SKC—sky is clear

(PLT288, CA.I.C.K2) — AIM ¶7-1-29

Answers

| 5989 | [C] | 5409 | [B] | 5410 | [C] | 5411 | [C] |

Chapter 7 **Weather Services**

ALL
5412. In the following METAR/TAF for HOU, what is the ceiling and visibility forecast on the 7th day of the month at 0600Z?

KHOU 061734Z 0618/0718 16014G22KT P6SM VCSH BKN018 BKN035
FM070100 17010KT P6SM BKN015 OVC025
FM070500 17008KT 4SM BR SCT008 OVC012
FM071000 18005KT 3SM BR OVC007
FM071500 23008KT 5SM BR VCSH SCT008 OVC015

A—Visibility 6 miles with a broken ceiling at 15,000 feet MSL.
B—4 nautical miles of visibility and an overcast ceiling at 700 feet MSL.
C—4 statute miles visibility and an overcast ceiling at 1,200 feet AGL.

The third line of the TAF reads from the 7th at 0500 wind 170 at 8 knots, visibility 4 statute miles in mist, scattered 800 AGL, overcast 1,200 AGL. Because the next weather forecast is not given until the 7th at 1000, you would use the information from the forecast for the 7th at 0500 to answer the question, "FM070500 17008KT 4SM BR SCT008 OVC012." Remember that a scattered layer does not signify a ceiling (PLT288, CA.I.C.K2) — FAA-H-8083-25

ALL
5413. Terminal Aerodrome Forecasts (TAF) are issued how many times a day and cover what period of time?

A—Four times daily and are usually valid for a 24 hour period.
B—Six times daily and are usually valid for a 24 hour period including a 4-hour categorical outlook.
C—Four times daily and are valid for 12 hours including a 6-hour categorical outlook.

Terminal Aerodrome Forecast (TAF) is a concise statement of the expected meteorological conditions at an airport during a specified period (usually 24 hours). TAFs use the same codes as METAR weather reports. They are scheduled four times daily for 24-hour periods beginning at 0000Z, 0600Z, 1200Z, and 1800Z. (PLT288, CA.I.C.K2) — FAA-H-8083-25

Graphical Forecasts for Aviation (GFA)

The GFA is an interactive web-based display providing continuously updated observed and forecasted weather information over the continental United States (CONUS). It is intended to give users a complete picture of weather critical to aviation safety. The GFA display shows user-selected weather categories, each containing multiple fields of interest at altitudes from the surface up to FL480. Depending on the field of interest chosen, weather information is available from -6 in the past (observed) to +15 hours in the future (forecasted).

The GFA is not considered a weather product but an aggregate of several existing weather products. The information and data from the various weather products are overlaid on a high-resolution basemap of the United States: **aviationweather.gov/gfa**. The user selects flight levels and current time period for either observed or forecasted weather information. Mouse clicking or hovering over the map provides additional information in textual format, such as current METAR or TAF for a selected airport. The GFA replaces the textual Area Forecast (FA) for the CONUS and Hawaii with a more modern digital solution for obtaining weather information.

ALL
5414. To best determine general forecast weather conditions covering a flight information region, the pilot should refer to

A—Graphical Forecasts for Aviation (GFA).
B—Weather Depiction Charts.
C—Satellite Maps.

The Graphical Forecasts for Aviation (GFA) is intended to provide the necessary aviation weather information to give users a complete picture of the weather that may impact flight in the continental U.S. (CONUS). (PLT290, CA.I.C.K2) — AIM

Answers

5412 [C]   5413 [A]   5414 [A]

Chapter 7 **Weather Services**

Winds and Temperatures Aloft Forecast (FB)

The FB is displayed in a 6-digit format (DDffTT). It shows wind direction (DD), wind velocity (ff), and the temperature (TT) that is forecast to exist at specified levels. For example, "234502" decodes as: winds from 230° true north, at 45 knots, temperatures 02°C.

When the wind speed (ff) is between 100 and 199 knots, the wind direction (DD) portion of the code will be greater than 50. In cases such as this, you will need to subtract 50 from the coded wind direction, and add 100 to the coded wind speed in order to decipher the code. For example, "734502" decodes as: winds from 230° true north at 145 knots, temperature 02°C.

Temperatures with a negative symbol in front of them (DDff-37) are negative. For flight levels above FL240, temperatures are always negative and will not have a negative symbol. Light and variable winds or wind speeds below 5 knots are indicated by 9900, followed by the forecast temperature. For example, the coded winds aloft forecast for flight level FL270 is "990017" and decodes as: winds are light and variable, temperature -17°C.

The observed winds aloft chart shows temperature, wind direction, and speed at selected stations. Arrows with pennants and barbs indicate wind direction and speed. Each pennant is 50 knots, each barb is 10 knots, and each half barb is 5 knots. Wind direction is shown by an arrow drawn to the nearest 10 degrees, with the second digit of the coded direction entered at the outer end of the arrow. Thus, a wind in the northwest quadrant with the digit 3 indicates 330°, and a wind in the southwest quadrant with the digit 3 indicates 230°.

ALL
5424. What values are used for Winds Aloft Forecasts?

A—True direction and MPH.
B—True direction and knots.
C—Magnetic direction and knots.

Wind direction is with reference to true north and wind speed is given in knots on winds aloft forecast reports. (PLT076, CA.I.C.K2) — AC 00-45

Inflight Weather Advisories (WA, WS, WST)

Inflight Weather Advisories advise pilots en route of the possibility of encountering hazardous flying conditions that may not have been forecast at the time of the preflight weather briefing.

AIRMETs (WA) contain information on weather that may be hazardous to single engine, other light aircraft, and VFR pilots. The items covered are moderate icing or turbulence, sustained winds of 30 knots or more at the surface, widespread areas of IFR conditions, and extensive mountain obscurement.

SIGMETs (WS) advise of weather potentially hazardous to all aircraft. The items covered are severe icing, severe or extreme turbulence, and widespread sandstorms, dust storms or volcanic ash lowering visibility to less than 3 miles.

SIGMETs and AIRMETs are broadcast upon receipt and at 30-minute intervals (H + 15 and H + 45) during the first hour. If the advisory is still in effect after the first hour, an alert notice will be broadcast. Pilots may contact the nearest FSS to ascertain whether the advisory is pertinent to their flights.

Convective SIGMETs (WST) cover weather developments such as tornadoes, lines of thunderstorms, and embedded thunderstorms; they also imply severe or greater turbulence, severe icing, and low-level wind shear. When a SIGMET forecasts embedded thunderstorms, it indicates that the thunderstorms are obscured by massive cloud layers and cannot be seen. Convective SIGMET bulletins are issued hourly

Answers
5424 [B]

Chapter 7 Weather Services

at H + 55. Unscheduled convective sigmets are broadcast upon receipt and at 15-minute intervals for the first hour (H + 15; H + 30; H + 45).

Telephone Information Briefing Service (TIBS), provided by FSS, is a system of automated telephone recordings of meteorological and aeronautical information issued throughout the United States. Based on the specific needs of each area, TIBS provides route and/or area briefings in addition to airspace procedures and special announcements concerning aviation interests that may be available. Depending on user demand, other items may be supplied; for example, surface weather observations, terminal forecasts, wind and temperatures aloft forecasts, etc. TIBS is not intended to be a substitute for preflight briefings from the FSS specialists. TIBS is recommended as a preliminary briefing, accessible by calling 1-800-WX-BRIEF and often will be valuable in helping you to make a "go or no go" decision.

ALL
5422. SIGMETs are issued as a warning of weather conditions which are hazardous

A—to all aircraft.
B—particularly to heavy aircraft.
C—particularly to light airplanes.

A SIGMET advises of weather potentially hazardous to all aircraft, other than convective activity. In the conterminous U.S., items covered are:

1. *Severe icing;*
2. *Severe or extreme turbulence; and*
3. *Dust storms, sandstorms or volcanic ash lowering visibilities to less than 3 miles.*

(PLT290, CA.I.C.K2) — AC 00-45

ALL
5423. Which correctly describes the purpose of convective SIGMETs (WST)?

A—They consist of an hourly observation of tornadoes, significant thunderstorm activity, and large hailstone activity.
B—They contain both an observation and a forecast of all thunderstorm and hailstone activity. The forecast is valid for 1 hour only.
C—They consist of either an observation and a forecast or just a forecast for tornadoes, significant thunderstorm activity, or hail greater than or equal to 3/4 inch in diameter.

Convective SIGMETs are issued in the conterminous U.S. for any of the following:

1. *Severe thunderstorms due to surface winds greater than or equal to 50 knots or hail at the surface greater than or equal to 3/4 inches in diameter or tornadoes;*
2. *Embedded thunderstorms;*
3. *Line of thunderstorms; or*

4. *Thunderstorms greater than or equal to VIP level four affecting 40% or more of an area at least 3,000 square miles.*

(PLT290, CA.I.C.K2) — AC 00-45

Answer (A) is incorrect because SIGMETs are unscheduled forecasts. Answer (B) is incorrect because SIGMETs are issued only for severe thunderstorms and hail 3/4 inch or larger and they can be valid for up to 2 hours.

ALL
5417. What type of Inflight Weather Advisories provides an en route pilot with information regarding the possibility of moderate icing, moderate turbulence, winds of 30 knots or more at the surface and extensive mountain obscurement?

A—Convective SIGMETs and SIGMETs.
B—Severe Weather Forecast Alerts (AWW) and SIGMETs.
C—AIRMETs and Center Weather Advisories (CWA).

AIRMETs and Center Weather Advisories (CWA) may be of significance to any pilot or aircraft operator and are issued for all domestic airspace. They are of particular concern to operators and pilots of aircraft sensitive to the phenomena described and to pilots without instrument ratings. They are issued for the following weather phenomena which are potentially hazardous to aircraft: moderate icing, moderate turbulence, sustained winds of 30 knots or more at the surface, widespread area of ceilings less than 1,000 feet and/or visibility less than three miles, and extensive mountain obscurement. (PLT294, CA.I.C.K2) — AIM ¶7-1-5

Answers

5422 [A]   5423 [C]   5417 [C]

Chapter 7 **Weather Services**

ALL
5418. What single reference contains information regarding a volcanic eruption, that is occurring or expected to occur?

A—In-Flight Weather Advisories.
B—Terminal Area Forecasts (TAF).
C—Weather Depiction Chart.

In-Flight Weather Advisories (SIGMETs) provide information regarding volcanic eruption, that is occurring or expected to occur. (PLT294, CA.I.C.K2) — AIM ¶7-1-5

Answer (B) is incorrect because Terminal Area Forecasts (TAF) is a concise statement of the expected meteorological conditions at an airport during a specified period. Answer (C) is incorrect because a Weather Depiction Chart is a report of weather as of the time of observation.

ALL
5560. Weather Advisory Broadcasts, including Severe Weather Forecast Alerts (AWW), SIGMETs and Convective SIGMETs, are provided by

A—ARTCCs on all frequencies, except emergency, when any part of the area described is within 150 miles of the airspace under their jurisdiction.
B—Flight Service on 122.2 MHz and adjacent VORs, when any part of the area described is within 200 miles of the airspace under their jurisdiction.
C—selected low-frequency and/or VOR navigational aids.

ARTCCs broadcast a Severe Weather Forecast Alert (AWW), SIGMET, Convective SIGMET, or CWA alert once on all frequencies, except emergency, when any part of the area described is within 150 miles of the airspace under their jurisdiction. These broadcasts contain a SIGMET or CWA (identification) and a brief description of the weather activity and general area affected. (PLT294, CA.I.C.K1) — AIM ¶7-1-9

Surface Analysis Chart

A surface analysis chart depicts frontal positions, pressure patterns, temperature, dew point, wind, weather, and obstructions to vision as of the valid time of the chart. Pressure patterns are shown with isobar lines around the highs and lows. Isobars are solid lines depicting sea level pressure patterns. They are usually spaced at 4-millibar intervals; close spacing of the isobars indicates a strong pressure gradient. When the pressure gradient is weak, dashed isobars are sometimes inserted at 2-millibar intervals to more clearly define the pressure pattern.

ALL
5425. On a Surface Analysis Chart, the solid lines that depict sea level pressure patterns are called

A—isobars.
B—isogons.
C—millibars.

Isobars are solid lines depicting the pressure pattern. They are usually spaced at four-millibar intervals on a surface analysis chart. (PLT287, CA.I.C.K2) — AC 00-45

Answer (B) is incorrect because isogons are lines of magnetic variation, found on navigational charts. Answer (C) is incorrect because millibars are units of pressure.

ALL
5426. Dashed lines on a Surface Analysis Chart, if depicted, indicate that the pressure gradient is

A—weak.
B—strong.
C—unstable.

When a pressure gradient is weak, dashed isobars are sometimes inserted at two-millibar intervals to more clearly define the pressure pattern. (PLT287, CA.I.C.K2) — AC 00-45

Answer (B) is incorrect because strong pressure gradients are indicated by closely-spaced solid isobars at 4-mb intervals. Answer (C) is incorrect because stability is concerned with temperature lapse rates.

Answers

5418 [A]   5560 [A]   5425 [A]   5426 [A]

ALL
5427. Which chart provides a ready means of locating observed frontal positions and pressure centers?

A—Surface Analysis Chart.
B—Constant Pressure Analysis Chart.
C—Weather Depiction Chart.

Surface Analysis Charts are used to denote pressure systems and fronts. (PLT287, CA.I.C.K2) — AC 00-45

Answer (B) is incorrect because Constant Pressure Analysis Charts provide observed moisture content, temperatures, and winds aloft. Answer (C) is incorrect because the Weather Depiction Chart depicts frontal location, cloud coverage and height, and VFR/MVFR/IFR.

ALL
5428. On a Surface Analysis Chart, close spacing of the isobars indicates

A—weak pressure gradient.
B—strong pressure gradient.
C—strong temperature gradient.

Close spacing of isobars indicate that a strong pressure gradient exists. (PLT071, CA.I.C.K2) — AC 00-45

Answer (A) is incorrect because farther spaced isobars indicate a weaker pressure gradient. Answer (C) is incorrect because isotherms indicate changing temperatures.

ALL
5429. The Surface Analysis Chart depicts

A—frontal locations and expected movement, pressure centers, cloud coverage, and obstructions to vision at the time of chart transmission.
B—actual frontal positions, pressure patterns, temperature, dewpoint, wind, weather, and obstructions to vision at the valid time of the chart.
C—actual pressure distribution, frontal systems, cloud heights and coverage, temperature, dewpoint, and wind at the time shown on the chart.

The Surface Analysis Chart depicts frontal system positions, pressure patterns, and the temperature, dew point, wind, weather and obstructions to vision at individual stations on the surface chart valid for the time given. (PLT287, CA.I.C.K2) — AC 00-45

Answer (A) is incorrect because the Surface Analysis Chart reports weather as of the time of observation. Answer (C) is incorrect because Surface Analysis Charts do not indicate cloud heights.

Constant Pressure Chart

A constant pressure analysis chart is an upper air weather map where all the information depicted is at the specified pressure-level of the chart. Each of the constant pressure analysis charts (850 MB, 700 MB, 500 MB, 300 MB, 250 MB, and 200 MB) can provide observed temperature/dewpoint spread, wind, height of the pressure surface, and the height changes over the previous 12-hour period.

ALL
5440. Hatching on a Constant Pressure Analysis Chart indicates

A—hurricane eye.
B—windspeed 70 knots to 110 knots.
C—windspeed 110 knots to 150 knots.

To aid in identifying areas of strong winds, hatching denotes wind speeds of 70 to 110 knots, a clear area within a hatched area indicates wind of 110 to 150 knots, and an area of 150 to 190 knots of wind is hatched. (PLT283, CA.I.C.K2) — AC 00-45

Answer (A) is incorrect because the hurricane eye has very low winds. Answer (C) is incorrect because a clear area within a hatched area indicates wind of 110 to 150 knots.

ALL
5441. What flight planning information can a pilot derive from Constant Pressure Analysis Charts?

A—Winds and temperatures aloft.
B—Clear air turbulence and icing conditions.
C—Frontal systems and obstructions to vision aloft.

The Constant Pressure Analysis Chart is a source of observed temperature, temperature/dewpoint spread, moisture and wind. (PLT283, CA.I.C.K2) — AC 00-45

Answer (B) is incorrect because clear air turbulence can be found on prognostic charts and in area forecasts. Answer (C) is incorrect because frontal systems and obstructions to vision aloft can be found on Surface Analysis and Weather Depiction charts.

Answers

5427 [A]   5428 [B]   5429 [B]   5440 [B]   5441 [A]

Chapter 7 **Weather Services**

ALL
5442. From which of the following can the observed temperature, wind, and temperature/dewpoint spread be determined at a specified altitude?

A—Stability Charts.
B—Winds Aloft Forecasts.
C—Constant Pressure Analysis Charts.

The Constant Pressure Analysis Chart is a source of observed temperature, temperature/dewpoint spread, moisture, and wind. (PLT283, CA.I.C.K2) — AC 00-45

Answer (A) is incorrect because Stability Charts provide information on stability, freezing level, precipitation, and average relative humidity. Answer (B) is incorrect because Winds Aloft Forecasts do not provide information about temperature/dewpoint spread.

Tropopause Height/Vertical Wind Shear Prognostic Chart

A tropopause height/vertical wind shear prognostic chart is a two-panel chart containing a maximum wind prognostic chart and a vertical wind shear prognostic chart. The chart is prepared for the contiguous 48 states and is available once a day with a valid time of 18Z. It shows the temperature, pressure, and wind at the tropopause.

ALL
5443. The minimum vertical wind shear value critical for probable moderate or greater turbulence is

A—4 knots per 1,000 feet.
B—6 knots per 1,000 feet.
C—8 knots per 1,000 feet.

The vertical shear critical for probable turbulence is 6 knots per 1,000 feet. (PLT518, CA.I.C.K2) — AC 00-45

Significant Weather Prognostics

A low-level significant weather prognostic chart (surface to 24,000 feet) portrays forecast weather which may influence flight planning, including those areas or activities of most significant turbulence and icing. It is a four-panel chart; the two lower panels are 12- and 24-hour surface progs. The chart is issued four times daily. The chart uses standard weather symbols as shown in Figure 7-5.

The high-level significant weather prognostic chart (24,000 feet to 63,000 feet) outlines areas of forecast turbulence and cumulonimbus clouds, shows the expected height of the tropopause, and predicts jet stream location and velocity. The chart depicts clouds and turbulence as shown in Figure 7-6.

The height of the tropopause is depicted in hundreds of feet MSL and is enclosed in a rectangular box. Areas of forecast moderate or greater CAT are bounded by heavy dashed lines and are labeled with the appropriate symbol and the vertical extent in hundreds of feet MSL. Cumulonimbus clouds imply moderate or greater turbulence and icing.

Answers

5442 [C]   5443 [B]

Chapter 7 **Weather Services**

Symbol	Meaning	Symbol	Meaning	Depiction	Meaning
◠△◠	Moderate Turbulence	▽̇	Rain Shower	(oval with dashes, ℞/▽̇)	Showery precipitation (Thunderstorms/rain showers) covering half or more of the area.
◠△△◠	Severe Turbulence	▽⁎	Snow Shower	(oval with dashes, ● ●)	Continuous precipitation (rain) covering half or more of the area.
⼁⼁⼁	Moderate Icing	℞	Thunderstorm	(oval, ⁎ over ▽)	Showery precipitation (snow showers) covering less than half of the area.
⼁⼁⼁	Severe Icing	⌒⌢	Freezing Rain		
●	Rain	𝅘𝅥	Tropical Storm	(oval, ,)	Intermittent precipitation (drizzle) covering less than half of the area.
⁎	Snow	𝅘𝅥	Hurricane (typhoon)		
,	Drizzle			(oval with dashes, ●● /▽̇)	Showery precipitation (rain showers) embedded in an area of continuous rain covering more than half of the area.

Note: Character of stable precipitation is the manner in which it occurs. It may be intermittent or continuous.

Examples:

	Intermittent	Continuous
Rain	●	●●
Drizzle	,	,,
Snow	⁎	⁎⁎

Figure 7-5. Significant weather prognostics

Depiction	Meaning	Depiction	Meaning
ISOL EMBD CB 420/XXX	Embedded cumulonimbus, less than 1/8 coverage, bases below 24,000 feet, tops 42,000 feet	TO △△ 330/XXX	Moderate to severe turbulence, below 24,000 feet to 33,000 feet (for turbulence below 24,000 feet see low-level prog)
OCNL EMBD CB 520/XXX	Embedded cumulonimbus, 1/8 to 4/8 coverage, bases below 24,000 feet, tops 52,000 feet	△ ABV 630/350	Moderate turbulence from 35,000 feet to above upper limit of the prog
FRQ CB 330/XXX	Cumulonimbus, 5/8 to 8/8 coverage, bases below 24,000 feet, tops 33,000 feet	(volcano symbol)	Volcanic Eruption Mt. Spurr 61.3 N 152.3 W At 15/1325Z CHECK SIGMETS FOR VOLCANIC ASH

Figure 7-6. Prognostic chart depictions

Chapter 7 **Weather Services**

ALL
5433. Which weather chart depicts conditions forecast to exist at a specific time in the future?

A—Freezing Level Chart.
B—Weather Depiction Chart.
C—12-Hour Significant Weather Prognostic Chart.

Prog (prognostic) charts portray weather forecasts for sometime in the future for the conterminous U.S. and adjacent areas. (PLT286, CA.I.C.K2) — AC 00-45

Answer (A) is incorrect because there is no chart named the Freezing Level Chart. Answer (B) is incorrect because the Weather Depiction Charts show conditions valid only for the time given for the chart.

ALL
5436. What is the upper limit of the Low Level Significant Weather Prognostic Chart?

A—30,000 feet.
B—24,000 feet.
C—18,000 feet.

The U.S. Low-Level Significant Weather Prog includes significant weather from the surface to 24,000 feet (400 millibars). (PLT286, CA.I.C.K2) — AC 00-45

ALL
5434. What weather phenomenon is implied within an area enclosed by small scalloped lines on a U.S. High-Level Significant Weather Prognostic Chart?

A—Cirriform clouds, light to moderate turbulence, and icing.
B—Cumulonimbus clouds, icing, and moderate or greater turbulence.
C—Cumuliform or standing lenticular clouds, moderate to severe turbulence, and icing.

Small-scalloped lines enclose areas of expected cumulonimbus development. Cumulonimbus clouds imply moderate or greater turbulence and icing. (PLT068, CA.I.C.K2) — AC 00-45

ALL
5435. The U.S. High-Level Significant Weather Prognostic Chart forecasts significant weather for what airspace?

A—18,000 feet to 45,000 feet.
B—24,000 feet to 45,000 feet.
C—24,000 feet to 63,000 feet.

The U.S. High-Level Significant Weather Prognostic Chart forecasts significant weather encompassing airspace from 24,000 feet to 63,000 feet pressure altitude (400 to 70 millibars). (PLT286, CA.I.C.K2) — AC 00-45

Lifted Index Chart

The lifted index is the temperature difference between an air parcel lifted adiabatically and the temperature of the environment at a given pressure height in the troposphere of the atmosphere, usually 500 mb. The lifted index chart is often used as an indicator of severe weather. When the value is positive, the atmosphere (at the respective height) is stable, and when the value is negative, the atmosphere is unstable.

ALL
5439. The difference found by subtracting the temperature of a parcel of air theoretically lifted from the surface to 500 millibars and the existing temperature at 500 millibars is called the

A—lifted index.
B—negative index.
C—positive index.

The lifted index is computed as if a parcel of air near the surface were lifted to 500 millibars. As the air is "lifted," it cools by expansion. The temperature the parcel would have at 500 millibars is then subtracted from the existing 500 millibar (mb) temperature. The difference is the lifted index; it may be positive, zero, or negative. (PLT070, CA.I.C.K2) — AC 00-45

Answer (B) is incorrect because a positive index means the lifted parcel of air is colder than the existing air at 500 mb, and the air is stable. Answer (C) is incorrect because a negative index means the lifted parcel of air is warmer than the existing air at 500 mb, and the air is unstable.

Answers

| 5433 | [C] | 5436 | [B] | 5434 | [B] | 5435 | [C] | 5439 | [A] |

Chapter 8
Aircraft Performance

Weight and Balance   *8–3*

    Computing Weight and Balance   *8–4*

    Graph Weight and Balance Problems   *8–4*

    Weight Change   *8–5*

    Weight Shift   *8–6*

Rotorcraft Weight and Balance   *8–12*

Glider Weight and Balance   *8–15*

Headwind and Crosswind Components   *8–17*

Density Altitude   *8–19*

Takeoff and Landing Considerations   *8–20*

Takeoff and Landing Distance   *8–22*

Fuel Consumption vs. Brake Horsepower   *8–26*

Time, Fuel, and Distance to Climb   *8–28*

    Table Method   *8–28*

    Graph Method   *8–29*

Cruise Performance Table   *8–33*

Cruise and Range Performance Table   *8–35*

Maximum Rate of Climb   *8–36*

Glide Distance   *8–37*

Rotorcraft Performance   *8–38*

Glider Performance   *8–40*

Balloon Performance   *8–43*

Chapter 8 **Aircraft Performance**

Weight and Balance

Even though an aircraft has been certificated for flight at a specified maximum gross weight, it may not be safe to take off with that load under all conditions. High altitude, high temperature, and high humidity are additional factors which may require limiting the load to be carried.

In addition to considering the weight, the pilot must ensure the load is arranged to keep the aircraft in balance. The balance point, or **center of gravity (CG)**, is the point at which all of the weight of the system is considered to be concentrated. For an aircraft to be safe to fly, the center of gravity must fall between specified limits. To keep the CG within safe limits, it may be necessary to move weight toward the nose of the aircraft (forward) which moves the CG forward, or toward the tail (aft) which moves the CG aft. The aircraft and the various compartments of the aircraft are designed for specific maximum weights and critical load factors. Compartments placarded for a given weight may be loaded to the maximum allowable load only if the CG is kept within limits and the aircraft is flown safely within critical load factor limits.

The **datum** is an imaginary vertical reference line from which locations on/in an aircraft are measured. The datum is established by the manufacturer and may vary in location in different aircraft. See Figure 8-1.

The **arm** (or station) is the horizontal distance measured in inches from the datum line to a point on the aircraft. If measured aft toward the tail, the arm is given a positive value; if measured forward toward the nose, the arm is given a negative value. When all arms are positive, the datum is located at the nose or in front of the airplane. See Figure 8-2.

The **moment** is the product of the weight of an object multiplied by its arm and is expressed in pound-inches (lbs-in): Weight × Arm = Moment. The moment index is a moment divided by a constant such as 100 or 1,000. It is used to simplify computations where heavy items and long arms result in large, unmanageable numbers.

The position of the CG is expressed in inches from datum, and is found by dividing the total moments by the total weight:

$$\text{CG (inches aft of datum)} = \frac{\text{Total Moment}}{\text{Total Weight}}$$

Figure 8-1. Datum lines

The specified forward and aft points within which the CG must be located for safe flight are called the **center of gravity limits**. These limits are specified by the manufacturer. The distance between the forward and aft CG limits is called the **center of gravity range**. The empty weight includes the airframe, engine(s), all items of equipment, unusable fuel, hydraulic fluid, and undrainable oil, or, in some aircraft, all of the oil. The useful load includes the pilot, passengers, baggage, fuel,

Figure 8-2. Positive and negative arms

and oil. The takeoff weight is the empty weight plus the useful load. The landing weight is the takeoff weight minus any fuel used.

Computing Weight and Balance

Problem:

Calculate the weight and balance and determine where the CG would be located for three weights given the following:

Weight D—160 lbs at 45 inches aft of datum

Weight E—170 lbs at 145 inches aft of datum

Weight F—105 lbs at 185 inches aft of datum

Solution:

1. Construct a table, with column headings as follows:

    | Item | Weight | Arm | Moment |

2. Find the moment for each item by multiplying the weight times the arm:

Item	Weight	Arm	Moment
Weight D	160	45	7,200
Weight E	170	145	24,650
Weight F	105	185	19,425

3. Total the weights and moments:

Weight	Moment
160	7,200
170	24,650
+ 105	+ 19,425
435 lbs	51,275 lbs-in

4. Determine the CG by dividing the total moment by the total weight:

    $$CG = \frac{\text{Total moment}}{\text{Total weight}}$$

    CG = 51,275 ÷ 435 = 117.8 inches

Graph Weight and Balance Problems

Airplane manufacturers use one of several available systems to provide loading information. Weight and balance computations are greatly simplified by two graphic aids: the loading graph and the center of gravity moment envelope. The graphs shown in FAA Figure 38 are typical of those found in a POH.

Problem:

Determine if the airplane is loaded within limits, given the following:

Empty weight (oil included) .... 1,271 lbs
Empty weight moment (lbs-in/1,000) .... 102.04 lbs-in
Pilot and copilot .... 400 lbs
Rear seat passenger .... 140 lbs
Cargo .... 100 lbs
Fuel .... 37 gallons

Solution:

1. Construct a table with the Item, Weight, and Moment. The moment of each item is found by using the loading graph in FAA Figure 38. Locate the weight of each item on the left side of the chart, and proceed to the right to intersect the correct item line. At point of intersection, proceed downward to find the moment for that item at the specified weight.

Item	Weight	Moment/1,000
Aircraft empty weight	1,271	102.04
Pilot and copilot	400	36.00
Aft passenger	140	18.00
Cargo	100	11.50
Fuel (37.0 gal × 6 lbs/gal)	+ 222	+ 20.00
Totals	2,133	187.54

2. Compare the total weight and moment to the limits in the CG envelope in FAA Figure 38. Move up the loaded aircraft weight scale to 2,133, then across to 187.54 on the moment/1,000 scale. The weight and CG are within limits.

Weight Change

There are a number of additional weight and balance formulas that may be used to determine the effect on the CG due to a weight change. Use the following formula to find the change in CG, if weight has been added or subtracted. The amount of weight changed and the new total weight must be known, in addition to the distance between the original CG and the point where the weight is being added or subtracted.

$$\frac{\text{Weight lost or gained}}{\text{New total weight}} = \frac{\text{Change in CG}}{\text{Distance between original CG and point of weight removed or added}}$$

Problem:

Determine the new CG location after 1 hour 45 minutes of flight time, given the following:

Total weight .... 4,037 lbs
CG location .... Station 67.8
Fuel consumption .... 14.7 GPH
Fuel CG .... Station 68.0

Solution:

1. Find the amount of weight change. The aircraft has consumed 14.7 GPH for 1 hour 45 minutes. The total fuel consumed is:

    14.7 GPH × 1.75 hr = 25.7 gal

    Which weighs:

    25.7 gal × 6 lbs/gal = 154 lbs

2. Determine the new total weight by subtracting the weight of the fuel consumed (154 lbs) from the total weight (4,037 lbs):

    4,037 − 154 = 3,883 lbs new total weight

3. Find the distance between the original CG (67.8) and the point weight removed (fuel CG = 68.0):

    68.0 − 67.8 = 0.2 inches

4. Place the three known values into the formula:

    $$\frac{154 \text{ lbs}}{3,883 \text{ lbs}} = \frac{\text{Change in CG}}{0.2 \text{ in}}$$

    $$\text{Change in CG} = \frac{154 \text{ lbs} \times 0.2 \text{ in}}{3,883 \text{ lbs}} = 0.01 \text{ in}$$

5. The CG was found to shift approximately 0.01 in. Since the weight was removed aft (68.0 in) of the CG (67.8 in), the CG shifted forward 0.01 in.

    $$\begin{array}{rl} 67.80 & \text{original CG} \\ -\,0.01 & \text{forward shift} \\ \hline 67.79 & \text{new CG} \end{array}$$

Weight Shift

A shift in weight may have a great affect on the CG location even though the total weight may not have changed. The change in CG caused by a weight shift, or the amount of weight to shift in order to move the CG within limits, may be found by the formula below:

$$\frac{\text{Weight shifted}}{\text{Total weight}} = \frac{\text{Change in CG}}{\text{Distance shifted}}$$

Problem:

Determine the new CG after luggage has been shifted, given the following:

Gross weight.. 5,000 lbs (including three pieces of luggage)
CG .... 98 inches aft of datum (2 inches aft of limits)
2 pieces of luggage .... 100 lbs (weighed together)

The luggage is moved from the rear baggage compartment (145 inches aft of datum) to the front compartment (45 inches aft of datum).

Chapter 8 Aircraft Performance

Solution:

1. Find the distance shifted by taking the difference between the original location (baggage compartment 145 inches) and the new location (front compartment 45 inches):

   ```
   145 in   baggage compartment
   - 45 in  front compartment
   100 in   distance shifted
   ```

2. Determine the change in CG by substituting the values into the formula:

   $$\frac{100 \text{ lbs}}{5{,}000 \text{ lbs}} = \frac{\text{Change in CG}}{100 \text{ in}}$$

   $$\frac{100 \text{ lbs} \times 100 \text{ in}}{5{,}000 \text{ lbs}} = \text{Change in CG} = 2 \text{ inches}$$

3. The CG is moved 2 inches. Since the weight was shifted from the rear compartment (145 inches) to the front compartment (45 inches), the CG moved forward by 2 inches.

   ```
   98 in   original CG
   - 2 in  CG shift
   96 in   new CG
   ```

The new CG is located 96 inches aft of datum, which places it on the aft limit.

ALL
5632. When computing weight and balance, the basic empty weight includes the weight of the airframe, engine(s), and all installed optional equipment. Basic empty weight also includes

A—the unusable fuel, full operating fluids, and full oil.
B—all usable fuel, full oil, hydraulic fluid, but does not include the weight of pilot, passengers, or baggage.
C—all usable fuel and oil, but does not include any radio equipment or instruments that were installed by someone other than the manufacturer.

Basic empty weight includes unusable fuel, full operating fluids, and full oil. (PLT021, CA.I.F.K2f) — FAA-H-8083-1

ALL
5633. If all index units are positive when computing weight and balance, the location of the datum would be at the

A—centerline of the main wheels.
B—nose, or out in front of the airplane.
C—centerline of the nose or tailwheel, depending on the type of airplane.

In general, the arm (index unit) of a location in the aircraft is in inches aft of the datum. A positive arm indicates the position of the object is aft of the datum. If all index units are positive, the datum must be at least at the nose of the aircraft. (PLT021, CA.I.F.K2f) — FAA-H-8083-1

Answer (A) is incorrect because the engine would have a negative arm if the datum was at the centerline of the main wheels. Answer (C) is incorrect because the propeller would have a negative arm if the datum were at the centerline of the nose or tailwheel.

ALL
5634. The CG of an aircraft can be determined by which of the following methods?

A—Dividing total arms by total moments.
B—Multiplying total arms by total weight.
C—Dividing total moments by total weight.

Total moment is the weight of the airplane multiplied by the distance between the datum and the CG. Therefore:

$$CG = \frac{\text{Total Moment}}{\text{Total Weight}}$$

(PLT003, CA.I.F.K2e) — FAA-H-8083-1

Answers

5632 [A]   5633 [B]   5634 [C]

Chapter 8 **Aircraft Performance**

ALL
5636. GIVEN:

Weight A: 155 pounds at 45 inches aft of datum
Weight B: 165 pounds at 145 inches aft of datum
Weight C: 95 pounds at 185 inches aft of datum

Based on this information, where would the CG be located aft of datum?

A—86.0 inches.
B—116.8 inches.
C—125.0 inches.

1. Arm is the aft of datum value for each item:

Weight	x	Arm	=	Moment	
155	x	45	=	6,975	for A
165	x	145	=	23,925	for B
+ 95	x	185	=	+ 17,575	for C
415 lbs				48,475 lbs-in	

2. Moments ÷ Total Weight = CG Location

    48,475 ÷ 415 = 116.8 inches

(PLT003, CA.I.F.K2e) — FAA-H-8083-1

ALL
5637. GIVEN:

Weight A: 140 pounds at 17 inches aft of datum
Weight B: 120 pounds at 110 inches aft of datum
Weight C: 85 pounds at 210 inches aft of datum

Based on this information, the CG would be located how far aft of datum?

A—89.11 inches.
B—96.89 inches.
C—106.92 inches.

1. Arm is the aft of datum value for each item:

Weight	x	Arm	=	Moment	
140	x	17	=	2,380	for A
120	x	110	=	13,200	for B
+ 85	x	210	=	+ 17,850	for C
345 lbs				33,430 lbs-in	

2. Moments ÷ Total Weight = CG Location

    33,430 ÷ 345 = 96.89 inches

(PLT003, CA.I.F.K2e) — FAA-H-8083-1

ALL
5638. GIVEN:

Weight A: 135 pounds at 15 inches aft of datum
Weight B: 205 pounds at 117 inches aft of datum
Weight C: 85 pounds at 195 inches aft of datum

Based on this information, the CG would be located how far aft of datum?

A—100.2 inches.
B—109.0 inches.
C—121.7 inches.

1. Arm is the aft of datum value for each item:

Weight	x	Arm	=	Moment	
135	x	15	=	2,025	for A
205	x	117	=	23,985	for B
+ 85	x	195	=	+ 16,575	for C
425 lbs				42,585 lbs-in	

2. Moments ÷ Total Weight = CG Location

    42,585 ÷ 425 = 100.2 inches

(PLT003, CA.I.F.K2e) — FAA-H-8083-1

ALL
5639. GIVEN:

Weight A: 175 pounds at 135 inches aft of datum
Weight B: 135 pounds at 115 inches aft of datum
Weight C: 75 pounds at 85 inches aft of datum

The CG for the combined weights would be located how far aft of datum?

A—91.76 inches.
B—111.67 inches.
C—118.24 inches.

1. Arm is the aft of datum value for each item:

Weight	x	Arm	=	Moment	
175	x	135	=	23,625	for A
135	x	115	=	15,525	for B
+ 75	x	85	=	+ 6,375	for C
385 lbs				45,525 lbs-in	

2. Moments ÷ Total Weight = CG Location

    45,525 ÷ 385 = 118.25 inches

(PLT003, CA.I.F.K2e) — FAA-H-8083-1

Answers

5636 [B]   5637 [B]   5638 [A]   5639 [C]

ALL
5164. Baggage weighing 90 pounds is placed in a normal category airplane's baggage compartment which is placarded at 100 pounds. If this airplane is subjected to a positive load factor of 3.5 Gs, the total load of the baggage would be

A—315 pounds and would be excessive.
B—315 pounds and would not be excessive.
C—350 pounds and would not be excessive.

Each cargo compartment must be designed for its placarded maximum weight of contents in relation to the critical load factors. Normal category aircraft having a gross weight of less than 4,000 pounds are designed for a maneuvering load factor of 3.8 times the aircraft weight or 3.8 Gs. Thus a load factor of 3.5 Gs would not be excessive. Load factor is the ratio of a given load to its weight. Thus:

```
   90.0  lbs weight
 × 3.5   Gs
 ─────
  315.0  lbs loading
```

(PLT018, CA.I.F.K2f) — FAA-H-8083-25

AIR
5650. (Refer to Figure 38.)
GIVEN:

Empty weight (oil is included)	1,271 lb
Empty weight moment (in-lb/1,000)	102.04
Pilot and copilot	400 lb
Rear seat passenger	140 lb
Cargo	100 lb
Fuel	37 gal

Is the airplane loaded within limits?

A—Yes, the weight and CG is within limits.
B—No, the weight exceeds the maximum allowable.
C—No, the weight is acceptable, but the CG is aft of the aft limit.

1. *Construct a table with the Item, Weight, and Moment. The moment of each item is found by using the Loading Graph in FAA Figure 38. Locate the weight of each item on the left side of the chart, and proceed to the right to intersect the correct item line. At point of intersection, proceed downward to find the moment for that item at the specified weight.*

Item	Weight	Moment
Aircraft empty weight	1,271	102.04
Pilot and copilot	400	36.00
Aft passenger	140	18.00
Cargo	100	11.50
Fuel (37.0 gal × 6 lbs/gal)	+ 222	+ 20.00
Totals	2,133	187.54

2. *Compare the total weight and moment to the limits in the center of gravity envelope in FAA Figure 38. Move up the loaded aircraft weight scale to 2,133, then across to 187.54 on the moment/1,000 scale. The weight and CG are within limits.*

(PLT021, CA.I.F.K2f) — FAA-H-8083-25

AIR
5651. (Refer to Figure 38.)
GIVEN:

Empty weight (oil is included)	1,271 lb
Empty weight moment (in-lb/1,000)	102.04
Pilot and copilot	260 lb
Rear seat passenger	120 lb
Cargo	60 lb
Fuel	37 gal

Under these conditions, the CG is determined to be located

A—within the CG envelope.
B—on the forward limit of the CG envelope.
C—within the shaded area of the CG envelope.

1. *Construct a table with the Item, Weight, and Moment. The moment of each item is found by using the Loading Graph in FAA Figure 38. Locate the weight of each item on the left side of the chart, and proceed to the right to intersect the correct item line. At point of intersection, proceed downward to find the moment for that item at the specified weight.*

Item	Weight	Moment
Aircraft empty weight	1,271	102.04
Pilot and copilot	260	23.30
Aft passenger	120	15.00
Cargo	60	6.80
Fuel (37.0 gal × 6 lbs/gal)	+ 222	+ 20.00
Totals	1,933	167.14

2. *Compare to the limits in FAA Figure 38. Using the CG Envelope Graph, move up the loaded aircraft weight scale to 1,933, then across to 167.14 on the moment/1,000 scale. The weight and CG are within limits.*

(PLT003, CA.I.F.K2f) — FAA-H-8083-1

Answers

5164 [B]   5650 [A]   5651 [A]

Chapter 8 **Aircraft Performance**

AIR
5652. (Refer to Figure 38.)
GIVEN:

Empty weight (oil is included)	1,271 lb
Empty weight moment (in-lb/1,000)	102.04
Pilot and copilot	360 lb
Cargo	340 lb
Fuel	37 gal

Will the CG remain within limits after 30 gallons of fuel has been used in flight?

A—Yes, the CG will remain within limits.
B—No, the CG will be located aft of the aft CG limit.
C—Yes, but the CG will be located in the shaded area of the CG envelope.

1. Subtract your fuel burn of 30 gallons from your total fuel of 37 gallons to find fuel remaining, 7 gallons.
2. Construct a table with the Item, Weight, and Moment. The moment of each item is found by using the Loading Graph in FAA Figure 38. Locate the weight of each item on the left side of the chart, and proceed to the right to intersect the correct item line. At point of intersection, proceed downward to find the moment for that item at the specified weight.

Item	Weight	Moment
Aircraft empty weight	1,271	102.04
Pilot and copilot	360	32.80
Cargo	340	39.50
Fuel (7.0 gal × 6 lbs/gal)	+ 42	+ 4.00
Totals	2,013	178.34

3. Compare to the limits in FAA Figure 38. Using the CG Envelope Graph, move up the loaded aircraft weight scale to 2,013, then across to 178.34 on the moment/1,000 scale. The CG will remain within limits.

(PLT003, CA.I.F.K2f) — FAA-H-8083-1

AIR
5646. GIVEN:

Total weight	4,137 lb
CG location station	67.8
Fuel consumption	13.7 GPH
Fuel CG station	68.0

After 1 hour 30 minutes of flight time, the CG would be located at station

A—67.79.
B—68.79.
C—70.78.

1. Find the weight change: 13.7 GPH for 1.5 hours = 20.55 gal

    20.55 gal × 6 lbs/gal = 123.3 lbs

2. New total weight is 4,137 – 123.3 = 4,013.7
3. The distance between the CG and the fuel arm is 68.0 – 67.8 = .2
4. Place the values in the formula and cross multiply:

    $$\frac{123.3}{4,013.7} = \frac{CG\ change}{.2}$$

    24.66 = 4,013.7 (CG change)

5. Divide to determine CG change:

    $$\frac{24.66}{4,013.7} = CG\ change = .00614\ inches$$

6. Calculate the new CG:

Original CG	67.80000
CG change	– .00614
New CG	67.79386

(PLT003, CA.I.F.K2e) — FAA-H-8083-1

Answers

5652 [A]   5646 [A]

AIR
5649. GIVEN:

Total weight .... 3,037 lb
CG location station 68.8
Fuel consumption .... 12.7 GPH
Fuel CG station.. 68.0

After 1 hour 45 minutes of flight time, the CG would be located at station

A—68.77.
B—68.83.
C—69.77.

1. Find the weight change: 12.7 GPH for 1.75 hours = 22.23 gal

    22.23 gal × 6 lbs/gal = 133.35 lbs

2. New total weight is 3,037 − 133.35 = 2,903.65

3. The distance between the CG and the fuel arm is 68.8 − 68.0 = .8

4. Place the values in the formula and cross mulitply:

$$\frac{133.35}{2,903.65} = \frac{CG\ change}{.8}$$

5. Divide to determine CG change:

$$\frac{106.68}{2,903.65} = CG\ change = .03674\ inches$$

6. Calculate the new CG:

    Original CG   68.80000
    CG change   + .03674
    New CG   68.83674

(PLT003, CA.I.F.K2e) — FAA-H-8083-1

AIR
5647. An aircraft is loaded with a ramp weight of 3,650 pounds and having a CG of 94.0, approximately how much baggage would have to be moved from the rear baggage area at station 180 to the forward baggage area at station 40 in order to move the CG to 92.0?

A—52.14 pounds.
B—62.24 pounds.
C—78.14 pounds.

Determine the amount of weight to be moved:

$$\frac{Weight\ shifted}{Total\ weight} = \frac{\Delta\ CG\ (94 - 92)}{Dist.\ Wt.\ shifted\ (180 - 40)}$$

$$\frac{Weight\ to\ be\ shifted}{3,650\ lbs} = \frac{2.0}{140}$$

$$\frac{3,650 \times 2}{140} = \frac{7,300}{140} = 52.143$$

(PLT003, CA.I.F.K2f) — FAA-H-8083-1

AIR
5648. An airplane is loaded to a gross weight of 4,800 pounds, with three pieces of luggage in the rear baggage compartment. The CG is located 98 inches aft of datum, which is 1 inch aft of limits. If luggage which weighs 90 pounds is moved from the rear baggage compartment (145 inches aft of datum) to the front compartment (45 inches aft of datum), what is the new CG?

A—96.13 inches aft of datum.
B—95.50 inches aft of datum.
C—99.87 inches aft of datum.

1. Change in CG = Weight shifted × Distance shifted ÷ Total weight

    90 × (145 − 45) ÷ 4,800 = 1.875 inches

2. Since the weight shifted forward, the CG also moves forward. The 1.875-inch change is subtracted from the original CG.

    New CG = 98.0 − 1.875 = 96.13 inches

(PLT003, CA.I.F.K2f) — FAA-H-8083-1

Answers

5649   [B]   5647   [A]   5648   [A]

Rotorcraft Weight and Balance

RTC
5682. With respect to using the weight information given in a typical aircraft owner's manual for computing gross weight, it is important to know that if items have been installed in the aircraft in addition to the original equipment, the

A—allowable useful load is decreased.
B—allowable useful load remains unchanged.
C—maximum allowable gross weight is increased.

The empty weight and moment given in most manufacturers' handbooks are for the basic aircraft prior to the installation of additional optional equipment. When the owner later adds items such as radio navigation equipment, autopilot, deicers, etc., the empty weight and the moment are changed. These changes must be recorded in the aircraft's weight and balance data and used in all computations. (PLT328) — FAA-H-8083-1

RTC
5536. The weight placed on a helicopter is
A—blade loading.
B—load limit.
C—useful load.

Load limit is the maximum load, expressed as multiples of positive and negative G (force of gravity), that an aircraft can sustain before structural damage becomes possible. (PLT328) — FAA-H-8083-1

Answer (A) is incorrect because blade loading is the load imposed on rotor blades, determined by dividing the total weight of the helicopter by the combined area of all the rotor blades. Answer (C) is incorrect because useful load is the difference between takeoff weight, or ramp weight if applicable, and basic empty weight.

RTC
5677. (Refer to Figure 39.)
GIVEN:

	WEIGHT	ARM (IN)	MOMENT (IN.-LBS)
Empty weight	1,700	+6.0	+10,200
Pilot weight	200	-31.0	?
Oil (8 qt, all usable)	?	+1.0	?
Fuel (50 gal, all usable)	?	+2.0	?
Baggage	30	-31.0	?
TOTALS	?	?	?

If the datum line is located at station 0, the CG is located approximately

A—1.64 inches aft of datum.
B—1.64 inches forward of datum.
C—1.66 inches forward of datum.

1. Calculate the total weight and moment:

Item	Weight (lbs)	Arm (in)	Moment (lbs-in)
Empty weight	1,700	+6.0	+10,200
Pilot	200	-31.0	-6,200
Oil (8 qt.) × 7.5 lbs	15	+1.0	+15
Fuel (50 gal) × 6 lbs	300	+2.0	+600
Baggage	+ 30	-31.0	-930
Totals	2,245		3,685

2. Calculate CG by dividing total moment by total weight:
$$CG = \frac{\text{Total Moment}}{\text{Total Weight}} = \frac{3,685}{2,245} = 1.64'' \text{ aft of datum}$$

(PLT021) — FAA-H-8083-21

RTC
5678. (Refer to Figure 40.)
GIVEN:

Basic weight (oil is included) .... 830 lb
Basic weight moment (1,000/in.-lb) 104.8
Pilot weight .... 175 lb
Passenger weight .... 160 lb
Fuel .... 19.2 gal

The CG is located

A—well aft of the aft CG limit.
B—within the CG envelope.
C—forward of the forward CG limit.

Answers

| 5682 | [A] | 5536 | [B] | 5677 | [A] | 5678 | [A] |

1. Calculate the total weight and moments:

Item	Weight (lbs)	Arm (in)	Moment /1,000
Aircraft	830	(given in problem)	104.8
Pilot	175	79.0	13.8
Passenger	160	79.0	12.6
Fuel (19.2 gal × 6)	+ 115.2	108.6	+ 12.5
Totals	1,280.2		143.7

2. Locate the weight and moment in the center of gravity chart. The values fall aft of the CG envelope.

(PLT021) — FAA-H-8083-21

RTC
5679. GIVEN:

	WT	LNG. ARM	LNG. MOM.	LAT. ARM	LAT. MOM.
Empty weight	1700	116.1	?	+0.2	—
Fuel (75 gal at 6.8 ppg)	?	110.0	?	—	—
Oil	12	179.0	?	—	—
Pilot (right seat)	175	65.0	?	+12.5	?
Passenger (left seat)	195	104.0	?	-13.3	?
TOTALS	?		?		?

Determine the longitudinal and lateral CG respectively.

A— 109.35" and -.04".
B— 110.43" and +.02".
C— 110.83" and -.02".

1. Determine weight and moments for both the longitudinal and the lateral weight distributions:

   a. Longitudinal

Item	Weight (lbs)	Arm (in)	Moment (lbs-in)
Empty weight	1,700	116.1	197,370
Fuel (75 × 6.8)	510	110.0	56,100
Oil	12	179.0	2,148
Pilot	175	65.0	11,375
Passenger	+ 195	104.0	+20,280
Totals	2,592		287,273

   b. Lateral

Item	Weight (lbs)	Arm (in)	Moment (lbs-in)
Empty weight	1,700	+0.2	+340
Fuel	510		
Oil	12		
Pilot	175	+12.5	+2,188
Passenger	+ 195	-13.3	-2,594
Totals	2,592		-66

2. Calculate the longitudinal and lateral CGs by dividing total moment by total weight:

$$CG = \frac{\text{Total Moment}}{\text{Total Weight}}$$

   a. Longitudinal

$$CG = \frac{287,273}{2,592} = 110.83 \text{ in}$$

   b. Lateral

$$CG = \frac{-66}{2,592} = -0.02546 \text{ in}$$

(PLT021) — FAA-H-8083-21

RTC
5644. (Refer to Figure 37.)
GIVEN:

	WEIGHT	MOMENT
Gyroplane basic weight (oil included)	1,315	150.1
Pilot weight	140	?
Passenger weight	150	?
27 gal fuel	162	?

The CG is located

A—outside the CG envelope; the maximum gross weight is exceeded.
B—outside the CG envelope; the maximum gross weight and the gross-weight moment are exceeded.
C—within the CG envelope; neither maximum gross weight nor gross-weight moment is exceeded.

Total the weights and moments to determine if the CG is within limits.

Item	Weight	Moment
Gyroplane	1,315	150.1
Pilot	140	7.2
Passenger	150	12.6
27 gallons gas	+ 162	+ 17.8
Total	1,767	187.7

These figures fall within permitted weight and CG.

(PLT003) — FAA-H-8083-1

Answers

5679 [C]   5644 [C]

Chapter 8 Aircraft Performance

RTC

5645. (Refer to Figure 37.)

GIVEN:

	WEIGHT	MOMENT
Gyroplane basic weight (oil included)	1,315	154.0
Pilot weight	145	?
Passenger weight	153	?
27 gal fuel	162	?

The CG is located

A—outside the CG envelope; the maximum gross weight is exceeded.
B—outside the CG envelope; but the maximum gross weight is not exceeded.
C—within the CG envelope; neither maximum gross weight nor gross-weight moment is exceeded.

Total the weights and moments to determine if the CG is within limits.

Item	Weight	Moment
Gyroplane	1,315	154.0
Pilot	145	7.4
Passenger	153	12.8
27 gallons gas	+ 162	+ 17.6
Total	1,775	191.8

These figures fall within permitted weight but outside CG.

(PLT003) — FAA-H-8083-1

RTC

5680. A helicopter is loaded in such a manner that the CG is located aft of the aft allowable CG limit. Which is true about this situation?

A—In case of an autorotation, sufficient aft cyclic control may not be available to flare properly.
B—This condition would become more hazardous as fuel is consumed, if the main fuel tank is located aft of the rotor mast.
C—If the helicopter should pitchup due to gusty winds during high-speed flight, there may not be sufficient forward cyclic control available to lower the nose.

If flight is continued in this condition, the pilot may find it impossible to fly in the upper allowable airspeed range due to insufficient forward cyclic displacement to maintain a nose-low attitude. This particular condition may become quite dangerous if gusty or rough air accelerates the helicopter to a higher airspeed than forward cyclic control will allow. The nose will start to rise and full forward cyclic stick may not be sufficient to hold it down or to lower it once it rises. (PLT240) — FAA-H-8083-21

RTC

5681. A helicopter is loaded in such a manner that the CG is located forward of the allowable CG limit. Which is true about this situation?

A—This condition would become less hazardous as fuel is consumed if the fuel tank is located aft of the rotor mast.
B—In case of engine failure and the resulting autorotation, you may not have enough cyclic control to flare properly for the landing.
C—Should the aircraft pitchup during cruise flight due to gusty winds, there may not be enough forward cyclic control available to lower the nose.

Flight under this condition should not be continued, since the possibility of running out of rearward cyclic control will increase rapidly as fuel is consumed, and the pilot may find it impossible to decelerate sufficiently to bring the helicopter to a stop. Also, in case of engine failure and the resulting autorotation, sufficient cyclic control may not be available to flare properly for the landing. (PLT240) — FAA-H-8083-21

Answers

5645 [B]   5680 [C]   5681 [B]

Glider Weight and Balance

GLI
5287. In regard to the location of the glider's CG and its effect on glider spin characteristics, which is true? If the CG is too far

A—aft, a flat spin may develop.
B—forward, spin entry will be impossible.
C—aft, spins will degenerate into CG high-speed spirals.

The location of the center of gravity of the glider critically affects its spin characteristics. If the CG is too far back a flat spin will develop and recovery may be impossible. (PLT021) — FAA-H-8083-13

GLI
5288. The CG of most gliders is located

A—ahead of the aerodynamic center of the wing to increase lateral stability.
B—ahead of the aerodynamic center of the wing to increase longitudinal stability.
C—behind the aerodynamic center of the wing to increase longitudinal stability.

Sailplanes are designed to achieve longitudinal stability by making the aircraft slightly nose heavy with the center of gravity ahead of the center of lift. (PLT256) — FAA-H-8083-13

GLI
5289. Loading a glider so that the CG exceeds the aft limits results in

A—excessive load factor in turns.
B—excessive upward force on the tail, and causes the nose to pitch down.
C—loss of longitudinal stability, and causes the nose to pitch up at slow speeds.

If the CG is displaced too far aft on the longitudinal axis, a tail-heavy condition will result. As the CG moves aft, a less stable condition occurs. (PLT256) — FAA-H-8083-13

GLI
5640. (Refer to Figure 36.)
GIVEN:

	WEIGHT	ARM	MOMENT
Empty weight	610	96.47	?
Pilot (fwd seat)	150	?	?
Passenger (aft seat)	180	?	?
Radio and batteries	10	23.20	?
TOTALS	?		?

The CG is located at station

A—33.20.
B—59.55.
C—83.26.

1. Determine the center of gravity under these conditions:

Item	Weight	× Arm	= Moment
Empty weight	610	96.47	58,846.7
Pilot (fwd seat)	150	43.80	6,570.0
Passenger (aft seat)	180	74.70	13,446.0
Radio & batteries	+ 10	23.20	+ 232.0
Totals	950		79,094.7

2. Calculate the CG location by dividing the total moment by the total weight:

$$CG = \frac{\text{Total Moment}}{\text{Total Weight}} = \frac{79,094.7}{950} = 83.26 \text{ in}$$

(PLT003) — FAA-H-8083-1

Answers

5287 [A]   5288 [B]   5289 [C]   5640 [C]

Chapter 8 Aircraft Performance

GLI

5641. (Refer to Figure 36.)
GIVEN:

	WEIGHT	ARM	MOMENT
Empty weight	612	96.47	?
Pilot (fwd seat)	170	?	?
Passenger (aft seat)	160	?	?
Radio and batteries	10	23.20	?
Ballast	20	14.75	?
TOTALS	?	?	?

The CG is located at station

A—81.23.
B—82.63.
C—83.26.

1. Determine the center of gravity under these conditions:

Item	Weight	x Arm	= Moment
Empty weight	612	96.47	59,040
Pilot (fwd seat)	170	43.80	7,446
Passenger (aft seat)	160	74.70	11,952
Radio & batteries	10	23.20	232
Ballast	+ 20	14.75	+ 295
Totals	972		78,965

2. Calculate the CG location by dividing total moment by total weight:

$$CG = \frac{\text{Total Moment}}{\text{Total Weight}} = \frac{78,965}{972} = 81.24 \text{ in}$$

(PLT003) — FAA-H-8083-1

GLI

5642. (Refer to Figure 36.)
GIVEN:

	WEIGHT	ARM	MOMENT
Empty weight	605	96.47	?
Pilot (fwd seat)	120	?	?
Passenger (aft seat)	160	?	?
Radio and batteries	20	23.20	?
Ballast	40	14.75	?
TOTALS	?	?	?

The CG is located at station

A—79.77.
B—80.32.
C—81.09.

1. Determine the center of gravity under these conditions:

Item	Weight	x Arm	= Moment
Empty weight	605	96.47	58,364.4
Pilot (fwd seat)	120	43.80	5,256.0
Passenger (aft seat)	160	74.70	11,952.0
Radio & batteries	20	23.20	464.0
Ballast	+ 40	14.75	+ 590.0
Totals	945		76,626.4

2. Calculate the CG location by dividing the total moment by the total weight:

$$CG = \frac{\text{Total Moment}}{\text{Total Weight}} = \frac{76,626.4}{945} = 81.09 \text{ in}$$

(PLT003) — FAA-H-8083-1

GLI

5643. GIVEN:

	WEIGHT	ARM	MOMENT
Empty weight	957	29.07	?
Pilot (fwd seat)	140	-45.30	?
Passenger (aft seat)	170	+1.60	?
Ballast	15	-45.30	?
TOTALS	?	?	?

The CG is located at station

A— -6.43.
B— +16.43.
C— +27.38.

1. Calculate the moments, and the total weight and moment:

Item	Weight	x Arm	= Moment
Empty weight	957	29.07	27,820.0
Pilot (fwd seat)	140	- 45.30	- 6,342.0
Passenger (aft seat)	170	1.60	272.0
Ballast	+ 15	- 45.30	- 679.5
Totals	1,282		21,070.5

2. CG station = Moment ÷ Weight

21,070.5 ÷ 1,282 = 16.4356

(PLT021) — FAA-H-8083-1

Answers

5641 [A]   5642 [C]   5643 [B]

Chapter 8 **Aircraft Performance**

Headwind and Crosswind Components

In general, taking off into a wind improves aircraft performance, and reduces the runway distance required to become airborne. The stronger the wind, the better the aircraft performs. Crosswinds, however, may make the aircraft difficult or impossible to control. The magnitudes of headwind and crosswind components produced by a wind of a given direction and speed can be determined by using the chart as shown in FAA Figure 31.

Problem:

The wind is reported to be from 190° at 15 knots, and you plan to land on runway 13. What will the headwind and crosswind components be?

Solution:

1. Compute the angle between the wind and the runway:

190°	wind direction
– 130°	runway heading
60°	wind angle across runway

2. Find the intersection of the 60° angle radial line and the 15-knot wind velocity arc on the graph. From the intersection move downward and read the crosswind component of 13 knots. From the point of intersection move to the left and read the headwind component of 7 knots. See Figure 8-3.

Figure 8-3. Wind components

AIR
5615. (Refer to Figure 31.) Rwy 30 is being used for landing. Which surface wind would exceed the airplane's crosswind capability of 0.2 V_{S0}, if V_{S0} is 60 knots?

A—260° at 20 knots.
B—275° at 25 knots.
C—315° at 35 knots.

1. Compute 0.2 V_{S0}:

   60 × 0.2 = 12 KIAS crosswind component

2. Compute the angle between the wind and the runway:

300°	runway direction
– 260°	wind direction
040°	wind angle across runway

3. Determine the crosswind component of 20 knots at 40° crossing angle.

(PLT013, CA.IV.B.K2) — FAA-H-8083-25

Answers
5615 [A]

Chapter 8 **Aircraft Performance**

AIR, RTC, GLI

5616. (Refer to Figure 31.) If the tower-reported surface wind is 010° at 18 knots, what is the crosswind component for a Rwy 08 landing?

A—7 knots.
B—15 knots.
C—17 knots.

1. Compute the angle between the wind and each runway:

   $\quad$ 080°$\quad$ runway direction
   $\quad$ −010°$\quad$ wind direction
   $\quad$ 070°$\quad$ wind angle across runway

2. Determine the crosswind component of 18 knots at 070°, 17 KIAS.

(PLT013, CA.IV.B.K2) — FAA-H-8083-25

AIR, RTC, GLI

5617. (Refer to Figure 31.) The surface wind is 180° at 25 knots. What is the crosswind component for a Rwy 13 landing?

A—19 knots.
B—21 knots.
C—23 knots.

1. Compute the angle between the wind and each runway:

   $\quad$ 180°$\quad$ wind direction
   $\quad$ −130°$\quad$ runway direction
   $\quad$ 050°$\quad$ wind angle across runway

2. Determine the crosswind component of 25 knots at 050°, 19 KIAS.

(PLT013, CA.IV.B.K2) — FAA-H-8083-25

AIR, RTC, GLI

5618. (Refer to Figure 31.) What is the headwind component for a Rwy 13 takeoff if the surface wind is 190° at 15 knots?

A—7 knots.
B—13 knots.
C—15 knots.

1. Compute the angle between the wind and each runway:

   $\quad$ 190°$\quad$ wind direction
   $\quad$ −130°$\quad$ runway direction
   $\quad$ 060°$\quad$ wind angle across runway

2. Determine the headwind component for 15 knots at 060°, 7 KIAS.

(PLT013, CA.IV.A.K1) — FAA-H-8083-25

Answers

5616 [C]$\qquad$5617 [A]$\qquad$5618 [A]

Density Altitude

Aircraft performance charts indicate what performance (rate of climb, takeoff roll, etc.) can be expected of an aircraft under stipulated conditions. Prediction of performance is based upon standard atmospheric conditions, or the International Standard Atmosphere, which at sea level is a temperature of +15°C (+59°F) and an atmospheric pressure of 29.92" Hg (1013.2 hectopascals).

In a standard atmosphere, temperature changes at a rate of 2°C (3.5°F) per 1,000 feet, and pressure changes approximately 1" Hg per 1,000 feet. Temperature and/or pressure deviations from standard will change the air density. The result is a value for density altitude, which affects aircraft performance. Performance charts based on density altitude allow the pilot to predict how an aircraft will perform.

Relative humidity also affects density altitude but is not considered when the performance charts are formulated. A combination of high temperature, high humidity, and high altitude will result in a density altitude higher than the pressure altitude, which results in reduced aircraft performance.

ALL
5302. What is the standard temperature at 10,000 feet?

A— -5°C.
B— -15°C.
C— +5°C.

Standard temperature at sea level is 15°C. The standard lapse rate is 2°C/1,000 feet.

10 × 2 = -20°C temperature decrease to 10,000 feet
+15° − 20° = -5°C standard temperature at 10,000 feet

(PLT492, CA.I.C.K3c) — AC 00-6

ALL
5303. What is the standard temperature at 20,000 feet?

A— -15°C.
B— -20°C.
C— -25°C.

Standard temperature at sea level is 15°C. The average lapse rate is 2°C/1,000 feet.

20 × -2 = -40°C temperature decrease to 20,000 feet
15°C − 40°C = -25°C standard temperature at 20,000 feet

(PLT492, CA.I.C.K3c) — AC 00-6

ALL
5305. What are the standard temperature and pressure values for sea level?

A— 15°C and 29.92" Hg.
B— 59°F and 1013.2" Hg.
C— 15°C and 29.92 Mb.

In the standard atmosphere, sea level pressure is 29.92 inches of mercury or 1013.2 hectopascals. The temperature at mean sea level is 15°C (59°F). (PLT492, CA.I.C.K3c) — AC 00-6

AIR, RTC
5234. The performance tables of an aircraft for takeoff and climb are based on

A— pressure/density altitude.
B— cabin altitude.
C— true altitude.

Pressure and density altitude are the factors used in the performance tables of the aircraft for takeoff and climb. (PLT134, CA.I.F.K2a) — FAA-H-8083-25

Answer (B) is incorrect because the cabin altitude is the altitude that is in the pressurized cabin. Answer (C) is incorrect because true altitude is the height above sea level. Aeronautical charts depict obstacle elevations in true altitude.

AIR, RTC
5300. What effect, if any, would a change in ambient temperature or air density have on gas turbine engine performance?

A— As air density decreases, thrust increases.
B— As temperature increases, thrust increases.
C— As temperature increases, thrust decreases.

An increase in altitude causes the engine air flow to decrease in a manner nearly identical to the altitude density ratio. This causes a significant decrease in thrust at altitude versus thrust at sea level as altitude increases. An increase in inlet air temperature will provide a lower combustion gas energy and cause a lower jet velocity. (PLT237, CA.I.F.K2a) — FAA-H-8083-25

Answers

5302 [A]   5303 [C]   5305 [A]   5234 [A]   5300 [C]

Takeoff and Landing Considerations

During takeoff with a crosswind, rudder is used to maintain directional control and aileron pressure to counter the wind. For both conventional and nosewheel-type airplanes, a higher than normal liftoff airspeed is used. Landing under crosswind conditions requires the direction of motion of the airplane and its longitudinal axis to be parallel to the runway at the moment of touchdown. During gusty wind conditions, both the approach and landing should be with power on.

Operating with an uphill runway slope has no effect on the takeoff speed but will increase the takeoff distance.

In the event of an actual engine failure immediately after takeoff and before a safe maneuvering altitude is attained, it is not recommended to attempt to turn back to the airport. Instead, it is generally safer to maintain a safe airspeed, and select a field directly ahead or slightly to either side of the takeoff path.

While diverting to an alternate airport due to an emergency, the heading should be changed to establish the new course immediately. Apply rule-of-thumb computations, estimates, and appropriate shortcuts to calculate wind correction, actual distance, and estimated time and fuel required.

When takeoff power is applied, it is usually necessary to hold considerable pressure on the controls to maintain straight flight and a safe climb attitude. Since the airplane is trimmed for the approach (a low power and low airspeed condition), application of maximum allowable power requires considerable control pressure to maintain a climb pitch attitude. The addition of power tends to raise the airplane's nose suddenly and it veers to the left.

ALL

5503. When diverting to an alternate airport because of an emergency, pilots should

A—rely upon radio as the primary method of navigation.
B—climb to a higher altitude because it will be easier to identify checkpoints.
C—apply rule-of-thumb computations, estimates, and other appropriate shortcuts to divert to the new course as soon as possible.

Course, time, speed and distance computations in flight require the same basic procedures as those used in preflight planning. However, because of cockpit space limitations and available equipment, and because the pilot's attention must be divided between solving the problem and operating the aircraft, the pilot must take advantage of all possible shortcuts and rule-of-thumb computations. (PLT208, CA.VI.C.R5) — FAA-H-8083-3

Answer (A) is incorrect because any form of navigation is appropriate. Answer (B) is incorrect because climbs may consume time and fuel.

AIR

5661. With regard to the technique required for a crosswind correction on takeoff, a pilot should use

A—aileron pressure into the wind and initiate the lift-off at a normal airspeed in both tailwheel- and nosewheel-type airplanes.
B—right rudder pressure, aileron pressure into the wind, and higher than normal lift-off airspeed in both tricycle- and conventional-gear airplanes.
C—rudder as required to maintain directional control, aileron pressure into the wind, and higher than normal lift-off airspeed in both conventional- and nosewheel-type airplanes.

Rudder is required at all times to maintain directional control. Aileron pressure into the wind will keep the wing down and prevent side skipping. A slightly higher than normal takeoff speed is desirable to ensure a very definite liftoff with no settling. (PLT221, CA.IV.A.R2a) — FAA-H-8083-3

Answer (A) is incorrect because the lift-off speed should be increased slightly and rudder pressure should be applied to maintain directional control. Answer (B) is incorrect because rudder pressure should be applied to maintain directional control, this can be both right or left deflection.

Answers

5503 [C]   5661 [C]

Chapter 8 **Aircraft Performance**

AIR

5662. When turbulence is encountered during the approach to a landing, what action is recommended and for what primary reason?

A—Increase the airspeed slightly above normal approach speed to attain more positive control.
B—Decrease the airspeed slightly below normal approach speed to avoid overstressing the airplane.
C—Increase the airspeed slightly above normal approach speed to penetrate the turbulence as quickly as possible.

Power-on approaches at an airspeed slightly above the normal approach speed should be used for landing in significantly turbulent air. This provides for more positive control of the airplane when strong horizontal wind gusts, or up- and downdrafts, are experienced. (PLT221, CA.IV.B.R3a) — FAA-H-8083-3

Answer (B) is incorrect because, since approach speed is well below V_A, no structural damage will occur. Answer (C) is incorrect because increased approach speed is to increase control effectiveness, not to fly through turbulence faster.

AIR

5663. If you experience an engine failure in a single-engine aircraft after takeoff, you should

A—establish the proper glide attitude.
B—turn into the wind.
C—adjust the pitch to maintain V_Y.

In the event of an engine failure on initial climb-out, the pilot's first responsibility is to maintain aircraft control. At a climb pitch attitude without power, the airplane is at or near a stalling AOA. At the same time, the pilot may still be holding right rudder. The pilot must immediately lower the nose to prevent a stall while moving the rudder to ensure coordinated flight. Attempting to turn back to the takeoff runway should not be attempted. The pilot should establish a controlled glide toward a plausible landing area, preferably straight ahead. (PLT208, CA.IV.A.R3b) — FAA-H-8083-3

AIR

5664. Which type of approach and landing is recommended during gusty wind conditions?

A—A power-on approach and power-on landing.
B—A power-off approach and power-on landing.
C—A power-on approach and power-off landing.

Power-on approaches at an airspeed slightly above the normal approach speed should be used for landing in significantly turbulent air. These landing approaches are usually performed at the normal approach speed plus one-half of the wind gust factor. An adequate amount of power should be used to maintain the proper airspeed throughout. (PLT221, CA.IV.B.R3a) — FAA-H-8083-3

AIR

5665. A proper crosswind landing on a runway requires that, at the moment of touchdown, the

A—direction of motion of the airplane and its lateral axis be perpendicular to the runway.
B—direction of motion of the airplane and its longitudinal axis be parallel to the runway.
C—downwind wing be lowered sufficiently to eliminate the tendency for the airplane to drift.

Direction of motion and the longitudinal axis must be parallel to the runway or skidding will occur, with possible damage to the aircraft. (PLT221, CA.IV.B.R2a) — FAA-H-8083-3

Answer (A) is incorrect because the direction of motion of the airplane must be parallel to the runway. Answer (C) is incorrect because the upwind wing should be lowered to eliminate drift.

AIR, GLI

5614. What effect does an uphill runway slope have on takeoff performance?

A—Increases takeoff speed.
B—Increases takeoff distance.
C—Decreases takeoff distance.

The effect of runway slope on takeoff distance is due to the component of weight along the inclined path of the aircraft. An upslope would contribute a retarding force component while a downslope would contribute an accelerating force component. In the case of an up-slope, the retarding force component adds to drag and rolling friction to reduce the net accelerating force. (PLT129, CA.IV.A.R2e) — FAA-H-8083-25

Answers

| 5662 [A] | 5663 [A] | 5664 [A] | 5665 [B] | 5614 [B] |

Chapter 8 **Aircraft Performance**

AIR, GLI

5614-1. When conducting a go-around, the pilot must be aware that

A—radio communications are key to alerting other aircraft in the pattern that a go-around maneuver is being conducted.
B—the airplane is trimmed for a power-off condition, and application of takeoff power will cause the nose to rise rapidly.
C—flaps should be raised as quickly as possible to reduce drag and increase airspeed for a successful go-around.

When takeoff power is applied, it is usually necessary to hold considerable pressure on the controls to maintain straight flight and a safe climb attitude. Since the airplane is trimmed for the approach (a low power and low airspeed condition), application of maximum allowable power requires considerable control pressure to maintain a climb pitch attitude. The addition of power tends to raise the airplane's nose suddenly and it veers to the left. (PLT221, CA.IV.B.R3a) — FAA-H-8083-3

Answer (A) is incorrect because power is the pilot's first concern in a go-around situation; aviate before you communicate. Answer (C) is incorrect because flaps should only be retracted once power has been applied and the proper climb attitude established.

Takeoff and Landing Distance

The takeoff distance graph such as the graph shown in FAA Figure 32, allows the pilot to determine the ground roll and takeoff distance over a 50-foot obstacle.

Problem:

Using the Obstacle Takeoff Graph (FAA Figure 32), determine the total takeoff distance over a 50-foot obstacle under the following conditions:

Temperature	30°F
Pressure Altitude	6,000 feet
Weight	3,300 lbs
Headwind component	20 knots

Solution:

1. Enter the chart at 30°F. Proceed upward until intersecting the 6,000-foot pressure altitude. From this point, proceed to the right until intersecting the first reference line.

2. From this point on the reference line, proceed diagonally upward to the right (on a line spaced proportionally between the existing guide lines) to the vertical line representing 3,300 pounds. From there, proceed to the right until intersecting the second reference line.

3. From this point, proceed diagonally downward and to the right (remaining proportionally between the existing guide lines) to the vertical line representing the 20-knot headwind component. From there, proceed to the far right scale and read the total takeoff distance over a 50-foot obstacle of 1,500 feet.

The takeoff distance graph is often used to find the required takeoff distance based on temperature, pressure altitude, weight and wind. The graph may also be used however, to find the maximum weight allowable under certain conditions for a particular takeoff distance.

Problem:

Using the information shown in FAA Figure 32, determine the maximum weight allowable to take off over a 50-foot obstacle in 1,500 feet under the following conditions:

Temperature	30°F
Pressure Altitude	6,000 feet
Headwind component	20 knots

Answers

5614-1 [B]

Chapter 8 **Aircraft Performance**

Solution:

1. Enter the chart at 30°F. Proceed upward until intersecting the 6,000-foot pressure altitude line. From this point, proceed to the right until intersecting the first reference line.
2. From this point, draw a line diagonally upward and to the right (remaining proportionally spaced between the existing guide lines) until intersecting the second reference line.
3. Re-enter the graph from the right at the 1,500-foot takeoff distance over a 50-foot obstacle. Proceed to the left until intersecting the vertical line representing a 20-knot headwind component. From there, proceed diagonally upward and to the left (remaining proportionally spaced between the existing guide lines) until intersecting the second reference line.
4. From this point, proceed to the left until intersecting the previously drawn diagonal line. From there, proceed vertically downward and read the maximum allowable takeoff weight of 3,300 pounds.

Use the same procedure for landing distance graphs as for the takeoff distance graph.

ALL
5208. At higher elevation airports the pilot should know that indicated airspeed

A—will be unchanged, but groundspeed will be faster.
B—will be higher, but groundspeed will be unchanged.
C—should be increased to compensate for the thinner air.

An airplane at altitude will land at the same indicated airspeed as at sea level but, because of the reduced air density, will have a greater true airspeed. If the true airspeed is greater, the ground speed will be greater. (PLT012, CA.I.D.K3a) — FAA-H-8083-25

AIR, GLI
5813. What should be expected when making a downwind landing? The likelihood of

A—undershooting the intended landing spot and a faster airspeed at touchdown.
B—overshooting the intended landing spot and a faster groundspeed at touchdown.
C—undershooting the intended landing spot and a faster groundspeed at touchdown.

In this situation, the pilot should aim at the near end of the runway, because of the tailwind increasing the aircraft's ground speed. (PLT170, CA.IV.B.K2) — FAA-H-8083-13

AIR
5619. (Refer to Figure 32.)
GIVEN:

Temperature	75°F
Pressure altitude	6,000 ft
Weight	2,900 lb
Headwind	20 kts

To safely take off over a 50-foot obstacle in 1,000 feet, what weight reduction is necessary?

A—50 pounds.
B—100 pounds.
C—300 pounds.

1. Start at the right side of the chart and find the 1,000-foot takeoff distance mark. From there, draw a horizontal line to the 20-knot headwind mark, and following the sloped lines, draw a line to the reference line.
2. Draw a horizontal line all the way across the weight section to the other reference line.
3. Starting from the left side of the chart, find the 75°F mark and draw a line up to the 6,000-foot pressure altitude line, and follow that sloped line across to the reference line. Follow the sloped reference lines to the right, up to where your line intercepts the horizontal line drawn previously across that section.
4. Draw a vertical line down from where they meet and read the maximum weight (2,600 pounds) for the aircraft to be able to clear the 50-foot obstacle.
5. Subtract that weight from 2,900 pounds to get 300 pounds.

(PLT011, CA.I.F.K1) — FAA-H-8083-25

Answers

5208 [A]   5813 [B]   5619 [C]

Chapter 8 **Aircraft Performance**

AIR
5620. (Refer to Figure 32.)
GIVEN:

Temperature	50°F
Pressure altitude	2,000 feet
Weight	2,700 lb
Wind	Calm

What is the total takeoff distance over a 50-foot obstacle?

A—800 feet.
B—650 feet.
C—1,050 feet.

1. Enter chart at 50°F, proceed up to the 2,000 foot pressure altitude line.
2. From this point, go to the right, to the weight reference line.
3. From this point, proceed up and to the right on the trend lines, until intercepting the 2,700 pound weight line. Then proceed to the right, to the wind reference line.
4. From this point, since the winds are calm, proceed to the right and read 800 feet.

(PLT011, CA.I.F.K1) — FAA-H-8083-25

AIR
5997. (Refer to Figure 32.) Determine the approximate runway length necessary for takeoff.
GIVEN:

Temperature	40°F
Pressure altitude	4,000 ft
Weight	3,200 lbs
Headwind	15 kts

A—1,300 feet.
B—850 feet.
C—950 feet.

1. Enter chart at 40°F, proceed up to the 4,000-foot pressure altitude line.
2. From this point, go to the right, to the weight reference line.
3. From this point, proceed up and to the right on the trend lines, until intercepting the 3,200 pound weight line. Then proceed to the right, to the wind reference line.
4. From this point, proceed to the right on the trend lines until intercepting 15 kts and read 1,300 feet.

(PLT011, CA.I.F.K1) — FAA-H-8083-25

AIR
5621. (Refer to Figure 32.)
GIVEN:

Temperature	100°F
Pressure altitude	4,000 ft
Weight	3,200 lb
Wind	Calm

What is the ground roll required for takeoff over a 50-foot obstacle?

A—1,180 feet.
B—1,350 feet.
C—1,850 feet.

1. Enter chart at 100°F, proceed up to the 4,000-foot pressure altitude line.
2. From this point, go to the right, to the weight reference line.
3. From this point, proceed up and to the right on a line spaced proportionally between the trend lines, until intercepting the 3,200-pound weight line. Then proceed to the right, to the wind reference line.
4. From this point, since the winds are calm, proceed to the right and read 1,850 feet.
5. Calculate the ground roll using the note that the ground roll is approximately 73% of total take-off distance over a 50-foot obstacle:

    1,850 × .73 = 1,350 feet ground roll

(PLT011, CA.I.F.K1) — FAA-H-8083-25

AIR
5622. (Refer to Figure 32.)
GIVEN:

Temperature	30°F
Pressure altitude	6,000 ft
Weight	3,300 lb
Headwind	20 kts

What is the total takeoff distance over a 50-foot obstacle?

A—1,100 feet.
B—1,300 feet.
C—1,500 feet.

1. Enter chart at 30°F, proceed up to the 6,000-foot pressure altitude line.
2. From this point, go to the right to the weight reference line.

Answers

5620 [A]   5997 [A]   5621 [B]   5622 [C]

3. From this point, proceed up and to the right on a line spaced proportionally between the trend lines, until intercepting the 3,300-pound weight line. Then proceed to the right, to the wind reference line.
4. From this point, proceed down and to the right (maintain proportional spacing), to the 20-knot headwind line. From this point, proceed to the right and read 1,500 feet.

(PLT011, CA.I.F.K1) — FAA-H-8083-25

AIR
5628. (Refer to Figure 35.)
GIVEN:

Temperature ....70°F
Pressure altitude... Sea level
Weight .... 3,400 lb
Headwind ....16 kts

Determine the approximate ground roll.

A—689 feet.
B—716 feet.
C—1,275 feet.

1. Enter the chart at the 70°F OAT point and proceed upward to intercept the sea level pressure altitude line. Proceed right to the intersection with the vertical reference line.
2. From the reference line, proceed upward to the right following the trend line, until reaching a vertical line representing the weight of 3,400 pounds.
3. Draw a line to the right from the intercept with the weight line to the intercept with the right vertical reference line.
4. Construct a vertical line to represent the headwind, 16 KIAS. Draw a line from the intercept with the reference line to the intersect with the headwind line. Proceed to the right and read the total distance over a 50-foot obstacle: 1,275 feet.
5. Apply the note to calculate the ground roll (53% of the landing distance):

    1,275 × 0.53 = 676 feet ground roll

Select the answer choice closest to this computation.

(PLT008, CA.I.F.K1) — FAA-H-8083-25

AIR
5629. (Refer to Figure 35.)
GIVEN:

Temperature ....85°F
Pressure altitude...6,000 ft
Weight .... 2,800 lb
Headwind ....14 kts

Determine the approximate ground roll.

A—742 feet.
B—1,280 feet.
C—1,480 feet.

1. Enter the chart at the 85°F OAT point and proceed upward to intercept the 6,000-foot pressure altitude line. Proceed right to the intersection with the vertical reference line.
2. From the reference line, proceed upward to the right following the trend line, until reaching a vertical line representing the weight of 2,800 pounds.
3. Draw a line to the right from the intercept with the weight line, to the intercept with the right vertical reference line.
4. Construct a vertical line to represent the headwind, 14 KIAS. Draw a line from the intercept with the reference line to the intersect with the headwind line. Proceed to the right and read the total distance over a 50-foot obstacle: 1,400 feet.
5. Apply the note to calculate the ground roll (53% of the landing distance):

    1,400 × 0.53 = 742 feet ground roll

(PLT008, CA.I.F.K1) — FAA-H-8083-25

Answers

5628 [A]   5629 [A]

Chapter 8 **Aircraft Performance**

AIR
5630. (Refer to Figure 35.)
GIVEN:

Temperature .... 50°F
Pressure altitude... Sea level
Weight .... 3,000 lb
Headwind ....10 kts

Determine the approximate ground roll.

A—425 feet.
B—636 feet.
C—836 feet.

1. Enter the chart at the 50°F OAT point and proceed upward to intercept the sea level pressure altitude line. Proceed right to the intersection with the vertical reference line.

2. From the reference line, proceed upward to the right following the trend line, until reaching a vertical line representing the weight of 3,000 pounds.

3. Draw a line to the right from the intercept with the weight line, to the intercept with the right vertical reference line.

4. Construct a vertical line to represent the headwind, 10 knots. Draw a line from the intercept with the reference line to the intersect with the headwind line. Proceed to the right and read the total distance over a 50-foot obstacle: 1,200 feet.

5. Apply the note to calculate the ground roll (53% of the landing distance):

    1,200 × 0.53 = 636 feet ground roll

(PLT008, CA.I.F.K1) — FAA-H-8083-25

AIR
5631. (Refer to Figure 35.)
GIVEN:

Temperature .... 80°F
Pressure altitude... 4,000 ft
Weight .... 2,800 lb
Headwind ....24 kts

What is the total landing distance over a 50-foot obstacle?

A—1,125 feet.
B—1,250 feet.
C—1,325 feet.

1. Enter the chart at the 80°F OAT point and proceed upward to intercept the 4,000-foot pressure altitude line. Proceed right to the intersection with the vertical reference line.

2. From the reference line, proceed upward to the right following the trend line, until reaching a vertical line representing the weight of 2,800 pounds.

3. Draw a line to the right from the intercept with the weight line, to the intercept with the right vertical reference line.

4. Construct a vertical line to represent the headwind, 24 knots. Draw a line from the intercept with the reference line to the intercept with the headwind line. Proceed to the right and read the total distance over a 50-foot obstacle: 1,125 feet.

(PLT011, CA.I.F.K1) — FAA-H-8083-25

Fuel Consumption vs. Brake Horsepower

The fuel consumption vs. brake horsepower graph allows the pilot to determine the gallons per hour used, based on percent of power and mixture settings. See FAA Figure 8.

Problem:

How much flight time is available with a 45-minute fuel reserve under the following conditions?

Fuel on board .... 38 gallons
Mixture.. Cruise (lean)
Percent power... 55%

Answers

5630 [B]   5631 [A]

Solution:

1. Determine the fuel consumption (GPH) based on a cruise (lean) setting of 55% power. Locate the point where the diagonal cruise (lean) line and the vertical 55% power line intersect. From the point of intersection, proceed to the left and read the fuel consumption: 11.4 GHP.
2. Find the total endurance possible with 38 gallons at 11.4 GHP.

    38 ÷ 11.4 = 3.33 hr (no reserve)
3. Determine the flight time available with a 45-minute (0.75 hours) fuel reserve remaining:

    3.33 hr   no reserve
    − 0.75 hr 45-minute reserve

    2.58 hr   with 45-minute reserve

    2.58 hr = 2 hours, 34 minutes

AIR
5451. (Refer to Figure 8.)
GIVEN:

Fuel quantity .... 47 gal
Power-cruise (lean) .... 55 percent

Approximately how much flight time would be available with a night VFR fuel reserve remaining?

A—3 hours 8 minutes.
B—3 hours 22 minutes.
C—3 hours 43 minutes.

1. Enter chart at the point where the 55% maximum continuous power line intersects the curved cruise (lean) line.
2. From that point, proceed to the left and read fuel flow: 11.4 GPH
3. Compute time of flight:

    47 ÷ 11.4 = 4.12 hours
4. Compute available flight time with a 45-minute (0.75 hour) reserve:

    4.12 − 0.75 = 3.37 = 3 hours, 22 minutes

(PLT012, CA.I.D.K3a) — FAA-H-8083-25

AIR
5452. (Refer to Figure 8.)
GIVEN:

Fuel quantity .... 65 gal
Best power (level flight) .... 55 percent

Approximately how much flight time would be available with a day VFR fuel reserve remaining?

A—4 hours 17 minutes.
B—4 hours 30 minutes.
C—5 hours 4 minutes.

1. Enter chart at the point where the 55% maximum continuous power line intersects the curved best power level flight line.
2. From that point, proceed to the left and read fuel flow: 13.0 GPH
3. Compute time of flight:

    65 gal ÷ 13.0 = 5.0 hours
4. Compute available flight time with a 30-minute (0.5 hour) reserve:

    5.0 − 0.5 = 4.5 = 4 hour, 30 minutes

(PLT012, CA.I.D.K3a) — FAA-H-8083-25

AIR
5453. (Refer to Figure 8.) Approximately how much fuel would be consumed when climbing at 75 percent power for 7 minutes?

A—1.82 gallons.
B—1.97 gallons.
C—2.15 gallons.

1. Enter chart at point where the 75% maximum continuous power line intersects the curved take off and climb line.
2. From that point, proceed to the left and read fuel flow: 18.4 GPH.
3. Compute fuel burn:

    (18.4 × 7) ÷ 60 = 2.1 gallons

(PLT012, CA.I.D.K3a) — FAA-H-8083-25

Answers

5451 [B]   5452 [B]   5453 [C]

Chapter 8 **Aircraft Performance**

AIR
5454. (Refer to Figure 8.) Determine the amount of fuel consumed during takeoff and climb at 70 percent power for 10 minutes.
A—2.66 gallons.
B—2.88 gallons.
C—3.2 gallons.

1. Interpolate a vertical line for 70% power vertically between the 65% and 75% power lines.
2. From the point of intersection of the 70% line with the takeoff and climb curve, draw a line to the left and read the fuel flow: 17.3 GPH.
3. Compute the fuel burned:

   (17.3 × 10) ÷ 60 = 2.88 gallons

(PLT012, CA.I.D.K3a) — FAA-H-8083-25

AIR
5455. (Refer to Figure 8.) With 38 gallons of fuel aboard at cruise power (55 percent), how much flight time is available with night VFR fuel reserve still remaining?
A—2 hours 34 minutes.
B—2 hours 49 minutes.
C—3 hours 18 minutes.

1. Enter chart at the point where the 55% maximum continuous power line intersects the curved cruise (lean) line.
2. From that point, proceed to the left and read fuel flow: 11.4 GPH.
3. Compute time of flight:

   38 gal ÷ 11.4 GPH = 3.33 hours
4. Compute available flight time with a 45-minute (0.75 hour) reserve:

   3.33 − 0.75 = 2.58 = 2 hours, 34 minutes

(PLT012, CA.I.D.K3a) — FAA-H-8083-25

Time, Fuel, and Distance to Climb

The time, fuel and distance to climb tables and graphs allow the pilot to calculate the time required, fuel used and distance covered during a climb to a specified altitude.

Table Method

Problem:

Referring to the time, fuel and distance to climb table (FAA Figure 9), determine the amount of fuel used from engine start to a pressure altitude (PA) of 12,000 feet using a normal rate of climb under the following conditions:

Weight .... 3,800 lbs

Airport Pressure altitude .... 4,000 feet

Temperature at 4,000 feet.. 26°C

Solution:

1. Locate the section appropriate to 3,800 pounds weight. Read across the 4,000-foot pressure altitude line to the entry under fuel used: 12 pounds.
2. Read across the 12,000-foot pressure altitude line to the entry under fuel used: 51 pounds.
3. Calculate the fuel required to climb:

   51 − 12 = 39 lbs
4. Apply Note #2. (A temperature of 26°C is +19°C, with respect to the standard atmosphere at 4,000 feet.)

   39 × 1.19 = 46.4 lbs
5. Apply Note #1:

   46.4 lbs + 12.0 lbs start and taxi = 58.4 lbs total

Answers

5454 [B]   5455 [A]

Chapter 8 **Aircraft Performance**

Graph Method

Problem:

Using the time, fuel, and distance to climb graph shown in FAA Figure 15, determine the fuel, time, and distance required to climb to cruise altitude under the following conditions:

Airport pressure altitude .... 2,000 feet
Airport temperature... 20°C
Cruise pressure altitude.. 10,000 feet
Cruise temperature .... 0°C

Solution:

1. Determine the fuel, time and distance to climb to 10,000 feet at 0°C. Locate the temperature at 0°C on the bottom left side of the graph. Proceed upward to the diagonal line representing the pressure altitude of 10,000 feet.
2. From this point proceed to the right and stop at each of the lines, forming three points of intersection.
3. From each of the three points, draw a line downward to read the fuel used (6 gals), time (11 min) and distance (16 NM). These are the values for a climb from sea level to 10,000 feet.
4. Repeat the steps to find the values for a climb from sea level to 2,000 feet. The fuel used is 1 gallon, time is 2 minutes, and distance is 3 NM.
5. Find the fuel, time and distance values for a climb from 2,000 feet to 10,000 feet, by taking the differences for the two altitudes:

    Fuel   6 (for 10,000 feet) − 1 (for 2,000 feet) = 5 gallons
    Time   11 (for 10,000 feet) − 2 (for 2,000 feet) = 9 minutes
    Distance   16 (for 2,000 feet) − 3 (for 2,000 feet) = 13 NM

AIR
5456. (Refer to Figure 9.) Using a normal climb, how much fuel would be used from engine start to 12,000 feet pressure altitude?

Aircraft weight... 3,800 lb
Airport pressure altitude .... 4,000 ft
Temperature .... 26°C

A—46 pounds.
B—51 pounds.
C—58 pounds.

1. Locate the section for 3,800 pounds weight. Read across the 4,000-foot PA line to the entry under fuel used: 12 pounds.
2. Read across the 12,000-foot PA line to the entry under fuel used: 51 pounds.
3. Calculate the fuel required to climb:

    51 − 12 = 39 lbs

4. Apply Note #2 before adding the fuel in Note #1. (A temperature of 26°C is +19°C, relative to the standard atmosphere at 4,000 feet.)

    39 × 1.19 = 46.4 lbs

5. Apply Note #1:

    46.4 lbs + 12.0 lbs start and taxi = 58.4 lbs total

(PLT004, CA.I.D.K3a) — FAA-H-8083-25

Answers

5456 [C]

Chapter 8 **Aircraft Performance**

AIR
5457. (Refer to Figure 9.) Using a normal climb, how much fuel would be used from engine start to 10,000 feet pressure altitude?

Aircraft weight .... 3,500 lb
Airport pressure altitude .... 4,000 ft
Temperature .... 21°C

A—23 pounds.
B—31 pounds.
C—35 pounds.

1. Locate the section for 3,500 pounds weight. Read across the 4,000-foot PA line to the entry under fuel used: 11 pounds.

2. Read across the 10,000-foot PA line to the entry under fuel used: 31 pounds.

3. Calculate the fuel required to climb:

    31 − 11 = 20 lbs

4. Apply Note #1. (A temperature of 21°C is +14°C, with respect to the standard atmosphere at 4,000 feet.)

    20 × 1.14 = 22.8 lbs

5. Apply Note #2:

    22.8 lbs + 12.0 lbs start and taxi = 34.8 lbs total

(PLT004, CA.I.D.K3a) — FAA-H-8083-25

AIR
5458. (Refer to Figure 10.) Using a maximum rate of climb, how much fuel would be used from engine start to 6,000 feet pressure altitude?

Aircraft weight .... 3,200 lb
Airport pressure altitude .... 2,000 ft
Temperature .... 27°C

A—10 pounds.
B—14 pounds.
C—24 pounds.

1. Locate the section for 3,200 pounds weight. Read across the 2,000-foot PA line to the entry under fuel used: 4 pounds.

2. Read across the 6,000-foot PA line to the entry under fuel used: 14 pounds.

3. Calculate the fuel required to climb:

    14 − 4 = 10 lbs

4. Apply Note #2 before adding the fuel in Note #1. (A temperature of 27°C is +16°C, with respect to the standard atmosphere at 2,000 feet.)

    10 × 1.16 = 11.6 lbs

5. Apply Note #1:

    11.6 lbs + 12.0 lbs start and taxi = 23.6 lbs total

(PLT004, CA.I.D.K3a) — FAA-H-8083-25

AIR
5459. (Refer to Figure 10.) Using a maximum rate of climb, how much fuel would be used from engine start to 10,000 feet pressure altitude?

Aircraft weight .... 3,800 lb
Airport pressure altitude .... 4,000 ft
Temperature .... 30°C

A—28 pounds.
B—35 pounds.
C—40 pounds.

1. Locate the section for 3,800 pounds weight. Read across the 4,000-foot PA line to the entry under fuel used: 12 pounds.

2. Read across the 10,000-foot PA line to the entry under fuel used: 35 pounds.

3. Calculate the fuel required to climb:

    35 − 12 = 23 lbs

4. Apply Note #2 before adding the fuel in Note #1. (A temperature of 30°C is +23°C, with respect to the standard atmosphere at 4,000 feet.)

    23 × 1.23 = 28.3 lbs

5. Apply Note #1:

    28.3 lbs +12.0 lbs start and taxi = 40.3 lbs total

(PLT004, CA.I.D.K3a) — FAA-H-8083-25

AIR
5482. (Refer to Figure 13.)
GIVEN:

Aircraft weight .... 3,400 lb
Airport pressure altitude .... 6,000 ft
Temperature at 6,000 feet .... 10°C

Using a maximum rate of climb under the given conditions, how much fuel would be used from engine start to a pressure altitude of 16,000 feet?

A—43 pounds.
B—45 pounds.
C—49 pounds.

Answers

5457 [C]   5458 [C]   5459 [C]   5482 [A]

Chapter 8 **Aircraft Performance**

1. Determine the weight of the fuel required to climb from sea level to the PA of the airport (6,000 feet) by interpolating between the 4,000- and 8,000-foot values (for an aircraft weight of 3,400 pounds):

    (9 + 19) ÷ 2 = 14 lbs

2. Determine the weight of fuel required to climb from sea level to 16,000 feet PA: 39 lbs.

3. Determine the weight of fuel required to climb from 6,000 feet to 16,000 feet, uncorrected for nonstandard temperature:

    39 − 14 = 25 lbs

4. Correct for nonstandard temperature, Note 2, using 7% increase (+10°C is 7°C relative to the standard atmosphere at 6,000 feet):

    1.07 × 25 = 26.7 lbs

5. Apply Note #1 to determine the total fuel requirement:

    26.7 lbs + 16.0 lbs start and taxi = 42.7
    = 43 lbs total

(PLT012, CA.I.D.K3a) — FAA-H-8083-25

AIR
5483. (Refer to Figure 13.)
GIVEN:

Aircraft weight.. 4,000 lb
Airport pressure altitude .... 2,000 ft
Temperature at 2,000 feet .... 32°C

Using a maximum rate of climb under the given conditions, how much time would be required to climb to a pressure altitude of 8,000 feet?

A—7 minutes.
B—8.4 minutes.
C—11.2 minutes.

1. Determine the time required to climb from sea level to the PA of the airport (2,000 feet) by interpolating between the sea level and the 4,000-foot values (for an aircraft weight of 4,000 lbs):

    (0 + 4) ÷ 2 = 2 minutes

2. Determine the time required to climb from sea level to 8,000-foot pressure altitude: 9 minutes

3. Determine the time required to climb from 2,000 feet to 8,000-foot pressure altitude (uncorrected, for nonstandard temperature):

    9 − 2 = 7 minutes

4. Correct the time required for nonstandard temperature by applying Note #2, using 21% increase (+32°C is +21°C relative to the standard atmosphere at 2,000 feet):

    1.21 × 7 = 8.4 min

(PLT004, CA.I.D.K3a) — FAA-H-8083-25

AIR
5484. (Refer to Figure 14.)
GIVEN:

Aircraft weight.. 3,700 lb
Airport pressure altitude .... 4,000 ft
Temperature at 4,000 feet .... 21°C

Using a normal climb under the given conditions, how much fuel would be used from engine start to a pressure altitude of 12,000 feet?

A—30 pounds.
B—37 pounds.
C—46 pounds.

1. Determine the weight of the fuel required to climb from sea level to the PA of the airport (4,000 feet) for an aircraft weight of 3,700 lbs: 12 lbs.

2. Determine the weight of the fuel required to climb from sea level to 12,000-foot PA: 37 lbs.

3. Determine the weight of fuel required to climb from 4,000 to 12,000 feet, uncorrected for non-standard temperature:

    37 − 12 = 25 lbs

4. Correct the fuel requirement for nonstandard temperature by applying Note 2, using 20% increase (+21°C is +14°C, relative to the standard atmosphere at 4,000 feet):

    1.20 × 25 = 30 lbs

5. Apply Note #1 to determine the total fuel requirement:

    30 lbs + 16 lbs start and taxi = 46 lbs total

(PLT012, CA.I.D.K3a) — FAA-H-8083-25

Answers

5483 [B]   5484 [C]

Chapter 8 **Aircraft Performance**

AIR
5485. (Refer to Figure 14.)
GIVEN:

Aircraft weight	3,400 lb
Airport pressure altitude	4,000 ft
Temperature at 4,000 feet	14°C

Using a normal climb under the given conditions, how much time would be required to climb to a pressure altitude of 8,000 feet?

A—4.8 minutes.
B—5 minutes.
C—5.5 minutes.

1. Determine the time which would have been required, using a 3,400 pounds weight, to climb from sea level to the airport pressure altitude of 4,000 feet: 5 minutes.
2. Determine the time to climb to 8,000 feet from sea level: 10 minutes.
3. The time required for climb, uncorrected for temperature, is 10 − 5 = 5 minutes.
4. Correct for non-standard temperature (+14°C is +7°C, relative to the standard atmosphere.).
5. Apply Note #2 using a 10% increase.

    1.1 × 5 = 5.5 minutes.

(PLT012, CA.I.D.K3a) — FAA-H-8083-25

AIR
5486. (Refer to Figure 15.)
GIVEN:

Airport pressure altitude	4,000 ft
Airport temperature	12°C
Cruise pressure altitude	9,000 ft
Cruise temperature	-4°C

What will be the distance required to climb to cruise altitude under the given conditions?

A—6 miles.
B—8.5 miles.
C—11 miles.

1. Enter the chart at -4°C and proceed upward until intersecting the 9,000-foot PA line. From this point, proceed to the right until intersecting the Dist-Nautical Miles curved line. From this point proceed downward and read the distance: 14.5 NM.

2. Enter chart at +12°C and proceed upward until intersecting the 4,000-foot PA line. From this point, proceed to the right until intersecting the Dist-Nautical Miles curved line. From this point, proceed downward and read the distance: 6 NM.
3. The difference is the distance required to climb:

    14.5 − 6 = 8.5 NM.

(PLT012, CA.I.D.K3a) — FAA-H-8083-25

AIR
5487. (Refer to Figure 15.)
GIVEN:

Airport pressure altitude	2,000 ft
Airport temperature	20°C
Cruise pressure altitude	10,000 ft
Cruise temperature	0°C

What will be the fuel, time, and distance required to climb to cruise altitude under the given conditions?

A—5 gallons, 9 minutes, 13 NM.
B—6 gallons, 11 minutes, 16 NM.
C—7 gallons, 12 minutes, 18 NM.

1. Enter the chart at 0°C and proceed to the 10,000-foot PA curve. From this point proceed to the right. Note the intersections with the fuel, time and distance curves. From these intersections, proceed downward and read:

    Fuel = 6 gal, Time = 11 min, Dist = 16 NM

2. Enter the chart at +20°C and proceed upward to intercept the 2,000-foot PA line, then right to the intersections with the fuel, time and distance curves. From these intersections proceed downward and read:

    Fuel = 1 gal, Time + 2 min, Dist = 3 NM

3. The differences are the fuel, time and distance to climb to cruise altitude:

    Fuel = 6 − 1 = 5 gallons
    Time = 11 − 2 = 9 minutes
    Distance = 16 − 3 = 13 NM

(PLT012, CA.I.D.K3a) — FAA-H-8083-25

Answers

5485 [C]   5486 [B]   5487 [A]

Chapter 8 **Aircraft Performance**

Cruise Performance Table

The cruise performance table may be used to determine the expected percent power, true airspeed and fuel flow for a particular altitude and power setting. Based on this information, the pilot can find the estimated time en route and fuel required.

Problem:

Using the Cruise Performance Table (FAA Figure 12), find the approximate flight time available under the following conditions allowing for VFR day fuel reserve:

Pressure Altitude .... 18,000 feet
Temperature .... -1°C
Power (Best fuel economy).. 22 RPM — 20 in. manifold pressure
Usable fuel... 344 lbs

Solution:

1. Determine the flight time available by finding the rate of fuel consumption. Enter the table on the left column (RPM) and read down to 2,200 RPM.
2. Find line for 20 in. MP under the second column (MP). Follow to the right, to the column that represents a temperature of -1°C (20°C above standard temperature).
3. Continue to the right, noting 43% BHP, and in the next column, read the true airspeed of 124 knots, and a fuel flow of 59 pounds per hour (pph).
4. Find the fuel rate for best fuel economy. The chart notes in the upper right-hand corner state for best fuel economy at 70% power or less, operate at 6 pph leaner than shown in chart. For the given conditions, the engine is operating at 43% BHP, so the note does apply. The fuel burn for best fuel economy is brought down to:

    59 − 6 = 53 pph

5. Determine the approximate flight time based on 344 lbs of usable fuel and a fuel rate of 53 pph:

    344 ÷ 53 = 6.50 hours (no reserve)

6. Find the flight time with VFR day fuel reserve (30 minutes):

    6.50   no reserve
    − 0.50 VFR day reserve
    6.00   with reserve

AIR
5463. (Refer to Figure 12.)
GIVEN:

Pressure altitude.. 18,000 ft
Temperature .... -21°C
Power ....2,400 RPM — 28" MP
Recommended lean mixture usable fuel........... 425 lb

What is the approximate flight time available under the given conditions? (Allow for VFR day fuel reserve.)

A—3 hours 46 minutes.
B—4 hours 1 minute.
C—4 hours 31 minutes.

1. Find the 2,400 RPM section and 28" MP row.
2. Follow to the right in the 28" MP row and read 94 pph under the -21°C columns.
3. Compute the time available (note does not apply in this case because BHP = 72%):

    Time = 425 ÷ 94 = 4.52 hr

4. Allowing 30 minutes for day reserve (30 minutes):

    4.52 − 0.50 = 4.02 hr = 4 hours, 1 minute

(PLT015, CA.I.D.K3a) — FAA-H-8083-25

Answers

5463 [B]

Chapter 8 **Aircraft Performance**

AIR
5464. (Refer to Figure 12.)
GIVEN:

Pressure altitude	18,000 ft
Temperature	-41°C
Power	2,500 RPM — 26" MP
Recommended lean mixture usable fuel	318 lb

What is the approximate flight time available under the given conditions? (Allow for VFR night fuel reserve.)

A—2 hours 27 minutes.
B—3 hours 12 minutes.
C—3 hours 42 minutes.

1. Find the 2,500 RPM section and 26" MP row.
2. Follow to the right in 26" MP row, and read 99 pph under the -41°C columns.
3. Compute the time available (note does not apply in this case because BHP = 75%):

    Time = 318 ÷ 99 = 3.21 hours

4. Allowing 45 minutes for night reserve (0.75 hour):

    3.21 – 0.75 = 2.46 = 2 hours, 27 minutes

(PLT015, CA.I.D.K3a) — FAA-H-8083-25

AIR
5465. (Refer to Figure 12.)
GIVEN:

Pressure altitude	18,000 ft
Temperature	-1°C
Power	2,200 RPM — 20" MP
Best fuel economy usable fuel	344 lb

What is the approximate flight time available under the given conditions? (Allow for VFR day fuel reserve.)

A—4 hours 50 minutes.
B—5 hours 20 minutes.
C—5 hours 59 minutes.

1. Find the 2,200 RPM section and 20" MP row.
2. Follow to the right in the 20" MP row, and read 59 under the -1°C columns.
3. Since best fuel economy is required, apply the note:

    59 – 6 = 53 lbs/hr best economy

4. Compute the time available:

    Time = 344 ÷ 53 = 6.49 hours

5. Allowing 30 minutes for day reserve (0.5 hour):

    6.49 – 0.50 = 5.99 hours

(PLT015, CA.I.D.K3a) — FAA-H-8083-25

AIR
5625. (Refer to Figure 34.)
GIVEN:

Pressure altitude	6,000 ft
Temperature	+3°C
Power	2,200 RPM — 22" MP
Usable fuel available	465 lb

What is the maximum available flight time under the conditions stated?

A—6 hours 27 minutes.
B—6 hours 39 minutes.
C—6 hours 56 minutes.

1. Enter the Cruise Performance Chart at the 2,200 RPM section (the left-hand column). In that section, move right and find the 22" MP row. Follow that row to the right and read 70 pph under the 3°C columns.
2. Calculate the available flight endurance using:

    Time = Fuel ÷ Fuel Burn Rate = 465 ÷ 70
    = 6.643 hours

3. Convert .643 hours into minutes:

    0.643 × 60 = 38.6 minutes

4. Therefore, the flight time is 6 hours, 39 minutes.

(PLT015, CA.I.D.K3a) — FAA-H-8083-25

AIR
5626. (Refer to Figure 34.)
GIVEN:

Pressure altitude	6,000 ft
Temperature	-17°C
Power	2,300 RPM — 23" MP
Usable fuel available	370 lb

What is the maximum available flight time under the conditions stated?

A—4 hours 20 minutes.
B—4 hours 30 minutes.
C—4 hours 50 minutes.

1. Enter the Cruise Performance Chart at the 2,300 RPM section (the left-hand column). In that section move right and find the 23" MP row. Follow that row right and read 82 pph under the -17°C columns.
2. Calculate the available flight endurance using:

    Time = Fuel ÷ Fuel Burn Rate = 370 ÷ 82
    = 4.51 hours

Answers

5464 [A]   5465 [C]   5625 [B]   5626 [B]

3. Convert 0.51 hour to minutes.

   .51 × 60 = 30.6 minutes

4. Therefore, the flight time is 4 hours, 30 minutes.

(PLT015, CA.I.D.K3a) — FAA-H-8083-25

AIR
5627. (Refer to Figure 34.)
GIVEN:

Pressure altitude..6,000 ft
Temperature ....+13°C
Power ....2,500 RPM — 23" MP
Usable fuel available .... 460 lb

What is the maximum available flight time under the conditions stated?

A—4 hours 58 minutes.
B—5 hours 7 minutes.
C—5 hours 12 minutes.

1. Enter the Cruise Performance Chart at the 2,500 RPM section (the left-hand column). In that section, move right and find the 23" MP row. Follow that row to the right until intersecting the 3°C conditions and read 90 pph.

2. Determine the fuel flow at 2,500 RPM, 23" MP and +23°C, 87 pph.

3. Average to determine fuel flow at +13°C, 2,500 RPM and 23" MP:

   (90 + 87) ÷ 2 = 88.5 pph

4. Calculate the available flight endurance using:

   Time = Fuel ÷ Fuel Burn Rate = 460 ÷ 88.5
   = 5.2 hours

5. Convert 0.2 hour into minutes:

   0.2 × 60 = 12 minutes

6. Therefore, the flight time is 5 hours, 12 minutes.

(PLT015, CA.I.D.K3a) — FAA-H-8083-25

Cruise and Range Performance Table

Referring to the cruise and range performance table, a pilot can determine true airspeed, fuel consumption, endurance, and range based on altitude and power setting.

Problem:

Using FAA Figure 11, find the approximate true airspeed and fuel consumption per hour at an altitude of 7,500 feet, 52 percent power.

Solution:

1. Enter the chart at the altitude to be flown (7,500 feet) on the left.

2. Under the percent brake horsepower (BHP) column, refer to the line representing 52 percent power. Read to the right and find the true airspeed (105 MPH) and fuel consumption (6.2 GPH).

AIR
5460. (Refer to Figure 11.) If the cruise altitude is 7,500 feet, using 64 percent power at 2,500 RPM, what would be the range with 48 gallons of usable fuel?

A—635 miles.
B—645 miles.
C—810 miles.

1. Find 7,500 feet in the first column.

2. Go across to third column to find 64% BHP.

3. Using the proper column according to the amount of fuel specified in the question, go across from 64% to find 810 miles endurance under the range column.

(PLT015, CA.I.D.K3a) — FAA-H-8083-25

Answers

5627 [C]   5460 [C]

Chapter 8 **Aircraft Performance**

AIR
5461. (Refer to Figure 11.) What would be the endurance at an altitude of 7,500 feet, using 52 percent power?

NOTE: (With 48 gallons fuel-no reserve.)

A—6.1 hours.
B—7.7 hours.
C—8.0 hours.

1. Find 7,500 feet in the first column.
2. Go across to third column to find 52% BHP.
3. Using the proper column according to the amount of fuel specified in the question, go across from 52% to find 7.7 hours endurance under the Endr. Hours column.

(PLT015, CA.I.D.K3a) — FAA-H-8083-25

AIR
5462. (Refer to Figure 11.) What would be the approximate true airspeed and fuel consumption per hour at an altitude of 7,500 feet, using 52 percent power?

A—103 MPH TAS, 6.3 GPH.
B—105 MPH TAS, 6.2 GPH.
C—105 MPH TAS, 6.6 GPH.

1. Find 7,500 feet in first column.
2. Go across to third column to find 52% BHP.
3. Read 105 TAS in TAS column and 6.2 GPH under the Gal/Hour column.

(PLT012, CA.I.D.K3a) — FAA-H-8083-25

Maximum Rate of Climb

The maximum rate of climb table illustrates the expected climb performance based on pressure altitude and temperature.

Problem:

Determine the maximum rate of climb under the given conditions:

Weight .... 3,400 lbs
Pressure altitude... 7,000 feet
Temperature .... +15°C

Solution:

To find the maximum rate of climb for 7,000 feet at 15°C, interpolation is necessary for both altitude and temperature. The interpolation may be accomplished in any order.

1. To find the value for 15°C, interpolation is used between 0° and 20°C. The difference between the two temperatures at 4,000 feet is 155 fpm (1,220 fpm – 1,065 fpm). The temperature of 15°C is 3/4 of the way between the 0°C and 20°C value. At 15°C for 4,000 feet, the rate of climb is 1,104 fpm.

    1,220 – 116-3/4 = 1,104

    or 1,065 + 39-1/4 = 1,104

2. The same method is applied to 8,000 feet to find the value for 15°C. The difference between 0°C and 20°C is 155 fpm (1,110 fpm – 955 fpm). Taking 3/4 of 155 fpm also gives 116 fpm. The rate of climb at 8,000 feet is 994 fpm.

    1,110 – 116 = 994 or 955 + 39 = 994

3. Interpolate for an altitude of 7,000 feet. The altitude of 7,000 feet is 3/4 of the way between 4,000 feet and 8,000 feet. The overall difference is 110 fpm, 3/4 of which would be 82.5 fpm. The rate for 7,000 feet is 1,021 fpm.

    1,114 – 82.5 = 1,031

    or 994 + 27.5 = 1,021

Answers

5461 [B]   5462 [B]

Chapter 8 **Aircraft Performance**

AIR
5623. (Refer to Figure 33.)
GIVEN:

Weight .... 4,000 lb
Pressure altitude.................................. 5,000 ft
Temperature .... 30°C

What is the maximum rate of climb under the given conditions?

A—655 ft/min.
B—702 ft/min.
C—774 ft/min.

1. Interpolate the rate of climb for 4,000 feet, altitude at 30°C:

   (800 + 655) ÷ 2 = 728 fpm

2. Interpolate the rate of climb for 8,000 feet, altitude at 30°C:

   (695 + 555) ÷ 2 = 625 fpm

3. Use linear interpolation, in ratio form, to deter-mine the rate of climb valid at 5,000 feet and 30°C. The gap between figure altitudes is four 1,000-foot sections.

   (728 ÷ 4) – (625 ÷ 4) = 26 fpm

4. Subtract this increment from the temperature-adjusted base altitude figure (4,000 feet MSL) and get your maximum rate of climb for all the given conditions:

   728 – 26 = 702 fpm

(PLT004, CA.I.D.K3a) — FAA-H-8083-25

AIR
5624. (Refer to Figure 33.)
GIVEN:

Weight .... 3,700 lb
Pressure altitude................................22,000 ft
Temperature .... -10°C

What is the maximum rate of climb under the given conditions?

A—305 ft/min.
B—320 ft/min.
C—384 ft/min.

1. Interpolate or average to determine the rate of climb at 20,000 feet, -10°C:

   (600 + 470) ÷ 2 = 535 fpm

2. Interpolate or average to determine the rate of climb at 24,000 feet, -10°C:

   (170 + 295) ÷ 2 = 233 fpm

3. Interpolate or average to determine the rate of climb at 22,000 feet and -10°C; incorporate the results for 20,000 and 24,000 feet obtained in Steps 1 and 2:

   (535 + 233) ÷ 2 = 384 fpm

(PLT004, CA.I.D.K3a) — FAA-H-8083-25

Glide Distance

Glide distance can be found by using a chart such as FAA Figure 3A.

Problem:

Find the distance you can glide from 5,500 feet above the terrain with a 10-knot tailwind.

Solution:

1. Follow a line to the right from the height above terrain of 5,500 feet until it intersects the slanted line.
2. From this intersection, draw a line downward until it intersects the glide distance. This intersection is at 8 nautical miles.

AIR
5537. (Refer to Figure 3A.) What is the approximate glide distance if you are operating at 5,500 feet?

A—10 NM.
B—8 NM.
C—6 NM.

Follow a line to the right from the height above terrain of 5,500 feet until it intersects the slanted line. From this intersection, draw a line downward until it intersects the glide distance. This intersection is at 8 nautical miles. (PLT006, CA.I.D.K2) — FAA-H-8083-25

Answers

5623 [B]   5624 [C]   5537 [B]

Chapter 8 Aircraft Performance

AIR

5538. (Refer to Figure 3A.) What is the approximate glide distance if you are operating at 8,000 feet?
A—12 NM.
B—10 NM.
C—14 NM.

Follow a line to the right from the height above terrain of 8,000 feet until it intersects the slanted line. From this intersection, draw a line downward until it intersects the glide distance. This intersection is at 12 nautical miles. (PLT006, CA.I.D.K2) — FAA-H-8083-25

Rotorcraft Performance

RTC
5683. (Refer to Figure 41.)
GIVEN:

Helicopter gross weight .... 1,225 lb
Ambient temperature .... 77°F

Determine the in-ground-effect hover ceiling.

A—6,750 feet.
B—7,250 feet.
C—8,000 feet.

1. Enter the "in ground effect" chart at the 1,225-pound point and proceed upward to the 25°C line (visualize midway between 20 and 30).
2. From that intersection proceed left and read the hovering ceiling, 6,750 feet.

(PLT021) — FAA-H-8083-21, Chapter 8

RTC
5684. (Refer to Figure 41.)
GIVEN:

Helicopter gross weight .... 1,175 lb
Ambient temperature .... 95°F

Determine the out-of-ground effect hover ceiling.

A—5,000 feet.
B—5,250 feet.
C—6,250 feet.

1. Enter the "out of ground effect" chart at the 1,175-pound point and proceed upward to the 35°C line (visualize midway between 30 and 40).
2. From that intersection proceed left and read the hovering ceiling, 5,250 feet.

(PLT048) — FAA-H-8083-21, Chapter 8

RTC
5685. (Refer to Figure 41.)
GIVEN:

Helicopter gross weight .... 1,275 lb
Ambient temperature .... 9°F

Determine the in ground effect hover ceiling.

A—6,600 feet.
B—7,900 feet.
C—8,750 feet.

1. Enter the "in ground effect" chart at the 1,275-pound point and proceed upward to the -12.8°C line (visualize between -10 and -20°C).
2. From that intersection proceed left and read the hovering ceiling, 7,900 feet.

(PLT011) — FAA-H-8083-21

RTC
5687. (Refer to Figure 42.) Departure is planned from a heliport that has a reported pressure altitude of 4,100 feet. What rate of climb could be expected in this helicopter if the ambient temperature is 90°F?

A—210 ft/min.
B—250 ft/min.
C—390 ft/min.

1. Visualize, or trace on the plastic overlay, a line midway between and parallel to the 80° and 100° lines. Enter the chart at the 4,100-foot pressure altitude point and proceed to the right until intersecting the 90°F OAT line.
2. From that point of intersection, proceed downward to the rate of climb axis and read 250 fpm.

(PLT004) — FAA-H-8083-21

Answers

5538 [A]   5683 [A]   5684 [B]   5685 [B]   5687 [B]

RTC
5688. (Refer to Figure 42.) Departure is planned for a flight from a heliport with a pressure altitude of 3,800 feet. What rate of climb could be expected in this helicopter during departure if the ambient temperature is 70°F?

A—330 ft/min.
B—360 ft/min.
C—400 ft/min.

1. Visualize, or trace on the plastic overlay, a line midway between and parallel to the 60° and 80° lines. Enter the chart at the 3,800-foot pressure altitude point and proceed to the right until intersecting your 70°F OAT line.
2. From that point of intersection, proceed downward to the rate of climb axis and read 338 fpm.

(PLT004) — FAA-H-8083-21

RTC
5689. (Refer to Figure 43.)
GIVEN:

Ambient temperature .... 60°F
Pressure altitude .... 2,000 ft

What is the rate of climb?

A—480 ft/min.
B—515 ft/min.
C—540 ft/min.

1. Enter the chart at the 2,000-foot pressure altitude point and proceed to the right until intersecting the 60°F OAT curve.
2. From that point of intersection, proceed downward to the scale and read the rate of climb, 515 fpm.

(PLT004) — FAA-H-8083-21

RTC
5690. (Refer to Figure 43.)
GIVEN:

Ambient temperature .... 80°F
Pressure altitude .... 2,500 ft

What is the rate of climb?

A—350 ft/min.
B—395 ft/min.
C—420 ft/min.

1. Enter the chart at the 2,500-foot pressure altitude point and proceed to the right until intersecting the 80°F OAT curve.
2. From that point of intersection, proceed downward to the scale and read the rate of climb, 395 fpm.

(PLT004) — FAA-H-8083-21

RTC
5691. (Refer to Figure 44.)
GIVEN:

Ambient temperature .... 40°F
Pressure altitude .... 1,000 ft

What is the rate of climb?

A—810 ft/min.
B—830 ft/min.
C—860 ft/min.

1. Enter the chart at the 1,000-foot pressure altitude point and proceed to the right until intersecting the 40°F OAT curve.
2. From that point of intersection proceed downward to the scale and read the rate of climb, 860 fpm.

(PLT004) — FAA-H-8083-21

RTC
5692. (Refer to Figure 44.)
GIVEN:

Ambient temperature .... 60°F
Pressure altitude .... 2,000 ft

What is the rate of climb?

A—705 ft/min.
B—630 ft/min.
C—755 ft/min.

1. Enter the chart at the 2,000-foot pressure altitude point and proceed to the right until intersecting the 60°F OAT curve.
2. From that point of intersection, proceed downward to the scale and read the rate of climb, 705 fpm.

(PLT004) — FAA-H-8083-21

Answers

5688 [A]   5689 [B]   5690 [B]   5691 [C]   5692 [A]

Chapter 8 **Aircraft Performance**

RTC
5693. (Refer to Figures 45 and 46.)
GIVEN:

Pressure altitude .... 4,000 ft
Ambient temperature .... 80°F

To clear a 50-foot obstacle, a jump takeoff would require

A—more distance than a running takeoff.
B—less distance than a running takeoff.
C—the same distance as a running takeoff.

1. Determine the running takeoff distance:
   a. Enter the chart at the 4,000-foot pressure altitude and proceed to the right to intersect the 80°F curve.
   b. From the point of intersection move down to the scale and read the total takeoff distance to clear a 50-foot obstacle, 1,230 feet.
2. In the same way as in Step 1, determine the jump takeoff distance to clear a 50-foot obstacle:1,440 feet.
3. The jump takeoff distance exceeds the running takeoff distance by 210 feet (1,440 – 1,230).

(PLT011) — FAA-H-8083-21

RTC
5694. (Refer to Figures 45 and 46.)
GIVEN:

Pressure altitude .... 4,000 ft
Ambient temperature .... 80°F

The takeoff distance to clear a 50-foot obstacle is

A—1,225 feet for a jump takeoff.
B—1,440 feet for a running takeoff.
C—less for a running takeoff than for a jump takeoff.

1. Move right from the 4,000-foot pressure altitude line until meeting the 80°F arc.
2. Go down from this intersection by continuing one and one-half small squares off the heavy line.
3. You arrive at the running takeoff line one and one-half squares to the right of 1,200 feet (12 × 100) with each square representing 20 = 1,230 feet.
4. Using FAA Figure 46, move right from the 4,000-foot pressure altitude line until meeting the 80°F arc.
5. Continue down from this intersection, two small squares away from the heavy line.
6. You arrive at the jump takeoff line at 1,440 feet.

(PLT011) — FAA-H-8083-21

Glider Performance

GLI
5773. (Refer to Figure 48.) If a dual glider weighs 1,040 pounds and an indicated airspeed of 55 MPH is maintained, how much altitude will be lost while traveling 1 mile?

A—120 feet.
B—240 feet.
C—310 feet.

Note that a weight of 1,040 pounds is associated with dual flight.

1. Enter the chart at 55 MPH and proceed vertically to intercept the "L/D Dual" curve.
2. From the intersection, proceed to the left and read the L/D 22.
3. Calculate the altitude loss using the relation:

   L/D = Glide Ratio = Horizontal Distance Traveled ÷ Vertical Distance Traveled

   $$\frac{22}{1} = \frac{5,280}{X}$$

   X = 240 feet

(PLT054) — FAA-H-8083-13

Answers

5693 [A]   5694 [C]   5773 [B]

Chapter 8 **Aircraft Performance**

GLI
5774. (Refer to Figure 48.) If a dual glider weighs 1,040 pounds, what is the minimum sink speed and rate of sink?

A—38 MPH and 2.6 ft/sec.
B—42 MPH and 3.1 ft/sec.
C—38 MPH and 3.6 ft/sec.

The gross weight of the glider is 1,040 pounds, therefore the sink speed "dual" would be used. The table at the top of the graph shows this value to be 3.1 fps at 42 MPH. (PLT054) — FAA-H-8083-13

GLI
5775. (Refer to Figure 48.) If the airspeed of a glider is increased from 54 MPH to 60 MPH, the L/D ratio would

A—decrease and the rate of sink would increase.
B—increase and the rate of sink would decrease.
C—decrease and the rate of sink would decrease.

1. Draw a vertical line representing a speed of 54 MPH to intersect the L/D curves.

2. Draw two lines to the left from the points of intersection to determine the L/D values.

3. In a fashion similar to Steps 1 and 2, determine the L/D values for a speed of 60 MPH.

4. Calculate the changes in L/D for single and dual operation. Single operation L/D decreases from 20.25 to 18.4. Dual operation L/D decreases from 22.1 to 20.8.

5. Note the rate of sink values, V_S, increase with an increase in airspeed for both single and dual curves.

(PLT054) — FAA-H-8083-13

GLI
5776. Minimum sink speed is the airspeed which results in the

A—least loss of altitude in a given time.
B—least loss of altitude in a given distance.
C—shallowest glide angle in any convective situation.

Minimum sink speed is the speed (indicated) at which the glider loses altitude most slowly. (PLT123) — FAA-H-8083-13

GLI
5777. (Refer to Figure 49.) If the airspeed is 70 MPH and the sink rate is 5.5 ft/sec, what is the effective L/D ratio with respect to the ground?

A—19:1.
B—20:1.
C—21:1.

1. Enter the chart at the 70 MPH airspeed point and draw a line vertically to intercept the L/D curve.

2. From that intersection proceed to the left to read the value of L/D 19:1.

(PLT054) — FAA-H-8083-13

GLI
5778. (Refer to Figure 49.) If the airspeed is 50 MPH and the sink rate is 3.2 ft/sec, what is the effective L/D ratio with respect to the ground?

A—20:1.
B—21:1.
C—23:1.

1. Enter the chart at the 50 MPH airspeed point and draw a line vertically to intercept the L/D curve.

2. From that intersection proceed to the left to read the value of L/D, 23:1.

(PLT054) — FAA-H-8083-13

GLI
5779. The glider has a normal L/D ratio of 23:1 at an airspeed of 50 MPH. What would be the effective L/D ratio with respect to the ground with a 10 MPH tailwind?

A—23:1.
B—25:1.
C—27.6:1.

Glide Ratio = Horizontal Distance Traveled ÷ Vertical Distance Traveled

A tailwind will increase the horizontal distance traveled, in any given time period, but will not affect the vertical distance (sink). Therefore, the new horizontal distance for a 10 MPH tailwind is:

$$\frac{23 \times (50 + 10)}{50} = 27.6$$

Therefore, the effective glide ratio is about 27.6:1.

(PLT054) — FAA-H-8083-13

Answers

5774 [B]   5775 [A]   5776 [A]   5777 [A]   5778 [C]   5779 [C]

Chapter 8 **Aircraft Performance**

GLI
5780. If the glider has drifted a considerable distance from the airport while soaring, the best speed to use to reach the airport when flying into a headwind is the

A—best glide speed.
B—minimum sink speed.
C—speed-to-fly plus half the estimated windspeed at the glider's altitude.

If maximum distance over the ground is desired, the airspeed for best L/D should be used. When gliding into a headwind, maximum distance will be achieved by adding approximately one-half of the estimated headwind velocity to the best L/D speed. (PLT132) — FAA-H-8083-13

GLI
5781. The maximum airspeed at which abrupt and full deflection of the controls would not cause structural damage to a glider is called the

A—speed-to-fly.
B—maneuvering speed.
C—never-exceed speed.

The speed at which full abrupt control travel at maximum gross weight may be used without exceeding the load limits is called maneuvering speed. (PLT257) — FAA-H-8083-13

GLI
5782. Which is true regarding minimum control airspeed while thermalling? Minimum control airspeed

A—may coincide with minimum sink airspeed.
B—is greater than minimum sink airspeed.
C—never coincides with minimum sink airspeed.

Minimum control airspeed is the speed at which an increase of either the angle of attack or load factor would result in an immediate stall. Therefore, minimum control speed is only a few miles per hour above the stall speed, nearly coinciding with minimum sink speed. (PLT132) — FAA-H-8083-13

GLI
5783. (Refer to Figure 50.) Which is true when the glider is operated in the high-performance category and the dive brakes/spoilers are in the closed position? The

A—design dive speed is 150 MPH.
B—never-exceed speed is 150 MPH.
C—design maneuvering speed is 76 MPH.

1. Locate the key showing high performance category (dark lines).
2. Note the V_{NE} for no brake operation (brakes/spoilers closed).
3. Read the intercept of the V_{NE} line with the speed ordinate, 150 MPH.

(PLT054) — FAA-H-8083-13

GLI
5784. (Refer to Figure 50.) If the glider's airspeed is 70 MPH and a vertical gust of +30 ft/sec is encountered, which would most likely occur? The

A—glider would momentarily stall.
B—maximum load factor would be exceeded.
C—glider would gain 1,800 feet in 1 minute.

1. Enter the chart at 70 MPH velocity.
2. Proceed vertically to an estimated position for a +30 fps gust. The position will be outside the envelope.
3. Note the maneuvering speed V_A, is greater than 70 MPH. Since the flight speed is less than V_A turbulence will not impose a damaging structural load and the glider will momentarily stall.

(PLT054) — FAA-H-8083-13

GLI
5785. Regarding the effect of loading on glider performance, a heavily loaded glider would

A—have a lower glide ratio than when lightly loaded.
B—have slower forward speed than when lightly loaded.
C—make better flight time on a cross-country flight between thermals than when lightly loaded.

Increasing the weight of the glider increases the airspeed at which the best glide ratio is obtained. Weight does not affect the maximum glide ratio, only the airspeed at which it is attained. (PLT256) — FAA-H-8083-13

GLI
5786. When flying into a strong headwind on a long final glide or a long glide back to the airport, the recommended speed to use is the

A—best glide speed.
B—minimum sink speed.
C—speed-to-fly plus half the estimated windspeed at the glider's flight altitude.

Answers

| 5780 | [C] | 5781 | [B] | 5782 | [A] | 5783 | [B] | 5784 | [A] | 5785 | [C] |
| 5786 | [C] |

If maximum distance over the ground is desired, the airspeed for best L/D should be used. When gliding into a headwind, maximum distance will be achieved by adding approximately one-half of the estimated headwind velocity to the best L/D speed. (PLT257) — FAA-H-8083-13

GLI
5787. Which procedure can be used to increase forward speed on a cross-country flight?

A—Maintain minimum sink speed plus or minus one-half the estimated wind velocity.
B—Use water ballast while thermals are strong and dump the water when thermals are weak.
C—Use water ballast while thermals are weak and dump the water when thermals are strong.

As the weight of the glider increases, the airspeed must be increased to maintain the same glide ratio. During a contest situation, it is desirable to fly faster. (PLT132) — FAA-H-8083-13

GLI
5788. The reason for retaining water ballast while thermals are strong, is to

A—decrease forward speed.
B—decrease cruise performance.
C—increase cruise performance.

As the weight of the glider increases, the airspeed must be increased to maintain the same glide ratio. (PLT257) — FAA-H-8083-13

GLI
5789. When flying into a headwind, penetrating speed is the glider's

A—speed-to-fly.
B—minimum sink speed.
C—speed-to-fly plus half the estimated wind velocity.

If maximum distance over the ground is desired, the airspeed for best L/D should be used. When gliding into a headwind, maximum distance will be achieved by adding approximately one-half of the estimated headwind velocity to the best L/D speed. (PLT132) — FAA-H-8083-13

GLI
5790. Which is true regarding the effect on a glider's performance by the addition of ballast or weight?

A—The glide ratio at a given airspeed will increase.
B—The heavier the glider is loaded, the less the glide ratio will be at all airspeeds.
C—A higher airspeed is required to obtain the same glide ratio as when lightly loaded.

As the weight of the glider increases, the airspeed must be increased to maintain the same glide ratio. (PLT257) — FAA-H-8083-13

Balloon Performance

LTA
5480. (Refer to Figure 52, point 1.)
GIVEN:

Departure point.................Georgetown Airport (Q61)
Departure time..0637
Winds aloft forecast (FD) at your altitude...........1008

At 0755, the balloon should be

A—over Auburn Airport (AUN).
B—over the town of Auburn.
C—slightly west of the town of Garden Valley.

1. Calculate time en route:

    0735 − 0637 = 1:18 = 1.3 hours

2. Compute distance traveled:

    Distance = Speed × Time
    8 × 1.3 = 10.4 NM

3. Plot course of 100° + 180° = 280° out to a distance of 10.4 NM from Georgetown Airport (Q61), point 1. The balloon should be just south of there.

(PLT012) — FAA-H-8083-25

Answers

5787 [B]   5788 [C]   5789 [C]   5790 [C]   5480 [A]

Chapter 8 Aircraft Performance

LTA

5571. (Refer to Figure 53, point 3.) If at 1,000 feet MSL and drifting at 10 knots toward Firebaugh Airport (F34), at what approximate distance from the airport should you begin a 100 ft/min ascent to arrive at the center of the airport at 3,000 feet?

A—3.5 NM.
B—5 NM.
C—8 NM.

3,000 feet − 1,000 feet = 2,000 feet to climb.

2,000 feet ÷ 100 fpm = 20 minutes

(10 KTS ÷ 60 min) × 20 minutes = 3.33 NM

(PLT012) — Sectional Chart Legend

LTA

5573. (Refer to Figure 54, point 5.) A balloon drifts over the town of Brentwood on a magnetic course of 185° at 10 knots. If wind conditions remain the same, after 1 hour 30 minutes the pilot

A—with no radio aboard, must be above 2,900 feet MSL and must have an operating transponder aboard.
B—must remain above 600 feet MSL for national security reasons.
C—with no radio aboard, must be above 2,900 feet MSL.

The balloon traveled a distance of 15 NM, and is located within controlled airspace. With no radio on board, the balloon must be above 2,900 feet MSL. Balloons are not certified with an electrical system, and therefore are not required to have a transponder. (PLT161) — Sectional Chart Legend, 14 CFR §91.215

LTA

5578. (Refer to Figure 53, point 4.) A balloon departs the town of Mendota and drifts for a period of 1 hour and 30 minutes in a wind of 230° at 10 knots. What maximum elevation figure would assure obstruction clearance during the next 1-1/2 hours of flight?

A—1,600 feet MSL.
B—3,200 feet MSL.
C—9,400 feet MSL.

The Maximum Elevation Figures are larger bold-faced blue numbers. They are shown in quadrangles bounded by ticked lines of latitude and longitude and are in thousands and hundreds of feet MSL. They are based on the highest known feature in each quadrangle, including terrain and obstructions. 3 hours into the flight at 10 knots would put the balloon in the upper right grid, which has a maximum altitude of 9,400 feet. (PLT064) — Sectional Chart Legend

LTA

5579. (Refer to Figure 52, point 4.) If Lincoln Regional Airport (LHM) is departed at 0630, and at 0730 the town of Newcastle is reached, the wind direction and speed would be approximately

A—082° at 6 knots.
B—262° at 11 knots.
C—082° at 17 knots.

The aircraft traveled 13 NM west-to-east. (PLT012) — Section Chart Legend

LTA

5580. (Refer to Figure 52, point 4.) If you depart Lincoln Regional Airport (LHM) and track a true course of 075° with a groundspeed of 12 knots, your position after 1 hour 20 minutes of flight would be over the town of

A—Foresthill.
B—Clipper Gap.
C—Weimar.

With a ground speed of 12 knots, the distance traveled after 1 hour 20 minutes would be:

12 knots × 1:20 = 16.08 NM

On a course of 075°, and a distance of 16.08 NM, your position would be over the town of Clipper Gap.

(PLT012) — Sectional Chart Legend

Answers

| 5571 | [A] | 5573 | [C] | 5578 | [C] | 5579 | [B] | 5580 | [B] |

LTA

5582. (Refer to Figure 53, point 4.) While drifting above the Johnston Airport (M90) with a northwesterly wind of 8 knots, you

A—are required to contact ATC on frequency 122.9 Mhz.
B—should remain higher than 2,000 feet AGL until you are at least 8 NM southeast of that airport.
C—will be over Firebaugh Airport (Q49) in approximately 1 hour.

With a northwesterly wind you will be drifting toward the southeast. Just southeast of Johnston Airport is the Mendota State Wildlife Area, which you should overfly at 2,000 feet AGL or higher. (PLT101) — Sectional Chart Legend

LTA

5586. (Refer to Figure 54, point 3.)

GIVEN:

Departure point	Meadowlark Airport
Departure time	0710
Wind	180°, 8 kts

At 0917 the balloon should be

A—east of VINCO intersection.
B—over the town of Brentwood.
C—3 miles south of the town of Brentwood.

Wind is from 180° pushing the balloon to the north at 8 NM/hr. The time elapsed from 0710 to 0917, which is 2 hours 7 minutes. Therefore, the balloon will travel 17 NM to the north. Using a plotter, measure 17 north, i.e., over Brentwood. (PLT012) — Sectional Chart Legend

LTA

5589. (Refer to Figure 52, point 5.) A balloon is launched at University Airport (0O5) and drifts south-southwesterly toward the depicted obstruction. If the altimeter was set to the current altimeter setting upon launch, what should it indicate if the balloon is to clear the obstruction by 500 feet above its top?

A—510 feet MSL.
B—813 feet MSL.
C—881 feet MSL.

The field elevation at University Airport is 68 feet MSL. A 381-foot obstacle southwest of the airport must be cleared by 500 feet.

68 + 313 + 500 = 881

Therefore, the altimeter would read 881 feet MSL.

(PLT041) — Sectional Chart Legend

Answers

5582	[B]	5586	[B]	5589	[C]

Chapter 9
Navigation

The Flight Computer   *9–3*

    Finding True Course, Time, Rate, Distance, and Fuel   *9–3*

    Finding Density Altitude   *9–10*

    Finding Wind Direction and Velocity   *9–12*

VHF Omni-Directional Range (VOR)   *9–14*

Horizontal Situation Indicator (HSI)   *9–18*

The Flight Computer

ASA's CX-3 is an electronic flight computer and can be used in place of the E6-B. This aviation computer can solve all flight planning problems, as well as perform standard mathematical calculations.

Finding True Course, Time, Rate, Distance, and Fuel

True course is expressed as an angle between the course line and true (geographic) north. Lines of longitude (meridians) designate the direction of north-south at any point on the surface of the Earth and converge at the poles. Because meridians converge toward the poles, true course measurement should be taken at a meridian near the midpoint of the course rather than at the point of departure.

The flight computer can be used to solve problems of time, rate and distance. When two factors are known, the third can be found using the proportion:

$$\text{Rate (speed)} = \frac{\text{Distance}}{\text{Time}}$$

Problem:

Find the time en route and fuel consumption based on the following information:

Wind	175° at 20 knots
Distance	135 NM
True course	075°
True airspeed	80 knots
Fuel consumption	105.0 pounds/hour

Solution using the E6-B:

1. Using the wind face side of the E6-B computer, set the true wind direction (175°) under the true index.
2. Place a wind dot 20 units (wind speed) directly above the grommet.
3. Rotate the plotting disk to set the true course (075°) under the true index.
4. Adjust the sliding grid so that the TAS arc (80 knots) is under the wind dot. Note that the wind dot is 15° right of centerline, so the wind correction angle (WCA) = 15°R.
5. Read the ground speed under the grommet: 81.0 knots.
6. a. Determine the time en route, using the formula:

    $$\frac{\text{Distance}}{\text{Ground speed}} = \text{Time}$$

    135 ÷ 81 = 1.67 hour

    b. The E6-B may also be used to find the time en route:
    i. Set the 60 (speed) index under 81 knots (outer scale).
    ii. Under 135 NM (outer scale) read the time of 100 minutes or 1 hour 40 minutes (inner scale).
7. Find the amount of fuel consumed, using the formula:

    Time × fuel consumption rate = total consumed

    1.67 hours × 105.0 pounds/hour = 175.35 pounds

Chapter 9 **Navigation**

The E6-B may also be used to find the amount of fuel consumed:
   a. Set the 60 (speed) index under 105.0 pounds/hour.
   b. Over 100 minutes or 1 hour 40 minutes (inner scale) read 175 pounds required (outer scale).

Solution using the CX-3:
1. Select Wind Correction from FLT menu and enter the given information:

   True Airspeed (TAS) .... 80 KTS
   True Course (TCrs) .... 0.075°
   Wind Speed (Wspd) .... 20 KTS
   Wind Direction (WDir) .... 175°

   Find a ground speed (GS) of 81 knots.

2. Select Ground Speed from the FLT menu and enter the given information:

   Distance (Dist) .... 135 NM
   Ground Speed (GS) .... 81 KTS

   Find a duration of 1 hour, 40 minutes.

3. Select Fuel from the FLT menu and enter the given information:

   Duration (Dur) .... 1:40:00 HMS
   Fuel Burn (Rate) .... 105 US GPH

   Find a total fuel consumed (Wt) of 175 pounds.

Problem:

Based on the following information, determine the approximate time, fuel consumed, compass headings, and distance traveled during the descent to the airport:

Cruising Altitude .... 10,500 feet
Airport elevation .... 1,700 feet
Descent to .... 1,000 feet AGL
Rate of descent .... 600 ft/min
Average true airspeed .... 135 knots
True course .... 263°
Average wind velocity .... 330° at 30 knots
Variation .... 7° east
Deviation .... +3°
Average fuel consumption .... 11.5 gal/hr

Solution using the E6-B:
1. Find the time en route. The time to descend is based on the vertical distance from the cruising altitude of 10,500 feet down to the lower altitude of 2,700 feet MSL (1,000 feet AGL + 1,700 feet MSL):

   ```
     10,500   feet cruising altitude
   – 2,700    feet lower altitude
     7,800    feet altitude change
   ```

$$\frac{\text{Distance}}{\text{Rate}} = \text{Time}$$

7,800 feet ÷ 600 feet/min = 13 minutes

2. Find the amount of fuel consumed using the formula:

   Time × fuel consumption rate = fuel consumed

   $$\frac{13 \text{ minutes} \times 11.5 \text{ gal/hr}}{60 \text{ min/hr}} = 2.5 \text{ gallons}$$

3. Use the wind face of the E6-B to find the ground speed (120 knots) and wind correction angle (+ 12°R). Due to wind being present, the TAS is not the ground speed. The speed used to calculate the distance covered must be the ground speed.

4. Calculate the distance:

   Time × speed = distance

   $$\frac{13 \text{ min} \times 120 \text{ knots}}{60 \text{ min/hr}} = 26 \text{ NM}$$

5. Determine the compass heading, by applying the wind correction angle that was found on the wind face of E6-B to the true course, which gives the true heading. The true heading is corrected by variation to give the magnetic heading. Finally, the deviation is used to correct magnetic heading to give the compass heading as follows:

263°	TC
+ 12°R	±WCA
275°	TH
− 7° E	±VAR
268°	MH
+ 3°	±DEV
271°	CH

Solution using the CX-3:

1. The time to descend is based on the vertical distance from the cruising altitude of 10,500 feet down to the lower altitude of 2,700 feet MSL (1,000 feet AGL + 1,700 feet MSL):

10,500	feet cruising altitude
− 2,700	feet lower altitude
7,800	feet altitude change

2. Determine your time of descent:

   $$\frac{\text{Distance}}{\text{Rate}} = \text{Time}$$

   7,800 feet ÷ 600 feet/min = 13 minutes

(continued)

Chapter 9 **Navigation**

3. Select Wind Correction from the FLT menu:

   True Airspeed (TAS) .... 135 KTS

   True Course (TCrs) .... 263°

   Wind Speed (WSpd) .... 30 KTS

   Wind Direction (WDir) .... 330 KTS

   Find a ground speed (GS) of 120 knots and a true heading (THdg) of 275°.

4. Subtract the variation of 7° east and add the deviation of 3° to get a compass heading of 271°.

5. Select Fuel from the FLT menu:

   Duration (Dur) .... 13 MIN

   Fuel Consumption (Rate) .... 11.5 US GPH

   Find a volume of total fuel consumed (Vol) of 2.49 U.S. gallons.

6. Select Ground Speed from the FLT menu:

   Duration (DUR) .... 13 MIN

   Ground Speed (GS) .... 120 KTS

   Find a distance (Dist) of 26 NM.

ALL
5479. True course measurements on a Sectional Aeronautical Chart should be made at a meridian near the midpoint of the course because the

A—values of isogonic lines change from point to point.
B—angles formed by isogonic lines and lines of latitude vary from point to point.
C—angles formed by lines of longitude and the course line vary from point to point.

Meridians (lines of longitude) converge toward the poles, so course measurement should be taken at a meridian near the midpoint of the course rather than at the point of departure. (PLT064, CA.VI.A.K1) — FAA-H-8083-25

Answers (A) and (B) are incorrect because isogonic lines are used to find magnetic course.

ALL
5999-1. What procedure could a pilot use to navigate under VFR from one point to another when ground references are not visible?

A—Dead reckoning.
B—Pilotage.
C—VFR is not allowed in these circumstances.

Pilotage is navigation by reference to landmarks or checkpoints. Dead reckoning is navigation solely by means of computations based on time, airspeed, distance, and direction. (PLT200, CA.VI.A.K1) — FAA-H-8083-25

AIR
5469. If fuel consumption is 80 pounds per hour and groundspeed is 180 knots, how much fuel is required for an airplane to travel 460 NM?

A—205 pounds.
B—212 pounds.
C—460 pounds.

1. Calculate the time en route:

   460 NM ÷ 180 knots = 2.556 hours

2. Determine the fuel burn:

   80 lbs/hr × 2.56 hours = 204.8 pounds

(PLT015, CA.VI.A.K7) — FAA-H-8083-25

Answers

5479 [C]   5999-1 [A]   5469 [A]

Chapter 9 **Navigation**

AIR
5470. If an airplane is consuming 95 pounds of fuel per hour at a cruising altitude of 6,500 feet and the groundspeed is 173 knots, how much fuel is required to travel 450 NM?

A—248 pounds.
B—265 pounds.
C—284 pounds.

1. Calculate the time en route:
   450 NM ÷ 173 knots = 2.6 hour
2. Determine the fuel burn:
   95 lbs/hr × 2.6 hours = 247 pounds

(PLT012, CA.I.D.K3a) — FAA-H-8083-25

AIR
5471. If an airplane is consuming 12.5 gallons of fuel per hour at a cruising altitude of 8,500 feet and the groundspeed is 145 knots, how much fuel is required to travel 435 NM?

A—27 gallons.
B—34 gallons.
C—38 gallons.

1. Calculate the time en route:
   435 NM ÷ 145 knots = 3 hours
2. Determine the fuel burn:
   12.5 GPH × 3 hours = 37.5 gallons

(PLT015, CA.I.D.K3c) — FAA-H-8083-25

AIR
5472. If an aircraft is consuming 9.5 gallons of fuel per hour at a cruising altitude of 6,000 feet and the groundspeed is 135 knots, how much fuel is required to travel 420 NM?

A—27 gallons.
B—30 gallons.
C—35 gallons.

1. Calculate the time en route:
   420 NM ÷ 135 knots = 3.11 hours
2. Determine the fuel burn:
   9.5 GPH × 3.11 hours = 29.5 gallons.

(PLT012, CA.VI.A.K7) — FAA-H-8083-25

AIR
5473. If an airplane is consuming 14.8 gallons of fuel per hour at a cruising altitude of 7,500 feet and the groundspeed is 167 knots, how much fuel is required to travel 560 NM?

A—50 gallons.
B—53 gallons.
C—57 gallons.

1. Calculate the time en route:
   560 NM ÷ 167 knots = 3.35 hours
2. Determine the fuel burn:
   14.8 GPH × 3.35 hours = 49.6 gallons

(PLT012, CA.I.D.K3a) — FAA-H-8083-25

AIR
5474. If fuel consumption is 14.7 gallons per hour and groundspeed is 157 knots, how much fuel is required for an airplane to travel 612 NM?

A—58 gallons.
B—60 gallons.
C—64 gallons.

1. Calculate the time en route:
   612 NM ÷ 157 knots = 3.9 hours
2. Determine the fuel burn:
   14.7 GPH × 3.9 = 57.33 gallons

(PLT012, CA.I.D.K3a) — FAA-H-8083-25

AIR, RTC
5481. GIVEN:
Wind .... 175° at 20 kts
Distance ....135 NM
True course...075°
True airspeed... 80 kts
Fuel consumption .... 105 lb/hr

Determine the time en route and fuel consumption.

A—1 hour 28 minutes and 73.2 pounds.
B—1 hour 38 minutes and 158 pounds.
C—1 hour 40 minutes and 175 pounds.

1. Compute the ground speed:
   Wind direction.. 175°
   Wind speed .... 20 knots
   Course..075°
   True airspeed .... 80 knots
   Ground speed..81.0 knots

(continued)

Answers

5470 [A]   5471 [C]   5472 [B]   5473 [A]   5474 [A]   5481 [C]

Chapter 9 Navigation

2. Determine the time en route:

    135 NM ÷ 81 knots = 1.67 hours
    = 1 hour 40 minutes

3. Calculate fuel consumed:

    105.0 lbs/hr × 1.67 hours = 175.0 pounds

(PLT012, CA.I.D.K3a) — FAA-H-8083-25

AIR
5466. An airplane descends to an airport under the following conditions:

Cruising altitude	6,500 ft
Airport elevation	700 ft
Descends to	800 ft AGL
Rate of descent	500 ft/min
Average true airspeed	110 kts
True course	335°
Average wind velocity	060° at 15 kts
Variation	3°W
Deviation	+2°
Average fuel consumption	8.5 gal/hr

Determine the approximate time, compass heading, distance, and fuel consumed during the descent.

A—10 minutes, 348°, 18 NM, 1.4 gallons.
B—10 minutes, 355°, 17 NM, 2.4 gallons.
C—12 minutes, 346°, 18 NM, 1.6 gallons.

1. Calculate the time to descend:

    Time = vertical distance ÷ vertical speed

    Where vertical distance = 6,500 – 1,500
    = 5,000 feet

    Time = 5,000 feet ÷ 500 FPM = 10 minutes
    = 0.1667 hr

2. Compute the fuel requirement:

    8.5 gal/hr × 0.1667 hr = 1.42 gallons

3. Calculate the wind correction angle and ground speed using a wind triangle:

    WCA = 8° right
    Ground speed = 108 knots

4. Calculate true heading (TH = TC + WCA):

    335° + 8° = 343° TH

5. Calculate compass heading (CH = TH + Var + Dev):

    343° + 3° + 2° = 348° CH

6. Compute distance flown:

    Distance = 108 knots × 0.1667 hour = 18 NM

(PLT004, CA.VI.A.K5b) — FAA-H-8083-25

AIR
5467. An airplane descends to an airport under the following conditions:

Cruising altitude	7,500 ft
Airport elevation	1,300 ft
Descends to	800 ft AGL
Rate of descent	300 ft/min
Average true airspeed	120 kts
True course	165°
Average wind velocity	240° at 20 kts
Variation	4°E
Deviation	-2°
Average fuel consumption	9.6 gal/hr

Determine the approximate time, compass heading, distance, and fuel consumed during the descent.

A—16 minutes, 168°, 30 NM, 2.9 gallons.
B—18 minutes, 164°, 34 NM, 3.2 gallons.
C—18 minutes, 168°, 34 NM, 2.9 gallons.

1. Calculate the time to descend:

    Time = vertical distance ÷ vertical speed

    Where vertical distance = 7,500 – 2,100
    = 5,400 feet

    Time = 5,400 feet ÷ 300 FPM = 18 minutes
    = 0.3 hour

2. Compute the fuel requirement:

    9.6 gal/hr × 0.3 hour = 2.88 gallons

3. Calculate the wind correction angle and ground speed using a wind triangle:

    WCA = 9° right
    Ground speed = 113 knots

4. Calculate true heading (TH = TC + WCA):

    165° + 9° = 174° TH

5. Calculate compass heading (CH = TH + Var + Dev):

    174° – 4° – 2° = 168° CH

6. Compute distance flown:

    Distance = 113 knots × 0.3 hour = 33.9 NM

(PLT004, CA.VI.A.K5b) — FAA-H-8083-25

Answers

5466 [A]   5467 [C]

AIR
5468. An airplane descends to an airport under the following conditions:

Cruising altitude... 10,500 ft
Airport elevation .... 1,700 ft
Descends to .... 1,000 ft AGL
Rate of descent .... 600 ft/min
Average true airspeed .... 135 kts
True course..263°
Average wind velocity............................ 330° at 30 kts
Variation .... 7°E
Deviation...+3°
Average fuel consumption ....11.5 gal/hr

Determine the approximate time, compass heading, distance, and fuel consumed during the descent.

A—9 minutes, 274°, 26 NM, 2.8 gallons.
B—13 minutes, 274°, 28 NM, 2.5 gallons.
C—13 minutes, 271°, 26 NM, 2.5 gallons.

1. Calculate the time to descend:

    Time = vertical distance ÷ vertical speed

    Where vertical distance = 10,500 – 2,700
    = 7,800 feet

    Time = 7,800 feet ÷ 600 FPM = 13 minutes
    = 0.2167 hour

2. Compute the fuel requirement:

    11.5 gal/hr × 0.2167 hour = 2.49 gallon

3. Calculate the wind correction angle and ground speed using a wind triangle:

    WCA = 12° right
    Ground speed = 120 knots

4. Calculate true heading (TH = TC + WCA):

    263° + 12° = 275° TH

5. Calculate compass heading (CH = TH + Var + Dev):

    275° – 7° + 3° = 271° CH

6. Compute distance flown:

    120 knots × 0.2167 hour = 26 NM

(PLT004, CA.VI.A.K5b) — FAA-H-8083-25

AIR
5488. An airplane departs an airport under the following conditions:

Airport elevation .... 1,000 ft
Cruise altitude ....9,500 ft
Rate of climb... 500 ft/min
Average true airspeed .... 135 kts
True course..215°
Average wind velocity............................ 290° at 20 kts
Variation .... 3°W
Deviation... -2°
Average fuel consumption .... 13 gal/hr

Determine the approximate time, compass heading, distance, and fuel consumed during the climb.

A—14 minutes, 234°, 26 NM, 3.9 gallons.
B—17 minutes, 224°, 36 NM, 3.7 gallons.
C—17 minutes, 242°, 31 NM, 3.5 gallons.

1. Calculate the time to climb:

    Time = vertical distance ÷ vertical speed

    Where vertical distance = 9,500 – 1,000
    = 8,500 feet

    Time = 8,500 feet ÷ 500 FPM = 17 minutes
    = 0.283 hour

2. Compute the fuel requirement:

    13 gal/hr × 0.283 hour = 3.679 gallons

3. Calculate the wind correction angle and ground speed using a wind triangle:

    WCA = 8° right
    Ground speed = 128 knots

4. Calculate true heading (TH = TC + WCA):

    215 + 8° = 223° TH

5. Calculate compass heading (CH = TH + Var + Dev):

    223° + 3° – 2° = 224° CH

6. Compute distance flown:

    Distance = 128 knots × 0.283 hour = 36.2 NM

(PLT012, CA.VI.A.K5c) — FAA-H-8083-25

Answers

5468 [C]   5488 [B]

Chapter 9 **Navigation**

AIR

5489. An airplane departs an airport under the following conditions:

Airport elevation .... 1,500 ft
Cruise altitude .... 9,500 ft
Rate of climb.. 500 ft/min
Average true airspeed .... 160 kts
True course.. 145°
Average wind velocity........................ 080° at 15 kts
Variation .... 5°E
Deviation... -3°
Average fuel consumption .... 14 gal/hr

Determine the approximate time, compass heading, distance, and fuel consumed during the climb.

A—14 minutes, 128°, 35 NM, 3.2 gallons.
B—16 minutes, 132°, 41 NM, 3.7 gallons.
C—16 minutes, 128°, 32 NM, 3.8 gallons.

1. Calculate the time to climb:

    Time = vertical distance ÷ vertical speed

    Where vertical distance = 9,500 – 1,500
    = 8,000 feet

    Time = 8,000 feet ÷ 500 FPM = 16 minutes
    = 0.27 hour

2. Compute the fuel requirement:

    14 gal/hr × 0.2666 hour = 3.73 gallons

3. Calculate the wind correction angle and ground speed using a wind triangle:

    WCA = 5° left
    Ground speed = 153 knots

4. Calculate true heading (TH = TC + WCA):

    145° – 5° = 140° TH

5. Calculate compass heading (CH = TH + Var + Dev):

    140° – 5° – 3° = 132° CH

6. Compute distance flown:

    Distance = 153 knots × 0.27 hour = 41.31 NM

(PLT012, CA.VI.A.K5c) — FAA-H-8083-25

Finding Density Altitude

Density altitude is the altitude in standard air where the density is the same as the existing density. It is affected by the pressure, temperature, and moisture content of the air. Both a decrease in pressure and an increase in temperature decrease the density of the air and increase the density altitude.

To find density altitude, refer to the right-hand window on the computer side of the E6-B.

Problem:

Find the density altitude from the following conditions:

Pressure Altitude .... 5,000 feet

True air temperature .... + 40°C

Solution using the E6-B:

1. Refer to the right-hand "Density Altitude" window. Note that the scale above the window is labeled air temperature (°C). The scale inside the window itself is labeled pressure altitude (in thousands of feet). Rotate the disc and place the pressure altitude of 5,000 feet opposite an air temperature of +40°C.

2. The density altitude shown in the window is 8,800 feet.

Solution using the CX-3:

Select Altitude from the FLT menu:

Pressure Altitude (PAlt).. 5,000 FT

Temperature (OAT) .... 40°C

Find a density altitude (Dalt) of 8,846 feet.

Answers

5489 [B]

Chapter 9 **Navigation**

ALL
5306. GIVEN:

Pressure altitude... 12,000 ft
True air temperature .... +50°F

From the conditions given, the approximate density altitude is

A—11,900 feet.
B—14,130 feet.
C—18,150 feet.

Using an E6-B:
1. Convert 50°F to °C using the temperature conversion table at the bottom of the E6-B. The result is 10°C.

2. Refer to the right-hand "Density Altitude" window. Note that the scale above the window is labeled air temperature (°C). The scale inside the window itself is labeled pressure altitude (in thousands of feet). Rotate the disc and place the pressure altitude of 12,000 feet opposite an air temperature of 10°C. The density altitude shown in the density altitude window is 14,130 feet.

Using a CX-3:
1. From the FLT menu select Altitude.
2. Enter a PAlt of 12,000 FT and OAT of 50°F to get a DAlt of 14,134 FT or approximately 14,130 feet.

(PLT005, CA.VI.A.K5d) — AC 00-6

ALL
5307. GIVEN:

Pressure altitude... 5,000 ft
True air temperature .... +30°C

From the conditions given, the approximate density altitude is

A—7,200 feet.
B—7,800 feet.
C—9,000 feet.

1. Refer to the right-hand "Density Altitude" window. Note that the scale above the window is labeled air temperature (°C). The scale inside the window itself is labeled pressure altitude (in thousands of feet). Rotate the disc and place the pressure altitude of 5,000 feet opposite an air temperature of 30°C.

2. The density altitude shown in the density altitude window is 7,800 feet.

(PLT005, CA.VI.A.K5d) — AC 00-6

ALL
5308. GIVEN:

Pressure altitude.. 6,000 ft
True air temperature .... +30°F

From the conditions given, the approximate density altitude is

A—9,000 feet.
B—5,500 feet.
C—5,000 feet.

Using an E6-B:
1. Convert 30°F to °C using the temperature conversion table at the bottom of the E6-B. The result is -1°C.

2. Refer to the right-hand "Density Altitude" window. Note that the scale above the window is labeled air temperature (°C). The scale inside the window itself is labeled pressure altitude (in thousands of feet). Rotate the disc and place the pressure altitude of 6,000 feet opposite an air temperature of -1°C. The density altitude shown in the window is 5,500 feet.

Using a CX-3:
1. From the FLT menu select Altitude.
2. Enter a PAlt of 6,000 FT and OAT of 30°F to get a DAlt of 5,494 FT or approximately 5,500 feet.

(PLT005, CA.VI.A.K5d) — AC 00-6

ALL
5309. GIVEN:

Pressure altitude.. 7,000 ft
True air temperature .... +15°C

From the conditions given, the approximate density altitude is

A—5,000 feet.
B—8,500 feet.
C—9,500 feet.

1. Refer to the right-hand "Density Altitude" window. Note that the scale above the window is labeled air temperature (°C). The scale inside the window itself is labeled pressure altitude (in thousands of feet). Rotate the disc and place the pressure altitude of 7,000 feet opposite an air temperature of 15°C.

2. The density altitude shown in the window is 8,500 feet.

(PLT005, CA.VI.A.K5d) — AC 00-6

Answers

5306 [B]   5307 [B]   5308 [B]   5309 [B]

Chapter 9 **Navigation**

ALL
5990. As air temperature increases, density altitude will

A—decrease.
B—increase.
C—remain the same.

Density altitude is the altitude in standard air where the density is the same as the existing density. It is affected by the pressure, temperature, and moisture content of the air. Both a decrease in pressure and an increase in temperature decrease the density of the air and increase the density altitude. (PLT206, CA.I.C.K3c) — AC 00-6

Finding Wind Direction and Velocity

The E6-B can be used to solve for an unknown wind. To determine wind direction and wind speed, the true course, wind correction angle, true airspeed and ground speed are necessary. The WCA may not be given directly in a problem, but can be determined from the true course (TC) and true heading (TH).

Problem:
Determine the wind direction and wind speed under the following conditions:

True course	095°
True heading	075°
True airspeed	90 knots
Ground speed	77 knots

Solution using the E6-B:

1. Set the true course (095°) under the true index located at the top of the computer.
2. Move the sliding grid to place the ground speed (77 knots) under the center grommet.
3. Determine the wind correction angle. Above the true heading (075°) read the wind correction angle, 20°L. Draw the wind dot over the true airspeed arc (90 knots) and 20° (wind correction angle) to the left.
4. Finally, rotate the window until the wind dot is lined up directly above the grommet. The wind direction is read under the true index (020°). For convenience, the sliding grid may be moved so that 100 knots is placed under the grommet. The difference between the grommet and the wind dot indicates the wind speed (31 knots).

Solution using the CX-3:

Select Wind Correction from the FLT menu:

Ground Speed (GS)	77 KTS
True Airspeed (TAS)	90 KTS
True Course (TCrs)	95°
True Heading (THdg)	75°

Find a wind direction (WDir) of 019° and wind speed (WSpd) of 31.7 knots.

Answers

5990 [B]

AIR, RTC
5475. GIVEN:

True course..105°
True heading..085°
True airspeed... 95 kts
Groundspeed.. 87 kts

Determine the wind direction and speed.

A—020° and 32 knots.
B—030° and 38 knots.
C—200° and 32 knots.

Using an E6-B computer:

1. Turn the compass azimuth so 105° is at the true index.
2. Slide board so grommet is on the ground speed arc: 87 knots.
3. Determine the WCA by comparing course to heading.

    105° − 085° = 20° left

4. Plot WCA at TAS arc with a pencil dot: 95 knots.
5. Rotate compass azimuth so pencil dot is on the centerline.
6. Read wind direction under true index and wind speed as number of units between grommet and pencil dot: 020° and 32 knots.

(PLT012, CA.I.D.K3a) — FAA-H-8083-25

AIR, RTC
5476. GIVEN:

True course..345°
True heading..355°
True airspeed... 85 kts
Groundspeed.. 95 kts

Determine the wind direction and speed.

A—095° and 19 knots.
B—113° and 19 knots.
C—238° and 18 knots.

Using an E6-B computer:

1. Turn compass azimuth so 345° is at the true index.
2. Slide board so grommet is on the ground speed arc: 95 knots.
3. Determine the WCA by comparing course to heading:

    345° − 355° = 10° right

4. Plot WCA at TAS arc with a pencil dot: 85 knots.
5. Rotate compass azimuth so pencil dot is on the centerline.
6. Read wind direction under true index and wind speed as number of units between grommet and pencil dot: 114° and 19 knots.

(PLT012, CA.I.D.K3a) — FAA-H-8083-25

ALL
5478. GIVEN:

Distance off course .... 9 mi
Distance flown .... 95 mi
Distance to fly..125 mi

To converge at the destination, the total correction angle would be

A—4°.
B—6°.
C—10°.

1. Determine the number of degrees correction required to parallel the desired course:

    $$\frac{\text{Miles off Course} \times 60}{\text{Number of Miles Flown}} = \text{Correction to Parallel}$$

    $$\frac{9 \times 60}{95} = 5.68° \text{ to parallel}$$

2. Determine the number of additional degrees correction required to intercept the course:

    $$\frac{\text{Miles off Course} \times 60}{\text{Number of Miles Remaining}} = \text{Correction to Intercept}$$

    $$\frac{9 \times 60}{125} = 4.32° \text{ additional to intercept}$$

3. Add the number of degrees required to parallel the course and the number of degrees required to intercept the course to find the total correction angle required to converge at destination:

    5.68° to parallel + 4.32° to intercept
    = 10.00° total to converge

(PLT001, CA.VI.A.K5b) — FAA-H-8083-25

Answers

5475 [A]   5476 [B]   5478 [C]

Chapter 9 **Navigation**

VHF Omni-Directional Range (VOR)

All VOR stations transmit an identifier. It is a three-letter Morse code signal interrupted only by a voice identifier on some stations, or to allow the controlling flight service station to speak on the frequency. Absence of a VOR identifier indicates maintenance is being performed on the station and the signal may not be reliable.

Figure 9-1. VOR indicators

All VOR receivers have at least the essential components shown in Figure 9-1. The pilot may select the desired course or radial by turning the omni-bearing selector (OBS). The course deviation indicator (CDI) centers when the aircraft is on the selected radial or its reciprocal. A full-scale deflection of the CDI from the center represents a deviation of approximately 10° to 12°.

The TO/FROM Indicator (ambiguity indicator) shows whether the selected course will take the aircraft TO or FROM the station. A TO indication shows that the OBS selection is on the other side of the VOR station. A FROM indication shows that the OBS selection and the aircraft are on the same side of the VOR station. When an aircraft flies over a VOR, the TO/FROM indicator will reverse, indicating station passage.

The position of the aircraft can always be determined by rotating the OBS until the CDI centers with a FROM indication. The course displayed indicates the radial FROM the station. The VOR indicator displays information as though the aircraft were going in the direction of the course selected. However, actual heading does not influence the display. See Figure 9-2.

VOR radials, all of which originate at the VOR antenna, diverge as they radiate outward. For example, while the 011° radial and the 012° radial both start at the same point, 1 NM from the antenna, they are 100 feet apart. When they are 2 NM from the antenna, they are 200 feet apart. So at 60 NM, the radials would be 1 NM (6,000 feet) apart. See Figure 9-3.

The VOR indicator uses a series of dots to indicate any deviation from the selected course, with each dot equal to approximately 2° of deviation. Thus, a one-dot deviation at a distance of 30 NM from the station would indicate that the aircraft was 1 NM from the selected radial (200 feet × 30 = 6,000 feet).

To orient where the aircraft is in relation to the VOR, first determine which radial is selected (look at the OBS setting). Next, determine whether the aircraft is flying to or away from the station (look at the TO/FROM indicator), to find which hemisphere the aircraft is in. Last, determine how far off course the aircraft is from the selected course (look at the CDI needle deflection) to find which quadrant the aircraft is in. Remember that aircraft heading does not affect orientation to the VOR.

VOR accuracy may be checked by means of a VOR Test Facility (VOT), ground or airborne checkpoints, or by checking dual VORs against each other. A VOT location and frequency can be found in the *Chart Supplements U.S.* and on the Air-to-Ground Communications Panel of the Low Altitude Enroute Chart.

Figure 9-2. VOR display

Figure 9-3. Radial divergence

Note:
Angular divergence is exaggerated for illustrative purposes.

To use the VOT, tune to the appropriate frequency and center the CDI. The omni-bearing selector should read 0° with a FROM indication, or 180° with a TO indication. The allowable error is ±4°. VOR receiver checkpoints are listed in the Chart Supplements U.S. With the appropriate frequency tuned and the OBS set to the published certified radial, the CDI should center with a FROM indication when the aircraft is over the designated checkpoint. Allowable accuracy is ±4° for a ground check, and ±6° for an airborne check. If the aircraft is equipped with dual VORs, they may be checked against each other. The maximum permissible variation when tuned to the same VOR is 4°.

The pilot must log the results of the VOR accuracy test in the aircraft logbook or other record. The log must include the date, place, bearing error if any, and a signature.

Chapter 9 **Navigation**

ALL
5532. When checking the course sensitivity of a VOR receiver, how many degrees should the OBS be rotated to move the CDI from the center to the last dot on either side?

A—5° to 10°.
B—10° to 12°.
C—18° to 20°.

Course sensitivity may be checked by noting the number of degrees of change in course selection as you rotate the OBS to move the CDI from center to the last dot on either side. This should be between 10° and 12°. (PLT276, CA.VI.B.K1) — FAA-H-8083-15

ALL
5533. An aircraft 60 miles from a VOR station has a CDI indication of one-fifth deflection, this represents a course centerline deviation of approximately

A—6 miles.
B—2 miles.
C—1 mile.

Aircraft displacement from course is approximately 200 feet per dot per nautical mile. The CDI deflection indication is one-fifth deflection at 60 miles from the station, and a one-fifth or one-dot deflection indicates a 2-mile displacement of the aircraft from the course centerline. (PLT090, CA.VI.B.K1) — FAA-H-8083-15

ALL
5500. Which situation would result in reverse sensing of a VOR receiver?

A—Flying a heading that is reciprocal to the bearing selected on the OBS.
B—Setting the OBS to a bearing that is 90° from the bearing on which the aircraft is located.
C—Failing to change the OBS from the selected inbound course to the outbound course after passing the station.

With the reciprocal of the inbound course set on the OBS and the indicator showing FROM, the aircraft will be turned away from the needle for direct return to course centerline. This is called reverse sensing. (PLT091, CA.VI.B.K1) — FAA-H-8083-25

ALL
5501. To track outbound on the 180 radial of a VOR station, the recommended procedure is to set the OBS to

A—360° and make heading corrections toward the CDI needle.
B—180° and make heading corrections away from the CDI needle.
C—180° and make heading corrections toward the CDI needle.

Tracking involves drift correction that is sufficient to maintain a direct course to or from a transmitting station. The course selected for tracking outbound is the course shown under the course index with the TO/FROM indicator showing FROM. Turning toward the needle returns the aircraft to the course centerline and centers the needle. (PLT091, CA.VI.B.K1) — FAA-H-8083-25

ALL
5502. To track inbound on the 215 radial of a VOR station, the recommended procedure is to set the OBS to

A—215° and make heading corrections toward the CDI needle.
B—215° and make heading corrections away from the CDI needle.
C—035° and make heading corrections toward the CDI needle.

Tracking involves drift correction that is sufficient to maintain a direct course to or from a transmitting station. The course selected for tracking outbound is the course shown under the course index with the TO/FROM indicator showing FROM. Turning toward the needle returns the aircraft to the course centerline and centers the needle. (PLT091, CA.VI.B.K1) — FAA-H-8083-25

ALL
5551. How should the pilot make a VOR receiver check when the aircraft is located on the designated checkpoint on the airport surface?

A—Set the OBS on 180° plus or minus 4°; the CDI should center with a FROM indication.
B—Set the OBS on the designated radial. The CDI must center within plus or minus 4° of that radial with a FROM indication.
C—With the aircraft headed directly toward the VOR and the OBS set to 000°, the CDI should center within plus or minus 4° of that radial with a TO indication.

Airborne and ground checkpoints consist of certified radials that should be received at specific points on the

Answers

| 5532 | [B] | 5533 | [B] | 5500 | [A] | 5501 | [C] | 5502 | [C] | 5551 | [B] |

airport surface or over specific landmarks while airborne in the immediate vicinity of the airport. Should an error in excess of ±4° be indicated through use of a ground check, or ±6° using the airborne check, IFR flight shall not be attempted without first correcting the source of the error. Caution: No correction other than the correction card figures supplied by the manufacturer should be applied in making these VOR receiver checks. (PLT507, CA.VI.B.K1) — AIM ¶1-1-4*

ALL
5552. When using VOT to make a VOR receiver check, the CDI should be centered and the OBS should indicate that the aircraft is on the

A—090 radial.
B—180 radial.
C—360 radial.

To use the VOT service, tune in the VOT frequency on your VOR receiver. With the Course Deviation Indicator (CDI) centered, the omni-bearing selector (OBS) should read 0° with the TO/FROM indication showing FROM, or the OBS should read 180° with the TO/FROM indication showing TO. Since VOR radials are always expressed as FROM the station, the OBS should indicate the aircraft is on the 360° radial FROM. (PLT507, CA.VI.B.K1) — AIM ¶1-1-4

ALL
5553. When the CDI needle is centered during an airborne VOR check, the omnibearing selector and the TO/FROM indicator should read

A—within 4° of the selected radial.
B—within 6° of the selected radial.
C—0° TO, only if you are due south of the VOR.

If neither a test signal nor a designated checkpoint on the surface is available, use an airborne checkpoint designated by the Administrator or, outside the United States, by appropriate authority. The maximum permissible bearing error is ±6°. (PLT507, CA.VI.B.K1) — 14 CFR §91.171

ALL
5555. For IFR operations off established airways, ROUTE OF FLIGHT portion of an IFR flight plan should list VOR navigational aids which are no more than

A—40 miles apart.
B—70 miles apart.
C—80 miles apart.

Operation off established airways below 18,000 feet MSL use aids not more than 80 NM apart. These aids are depicted on Enroute Low-Altitude Charts. (PLT224, CA.VI.B.K1) — AIM ¶5-1-8

AIR, RTC, LTA
5062. What is the maximum bearing error (+ or -) allowed for an operational VOR equipment check when using an FAA-approved ground test signal?

A—4 degrees.
B—6 degrees.
C—8 degrees.

The maximum permissible bearing error is ±4° when using a VOT. (PLT508, CA.VI.B.K1) — 14 CFR §91.171

AIR, RTC, LTA
5122-1. When must an operational check on the aircraft VOR equipment be accomplished to operate under IFR? Within the preceding

A—30 days or 30 hours of flight time.
B—10 days or 10 hours of flight time.
C—30 days.

No person may operate a civil aircraft under IFR using the VOR system of radio navigation unless the VOR equipment of that aircraft has been operationally checked within the preceding 30 days, and was found to be within permissible limits. (PLT508, CA.VI.B.K1) — 14 CFR §91.171

AIR, RTC, LTA
5122-2. Which data must be recorded in the aircraft logbook or other record by a pilot making a VOR operational check for IFR operations?

A—VOR name or identification, place of operational check, amount of bearing error, and date of check.
B—Date of check, place of operational check, bearing error, and signature.
C—VOR name or identification, amount of bearing error, date of check, and signature.

Each person making a VOR operational check shall enter the date, place, bearing error, and sign the aircraft log or other record. (PLT508, CA.VI.B.K1) — 14 CFR §91.171

Answers

| 5552 | [C] | 5553 | [B] | 5555 | [C] | 5062 | [A] | 5122-1 | [C] | 5122-2 | [B] |

Chapter 9 **Navigation**

AIR, RTC, LTA

5122-3. When navigating using only VOR/DME based RNAV, selection of a VOR NAVAID that does not have DME service will

A—result in loss of RNAV capability.
B—have no effect on navigation capability.
C—not impact navigation provided enough of the GPS is operating.

VOR/DME-based RNAV units need both VOR and DME signals to operate in RNAV mode. If the NAVAID selected is a VOR without DME, RNAV mode will not function. When DME is not available the RNAV unit will function as a VOR receiver with DME capability in VOR (or non-RNAV) mode. (PLT354, CA.VI.B.K1) — FAA-H-8083-25

Horizontal Situation Indicator (HSI)

The HSI is a combination of two instruments: the heading indicator and the VOR. See Figure 9-4.

The aircraft heading displayed on the rotating azimuth card under the upper lubber line in Figure 9-4 is 330°. The course indicating arrowhead that is shown is set to 300°. The tail of the course indicating arrow indicates the reciprocal, or 120°.

The course deviation bar operates with a VOR/LOC navigation receiver to indicate either left or right deviations from the course that is selected with the course indicating arrow. It moves left or right to indicate deviation from the centerline in the same manner that the angular movement of a conventional VOR/LOC needle indicates deviation from course.

The desired course is selected by rotating the course indicating arrow in relation to the azimuth card by means of the course set knob. This gives the pilot a pictorial presentation. The fixed aircraft symbol and the course deviation bar display the aircraft relative to the selected course as though the pilot was above the aircraft looking down.

The TO/FROM indicator is a triangular-shaped pointer. When this indicator points to the head of the course arrow, it indicates that the course selected, if properly intercepted and flown, will take the aircraft TO the selected facility, and vice versa.

The glide slope deviation pointer indicates the relationship of the aircraft to the glide slope. When the pointer is below the center position, the aircraft is above the glide slope, and an increased rate of descent is required.

To orient where the aircraft is in relation to the facility, first determine which radial is selected (look at the arrowhead). Next, determine whether the aircraft is flying to or away from the station (look at the TO/FROM indicator) to find which hemisphere the aircraft is in. Then, determine how far from the selected course the aircraft is (look at the deviation bar) to find which quadrant the aircraft is in. Finally, consider the aircraft heading (under the lubber line) to determine the aircraft's position within the quadrant.

Figure 9-4. Horizontal situation indicator (HSI)

Answers

5122-3 [A]

ALL
5506. (Refer to Figure 17.) Which illustration indicates that the airplane will intercept the 060 radial at a 60° angle inbound, if the present heading is maintained?

A—6.
B—4.
C—5.

To intercept the 060° radial inbound (TO), the reciprocal (240°) would be selected. Only illustrations 4, 5, and 6 have the 240° course selected. The 240° course may be intercepted at a 60° angle with either a heading of 300° (240° + 60°) or 180° (240° − 60°). The only illustration showing either is 6. (PLT014, CA.VI.B.K1) — FAA-H-8083-15

AIR, RTC, LTA
5507. (Refer to Figure 17.) Which statement is true regarding illustration 2, if the present heading is maintained? The airplane will

A—cross the 180 radial at a 45° angle outbound.
B—intercept the 225 radial at a 45° angle.
C—intercept the 360 radial at a 45° angle inbound.

Illustration 2 shows the aircraft heading 225°. The bearing pointer indicates a heading of 235° will take the aircraft to the station; therefore, you are on the 055° radial. If the present heading is maintained, the station will remain to the right of the aircraft and you will cross the 180° radial at approximately a 45° angle outbound (225° − 180° = 45°). (PLT056, CA.VI.B.K1) — FAA-H-8083-15

AIR, RTC, LTA
5508. (Refer to Figure 17.) Which illustration indicates that the airplane will intercept the 060 radial at a 75° angle outbound, if the present heading is maintained?

A—4.
B—5.
C—6.

Only two possible headings will intercept the 060° radial at a 75° angle outbound: 135° and 345°. The only one of those shown is illustration 5. The illustration shows that if the aircraft turned to 060°, it would be going FROM the station and would have to fly left to get on the 060 radial. (PLT014, CA.VI.B.K1) — FAA-H-8083-15

AIR, RTC, LTA
5509. (Refer to Figure 17.) Which illustration indicates that the airplane should be turned 150° left to intercept the 360 radial at a 60° angle inbound?

A—1.
B—2.
C—3.

Only two headings intercept the 360° radial inbound at a 60° angle: 120° and 240°. An aircraft heading 270° could turn left 150° to intercept at a 60° angle on a heading of 120°. An aircraft heading 030° could turn left 150° to intercept at a 60° angle on a heading of 240°. Illustration 1 shows the aircraft flying one of the two possible headings. (PLT014, CA.VI.B.K1) — FAA-H-8083-15

AIR, RTC, LTA
5510. (Refer to Figure 17.) Which is true regarding illustration 4, if the present heading is maintained? The airplane will

A—cross the 060 radial at a 15° angle.
B—intercept the 240 radial at a 30° angle.
C—cross the 180 radial at a 75° angle.

Illustration 4 shows the aircraft heading 255° with a magnetic bearing of 275° to the station. The aircraft will pass south of the station and cross the 180° radial at a 75° angle (255° − 180° = 75°). (PLT014, CA.VI.B.K1) — FAA-H-8083-15

Answers

5506 [A]   5507 [A]   5508 [B]   5509 [A]   5510 [C]

Cross-Reference A
Question Number and Page Number

This cross-reference lists all of the questions in this book in sequential order. Use this list in combination with Cross-Reference B to find specific questions to aid your studies. For more information about the questions included in ASA Test Preps, please see pages vi–vii and xvii.

Question Number	Page Number	Question Number	Page Number	Question Number	Page Number	Question Number	Page Number
5001	4–38	5032	4–11	5061	4–21	5082-4	5–6
5002	4–39	5033	4–12	5061-1	4–21	5083	5–14
5003-1	4–39	5034	4–12	5061-2	4–21	5083-1	5–14
5003-2	4–39	5035-1	4–43	5061-3	4–22	5084	4–43
5004-1	4–39	5035-2	4–43	5061-4	4–22	5085	5–15
5004-2	4–39	5036	4–43	5062	9–17	5086	4–42
5004-3	4–39	5037	4–43	5063	4–22	5087	4–42
5005	4–40	5038	4–43	5064	4–23	5088	5–12
5006	4–40	5039	4–5	5065	4–31	5089	5–12
5007	4–40	5040	4–44	5066	4–23	5090	5–12
5008	4–40	5041	4–44	5067	4–23	5091	5–22
5009	5–6	5042	4–44	5068-1	4–42	5092	4–31
5010	4–14	5043	5–5	5068-2	4–24	5093	4–33
5011	4–13	5044	4–13	5068-3	4–24	5094	4–37
5012	4–13	5045	4–15	5068-4	4–24	5095	4–35
5013	3–5	5046	4–16	5069	4–24	5096	4–34
5014	3–5	5046-1	4–16	5070	4–25	5096-1	4–34
5015-1	3–5	5046-2	4–16	5071	4–25	5097	4–33
5015-2	3–5	5047	4–13	5072-1	4–42	5098	4–37
5016-1	3–6	5048	4–45	5072-2	4–21	5099	4–34
5016-2	3–5	5049-1	4–16	5073-1	4–26	5100	4–34
5016-3	3–5	5049-2	4–16	5073-2	4–27	5101	4–34
5016-4	3–6	5049-3	4–17	5073-3	4–27	5102	4–36
5017	1–22	5050	4–17	5074	4–27	5103	4–37
5018	4–4	5050-1	4–17	5075	4–27	5104	4–36
5019	4–5	5051-1	4–18	5076-1	4–28	5105	4–34
5020	4–4	5051-2	4–18	5076-2	4–28	5106	4–9
5021	4–7	5051-3	4–19	5076-3	4–28	5107	4–9
5021-1	4–7	5051-4	4–19	5076-4	4–28	5108	4–9
5021-2	4–7	5052	4–18	5076-5	4–28	5109	4–14
5022	4–3	5053	1–30	5077	4–29	5110-1	4–18
5023	4–5	5054	1–30	5078	4–30	5110-2	4–18
5024	4–8	5055	4–12	5080-1	4–30	5111	4–4
5025	4–8	5056-1	4–19	5080-2	4–30	5112	4–29
5026	4–8	5056-2	4–19	5080-3	4–30	5113-1	4–31
5027	4–10	5057	4–45	5080-4	4–31	5113-2	4–32
5028	4–10	5058	4–42	5081	4–45	5114	3–7
5029	4–42	5059	4–20	5082-1	5–6	5115	5–5
5030	4–11	5060	4–21	5082-2	5–6	5116-1	5–12
5031	4–11	5060-1	4–21	5082-3	5–6	5116-2	5–13

Cross-Reference A Question Number and Page Number

Question Number	Page Number	Question Number	Page Number	Question Number	Page Number	Question Number	Page Number
5117	5–7	5164	8–9	5210	1–18	5256	2–16
5118	5–7	5165	1–11	5210-1	1–18	5257	2–16
5119-1	5–7	5166	1–11	5211	1–23	5258	2–16
5119-2	5–7	5167	1–10	5212	1–15	5259	2–17
5119-3	5–8	5168	2–13	5213	1–12	5260	2–17
5120-1	5–8	5169	2–3	5214	1–12	5261	2–17
5120-2	5–8	5170	2–6	5215	1–12	5262	2–17
5121	5–14	5171	2–3	5216	1–27	5263	2–17
5122-1	9–17	5172	2–4	5217	1–12	5264	2–17
5122-2	9–17	5173	2–3	5218	1–10	5265	2–18
5122-3	9–18	5174	2–4	5219	1–10	5266-1	2–18
5124-2	4–41	5175	2–9	5220	1–9	5266-2	2–18
5124-3	4–41	5176	2–4	5220-1	1–9	5267	2–18
5125-2	4–41	5177	3–6	5221	1–20	5268	3–9
5126	4–4	5177-1	3–6	5221-1	1–20	5269	3–9
5127	4–12	5177-2	3–6	5222	1–22	5270	3–9
5128	4–9	5178	3–7	5223	1–8	5271	2–9
5129	4–24	5179	1–19	5224	1–27	5272	5–23
5131	4–44	5180	1–20	5225	1–21	5273	2–29
5132	4–44	5181	1–21	5226	1–16	5274	2–29
5133	5–23	5182	1–24	5227	1–16	5275	2–29
5134	5–23	5183	2–10	5228	1–15	5276	1–25
5135	5–23	5184	2–10	5229	1–8	5277	1–30
5138	5–16	5185-1	2–7	5230	1–16	5278	1–30
5139	5–16	5186	2–8	5231	1–13	5279	1–30
5139-1	5–16	5187	2–5	5232	1–13	5280	1–10
5140	5–16	5188	2–5	5233	3–5	5281	1–30
5141	4–14	5189	2–6	5234	8–19	5282	1–25
5142	4–14	5190	2–8	5235	2–10	5283	1–31
5143	4–14	5191	3–9	5236	2–10	5284	1–31
5144	4–15	5192	1–20	5237	2–11	5285	1–31
5145	5–19	5193	1–18	5238	1–26	5286	1–31
5146	2–33	5194	1–18	5239	1–5	5287	8–15
5151	1–21	5195	1–18	5240	2–13	5288	8–15
5152	1–21	5196	1–23	5241	2–14	5289	8–15
5152-1	1–21	5197	1–26	5242	2–14	5290	1–31
5153	1–19	5198	1–4	5243	2–14	5291	1–31
5154	1–19	5198-1	1–4	5244	2–14	5292	1–31
5155	1–22	5199	1–5	5245	2–14	5293	1–32
5156	1–22	5200	1–8	5246	2–14	5294	1–32
5157	1–22	5201	1–9	5247	2–15	5295	1–32
5158	1–9	5202	1–10	5248	2–15	5296	1–32
5159	1–22	5203	1–8	5249	2–15	5297	2–29
5160	1–24	5204	1–24	5250	2–15	5298	2–5
5161	1–8	5205	1–15	5251	2–15	5299	2–8
5161-1	1–8	5206	1–23	5252	2–15	5300	8–19
5162	1–9	5207	1–15	5253	2–16	5301	6–4
5163	1–19	5208	8–23	5254	2–16	5302	8–19
5163-1	1–19	5209	1–27	5255	2–16	5303	8–19

A–2   ASA   **Commercial Pilot Test Prep**

Cross-Reference A Question Number and Page Number

Question Number	Page Number	Question Number	Page Number	Question Number	Page Number	Question Number	Page Number
5304	6-6	5350	6-25	5396	6-31	5457	8-30
5305	8-19	5351	6-27	5397	6-31	5458	8-30
5306	9-11	5352	6-28	5398	7-3	5459	8-30
5307	9-11	5353	6-28	5399	7-4	5460	8-35
5308	9-11	5354	6-28	5402	7-4	5461	8-36
5309	9-11	5355	6-28	5403	7-4	5462	8-36
5310	6-4	5356	6-5	5404	7-4	5463	8-33
5310-1	6-4	5357	6-18	5405	7-4	5464	8-34
5311	6-4	5358	6-29	5406	7-7	5465	8-34
5312	6-4	5359	6-28	5407	7-7	5466	9-8
5313	6-7	5360	6-20	5408	3-7	5467	9-8
5314	6-8	5361	6-22	5409	7-8	5468	9-9
5315	6-5	5362	6-22	5410	7-8	5469	9-6
5316	6-8	5363	6-22	5411	7-8	5470	9-7
5317	6-8	5364	6-22	5412	7-9	5471	9-7
5318	6-8	5365	6-22	5413	7-9	5472	9-7
5319	6-8	5366	6-22	5414	7-9	5473	9-7
5320	6-10	5367	6-23	5417	7-11	5474	9-7
5321	6-8	5368	6-23	5418	7-12	5475	9-13
5322	6-22	5369	6-23	5422	7-11	5476	9-13
5323	6-10	5370	6-23	5423	7-11	5477	4-11
5324	6-19	5371	6-23	5424	7-10	5478	9-13
5325	6-20	5372	6-23	5425	7-12	5479	9-6
5326	6-20	5373	6-24	5426	7-12	5480	8-43
5327	6-13	5373-1	6-24	5427	7-13	5481	9-7
5328	6-16	5373-2	6-24	5428	7-13	5482	8-30
5329	6-13	5373-3	6-24	5429	7-13	5483	8-31
5330	6-13	5374	6-25	5433	7-16	5484	8-31
5331	6-16	5375	6-24	5434	7-16	5485	8-32
5332	6-14	5376	6-25	5435	7-16	5486	8-32
5333	6-10	5377	6-25	5436	7-16	5487	8-32
5334	6-11	5378	6-26	5439	7-16	5488	9-9
5335	6-14	5379	6-26	5440	7-13	5489	9-10
5336	6-11	5380	6-26	5441	7-13	5490	5-23
5337	6-14	5381	6-5	5442	7-14	5491-2	5-23
5338	6-14	5382	6-5	5443	7-14	5493	5-24
5339	6-18	5383	6-5	5444	7-7	5494	5-24
5340	6-13	5384	6-5	5445	7-7	5500	9-16
5341	6-14	5385	6-6	5446	7-7	5501	9-16
5342	6-14	5386	6-29	5447	6-6	5502	9-16
5343	6-15	5387	6-30	5448	6-29	5503	8-20
5343-1	6-15	5388	6-30	5449	6-27	5505	1-11
5344	6-15	5389	6-30	5450	6-18	5506	9-19
5345	6-15	5390	6-30	5451	8-27	5507	9-19
5346	6-15	5391	6-30	5452	8-27	5508	9-19
5347	6-17	5392	6-32	5453	8-27	5509	9-19
5347-1	6-17	5393	6-18	5454	8-28	5510	9-19
5348	6-15	5394	6-30	5455	8-28	5532	9-16
5349	6-16	5395	6-31	5456	8-29	5533	9-16

Cross-Reference A Question Number and Page Number

Question Number	Page Number	Question Number	Page Number	Question Number	Page Number	Question Number	Page Number
5534	4-35	5601	3-4	5649	8-11	5695	2-19
5535	4-36	5602	3-4	5650	8-9	5696	2-20
5535-1	4-36	5603	2-45	5651	8-9	5697	2-20
5536	8-12	5604	3-3	5652	8-10	5698	2-20
5539	4-10	5604-1	3-4	5653	2-12	5699	2-20
5545	4-6	5605	3-4	5654	2-11	5700	2-20
5547	4-35	5606	2-7	5655	1-29	5701	2-21
5551	9-16	5607	2-9	5656-1	5-16	5702	2-21
5552	9-17	5608	2-5	5656-2	5-17	5703	2-21
5553	9-17	5609	2-5	5656-3	5-17	5703-1	2-21
5554	4-45	5610	2-5	5657	5-19	5704	2-21
5555	9-17	5611	2-6	5658	5-19	5705	2-22
5560	7-12	5612	2-30	5659-1	5-19	5706	2-22
5562	2-45	5613	2-30	5659-2	5-19	5707	2-22
5563	2-45	5614	8-21	5660	5-19	5708	2-22
5564	5-7	5614-1	8-22	5661	8-20	5709	2-22
5565	5-10	5615	8-17	5662	8-21	5710	2-22
5566	5-10	5616	8-18	5663	8-21	5711	2-23
5567	5-10	5617	8-18	5664	8-21	5712	2-23
5568	5-10	5618	8-18	5665	8-21	5713	2-23
5569	5-9	5619	8-23	5666	4-30	5714	2-23
5569-1	5-9	5620	8-24	5667	2-11	5715	2-23
5570	5-10	5621	8-24	5668	2-11	5716	2-23
5570-1	5-11	5622	8-24	5669	3-4	5717	2-24
5571	8-44	5623	8-37	5670	3-4	5718	2-24
5572	5-8	5624	8-37	5671	2-18	5719	2-24
5572-1	5-8	5625	8-34	5672	2-18	5720	2-24
5573	8-44	5626	8-34	5673	2-19	5721	2-25
5574-1	5-13	5627	8-35	5674	2-19	5722	2-25
5574-2	5-13	5628	8-25	5675	2-19	5723	2-25
5574-3	5-13	5629	8-25	5676	2-19	5724	2-25
5575	5-9	5630	8-26	5677	8-12	5725	2-25
5575-1	5-10	5631	8-26	5678	8-12	5726	2-26
5576	5-8	5632	8-7	5679	8-13	5727	2-26
5577	5-12	5633	8-7	5680	8-14	5728	2-26
5578	8-44	5634	8-7	5681	8-14	5729	2-26
5579	8-44	5636	8-8	5682	8-12	5730	2-26
5580	8-44	5637	8-8	5683	8-38	5731	2-26
5581	5-11	5638	8-8	5684	8-38	5732	2-27
5581-1	5-11	5639	8-8	5685	8-38	5733	2-27
5582	8-45	5640	8-15	5686	2-19	5734	2-27
5583	5-9	5641	8-16	5687	8-38	5735	2-27
5584	5-9	5642	8-16	5688	8-39	5736	2-27
5585	5-11	5643	8-16	5689	8-39	5737	2-28
5586	8-45	5644	8-13	5690	8-39	5737-1	2-28
5587	5-9	5645	8-14	5691	8-39	5738	2-28
5588	5-15	5646	8-10	5692	8-39	5739	6-20
5589	8-45	5647	8-11	5693	8-40	5740	3-7
5590	4-45	5648	8-11	5694	8-40	5741	3-4

Cross-Reference A Question Number and Page Number

Question Number	Page Number
5742	6–31
5744	6–31
5745	6–31
5746	6–32
5747	6–32
5748	5–20
5749	5–24
5750	1–29
5751	1–29
5752	1–29
5753	1–29
5754	1–29
5755	2–28
5756	2–28
5757	5–26
5758	5–24
5759	5–26
5760	5–26
5761	5–26
5762	5–27
5763	5–27
5763-1	5–27
5763-2	5–27
5763-3	5–27
5763-4	5–27
5764	5–28
5765	5–28
5765-1	5–28
5765-2	5–28
5766	2–12
5767	2–12
5768	5–15
5769	2–30
5770	2–31
5771	2–31
5772	2–31
5773	8–40
5774	8–41
5775	8–41
5776	8–41
5777	8–41
5778	8–41
5779	8–41
5780	8–42
5781	8–42
5782	8–42
5783	8–42
5784	8–42
5785	8–42

Question Number	Page Number
5786	8–42
5787	8–43
5788	8–43
5789	8–43
5790	8–43
5791	2–31
5792	2–30
5793	2–31
5794	2–30
5795	2–31
5796	2–31
5797	2–32
5798	2–32
5799	2–32
5800	2–32
5801	2–32
5802	2–32
5803	2–33
5804	2–33
5805	2–33
5806	2–33
5807	2–33
5808	2–34
5809	2–34
5810	2–34
5811	2–34
5812	2–34
5813	8–23
5814	2–35
5815	2–35
5816	2–35
5817	2–35
5818	2–35
5819	2–35
5820	2–36
5821	2–36
5822	2–36
5823	2–36
5824	2–36
5825	2–37
5826	2–37
5827	2–37
5828	2–37
5829	2–37
5830	2–37
5831	2–38
5832	2–38
5833	2–38
5834	2–38

Question Number	Page Number
5835	2–38
5836	2–38
5837	2–38
5838	2–38
5839	2–39
5840	2–39
5841	2–39
5842	2–39
5843	2–39
5844	2–39
5845	2–39
5846	2–40
5847	2–40
5848	2–40
5849	2–40
5850	2–40
5851	2–40
5852	2–41
5853	2–41
5854	2–41
5855	2–41
5856	2–41
5857	2–41
5858	2–41
5859	2–42
5860	2–42
5861	2–42
5862	2–42
5863	2–42
5864	2–42
5865	2–42
5866	2–43
5867	2–43
5868	2–43
5869	2–43
5870	2–43
5871	2–43
5872	2–43
5873	2–43
5874	2–44
5875	2–44
5876	2–44
5877	2–44
5878	2–44
5879	2–44
5880	2–45
5881	2–45
5882	4–46
5883	4–46

Question Number	Page Number
5884	4–46
5885	4–46
5886	4–46
5887	4–46
5888	4–46
5889	4–47
5890	4–47
5891	4–47
5892	4–47
5893	4–47
5894	4–47
5895	4–47
5896	4–47
5897	4–48
5898	4–48
5899	4–48
5900	4–48
5901	4–48
5902	4–48
5903	4–48
5904	4–48
5905	4–49
5906	4–49
5907	4–49
5908	4–49
5909	4–49
5910	4–49
5911	4–50
5912	4–50
5913	4–50
5914	4–50
5915	4–50
5916	4–50
5917	4–50
5918	4–51
5919	4–51
5920	4–51
5921	4–51
5922	4–51
5923	4–51
5924	4–51
5925	4–51
5926	4–52
5927	4–52
5928	4–52
5929	4–52
5930	4–52
5931	4–52
5932	4–53

Cross-Reference A Question Number and Page Number

Question Number	Page Number	Question Number	Page Number	Question Number	Page Number	Question Number	Page Number
5933	4–53	5951	5–33	5970	5–18	5986	4–40
5934	4–53	5952	5–34	5971	6–20	5987	4–37
5935	4–53	5953	5–34	5972	5–16	5988	7–5
5936	4–53	5954	5–34	5973	2–30	5989	7–8
5937	4–53	5955	5–34	5974	1–15	5990	9–12
5938	4–54	5956	5–34	5975	5–20	5991	6–9
5939	4–54	5957	5–34	5976	5–17	5992	4–32
5940	4–54	5958	5–35	5977	1–21	5993	5–11
5941	5–31	5959	5–35	5978	1–20	5994	5–11
5941-1	5–32	5960	5–35	5978-1	1–20	5995	5–13
5942	5–32	5961	5–35	5979	1–13	5996	5–13
5943	5–32	5962	5–35	5980	5–20	5997	8–24
5944	5–32	5963	5–36	5981	5–20	5998	5–28
5945	5–32	5964	5–18	5982	5–20	5999	5–21
5946	5–33	5965	4–38	5983	5–20	5999-1	9–6
5947	5–33	5966	4–4	5983-1	5–21	5999-2	3–10
5948	5–33	5967	4–4	5983-2	5–21	5999-3	3–10
5949	5–33	5968	4–5	5984	5–21	5999-4	5–21
5950	5–33	5969	4–5	5985	4–40		

Cross-Reference B
Airman Knowledge Test Report Codes and Question Numbers

When you take the applicable FAA Knowledge Exam required for an airman certificate or rating, you will receive an Airman Knowledge Test Report (AKTR). This test report will list the Learning Statement Codes (LSC) or Airman Certification Codes (ACS) for questions you have answered incorrectly. Match the codes given on your AKTR to the ones listed in this cross-reference. Use Cross-Reference A in this book to find the page number for the question numbers listed below.

Your AKTR will list the codes accordingly:

- If an ACS exists for the certificate or rating you're seeking, the report will list an ACS code. Reference the ACS specific to the certificate or rating to determine the subject you missed on the test: **faa.gov/training_testing/testing/acs/**
- If an ACS does not yet exist for the certificate or rating you're seeking, the report will list an LSC. Reference the Learning Statement Reference Guide to determine the subject you missed on the test: **faa.gov/training_testing/testing/media/LearningStatementReferenceGuide.pdf**

Your instructor is required to provide instruction on each of the areas of deficiency listed on your AKTR and give you an endorsement for this instruction. The AKTR must be presented to the examiner conducting your practical test. During the oral portion of the practical test, the examiner is required to evaluate the noted areas of deficiency.

If you received a code on your AKTR that is not listed in this cross-reference, email ASA at **cfi@asa2fly.com**. We will provide the definition so you can review that subject area.

Learning Statement Codes and Question Numbers

Learning Statement Code	FAA Reference	Subject Description (or Topic 〉 Content 〉 Specific classification) Question Numbers
PLT001	AC 00-30 FAA-H-8083-15 FAA-H-8083-25	Calculate a course intercept *5478*
PLT002	FAA-H-8083-25	Aircraft Performance 〉 Charts 〉 Stall Speed *5179, 5180, 5221, 5221-1*
PLT003	FAA-H-8083-1	Weight and Balance 〉 Center of Gravity 〉 Computations *5634, 5636, 5637, 5638, 5639, 5640, 5641, 5642, 5644, 5645, 5646, 5647, 5648, 5649, 5651, 5652*
PLT004	FAA-H-8083-25	Aircraft Performance 〉 Charts 〉 Climb; Fuel Used; Rate of Climb vs. PA and Temp *5456, 5457, 5458, 5459, 5466, 5467, 5468, 5483, 5623, 5624, 5687, 5688, 5689, 5690, 5691, 5692*
PLT005	AC 00-6	Calculate aircraft performance—density altitude *5306, 5307, 5308, 5309*
PLT006	FAA-H-8083-25	Aircraft Performance 〉 Charts 〉 Glide Distance *5537, 5538*
PLT008	FAA-H-8083-25	Aircraft Performance 〉 Charts 〉 Landing Distance *5628, 5629, 5630*

Cross-Reference B Learning Statement Codes and Question Numbers

Learning Statement Code	FAA Reference	Subject Description (or Topic ⟩ Content ⟩ Specific classification) Question Numbers
PLT011	FAA-H-8083-25	Aircraft Performance ⟩ Charts ⟩ Ground Roll; Takeoff Distance *5619, 5620, 5621, 5622, 5631, 5685, 5693, 5694, 5793, 5997*
PLT012	FAA-H-8083-25	Aircraft Performance ⟩ Charts ⟩ Climb; Fuel Used Aircraft Performance ⟩ Computations ⟩ Flight Time; Fuel Navigation ⟩ Dead Reckoning ⟩ Calculations; Wind Navigation ⟩ Radio ⟩ Bearing Change Rule-of-Thumb Calculation *5208, 5451, 5452, 5453, 5454, 5455, 5462, 5470, 5472, 5473, 5474, 5475, 5476, 5480, 5481, 5482, 5484, 5485, 5486, 5487, 5488, 5489, 5571, 5579, 5580, 5586, 5808*
PLT013	FAA-H-8083-25	Aircraft Performance ⟩ Charts ⟩ Wind Components *5615, 5616, 5617, 5618*
PLT014	FAA-H-8083-25	Navigation ⟩ Radio ⟩ ADF/NDB; Bearing Change Rule-of-Thumb Calculation *5506, 5508, 5509, 5510*
PLT015	FAA-H-8083-25	Aerodynamics ⟩ Principles of Flight ⟩ L/D Ratio Aircraft Performance ⟩ Charts ⟩ Endurance; Maximum Range Aircraft Performance ⟩ Computations ⟩ Fuel *5213, 5214, 5215, 5460, 5461, 5463, 5464, 5465, 5469, 5471, 5625, 5626, 5627*
PLT017	FAA-H-8083-25	Aerodynamics ⟩ Principles of Flight ⟩ Angle of Attack *5165, 5166, 5505*
PLT018	FAA-H-8083-25	Aerodynamics ⟩ Load Factor ⟩ Flight Envelope; Variation Aircraft Performance ⟩ Charts ⟩ Stall Speed vs. Angle of Attack *5156, 5163, 5164, 5222, 5978, 5978-1*
PLT021	FAA-H-8083-1 FAA-H-8083-25	Weight and Balance ⟩ Aircraft Loading ⟩ Shifting Weight Weight and Balance ⟩ Center of Gravity ⟩ Computations; Definitions; Shifting Weight *5287, 5632, 5633, 5643, 5650, 5677, 5678, 5679, 5683, 5841*
PLT022	AC 60-22	Human Factors ⟩ ADM ⟩ Process; Risk Management *5941, 5942, 5943, 5947, 5949, 5961, 5962, 5963*
PLT027	FAA-H-8083-21 FAA-H-8083-25	Aerodynamics ⟩ Principles of Flight ⟩ Forces Acting on Aircraft *5240*
PLT030	FAA-H-8083-11	Aerodynamics ⟩ Principles of Flight ⟩ Forces Acting on Aircraft *5854, 5855*
PLT040	SAC	Airspace ⟩ Cloud Clearances/Visibility ⟩ Class G Airspace ⟩ Controlled ⟩ Class E Airspace ⟩ Special Use ⟩ Alert Areas *5554, 5564, 5565, 5566, 5567, 5568, 5572, 5572-1, 5574-1, 5574-2, 5575, 5587, 5588*
PLT041	FAA-H-8083-25	Aircraft Performance ⟩ Charts ⟩ L/D vs. Gliding Distance and Altitude Lost *5114, 5589*
PLT044	14 CFR 91 AIM	Airspace ⟩ Controlled ⟩ Class D Instrument Procedures ⟩ Communications ⟩ Terminology *5118, 5563*
PLT048	FAA-H-8083-21	Interpret Hovering Ceiling Chart *5684*

Cross-Reference B Learning Statement Codes and Question Numbers

Learning Statement Code	FAA Reference	Subject Description (or Topic 〉 Content 〉 Specific classification) Question Numbers
PLT054	FAA-H-8082-13	Interpret information on a Glider Performance Graph *5773, 5774, 5775, 5777, 5778, 5779, 5783, 5784*
PLT056	FAA-H-8083-15 FAA-H-8083-25	Navigation 〉 Radio 〉 Bearing/Radial Intercepts *5507*
PLT059	AIM FAA-H-8083-25	Weather 〉 Aeronautical Weather Reports 〉 METAR Weather 〉 Meteorology 〉 Clouds *5331, 5402, 5403, 5404, 5988*
PLT061	FAA-H-8083-25	Weather 〉 Aeronautical Weather Reports 〉 PIREP *5406, 5989*
PLT062	AC 00-6	Weather 〉 Charts/Maps 〉 Adiabatic Charts *5396, 5397, 5742, 5744*
PLT064	FAA-H-8083-25 SAC	Airspace 〉 Controlled 〉 Class D Navigation 〉 Pilotage 〉 Charts *5479, 5570, 5577, 5578, 5581, 5584, 5585*
PLT068	AC 00-45	Weather 〉 Charts/Maps 〉 High-Level Significant Weather Prog; Low-Level Significant Weather Prog *5434*
PLT070	AC 00-45	Interpret information on a Stability Chart *5439*
PLT071	AC 00-45	Interpret information on a Surface Analysis Chart *5428*
PLT074	FAA-H-8083-25	Aerodynamics 〉 Load Factor 〉 Flight Envelope *5232, 5979*
PLT076	AC 00-6 AC 00-45	Interpret information on a Winds and Temperatures Aloft Forecast (FD) *5383, 5424*
PLT088	FAA-H-8083-25	Aircraft Systems 〉 Flight Instruments 〉 Airspeed Indicator *5016-4, 5177*
PLT090	AIM FAA-H-8083-15 FAA-H-8083-25	Navigation 〉 Radio 〉 Bearing Change Rule-of-Thumb Calculation; Bearing/Radial Intercepts; VOR *5533*
PLT091	FAA-H-8083-15 FAA-H-8083-25	Navigation 〉 Radio 〉 ADF/NDB; Bearing/Radial Intercepts *5500, 5501, 5502*
PLT096	AIM	Human Factors 〉 Aeromedical 〉 Hypoxia *5761*
PLT101	SAC	Navigation 〉 Pilotage 〉 Charts *5569, 5582, 5583*
PLT103	AC 60-22	Human Factors 〉 ADM 〉 Attitude Management; Judgment *5944, 5945, 5946, 5948, 5950, 5951, 5952, 5955, 5956, 5957, 5959, 5960*
PLT104	AC 60-22 FAA-H-8083-25	Human Factors 〉 ADM, CRM 〉 Judgment; Process *5765-2, 5941-1, 5958*

Cross-Reference B Learning Statement Codes and Question Numbers

Learning Statement Code	FAA Reference	Subject Description (or Topic 〉 Content 〉 Specific classification) Question Numbers
PLT105	AC 00-6	Aircraft Systems 〉 Avionics 〉 Radar *5365, 5375*
PLT112	FAA-H-8083-21 FAA-S-8081-16	Aircraft Systems 〉 Flight Controls/Primary 〉 Helicopter Flight Operations 〉 Climb 〉 Helicopter Flight Operations 〉 Maneuvers 〉 Helicopter *5673, 5674, 5675, 5709, 5710, 5711*
PLT113	14 CFR 23 FAA-H-8083-25	Aircraft Performance 〉 Limitations 〉 Airspeeds; Utility Category *5017, 5604-1, 5716*
PLT115	FAA-H-8083-25	Aircraft Systems 〉 Powerplant 〉 Combustion *5185-1, 5186, 5190*
PLT118	FAA-H-8083-25	Aircraft Systems 〉 Flight Instruments 〉 Turn Indicators *5210-1, 5269*
PLT119	14 CFR 91	Regulations 〉 14 CFR Part 91 〉 Instrument and Equipment Requirements *5666*
PLT120	FAA-H-8083-25	Aircraft Performance 〉 Atmospheric Effects 〉 Turbulence Weather 〉 Hazardous 〉 Turbulence *5160, 5669, 5670*
PLT123	14 CFR 91 FAA-H-8083-25	Aerodynamics 〉 Airspeed 〉 High Aircraft Systems 〉 Pitot/Static 〉 Airspeed Indicator Regulations 〉 14 CFR Part 91 〉 Aircraft Speed *5601, 5177-2, 5602, 5735, 5736, 5776*
PLT124	FAA-H-8083-11 FAA-H-8083-13	Aerodynamics 〉 Atmospheric Effects 〉 Wind Aerodynamics 〉 Principles of Flight 〉 Forces Acting on Aircraft *5296*
PLT126	AC 91-13	Aircraft Systems 〉 Landing Gear 〉 Cold Weather Operation *5767, 5768*
PLT127	AIM	Aircraft Performance 〉 Density Altitude 〉 Effects *5258, 5259, 5260, 5310-1, 5686*
PLT129	FAA-H-8083-25	Aircraft Performance 〉 Charts 〉 Takeoff Distance *5614, 5719*
PLT130	FAA-H-8083-11	Aircraft Systems 〉 Fuel/Oil 〉 Hot Air Balloon/Propane *5826*
PLT131	FAA-H-8083-25	Aerodynamics 〉 Principles of Flight 〉 Ground Effect *5209, 5216, 5224*
PLT132	FAA-H-8083-25	Aerodynamics 〉 Airspeed 〉 High Aerodynamics 〉 Load Factor 〉 Flight Envelope *5177-1, 5780, 5782, 5787, 5789*
PLT133	Goodyear Airship Op. Manual	Recall aircraft performance—normal climb/descent rates *5877*
PLT134	FAA-H-8083-25	Recall aircraft performance—takeoff *5234*

Cross-Reference B Learning Statement Codes and Question Numbers

Learning Statement Code	FAA Reference	Subject Description (or Topic 〉 Content 〉 Specific classification) Question Numbers
PLT136	AC 91-13	Aircraft Systems 〉 Fuel/Oil 〉 Crankcase Breather Lines 5766
PLT140	AIM	Airport Operations 〉 LAHSO 〉 Responsibilities 5139, 5139-1, 5140, 5656-1, 5656-2, 5656-3, 5972, 5976, 5977
PLT141	AIM FAA-H-8083-3	Airport Operations 〉 Marking/Signs 〉 Runway Incursions; Taxiway Flight Operations 〉 Night 〉 Planning 5133, 5134, 5145, 5491-2, 5657, 5658, 5659-1, 5659-2, 5660, 5964, 5970, 5975, 5980, 5981, 5982, 5983, 5983-1, 5983-2, 5984, 5999-4
PLT149	FAA-H-8083-21	Flight Operations 〉 Normal Procedures 〉 Flight Control Positioning 5738
PLT152	FAA-H-8083-21	Flight Operations 〉 Emergency Procedures 〉 Helicopter 5869, 5871
PLT153	Goodyear Airship Op. Manual	Recall airship—flight operations 5866, 5870, 5879, 5865
PLT154	Goodyear Airship Op. Manual	Recall airship—ground weigh-off/static/trim condition 5875
PLT157	Goodyear Airship Op. Manual	Recall airship—pressure height/dampers/position 5873
PLT159	Goodyear Airship Op. Manual	Recall airship—pressure height/super heat/valving gas 5864, 5867
PLT161	14 CFR 91	Airport Operations 〉 Traffic Patterns 〉 Standard Procedure Airspace 〉 Controlled 〉 Class B Regulations 〉 14 CFR Part 91 〉 Aircraft Speed; ATC Transponder/Altitude Reporting Equipment; Instrument and Equipment Requirements; Visual Flight Rules 5009, 5060-1, 5072-1, 5072-2, 5077, 5078, 5082-2, 5082-4, 5083, 5112, 5119-3, 5573, 5576, 5590, 5870-1
PLT162	14 CFR 91	Airspace 〉 Controlled 〉 Class B; Class C 5082-1, 5082-3, 5120-1, 5120-2, 5569-1
PLT163	14 CFR 91	Regulations 〉 14 CFR Part 91 〉 Visual Flight Rules 5083-1, 5084, 5085, 5086, 5087, 5088, 5993
PLT166 PLT167	FAA-H-8083-25	Aircraft Systems 〉 Flight Instruments 〉 Altimeter 5408, 5740
PLT168	FAA-H-8083-3 FAA-H-8083-25	Aerodynamics 〉 Airspeed 〉 Angle of Attack Aerodynamics 〉 Principles of Flight 〉 Angle of Attack; Forces Acting on Aircraft; Ground Effect; Thrust 5167, 5198, 5199, 5200, 5204, 5210, 5220, 5220-1
PLT169	FAA-H-8083-21	Flight Operations 〉 Emergency Procedures 〉 Helicopter 5695, 5696
PLT170	FAA-H-8083-3	Flight Operations 〉 Landing 〉 Touchdown 5124-2, 5727, 5730, 5732, 5769, 5813, 5815, 5853

Cross-Reference B Learning Statement Codes and Question Numbers

Learning Statement Code	FAA Reference	Subject Description (or Topic 〉 Content 〉 Specific classification) Question Numbers
PLT173	AC 00-6	Weather 〉 Meteorology 〉 Stability 5332, 5333, 5335, 5336, 5341, 5342, 5344, 5345, 5346
PLT175	FAA-H-8083-21	Flight Operations 〉 Emergency Procedures 〉 Approach/Landing; Helicopter 5714, 5715, 5722, 5723
PLT177	FAA-H-8083-11	Recall balloon—flight operations 5857, 5858
PLT180	FAA-H-8083-11	Aerodynamics 〉 Principles of Flight 〉 Balloon 5829, 5830, 5831, 5838, 5851
PLT182	FAA-H-8083-11	Aircraft Systems 〉 Flight Controls/Primary 〉 Balloon 5825
PLT183	FAA-H-8083-11	Flight Operations 〉 Descent 〉 Gas Balloon 5836, 5837
PLT184	FAA-H-8083-11 Powerline Excerpts	Recall balloon flight operations—launch/landing 5852, 5862, 5863
PLT187	FAA-H-8083-25	Aircraft Systems 〉 Flight Instruments 〉 Gyroscopic; Turn Indicators 5268, 5270
PLT189	FAA-H-8083-25	Aircraft Systems 〉 Powerplant 〉 Carburetor Heat 5170, 5189
PLT190	FAA-H-8083-25	Aircraft Systems 〉 De-icing/Anti-icing 〉 Carburetor Heat 5676
PLT192	AC 00-6 FAA-H-8083-25	Weather 〉 Meteorology 〉 Clouds; Moisture; Stability 5327, 5328, 5329, 5330, 5337, 5338, 5339, 5340, 5349
PLT194	AC 90-48 AIM FAA-H-8083-3	Flight Operations 〉 Collision Avoidance 〉 Judging Threats; Vision in Flight 5272, 5749, 5758
PLT197	AC 00-6 FAA-H-8083-3	Weather 〉 Meteorology 〉 Circulation; Wind 5311, 5312, 5315
PLT200	FAA-H-8083-25	Recall dead reckoning—calculations/charts 5999-1
PLT201	FAA-H-8083-13	Recall departure procedures—ODP/SID 5728
PLT203	AC 00-6	Weather 〉 Meteorology 〉 High Altitude 5381
PLT204	FAA-H-8083-9	Fundamentals of Instruction 〉 Effective Communication 〉 Barriers to Effective Communication; Basic Elements; Presentation 5903, 5904, 5905
PLT205	AIM	Recall effects of alcohol on the body 5763-1, 5763-2
PLT206	AC 00-6	Recall effects of temperature—density altitude/icing 5990

Cross-Reference B Learning Statement Codes and Question Numbers

Learning Statement Code	FAA Reference	Subject Description (or Topic 〉 Content 〉 Specific classification) Question Numbers
PLT208	FAA-H-8083-3 FAA-H-8083-25	Flight Operations 〉 Emergency Procedures 〉 Approach/Landing; Flight Diversion; Lost Procedures; Night *5503, 5663, 5713, 5821, 5839, 5845, 5861, 5868, 5880*
PLT211	FAA-H-8083-9	Fundamentals of Instruction 〉 Critique/Evaluation 〉 Testing *5921, 5922, 5923*
PLT213	FAA-H-8083-25	Aerodynamics 〉 Stability/Control 〉 Longitudinal; Negative Dynamic *5226, 5227, 5228*
PLT214	FAA-H-8083-25	Recall flight characteristics—structural/wing design *5974*
PLT215	FAA-H-8083-15 FAA-H-8083-25	Aircraft Systems 〉 Flight Instruments 〉 Compass Navigation 〉 Radio 〉 Bearing/Radial Intercepts *5178, 5612, 5613, 5791*
PLT216	FAA-H-8083-13	Aircraft Systems 〉 Flight Instruments 〉 Variometer *5273, 5274, 5275, 5297*
PLT217	FAA-H-8083-21	Flight Operations 〉 Maneuvers 〉 Helicopter *5267, 5724*
PLT219	FAA-H-8083-3	Flight Operations 〉 Maneuvers 〉 Basic *5191, 5248, 5828*
PLT220	14 CFR 61	Regulations 〉 14 CFR Part 61 〉 Night *5027, 5080-1, 5080-2, 5080-3, 5080-4, 5081, 5135, 5493, 5494*
PLT221	FAA-H-8083-11	Flight Operations 〉 Landing 〉 Balloon Flight Operations 〉 Launch Procedures 〉 Balloon Flight Operations 〉 Takeoff 〉 Balloon *5614-1, 5661, 5662, 5664, 5665, 5834, 5850, 5856, 5874, 5878*
PLT222	FAA-H-8083-3	Aircraft Systems 〉 Propeller 〉 Adjustable-Pitch *5801*
PLT224	AIM	Instrument Procedures 〉 Flight Planning 〉 Flight Plan *5059, 5092, 5555*
PLT226	AC 00-6 FAA-H-8083-25	Weather 〉 Meteorology 〉 Fog *5350, 5376, 5378, 5379, 5380*
PLT227	FAA-H-8083-9	Fundamentals of Instruction 〉 Instructor Responsibilities 〉 Student Piloting Ability Evaluation *5934*
PLT229	FAA-H-8083-9	Fundamentals of Instruction 〉 Professionalism 〉 Acceptance of the Student; Sincerity *5926, 5927*
PLT231	FAA-H-8083-9	Fundamentals of Instruction 〉 Human Behavior 〉 Control of Human Behavior; Flight Instructor as a Practical Psychologist Fundamentals of Instruction 〉 Learning Process 〉 Laws of Learning *5935, 5936, 5937*
PLT232	FAA-H-8083-9	Fundamentals of Instruction 〉 Instructor Responsibilites 〉 Providing Adequete Instruction *5929, 5930, 5932*

Cross-Reference B Learning Statement Codes and Question Numbers

Learning Statement Code	FAA Reference	Subject Description (or Topic 〉 Content 〉 Specific classification) Question Numbers
PLT233	FAA-H-8083-9	Fundamentals of Instruction 〉 Human Behavior 〉 Defense Mechanisms *5900, 5901*
PLT235	FAA-H-8083-25	Aerodynamics 〉 Principles of Flight 〉 Forces Acting on Aircraft *5241, 5244, 5246, 5249, 5250, 5292*
PLT236	FAA-H-8083-21	Aerodynamics 〉 Principles of Flight 〉 Forces Acting on Aircraft *5239, 5285*
PLT237	FAA-H-8083-25	Aerodynamics 〉 Principles of Flight 〉 Angle of Attack; Forces Acting on Aircraft *5161, 5161-1, 5162, 5229, 5281, 5283, 5284, 5300*
PLT238	FAA-H-8083-13	Aerodynamics 〉 Principles of Flight 〉 Forces Acting on Aircraft *5293, 5294*
PLT240	FAA-H-8083-25	Weight and Balance 〉 Aircraft Loading 〉 Limitations Weight and Balance 〉 Center of Gravity 〉 Stability *5205, 5206, 5207, 5212, 5680, 5681*
PLT241	Soaring Flight Manual	Recall forces acting on aircraft—drag/gravity/thrust/lift *5280*
PLT242	FAA-H-8083-25	Aerodynamics 〉 Principles of Flight 〉 Forces Acting on Aircraft *5158, 5196, 5197, 5198-1, 5201, 5202, 5218, 5219, 5223, 5245, 5291*
PLT243	FAA-H-8083-25	Recall forces acting on aircraft—propeller/torque *5237, 5238*
PLT244	FAA-H-8083-11 FAA-H-8083-13	Aerodynamics 〉 Stability/Control 〉 Glide Control Flutter Flight Operations 〉 Maneuvers 〉 Balloon *5835, 5881*
PLT245	FAA-H-8083-13	Recall forces acting on aircraft—stalls/spins *5772*
PLT246	FAA-H-8083-25	Recall forces acting on aircraft/steady state climb/flight *5203*
PLT249	FAA-H-8083-25	Aircraft Systems 〉 Powerplant 〉 Mixture Control *5176, 5187, 5298, 5608, 5609, 5610*
PLT251	FAA-H-8083-11 FAA-H-8083-25	Aircraft Systems 〉 Fuel/Oil 〉 Hot Air Balloon/Propane Aircraft Systems 〉 Powerplant 〉 Combustion *5299, 5833, 5840, 5844, 5846*
PLT253	FAA-H-8083-25	Aircraft Systems 〉 Powerplant 〉 Mixture Control *5168, 5842, 5843, 5847, 5848, 5849*
PLT254	FAA-H-8083-11	Aircraft Systems 〉 Fuel/Oil 〉 Hot Air Balloon/Propane *5832*
PLT256	FAA-H-8083-13	Aircraft Performance 〉 Charts 〉 Ballast/Weight vs. Airspeeds/Performance *5288, 5289, 5785*
PLT257	FAA-H-8083-13	Aerodynamics 〉 Airspeed 〉 Angle of Attack Aerodynamics 〉 Principles of Flight 〉 Forces Acting on Aircraft Flight Operations 〉 Soaring Techniques 〉 Speed-to-Fly *5277, 5278, 5279, 5781, 5786, 5788, 5790, 5797, 5814*

Learning Statement Code	FAA Reference	Subject Description (or Topic 〉 Content 〉 Specific classification) Question Numbers
PLT259	FAA-H-8083-21	Flight Operations 〉 Emergency Procedures 〉 Helicopter *5266-1, 5266-2*
PLT261	AC 00-6	Weather 〉 Meteorology 〉 Thunderstorms *5361, 5362*
PLT262	FAA-H-8083-21	Recall helicopter hazards—dynamic rollover / Low G / LT *5703-1*
PLT263	AC 00-6 AIM FAA-H-8083-3	Flight Operations 〉 Landing 〉 Turbulence Weather 〉 Hazardous 〉 Turbulence Weather 〉 Meteorology 〉 Fog; Fronts; High Altitude *5374, 5377, 5382*
PLT264	FAA-H-8083-21 FAA-S-8081-16	Flight Operations 〉 Emergency Procedures 〉 Helicopter *5698, 5699, 5700, 5702, 5703*
PLT265	FAA-H-8083-21	Flight Operations 〉 Emergency Procedures 〉 Ground Emergencies *5697, 5733*
PLT268	FAA-H-8083-21	Aerodynamics 〉 Performance 〉 Helicopter Flight Operations 〉 Maneuvers 〉 Helicopter *5242, 5247, 5707, 5712, 5720, 5721*
PLT269	FAA-H-8083-9	Recall human behavior—defense mechanism *5896, 5897, 5898, 5899*
PLT270	FAA-H-8083-9	Fundamentals of Instruction 〉 Human Behavior 〉 Human Needs *5895*
PLT272	AC 60-22	Human Factors 〉 ADM 〉 Stress Management *5953, 5954*
PLT276	AIM FAA-H-8083-15 FAA-H-8083-25	Navigation 〉 Radio 〉 VOR *5532*
PLT280	FAA-H-8083-25	Recall inflight illusions—causes/sources *5765-1*
PLT281	FAA-H-8083-25	Recall information in a *Chart Supplements U.S.* *5999*
PLT283	AC 00-45	Weather 〉 Charts/Maps 〉 Constant Pressure Analysis Charts *5440, 5441, 5442*
PLT286	AC 00-45	Weather 〉 Charts/Maps 〉 Low-Level Significant Weather Prog *5433, 5435, 5436*
PLT287	AC 00-6 AC 00-45 FAA-H-8083-25	Weather 〉 Charts/Maps 〉 Surface Analysis Charts Weather 〉 Meteorology 〉 Wind *5314, 5425, 5426, 5427, 5429*
PLT288	AIM FAA-H-8083-25	Weather 〉 Aeronautical Weather Forecasts 〉 Aerodrome Forecast (TAF) *5409, 5410, 5411, 5412, 5413*
PLT290	AIM	Weather 〉 Aeronautical Weather Forecasts 〉 Inflight Aviation Weather Advisories; Weather Advisory Broadcasts *5414, 5422, 5423*

Cross-Reference B Learning Statement Codes and Question Numbers

Learning Statement Code	FAA Reference	Subject Description (or Topic 〉 Content 〉 Specific classification) Question Numbers
PLT294	AIM	Weather 〉 Aeronautical Weather Forecasts 〉 Inflight Aviation Weather Advisories *5417, 5418, 5560*
PLT295	FAA-H-8083-9	Fundamentals of Instruction 〉 Critique/Evaluation 〉 Instructor as a Critic Fundamentals of Instruction 〉 Techniques-Flight Instruction 〉 Obstacles to Learning during Flight Instruction *5894, 5938, 5939*
PLT298	14 CFR 91	Intrument Procedures 〉 En Route 〉 VFR on Top *5562, 5795, 5803*
PLT301	AC 00-6	Weather 〉 Meteorology 〉 Temperature *5304*
PLT302	AC 00-6 AC 00-30	Weather 〉 Meteorology 〉 High Altitude; Wind *5384, 5385, 5447, 5448*
PLT303	FAA-H-8083-13	Aerodynamics 〉 Performance 〉 Glider *5295*
PLT304	FAA-H-8083-13	Flight Operations 〉 Launch Procedures 〉 Glider *5146, 5802, 5805, 5807, 5809, 5810, 5811, 5812*
PLT305	FAA-H-8083-25	Aircraft Systems 〉 Flight Controls/Secondary 〉 Airplane *5181*
PLT306	FAA-H-8083-9	Fundamentals of Instruction 〉 Learning Process 〉 Characteristics of Learning; Levels of Learning *5883, 5886, 5892, 5893*
PLT308	FAA-H-8083-9	Fundamentals of Instruction 〉 Learning Process 〉 Definition of Learning; Perceptions *5882, 5884, 5885, 5887, 5888, 5889*
PLT309	FAA-H-8083-25	Aerodynamics 〉 Load Factor 〉 Flight Envelope; Variation Aerodynamics 〉 Principles of Flight 〉 Forces Acting on Aircraft *5153, 5154, 5157, 5159, 5225, 5286*
PLT310	FAA-H-8083-25	Aerodynamics 〉 Load Factor 〉 Definition; Flight Envelope *5151, 5152, 5152-1, 5163-1*
PLT312	AC 00-6 FAA-H-8083-25	Aerodynamics 〉 Load Factor 〉 Stall Speed; Variation Weather 〉 Hazardous 〉 Turbulence *5155, 5231, 5233*
PLT323	14 CFR 91	Regulations 〉 14 CFR Part 91 〉 General *5121*
PLT326	FAA-H-8083-25	Aircraft Systems 〉 Environmental 〉 Oxygen *5792*
PLT328	FAA-H-8083-21	Weight and Balance 〉 Aircraft Loading 〉 Definitions *5536, 5682*
PLT330	AIM	Human Factors 〉 Aeromedical 〉 Hypoxia *5764*
PLT332	FAA-H-8083-25	Human Factors 〉 Aeromedical 〉 Hyperventilation *5757, 5759, 5760, 5762*

Cross-Reference B Learning Statement Codes and Question Numbers

Learning Statement Code	FAA Reference	Subject Description (or *Topic* 〉 *Content* 〉 *Specific* classification) / Question Numbers
PLT333	FAA-H-8083-3	Flight Operations 〉 Night 〉 Orientation & Navigation *5490*
PLT334	FAA-H-8083-25	Recall physiological factors—spatial disorientation *5765, 5998*
PLT336	FAA-H-8083-21	Flight Operations 〉 Approach 〉 Helicopter Flight Operations 〉 Landing 〉 Helicopter *5717, 5725, 5726*
PLT337	FAA-H-8083-25	Recall pitot-static systems *5999-3*
PLT341	FAA-H-8083-21	Flight Operations 〉 Approach 〉 Helicopter *5701*
PLT343	AC 20-103 AC 91-13 FAA-H-8083-25	Aircraft Systems 〉 Powerplant 〉 Carburetor Heat; Combustion; Ignition System; Mixture Control; Preheating; Throttle Operation *5171, 5172, 5173, 5174, 5175, 5188, 5254, 5271, 5606, 5607, 5611, 5653*
PLT344	AC 00-6	Weather 〉 Meteorology 〉 Fronts; Precipitation *5322, 5324*
PLT346	FAA-H-8083-11	Aircraft Systems 〉 Flight Controls/Primary 〉 Balloon *5827*
PLT348	FAA-H-8083-3 FAA-8083-25	Aerodynamics 〉 Principles of Flight 〉 Turn Rate/Radius *5192, 5193, 5194, 5195*
PLT349	FAA-H-8083-21	Flight Operations 〉 Landing 〉 Helicopter *5729*
PLT350	FAA-H-8083-3 FAA-H-8083-25	Aircraft Systems 〉 Propeller 〉 Adjustable-Pitch; Fixed-Pitch *5183, 5184, 5654, 5667, 5668*
PLT351	FAA-H-8083-25	Aerodynamics 〉 Principles of Flight 〉 L/D Ratio Aircraft Systems 〉 Propeller 〉 Principles *5217, 5235, 5236*
PLT354	FAA-H-8083-25	Recall radio—GPS, RNAV, RAIM *5999-2, 5122-3*
PLT366	49 CFR 830	Regulations 〉 NTSB Part 830 〉 Accident Report; Incident Report; Notification *5001, 5004-1, 5004-2, 5004-3, 5005, 5007, 5008*
PLT370	AIM	Recall regulations—ATC authorization, clearances *5994*
PLT371	14 CFR 61	Regulations 〉 14 CFR Part 61 〉 Aircraft Class Ratings *5019*
PLT372	14 CFR 91	Regulations 〉 14 CFR Part 91 〉 Maintenance *5099, 5100*
PLT373	14 CFR 91 FAA-H-8083-21	Regulations 〉 14 CFR Part 91 〉 Special Flight Operations Aircraft Performance 〉 Limitations 〉 Gyroplane *5053, 5054, 5068-1, 5068-2, 5068-3, 5068-4, 5069, 5129, 5734*

Cross-Reference B Learning Statement Codes and Question Numbers

Learning Statement Code	FAA Reference	Subject Description (or Topic 〉 Content 〉 Specific classification) Question Numbers
PLT374	14 CFR 1 14 CFR 91	Regulations 〉 14 CFR Part 1 〉 Definitions Regulations 〉 14 CFR Part 91 〉 Maintenance *5093, 5094*
PLT376	AIM	Recall regulations—airspace, other special use, TFRs *5575-1, 5995, 5996*
PLT377	14 CFR 91 49 CFR 830	Regulations 〉 NTSB Part 830 〉 Accident Report Regulations 〉 14 CFR Part 91 〉 Aircraft Certificate Requirements; Maintenance *5006, 5096, 5096-1, 5547, 5987*
PLT378	14 CFR 91	Regulations 〉 14 CFR Part 91 〉 Maintenance *5103*
PLT384	14 CFR 61	Recall regulations—briefing of passengers *5048*
PLT386	14 CFR 61	Regulations 〉 14 CFR Part 61 〉 Pilot Certificate *5020*
PLT387	14 CFR 61	Regulations 〉 14 CFR Part 61 〉 Current Address *5032*
PLT389	14 CFR 91	Regulations 〉 14 CFR Part 91 〉 Special Flight Operations *5055, 5967, 5968, 5969*
PLT391	14 CFR 61	Instrument Procedures 〉 Communications 〉 Failure *5603*
PLT392	14 CFR 91	Regulations 〉 14 CFR Part 91 〉 General *5056-1, 5056-2, 5071*
PLT393	14 CFR 91	Instrument Procedures 〉 Communications 〉 Reports *5043, 5125-2, 5574-3*
PLT395	14 CFR 1	Regulations 〉 14 CFR Part 1 〉 Definitions *5010, 5011, 5012, 5015-1, 5015-2, 5016-1, 5016-3, 5965*
PLT400	14 CFR 91	Regulations 〉 14 CFR Part 91 〉 Preflight Action *5046, 5050-1*
PLT401	14 CFR 91	Regulations 〉 14 CFR Part 91 〉 General *5047, 5796, 5804*
PLT405	14 CFR 91	Regulations 〉 14 CFR Part 91 〉 Instrument and Equipment Requirements *5060, 5065, 5066*
PLT413	14 CFR 91	Regulations 〉 14 CFR Part 91 〉 Visual Flight Rules *5058*
PLT414	14 CFR 91	Regulations 〉 14 CFR Part 91 〉 Right-of-Way *5074, 5075, 5076-1, 5076-2, 5076-3, 5076-4, 5076-5*
PLT415	14 CFR 91	Regulations 〉 14 CFR Part 91 〉 Instrument and Equipment Requirements *5057*
PLT416	49 CFR 830	Regulations 〉 NTSB Part 830 〉 Immediate Notification; Notification *5002, 5003-1, 5003-2*

Learning Statement Code	FAA Reference	Subject Description (or Topic 〉 Content 〉 Specific classification) Question Numbers
PLT417	14 CFR 91	Regulations 〉 14 CFR Part 91 〉 Instrument and Equipment Requirements 5067
PLT419	14 CFR 61	Regulations 〉 14 CFR Part 61 〉 Flight Instructor 5040, 5041, 5902
PLT420	14 CFR 91	Instrument Procedures 〉 Approach Procedures 〉 Procedure Turns 5124-3, 5731
PLT425	14 CFR 91	Regulations 〉 14 CFR Part 91 〉 Maintenance 5095, 5102, 5104, 5535, 5535-1
PLT426	14 CFR 91	Regulations 〉 14 CFR Part 91 〉 Maintenance 5097
PLT427	14 CFR 61, 68	Recall regulations medical certification requirements 5021-1
PLT430	14 CFR 91	Regulations 〉 14 CFR Part 91 〉 Flight Rules 5113-1, 5113-2, 5992
PLT431	14 CFR 91	Regulations 〉 14 CFR Part 91 〉 Flight Rules; General 5073-1, 5073-2, 5073-3
PLT434	14 CFR 91	Airspace 〉 Controlled 〉 Class E 5117, 5119-1, 5119-2
PLT435	14 CFR 91	Airport Operations 〉 Traffic Patterns 〉 Standard Procedure 5116-1, 5116-2
PLT438	14 CFR 91	Regulations 〉 14 CFR Part 91 〉 Instrument and Equipment Requirements 5063, 5064
PLT442	14 CFR 61	Regulations 〉 14 CFR Part 61 〉 Night 5028, 5029, 5030, 5031, 5033, 5034, 5477
PLT443	14 CFR 61	Regulations 〉 14 CFR Part 61 〉 Pilot Certificate 5022, 5023, 5039
PLT444	14 CFR 61 14 CFR 91 14 CFR 119	Regulations 〉 14 CFR Part 61 〉 Flight Review; Pilot-in-Command; Tailwheel Airplane Regulations 〉 14 CFR Part 91 〉 General; Preflight Action Regulations 〉 14 CFR Part 119 〉 Less Than 25 NM Radius 5018, 5044, 5045, 5046-1, 5046-2, 5049-1, 5049-2, 5050, 5109, 5111, 5115, 5138, 5966, 5967
PLT445	14 CFR 91	Regulations 〉 14 CFR Part 91 〉 Preflight Action 5049-3, 5794, 5973
PLT446	14 CFR 91	Regulations 〉 14 CFR Part 91 〉 Emergency Locator Transmitters 5070, 5098
PLT447	14 CFR 61	Regulations 〉 14 CFR Part 61 〉 Medical Certificates 5021, 5021-2, 5037, 5038
PLT448	14 CFR 61	Regulations 〉 14 CFR Part 61 〉 Pilot Certificate; Pilot-in-Command 5024, 5025, 5026, 5106, 5107, 5108, 5126, 5127, 5128, 5131, 5132, 5545

Cross-Reference B Learning Statement Codes and Question Numbers

Learning Statement Code	FAA Reference	Subject Description (or Topic ⟩ Content ⟩ Specific classification) Question Numbers
PLT451	14 CFR 61	Recall regulations—ratings issued, experience requirements, limitations *5539*
PLT454	14 CFR 91	Regulations ⟩ 14 CFR Part 91 ⟩ Maintenance *5101, 5105, 5534*
PLT457	14 CFR 61	Regulations ⟩ 14 CFR Part 61 ⟩ Student Pilot *5035-1, 5035-2, 5036, 5042*
PLT461	AIM	Regulations ⟩ 14 CFR Part 91 ⟩ Instrument and Equipment Requirements *5748*
PLT463	14 CFR 61 14 CFR 91	Human Factors ⟩ Aeromedical ⟩ Alcohol Regulations ⟩ 14 CFR Part 61 ⟩ Drugs and/or Alcohol *5141, 5142, 5143, 5144, 5763-3, 5763-4*
PLT464	14 CFR 91	Regulations ⟩ 14 CFR Part 91 ⟩ Flight Crewmembers at Station *5051-1, 5051-2, 5051-3, 5051-4, 5110-2*
PLT465	14 CFR 91	Regulations ⟩ 14 CFR Part 91 ⟩ Flight Rules *5052*
PLT466	14 CFR 1	Regulations ⟩ 14 CFR Party 1 ⟩ Definitions *5013, 5014, 5016-2, 5604, 5605*
PLT467	14 CFR 91	Regulations ⟩ 14 CFR Part 91 ⟩ Visual Flight Rules *5089, 5090, 5091*
PLT470	FAA-H-8083-21 FAA-H-8083-21	Aerodynamics ⟩ Principles of Flight ⟩ Forces Acting on Aircraft; Gyroplane Rotor; Helicopter Rotor Aircraft Systems ⟩ Flight Controls/Primary ⟩ Antitorque Pedals Aircraft Systems ⟩ Rotor ⟩ Full Articulated; Semirigid Flight Operations ⟩ Emergency Procedures ⟩ Helicopter *5243, 5251, 5252, 5253, 5257, 5671, 5672, 5704, 5705, 5706, 5737, 5737-1*
PLT471	FAA-8083-21	Aircraft Systems ⟩ Transmission ⟩ Clutch; Freewheeling Unit *5255, 5256*
PLT472	FAA-H-8083-21	Aircraft Systems ⟩ Flight Controls/Primary ⟩ Vibrations Aircraft Systems ⟩ Rotor ⟩ Tail Rotor; Vibrations Aircraft Systems ⟩ Transmission ⟩ Emergencies *5261, 5262, 5263, 5264, 5265*
PLT473	FAA-H-8083-25	Aircraft Systems ⟩ Flight Controls/Secondary ⟩ Airplane *5182, 5276, 5859, 5860, 5872, 5876*
PLT474	AC 00-6 FAA-H-8083-13	Flight Operations ⟩ Collision Avoidance ⟩ Soaring Gliders Flight Operations ⟩ Meteorology ⟩ Waves for Soaring Flight Operations ⟩ Soaring Techniques ⟩ Ballast; Ridge Soaring *5816, 5818, 5819, 5820, 5822, 5823, 5824*
PLT475	AC 00-6	Weather ⟩ Meteorology ⟩ Thunderstorms *5363, 5366, 5367, 5405*
PLT477	FAA-H-8083-25	Aerodynamics ⟩ Principles of Flight ⟩ Angle of Attack; Stall Speed *5211, 5817*
PLT478	FAA-H-8083-25	Aircraft Systems ⟩ Powerplant ⟩ Ignition System *5169*

Cross-Reference B Learning Statement Codes and Question Numbers

Learning Statement Code	FAA Reference	Subject Description (or Topic ⟩ Content ⟩ Specific classification) / Question Numbers
PLT480	FAA-H-8083-25	Aerodynamics ⟩ Stability/Control ⟩ Nuetral Static; Positive Static *5230*
PLT481	FAA-H-8083-9	Fundamentals of Instruction ⟩ Critique/Evaluation ⟩ Instructor as a Critic Fundamentals of Instruction ⟩ Teaching Process ⟩ Basic Steps *5906, 5917*
PLT482	FAA-H-8083-9	Fundamentals of Instruction ⟩ Critique/Evaluation ⟩ Instructor as a Critic; Quizzing *5908, 5916, 5918, 5919, 5920*
PLT484	Sectional Chart Legend	Recall symbols—chart/navigation *5581-1*
PLT486	FAA-H-8083-3	Flight Operations ⟩ Takeoff ⟩ Crosswind *5708, 5718*
PLT487	FAA-H-8083-9	Fundamentals of Instruction ⟩ Teaching Methods ⟩ Demonstration-Performance Method *5915*
PLT488	FAA-H-8083-9	Fundamentals of Instruction ⟩ Teaching Methods ⟩ Guided Discussion Method; Lecture Method *5913, 5914*
PLT489	FAA-H-8083-9	Fundamentals of Instruction ⟩ Teaching Methods ⟩ Organizing Material *5909, 5910*
PLT490	FAA-H-8083-9	Fundamentals of Instruction ⟩ Instructor Responsibilities ⟩ Providing Adequete Instruction; Student Motivation Fundamentals of Instruction ⟩ Learning Process ⟩ Laws of Learning; Motivation *5890, 5891, 5928, 5931, 5933*
PLT491	FAA-H-8083-9	Fundamentals of Instruction ⟩ Teaching Methods ⟩ Lecture Method; Organizing Material *5907, 5911, 5912, 5940*
PLT492	AC 00-6	Weather ⟩ Meteorology ⟩ Stability; Temperature; Temperature and Pressure *5301, 5302, 5303, 5305, 5320, 5334*
PLT493	AC 00-6	Weather ⟩ Meteorology ⟩ Icing *5739*
PLT494	AC 00-6 FAA-H-8083-13	Flight Operations ⟩ Soaring Techniques ⟩ Thermal Soaring Weather ⟩ Meteorology ⟩ Thermals *5386, 5387, 5389, 5390, 5394, 5395, 5745, 5747*
PLT495	AC 00-6	Weather ⟩ Meteorology ⟩ Thunderstorms *5364, 5368, 5369, 5370, 5371, 5372, 5373, 5373-1, 5373-2, 5373-3*
PLT496	FAA-H-8083-13	Flight Operations ⟩ Launch Procedures ⟩ Glider *5770, 5771, 5798, 5799, 5800, 5806*
PLT497	14 CFR 91	Regulations ⟩ 14 CFR Part 91 ⟩ ATC Transponder/Altitude Reporting Equipment *5061, 5061-1, 5061-2, 5061-3, 5061-4*
PLT501	AIM AC 00-6	Weather ⟩ Hazardous ⟩ Turbulence; Windshear *5357, 5444, 5445, 5446, 5450, 5741*

Cross-Reference B Learning Statement Codes and Question Numbers

Learning Statement Code	FAA Reference	Subject Description (or *Topic* ⟩ *Content* ⟩ *Specific* classification) Question Numbers
PLT503	AIM	Human Factors ⟩ Aeromedical ⟩ Alcohol *5763*
PLT505	FAA-H-8083-9	Fundamentals of Instruction ⟩ Instructional Aids ⟩ Use *5924, 5925*
PLT507	AIM FAA-H-8083-25	Navigation ⟩ Radio ⟩ VOR *5551, 5552, 5553*
PLT508	14 CFR 91	Regulations ⟩ 14 CFR Part 91 ⟩ Preflight Action *5062, 5122-1, 5122-2*
PLT509	AIM FAA-H-8083-25	Flight Operations ⟩ Wake Turbulence ⟩ Helicopter Vortices; Vortex Avoidance; Vortex Hazards *5655, 5750, 5751, 5752, 5753, 5754, 5755, 5756*
PLT510	AC 00-6	Weather ⟩ Meteorology ⟩ Wind *5388, 5392, 5393*
PLT511	AC 00-6 FAA-H-8083-25	Weather ⟩ Meteorology ⟩ Air Masses; Circulation; Fronts; Icing; Stability; Wind *5313, 5317, 5318, 5321, 5325, 5326, 5343, 5343-1, 5347, 5347-1, 5348, 5360, 5391, 5746, 5971*
PLT512	AC 00-6	Weather ⟩ Meteorology ⟩ Moisture *5323*
PLT514	AC 00-45	Recall weather reporting systems—briefings/forecasts/reports *5398, 5407*
PLT515	AC 00-45 AIM FAA-H-8083-25	Weather ⟩ Aeronautical Weather Forecasts ⟩ Inflight Aviation Weather Advisories; Preflight Planning Weather ⟩ Aeronautical Weather Reports ⟩ TIBS *5399*
PLT516	AC 00-6	Weather ⟩ Meteorology ⟩ Wind *5310, 5356*
PLT517	AC 00-6	Weather ⟩ Meteorology ⟩ Circulation *5316, 5319, 5991*
PLT518	AC 00-6 AC 00-30 AIM FAA-H-8083-25	Weather ⟩ Hazardous ⟩ Windshear Weather ⟩ Meteorology ⟩ High Altitude *5351, 5352, 5353, 5354, 5355, 5358, 5359, 5443, 5449*
PLT519	FAA-H-8083-13	Recall wing spoilers—purpose/operation *5282, 5290*
PLT526	AIM	Recall near midair collision report *5985, 5986*

Airman Certification Codes and Question Numbers

ACS Code	Question Numbers
CA.I.A.K1	5027, 5028, 5030, 5031, 5032, 5033, 5034, 5477, 5539
CA.I.A.K2	5010, 5011, 5012, 5019, 5020, 5022, 5023, 5024, 5025, 5026, 5039, 5044, 5047, 5055, 5068-2, 5068-3, 5068-4, 5069, 5071, 5073-1, 5073-2, 5073-3, 5106, 5107, 5108, 5109, 5111, 5126, 5128, 5129, 5545, 5966, 5967
CA.I.A.K3	5021, 5021-2
CA.I.A.K4	5018
CA.I.A.K5	5021-1
CA.I.B.K1a	5046, 5046-1, 5046-2, 5050-1, 5096, 5096-1, 5535
CA.I.B.K1b	5095, 5097, 5099, 5100, 5101, 5102, 5105, 5535-1, 5547
CA.I.B.K1c	5094, 5103, 5104, 5987
CA.I.B.K2	5098
CA.I.B.K3	5065, 5066, 5080-1, 5080-2, 5666
CA.I.C.K1	5398, 5399, 5560
CA.I.C.K2	5331, 5402, 5403, 5404, 5406, 5407, 5409, 5410, 5411, 5412, 5413, 5414, 5417, 5418, 5422, 5423, 5424, 5425, 5426, 5427, 5428, 5429, 5433, 5434, 5435, 5436, 5439, 5440, 5441, 5442, 5443, 5444, 5445, 5446, 5988, 5989
CA.I.C.K3	5049-3, 5301, 5310-1
CA.I.C.K3a	5313, 5314, 5317, 5318, 5319, 5321, 5332, 5333, 5334, 5336, 5342, 5342, 5343-1, 5344, 5345, 5346, 5348, 5381, 5384, 5385
CA.I.C.K3b	5310, 5311, 5312, 5315, 5316, 5351, 5352, 5353, 5354, 5356, 5393, 5405, 5448, 5450
CA.I.C.K3c	5302, 5303, 5304, 5305, 5990
CA.I.C.K3d	5320, 5322, 5323, 5362
CA.I.C.K3e	5347, 5347-1
CA.I.C.K3f	5327, 5328, 5329, 5330, 5335, 5337, 5338, 5340, 5341, 5349
CA.I.C.K3g	5339, 5357, 5382, 5383, 5447, 5669
CA.I.C.K3h	5363, 5364, 5366, 5367, 5368, 5369, 5370, 5371, 5372, 5373, 5373-1, 5373-2, 5373-3
CA.I.C.K3i	5324, 5325, 5326, 5360
CA.I.C.K3j	5350, 5374, 5376, 5377, 5378, 5379, 5380
CA.I.C.K3l	5135
CA.I.C.K4	5365, 5375, 5449
CA.I.C.R1c	5361, 5739, 5971
CA.I.D.K1	5491-2
CA.I.D.K2	5091, 5092, 5537, 5538, 5991, 5992
CA.I.D.K3a	5208, 5451, 5452, 5453, 5454, 5455, 5456, 5457, 5458, 5459, 5460, 5461, 5462, 5463, 5464, 5465, 5470, 5473, 5474, 5475, 5476, 5481, 5482, 5483, 5484, 5485, 5486, 5487, 5623, 5624, 5625, 5626, 5627
CA.I.D.K3c	5059, 5471
CA.I.D.R3	5049-1, 5049-2

Cross-Reference B Airman Certification Codes and Question Numbers

ACS Code	Question Numbers
CA.I.E.K1	5009, 5043, 5060, 5060-1, 5061, 5061-4, 5072-2, 5077, 5078, 5082-1, 5082-2, 5082-4, 5083, 5083-1, 5085, 5088, 5089, 5090, 5112, 5116-1, 5117, 5118, 5119-1, 5119-2, 5119-3, 5120-1, 5120-2, 5121
CA.I.E.K2	5082-3, 5564, 5565, 5566, 5567, 5568, 5569, 5569-1, 5570, 5570-1, 5572, 5572-1, 5575, 5576, 5577, 5581, 5581-1, 5583, 5584, 5585, 5587, 5588, 5993, 5994
CA.I.E.K3	5575-1, 5995, 5996
CA.I.F.K1	5231, 5232, 5619, 5620, 5621, 5622, 5628, 5629, 5630, 5631, 5979, 5997
CA.I.F.K2a	5234, 5300
CA.I.F.K2e	5207, 5634, 5636, 5637, 5638, 5639, 5646, 5649
CA.I.F.K2f	5164, 5632, 5633, 5647, 5648, 5650, 5651, 5652
CA.I.F.K3	5015-1, 5151, 5152, 5152-1, 5153, 5154, 5156, 5157, 5158, 5159, 5160, 5161, 5161-1, 5162, 5163-1, 5165, 5166, 5167, 5177-1, 5177-2, 5181, 5182, 5192, 5194, 5195, 5196, 5197, 5198, 5198-1, 5199, 5200, 5201, 5202, 5203, 5204, 5206, 5209, 5210, 5211, 5213, 5214, 5215, 5216, 5217, 5218, 5219, 5220, 5220-1, 5221, 5221-1, 5223, 5224, 5225, 5226, 5227, 5228, 5229, 5230, 5238, 5505, 5601, 5602, 5974, 5977
CA.I.F.R2	5015-2, 5016-1, 5016-2, 5016-4, 5017, 5233, 5604, 5604-1, 5605, 5670, 5741
CA.I.G.K1	5767
CA.I.G.K1c	5183, 5184, 5190, 5235, 5236, 5237, 5298, 5299, 5608, 5609, 5610, 5611, 5654, 5667, 5668
CA.I.G.K1d	5768
CA.I.G.K1e	5170, 5176, 5185-1, 5186, 5187, 5189, 5606
CA.I.G.K1h	5114, 5177, 5268, 5269, 5408, 5740
CA.I.G.K1i	5653
CA.I.G.R1	5169, 5171, 5172, 5173, 5174, 5175, 5188, 5271, 5607, 5766
CA.I.H.K1	5490
CA.I.H.K1a	5761, 5764
CA.I.H.K1b	5757, 5759, 5760, 5762
CA.I.H.K1d	5765, 5765-1, 5998
CA.I.H.K1g	5953, 5954
CA.I.H.K1h	5765-2
CA.I.H.K2	5141, 5142, 5143, 5144
CA.I.H.K3	5763, 5763-1, 5763-2, 5763-3, 5763-4
CA.I.H.K4	5941, 5941-1, 5942, 5943, 5961, 5962, 5963
CA.I.H.R2	5944, 5945, 5946, 5947, 5948, 5949, 5950, 5951, 5952, 5955, 5956, 5957, 5958, 5959, 5960
CA.II.A.K2	5045
CA.II.A.K3d	5093
CA.II.A.K4	5050
CA.II.B.K1	5051-1, 5051-2, 5051-3, 5051-4, 5052, 5110-1
CA.II.B.R1	5056-1, 5056-2
CA.II.D.K1	5999
CA.II.D.K2	5970

ACS Code	Question Numbers
CA.II.D.K3	5133, 5134, 5145, 5657, 5658, 5659-1, 5659-2, 5660, 5964, 5975, 5980, 5981, 5982, 5983, 5983-1, 5983-2, 5984, 5999-4
CA.II.D.K5	5748
CA.III.A.K2	5115
CA.III.A.K8	5001, 5002, 5003-1, 5003-2, 5004-1, 5004-2, 5004-3, 5005, 5006, 5007, 5008, 5965, 5985, 5986
CA.III.B.K3	5074, 5075, 5076-1, 5076-2, 5076-3, 5076-4, 5076-5
CA.IV.A.K1	5618
CA.IV.A.K2	5016-3
CA.IV.A.R2a	5661
CA.IV.A.R2b	5359
CA.IV.A.R2d	5655, 5750, 5751, 5752, 5753, 5754
CA.IV.A.R2e	5614
CA.IV.A.R3b	5663
CA.IV.B.K2	5615, 5616, 5617, 5813
CA.IV.B.R2a	5665
CA.IV.B.R2b	5355, 5358
CA.IV.B.R3a	5662, 5664, 5614-1
CA.IV.B.R3b	5138, 5139, 5139-1, 5140, 5656-1, 5656-2, 5656-3, 5972, 5976
CA.IX.B.K1	5494
CA.IX.C.K1	5493
CA.IX.C.K2	5125-2
CA.IX.C.K2d	5999-3
CA.IX.D.K1	5070
CA.IX.D.K3c	5067
CA.V.A.K2	5163
CA.V.A.K2d	5222, 5978, 5978-1
CA.V.A.K2e	5191, 5193, 5210-1, 5270
CA.VI.A.K1	5479, 5999-1
CA.VI.A.K2	5178
CA.VI.A.K5b	5466, 5467, 5468, 5478
CA.VI.A.K5c	5488, 5489
CA.VI.A.K5d	5306, 5307, 5308, 5309
CA.VI.A.K7	5469, 5472
CA.VI.A.R1	5272, 5749, 5758
CA.VI.B.K1	5122-1, 5122-2, 5122-3, 5062, 5500, 5501, 5502, 5506, 5507, 5508, 5509, 5510, 5532, 5533, 5551, 5552, 5553, 5555
CA.VI.B.K2	5999-2
CA.VI.B.K4	5534

Cross-Reference B: Airman Certification Codes and Question Numbers

ACS Code	Question Numbers
CA.VI.C.R5	5503
CA.VII.B.K1	5013, 5014
CA.VII.C.K1	5179, 5180, 5212
CA.VII.C.K4	5155
CA.VII.E.K1	5205
CA.VIII.A.K1	5063, 5064
MC.I.A.K3	5110-2
MC.II.A.K1	5116-2, 5574-3
MC.II.A.K4	5113-1, 5113-2

FAA-CT-8080-1E

Airman Knowledge Testing Supplement for Commercial Pilot

2018

U.S. Department of Transportation
FEDERAL AVIATION ADMINISTRATION
Flight Standards Service

Preface

This testing supplement supersedes FAA-CT-8080-1D, Airman Knowledge Testing Supplement for Commercial Pilot, dated 2016.

This Airman Knowledge Testing Supplement is designed by the Federal Aviation Administration (FAA) Flight Standards Service. It is intended for use by Airman Knowledge Testing (AKT) Organization Designation Authorization (ODA) Holders and other entities approved and/or authorized to administer airman knowledge tests on behalf of the FAA in the following knowledge areas:

Commercial Pilot—Airplane (CAX)
Commercial Pilot—Glider (CGX)
Commercial Pilot—Lighter-Than-Air–Airship (CLA)
Commercial Pilot—Rotorcraft/Gyroplane (CRG)
Commercial Pilot—Rotorcraft/Helicopter (CRH)
Commercial Pilot—Balloon Gas (CBG)
Commercial Pilot—Balloon–Hot Air (CBH)
Military Competence for Commercial Pilot Certification, Non-Category Specific (MCN)

Comments regarding this supplement, or any Airman Testing publication, should be emailed to AFS630comments@faa.gov .

Contents

Preface iii
Contents v

Appendix 1

Legend 1. Sectional Aeronautical Chart. 1-1
Legend 2. Chart Supplement. 1-2
Legend 3. Chart Supplement. 1-3
Legend 4. Chart Supplement. 1-4
Legend 5. Chart Supplement. 1-5
Legend 6. Chart Supplement. 1-6
Legend 7. Chart Supplement. 1-7
Legend 8. Chart Supplement. 1-8
Legend 9. Chart Supplement. 1-9
Legend 10. Chart Supplement. 1-10
Legend 11. Chart Supplement. 1-11
Legend 12. Chart Supplement. 1-12
Legend 13. Chart Supplement. 1-13
Legend 14. Chart Supplement. 1-14
Legend 15. Chart Supplement. 1-15
Legend 16. Chart Supplement. 1-16

Appendix 2

Figure 1. Drag vs. Velocity. 2-1
Figure 2. Stall Speeds. 2-1
Figure 3. Angle of Attack vs. Lift. 2-2
Figure 3A. Maximum Glide Distance. 2-3
Figure 4. Stall Speed vs. Load Factor. 2-3
Figure 5. Velocity vs. Load Factor. 2-4
Figure 6. Adiabatic Chart. 2-5
Figure 8. Fuel Consumption vs. Brake Horsepower. 2-6
Figure 9. Fuel, Time, and Distance to Climb. 2-7
Figure 10. Fuel, Time, and Distance to Climb. 2-8
Figure 11. Cruise and Range Performance. 2-9
Figure 12. Cruise Performance. 2-10
Figure 13. Fuel, Time, and Distance to Climb. 2-11
Figure 14. Fuel, Time, and Distance to Climb. 2-12
Figure 15. Fuel, Time, and Distance to Climb. 2-13
Figure 17. Horizontal Situation Indicator (HSI). 2-14
Figure 26. ILS or LOC RWY 24R (LAX). 2-15
Figure 27. ILS or LOC RWY 35R (DEN). 2-16
Figure 28. ILS or LOC RWY 31 (DSM). 2-17
Figure 29. ILS or LOC RWY 8L (ATL). 2-18
Figure 30. VOR/DME or GPS-A (7D3). 2-19
Figure 31. Wind Component Chart. 2-20
Figure 32. Obstacle Take-off Chart. 2-21
Figure 33. Maximum Rate of Climb Chart. 2-22
Figure 34. Cruise Performance Chart. 2-23

v

Figure 35. Normal Landing Chart. 2-24
Figure 36. Stations Diagram. 2-25
Figure 37. Center of Gravity Envelope and Loading Graph. 2-26
Figure 38. Loading Graph and Center of Gravity Envelope. 2-27
Figure 39. Stations Diagram. 2-28
Figure 40. Weight and Balance Chart. 2-29
Figure 41. Hover Ceiling vs. Gross Weight. 2-30
Figure 42. Rate of Climb (FT/MIN). 2-31
Figure 43. Best Rate of Climb Speed. 2-32
Figure 44. Rate of Climb. 2-33
Figure 45. Running Takeoff. 2-34
Figure 46. Jump Takeoff. 2-35
Figure 48. Performance Curves Chart. 2-36
Figure 49. Performance Curves Chart. 2-37
Figure 50. Flight Envelope. 2-38
Figure 51. Airport Signs. 2-39
Figure 52. Sectional Chart Excerpt. 2-40
Figure 53. Sectional Chart Excerpt. 2-41
Figure 54. Sectional Chart Excerpt. 2-42
Figure 55. En Route Low Altitude Segment. 2-43
Figure 55A. En Route Low Altitude Segment. 2-44
Figure 56. Two signs. 2-45
Figure 57. Sign. 2-45
Figure 58. Airport Diagram and Sign. 2-45
Figure 59. Taxiway Diagram and Sign. 2-46
Figure 60. Two Signs. 2-46
Figure 61. Sign. 2-47
Figure 62. Sign. 2-47
Figure 63. Sign and Intersection Diagram. 2-47
Figure 64. Sign. 2-48
Figure 65. Sign. 2-48
Figure 66. Chart Supplement. 2-49
Figure 67. Chart Supplement. 2-50
Figure 68. Chart Supplement. 2-51
Figure 69. Weather Prediction Center (WPC) Surface Prog Chart. 2-52
Figure 70. Weather Prediction Center (WPC) Surface Prog Chart. 2-53
Figure 71. Low-level Significant Weather Chart. 2-54

Appendix 1

Appendix 1

SECTIONAL AERONAUTICAL CHART
SCALE 1:500,000

LEGEND — Airports having Control Towers are shown in Blue, all others in Magenta. Consult Airport/Facility Directory (A/FD) for details involving airport lighting, navigation aids, and services. For additional symbol information refer to the Chart User's Guide.

AIRPORTS

- ○ Other than hard-surfaced runways
- ⊗ Seaplane Base
- ⦸ Hard-surfaced runways 1500 ft. to 8069 ft. in length
- ⟋ Hard-surfaced runways greater than 8069 ft., or same multiple runways less than 8069 ft.
- ⟋⊙ Open dot within hard-surfaced runway configuration indicates approximate VOR, VOR-DME, or VORTAC location.

All recognizable hard-surfaced runways, including those closed, are shown for visual identification. Airports may be public or private.

ADDITIONAL AIRPORT INFORMATION

- Ⓡ Private "(Pvt)" – Non-public use having emergency or landmark value.
- ◎ Military – Other than hard-surfaced. All military airports are identified by abbreviations AFB, NAS, AAF, etc. For complete airport information consult DOD FLIP.
- ⊗ Abandoned—paved, having landmark value, 3000 ft. or greater
- Ⓗ Heliport Selected
- Ⓕ Ultralight Flight Park Selected
- ⊗ Unverified

Services—fuel available and field attended during normal working hours depicted by use of ticks around basic airport symbol. (Normal working hours are Mon thru Fri 10:00 A.M. to 4:00 P.M. local time. Consult A/FD for service availability at airports with hard-surfaced runways greater than 8069 ft.

★ Rotating airport beacon in operation Sunset to Sunrise

AIRPORT DATA

Box indicators FAR 93 Special Air Traffic Rules & Airport Traffic Patterns

```
         FSS      FAR 91       Location
         |        NO SVFR      Identifier
         |        |            |
         NAME (NAM)(PNAM)  ATIS 123.8
         CT – 118.3 *
         285 L72  122.95       ICAO
                  RP 23, 34    Location
         VFR Advsy 125.0       Indicator
         AOE       UNICOM      shown
                   Airport     outside
                   of Entry    contiguous
                               U.S.
```

Runways with Right Traffic Patterns (public use)
RP Special conditions exist - see A/FD

FSS – Flight Service Station
NO SVFR – Fixed wing special VFR flight is prohibited.
CT - 118.3 – Control Tower (CT) primary frequency
★ – Star indicates operation part-time (see tower frequencies tabulation for hours of operation).
ⓒ – Indicates Common Traffic Advisory Frequencies (CTAF)
ATIS 123.8 – Automatic Terminal Information Service
ASOS/AWOS 135.42 – Automated Surface Weather Observing Systems (shown where full-time ATIS is not available).
Some ASOS/AWOS facilities may not be located at airports.
UNICOM – Aeronautical advisory station
VFR Advsy – VFR Advisory Service shown where full-time ATIS not available and frequency is other than primary CT frequency.
285 – Elevation in feet
*L – Lighting in operation sunset to sunrise
*L – Lighting limitations exist, refer to Airport/Facility Directory.
72 – Length of longest runway in hundreds of feet; usable length may be less.

When information is lacking, the respective character is replaced by a dash. Lighting codes refer to runway edge lights and may not represent the longest runway or full length lighting.

AIRPORT TRAFFIC SERVICE AND AIRSPACE INFORMATION

Only the controlled and reserved airspace effective below 18,000 ft. MSL are shown on this chart. All times are local.

- Class B Airspace
- Class C Airspace (mode C See FAR 91.215/AIM.)
- Class D Airspace
- [40] Ceiling of Class D Airspace in hundreds of feet. (A minus ceiling value indicates surface up to but not including that value.)
- Class E (sfc) Airspace
- Class E Airspace with floor 700 ft. above surface.
- Class E Airspace with floor 1200 ft. or greater above surface that abuts Class G Airspace.

- Prohibited, Restricted, and Warning Areas; Canadian Advisory, Danger, and Restricted Areas.
- Alert Area and MOA - Military Operations Area
- Special Airport Traffic Area (See FAR Part 93 for details)
- Mode C (See FAR 91.215/AIM.)
- ADIZ - Air Defense Identification Zone
- National Security Area
- Terminal Radar Service Area (TRSA)
- IR211→ MTR - Military Training Route

MISCELLANEOUS

- −1° E − Isogonic Line (2010 VALUE)
- Ⓤ Ultralight Activity
- Ⓗ Hang Glider Activity
- Ⓖ Glider Operations
- Ⓤ̲Ⓐ̲ Unmanned Aircraft Activity
- Parachute Jumping Area (See Airport/Facility Directory).
- • Marine Light
- ◆ NAME (VPXYZ) VFR Waypoints (See Airport/Facility Directory for latitude/longitude).

OBSTRUCTIONS

- ⋏ below 1000 ft. AGL
- ⋏ or 𝘈 Group Obstruction
- ⋆ Obstruction with high-intensity lights May operate part-time
- 𝘈 1000 ft. and higher AGL
- 2049 Elevation of the top above mean sea level
- (1149) Height above ground
- UC — Under construction or reported; position and elevation unverified.

NOTICE: Guy wires may extend outward from structures.

Differentiates floors of Class E Airspace greater than 700 ft. above surface. Class E Airspace exists at 1200 ft AGL unless otherwise designated as shown above. Class E Airspace low altitude Federal Airways are indicated by center line. Intersection - Arrows are directed towards facilities which establish intersection.

- 2400 MSL
- 4500 MSL
- 132° V 69
- Total mileage between NAVAID, on direct Airways and Class E Airspace low altitude RNAV routes are indicated by center line.
- 169 TK313 (helicopter only)
- ◆ RNAV waypoint

RADIO AIDS TO NAVIGATION

- ⬡ VHF OMNI RANGE (VOR)
- ⬡ VORTAC
- ⬡ VOR-DME
- Non-Directional Radiobeacon (NDB)
- NDB-DME
- · Other facilities, i.e., FSS Outlet, RCO, etc.

COMMUNICATION BOXES

```
122.1R 122.6 123.6
  OAKDALE
382  OAK
```

Underline indicates no voice on this frequency.
Crosshatch indicates Shutdown Status

- ∗ Operates less than continuous or On-Request.
- Ⓗ ASOS/AWOS
- Ⓗ HIWAS
- Ⓔ FSS radio providing voice communication

Heavy line box indicates Flight Service Station (FSS). Frequencies 121.5, 122.2, 243.0 and 255.4 (Canada - 121.5, 126.7 and 243.0) are available at many FSSs and are not shown above boxes. All other frequencies are shown.

Certain FSSs provide Airport Advisory Service, see Chart Supplement.
R - Receive Only.

```
122.1R
MIAMI
```

Frequencies above this line box are remoted to NAVAID site. Other FSS frequencies providing voice communication may be available as determined by altitude and terrain. Consult Chart Supplement for complete information.

```
122.1R
CHICAGO CHI
```

TOPOGRAPHIC INFORMATION

- ══65══ Roads & Road Markers
- ┼┼┼┼┼ Railroad
- ╌╌╌╌╌ Power Transmission Lines
- ─ ─ ─ ─ Aerial Cable
- ■ Landmark Feature - stadium, factory, school, golf course, etc.
- ⌂ Outdoor Theatre
- ◉ Lookout Tower
- 618 (Elevation Base of Tower)
- ✚CG Coast Guard Station
- ◯ Race Track
- • Tank-water, oil or gas
- ○ Oil Well • Water Well
- ✱ Mine or Quarry
-)(Mountain Pass 11823 (Elevation of Pass)

(Pass symbol does not indicate a recommended route or direction of flight and pass elevation does not indicate a recommended clearance altitude. Hazardous flight conditions may exist within and near mountain passes).

Dams Bridges and Viaducts
Perennial Lake   Non-Perennial Lake

Legend 1. Sectional Aeronautical Chart.

1-1

Appendix 1

12   AIRPORT/FACILITY DIRECTORY LEGEND

SAMPLE

① **CITY NAME**

② **AIRPORT NAME** ③ (ALTERNATE NAME) (LTS)(KLTS) ④ CIV/MIL ⑤ 3 N ⑥ UTC–6(–5DT) ⑦ N34°41.93′ W99°20.20′ ⑧ JACKSONVILLE COPTER
200 B TPA—1000(800) AOE LRA Class IV, ARFF Index A NOTAM FILE ORL Not insp. H–4G, L–19C
⑪ ⑫ ⑬ ⑭ ⑮ ⑯ ⑰ IAP, DIAP, AD
⑨

⑱ → **RWY 18–36:** H12004X200 (ASPH–CONC–GRVD)
    S–90, D–160, 2D–300 PCN 80 R/B/W/T   HIRL   CL
    RWY 18: RLLS. MALSF. TDZL. REIL. PAPI(P2R)—GA 3.0° TCH 36′.
      RVR–TMR. Thld dsplcd 300′.   Trees. Rgt tfc.   0.3% up.
    RWY 36: ALSF1.   0.4% down.
  RWY 09–27: H6000X150 (ASPH)   MIRL
  RWY 173–353: H3515X150 (ASPH–PFC)   AUW PCN 59 F/A/W/T

⑲ → **LAND AND HOLD–SHORT OPERATIONS**
    LDG RWY   HOLD–SHORT POINT   AVBL LDG DIST
    RWY 18   09–27   6500
    RWY 36   09–27   5400

⑳ → **RUNWAY DECLARED DISTANCE INFORMATION**
    RWY 18: TORA–12004 TODA–12004 ASDA–11704 LDA–11504
    RWY 36: TORA–12004 TODA–12004 ASDA–12004 LDA–11704

㉑ → **ARRESTING GEAR/SYSTEM**
    RWY 18 HOOK E5 (65′ OVRN) BAK–14 BAK–12B (1650′)
              BAK–14 BAK–12B (1087′) HOOK E5 (74′ OVRN) **RWY 36**

㉒ → **SERVICE:** S4 **FUEL** 100LL, JET A   **OX** 1, 3 **LGT** ACTIVATE MALSR Rwy
    29, REIL Rwy 11, VASI Rwy 11, HIRL Rwy 11–29, PAPI Rwy 17
    and Rwy 35, MIRL Rwy 17–35—**CTAF. MILITARY—A–GEAR** E–5
    connected on dep end, disconnected on apch end.
    JASU 3(AM32A–60) 2(A/M32A–86) **FUEL** J8(Mil)(NC–100, A)
    FLUID W SP PRESAIR LOX **OIL** O–128 **MAINT** S1 Mon–Fri 1000–2200Z‡
    TRAN ALERT Avbl 1300–0200Z‡ svc limited weekends.

㉓ → **AIRPORT REMARKS:** Special Air Traffic Rules—Part 93, see Regulatory Notices. Attended 1200–0300Z‡. Parachute Jumping.
    Deer invof arpt. Heavy jumbo jet training surface to 9000′. Twy A clsd indef. Flight Notification Service (ADCUS) avbl.

㉔ → **MILITARY REMARKS:** ANG PPR/Official Business Only. Base OPS DSN 638–4390, C503–335–4222. Ctc Base OPS 15 minutes
    prior to ldg and after dep. Limited tran parking.

㉕ → **AIRPORT MANAGER:** (580) 481–5739

㉖ → **WEATHER DATA SOURCES:** AWOS–1 120.3   (202) 426–8000. LAWRS.

㉗ → **COMMUNICATIONS: SFA CTAF** 122.8   **UNICOM** 122.95   **ATIS** 127.25 273.5 (202) 426–8003   **PTD** 372.2
    NAME **FSS** (ORL) on arpt. 123.65 122.65 122.2
    NAME **RCO** 112.2T 112.1R (NAME RADIO)
    ®NAME **APP/DEP CON** 128.35 257.725 (1200–0400Z‡)
      TOWER 119.65 255.6 (1200–0400Z‡)   **GND CON** 121.7   **GCO** 135.075 (ORLANDO CLNC)   **CLNC DEL** 125.55
      CPDLC D–HZWXR, D–TAXI, DCL (LOGON KMEM)
    NAME **COMD POST** (GERONIMO) 311.0 321.4 6761   **PMSV METRO** 239.8   NAME **OPS** 257.5

㉘ → **AIRSPACE: CLASS B** See VFR Terminal Area Chart.
㉙ → **VOR TEST FACILITY (VOT):** 116.7
㉚ → **RADIO AIDS TO NAVIGATION:** NOTAM FILE ORL. VHF/DF ctc FSS.
    (H) **VORTAC**   112.2   MCO   Chan 59   N28°32.55′ W81°20.12′   at fld. 1110/8E.
    (H) **TACAN**   Chan 29   CBU   (109.2)   N28°32.65′ W81°21.12′   at fld. 1115/8E.
    HERNY NDB (LOM)   221   OR   N28°37.40′ W81°21.05′   177° 5.4 NM to fld.
    ILS/DME 108.5   I–ORL   Chan 22   Rwy 18.   Class IIE.   LOM HERNY NDB.
    ASR/PAR (1200–0400Z‡)

㉛ → **COMM/NAV/WEATHER REMARKS:** Emerg frequency 121.5 not avbl at twr.

• • • • • • • • • • • • • • •

HELIPAD H1: H100X75 (ASPH)
HELIPAD H2: H60X60 (ASPH)
HELIPORT REMARKS: Helipad H1 lctd on general aviation side and H2 lctd on air carrier side of arpt.

• • • • • • • • • • • • • • •

187   TPA 1000(813)
WATERWAY 15–33: 5000X425 (WATER)
SEAPLANE REMARKS: Birds roosting and feeding areas along river banks. Seaplanes operating adjacent to SW side of arpt not
    visible from twr and are required to ctc twr.

All bearings and radials are magnetic unless otherwise specified. All mileages are nautical unless otherwise noted.
All times are Coordinated Universal Time (UTC) except as noted. All elevations are in feet above/below Mean Sea Level (MSL) unless otherwise noted.
The horizontal reference datum of this publication is North American Datum of 1983 (NAD83), which for charting purposes is considered equivalent to World Geodetic System 1984 (WGS 84).

SC, 1 FEB 20XX to 29 MAR 20XX

Legend 2. Chart Supplement.

Appendix 1

AIRPORT/FACILITY DIRECTORY LEGEND 13

SKETCH LEGEND

⑩

RUNWAYS/LANDING AREAS

- Hard Surfaced
- Metal Surface
- Sod, Gravel, etc.
- Light Plane, Ski Landing Area or Water
- Under Construction
- Closed Rwy
- Closed Pavement
- Helicopter Landings Area
- Displaced Threshold
- Taxiway, Apron and Stopways

RADIO AIDS TO NAVIGATION

- VORTAC
- VOR
- VOR/DME
- NDB
- TACAN
- NDB/DME
- DME

MISCELLANEOUS AERONAUTICAL FEATURES

- Airport Beacon
- Wind Cone
- Landing Tee
- Tetrahedron
- Control Tower .... or TWR

When control tower and rotating beacon are co-located beacon symbol will be used and further identified as TWR.

MISCELLANEOUS BASE AND CULTURAL FEATURES

- Buildings
- Power Lines
- Fence
- Towers
- Wind Turbine
- Tanks
- Oil Well
- Smoke Stack
- Obstruction 5812
- Controlling Obstruction .... +5812
- Trees
- Populated Places
- Cuts and Fills ..... Cut   Fill
- Cliffs and Depressions
- Ditch
- Hill

APPROACH LIGHTING SYSTEMS

A dot "•" portrayed with approach lighting letter identifier indicates sequenced flashing lights (F) installed with the approach lighting system e.g. (A1) Negative symbology, e.g., (A1). (V) indicates Pilot Controlled Lighting (PCL).

- Runway Centerline Lighting
- (A) Approach Lighting System ALSF-2
- (A1) Approach Lighting System ALSF-1
- (A2) Short Approach Lighting System SALS/SALSF
- (A3) Simplified Short Approach Lighting System (SSALR) with RAIL
- (A4) Medium Intensity Approach Lighting System (MALS and MALSF)/(SSALS and SSALF)
- (A5) Medium Intensity Approach Lighting System (MALSR) and RAIL
- Omnidirectional Approach Lighting System (ODALS)
- (D) Navy Parallel Row and Cross Bar
- (†) Air Force Overrun
- (V) Visual Approach Slope Indicator with Standard Threshold Clearance provided
- (V2) Pulsating Visual Approach Slope Indicator (PVASI)
- (V3) Visual Approach Slope Indicator with a threshold crossing height to accomodate long bodied or jumbo aircraft
- (V4) Tri-color Visual Approach Slope Indicator (TRCV)
- (V5) Approach Path Alignment Panel (APAP)
- (P) Precision Approach Path Indicator (PAPI)

SC, 1 FEB 20XX to 29 MAR 20XX

Legend 3. Chart Supplement.

Appendix 1

14   **AIRPORT/FACILITY DIRECTORY LEGEND**

LEGEND

This directory is a listing of data on record with the FAA on public–use airports, military airports and selected private–use airports specifically requested by the Department of Defense (DoD) for which a DoD Instrument Approach Procedure has been published in the U.S. Terminal Procedures Publication. Additionally this listing contains data for associated terminal control facilities, air route traffic control centers, and radio aids to navigation within the conterminous United States, Puerto Rico and the Virgin Islands. Civil airports and joint Civil/Military airports which are open to the public are listed alphabetically by state, associated city and airport name and cross–referenced by airport name. Military airports and private–use (limited civil access) joint Military/Civil airports are listed alphabetically by state and official airport name and cross–referenced by associated city name. Navaids, flight service stations and remote communication outlets that are associated with an airport, but with a different name, are listed alphabetically under their own name, as well as under the airport with which they are associated.

The listing of an airport as open to the public in this directory merely indicates the airport operator's willingness to accommodate transient aircraft, and does not represent that the airport conforms with any Federal or local standards, or that it has been approved for use on the part of the general public. Military airports, private–use airports, and private–use (limited civil access) joint Military/Civil airports are open to civil pilots only in an emergency or with prior permission. See Special Notice Section, Civil Use of Military Fields.

The information on obstructions is taken from reports submitted to the FAA. Obstruction data has not been verified in all cases. Pilots are cautioned that objects not indicated in this tabulation (or on the airports sketches and/or charts) may exist which can create a hazard to flight operation. Detailed specifics concerning services and facilities tabulated within this directory are contained in the Aeronautical Information Manual, Basic Flight Information and ATC Procedures.

The legend items that follow explain in detail the contents of this Directory and are keyed to the circled numbers on the sample on the preceding pages.

① CITY/AIRPORT NAME

Civil and joint Civil/Military airports which are open to the public are listed alphabetically by state and associated city. Where the city name is different from the airport name the city name will appear on the line above the airport name. Airports with the same associated city name will be listed alphabetically by airport name and will be separated by a dashed rule line. A solid rule line will separate all others. FAA approved helipads and seaplane landing areas associated with a land airport will be separated by a dotted line. Military airports and private–use (limited civil access) joint Military/Civil airports are listed alphabetically by state and official airport name.

② ALTERNATE NAME

Alternate names, if any, will be shown in parentheses.

③ LOCATION IDENTIFIER

The location identifier is a three or four character FAA code followed by a four–character ICAO code, when assigned, to airports. If two different military codes are assigned, both codes will be shown with the primary operating agency's code listed first. These identifiers are used by ATC in lieu of the airport name in flight plans, flight strips and other written records and computer operations. Zeros will appear with a slash to differentiate them from the letter "O".

④ OPERATING AGENCY

Airports within this directory are classified into two categories, Military/Federal Government and Civil airports open to the general public, plus selected private–use airports. The operating agency is shown for military, private–use and joint use airports. The operating agency is shown by an abbreviation as listed below. When an organization is a tenant, the abbreviation is enclosed in parenthesis. No classification indicates the airport is open to the general public with no military tenant.

A	US Army	MC	Marine Corps
AFRC	Air Force Reserve Command	MIL/CIV	Joint Use Military/Civil Limited Civil Access
AF	US Air Force	N	Navy
ANG	Air National Guard	NAF	Naval Air Facility
AR	US Army Reserve	NAS	Naval Air Station
ARNG	US Army National Guard	NASA	National Air and Space Administration
CG	US Coast Guard	P	US Civil Airport Wherein Permit Covers Use by Transient Military Aircraft
CIV/MIL	Joint Use Civil/Military Open to the Public		
DND	Department of National Defense Canada	PVT	Private Use Only (Closed to the Public)

⑤ AIRPORT LOCATION

Airport location is expressed as distance and direction from the center of the associated city in nautical miles and cardinal points, e.g., 4 NE.

⑥ TIME CONVERSION

Hours of operation of all facilities are expressed in Coordinated Universal Time (UTC) and shown as "Z" time. The directory indicates the number of hours to be subtracted from UTC to obtain local standard time and local daylight saving time UTC–5(–4DT). The symbol ‡ indicates that during periods of Daylight Saving Time (DST) effective hours will be one hour earlier than shown. In those areas where daylight saving time is not observed the (–4DT) and ‡ will not be shown. Daylight saving time is in effect from 0200 local time the second Sunday in March to 0200 local time the first Sunday in November. Canada and all U.S. Conterminous States observe daylight saving time except Arizona and Puerto Rico, and the Virgin Islands. If the state observes daylight saving time and the operating times are other than daylight saving times, the operating hours will include the dates, times and no ‡ symbol will be shown, i.e., April 15–Aug 31 0630–1700Z, Sep 1–Apr 14 0600–1700Z.

SC, 1 FEB 20XX to 29 MAR 20XX

Legend 4. Chart Supplement.

AIRPORT/FACILITY DIRECTORY LEGEND

⑦ GEOGRAPHIC POSITION OF AIRPORT—AIRPORT REFERENCE POINT (ARP)
Positions are shown as hemisphere, degrees, minutes and hundredths of a minute and represent the approximate geometric center of all usable runway surfaces.

⑧ CHARTS
Charts refer to the Sectional Chart and Low and High Altitude Enroute Chart and panel on which the airport or facility is depicted. Helicopter Chart depictions will be indicated as COPTER. IFR Gulf of Mexico West and IFR Gulf of Mexico Central will be referenced as GOMW and GOMC.

⑨ INSTRUMENT APPROACH PROCEDURES, AIRPORT DIAGRAMS
IAP indicates an airport for which a prescribed (Public Use) FAA Instrument Approach Procedure has been published. DIAP indicates an airport for which a prescribed DoD Instrument Approach Procedure has been published in the U.S. Terminal Procedures. See the Special Notice Section of this directory, Civil Use of Military Fields and the Aeronautical Information Manual 5–4–5 Instrument Approach Procedure Charts for additional information. AD indicates an airport for which an airport diagram has been published. Airport diagrams are located in the back of each Chart Supplement volume alphabetically by associated city and airport name.

⑩ AIRPORT SKETCH
The airport sketch, when provided, depicts the airport and related topographical information as seen from the air and should be used in conjunction with the text. It is intended as a guide for pilots in VFR conditions. Symbology that is not self-explanatory will be reflected in the sketch legend. The airport sketch will be oriented with True North at the top. Airport sketches will be added incrementally.

⑪ ELEVATION
The highest point of an airport's usable runways measured in feet from mean sea level. When elevation is sea level it will be indicated as "00". When elevation is below sea level a minus "–" sign will precede the figure.

⑫ ROTATING LIGHT BEACON
B indicates rotating beacon is available. Rotating beacons operate sunset to sunrise unless otherwise indicated in the AIRPORT REMARKS or MILITARY REMARKS segment of the airport entry.

⑬ TRAFFIC PATTERN ALTITUDE
Traffic Pattern Altitude (TPA)—The first figure shown is TPA above mean sea level. The second figure in parentheses is TPA above airport elevation. Multiple TPA shall be shown as "TPA—See Remarks" and detailed information shall be shown in the Airport or Military Remarks Section. Traffic pattern data for USAF bases, USN facilities, and U.S. Army airports (including those on which ACC or U.S. Army is a tenant) that deviate from standard pattern altitudes shall be shown in Military Remarks.

⑭ AIRPORT OF ENTRY, LANDING RIGHTS, AND CUSTOMS USER FEE AIRPORTS
U.S. CUSTOMS USER FEE AIRPORT—Private Aircraft operators are frequently required to pay the costs associated with customs processing.

AOE—Airport of Entry. A customs Airport of Entry where permission from U.S. Customs is not required to land. However, at least one hour advance notice of arrival is required.

LRA—Landing Rights Airport. Application for permission to land must be submitted in advance to U.S. Customs. At least one hour advance notice of arrival is required.

NOTE: Advance notice of arrival at both an AOE and LRA airport may be included in the flight plan when filed in Canada or Mexico. Where Flight Notification Service (ADCUS) is available the airport remark will indicate this service. This notice will also be treated as an application for permission to land in the case of an LRA. Although advance notice of arrival may be relayed to Customs through Mexico, Canada, and U.S. Communications facilities by flight plan, the aircraft operator is solely responsible for ensuring that Customs receives the notification. (See Customs, Immigration and Naturalization, Public Health and Agriculture Department requirements in the International Flight Information Manual for further details.)

U.S. CUSTOMS AIR AND SEA PORTS, INSPECTORS AND AGENTS

Northeast Sector (New England and Atlantic States—ME to MD)	407–975–1740
Southeast Sector (Atlantic States—DC, WV, VA to FL)	407–975–1780
Central Sector (Interior of the US, including Gulf states—MS, AL, LA)	407–975–1760
Southwest East Sector (OK and eastern TX)	407–975–1840
Southwest West Sector (Western TX, NM and AZ)	407–975–1820
Pacific Sector (WA, OR, CA, HI and AK)	407–975–1800

⑮ CERTIFICATED AIRPORT (14 CFR PART 139)
Airports serving Department of Transportation certified carriers and certified under 14 CFR part 139 are indicated by the Class and the ARFF Index; e.g. Class I, ARFF Index A, which relates to the availability of crash, fire, rescue equipment. Class I airports can have an ARFF Index A through E, depending on the aircraft length and scheduled departures. Class II, III, and IV will always carry an Index A.

AIRPORT CLASSIFICATIONS

Type of Air Carrier Operation	Class I	Class II	Class III	Class IV
Scheduled Air Carrier Aircraft with 31 or more passenger seats	X			
Unscheduled Air Carrier Aircraft with 31 or more passengers seats	X	X		X
Scheduled Air Carrier Aircraft with 10 to 30 passenger seats	X	X	X	

SC, 1 FEB 20XX to 29 MAR 20XX

Legend 5. Chart Supplement.

AIRPORT/FACILITY DIRECTORY LEGEND

16

INDICES AND AIRCRAFT RESCUE AND FIRE FIGHTING EQUIPMENT REQUIREMENTS

Airport Index	Required No. Vehicles	Aircraft Length	Scheduled Departures	Agent + Water for Foam
A	1	<90'	≥1	500#DC or HALON 1211 or 450#DC + 100 gal H_2O
B	1 or 2	≥90', <126'	≥5	Index A + 1500 gal H_2O
		≥126', <159'	<5	
C	2 or 3	≥126', <159'	≥5	Index A + 3000 gal H_2O
		≥159', <200'	<5	
D	3	≥159', <200'	≥5	Index A + 4000 gal H_2O
		>200'	<5	
E	3	≥200'	≥5	Index A + 6000 gal H_2O

> Greater Than; < Less Than; ≥ Equal or Greater Than; ≤ Equal or Less Than; H_2O–Water; DC–Dry Chemical.

NOTE: The listing of ARFF index does not necessarily assure coverage for non–air carrier operations or at other than prescribed times for air carrier. ARFF Index Ltd.—indicates ARFF coverage may or may not be available, for information contact airport manager prior to flight.

⑯ NOTAM SERVICE
All public use landing areas are provided NOTAM service. A NOTAM FILE identifier is shown for individual landing areas, e.g., "NOTAM FILE BNA". See the AIM, Basic Flight Information and ATC Procedures for a detailed description of NOTAMs. Current NOTAMs are available from flight service stations at 1–800–WX–BRIEF (992–7433) or online through the FAA PilotWeb at https://pilotweb.nas.faa.gov. Military NOTAMs are available using the Defense Internet NOTAM Service (DINS) at https://www.notams.faa.gov. Pilots flying to or from airports not available through the FAA PilotWeb or DINS can obtain assistance from Flight Service.

⑰ FAA INSPECTION
All airports not inspected by FAA will be identified by the note: Not insp. This indicates that the airport information has been provided by the owner or operator of the field.

⑱ RUNWAY DATA
Runway information is shown on two lines. That information common to the entire runway is shown on the first line while information concerning the runway ends is shown on the second or following line. Runway direction, surface, length, width, weight bearing capacity, lighting, and slope, when available are shown for each runway. Multiple runways are shown with the longest runway first. Direction, length, width, and lighting are shown for sea–lanes. The full dimensions of helipads are shown, e.g., 50X150. Runway data that requires clarification will be placed in the remarks section.

RUNWAY DESIGNATION
Runways are normally numbered in relation to their magnetic orientation rounded off to the nearest 10 degrees. Parallel runways can be designated L (left)/R (right)/C (center). Runways may be designated as Ultralight or assault strips. Assault strips are shown by magnetic bearing.

RUNWAY DIMENSIONS
Runway length and width are shown in feet. Length shown is runway end to end including displaced thresholds, but excluding those areas designed as overruns.

RUNWAY SURFACE AND SURFACE TREATMENT
Runway lengths prefixed by the letter "H" indicate that the runways are hard surfaced (concrete, asphalt, or part asphalt–concrete). If the runway length is not prefixed, the surface is sod, clay, etc. The runway surface composition is indicated in parentheses after runway length as follows:

(AFSC)—Aggregate friction seal coat
(AM2)—Temporary metal planks coated with nonskid material
(ASPH)—Asphalt
(CONC)—Concrete
(DIRT)—Dirt
(GRVD)—Grooved
(GRVL)—Gravel, or cinders
(MATS)—Pierced steel planking, landing mats, membranes
(PEM)—Part concrete, part asphalt
(PFC)—Porous friction courses
(PSP)—Pierced steel plank
(RFSC)—Rubberized friction seal coat
(SAND)—Sand
(TURF)—Turf
(TRTD)—Treated
(WC)—Wire combed

SC, 1 FEB 20XX to 29 MAR 20XX

Legend 6. Chart Supplement.

AIRPORT/FACILITY DIRECTORY LEGEND

RUNWAY WEIGHT BEARING CAPACITY

Runway strength data shown in this publication is derived from available information and is a realistic estimate of capability at an average level of activity. It is not intended as a maximum allowable weight or as an operating limitation. Many airport pavements are capable of supporting limited operations with gross weights in excess of the published figures. Permissible operating weights, insofar as runway strengths are concerned, are a matter of agreement between the owner and user. When desiring to operate into any airport at weights in excess of those published in the publication, users should contact the airport management for permission. Runway strength figures are shown in thousand of pounds, with the last three figures being omitted. Add 000 to figure following S, D, 2S, 2T, AUW, SWL, etc., for gross weight capacity. A blank space following the letter designator is used to indicate the runway can sustain aircraft with this type landing gear, although definite runway weight bearing capacity figures are not available, e.g., S, D. Applicable codes for typical gear configurations with S=Single, D=Dual, T=Triple and Q=Quadruple:

CURRENT	NEW	NEW DESCRIPTION
S	S	Single wheel type landing gear (DC3), (C47), (F15), etc.
D	D	Dual wheel type landing gear (BE1900), (B737), (A319), etc.
T	D	Dual wheel type landing gear (P3, C9).
ST	2S	Two single wheels in tandem type landing gear (C130).
TRT	2T	Two triple wheels in tandem type landing gear (C17), etc.
DT	2D	Two dual wheels in tandem type landing gear (B707), etc.
TT	2D	Two dual wheels in tandem type landing gear (B757, KC135).
SBTT	2D/D1	Two dual wheels in tandem/dual wheel body gear type landing gear (KC10).
None	2D/2D1	Two dual wheels in tandem/two dual wheels in tandem body gear type landing gear (A340-600).
DDT	2D/2D2	Two dual wheels in tandem/two dual wheels in double tandem body gear type landing gear (B747, E4).
TTT	3D	Three dual wheels in tandem type landing gear (B777), etc.
TT	D2	Dual wheel gear two struts per side main gear type landing gear (B52).
TDT	C5	Complex dual wheel and quadruple wheel combination landing gear (C5).

AUW—All up weight. Maximum weight bearing capacity for any aircraft irrespective of landing gear configuration.

SWL—Single Wheel Loading. (This includes information submitted in terms of Equivalent Single Wheel Loading (ESWL) and Single Isolated Wheel Loading).

PSI—Pounds per square inch. PSI is the actual figure expressing maximum pounds per square inch runway will support, e.g., (SWL 000/PSI 535).

Omission of weight bearing capacity indicates information unknown.

The ACN/PCN System is the ICAO standard method of reporting pavement strength for pavements with bearing strengths greater than 12,500 pounds. The Pavement Classification Number (PCN) is established by an engineering assessment of the runway. The PCN is for use in conjunction with an Aircraft Classification Number (ACN). Consult the Aircraft Flight Manual, Flight Information Handbook, or other appropriate source for ACN tables or charts. Currently, ACN data may not be available for all aircraft. If an ACN table or chart is available, the ACN can be calculated by taking into account the aircraft weight, the pavement type, and the subgrade category. For runways that have been evaluated under the ACN/PCN system, the PCN will be shown as a five-part code (e.g. PCN 80 R/B/W/T). Details of the coded format are as follows:

NOTE: Prior permission from the airport controlling authority is required when the ACN of the aircraft exceeds the published PCN or aircraft tire pressure exceeds the published limits.

(1) The PCN NUMBER—The reported PCN indicates that an aircraft with an ACN equal or less than the reported PCN can operate on the pavement subject to any limitation on the tire pressure.

(2) The type of pavement:
R — Rigid
F — Flexible

(3) The pavement subgrade category:
A — High
B — Medium
C — Low
D — Ultra-low

(4) The maximum tire pressure authorized for the pavement:
W — Unlimited, no pressure limit
X — High, limited to 254 psi (1.75 MPa)
Y — Medium, limited to 181 psi (1.25MPa)
Z — Low, limited to 73 psi (0.50 MPa)

(5) Pavement evaluation method:
T — Technical evaluation
U — By experience of aircraft using the pavement

RUNWAY LIGHTING

Lights are in operation sunset to sunrise. Lighting available by prior arrangement only or operating part of the night and/or pilot controlled lighting with specific operating hours are indicated under airport or military remarks. At USN/USMC facilities lights are available only during airport hours of operation. Since obstructions are usually lighted, obstruction lighting is not included in this code. Unlighted obstructions on or surrounding an airport will be noted in airport or military remarks. Runway lights nonstandard (NSTD) are systems for which the light fixtures are not FAA approved L-800 series: color, intensity, or spacing does not meet FAA standards. Nonstandard runway lights, VASI, or any other system not listed below will be shown in airport remarks or military

SC, 1 FEB 20XX to 29 MAR 20XX

Legend 7. Chart Supplement.

18   AIRPORT/FACILITY DIRECTORY LEGEND

service. Temporary, emergency or limited runway edge lighting such as flares, smudge pots, lanterns or portable runway lights will also be shown in airport remarks or military service. Types of lighting are shown with the runway or runway end they serve.

NSTD—Light system fails to meet FAA standards.
LIRL—Low Intensity Runway Lights.
MIRL—Medium Intensity Runway Lights.
HIRL—High Intensity Runway Lights.
RAIL—Runway Alignment Indicator Lights.
REIL—Runway End Identifier Lights.
CL—Centerline Lights.
TDZL—Touchdown Zone Lights.
ODALS—Omni Directional Approach Lighting System.
AF OVRN—Air Force Overrun 1000´ Standard Approach Lighting System.
MALS—Medium Intensity Approach Lighting System.
MALSF—Medium Intensity Approach Lighting System with Sequenced Flashing Lights.
MALSR—Medium Intensity Approach Lighting System with Runway Alignment Indicator Lights.
RLLS—Runway Lead–in Light System

SALS—Short Approach Lighting System.
SALSF—Short Approach Lighting System with Sequenced Flashing Lights.
SSALS—Simplified Short Approach Lighting System.
SSALF—Simplified Short Approach Lighting System with Sequenced Flashing Lights.
SSALR—Simplified Short Approach Lighting System with Runway Alignment Indicator Lights.
ALSAF—High Intensity Approach Lighting System with Sequenced Flashing Lights.
ALSF1—High Intensity Approach Lighting System with Sequenced Flashing Lights, Category I, Configuration.
ALSF2—High Intensity Approach Lighting System with Sequenced Flashing Lights, Category II, Configuration.
SF—Sequenced Flashing Lights.
OLS—Optical Landing System.
WAVE–OFF.

NOTE: Civil ALSF2 may be operated as SSALR during favorable weather conditions. When runway edge lights are positioned more than 10 feet from the edge of the usable runway surface a remark will be added in the "Remarks" portion of the airport entry. This is applicable to Air Force, Air National Guard and Air Force Reserve Bases, and those joint use airfields on which they are tenants.

VISUAL GLIDESLOPE INDICATORS

APAP—A system of panels, which may or may not be lighted, used for alignment of approach path.
    PNIL   APAP on left side of runway   PNIR   APAP on right side of runway

PAPI—Precision Approach Path Indicator
    P2L   2–identical light units placed on left side of runway   P4L   4–identical light units placed on left side of runway
    P2R   2–identical light units placed on right side of runway   P4R   4–identical light units placed on right side of runway

PVASI—Pulsating/steady burning visual approach slope indicator, normally a single light unit projecting two colors.
    PSIL   PVASI on left side of runway   PSIR   PVASI on right side of runway

SAVASI—Simplified Abbreviated Visual Approach Slope Indicator
    S2L   2–box SAVASI on left side of runway   S2R   2–box SAVASI on right side of runway

TRCV—Tri–color visual approach slope indicator, normally a single light unit projecting three colors.
    TRIL   TRCV on left side of runway   TRIR   TRCV on right side of runway

VASI—Visual Approach Slope Indicator
    V2L   2–box VASI on left side of runway   V6L   6–box VASI on left side of runway
    V2R   2–box VASI on right side of runway   V6R   6–box VASI on right side of runway
    V4L   4–box VASI on left side of runway   V12   12–box VASI on both sides of runway
    V4R   4–box VASI on right side of runway   V16   16–box VASI on both sides of runway

NOTE: Approach slope angle and threshold crossing height will be shown when available; i.e., –GA 3.5° TCH 37´.

PILOT CONTROL OF AIRPORT LIGHTING

Key Mike	Function
7 times within 5 seconds	Highest intensity available
5 times within 5 seconds	Medium or lower intensity (Lower REIL or REIL–Off)
3 times within 5 seconds	Lowest intensity available (Lower REIL or REIL–Off)

Available systems will be indicated in the Service section, e.g., **LGT** ACTIVATE HIRL Rwy 07–25, MALSR Rwy 07, and VASI Rwy 07—122.8.

Where the airport is not served by an instrument approach procedure and/or has an independent type system of different specification installed by the airport sponsor, descriptions of the type lights, method of control, and operating frequency will be explained in clear text. See AIM, "Basic Flight Information and ATC Procedures," for detailed description of pilot control of airport lighting.

RUNWAY SLOPE

When available, runway slope data will be provided. Runway slope will be shown only when it is 0.3 percent or greater. On runways less than 8000 feet, the direction of the slope up will be indicated, e.g., 0.3% up NW. On runways 8000 feet or greater, the slope will be shown (up or down) on the runway end line, e.g., RWY 13: 0.3% up., RWY 31: Pole. Rgt tfc. 0.4% down.

SC, 1 FEB 20XX to 29 MAR 20XX

Legend 8. Chart Supplement.

AIRPORT/FACILITY DIRECTORY LEGEND 19

RUNWAY END DATA

Information pertaining to the runway approach end such as approach lights, touchdown zone lights, runway end identification lights, visual glideslope indicators, displaced thresholds, controlling obstruction, and right hand traffic pattern, will be shown on the specific runway end. "Rgt tfc"—Right traffic indicates right turns should be made on landing and takeoff for specified runway end. Runway Visual Range shall be shown as "RVR" appended with "T" for touchdown, "M" for midpoint, and "R" for rollout; e.g., RVR-TMR.

⑲ LAND AND HOLD–SHORT OPERATIONS (LAHSO)

LAHSO is an acronym for "Land and Hold–Short Operations" These operations include landing and holding short of an intersection runway, an intersecting taxiway, or other predetermined points on the runway other than a runway or taxiway. Measured distance represents the available landing distance on the landing runway, in feet.

Specific questions regarding these distances should be referred to the air traffic manager of the facility concerned. The Aeronautical Information Manual contains specific details on hold–short operations and markings.

⑳ RUNWAY DECLARED DISTANCE INFORMATION

TORA—Take–off Run Available. The length of runway declared available and suitable for the ground run of an aeroplane take–off.
TODA—Take–off Distance Available. The length of the take–off run available plus the length of the clearway, if provided.
ASDA—Accelerate–Stop Distance Available. The length of the take–off run available plus the length of the stopway, if provided.
LDA—Landing Distance Available. The length of runway which is declared available and suitable for the ground run of an aeroplane landing.

㉑ ARRESTING GEAR/SYSTEMS

Arresting gear is shown as it is located on the runway. The a–gear distance from the end of the appropriate runway (or into the overrun) is indicated in parentheses. A–Gear which has a bi–direction capability and can be utilized for emergency approach end engagement is indicated by a (B). Up to 15 minutes advance notice may be required for rigging A–Gear for approach and engagement. Airport listing may show availability of other than US Systems. This information is provided for emergency requirements only. Refer to current aircraft operating manuals for specific engagement weight and speed criteria based on aircraft structural restrictions and arresting system limitations.

Following is a list of current systems referenced in this publication identified by both Air Force and Navy terminology:

BI–DIRECTIONAL CABLE (B)

TYPE	DESCRIPTION
BAK–9	Rotary friction brake.
BAK–12A	Standard BAK–12 with 950 foot run out, 1–inch cable and 40,000 pound weight setting. Rotary friction brake.
BAK–12B	Extended BAK–12 with 1200 foot run, 1¼ inch Cable and 50,000 pounds weight setting. Rotary friction brake.
E28	Rotary Hydraulic (Water Brake).
M21	Rotary Hydraulic (Water Brake) Mobile.

The following device is used in conjunction with some aircraft arresting systems:

BAK–14	A device that raises a hook cable out of a slot in the runway surface and is remotely positioned for engagement by the tower on request. (In addition to personnel reaction time, the system requires up to five seconds to fully raise the cable.)
H	A device that raises a hook cable out of a slot in the runway surface and is remotely positioned for engagement by the tower on request. (In addition to personnel reaction time, the system requires up to one and one–half seconds to fully raise the cable.)

UNI–DIRECTIONAL CABLE

TYPE	DESCRIPTION
MB60	Textile brake—an emergency one–time use, modular braking system employing the tearing of specially woven textile straps to absorb the kinetic energy.
E5/E5–1/E5–3	Chain Type. At USN/USMC stations E–5 A–GEAR systems are rated, e.g., E–5 RATING–13R–1100 HW (DRY), 31L/R–1200 STD (WET). This rating is a function of the A–GEAR chain weight and length and is used to determine the maximum aircraft engaging speed. A dry rating applies to a stabilized surface (dry or wet) while a wet rating takes into account the amount (if any) of wet overrun that is not capable of withstanding the aircraft weight. These ratings are published under Service/Military/A–Gear in the entry.

FOREIGN CABLE

TYPE	DESCRIPTION	US EQUIVALENT
44B–3H	Rotary Hydraulic (Water Brake)	
CHAG	Chain	E–5

UNI–DIRECTIONAL BARRIER

TYPE	DESCRIPTION
MA–1A	Web barrier between stanchions attached to a chain energy absorber.
BAK–15	Web barrier between stanchions attached to an energy absorber (water squeezer, rotary friction, chain). Designed for wing engagement.

NOTE: Landing short of the runway threshold on a runway with a BAK–15 in the underrun is a significant hazard. The barrier in the down position still protrudes several inches above the underrun. Aircraft contact with the barrier short of the runway threshold can cause damage to the barrier and substantial damage to the aircraft.

OTHER

TYPE	DESCRIPTION
EMAS	Engineered Material Arresting System, located beyond the departure end of the runway, consisting of high energy absorbing materials which will crush under the weight of an aircraft.

SC, 1 FEB 20XX to 29 MAR 20XX

Legend 9. Chart Supplement.

Appendix 1

20 AIRPORT/FACILITY DIRECTORY LEGEND

㉒ SERVICE

SERVICING—CIVIL

S1: Minor airframe repairs.
S2: Minor airframe and minor powerplant repairs.
S3: Major airframe and minor powerplant repairs.
S4: Major airframe and major powerplant repairs.
S5: Major airframe repairs.
S6: Minor airframe and major powerplant repairs.
S7: Major powerplant repairs.
S8: Minor powerplant repairs.

FUEL

CODE	FUEL	CODE	FUEL
80	Grade 80 gasoline (Red)	B	Jet B, Wide–cut, turbine fuel without FS–II*, FP** minus 50° C
100	Grade 100 gasoline (Green)		
100LL	100LL gasoline (low lead) (Blue)	B+	Jet B, Wide–cut, turbine fuel with FS–II*, FP** minus 50° C
115	Grade 115 gasoline (115/145 military specification) (Purple)	J4 (JP4)	(JP–4 military specification) FP** minus 58° C.
A	Jet A, Kerosene, without FS–II*, FP** minus 40° C.	J5 (JP5)	(JP–5 military specification) Kerosene with FS–II, FP** minus 46°C.
A+	Jet A, Kerosene, with FS–II*, FP** minus 40°C.	J8 (JP8)	(JP–8 military specification) Jet A–1, Kerosene with FS–II*, CI/LI#, SDA##, FP** minus 47°C.
A++	Jet A, Kerosene, with FS–II*, CI/LI#, SDA##, FP** minus 40°C.		
A++100	Jet A, Kerosene, with FS–II*, CI/LI#, SDA##, FP** minus 40°C, with +100 fuel additive that improves thermal stability characteristics of kerosene jet fuels.	J8+100	(JP–8 military specification) Jet A–1, Kerosene with FS–II*, CI/LI#, SDA##, FP** minus 47°C, with +100 fuel additive that improves thermal stability characteristics of kerosene jet fuels.
		J	(Jet Fuel Type Unknown)
A1	Jet A–1, Kerosene, without FS–II*, FP** minus 47°C.	MOGAS	Automobile gasoline which is to be used as aircraft fuel.
		UL91	Unleaded Grade 91 gasoline
A1+	Jet A–1, Kerosene with FS–II*, FP** minus 47° C.	UL94	Unleaded Grade 94 gasoline

*(Fuel System Icing Inhibitor)   **(Freeze Point)   # (Corrosion Inhibitors/Lubricity Improvers)   ## (Static Dissipator Additive)

NOTE: Certain automobile gasoline may be used in specific aircraft engines if a FAA supplemental type certificate has been obtained. Automobile gasoline, which is to be used in aircraft engines, will be identified as "MOGAS", however, the grade/type and other octane rating will not be published.

Data shown on fuel availability represents the most recent information the publisher has been able to acquire. Because of a variety of factors, the fuel listed may not always be obtainable by transient civil pilots. Confirmation of availability of fuel should be made directly with fuel suppliers at locations where refueling is planned.

OXYGEN—CIVIL

OX 1 High Pressure
OX 2 Low Pressure
OX 3 High Pressure—Replacement Bottles
OX 4 Low Pressure—Replacement Bottles

SERVICE—MILITARY

Specific military services available at the airport are listed under this general heading. Remarks applicable to any military service are shown in the individual service listing.

JET AIRCRAFT STARTING UNITS (JASU)—MILITARY

The numeral preceding the type of unit indicates the number of units available. The absence of the numeral indicates ten or more units available. If the number of units is unknown, the number one will be shown. Absence of JASU designation indicates non–availability.
The following is a list of current JASU systems referenced in this publication:

USAF JASU (For variations in technical data, refer to T.O. 35–1–7.)
ELECTRICAL STARTING UNITS:

A/M32A–86	AC: 115/200v, 3 phase, 90 kva, 0.8 pf, 4 wire
	DC: 28v, 1500 amp, 72 kw (with TR pack)
MC–1A	AC: 115/208v, 400 cycle, 3 phase, 37.5 kva, 0.8 pf, 108 amp, 4 wire
	DC: 28v, 500 amp, 14 kw
MD–3	AC: 115/208v, 400 cycle, 3 phase, 60 kva, 0.75 pf, 4 wire
	DC: 28v, 1500 amp, 45 kw, split bus
MD–3A	AC: 115/208v, 400 cycle, 3 phase, 60 kva, 0.75 pf, 4 wire
	DC: 28v, 1500 amp, 45 kw, split bus
MD–3M	AC: 115/208v, 400 cycle, 3 phase, 60 kva, 0.75 pf, 4 wire
	DC: 28v, 500 amp, 15 kw
MD–4	AC: 120/208v, 400 cycle, 3 phase, 62.5 kva, 0.8 pf, 175 amp, "WYE" neutral ground, 4 wire, 120v, 400 cycle, 3 phase, 62.5 kva, 0.8 pf, 303 amp, "DELTA" 3 wire, 120v, 400 cycle, 1 phase, 62.5 kva, 0.8 pf, 520 amp, 2 wire

SC, 1 FEB 20XX to 29 MAR 20XX

Legend 10. Chart Supplement.

AIRPORT/FACILITY DIRECTORY LEGEND

AIR STARTING UNITS
- AM32–95 — 150 +/– 5 lb/min (2055 +/– 68 cfm) at 51 +/– 2 psia
- AM32A–95 — 150 +/– 5 lb/min @ 49 +/– 2 psia (35 +/– 2 psig)
- LASS — 150 +/– 5 lb/min @ 49 +/– 2 psia
- MA–1A — 82 lb/min (1123 cfm) at 130° air inlet temp, 45 psia (min) air outlet press
- MC–1 — 15 cfm, 3500 psia
- MC–1A — 15 cfm, 3500 psia
- MC–2A — 15 cfm, 200 psia
- MC–11 — 8,000 cu in cap, 4000 psig, 15 cfm

COMBINED AIR AND ELECTRICAL STARTING UNITS:
- AGPU
  - AC: 115/200v, 400 cycle, 3 phase, 30 kw gen
  - DC: 28v, 700 amp
  - AIR: 60 lb/min @ 40 psig @ sea level
- AM32A–60*
  - AIR: 120 +/– 4 lb/min (1644 +/– 55 cfm) at 49 +/– 2 psia
  - AC: 120/208v, 400 cycle, 3 phase, 75 kva, 0.75 pf, 4 wire, 120v, 1 phase, 25 kva
  - DC: 28v, 500 amp, 15 kw
- AM32A–60A
  - AIR: 150 +/– 5 lb/min (2055 +/– 68 cfm at 51 +/– psia
  - AC: 120/208v, 400 cycle, 3 phase, 75 kva, 0.75 pf, 4 wire
  - DC: 28v, 200 amp, 5.6 kw
- AM32A–60B*
  - AIR: 130 lb/min, 50 psia
  - AC: 120/208v, 400 cycle, 3 phase, 75 kva, 0.75 pf, 4 wire
  - DC: 28v, 200 amp, 5.6 kw

*NOTE: During combined air and electrical loads, the pneumatic circuitry takes preference and will limit the amount of electrical power available.

USN JASU

ELECTRICAL STARTING UNITS:
- NC–8A/A1
  - DC: 500 amp constant, 750 amp intermittent, 28v;
  - AC: 60 kva @ .8 pf, 115/200v, 3 phase, 400 Hz.
- NC–10A/A1/B/C
  - DC: 750 amp constant, 1000 amp intermittent, 28v;
  - AC: 90 kva, 115/200v, 3 phase, 400 Hz.

AIR STARTING UNITS:
- GTC–85/GTE–85 — 120 lbs/min @ 45 psi.
- MSU–200NAV/A/U47A–5 — 204 lbs/min @ 56 psia.
- WELLS AIR START SYSTEM — 180 lbs/min @ 75 psi or 120 lbs/min @ 45 psi. Simultaneous multiple start capability.

COMBINED AIR AND ELECTRICAL STARTING UNITS:
- NCPP–105/RCPT — 180 lbs/min @ 75 psi or 120 lbs/min @ 45 psi. 700 amp, 28v DC. 120/208v, 400 Hz AC, 30 kva.

ARMY JASU
- 59B2–1B — 28v, 7.5 kw, 280 amp.

OTHER JASU

ELECTRICAL STARTING UNITS (DND):
- CE12 — AC 115/200v, 140 kva, 400 Hz, 3 phase
- CE13 — AC 115/200v, 60 kva, 400 Hz, 3 phase
- CE14 — AC/DC 115/200v, 140 kva, 400 Hz, 3 phase, 28vDC, 1500 amp
- CE15 — DC 22–35v, 500 amp continuous 1100 amp intermittent
- CE16 — DC 22–35v, 500 amp continuous 1100 amp intermittent soft start

AIR STARTING UNITS (DND):
- CA2 — ASA 45.5 psig, 116.4 lb/min

COMBINED AIR AND ELECTRICAL STARTING UNITS (DND)
- CEA1
  - AC 120/208v, 60 kva, 400 Hz, 3 phase DC 28v, 75 amp
  - AIR 112.5 lb/min, 47 psig

ELECTRICAL STARTING UNITS (OTHER)
- C–26 — 28v 45kw 115–200v 15kw 380–800 Hz 1 phase 2 wire
- C–26–B, C–26–C — 28v 45kw: Split Bus: 115–200v 15kw 380–800 Hz 1 phase 2 wire
- E3 — DC 28v/10kw

AIR STARTING UNITS (OTHER):
- A4 — 40 psi/2 lb/sec (LPAS Mk12, Mk12L, Mk12A, Mk1, Mk2B)
- MA–1 — 150 Air HP, 115 lb/min 50 psia
- MA–2 — 250 Air HP, 150 lb/min 75 psia

CARTRIDGE:
- MXU–4A — USAF

SC, 1 FEB 20XX to 29 MAR 20XX

Legend 11. Chart Supplement.

Appendix 1

22   **AIRPORT/FACILITY DIRECTORY LEGEND**

FUEL—MILITARY

Fuel available through US Military Base supply, DESC Into–Plane Contracts and/or reciprocal agreement is listed first and is followed by (Mil). At commercial airports where Into–Plane contracts are in place, the name of the refueling agent is shown. Military fuel should be used first if it is available. When military fuel cannot be obtained but Into–Plane contract fuel is available, Government aircraft must refuel with the contract fuel and applicable refueling agent to avoid any breach in contract terms and conditions. Fuel not available through the above is shown preceded by NC (no contract). When fuel is obtained from NC sources, local purchase procedures must be followed. The US Military Aircraft Identaplates DD Form 1896 (Jet Fuel), DD Form 1897 (Avgas) and AF Form 1245 (Avgas) are used at military installations only. The US Government Aviation Into–Plane Reimbursement (AIR) Card (currently issued by AVCARD) is the instrument to be used to obtain fuel under a DESC Into–Plane Contract and for NC purchases if the refueling agent at the commercial airport accepts the AVCARD. A current list of contract fuel locations is available online at https://cis.energy.dla.mil/ip_cis/. See legend item 14 for fuel code and description.

SUPPORTING FLUIDS AND SYSTEMS—MILITARY

CODE	
ADI	Anti–Detonation Injection Fluid—Reciprocating Engine Aircraft.
W	Water Thrust Augmentation—Jet Aircraft.
WAI	Water–Alcohol Injection Type, Thrust Augmentation—Jet Aircraft.
SP	Single Point Refueling.
PRESAIR	Air Compressors rated 3,000 PSI or more.
De–Ice	Anti–icing/De–icing/Defrosting Fluid (MIL–A–8243).

OXYGEN:

LPOX	Low pressure oxygen servicing.
HPOX	High pressure oxygen servicing.
LHOX	Low and high pressure oxygen servicing.
LOX	Liquid oxygen servicing.
OXRB	Oxygen replacement bottles. (Maintained primarily at Naval stations for use in acft where oxygen can be replenished only by replacement of cylinders.)
OX	Indicates oxygen servicing when type of servicing is unknown.

NOTE: Combinations of above items is used to indicate complete oxygen servicing available;

LHOXRB	Low and high pressure oxygen servicing and replacement bottles;
LPOXRB	Low pressure oxygen replacement bottles only, etc.

NOTE: Aircraft will be serviced with oxygen procured under military specifications only. Aircraft will not be serviced with medical oxygen.

NITROGEN:

LPNIT — Low pressure nitrogen servicing.
HPNIT — High pressure nitrogen servicing.
LHNIT — Low and high pressure nitrogen servicing.

OIL—MILITARY

US AVIATION OILS (MIL SPECS):

CODE	GRADE, TYPE
O–113	1065, Reciprocating Engine Oil (MIL–L–6082)
O–117	1100, Reciprocating Engine Oil (MIL–L–6082)
O–117+	1100, O–117 plus cyclohexanone (MIL–L–6082)
O–123	1065, (Dispersant), Reciprocating Engine Oil (MIL–L–22851 Type III)
O–128	1100, (Dispersant), Reciprocating Engine Oil (MIL–L–22851 Type II)
O–132	1005, Jet Engine Oil (MIL–L–6081)
O–133	1010, Jet Engine Oil (MIL–L–6081)
O–147	None, MIL–L–6085A Lubricating Oil, Instrument, Synthetic
O–148	None, MIL–L–7808 (Synthetic Base) Turbine Engine Oil
O–149	None, Aircraft Turbine Engine Synthetic, 7.5c St
O–155	None, MIL–L–6086C, Aircraft, Medium Grade
O–156	None, MIL–L–23699 (Synthetic Base), Turboprop and Turboshaft Engines
JOAP/SOAP	Joint Oil Analysis Program. JOAP support is furnished during normal duty hours, other times on request. (JOAP and SOAP programs provide essentially the same service, JOAP is now the standard joint service supported program.)

TRANSIENT ALERT (TRAN ALERT)—MILITARY

Tran Alert service is considered to include all services required for normal aircraft turn–around, e.g., servicing (fuel, oil, oxygen, etc.), debriefing to determine requirements for maintenance, minor maintenance, inspection and parking assistance of transient aircraft. Drag chute repack, specialized maintenance, or extensive repairs will be provided within the capabilities and priorities of the base. Delays can be anticipated after normal duty hours/holidays/weekends regardless of the hours of transient maintenance operation. Pilots should not expect aircraft to be serviced for TURN–AROUNDS during time periods when servicing or maintenance manpower is not available. In the case of airports not operated exclusively by US military, the servicing indicated by the remarks will not always be available for US military aircraft. When transient alert services are not shown, facilities are unknown. NO PRIORITY BASIS—means that transient alert services will be provided only after all the requirements for mission/tactical assigned aircraft have been accomplished.

SC, 1 FEB 20XX to 29 MAR 20XX

Legend 12. Chart Supplement.

Appendix 1

AIRPORT/FACILITY DIRECTORY LEGEND 23

㉓ AIRPORT REMARKS

The Attendance Schedule is the months, days and hours the airport is actually attended. Airport attendance does not mean watchman duties or telephone accessibility, but rather an attendant or operator on duty to provide at least minimum services (e.g., repairs, fuel, transportation).

Airport Remarks have been grouped in order of applicability. Airport remarks are limited to those items of information that are determined essential for operational use, i.e., conditions of a permanent or indefinite nature and conditions that will remain in effect for more than 30 days concerning aeronautical facilities, services, maintenance available, procedures or hazards, knowledge of which is essential for safe and efficient operation of aircraft. Information concerning permanent closing of a runway or taxiway will not be shown. A note "See Special Notices" shall be applied within this remarks section when a special notice applicable to the entry is contained in the Special Notices section of this publication.

Parachute Jumping indicates parachute jumping areas associated with the airport. See Parachute Jumping Area section of this publication for additional Information.

Landing Fee indicates landing charges for private or non-revenue producing aircraft. In addition, fees may be charged for planes that remain over a couple of hours and buy no services, or at major airline terminals for all aircraft.

Note: Unless otherwise stated, remarks including runway ends refer to the runway's approach end.

㉔ MILITARY REMARKS

Joint Civil/Military airports contain both Airport Remarks and Military Remarks. Military Remarks published for these airports are applicable only to the military. Military and joint Military/Civil airports contain only Military Remarks. Remarks contained in this section may not be applicable to civil users. When both sets of remarks exist, the first set is applicable to the primary operator of the airport. Remarks applicable to a tenant on the airport are shown preceded by the tenant organization, i.e., (A) (AF) (N) (ANG), etc. Military airports operate 24 hours unless otherwise specified. Airport operating hours are listed first (airport operating hours will only be listed if they are different than the airport attended hours or if the attended hours are unavailable) followed by pertinent remarks in order of applicability. Remarks will include information on restrictions, hazards, traffic pattern, noise abatement, customs/agriculture/immigration, and miscellaneous information applicable to the Military.

Type of restrictions:

CLOSED: When designated closed, the airport is restricted from use by all aircraft unless stated otherwise. Any closure applying to specific type of aircraft or operation will be so stated. USN/USMC/USAF airports are considered closed during non-operating hours. Closed airports may be utilized during an emergency provided there is a safe landing area.

OFFICIAL BUSINESS ONLY: The airfield is closed to all transient military aircraft for obtaining routine services such as fueling, passenger drop off or pickup, practice approaches, parking, etc. The airfield may be used by aircrews and aircraft if official government business (including civilian) must be conducted on or near the airfield and prior permission is received from the airfield manager.

AF OFFICIAL BUSINESS ONLY OR NAVY OFFICIAL BUSINESS ONLY: Indicates that the restriction applies only to service indicated.

PRIOR PERMISSION REQUIRED (PPR): Airport is closed to transient aircraft unless approval for operation is obtained from the appropriate commander through Chief, Airfield Management or Airfield Operations Officer. Official Business or PPR does not preclude the use of US Military airports as an alternate for IFR flights. If a non-US military airport is used as a weather alternate and requires a PPR, the PPR must be requested and confirmed before the flight departs. The purpose of PPR is to control volume and flow of traffic rather than to prohibit it. Prior permission is required for all aircraft requiring transient alert service outside the published transient alert duty hours. All aircraft carrying hazardous materials must obtain prior permission as outlined in AFJI 11-204, AR 95-27, OPNAVINST 3710.7.

Note: OFFICIAL BUSINESS ONLY AND PPR restrictions are not applicable to Special Air Mission (SAM) or Special Air Resource (SPAR) aircraft providing person or persons on aboard are designated Code 6 or higher as explained in AFJMAN 11-213, AR 95-11, OPNAVINST 3722-8J. Official Business Only or PPR do not preclude the use of the airport as an alternate for IFR flights.

㉕ AIRPORT MANAGER

The phone number of the airport manager.

㉖ WEATHER DATA SOURCES

Weather data sources will be listed alphabetically followed by their assigned frequencies and/or telephone number and hours of operation.

ASOS—Automated Surface Observing System. Reports the same as an AWOS-3 plus precipitation identification and intensity, and freezing rain occurrence;

AWOS—Automated Weather Observing System

AWOS-A—reports altimeter setting (all other information is advisory only).

AWOS-AV—reports altimeter and visibility.

AWOS-1—reports altimeter setting, wind data and usually temperature, dew point and density altitude.

AWOS-2—reports the same as AWOS-1 plus visibility.

AWOS-3—reports the same as AWOS-1 plus visibility and cloud/ceiling data.

AWOS-3P reports the same as the AWOS-3 system, plus a precipitation identification sensor.

AWOS-3PT reports the same as the AWOS-3 system, plus precipitation identification sensor and a thunderstorm/lightning reporting capability.

SC, 1 FEB 20XX to 29 MAR 20XX

Legend 13. Chart Supplement.

Appendix 1

24   **AIRPORT/FACILITY DIRECTORY LEGEND**

    AWOS–3T reports the same as AWOS–3 system and includes a thunderstorm/lightning reporting capability.
      See AIM, Basic Flight Information and ATC Procedures for detailed description of Weather Data Sources.
    AWOS–4—reports same as AWOS–3 system, plus precipitation occurrence, type and accumulation, freezing rain, thunderstorm and runway surface sensors.
    HIWAS—See RADIO AIDS TO NAVIGATION
    LAWRS—Limited Aviation Weather Reporting Station where observers report cloud height, weather, obstructions to vision, temperature and dewpoint (in most cases), surface wind, altimeter and pertinent remarks.
    LLWAS—indicates a Low Level Wind Shear Alert System consisting of a center field and several field perimeter anemometers.
    SAWRS—identifies airports that have a Supplemental Aviation Weather Reporting Station available to pilots for current weather information.
    SWSL—Supplemental Weather Service Location providing current local weather information via radio and telephone.
    TDWR—indicates airports that have Terminal Doppler Weather Radar.
    WSP—indicates airports that have Weather System Processor.
    When the automated weather source is broadcast over an associated airport NAVAID frequency (see NAVAID line), it shall be indicated by a bold ASOS, AWOS, or HIWAS followed by the frequency, identifier and phone number, if available.

㉗ COMMUNICATIONS

Airport terminal control facilities and radio communications associated with the airport shall be shown. When the call sign is not the same as the airport name the call sign will be shown. Frequencies shall normally be shown in descending order with the primary frequency listed first. Frequencies will be listed, together with sectorization indicated by outbound radials, and hours of operation. Communications will be listed in sequence as follows:
Single Frequency Approach (SFA), Common Traffic Advisory Frequency (CTAF), Aeronautical Advisory Stations (UNICOM) or (AUNICOM), and Automatic Terminal Information Service (ATIS) along with their frequency is shown, where available, on the line following the heading "COMMUNICATIONS." When the CTAF and UNICOM frequencies are the same, the frequency will be shown as CTAF/UNICOM 122.8.
The FSS telephone nationwide is toll free 1–800–WX–BRIEF (1–800–992–7433). When the FSS is located on the field it will be indicated as "on arpt". Frequencies available at the FSS will follow in descending order. Remote Communications Outlet (RCO) providing service to the airport followed by the frequency and FSS RADIO name will be shown when available. FSS's provide information on airport conditions, radio aids and other facilities, and process flight plans. Airport Advisory Service (AAS) is provided on the CTAF by FSS's for select non–tower airports or airports where the tower is not in operation.
(See AIM, Para 4–1–9 Traffic Advisory Practices at Airports Without Operating Control Towers or AC 90–42C.)
Aviation weather briefing service is provided by FSS specialists. Flight and weather briefing services are also available by calling the telephone numbers listed.
Remote Communications Outlet (RCO)—An unmanned air/ground communications facility that is remotely controlled and provides UHF or VHF communications capability to extend the service range of an FSS.
Civil Communications Frequencies–Civil communications frequencies used in the FSS air/ground system are operated on 122.0, 122.2, 123.6; emergency 121.5; plus receive–only on 122.1.

    a. 122.0 is assigned as the Enroute Flight Advisory Service frequency at selected FSS RADIO outlets.
    b. 122.2 is assigned as a common enroute frequency.
    c. 123.6 is assigned as the airport advisory frequency at select non–tower locations. At airports with a tower, FSS may provide airport advisories on the tower frequency when tower is closed.
    d. 122.1 is the primary receive–only frequency at VOR's.
    e. Some FSS's are assigned 50 kHz frequencies in the 122–126 MHz band (eg. 122.45). Pilots using the FSS A/G system should refer to this directory or appropriate charts to determine frequencies available at the FSS or remoted facility through which they wish to communicate.

Emergency frequency 121.5 and 243.0 are available at all Flight Service Stations, most Towers, Approach Control and RADAR facilities.

Frequencies published followed by the letter "T" or "R", indicate that the facility will only transmit or receive respectively on that frequency. All radio aids to navigation (NAVAID) frequencies are transmit only. In cases where communications frequencies are annotated with (R) or (E), (R) indicates Radar Capability and (E) indicates Emergency Frequency.

TERMINAL SERVICES

    SFA—Single Frequency Approach.
    CTAF—A program designed to get all vehicles and aircraft at airports without an operating control tower on a common frequency.
    ATIS—A continuous broadcast of recorded non–control information in selected terminal areas.
    D–ATIS—Digital ATIS provides ATIS information in text form outside the standard reception range of conventional ATIS via landline & data link communications and voice message within range of existing transmitters.
    AUNICOM—Automated UNICOM is a computerized, command response system that provides automated weather, radio check capability and airport advisory information selected from an automated menu by microphone clicks.
    UNICOM—A non–government air/ground radio communications facility which may provide airport information.
    PTD—Pilot to Dispatcher.
    APP CON—Approach Control. The symbol ⓡ indicates radar approach control.
    TOWER—Control tower.
    GCA—Ground Control Approach System.
    GND CON—Ground Control.

SC, 1 FEB 20XX to 29 MAR 20XX

Legend 14. Chart Supplement.

AIRPORT/FACILITY DIRECTORY LEGEND

GCO—Ground Communication Outlet—An unstaffed, remotely controlled, ground/ground communications facility. Pilots at uncontrolled airports may contact ATC and FSS via VHF to a telephone connection to obtain an instrument clearance or close a VFR or IFR flight plan. They may also get an updated weather briefing prior to takeoff. Pilots will use four "key clicks" on the VHF radio to contact the appropriate ATC facility or six "key clicks" to contact the FSS. The GCO system is intended to be used only on the ground.

DEP CON—Departure Control. The symbol ® indicates radar departure control.

CLNC DEL—Clearance Delivery.

CPDLC—Controller Pilot Data Link Communication. FANS ATC data communication capability from the aircraft to the ATC Data Link system.

PRE TAXI CLNC—Pre taxi clearance.

VFR ADVSY SVC—VFR Advisory Service. Service provided by Non-Radar Approach Control.
  Advisory Service for VFR aircraft (upon a workload basis) ctc APP CON.

COMD POST—Command Post followed by the operator call sign in parenthesis.

PMSV—Pilot-to-Metro Service call sign, frequency and hours of operation, when full service is other than continuous. PMSV installations at which weather observation service is available shall be indicated, following the frequency and/or hours of operation as "Wx obsn svc 1900–0000Z‡" or "other times" may be used when no specific time is given. PMSV facilities manned by forecasters are considered "Full Service". PMSV facilities manned by weather observers are listed as "Limited Service".

OPS—Operations followed by the operator call sign in parenthesis.

CON

RANGE

FLT FLW—Flight Following

MEDIVAC

NOTE: Communication frequencies followed by the letter "X" indicate frequency available on request.

㉘ AIRSPACE

Information concerning Class B, C, and part-time D and E surface area airspace shall be published with effective times, if available.

CLASS B—Radar Sequencing and Separation Service for all aircraft in CLASS B airspace.

CLASS C—Separation between IFR and VFR aircraft and sequencing of VFR arrivals to the primary airport.

TRSA—Radar Sequencing and Separation Service for participating VFR Aircraft within a Terminal Radar Service Area.

Class C, D, and E airspace described in this publication is that airspace usually consisting of a 5 NM radius core surface area that begins at the surface and extends upward to an altitude above the airport elevation (charted in MSL for Class C and Class D). Class E surface airspace normally extends from the surface up to but not including the overlying controlled airspace.

When part-time Class C or Class D airspace defaults to Class E, the core surface area becomes Class E. This will be formatted as:
AIRSPACE: CLASS C svc "times" ctc **APP CON** other times CLASS E:
or
AIRSPACE: CLASS D svc "times" other times CLASS E.

When a part-time Class C, Class D or Class E surface area defaults to Class G, the core surface area becomes Class G up to, but not including, the overlying controlled airspace. Normally, the overlying controlled airspace is Class E airspace beginning at either 700´ or 1200´ AGL and may be determined by consulting the relevant VFR Sectional or Terminal Area Charts. This will be formatted as:
AIRSPACE: CLASS C svc "times" ctc **APP CON** other times CLASS G, with CLASS E 700´ (or 1200´) AGL & abv:
or
AIRSPACE: CLASS D svc "times" other times CLASS G with CLASS E 700´ (or 1200´) AGL & abv:
or
AIRSPACE: CLASS E svc "times" other times CLASS G with CLASS E 700´ (or 1200´) AGL & abv.

NOTE: AIRSPACE SVC "TIMES" INCLUDE ALL ASSOCIATED ARRIVAL EXTENSIONS. Surface area arrival extensions for instrument approach procedures become part of the primary core surface area. These extensions may be either Class D or Class E airspace and are effective concurrent with the times of the primary core surface area. For example, when a part-time Class C, Class D or Class E surface area defaults to Class G, the associated arrival extensions will default to Class G at the same time. When a part-time Class C or Class D surface area defaults to Class E, the arrival extensions will remain in effect as Class E airspace.

NOTE: CLASS E AIRSPACE EXTENDING UPWARD FROM 700 FEET OR MORE ABOVE THE SURFACE, DESIGNATED IN CONJUNCTION WITH AN AIRPORT WITH AN APPROVED INSTRUMENT PROCEDURE.
Class E 700´ AGL (shown as magenta vignette on sectional charts) and 1200´ AGL (blue vignette) areas are designated when necessary to provide controlled airspace for transitioning to/from the terminal and enroute environments. Unless otherwise specified, these 700´/1200´ AGL Class E airspace areas remain in effect continuously, regardless of airport operating hours or surface area status. These transition areas should not be confused with surface areas or arrival extensions.

(See Chapter 3, AIRSPACE, in the Aeronautical Information Manual for further details)

SC, 1 FEB 20XX to 29 MAR 20XX

Legend 15. Chart Supplement.

26   **AIRPORT/FACILITY DIRECTORY LEGEND**

㉙ VOR TEST FACILITY (VOT)

The VOT transmits a signal which provided users a convenient means to determine the operational status and accuracy of an aircraft VOR receiver while on the ground. Ground based VOTs and the associated frequency shall be shown when available. VOTs are also shown with identifier, frequency and referenced remarks in the VOR Receiver Check section in the back of this publication.

㉚ RADIO AIDS TO NAVIGATION

The Airport/Facility Directory section of the Chart Supplement lists, by facility name, all Radio Aids to Navigation that appear on FAA, Aeronautical Information Services Visual or IFR Aeronautical Charts and those upon which the FAA has approved an Instrument Approach Procedure, with exception of selected TACANs. All VOR, VORTAC, TACAN and ILS equipment in the National Airspace System has an automatic monitoring and shutdown feature in the event of malfunction. Unmonitored, as used in this publication, for any navigational aid, means that monitoring personnel cannot observe the malfunction or shutdown signal. The NAVAID NOTAM file identifier will be shown as "NOTAM FILE IAD" and will be listed on the Radio Aids to Navigation line. When two or more NAVAIDS are listed and the NOTAM file identifier is different from that shown on the Radio Aids to Navigation line, it will be shown with the NAVAID listing. NOTAM file identifiers for ILSs and its components (e.g., NDB (LOM) are the same as the associated airports and are not repeated. Automated Surface Observing System (ASOS), Automated Weather Observing System (AWOS), and Hazardous Inflight Weather Advisory Service (HIWAS) will be shown when this service is broadcast over selected NAVAIDs.

NAVAID information is tabulated as indicated in the following sample:

```
                    TACAN/DME Channel    Geographical Position              Site Elevation   Magnetic Variation
                            ↓                    ↓                                ↓              ↓
NAME (L) ABVORTAC  117.55   ABE   Chan 122(Y)   N40°43.60' W75°27.30'   180° 4.1 NM to fld.   1110/8E   AWOS.  HIWAS.
    ↑         ↑      ↑                                                           ↑              ↑         ↑
  Class   Frequency  Identifier                            Bearing and distance           Automated   Hazardous
                                                         facility to center of airport     Weather     Inflight
                                                                                          Observing    Weather
                                                                                           System      Service

          VOR unusable 020°–060° byd 26 NM blo 3,500'
                          ↑
          Restriction within the normal altitude/range of the navigational aid
          (See primary alphabetical listing for restrictions on VORTAC and VOR/DME).
```

Note: Those DME channel numbers with a (Y) suffix require TACAN to be placed in the "Y" mode to receive distance information.

HIWAS—Hazardous Inflight Weather Advisory Service is a continuous broadcast of inflight weather advisories including summarized SIGMETs, convective SIGMETs, AIRMETs and urgent PIREPs. HIWAS is presently broadcast over selected VOR's throughout the U.S.

ASR/PAR—Indicates that Surveillance (ASR) or Precision (PAR) radar instrument approach minimums are published in the U.S. Terminal Procedures. Only part–time hours of operation will be shown.

SC, 1 FEB 20XX to 29 MAR 20XX

Legend 16. Chart Supplement.

Appendix 2

Appendix 2

Figure 1. Drag vs. Velocity.

GROSS WEIGHT 2,750 LB		ANGLE OF BANK			
		LEVEL	30°	45°	60°
POWER		GEAR AND FLAPS UP			
ON	MPH	62	67	74	88
	KTS	54	58	64	76
OFF	MPH	75	81	89	106
	KTS	65	70	77	92
		GEAR AND FLAPS DOWN			
ON	MPH	54	58	64	76
	KTS	47	50	56	66
OFF	MPH	66	71	78	93
	KTS	57	62	68	81

Figure 2. Stall Speeds.

2-1

Appendix 2

Figure 3. Angle of Attack vs. Lift.

Appendix 2

Figure 3A. Maximum Glide Distance.

Figure 4. Stall Speed vs. Load Factor.

Figure 5. Velocity vs. Load Factor.

Figure 6. Adiabatic Chart.

Figure 8. Fuel Consumption vs. Brake Horsepower.

Appendix 2

NORMAL CLIMB—100 KIAS

CONDITIONS:
FLAPS UP
GEAR UP
2,550 RPM
25 INCHES MP OR FULL THROTTLE
COWL FLAPS OPEN
STANDARD TEMPERATURE

MIXTURE SETTING	
PRESS ALT	PPH
S.L. to 4,000	108
8,000	96
12,000	84

NOTES:
1. INCREASE TIME, FUEL, AND DISTANCE BY 10% FOR EACH 10 °C ABOVE STANDARD TEMPERATURE.
2. ADD 12 POUNDS OF FUEL FOR ENGINE START, TAXI, AND TAKEOFF ALLOWANCE.
3. DISTANCES SHOWN ARE BASED ON ZERO WIND.

WEIGHT (LB)	PRESS ALT (FT)	RATE OF CLIMB (FPM)	FROM SEA LEVEL TIME (MIN)	FROM SEA LEVEL FUEL USED (LB)	FROM SEA LEVEL DISTANCE (NM)
3,800	S.L.	580	0	0	0
	2,000	580	3	6	6
	4,000	570	7	12	12
	6,000	470	11	19	19
	8,000	365	16	27	28
	10,000	265	22	37	40
	12,000	165	32	51	59
3,500	S.L.	685	0	0	0
	2,000	685	3	5	5
	4,000	675	6	11	10
	6,000	565	9	16	16
	8,000	455	13	23	23
	10,000	350	18	31	33
	12,000	240	25	41	46
3,200	S.L.	800	0	0	0
	2,000	800	2	4	4
	4,000	795	5	9	8
	6,000	675	8	14	13
	8,000	560	11	19	19
	10,000	445	15	25	27
	12,000	325	20	33	37

Figure 9. Fuel, Time, and Distance to Climb.

Appendix 2

MAXIMUM RATE OF CLIMB

CONDITIONS:
FLAPS UP
GEAR UP
2,700 RPM
FULL THROTTLE
MIXTURE SET AT PLACARD FUEL FLOW
COWL FLAPS OPEN
STANDARD TEMPERATURE

MIXTURE SETTING	
PRESS ALT	PPH
S.L.	138
4,000	126
8,000	114
12,000	102

NOTES:
1. ADD 12 POUNDS OF FUEL FOR ENGINE START, TAXI, AND TAKEOFF ALLOWANCE.
2. INCREASE TIME, FUEL, AND DISTANCE BY 10% FOR EACH 10 °C ABOVE STANDARD TEMPERATURE.
3. DISTANCES SHOWN ARE BASED ON ZERO WIND.

WEIGHT (LB)	PRESS ALT (FT)	CLIMB SPEED (KIAS)	RATE OF CLIMB (FPM)	FROM SEA LEVEL — TIME (MIN)	FROM SEA LEVEL — FUEL USED (LB)	FROM SEA LEVEL — DISTANCE (NM)
3,800	S.L.	97	860	0	0	0
	2,000	95	760	2	6	4
	4,000	94	660	5	12	9
	6,000	93	565	9	18	14
	8,000	91	465	13	26	21
	10,000	90	365	18	35	29
	12,000	89	265	24	47	41
3,500	S.L.	95	990	0	0	0
	2,000	94	885	2	5	3
	4,000	93	780	5	10	7
	6,000	91	675	7	16	12
	8,000	90	570	11	22	17
	10,000	89	465	15	29	24
	12,000	87	360	20	38	32
3,200	S.L.	94	1,135	0	0	0
	2,000	92	1,020	2	4	3
	4,000	91	910	4	9	6
	6,000	90	800	6	14	10
	8,000	88	685	9	19	14
	10,000	87	575	12	25	20
	12,000	86	465	16	32	26

Figure 10. Fuel, Time, and Distance to Climb.

Appendix 2

GROSS WEIGHT – 2,300 LB
STANDARD CONDITIONS
ZERO WIND LEAN MIXTURE

NOTE: MAXIMUM CRUISE IS NORMALLY LIMITED TO 75% POWER.

ALT.	RPM	% BHP	TAS MPH	GAL/ HOUR	38 GAL (NO RESERVE) ENDR (HOURS)	38 GAL (NO RESERVE) RANGE (MILES)	48 GAL (NO RESERVE) ENDR (HOURS)	48 GAL (NO RESERVE) RANGE (MILES)
2,500	2,700	86	134	9.7	3.9	525	4.9	660
	2,600	79	129	8.6	4.4	570	5.6	720
	2,500	72	123	7.8	4.9	600	6.2	760
	2,400	65	117	7.2	5.3	620	6.7	780
	2,300	58	111	6.7	5.7	630	7.2	795
	2,200	52	103	6.3	6.1	625	7.7	790
5,000	2,700	82	134	9.0	4.2	565	5.3	710
	2,600	75	128	8.1	4.7	600	5.9	760
	2,500	68	122	7.4	5.1	625	6.4	790
	2,400	61	116	6.9	5.5	635	6.9	805
	2,300	55	108	6.5	5.9	635	7.4	805
	2,200	49	100	6.0	6.3	630	7.9	795
7,500	2,700	78	133	8.4	4.5	600	5.7	755
	2,600	71	127	7.7	4.9	625	6.2	790
	2,500	64	121	7.1	5.3	645	6.7	810
	2,400	58	113	6.7	5.7	645	7.2	820
	2,300	52	105	6.2	6.1	640	7.7	810
10,000	2,650	70	129	7.6	5.0	640	6.3	810
	2,600	67	125	7.3	5.2	650	6.5	820
	2,500	61	118	6.9	5.5	655	7.0	830
	2,400	55	110	6.4	5.9	650	7.5	825
	2,300	49	100	6.0	6.3	635	8.0	800

Figure 11. Cruise and Range Performance.

Appendix 2

PRESSURE ALTITUDE – 18,000 FEET

CONDITIONS:
4,000 POUNDS
RECOMMENDED LEAN MIXTURE
COWL FLAPS CLOSED

NOTES:
FOR BEST FUEL ECONOMY AT 70% POWER OR LESS, OPERATE AT 6 PPH LEANER THAN SHOWN IN THIS CHART OR AT PEAK EGT.

RPM	MP	20 °C BELOW STANDARD TEMPERATURE −41 °C % BHP	KTAS	PPH	STANDARD TEMPERATURE −21 °C % BHP	KTAS	PPH	20 °C ABOVE STANDARD TEMP −1 °C % BHP	KTAS	PPH
2,500	30	---	---	---	81	188	106	76	185	100
	28	80	184	105	76	182	99	71	178	93
	26	75	178	99	71	176	93	67	172	88
	24	70	171	91	66	168	86	62	164	81
	22	63	162	84	60	159	79	56	155	75
2,400	30	81	185	107	77	183	101	72	180	94
	28	76	179	100	72	177	94	67	173	88
	26	71	172	93	67	170	88	63	166	83
	24	66	165	87	62	163	82	58	159	77
	22	61	158	80	57	155	76	54	150	72
2,300	30	79	182	103	74	180	97	70	176	91
	28	74	176	97	70	174	91	65	170	86
	26	69	170	91	65	167	86	61	163	81
	24	64	162	84	60	159	79	56	155	75
	22	58	154	77	55	150	73	51	145	65
2,200	26	66	166	87	62	163	82	58	159	77
	24	61	158	80	57	154	76	54	150	72
	22	55	148	73	51	144	69	48	138	66
	20	49	136	66	46	131	63	43	124	59

Figure 12. Cruise Performance.

Appendix 2

MAXIMUM RATE OF CLIMB

CONDITIONS:
FLAPS UP
GEAR UP
2,600 RPM
COWL FLAPS OPEN
STANDARD TEMPERATURE

MIXTURE SETTING		
PRESS ALT	MP	PPH
S.L. TO 17,000	35	162
18,000	34	156
20,000	32	144
22,000	30	132
24,000	28	120

NOTES:
1. ADD 16 POUNDS OF FUEL FOR ENGINE START, TAXI, AND TAKEOFF ALLOWANCE.
2. INCREASE TIME, FUEL, AND DISTANCE BY 10% FOR EACH 10 °C ABOVE STANDARD TEMPERATURE.
3. DISTANCES SHOWN ARE BASED ON ZERO WIND.

WEIGHT (LB)	PRESS ALT (FT)	CLIMB SPEED (KIAS)	RATE OF CLIMB (FPM)	FROM SEA LEVEL TIME (MIN)	FROM SEA LEVEL FUEL USED (LB)	FROM SEA LEVEL DISTANCE (NM)
4,000	S.L.	100	930	0	0	0
	4,000	100	890	4	12	7
	8,000	100	845	9	24	16
	12,000	100	790	14	38	25
	16,000	100	720	19	52	36
	20,000	99	515	26	69	50
	24,000	97	270	37	92	74
3,700	S.L.	99	1,060	0	0	0
	4,000	99	1,020	4	10	6
	8,000	99	975	8	21	13
	12,000	99	915	12	33	21
	16,000	99	845	17	45	30
	20,000	97	630	22	59	42
	24,000	95	370	30	77	60
3,400	S.L.	97	1,205	0	0	0
	4,000	97	1,165	3	9	5
	8,000	97	1,120	7	19	12
	12,000	97	1,060	11	29	18
	16,000	97	985	15	39	26
	20,000	96	760	19	51	36
	24,000	94	485	26	65	50

Figure 13. Fuel, Time, and Distance to Climb.

Appendix 2

NORMAL CLIMB – 110 KIAS

CONDITIONS:
FLAPS UP
GEAR UP
2,500 RPM
30 INCHES HG
120 PPH FUEL FLOW
COWL FLAPS OPEN
STANDARD TEMPERATURE

NOTES:
1. ADD 16 POUNDS OF FUEL FOR ENGINE START, TAXI, AND TAKEOFF ALLOWANCE.
2. INCREASE TIME, FUEL, AND DISTANCE BY 10% FOR EACH 7 °C ABOVE STANDARD TEMPERATURE.
3. DISTANCES SHOWN ARE BASED ON ZERO WIND.

WEIGHT (LB)	PRESS ALT (FT)	RATE OF CLIMB (FPM)	FROM SEA LEVEL TIME (MIN)	FROM SEA LEVEL FUEL USED (LB)	FROM SEA LEVEL DISTANCE (NM)
4,000	S.L.	605	0	0	0
	4,000	570	7	14	13
	8,000	530	14	28	27
	12,000	485	22	44	43
	16,000	430	31	62	63
	20,000	365	41	82	87
3,700	S.L.	700	0	0	0
	4,000	665	6	12	11
	8,000	625	12	24	23
	12,000	580	19	37	37
	16,000	525	26	52	53
	20,000	460	34	68	72
3,400	S.L.	810	0	0	0
	4,000	775	5	10	9
	8,000	735	10	21	20
	12,000	690	16	32	31
	16,000	635	22	44	45
	20,000	565	29	57	61

Figure 14. Fuel, Time, and Distance to Climb.

Figure 15. Fuel, Time, and Distance to Climb.

Appendix 2

UPPER LUBBER LINE
Indicates magnetic heading of aircraft.

BEARING POINTER
Indicates magnetic bearing from aircraft to navigational aid selected.

COURSE ARROW
Indicates course set in Course Selector window.

ROTATING COMPASS CARD
Actuated by Master Compass system and rotates as the aircraft turns.

HEADING MARKER
Rotates with the Compass Card. Can be manually set with the Heading Set knob.

TO/FROM INDICATOR
Shows whether the course selected, if intercepted and flown, will take you TO or FROM station.

COURSE SELECTOR WINDOW
Selected course is read in this window.

COURSE DEVIATION INDICATOR
Shows position of selected radial in relation to aircraft.

COURSE SET KNOB
Used to select any desired course.

Figure 17. Horizontal Situation Indicator (HSI).

2-14

Figure 26. ILS or LOC RWY 24R (LAX).

Figure 27. ILS or LOC RWY 35R (DEN).

Figure 28. ILS or LOC RWY 31 (DSM).

Figure 29. ILS or LOC RWY 8L (ATL).

Figure 30. VOR/DME or GPS-A (7D3).

Figure 31. Wind Component Chart.

Appendix 2

ASSOCIATED CONDITIONS:

POWER	TAKEOFF POWER SET BEFORE BRAKE RELEASE
FLAPS	20°
RUNWAY	PAVED, LEVEL, DRY SURFACE
TAKEOFF SPEED	IAS AS TABULATED

NOTE: GROUND ROLL IS APPROX 73% OF TOTAL TAKEOFF DISTANCE OVER A 50 FT OBSTACLE

EXAMPLE:

OAT	75 °F
PRESSURE ALTITUDE	4,000 FT
TAKEOFF WEIGHT	3,100 LB
HEADWIND	20 KNOTS
TOTAL TAKEOFF DISTANCE OVER A 50 FT OBSTACLE	1,350 FT
GROUND ROLL (73% OF 1,350)	986 FT
IAS TAKEOFF SPEED	
LIFT-OFF	74 MPH
AT 50 FT	74 MPH

WEIGHT (LB)	IAS TAKEOFF SPEED (ASSUMES ZERO INSTR ERROR)			
	LIFT-OFF		50 FEET	
	MPH	KNOTS	MPH	KNOTS
3,400	77	67	77	67
3,200	75	65	75	65
3,000	72	63	72	63
2,800	69	60	69	60
2,600	66	57	66	57
2,400	63	55	63	55

Figure 32. Obstacle Take-off Chart.

2-21

Appendix 2

CONDITIONS:
FLAPS UP
GEAR UP
2,600 RPM
COWL FLAPS OPEN

PRESS ALT	MP	PPH
S.L. TO 17,000	35	162
18,000	34	156
20,000	32	144
22,000	30	132
24,000	28	120

WEIGHT (LB)	PRESS ALT (FT)	CLIMB SPEED (KIAS)	RATE OF CLIMB (FPM) −20 °C	0 °C	20 °C	40 °C
4,000	S.L.	100	1,170	1,035	895	755
	4,000	100	1,080	940	800	655
	8,000	100	980	840	695	555
	12,000	100	870	730	590	---
	16,000	100	740	605	470	---
	20,000	99	485	355	---	---
	24,000	97	190	70	---	---
3,700	S.L.	99	1,310	1,165	1,020	875
	4,000	99	1,215	1,070	925	775
	8,000	99	1,115	965	815	670
	12,000	99	1,000	855	710	---
	16,000	99	865	730	590	---
	20,000	97	600	470	---	---
	24,000	95	295	170	---	---
3,400	S.L.	97	1,465	1,320	1,165	1,015
	4,000	97	1,370	1,220	1,065	910
	8,000	97	1,265	1,110	955	795
	12,000	97	1,150	995	845	---
	16,000	97	1,010	865	725	---
	20,000	96	730	595	---	---
	24,000	94	405	275	---	---

Figure 33. Maximum Rate of Climb Chart.

Appendix 2

PRESSURE ALTITUDE 6,000 FEET

CONDITIONS:
3,800 POUNDS
RECOMMENDED LEAN MIXTURE
COWL FLAPS CLOSED

RPM	MP	20 °C BELOW STANDARD TEMPERATURE −17 °C % BHP	KTAS	PPH	STANDARD TEMPERATURE 3 °C % BHP	KTAS	PPH	20 °C ABOVE STANDARD TEMPERATURE 23 °C % BHP	KTAS	PPH
2,550	24	---	---	---	78	173	97	75	174	94
	23	76	167	96	74	169	92	71	171	89
	22	72	164	90	69	166	87	67	167	84
	21	68	160	85	65	162	82	63	163	80
2,500	24	78	169	98	75	171	95	73	172	91
	23	74	166	93	71	167	90	69	169	87
	22	70	162	88	67	164	85	65	165	82
	21	66	158	83	63	160	80	61	160	77
2,400	24	73	165	91	70	166	88	68	167	85
	23	69	161	87	67	163	84	64	164	81
	22	65	158	82	63	159	79	61	160	77
	21	61	154	77	59	155	75	57	155	73
2,300	24	68	161	86	66	162	83	64	163	80
	23	65	158	82	62	159	79	60	159	76
	22	61	154	77	59	155	75	57	155	72
	21	57	150	73	55	150	71	53	150	68
2,200	24	63	156	80	61	157	77	59	158	75
	23	60	152	76	58	153	73	56	154	71
	22	57	149	72	54	149	70	53	149	67
	21	53	144	68	51	144	66	49	143	64
	20	50	139	64	48	138	62	46	137	60
	19	46	133	60	44	132	58	43	131	57

Figure 34. Cruise Performance Chart.

Appendix 2

ASSOCIATED CONDITIONS:

POWER — AS REQUIRED TO MAINTAIN 800 FT/MIN DESCENT ON APPROACH
FLAPS — DOWN
RUNWAY — PAVED, LEVEL, DRY SURFACE
APPROACH SPEED — IAS AS TABULATED

NOTE: GROUND ROLL IS APPROX 53% OF TOTAL LANDING DISTANCE OVER A 50 FT OBSTACLE.

EXAMPLE:

OAT	75 °F
PRESSURE ALTITUDE	4,000 FT
LANDING WEIGHT	3,200 LB
HEADWIND	10 KNOTS
TOTAL LANDING DISTANCE OVER A 50 FT OBSTACLE	1,475 FT
GROUND ROLL (53% OF 1,475)	782 FT
IAS TAKEOFF SPEED	87 MPH IAS

WEIGHT (LB)	IAS APPROACH SPEED (ASSUMES ZERO INSTR ERROR)	
	MPH	KNOTS
3,400	90	78
3,200	87	76
3,000	84	73
2,800	81	70
2,600	78	68
2,400	75	65

Figure 35. Normal Landing Chart.

Appendix 2

STA 0
REAR SEAT STA 74.70
FRONT SEAT STA 43.80

Figure 36. Stations Diagram.

Figure 37. Center of Gravity Envelope and Loading Graph.

Figure 38. Loading Graph and Center of Gravity Envelope.

Appendix 2

Figure 39. Stations Diagram.

Appendix 2

THE FOLLOWING CG LOCATIONS MAY BE USED WHEN DETERMINING THE HELICOPTER CG POSITION.

ITEM	LONG CG	LAT CG
PILOT & BAGGAGE UNDER "R" SEAT	79.0	+10.7
PASSENGER & BAGGAGE UNDER "L" SEAT	79.0	−9.3
MAIN FUEL	108.6	−11.0
AUX FUEL (OPTIONAL)	103.8	+11.2

Figure 40. Weight and Balance Chart.

Appendix 2

Figure 41. Hover Ceiling vs. Gross Weight.

Figure 42. Rate of Climb (FT/MIN).

Figure 43. Best Rate of Climb Speed.

Figure 44. Rate of Climb.

Figure 45. Running Takeoff.

Figure 46. Jump Takeoff.

Appendix 2

DESIGN DATA

WING SPAN	51'	EMPTY WEIGHT	600 LB
LENGTH	25' 9"	GROSS WEIGHT	1,040 LB
HEIGHT	9' 3-½"	WING AREA	219.5 SQ FT
ASPECT RATIO	11.85	WING LOADING	4.74 PSF

PERFORMANCE

MAX SPEED	98 MPH	STALL (DUAL)	35 MPH
AIRPLANE TOW	98 MPH	L/D MPH (SOLO)	22.25 TO 1 AT 45
AUTO WINCH	69 MPH	L/D MPH (DUAL)	22.25 TO 1 AT 52
DRIVE BRAKE			
EXTEND. MAX	98 MPH	SINK SPEED (SOLO)	2.6 FPS AT 38
STALL (SOLO)	31 MPH	SINK SPEED (DUAL)	3.1 FPS AT 42

Figure 48. Performance Curves Chart.

Figure 49. Performance Curves Chart.

Appendix 2

Figure 50. Flight Envelope.

Figure 51. Airport Signs.

Appendix 2

Figure 52. Sectional Chart Excerpt.

Note: Chart is not to scale and should not be used for navigation. Chart is for testing purposes only.

Figure 53. Sectional Chart Excerpt.

Note: Chart is not to scale and should not be used for navigation. Chart is for testing purposes only.

Appendix 2

Figure 54. Sectional Chart Excerpt.

Note: Chart is not to scale and should not be used for navigation. Chart is for testing purposes only.

Figure 55. En Route Low Altitude Segment.

Appendix 2

Figure 55A. En Route Low Altitude Segment.

Appendix 2

Figure 56. Two signs.

Figure 57. Sign.

Figure 58. Airport Diagram and Sign.

2-45

Appendix 2

Figure 59. Taxiway Diagram and Sign.

Figure 60. Two Signs.

2-46

Appendix 2

Figure 61. Sign.

Figure 62. Sign.

Figure 63. Sign and Intersection Diagram.

2-47

Appendix 2

Figure 64. Sign.

Figure 65. Sign.

2-48

OKLAHOMA

WILEY POST (PWA)(KPWA) 7 NW UTC–6(–5DT) N35°32.05´ W97°38.82´
1300 B TPA—See Remarks NOTAM FILE PWA
RWY 17L–35R: H7199X150 (CONC) S–35, D–50, 2D–90 HIRL
  RWY 17L: MALSR. PAPI(P4L)—GA 3.0° TCH 54´. Rgt tfc.
  RWY 35R: MALSR. PAPI(P4L)—GA 3.0° TCH 54´. Thld dsplcd 355´. Trees.
RWY 17R–35L: H5002X75 (ASPH–CONC) S–26, D–45 MIRL
  RWY 17R: REIL. PAPI(P4L)—GA 3.0° TCH 43´. Tree. Rgt tfc.
  RWY 35L: REIL. PAPI(P4L)—GA 3.0° TCH 42´.
RWY 13–31: H4214X100 (CONC) S–35, D–50, 2D–90 MIRL
0.6% up SE
  RWY 13: Rgt tfc.
RUNWAY DECLARED DISTANCE INFORMATION
  RWY 13: TORA–4214 TODA–4214 ASDA–4214 LDA–4214
  RWY 17L: TORA–7199 TODA–7199 ASDA–6844 LDA–6844
  RWY 17R: TORA–5002 TODA–5002 ASDA–5002 LDA–5002
  RWY 31: TORA–4214 TODA–4214 ASDA–4214 LDA–4214
  RWY 35L: TORA–5001 TODA–5001 ASDA–5001 LDA–5001
  RWY 35R: TORA–7198 TODA–7198 ASDA–7198 LDA–6844
SERVICE: S4 **FUEL** 100LL, JET A **OX** 1, 2, 3, 4 **LGT** Dusk–Dawn. When twr clsd ACTIVATE HIRL Rwy 17L–35R and MALSR Rwy 17L and Rwy 35R—CTAF.
AIRPORT REMARKS: Attended continuously. 100LL fuel avbl 24 hrs self serve with credit card. Surface conditions reported Mon–Fri 1400–2300Z‡. Rwy 13–31 CLOSED 0400–1300Z‡. Rwy 13–31 CLOSED to tkof and Rwy 31 CLOSED to acft over 12,500 lbs gross weight. Flocks of birds on and invof arpt all quadrants. Noise abatement procedure: Acft in excess of 12,500 pounds departing Rwy 17L–35R climb at a maximum rate consistent with safety to an altitude of 1500´ AGL then reduce power setting and climb rate to 3000´ AGL or 2 NM from arpt depending on air traffic control and safety conditions. TPA for Rwy 17R/35L 1900(600) 2300(1000) all other rwys. Rwy 13–31 unlighted 0400–1300Z‡. Touch & go or stop & go ldgs not authorized Rwy 13–31.
AIRPORT MANAGER: 405-316-4061
WEATHER DATA SOURCES: ASOS (405) 798-2013
COMMUNICATIONS: CTAF 126.9 **ATIS** 128.725 **UNICOM** 122.95
  RCO 122.65 (MC ALESTER RADIO)
® **OKE CITY APP/DEP CON** 124.6 (171°–360°) 120.45 (081°–170°) 124.2 (001°–080°)
  TOWER 126.9 (1300–0400Z‡) **GND CON** 121.7
AIRSPACE: CLASS D svc 1300–0400Z‡ other times CLASS E.
RADIO AIDS TO NAVIGATION: NOTAM FILE PWA.
  (T) VORW/DME 113.4 PWA Chan 81 N35°31.98´ W97°38.83´ at fld. 1271/8E.
  ILS 110.15 I–PWA Rwy 17L. Unmonitored when ATCT clsd. DME also serves Rwy 35R.
  ILS/DME 110.15 I–TFM Chan 38(Y) Rwy 35R. Class IT. DME also serves Rwy 17L.

DALLAS–FT WORTH
H–6H, L–15D
IAP, AD

Figure 66. Chart Supplement.

TEXAS 337

LUBBOCK

LUBBOCK EXECUTIVE AIRPARK (F82)   5 S   UTC–6(–5DT)   N33°29.14´ W101°48.76´   DALLAS–FT WORTH
3200   B   TPA—4200(1000)   NOTAM FILE FTW   L–6H
RWY 17–35: H3500X70 (ASPH)   S–13   HIRL
RWY 07–25: 1500X110 (TURF)
 RWY 07: P–line.
SERVICE: S4   **FUEL** 100LL, JET A
AIRPORT REMARKS: Attended 1400–0000Z‡. After hrs 806–789–6437, 806–589–8143. Fuel avbl 24 hrs with major credit card. Rwy 17 road located at thld. Farm equipment ops AER 17, Rwy 25 and Rwy 35.
AIRPORT MANAGER: 806–789–6437
COMMUNICATIONS: CTAF/UNICOM 122.8
RADIO AIDS TO NAVIGATION: NOTAM FILE LBB.
 (L) VORTACW 109.2   LBB   Chan 29   N33°42.30´ W101°54.84´   148° 14.1 NM to fld. 3310/11E.   **HIWAS.**
 VOR portion unusable:
  140°–190° byd 20 NM blo 5,100´

- -

LUBBOCK PRESTON SMITH INTL (LBB)(KLBB)   4 N   UTC–6(–5DT)   N33°39.82´ W101°49.23´   DALLAS–FT WORTH
3282   B   LRA   Class I, ARFF Index C   NOTAM FILE LBB   H–6G, L–6H
RWY 17R–35L: H11500X150 (CONC–GRVD)   S–100, D–170, 2S–175,   IAP, AD
 2D–350 PCN 65 R/B/W/T   HIRL
 RWY 17R: MALSR. PAPI(P4R)—GA 3.0° TCH 69´. RVR–T Rgt tfc. 0.4% down.
 RWY 35L: ODALS. VASI(V4L)—GA 3.0° TCH 54´. RVR–R 0.3% up.
RWY 08–26: H8003X150 (CONC–GRVD)   S–100, D–170, 2S–175,
 2D–350 PCN 71 R/B/W/T   HIRL
 RWY 08: REIL. PAPI(P4L)—GA 3.0° TCH 50´. RVR–R Rgt tfc.
 RWY 26: MALSR. PAPI(P4L)—GA 3.0° TCH 50´. RVR–T
RWY 17L–35R: H2891X74 (ASPH)   S–12.5
 RWY 35R: Road. Rgt tfc.
RUNWAY DECLARED DISTANCE INFORMATION
 RWY 08: TORA–8003   TODA–8003   ASDA–8003   LDA–8003
 RWY 17L: TORA–2891   TODA–2891   ASDA–2891   LDA–2891
 RWY 17R: TORA–11500 TODA–11500 ASDA–11500 LDA–11500
 RWY 26: TORA–8003   TODA–8003   ASDA–8003   LDA–8003
 RWY 35L: TORA–11500 TODA–11500 ASDA–11500 LDA–11500
 RWY 35R: TORA–2891   TODA–2891   ASDA–2891   LDA–2891
SERVICE: S4   **FUEL** 100LL, JET A, A1+   **OX** 1, 2, 3, 4
AIRPORT REMARKS: Attended continuously. Numerous birds on and invof arpt. PAEW adjacent Rwy 08–26 and Rwy 17R–35L. Passenger terminal ramp access rstd to air carriers and others with prior permission call 806–775–2044. Rwy 17L–35R rstd to general aviation acft 12,500 lbs or less. Rwy 17L–35R, Twy B, Twy D, and Twy E not avbl for air carrier acft with over 9 psgr seats. Twy B, Twy D, and Twy E rstd to acft weighing less than 50,000 lbs. Twy L between Twy F and Twy J clsd to more than 120,001 lbs. East ramp delineated taxilane and apron area rstd to 120,000 lbs dual tandem acft, 89,000 lbs dual single wheel acft and 60,000 lbs single wheel acft. All other east ramp pavements rstd to acft less than 12,500 lbs single wheel acft. Flight Notification Service (ADCUS) available.
AIRPORT MANAGER: 806–775–3126
WEATHER DATA SOURCES: ASOS 125.3 (806) 766–6432. **HIWAS** 109.2 LBB. WSP.
COMMUNICATIONS: ATIS 125.3   **UNICOM** 122.95
 RCO 122.55 (FORT WORTH RADIO)
Ⓡ **APP/DEP CON** 119.2 119.9
 TOWER 120.5   **GND CON** 121.9   **CLNC DEL** 125.8
AIRSPACE: CLASS C svc ctc APP CON
RADIO AIDS TO NAVIGATION: NOTAM FILE LBB.
 (L) VORTACW 109.2   LBB   Chan 29   N33°42.30´ W101°54.84´   107° 5.3 NM to fld. 3310/11E.   **HIWAS.**
 VOR portion unusable:
  140°–190° byd 20 NM blo 5,100´
 LUBBI NDB (LOMW) 272   LD   N33°39.76´ W101°43.39´   265° 4.9 NM to fld. 3198/6E.
 POLLO NDB (LOM) 219   LB   N33°44.26´ W101°49.76´   168° 4.5 NM to fld.
 ILS/DME 111.7   I–LBB   Chan 54   Rwy 17R.   Class IA.   LOM POLLO NDB.
 ILS 111.9   I–LDT   Rwy 26.   Class IA.   LOM LUBBI NDB.

SC, 1 FEB 20XX to 29 MAR 20XX

Figure 67. Chart Supplement.

TEXAS

DALLAS

ADDISON (ADS)(KADS)   9 N   UTC−6(−5DT)   N32°58.11′ W96°50.19′
645   B   TPA—See Remarks   LRA   NOTAM FILE ADS
RWY 15−33: H7203X100 (ASPH−GRVD)   S−60, D−120   HIRL
 RWY 15: MALSR. PAPI(P4R)—GA 3.0° TCH 60′. Thld dsplcd 979′. Tree.
 RWY 33: REIL. PAPI(P4L)—GA 3.0° TCH 60′. Thld dsplcd 772′. Bldg.
RUNWAY DECLARED DISTANCE INFORMATION
 RWY 15: TORA−7203   TODA−7203   ASDA−7203   LDA−6224
 RWY 33: TORA−7203   TODA−7203   ASDA−7203   LDA−6431
ARRESTING GEAR/SYSTEM
 RWY 15: EMAS
SERVICE: S4   **FUEL** 100LL, JET A   **OX** 2, 3   **LGT** ACTIVATE HIRL Rwy 15−33 and MALSR Rwy 15—CTAF.
AIRPORT REMARKS: Attended continuously. Birds on and invof arpt. No touch and go ldgs without arpt mgr apvl. Numerous 200′ bldgs within 1 mile east, and south of arpt, transmission twrs and water tanks west of arpt. Noise sensitive areas surround arpt. Pilots req to use NBAA std noise procedures. TPA—1601 (956) for light acft, 2001 (1356) for large acft. Be alert, rwy holding position markings lctd at the west edge of Twy A. Flight Notification Service (ADCUS) available.
AIRPORT MANAGER: 972−392−4850
WEATHER DATA SOURCES: AWOS−3 (972) 386−4855 LAWRS.
COMMUNICATIONS: CTAF 126.0   ATIS 133.4 972−628−2439
UNICOM 122.95
 ®**REGIONAL APP/DEP CON** 124.3
 TOWER 126.0 (1200−0400Z‡)   **GND CON** 121.6   **CLNC DEL** 119.55
AIRSPACE: CLASS D svc 1200−0400Z‡, other times CLASS G.
RADIO AIDS TO NAVIGATION: NOTAM FILE FTW.
 MAVERICK (H) VORW/DME 113.1   TTT   Chan 78   N32°52.15′ W97°02.43′   054° 11.9 NM to fld. 540/6E.
  All acft arriving DFW are requested to turn DME off until departure due to traffic overload of Maverick DME unusable:
   180°−190°
 ILS/DME 110.1   I−ADS   Chan 38   Rwy 15.   Class IT.   Unmonitored when ATCT closed. DME also serves Rwy 33.
 ILS/DME 110.1   I−TBQ   Chan 38   Rwy 33.   Class IB.   Localizer unmonitored when ATCT closed. DME also serves Rwy 15.

DALLAS−FT WORTH
COPTER
H−6H, L−17C, A
IAP, AD

- -

AIR PARK−DALLAS (F69)   16 NE   UTC−6(−5DT)   N33°01.41′ W96°50.22′
695   TPA—1890(1195)   NOTAM FILE FTW
RWY 16−34: H3080X30 (ASPH)   LIRL(NSTD)
 RWY 16: Thld dsplcd 300′. Pole.
 RWY 34: Tree. Rgt tfc.
SERVICE: S4   **FUEL** 100LL   **LGT** ACTIVATE LIRL Rwy 16−34—CTAF. Rwy 16−34 NSTD LIRL; 2780′ of rwy lgtd. Thld and dsplcd thld not lighted.
AIRPORT REMARKS: Uattended. For fuel call 972−248−4265 prior to arr. Rwy 16−34 pavement cracking, loose stones on rwy. Rwy 34 NSTD cntrln marking incorrect size and spacing. Rwy numbers 25′ tall, markings faded. Rwy number 34 not located at rwy end.
AIRPORT MANAGER: 972−248−4265
COMMUNICATIONS: CTAF 122.9
RADIO AIDS TO NAVIGATION: NOTAM FILE FTW.
 MAVERICK (H) VORW/DME 113.1   TTT   Chan 78   N32°52.15′ W97°02.43′   042° 13.8 NM to fld. 540/6E.
  All acft arriving DFW are requested to turn DME off until departure due to traffic overload of Maverick DME unusable:
   180°−190°
COMM/NAV/WEATHER REMARKS: For Clnc Del ctc Regional Apch at 972−615−2799.

DALLAS−FT WORTH
COPTER
L−17C, A

SC, 1 FEB 20XX to 29 MAR 20XX

Figure 68. Chart Supplement.

Appendix 2

Figure 69. Weather Prediction Center (WPC) Surface Prog Chart.

2-52

Appendix 2

Figure 70. Weather Prediction Center (WPC) Surface Prog Chart.

2-53

Appendix 2

Figure 71. Low-level Significant Weather Chart.

2-54